ECONOMIC INTEGRATION IN EASTERN EUROPE

ECONOMIC INTEGRATION IN EASTERN EUROPE

A Handbook

Jozef M. van Brabant

HARVESTER WHEATSHEAF

New York   London   Toronto   Sydney   Tokyo

First published 1989 by
Harvester Wheatsheaf,
66 Wood Lane End, Hemel Hempstead,
Hertfordshire, HP2 4RG
A division of
Simon & Schuster International Group

© 1989 Jozef M. van Brabant

Printed and bound in Great Britain by
BPCC Wheaton Ltd, Exeter

British Library Cataloguing in Publication Data

Brabant, Jozef M. van
    Economic integration in Eastern Europe: a reference
    book.
    1. Eastern Europe. Economic cooperation
    I. Title
    337.1'47

    ISBN 0-7450-0607-8

1 2 3 4 5   93 92 91 90 89

To Anja, Katja, and Miyuki – in gratitude

CONTENTS

FIGURES AND TABLES

PREFACE

This monograph derives largely from my earlier work on the economic integration efforts of the Eastern European economies, which has been a core topic of my intellectual curiosity and professional commitment since the mid-1960s. From long durations spent in half a dozen countries on two continents in yet a larger number of academic and other kinds of organizations, I have inevitably incurred a top-heavy bill of obligations.

For financial, bibliographical, secretarial, moral, professional and other support, I sincerely thank the Belgian National Foundation for Scientific Research, the Belgian Ministry of Education and Culture, the Center of Economic Research at the Catholic University of Louvain (Belgium), the Osteuropa-Institut an der Freien Universität Berlin (Federal Republic of Germany), the Department of International Economic and Social Affairs of the United Nations Secretariat (New York), the United Nations Economic Commission for Europe (Geneva, Switzerland), and the Istituto Universitario Europeo (San Domenico di Fiesole (Firenze), Italy). However great my indebtedness to these institutions and their staffs, some of whom have given me invaluable assistance over the years, no single one should be held responsible for the shortcomings of this product. Full responsibility for misinterpreting facts and figures, for ignoring advice, or for other kinds of errors, is solely mine.

Most portions of this book were written in my spare time while working officially as a staff member of the Department of International Economic and Social Affairs of the United Nations Secretariat in New York. The opinions expressed here are my own and do not necessarily reflect those of the United Nations Secretariat.

As with most of my earlier research efforts, I owe much to the women in my family and to their ingenuity in foisting 'spare writing time' onto me. I could have allocated that resource to pursuits other than drafting yet one more monograph. Under the circumstances, however, I was not allowed to choose. Once again, I am much obliged to my three women.

NOTE ON TRANSLITERATION, REFERENCING AND UNITS

Cyrillic-language publications or names of persons from Cyrillic-script regions are transliterated according to the so-called scientific transliteration system advocated by the USSR Academy of Sciences. A distinction is made between the three Russian *e*'s and, in the case of Bulgarian sources, the Russian *šč* is replaced by *št*. Whenever possible, names of writers, personalities or places are spelled according to the convention of the home country, possibly followed by transliteration as indicated. The affiliated organs of the Council for Mutual Economic Assistance (CMEA) are normally referred to by their Russian names or acronyms because their official or working language in most cases is Russian. I have followed this usage so as to minimize potential confusion in the spelling of proper names and to be able to refer to these organizations in a uniform format. I realize that this system of transliteration produces some unusual renditions of familiar names. These include Brežnev for Leonid I. Brezhnev, Chruščëv for Nikita S. Khrushchev and Gorbačëv for Mikhail S. Gorbachev.

Bibliographic references in the text are identified by author and date of publication. In the absence of a name, the reference consists of a simple acronym of the organization sponsoring the publication or of one key word from the title. Because they are meant to be codes to the Bibliography, where full details are given, name prefixes are deleted from text references.

Throughout the volume, a billion is understood to equal a thousand million, and all dollar magnitudes are expressed as US dollar values. References to the currency denominations of the Slavic countries, other than the ruble, follow the standards of the countries in question; that is, the inflection of the currency denomination depends on the magnitude of the preceding number. All dates are specified according to European custom: 1 April 1970.

ABBREVIATIONS

BIS	Bank for International Settlements
BTPA	bilateral trade and payments agreement
CC	Central Committee
CCP	Conference of First Secretaries of Communist and Workers' Parties and of the Heads of Government of the CMEA Member Countries
CCS	Central Committee Secretaries in charge of economic affairs
CMEA	Council for Mutual Economic Assistance
CoCom	Coordinating Committee for Multilateral Trade Controls
Cominform	Communist Information Bureau
Comintern	Communist International
CP	Communist Party
CPE	centrally planned economy
DE	developing economy
DME	developed market economy
EC	European Communities
ECPS	economic cooperation and production specialization
EEC	European Economic Community
EJR	economically justified requirement
EPU	European Payments Union
ERP	European Recovery Program
EWP	East-West price
FRG	Federal Republic of Germany
FTO	foreign trade organization
GATT	General Agreement on Tariffs and Trade
GDR	German Democratic Republic
IBEC	International Bank for Economic Cooperation
IBRD	International Bank for Reconstruction and Development
IEO	international economic organization
IIB	International Investment Bank
IMF	International Monetary Fund
IPO	international protection organization

IPS	independent price system
ISDL	international socialist division of labor
ITS	international trade system
JSC	joint-stock company
ME	market economy
MFN	most-favored nation
MFT	state monopoly of foreign trade and payments
MTPA	multilateral trade and payments agreement
NATO	North Atlantic Treaty Organization
NEM	new economic mechanism
NIC	newly industrializing developing country
OECD	Organization for Economic Co-operation and Development
OEEC	Organization for European Economic Co-operation
SCEP	Standing Commission on Economic Problems
SCFQ	Standing Commission on Currency and Financial Questions
SCFT	Standing Commission on Foreign Trade
SEI	socialist economic integration
STC	scientific-technological cooperation
TR	transferable ruble
TRP	transferable ruble price
WMP	world market price

INTRODUCTION

This volume is meant as an introductory, yet comprehensive, guide to the myriad economic problems associated with attempts to foster economic integration among the centrally planned economies (CPEs). I shall be concerned especially with the context of the trade, payments and economic cooperation arrangements that are within the purview of the Council for Mutual Economic Assistance (CMEA). In this brief introduction, I attempt to clarify the type of problems to be broached, the countries of principal concern, the level of sophistication being sought and the more general political setting of regional economic cooperation among the CPEs.

CMEA MEMBERSHIP AND THE AREA OF CONCERN

The CMEA includes countries from Africa, Asia, Europe and Latin America. If the discourse is restricted to the full members of the CMEA, then no African country should be included. Full members include the six Eastern European countries of Bulgaria, Czechoslovakia, the German Democratic Republic (GDR), Hungary, Poland and Rumania, all of which, except the GDR, are founder members. The Soviet Union is a full member as well as a founder. Albania has been a member since 1949 but is now inactive (since 1961). Other members are Cuba (since 1972), Mongolia (since 1962) and Vietnam (since 1978). These countries endorsed the CMEA's charter and thereby expressed their willingness to subscribe to the purposes and means of the CMEA as an organization entrusted with the promotion of, in effect, socialist economic integration (SEI), which will be discussed at length in Part II. The *Dogmengeschichte* of the aims of CMEA economic cooperation is explained in Part I.

In addition to full membership, the Council recognizes three other types of association. Associate membership applies only to Yugoslavia, which originally held only a simple observership. Yugoslavia's membership is based on a special agreement with the Council in which it pledged to participate fully in only some activities of the Council. This arrangement provided an acceptable way of luring Yugoslavia into the CMEA fold without flaunting the country's jealously guarded privileged position as a non-aligned, yet socialist, country.

Cooperant status presently applies to Afghanistan, Angola, Ethiopia, Finland, Iraq, Mexico, Mozambique, Nicaragua and Democratic Yemen. This status issues from a special framework agreement between the cooperant and the Council that permits closer cooperative ties. The promotion of regular commerce is chiefly envisaged, though bilateralism in relations between CPEs and developing economies (DEs) may confine the role of the framework agreement. Cooperant status is probably more significant for fostering scientific-technological cooperation and facilitating the reciprocal flow of pertinent economic information; it may even bolster the cooperant's access to the CMEA's development assistance programs.

Observer status has traditionally been reserved for CPEs that are not CMEA members, DEs increasingly and on occasion for international organizations. An observer literally takes part in some meetings, usually of the Council Session, but otherwise has no further obligations *vis-à-vis* the Council. Such status is typically issued for individual meetings. It does not obligate the parties involved to anything beyond diplomatic courtesy during that particular conference.

In this volume, I shall be particularly concerned with the seven active European members, who, for convenience, I shall occasionally refer to as Eastern Europe. In using the latter concept for the smaller countries, which I shall do to draw contrasts, the distinction between Eastern Europe proper and the group with the Soviet Union will always be made explicit. As a geographical expression, Eastern Europe also includes Albania and Yugoslavia, but I shall not use the term in that sense unless the theme at hand warrants it. Finally, I realize that Central and East Central Europe are terms with historical connotations. To minimize confusion, I shall largely avoid these terms.

When it comes to circumscribing the heartland of SEI, by necessity one is talking primarily about Eastern Europe as a group of countries on a comparatively medium level of industrial development. These countries share political institutions, geographical proximity, broad ideological convictions and, given their geopolitical situation in the postwar period, the need to ensure common security. Therefore, in what follows, I shall be mostly concerned with the seven European CPEs. I shall bring the other cooperating countries into the analysis when they really matter or at points where the Council may affect their economic policies.

By restricting the field of inquiry largely to the European members, I do not wish to deny importance to other CMEA participants. At the very least, their presence has been seen as an economic as well as political bonus for the European CPEs, particularly for the Soviet Union. The inclusion of these developing countries permits the CPEs to emphasize their international commitment and outlook. The economic benefits derive chiefly for these less-developed countries in terms of capital flows, price advantages and access to markets. Though these benefits should not be completely overlooked, they are not a focal concern of this monograph.

PURPOSES OF THE VOLUME

This volume has two broad purposes. First, I wish to present a succinct summary of the state of our knowledge about economic integration among the Eastern European countries, which seems appropriate at this time in that, in early 1989, the CMEA will have celebrated its fortieth anniversary. Moreover, I hope to compile and digest this information sufficiently so that it becomes fully accessible to the nonspecialist reader. The volume is, deliberately, not designed to provide an exhaustive analysis of the present state of affairs with SEI. Likewise, I do not present an economic history of postwar Eastern Europe or a detailed account of the present CMEA organizational setup. Finally, I have not attempted to resolve controversies inherent in the study of economies in which quantitative as well as qualitative information is exceedingly sparse. This imperfect information chain contains huge gaps, particularly for the early years of CMEA cooperation.

Primarily, I aim to introduce the nonspecialist reader with some knowledge of economics and international relations to a spectrum of institutional, organizational and analytical aspects of regional economic integration in Eastern Europe. For material beyond the scope of this inquiry, I provide a guide to the specialized literature. But I also hope that the specialist may find some useful references in this structured approach to the state of our knowledge about SEI and to the various ways in which these CPEs actually participate in regional and, to some extent, global economic affairs. To keep this discourse accessible to the average reader, I have purposefully avoided many topics that have remained controversial for years. So far, it has not been possible to resolve these issues, chiefly because of a lack of access to historical archives, an absence of empirical and reliable qualitative information, and because many of these controversies cannot be interpreted one way or the other with the information at hand. Although these controversial aspects will not forcibly be dodged, when needed I intend to present them in as simple a form as I can.

MAIN TOPICS

The topics to be dealt with here may be grouped under four headings. First, I offer a broad review of the principal circumstances in which the Council was conceived and the major markers of its evolution from the end of World War II to the late 1980s. I trace the story back to the end of World War II in order to convey a flavor of how the CMEA came about and to identify the principal motives that prevailed at that time. I then sketch the history and evolution of the CMEA over the past forty years. While this flashback is instructive for its own sake, perhaps more importantly, such a condensed historical review will help place current discussions about SEI into proper perspective.

Since about the mid-1980s the CMEA organization itself, as well as certain policies, instruments and institutions of its members that are crucial to the enhancement of SEI, has been undergoing a process of 'radical reform.' One could legitimately inquire into these transformations for their own sake, and some readers may even wish to evaluate the realism of these intentions, particularly as they relate to the creation of a common market. Although these issues do crop up in this volume, they are not its main purpose. I hope to provide at least a broad, if perhaps cursory, awareness and understanding of what has happened during the past forty years that will help the reader approach contemporary political and economic debates with an appropriate degree of realism, if not necessarily skepticism. I hope to instill in the reader an impartial appreciation of what these countries together can and cannot accomplish. Soviet policies in the postwar period relating to Eastern Europe will be placed centerstage here. Part I also sets forth the purposes of the organization as distilled from official documents and revealed policy stances of the individual members, the group as a whole and the regional organization as such.

Part II clarifies the organizational and institutional structure of the CMEA, the major policies pursued and the links between the Council and any member's economic policy instruments, institutions and development policies. Because these features have fluctuated over time, the interactions between the CMEA and its members need to be clarified against an historical backdrop. This is especially necessary in order to discuss the CMEA's links with the traditional CPE, the modified CPE as it emerged briefly in the 1960s and 1970s and the reforming CPE of the late 1980s. Part I will prove to be instructive in this context. The extent to which the CMEA as a regional organization can interface with the organization and macroeconomic management of the member economies is pivotal for the effective promotion of integration.

How the instruments and institutions of the CMEA blend in with the economic policy instruments and related institutions of the member countries forms the principal subject of Part III. There I shall discuss how the economic policies of the various CPEs can be harmonized with each other and with regional and third countries, especially industrial market economies (MEs).

Part IV has a dual purpose. I assess the impact of SEI on growth performance, regional economic cohesion, production specialization, economic interdependence and East-West economic relations. I also discuss the advantages and drawbacks of integration in terms of the cost of protection and of gearing output to dual markets. These elaborations are then used to assess what room exists for implementing changes in the purposes, institutions, instruments and impacts of integration on economic reforms in Eastern Europe.

THE CONCEPT OF INTEGRATION IN THE EASTERN EUROPEAN CONTEXT

Whether one can properly apply the notion of regional economic integration to the cooperation efforts of the CMEA member countries is not at all self-evident. In fact, observers from East and West alike, but chiefly the latter, have debated for years about whether or not one can legitimately speak of integration when these countries are, in fact, unwilling to attune their regional cooperation efforts to their major institutional and organizational features. Certainly, regional and national features need not necessarily be identical. However, given the organizational setup of the majority of the CPEs, their regional organization should logically have been patterned on the concept of strict central planning. Various mechanisms of regional planning should have been the counterparts of the organizational and decision-making systems that typically prevail in the member countries. But fierce controversy has at times raged about whether the CMEA should be geared toward planned integration.

The controversy surrounding the CMEA's aims at integration failed to be resolved either as a result of practical policy on the part of the CPEs or by the doctrine they claimed to have espoused until about 1969–71, when they finally adopted a major policy document that explicitly coined the term SEI. Before that momentous change, at least from an ideological perspective, the CPEs, particularly during the early part of the 1950s, tended to refer to their regional efforts as fraternal economic cooperation or as the international socialist division of labor (ISDL), the term preferred during the 1960s. The term integration was generally reserved for the cooperation efforts of market-type economies, chiefly those in Western Europe, and, before 1969, was generally used in a very negative or even derogatory sense. In the late 1950s and early 1960s, 'integration' certainly had a pronounced pejorative connotation, referring as it did to new means invented by monopoly capital to exploit workers and thereby deferring capitalism's inevitable demise.

Here, as in an earlier work, I want to define economic integration as a process aimed at the leveling up of differences in relative scarcities of goods and services by the conscious elimination of barriers to trade and other forms of interaction between at least two different states (Brabant, 1980, pp. 5–6). This definition is not the one that can be readily derived from formal, explicit statements by the CMEA members. Nonetheless, from reading official policy pronouncements it is inescapable to conclude that the CMEA countries have been aiming at a gradual reduction of differences in relative economic scarcities in the various member economies since the late 1940s.

The ISDL doctrine was pronounced in conjunction with the commitment to 'equalize levels of economic development' of the CMEA members. Although this may have been an important overt policy objective in the European context, and certainly Bulgaria and (to a lesser extent) Rumania benefited from the implied resource transfers, it put the CPEs in an awkward position *vis-à-vis* the less-developed CPEs, such as Cuba, Mongolia and Vietnam. Admittedly, these considerations about equalizing development levels from above – by deliberately holding down the buoyancy of economic performance in the most developed countries – or from below – by eliminating real relative economic scarcities – have not always played a pivotal role in the formulation and implementation of actual economic policies. Concerns about exploiting differences in economic scarcities were much more muted during the period of 'economic cooperation' than they appear to have been more recently. Nonetheless, I want to divorce the term from its official endorsement, if only because it is not inevitable that the acceptance of a political document on integration with that name will automatically entail the emergence of the relevant economic processes.

THE ECONOMICS AND POLITICS OF INTEGRATION

When the members of an economic union are sovereign states, their specific and separate interests will generate explicit or hidden conflicts about the advantages and drawbacks of the union that decision makers within a centralist organization can sidestep, if they so wish, by the authority vested in them. The potential for conflict is aggravated when the economic union is brought about with a host of circumstances that have little to do with the economics of regional integration. Because the CMEA was born in an exceedingly hostile regional and international environment and has matured until now against numerous political drawbacks emanating from centrifugal forces within individual member countries, within the region as a whole and in its wider international contacts, economic integration cannot be properly adjudicated only in an economic context.

Although SEI has a variety of strategic, military, political, social and other tangents, I shall bypass most of these issues and concentrate here on the economics of SEI processes. My apologies for doing so are numerous. For one, I am but an economist. I trust that others can take care of at least the metaeconomic issues in a more coherent, cogent and well-founded manner than I can possibly accomplish. There are, of course, other reasons that force me to compress my attention to the noneconomic issues, however interesting they may be in their own right or however much I, as a concerned economist, could contribute to them.

In summary, this monograph is primarily about the economics of international relations within the context of the CMEA as the regional organization of the the majority of CPEs. But the horizon will not necessarily blur types of economic cooperation among the members that are initiated, guided, regulated and controlled by forces other than those available to the organization. While other aspects may at times be touched upon to round off the economic discourse, no attempt will be made to be comprehensive or exhaustive on those topics.

PART I

THE BIRTH AND EVOLUTION OF THE COUNCIL

Part I paints on a rather broad canvas the origins of the Council at the end of World War II and the key features of its evolution up to the late 1980s. I will present a kaleidoscopic, modernistic picture executed with broad brush strokes and a painter's knife rather than a carefully proportioned Renaissance miniature because this review is not meant as a rounded economic history of Eastern Europe, an endeavor that would quickly have been stymied by too many unknown parameters of the CMEA's evolvement, particularly during the first twenty years of postwar cooperation. Although information for recent years is undoubtedly more ample, important gaps remain in our knowledge of what continues to be the Byzantine art of deliberations among nominally sovereign states.

Chapter 1 is concerned with the most important circumstances of the CMEA's creation in January 1949. It examines both the political and, especially, the economic aspects of that evolution. Politics will be brought in only to the extent that it helps clarify the economic events of the 1940s and early 1950s. The particulars of the Council's creation are detailed in chapter 2. The time dimension of the inquiry is the year and a half from early 1949 to about mid-1950, when a major change in the fortunes of the CMEA occurred. The activities of the next decade or so are the subject of chapter 3. The central topic of chapter 4 is the emergence of the CMEA organization from its dormant phase and its gradual blossoming into a functioning organ with an official charter, explicit policy goals, meaningful cooperation policies, institutional supports and some policy instruments that are, in principle, capable of influencing decision making about the level and composition of foreign economic exchanges. All discussion in this chapter is centered around the role of the first broad policy document on SEI and the environment within which it was negotiated and implemented. Chapter 5 does likewise for the second major policy document on SEI. Chapter 6 is particularly concerned with the unusual development circumstances of the CMEA during the early 1980s and the possible bearing these may have on the course of integration to be pursued in the next decade or so, now that the CMEA is formally aiming at the creation of a common market.

1 · THE ORIGINS OF THE CMEA

Sketching the economic, social, political and military atmosphere within which the CMEA was first conceived is a rather straightforward task. To precisely pinpoint, however, what exactly the founding countries were trying to accomplish with the CMEA is an entirely different, and daunting, matter. Anyone keenly interested in unraveling the CMEA's birth and evolution must first come to grips with one major characteristic of that organ. Today, as in the past, it is still impossible to identify with any reasonable degree of comfort the exact reasons for the creation of the CMEA or the circumstances of its gestation during the early part of 1949. The period itself was characterized by considerable uncertainty in economic, political and security matters. When the idea of creating a formal organization gradually crystallized in regional cooperation debates, not only was open rivalry between East and West, principally between the United States and the USSR, emerging but those first postwar years also witnessed rapid and at times violent transitions in Eastern European political regimes. The historiography of that period is still shrouded in too many ideological preconceptions to yield a solid foundation for reliable analysis.[1]

An even more complex assignment is how to set forth in a coherent and objective framework what was actually then being discussed among politicians, economists and diplomats. Most of the pertinent archival material, if the debates were recorded at all, remains inaccessible, certainly to an outside observer such as myself. But difficulty in accessing information applies as well to the vast majority of commentators and analysts from Eastern Europe. Apparently there are comprehensive archives in the CMEA Secretariat, but I do not know anyone who has ever obtained access to them.[2] From the few secondary sources who may legitimately claim having had access to some authentic documents, it is not always clear how their selection was conducted or what the precise purpose of their investigation was. In most cases, details about early CMEA discussions tend to surface as a casual by-product of investigations into interparty or intercountry relations rather than as a well-defined area of inquiry in its own right. The proper questions for such a framework are generally not those

that one would ask if the main aim was to investigate the origins of the
CMEA as an independent research project.

Sections 1.1 and 1.2 of this chapter detail several of the many political and
economic angles of the environment within which the Eastern European
models of central planning were forcibly established after World War II.
Section 1.3 zeroes in on the key elements of the immediate circumstances
within which the CMEA was set up in early 1949. Section 1.4 clarifies some
of the more cogent aspects of one strand of the discussions that allegedly led
to a founding treaty. Because this treaty is still based on conjecture and
CMEA historians have given it little more than casual reference, I include it
here among the circumstantial evidence of the CMEA's gestation. The last
section places in retrospect the debates of the late 1940s through January
1949.

1.1 POLITICAL ASPECTS OF COOPERATION IN THE 1940s

Although this book is not about politics *per se*, it would be counterproductive to attempt to dodge the political reality that prevailed when the
CMEA's establishment was first contemplated. Among the different issues
that could be considered, I shall stress the following themes:

1. Mostly divergent precepts about the reconstruction of the postwar
   world economic and political order among the wartime allies once
   hostilities ceased.
2. The fluid political situation in many of the Eastern European
   countries.
3. War reparations.
4. The challenge of the Marshall Plan.
5. Political mutations in Eastern Europe.
6. The Yugoslav affair.
7. The frustrated attempts to agree upon some kind of Eastern European
   regionalism.

1.1.1 The postwar economic and political order

One of the many outcomes of World War II was a vacuum in the economic
and political positioning of many European states. Among the erstwhile
world powers, Nazi Germany was defeated, but France and the United
Kingdom, who had been victorious, were paying a very high cost for their
victory in terms of economic resources, political stature and ability to
surmount the dislocations caused by the war. Because of their Pyrrhic
victory, France and the United Kingdom were not able to assume a leading
role in the reconstruction of the world economic and political order when
hostilities ended. That vacuum would be filled by the two largest countries

that had remained on the fringes of international economic cooperation in the interwar period. On the one hand, the United States emerged as the now-dominant global economic power. Complementing the newly won position of the United States was that of the Soviet Union. As one of the victors with considerable national and other resources, as well as with a tenaciously displayed formidable ability to overcome adversity, the USSR had become a major contender in steering global economic, security and political affairs in line with its perceived interests.

There were various matters to be settled in 1945 that are related to this shift in global power relations. During the war, allied cooperation had largely rested on the need to defeat the Axis powers, a concern that had taken nearly absolute precedence over other matters, including postwar peace settlements. Nonetheless, reconstruction of the world order had then been on the agenda of a number of bi- and multilateral conferences. The first of these high-level deliberations, chiefly between the governments of the United States and Great Britain, was convened soon after hostilities started; further consultations were initiated at regular intervals. Some of these, chiefly Anglo-American deliberations (Brabant, 1989), sought to lay the foundations for a postwar world economic order based on a multilaterally free trading system anchored to a common monetary institution, which would be the world's lender of last resort, and to another institution entrusted with reconstruction and development finance. These three pillars were to form integral components of a rearrangement of economic, social, political and security relations among the sovereign states within the rules and regulations of a global organization, the United Nations, whose tasks extended from ensuring economic health and prosperity in the world economy to maintaining political and military security, and, indeed, to guaranteeing the inalienable right of national independence and self-determination.

Although the UK–US alliance was critical in first charting the postwar global economic order, what was being sought was a reconstruction of the economic order on a global basis. Most other countries among the 'friendly' powers were to be invited to participate fully in the final negotiating stages on the new world economic system. Their particular concerns would have to be allayed if an agreement based on Anglo-American blueprints was to be forged. In particular, it meant facing the Soviet Union's need to accommodate the peculiarities of a CPE, including the associated sharp separation of domestic and external economic activities.

It has remained a highly contentious issue whether or not the Anglo-American alliance was then aiming at a genuine multilateral monetary and trading system. To encapsulate unambiguously the real motivating forces underlying the Western proposals is probably impossible. In later analyses, the Soviet Union certainly stressed the selfishness of the United States in seeking to create dollar hegemony, to strengthen its economic dominance abroad through free capital movements – particularly direct foreign investments by the emerging multinational or transnational corporations – and to exploit actors in the world economy who were structurally or temporarily weak partners in international economic relations. The fortuitous position of strength-by-default in which the US economy found itself by war's end, of course, constituted a critical facet of this perception. But Soviet anxieties stemmed from other factors as well. The military strength of the United States and the anticommunist crusading stance of many US policymakers undoubtedly contributed to wariness on the part of the dominant Stalin regime in formulating Soviet policymaking. Even when viewed through Western eyes, which then, of course, would not even have admitted the existence or importance of the *Pax Americana*, there is considerable doubt about whether the Western allies were genuinely trying to fuse the USSR into the global concert of nations as an equal partner with big-power status.

Incompatibilities in outlook about the postwar organization of the world may have been glossed over during the war, but the polarization of foreign policy deliberations could no longer be easily galvanized by the time Churchill pronounced his famous Fulton address, when the notion of the 'descending iron curtain' over Eastern Europe became a household word. But the chilling presumptions of dominance in world affairs by the 'English speaking peoples' under the nuclear umbrella that 'God had willed to the United States' must have been especially perturbing to the endemically paranoid Stalin. Churchill's call for a 'unity in Europe from which no nation should be permanently outcast,' but one that would not include the Soviet Union, sealed the fate of inter-Allied cooperation. The intrinsic antagonistic nature of these relations then erupted into the rapidly escalating cold war.[3]

There is little doubt that the majority of high-level officials in the British Foreign Office and the US State Department who were involved in negotiating the agreements were really serious about working out either a genuine multilateral world order or one based on spheres of interest (Fehér, 1988). The Soviet Union could have been allocated a role commensurate with its position in postwar politics and economic strengths. The Soviet Union would have fitted in, if at all, as a differentiated ally rather than as an adversary. These motivations lasted well into 1947, as demonstrated, for example, by the open-arms attitude toward Soviet participation in the stillborn International Trade Organization.

Whether the above characterization is a fair reflection of the many-sided and interrelated events that transpired at the time is debatable. There is no doubt, however, that the postwar cooperation planned for during World War II and immediately thereafter during several high-level conferences did not materialize. Rather than becoming homogeneous, a world was being created that became increasingly fragmented and polarized. Aside from the disagreements about economic matters, there were serious concerns about spheres of influence and the future of Eastern Europe. This situation led to a vexing quandary for the smaller Eastern European countries. Their economic reconstruction and postwar growth greatly depended on gaining access to comprehensive foreign economic cooperation, including within their own region (see section 1.2). Their traditional allies, especially during the interwar period, had been the major powers in Western and Central Europe. As noted, defeated and occupied as it was, Germany, the key player of the 1930s, could no longer be their economic and political mentor. France and the United Kingdom were too weak to fill the void left by Germany even had they desired to extend their traditional spheres of interest to Eastern Europe.

1.1.2 Unstable political transitions in Eastern Europe

The eventual fate of Eastern Europe figured prominently in key Allied deliberations at the height of the war, including the conferences of Moscow, Teheran and Yalta. If it appeared as if the postwar settlement of affairs in Eastern Europe would henceforth proceed smoothly, this presumption proved seriously flawed as deliberations over political, security and economic relations quickly deteriorated and were turned into a key bone of contention among the Allies. As seen from the wartime alliances with the powers in exile, this was more the case for the countries (Czechoslovakia and chiefly Poland)[4] that had sided with the victorious powers than for those that had been part of (the Soviet zone in Germany – the later GDR) or had sided with the Axis powers (Bulgaria, Hungary and Rumania). Western attitudes on solidifying spheres of influence in the latter countries were somewhat accommodating, although by no means did the Allies acquiesce to Stalin's ideological and political precepts, which were being catapulted into these countries through 'imported' Communist agitators. The Western powers were resolutely adamant on ensuring the democratization of Czechoslovakia and Poland. The Polish question, especially, became an exceedingly contentious issue over which many meetings of the Allied foreign ministers struggled and, in the end, miserably faltered.

1.1.3 War reparations

Following the end of hostilities, war reparations emerged as a thorny and divisive issue in the negotiations about reconstruction. Initially there had been full agreement within the alliance on the principle of exacting war reparations, especially in favor of the USSR because it had suffered the most extensive material damage and loss in human lives. But concerns about avoiding a repetition of the many dilemmas associated with the so-called transfer problem[5] after World War I, and other considerations, had left undetermined the precise sums eventually to be involved and how these transfers were to be effected without creating havoc for the conquered countries. Postwar negotiations were to have tackled those technical questions expeditiously. That the United States was not seeking war reparations, whereas France and the United Kingdom were too weak to press for substantial transfers, also played a role in setting up the asymmetric negotiating positions that prevailed after the war and that led to so much inter-Allied acrimony.

Reasons for seeking compensation for war damage varied. The economic objectives are touched upon in section 1.2. But there were also strategic and political considerations. Strategic justifications included the deliberate weakening of the erstwhile enemy, which the Soviet Union saw being accomplished primarily through effecting punishing war reparations. The Western allies preferred exercising control over the activities of the German administration rather than transferring wealth. If the Anglo-American alliance sought to support the Soviet economy during World War II, it was certainly not keen on prolonging it for very long thereafter. Churchill particularly was averse to buttressing the Stalin regime through large-scale economic support without obtaining concessions on European and, indeed, global cooperation. Political reasons should also be mentioned. The retribution that could be exacted for the damages sustained during the war was felt to be an almost self-evident aspect of peace settlements. Of course, what may have been politically expedient during hostilities ceased to be so in peacetime.

1.1.4 The challenge of the Marshall Plan

Steering the European economies back toward a civilian development track with full employment was one critical policy objective. Its rationale derived not only from the fact that sustained growth was deemed beneficial in itself but was also stressed as an alternative to the ruinous deflationary and beggar-thy-neighbor policies of the 1930s, which undoubtedly contributed to the rise of Nazi Germany and eventually to the outbreak of the war. The ability of the European countries to eliminate the war damage, to quickly restore a civilian economic setting, and to generate an autonomous economic dynamism sufficient to sustain the pace of recovery and economic development on the basis of own resources proved to be much more delicate assignments.

Under the circumstances, the US government saw no alternative but to engage in large-scale economic aid. While this served economic and strategic concerns, such aid also had a prominent political dimension in that it laid the foundation for the Atlantic Alliance, the formation of the North Atlantic Treaty Organization (NATO) and the ensuing military-strategic cooperation. Furthermore, aid created a degree of economic interdependence around the US economy from which it would be difficult to escape without incurring substantial adjustment costs. One option then entertained under various guises was to grant economic aid that would yield the greatest economic stimulus to recipient economies while simultaneously avoiding overburdening the US economy. This was essentially the concept underlying the Marshall Plan; that is, energizing the European economies by letting individual governments formulate a development plan with an external deficit financed through capital inflows from the United States.

Whether the Marshall Plan was originally intended to permit full-scale and equal participation of the Soviet Union and its allies is a matter still being debated by historians and diplomatic scholars (see Lundestad, 1986, and other papers in Harberl and Niethammer, 1986). No one denies that Eastern European governments were invited to participate in the concep-tualization of the Marshall Plan, that the Soviet Union took part in some of these deliberations, that especially Czechoslovakia, Hungary and Poland had expressed interest in participating, and that ultimately the Soviet Union was instrumental in the boycotting of the Paris conference, an action that, in fact, sealed the division of Europe into two parts with distinct ideological, economic, political and strategic ambitions.

The most frequently cited argument in the discussion about what led to the CMEA's creation derives from a basic incompatibility between the Marshall Plan and Soviet policy with respect to Eastern Europe. That is to say, Eastern Europe's fundamental interest in participating in the American-backed European recovery program (ERP) conflicted with Soviet objectives. Stalin's aims for Eastern Europe and his objectives with respect to the most desirable course of postwar development were irrecon-cilable with a large-scale American presence in Europe. In all this it is important to recall that when the US secretary of state, George C. Marshall, announced the program for the reconstruction of Europe with American aid on 5 June 1947, Stalin's stranglehold over Eastern Europe had not yet been completed and certainly not yet perfected. For example, the dominating influence of the Communist Parties (CPs), or the Popular Front coalitions, had not yet reached the level of final takeover and undivided subservience to Soviet policies, particularly not in Central Europe. Moreover, the actual position of the political leadership in those countries where political power had already been usurped by left-wing coalitions was still unsteady (by no means as monolithic as it was soon to become) and certainly not as supine to Soviet demands as would become the case a few years hence. In any event, the people's democracies could hardly be considered submissive vassals, entirely subservient to Stalin's pervasive influence.

1.1.5 Political mutations in Eastern Europe

By the end of World War II, the Soviet army had gained supreme influence throughout Eastern Europe, except in Albania and Yugoslavia. In the wake of this influence came shaky political coalitions and alliances, all of which had a more or less vibrant CP wing. In some cases, this leftish branch was homegrown as a result of resistance efforts during the war. In other instances, most notably in the later GDR and Poland, the political leadership-to-be had been raised in the Soviet Union, in some cases within the context of the (Third) Communist International (Comintern).

Whether Stalin had hatched a clear-cut plan regarding the future of postwar Eastern Europe is a matter on which the historical record is unclear and specialist opinion diverges widely. Some contend that Stalin had formulated a master plan, which he succeeded in implementing gradually (see Carrère d'Encausse, 1985). But many other observers emphasize that, though Stalin desired greater security for the Soviet Union, he had not decided how this could best be accomplished in terms of a *cordon sanitaire* on the western flank. By the late 1940s, however, little doubt remained about Stalin's penchant for securing a high degree of Soviet influence in these countries. But he had no particular desire to integrate the Eastern European countries individually or as a group into the Soviet federation as autonomous republics, even though some of these weak partners, including Bulgaria and Yugoslavia in 1945–6, may have aspired to this exalted status.

The jockeying for power in the bloc continued in the late 1940s. Also, inside the USSR forces were at work that sought to come to grips with an eventual rejuvenation of the Soviet-dominated economies. Is it possible that Stalin was deceived by his protégés when they formulated their case for Eastern European cooperation? Michael C. Kaser (1967, pp. 9ff.) has speculated most interestingly on such a possibility. He maintains that the CMEA's founding resulted from an enterprising move by Nikolaj A. Voznesenskij, then Gosplan chairman, and his supporters, who tended to be sympathetic to allocating a greater technical role to economic policy instruments and institutions. Once he was removed from office as the chief Soviet planner in early 1949, Stalin, according to Kaser, simply weakened the Council into impotence. Using this information, Peter Wiles (1968, p. 313) rationalized the CMEA as a 'carryover from the aggressive, expansionist, forward-looking policy of A. A. Ždanov, who had supported a forward, "Leningrad-type" policy in Europe and treated the [CPs] of both Eastern and Western Europe as responsible, semi-independent, agents.' He concludes that the CMEA was the last fling of the Ždanov-Voznesenskij policy, and that 'Stalin found himself saddled with an organ he had indeed allowed to be born, but could not personally work with.'

This is reading at the same time too much and too little into Kaser's careful reconstruction of what might have prompted the CMEA's foundation. Of course, it is quite legitimate to try to explain past history by subsequent events if information on the latter is ampler than on the former, which it most certainly is with the CMEA. But it seems futile to explain the origins of the CMEA by its inactivity up to 1954. Indeed, the question of why the

Council for all practical purposes did not function in the early years of its existence is quite different – at least it may be quite distinct – from that of why it was established at all, except in the trivial case in which it was set up not to function. The limited documentary evidence that is available, and which I shall examine in some detail in section 1.2 and chapter 2, does not corroborate the speculation that such a motive prevailed in early 1949.

1.1.6 The Yugoslav affair and propaganda

The conflict between Stalin and Tito was a most serious, fundamental one, fought largely on doctrinal and ideological grounds. But that overt scenario, in fact, emanated from conditions steeped in power politics. As the only country of Eastern Europe to liberate itself from fascism after having incurred great material and human losses during World War II, Tito saw no particular reason for emulating in economics and politics a path that was solely dictated by the economic, ideological and political interests of the USSR. In 1945–6, certainly, he might have bowed to such dictates simply by virtue of the terms of reference of communist international solidarity under Soviet 'democratic centralism.' But by 1947–8, this option had been downgraded as a result of real-life experience, including the actual needs of a country embarking on its own road to economic development and needs for societal organization. The Yugoslav affair touched the heart of as-yet-untested and uncharted questions pertaining to relations among nominally sovereign communist countries. Would dissent be tolerated? Or would there have to be widespread uniformity in economic affairs, perhaps to such an extent that the creation of a common organization, such as the CMEA, would become essential?

The Tito–Stalin rift also had a propaganda aspect. The CMEA could have been used to demonstrate an alleged unity in the socialist camp by creating an economic equivalent to the Communist Information Bureau (Cominform, founded in 1947). A concerted offensive to deny economic assistance and even ordinary trade of essential goods and services to undermine the Yugoslav economy may initially have been one of the principal rationales that led to the creation of the CMEA. But it cannot have been the sole motivation for setting up a common regional economic organization. The Yugoslav affair's share in the diverse considerations that contributed to the decision to initiate the CMEA is thus rather nebulous. Beyond doubt, however, is that the conflict with Yugoslavia halted all initial plans and endeavors for multilateral economic cooperation in the region.

1.1.7 Eastern European regionalism

During and after the war, several of the Eastern European countries hatched schemes for postwar regional economic cooperation in the context of federations, confederations, economic unions or other constitutional frameworks. The best-known examples are the Czechoslovak-Polish confederal or federal plans and the Balkan federation schemes, which consisted of various combinations among Albania, Bulgaria, Greece, Rumania, Turkey and Yugoslavia. The most important of the many Balkan plans, at least for our purposes here, was the Bulgarian-Yugoslav scheme that, in some of its versions, also envisaged the 'integration' of Albania in one way or another.

There was a central political component of these plans that derived from the demonstrated need to strengthen the framework within which the Eastern European countries might safeguard their political independence and enhance their fortunes through groupwide cooperation. These plans may have been the most important determinant of the concerns about regionalizing Central Europe. Stalin's nipping these efforts in the bud, as shown in section 1.2, may have stimulated the creation of an alternative political framework – perhaps the CMEA. Although thus political in nature, the CMEA could in fact have markedly strengthened the focus of regionalization as the key channel for pursuing other endeavors.

Most of these political factors may have played some role in the deliberations of late 1948 and early 1949. The Yugoslav affair, the Marshall Plan debacle, and frustrated federation or confederation plans may have elevated the need for an overt demonstration of political and economic unity to the critical-threshold level. But one must look beyond the preemptive political arguments to explain the creation and early activities of the CMEA. The economic component particularly has been left out of the traditional treatment of the CMEA's origins. Its importance will be assessed after presenting key pointers of the economic situation that prevailed at the time and of the industrialization and more general economic growth aspirations that were harbored by many of these countries.

1.2 ECONOMIC ASPECTS OF COOPERATION IN THE 1940s

The most significant topics that may have had a marked bearing on the birth of the CMEA in January 1949 can be grouped under the following headings:

1. Postwar reconstruction and development.
2. Trade patterns and economic aid.
3. Regional economic cooperation.
4. Trade and financial relations.
5. Countering the Western policy stances on economic embargo and sanctions.
6. Isolating Yugoslavia and thus reinforcing cohesion within the group.

1.2.1 Postwar reconstruction and development

The destruction wrought by World War II and by the immediate postwar adjustments in the sociopolitical landscape bequeathed to Eastern Europe a legacy perhaps much worse than that received by Western Europe. With the exception of Czechoslovakia, these countries were not well developed or even moderately industrialized, and they did not normally have fully integrated domestic markets. Furthermore, special problems had to be faced because these countries had to grapple with a burdensome, unskilled agricultural overpopulation in order to secure per capita economic growth and forestall a repetition of the turbulent events that had been characteristic of the interwar period. By themselves these legacies of prewar economic and related developments constituted a major inducement for the creation of institutions with sufficient power to initiate an embryonic form of regional economic integration (see Hertz, 1947; Marczewski, 1956, pp. 13ff.), possibly while concurrently seeking economic assistance from abroad. The prospect of obtaining foreign economic aid, such as ERP, provided an attractive injection of incentives for setting the backward economies in motion and reequilibrating those still suffering from structural imbalances. The cost of economic stabilization and of stimulating positive per capita income growth could in this way have been reduced to a more tolerable level than had growth been secured exclusively on the basis of native resources.

Whatever the political foils wielded to force the Eastern European countries into declining ERP, the initial enthusiasm of much of Eastern Europe proper for it was based not only, and perhaps not mainly, on political calculation. They also wished to speed up the process of economic recovery and accelerate the pace of economic development. A quick solution to their urgent economic needs required large-scale aid, possibly from the USSR.

Aside from the immediate urge to reactivate their economies, the more fundamental reality of Eastern European economic underdevelopment at the time should not be neglected, as it so often is in the CMEA literature. The interwar period had not been productive, particularly when placed in the context of regional cooperation and normalization of animated controversies that had been inherited from the past. These disputes had prevented the emergence of a regional effort to overcome the dislocations caused by World War I and its aftermath or to counter subsequent economic crises.

Certainly, the Eastern European countries were by and large competitors not only in terms of exports but also for resource outflows. As a result, during the interwar period, Central European countries traded more with Western Europe than among themselves. Some kind of triangular complementarity had been established among Central Europe, the Balkan states and Western Europe, but this level of economic interaction fell far short of what could have been achieved by a comprehensive endeavor to elaborate regional economic integration. It might therefore be reasonably expected that, as a result of the postwar fusion of the Eastern European countries into a single polity, the region's former international trade could have taken the form largely of intragroup trade, governed from a single center, with as much mobility of capital and labor as the costs of structural redeployment permitted or defense considerations justified.

1.2.2 Trade patterns and economic aid

Whatever the political conditions within which the Eastern European countries were forced to unfold their postwar identity and development, it is beyond doubt that they were ultimately sucked into the Soviet orbit. Growing isolation from and Stalin's paranoia toward the West inhibited the newly won 'partners' from resuming their prewar patterns of trade and economic relations. Yet, without such commercial and other economic ties with the outside world, these countries could not resume normal economic activity; they certainly could not have hoped to overcome the basic roots of their economic underdevelopment by themselves.

It should be recalled that a large share of the prewar trade of these countries was cleared in particular with the German Reich. At the end of the war, a political and economic vacuum was left that neither Germany nor the West could fill, and that, under the circumstances, the Soviet Union was all too willing and eager to exploit. In short, the USSR helped relieve the desperate shortage of food by loans of grain and other foodstuffs, provided other consumer goods and concluded trade agreements that secured the supply of raw materials and other essentials in exchange for whatever Eastern Europe had to offer. For the countries concerned, at that time their only alternative to the Soviet offer was no trade at all.

These initial trade agreements and loans, however, had been concluded to meet immediate requirements – not as the beginning of a comprehensive program of economic cooperation. They did not lead to a firm continuation of ties in the form of regular trade exchanges. For example, in 1947–8 the Soviet share of Czechoslovakia's, Hungary's and Poland's trade had fallen – it was just over 30 percent – and tended to decline further as trade with the West resumed and rapidly accelerated. If the USSR also wished to maintain its exclusive position in the economic domain, it would have to launch a meaningful alternative.

The need for changing gears became particularly urgent during 1947 when the prospect of maintaining supremacy over the region tended to be frustrated by the ERP's attractiveness. The Soviet Union had to provide a palliative. To pacify Eastern Europe, it made a series of gestures that included renegotiating credit agreements with Bulgaria, Czechoslovakia and Yugoslavia; writing off half of the Hungarian and Rumanian reparation debts; and initiating other measures that contributed to the easing of external payments pressures and generated popular goodwill toward the new political regimes.

1.2.3 Regional economic cooperation

Because the Eastern European countries are basically more competitive than complementary, most observers have looked skeptically at the usefulness of integrating them. However, several cogent arguments justify the expectation that an integrated regional economic policy could have exerted a more positive influence on the process of industrializing and restructuring the area. First, it is not immediately obvious why the competitive nature of most Eastern European countries, their different levels of development and the relative scarcity of basic primary raw materials and fuels in their domestic resource base should necessarily obviate positive results from cooperative efforts. The opportunities for intragroup cooperation were potentially considerable. The significant scope for gains from trade creation (that is, a rise in trade participation by substituting imports for high-cost domestic production) because of scale economies should have outweighed the disadvantages of anchoring regional cooperation primarily to trade diversion (that is, relocation of trade from low-cost third markets to intragroup relations). In particular this was to be expected in the postwar constellation of forces and the determination by leaders to foster industrialization as a remedy for disequilibriums.

Second, ever since the breakup of the Austro-Hungarian empire various proposals for regional economic integration in Eastern Europe had been launched. During and immediately after the war several such schemes were already in an advanced stage of preparation. One should recall, for instance, the then very topical Czechoslovak-Polish cooperation plan and the various alternatives for a Balkan federation. Clearly, the aims of many of these proposals, particularly those around the so-called *intermarium* idea (Meiß-ner, 1966) of constructing an integrated Central Europe as a wedge between Germany and the Soviet Union, surpassed pure economics. But the anticipated salutary economic effects were central to the debates; indeed, they had first been broached on the eve of World War II when Poland was directly threatened by the surrounding powers. That attempts to test the usefulness of these proposals were short-circuited, mainly as a result of the USSR's meddling, should not detract us from the high expectations that governments had placed on such channels for forging durable economic progress. Some of these intended unions were based on sound principles and could have led to quite a different pattern of development than the one actually pursued after the war.

The economic and political initiatives mooted in the aftermath of World War II had given rise to newly conceived projects, some of which had advanced to the preliminary agreement stage. Such projects promised a radical change in the trend toward autarky that tended to mar postwar recovery and growth. The negotiations held out bright prospects for sound economic growth not only for countries with limited natural resources but also for those that would waste scarce resources if parallel structural developments occurred. It was hoped that economic integration would enable each country to concentrate on developing those sectors best suited to its prevailing conditions and to attain high technical competence while relying on more extensive trading markets.

But, as with the desire to join the Marshall Plan or Western integration schemes, efforts designed to promote integration and regionalism without the USSR were prematurely scrapped, apparently on Stalin's personal orders. Stalin intensely distrusted the intentions of the Eastern European countries and feared that their economic strength through cooperation might lead to an anti-Soviet bulwark. Indeed, a regional effort to solve their most urgent shared problems without Soviet tutelage might have undermined the USSR's long-term interests in exercising its hegemony over Eastern Europe. Would a regional policy with the USSR then offer an alternative? Most observers refute this as a plausible scenario on the grounds that Stalin did not wish a regional economic policy. As Wiles (1968, p. 3) notes, 'His whole object was to hold the satellites down, but at arm's length. Unreliable and westernized, they must not be allowed too close.' That is also why Stalin balked at outright annexation, for which the USSR had the power but perhaps not the will, and why he forced each country to pursue autarky. I do not find this line of thought very convincing as an explanation of what occurred in late 1948 and early 1949, but it conceivably helps to explain other aspects of the CMEA's history until the mid-1950s.

1.2.4 Trade and financial relations

Some observers have indirectly stressed the parallel between the economics of the CMEA and the political purposes of the Cominform (see section 1.1). That is, that the main objective of the CMEA was the integration of Eastern Europe into a solid economic bloc or the creation of a *Großraumwirtschaft*, just as the Cominform had been set up to enforce ideological and political unity among the CPs. It is certain that the Cominform had been set up as a response to the challenge presented by the phase of mainly political diversity. The socialist bloc could only be tightened by placing greater emphasis on all-around unity, and this could hardly be secured in the political sphere if economic matters proceeded unchecked. It is likely that one of the goals of the Cominform concerned economic affairs. Whether or not in early 1947 Stalin intended to replace the bilateral treaties by a full-fledged, but gradual integration scheme to be patterned along the basic lines of the Cominform in political affairs has so far remained an unconfirmed speculation.

1.2.5 East-West embargo and sanctions

In 1948 perhaps the most central stimulus for establishing a common economic agency was provided by the growing open antagonisms between

East and West. In addition to the problems of adverse trade trends and the attractiveness of sizable US economic aid, the Soviet Union had to overcome Eastern European tensions that stemmed from Soviet intervention in both regional integration and interregional cooperation plans. Under these circumstances, then, it seems logical to expect that a program for mutual economic cooperation would have been launched, possibly under the supervision of the Cominform.[6] Two further factors, the Yugoslav affair and the emerging embargo under US prodding, must have further exacerbated these conflicts.

Yugoslavia's expulsion occurred suddenly in late June 1948 after a secret but nonetheless protracted and bitter debate on the possible roads to socialism. After the other Eastern European countries firmly joined the Soviet position denouncing Marshall aid and supporting the Berlin blockade, the West reinforced the isolation of Eastern Europe by boycotting economic relations, enforcing the initial stages of the strategic embargo that has been extant since 1948 and prohibiting capital exports. As of 1 March 1948, all American exports to Europe were subject to government licensing. The scope of the boycott was extended on 3 April 1948 by the statutes of the Marshall Plan. The participants of the ERP and the Organization of European Economic Co-operation (OEEC), which was founded as the key organ for fostering smooth Marshall Plan assistance, could not trade with Eastern Europe goods forbidden or subject to controls in the United States. This policy was formalized later with the creation of the Coordinating Committee for Multilateral Trade Controls (CoCom). The immediate impact of the West's retaliations affected the smaller Eastern European countries – particularly Czechoslovakia, Hungary and Poland, which still heavily relied on trade with the West – much more vitally than they could ever possibly have hurt the Soviet economy. This provides one additional argument favoring a more positive approach toward the elaboration of a regional economic policy and a common organization to administer it. Mutual assistance could also have been provided through channels other than those of a formalized regional apparatus.

Both developments most likely brought added pressure on the Soviet Union to take measures beyond those intrinsically available in an interparty agency such as the Cominform. Eastern European commentators argue that the Western boycott and export embargo were instrumental in spurring the creation of the CMEA. They fail to explain, though, that this position for Stalin and his protégés did little to ease Eastern Europe's economic problems. All it initially accomplished was a compression of trade and its diversion to the Soviet orbit. Although the West's beginning economic warfare was a welcome argument that fueled Soviet propaganda and strengthened the display of papered-up unity exhibited by the foundation of the CMEA, it hardly justified the creation of a common economic organization.

1.2.6 The isolation of Yugoslavia and strengthening economic cohesion

As a means of enhancing Eastern European resistance to the West's economic warfare and supporting the political isolation of Yugoslavia – and eventually bringing it back into the Soviet fold through economic pressures – the CMEA could also have had a third purpose, namely, the strengthening of groupwide economic cohesion with the explicit purpose of fostering economic growth within the group. As such it could have provided a platform far superior to the by-then-common bilateral trade and payments agreements (BTPAs). It would also have offered a more suitable alternative to the crude exploitation of Eastern Europe's resources. As a result of reparation claims, control over key activities, such as through the 'mixed' or joint-stock companies (JSCs), dismantling of factories on a large scale and regular trade agreements, the USSR sought to acquire a dominant position in the trade of Eastern European countries and managed to further strengthen its already paramount role in the region's policies, including in economic matters.

Admittedly, the above arguments fail to solve fully the riddle of why the CMEA was established. Obviously, political motivations inspired by the need to demonstrate unity against Western policies were of overwhelming importance. But the subsequent isolation of the communist world and the embargo imposed partly as a result of the Berlin blockade seem to strengthen the economic arguments for the gradual elaboration of a common regional economic policy for Eastern Europe, including the USSR. That economic issues were instrumental causes in the creation of the CMEA, or that they were at least as important as the political considerations associated with that action, does not represent the traditional approach to rationalizing the CMEA's foundation. That these played an important role in the early debates will be detailed in chapter 2. First, however, two other problems of historical fact must be settled.

1.3 THE FOUNDING DATE AND CONFERENCES ON THE CREATION OF THE CMEA

One might think that such a trivial question as the exact date the CMEA was founded could be unambiguously established. Unfortunately this is not the case and it is by no means clear why this is so. In and of itself, the founding date may seem an unimportant bit of information. But because of the conflicting interpretations of what in fact took place and when in 1949 and 1950, it is by no means superfluous to scrutinize the record once again in an attempt to reach at least minimal consensus. This will be important for my reconstruction in chapter 2 of the various fundamental economic aspects underlying the CMEA's creation.

The literature abounds with a variety of specifications of the CMEA's founding date (see Brabant, 1974a, pp. 192–3; Brabant, 1987a, pp. 31–2). Simple reasoning and an arbitrary proposition may help to dispose of the matter until an official inside history of largely intramural events becomes available. For now, we cannot specify a precise founding date because none can be ascertained from the genuine documentary evidence available.

It is public record that the communiqué announcing the CMEA's creation was published in all main Communist Party papers of 25 January 1949 (see *Pravda*, 25 January 1949, p. 1). The most satisfactory interim solution for the problem at hand, then, would be to accept this timing as the CMEA's founding date. Alternatively, one could accept the first conference (Moscow, 5–8 January 1949) known to have discussed the creation of the CMEA as setting the founding date. This would point to 5 January 1949, as most accounts of the events suggest that the participants were presented with a *fait accompli*, although Party and government officials were not entirely ignorant of the imminent formation of the CMEA. Information then diverges on substantive matters (see chapter 2). To the extent that the conference was a genuine deliberative meeting, as some commentators have suggested, the founding date would be the closing day, or 8 January 1949, as that was when the conference documents were adopted.

As to what actually took place between the end of the conference and the publication date of the communiqué, to the best of my knowledge no single satisfactory explanation has thus far been offered.[7] It is important to recall that the conference was attended mostly by the chief planners of the founding countries. Although some of the top political leadership participated in the Moscow meeting as well, formal approval may have required national ratification. It may be that between 8 and 25 January 1949 further political consultations on the plans for the creation of the CMEA took place. Or was it from the very beginning thought best not to divulge anything about the Council? According to M. Kaser this conference was characterized by so much disunity about the Council's functions and tasks that it was deemed useful to discreetly omit a founding date so as to mislead the outside world into believing the CMEA was unanimously acclaimed. Though this could still have provided a propaganda stunt and the sought declaration of unity in economic and other affairs, such objectives could have been achieved more easily by means other than delaying the founding communiqué's publication.

Because the concept of groupwide economic integration presented in January 1949 had not been thoroughly prepared, it is not surprising that key points of the project were left open for further discussion. There are some indications of secret (Kaser, 1966, p. 816) and other meetings (Čížkovský, 1970, 1971) that help to clarify the issues at stake. Before looking at them, however, a word on a secret treaty that was allegedly endorsed in January 1949.

1.4 THE PURPORTED TREATY OF CMEA COOPERATION

A number of the early Western sources dealing with the Eastern European cooperation movement (see Brabant, 1974a, pp. 196–7) mention the existence of some type of wide-ranging economic pact that the CMEA members signed on 18 January 1949, following their earlier summit, but apparently never ratified. This is said to have been concluded among the six Eastern European countries (Bulgaria, Czechoslovakia, Hungary, Poland, Rumania and the Soviet Union) that attended the January conference, signed the conference documents and endorsed the publication of the communiqué that disclosed the establishment of the Council. Until recently the available evidence was too conjectural to confirm that such a far-reaching comprehensive economic pact was negotiated or even seriously contemplated and that it had been decided to keep it secret.

Apparent agreement has now surfaced.[8] Whether the document is a genuine copy of the treaty, simply a hoax perpetrated on the US foreign service or a sham invented by a government agency will not be examined here. In the next paragraphs, I examine the salient features of the document and place it in its proper context.

1.4.1 Original purposes of CMEA cooperation

The Council's founders apparently contracted to create the common economic organization initially for a period of twenty years, starting 18 January 1949. Without explicit abrogation, the agreement would automatically be extended for another decade. This regional institution was to formulate a common economic plan for the harmonious development of the entire region, including the USSR, and the creation of far-reaching complementarity in economic profiles, planning approaches and supporting institutions. For those purposes, the Council was endowed with plenipotentiary economic powers.

The Council was to help dovetail the member economies through joint firms, especially so as to boost regional output of fuels, energy and basic raw materials from newly discovered deposits. The goal was to accelerate supplies of essential inputs for the region's industrialization. Through joint companies and the coordination of national economic plans, the Council was to promote standardization and regional complementarities, presumably to take advantage of economies of scale. Exchange of scientific and technical information and promotion of capital flows, including direct investments, were also to play an active role in bringing about harmonious growth anchored to industrialization. Initially, accommodation would be sought for whatever goods and services the member countries had to offer to the rest of the region.

1.4.2 The organization of regional cooperation

Organizationally, the Council would consist of a Secretariat General in Moscow endowed with its own fund, to be contributed by 1 April 1949, of 100 million rubles.[9] Half would be financed by the Soviet Union, with the remainder coming from equal shares by the other founder members. Subscriptions could be contributed in gold, freely convertible currencies or rubles (presumably applying only to the Soviet Union). The Secretariat General would be the executive arm of the Council Session – the highest organ of the organization. The Session's principal task would be to discuss the economic situation of each member separately and its relationships with the rest of the Council. It could be convened whenever warranted for ensuring smooth progress toward regional integration, but not less than quarterly. Any member could request an out-of-sequence convocation at any time. Meetings would be held in rotation in the various member countries in alphabetic order according to the Cyrillic alphabet of the country names.

Starting in 1950, the national economic development plans of the members would be drawn up in full conformity with the Council's advice. In the interim, members agreed to adapt their plans to the extent possible to regional requirements according to the Secretariat General's advice. This would apply particularly to investment decisions for which the then-operative plans still left some room for maneuvering. Its main purpose was to shorten the transition period toward a uniform approach to industrialization, which was to be fully in place by early 1950. Each member would be obliged to cooperate fully with the Council by making available all relevant statistical and other information as well as pertinent documents to permit timely policy initiatives and responses by the Council and the Secretariat General. Each member would at least have to furnish monthly reports documenting evidence of its economic and financial situation for the preceding month. This information would also be accessible to observers and technicians chosen by the Council to carry out fact-finding missions in any signatory country. Such investigations could be proposed by the Secretariat General, the Council Session or at the request of the member in question. The Secretariat General could accept any decision, subject only to ratification by the Council Session at its first subsequent meeting.

1.4.3 Supranational planning and regional economic cooperation

There is nothing in the document to indicate that the Council would be anything but a supranational organization in charge of enhancing regional economic interdependence by means of a common economic plan drawn up on the basis of instructions handed down by the Council Session and its Secretariat General to the national planning agencies of the individual members. The Secretariat General would in fact be a regional planning agency with full access to pertinent information and wide-ranging decision-making powers, subject only to approval by the formal Council Session. Although some of the formulations are notably vague, this planning agency would be entrusted with decision-making latitude and control powers that considerably transcend the authority normally vested with the national planning agencies. Its stature would also be enhanced because the relationship between the Secretariat General and the Session was inherently different from that between the national planning agencies and the respective government or CP level. Or was it assumed that overall decision-making authority would be entrusted to the Soviet Union or the Cominform to ensure political supremacy over economic affairs? The Council Session would chart overall policy for the region, formulate the key strategic goals of integration and translate them into concrete operative plan targets worked out by the Secretariat General in cooperation with the subordinate national planning agencies.

1.4.4 The fate of the treaty

The tasks stipulated in *Protocol* were never implemented, and the Council did not get off the ground in the way possibly envisaged at that early stage. Rather than drafting comprehensive development plans and welding the diverse interests of the members into operational development goals and instruments, the Council organs confined themselves to the preparation of a few mechanisms by which better coordination of national economic and trade policies could be secured.

But the actual course of events starting in late 1949 or early 1950 approximates rather closely what was apparently charted in *Protocol* if the general statements referring to the Secretariat General and Council are simply replaced by Gosplan and the Soviet Union's Politburo. Once the Eastern European countries were firmly ensconced in the Soviet orbit, and the Korean conflict galvanized whatever different approaches to industrialization still persisted in 1949–50, the Soviet Union closely supervised the region's economic policy. In fact, substantial components of national economic planning were entrusted to Soviet advisers and technicians primarily through the so-called Soviet embassy system of CMEA cooperation. Soviet advisers prevailed as well in the CMEA organization and national planning agencies.

1.5 THE FOUNDING TREATY AND THE COUNCIL'S CREATION IN RETROSPECT

Why was the treaty not enacted and why did SEI fail to take off until at least a decade later than originally planned, and then under quite different conditions? Recalling that the majority of the representatives of the smaller Eastern European countries at the founding conference were economic chiefs who were still clamoring for control over their economies, it is improbable that the Moscow conferees could have definitely settled the crucial issue at stake or that they were empowered to transfer a substantial component of their countries' economic and political sovereignty. The documents elaborated in Moscow were probably preliminary drafts that had to be approved by chief national policymakers and possibly formally ratified according to national parliamentary procedures. Were the agreements hammered out in principle by economists partially or entirely disowned by one or more CP heads? If so, this might help to explain the slow start and quick abandonment of the integration process. Or did the policymakers approve the agreement and mandate their ambassadors in Moscow to sign *Protocol* on 18 January? If so, what provoked the critical short circuit?

Until archives are opened up, these questions will remain. But it should be noted that *Protocol* is unusually incomplete. Certainly, the actual course of socialist economic cooperation has frequently deviated from legally contracted obligations if actual needs conflict with a course of action charted in a comprehensive formal or informal agreement. Incomplete as it was, the agreement could have formed the backbone of regional economic cooperation. It is, however, a fact that these countries generally prefer to draw up legal agreements that place the document in its proper international setting, stipulate the salient points of agreement and provide sufficient details regarding the intended functioning of the organs thereby established. These are now missing. Could *Protocol* have been an incomplete draft?

Although notably vague about organizational and substantive matters, surprisingly, the document discloses details about common funding and rules – an item usually omitted from published agreements – but does not amplify on the purpose(s) of the ruble fund, which would have been too large for operational expenses. But the ruble fund would have been far too small to permit the Secretariat General to exert a direct influence over investment strategies, which would have been superfluous in view of its virtually complete control over the member countries' appropriations. Even if confined to the establishment of joint companies, could such a meager endowment have exerted a major role in charting integration?

Could the fund have been intended as a ruble currency zone, paralleling the West's International Monetary Fund (IMF), with its prime goal being the financing of trade disequilibriums? Kaser (1967, p. 48) contends that the fund would have provided 'a reasonable lubricant for multilateralism,' although it could have financed at most 0.5 percent of the regional (except GDR) trade volume in 1949 and about 12 percent of half the sum of year-end absolute bilateral imbalances. Nonetheless, it might have constituted a useful starting point for farther-reaching cooperation endeavors in subsequent years, including a radical departure from the strictly bilateralized trade system.

Did the 1949 purported treaty embody elements of SEI that, if implemented, would have benefited the regional cooperation endeavors of the European CPEs? Because *Protocol* provided precisely for a counterpart at the regional level of the national planning offices, even though these had by that time not yet reached the all-powerful position they would assume beginning in the early 1950s, the answer is an unambiguous yes. Whether one advocates central planning or not is, of course, a different issue from ascertaining congruence between what is intended and what can be carried out. A regional planning institute would have constituted the element that, in retrospect, has been missing from CMEA cooperation ever since the organization was created.

NOTES

1. I myself have occasionally engaged in this type of analysis (see Brabant, 1974a, 1976, 1979a, 1980, 1987a) if only to make up in part for the widespread apathy in the profession, in East and West alike.
2. I for one have failed to obtain even permission in principle to access that source.
3. All quotes are from Churchill's address as reproduced in the *New York Times*, 6 March 1946, p. 1.
4. Yugoslavia was the only country that emerged from the war with a well-established, homegrown resistance movement that had made it to the apex of political power before the Soviet army 'liberated' the rest of Eastern Europe.
5. This is the issue of taking away part of the wealth of one country in favor of another through the generation of export revenues. The problem consists in the effects of such a transaction, if possible at all, on the productive capacity and competitiveness of both the country of transfer and the beneficiary.
6. Rudolf Slánský, then Czechoslovakia's CP General Secretary, reportedly proposed at the first session of the Cominform in September 1947 that such a task be entrusted to that organ, but he was apparently rebuffed (Sláma, 1979, p. 25).
7. A very interesting story about the founding of the CMEA was recently published in an interview in *Polityka* (see Rózański, 1987). Other useful renditions are Kaplan, 1977, 1978, 1979.
8. For details, see Brabant, 1979a, which also contains my English rendition of the treaty (pp. 263–5). In what follows, I shall refer to the treaty as *Protocol*.
9. At the official exchange rate then in force the fund would have amounted to about $18.9 million (pre-1971 US dollars). At the rate introduced in March 1950, it would have equaled some $25 million if all contributions had first been converted into rubles.

2 · CREATION OF THE CMEA AND ITS INITIAL AGENDA

Public knowledge of the circumstances surrounding the creation of the CMEA, as noted in chapter 1, is still very sketchy. Twenty years after the creation of the Council in 1967, it was revealed for the first time (Faddeev, 1976), in less oblique terms than those of the founding communiqué, that a high-level conference of the six founder countries had taken place in Moscow from 5–8 January 1949. It also disclosed that the meeting had adopted a number of documents and agreements, including on the Council's organization, its fundamental purposes and procedures and its role in protecting the cooperating countries directly or indirectly against outside interference.

The literature remains ambiguous about whether the actions taken in early 1949 can formally be equated with the Council's statutes or an early version of the charter that was finally endorsed in 1959. The founding communiqué published in January 1949 was the only policy document released until the emergence of the discussions around the endorsement of a formal charter and broadly based policy guidelines for the ISDL in the late 1950s (see chapter 3) and early 1960s (see chapter 4). But a strong case can be made that the members sought a more rounded organizational infrastructure, including early statutes, and that they engaged in more substantive deliberations than is usually admitted in the literature.

Before clarifying the early debates, I justify in section 2.1 why I emphasize the need for a concerted effort directed at clarifying the early history of the CMEA. Section 2.2 sets forth the key negotiations of the period. The major points of the debate are summarized in section 2.3. Section 2.4 looks at the programs then adopted. The roles of plan coordination and joint planning during that early phase are highlighted in section 2.5. Section 2.6 examines the indirect instruments of economic coordination and their supporting institutions that were then integral components of the deliberations. The final section indicates many of the factors that contributed to the cessation of discussions about regional integration and to the Council's dormancy over the next decade.

2.1 THE FOUNDING YEARS AS HISTORY

Nothing of the known activities of the Council until about the late 1950s indicates that the organization played any substantive role in charting the course of each country's economic development, in organizing the trade that the countries chose to engage in or in stimulating regional specialization beyond the requirements, including intended exports, of the individual producer in isolation, except on a strictly *ad hoc* basis (such as in the case of ball bearings). Yet a careful analysis of secondary sources on the Council's early activities suggests that, roughly from April 1949 until at least mid-1950, the members engaged in technical negotiations about the possibilities of SEI and in what ways this should be fostered. Had those early debates on the wherewithal of SEI been successfully concluded, the Council might have been transformed into a genuine institution, one entrusted with fostering regional economic integration as defined in the introduction to this work.

Without hindsight it is still difficult to clarify the early negotiations and assess their impact on the subsequent course of SEI. This is so because the sources, scanty as they unfortunately are, present conflicting facts and contradictory interpretations, often to suit contemporaneous sociopolitical currents. The seeming logic that I impart to the sequence of debates may well amount to reading too much into the disparate pieces of concrete information. Nonetheless, I consider it useful to highlight these features, if only because CMEA developments from the mid-1960s to recent transformations hark back to the debates in 1949–50 on the instruments and policies of indirect coordination of decision making and their supporting institutions. The similarities are more than casual, for in these endeavors to embrace new forms of economic cooperation among the CPEs 'we find nonetheless a first attempt [*Ansatz*] at solutions that were later set as goals on bi- and multilateral CMEA levels' (Neumann, 1980, p. 18).

Gerd Neumann's position is not generally supported in the specialized literature on the grounds, at best, that something that failed may be of historical interest but cannot contribute much to the current debates on integration. I disagree. Though it is admittedly difficult to isolate the most plausible reasons for the failures of these first steps toward SEI, as Neumann emphasizes (1980, p. 18), the set goals diverged from the prevailing possibilities for cooperation and thus underscored the urgent need to develop these relations. The present debates on radical CMEA reform warrant a similar position. A reexamination of the early history of the CMEA may therefore yield food for thought that is pertinent even to ongoing integration debates.

2.2 MAJOR VENUES OF THE NEGOTIATIONS

Between the January founding conference and the third Council Session held in Moscow on 24–25 November 1950, several important policy meetings occcurred. To better understand what may have germinated at the time, their respective agendas and preoccupations need to be kept apart and clarified one at a time. First, the Council Session was convened in Moscow from 26 to 28 April 1949 for its first, constitutional, Session, and in Sofia from 25 to 27 August 1949 for the second Session.[1] These meetings should be ranked highly because they were originally slated to be the first quarterly comprehensive consultations on economic policies (Lukin, 1974, pp. 46–7). These meetings should have dealt not only with broad policy objectives but also with the concrete economic situation of the community as a whole and selected members in particular. Second, the Bureau of the Council (formed in January 1949, as discussed later in this section) presumably debated the agenda points and prepared the various meetings of the Council Session, including several that did not materialize in late 1949 and early 1950 as originally scheduled; some in fact never convened. Third, the so-called working apparatus of the Bureau, the precursor of the Secretariat officially erected in 1954, must have investigated some aspects pertaining to the planned regional economic cooperation endeavors. Finally, there were relatively frequent contacts among the various governments, mostly revolving around the Soviet Union as effective center of the cooperation that was occurring at the time. But the early meetings among the other countries should not be denigrated.

The January 1949 conference decided to create the Council, agreed in principle on the organizational structure of the Council, which itself came about during the first inaugural Council Session in April 1949, and, according to Nikolaj V. Faddeev (1967, p. 195), adopted 'new principles of international political and economic collaboration' among the CPEs. The first issue is resolved in chapter 1; issues regarding the principles and goals of cooperation will be addressed later in this chapter. But a word on the broad features of the organization that was then envisaged may be useful at this juncture.

As a result of the first Session, the Bureau of the Council, also referred to as the 'central working apparatus,' was formally established, though its structure, composition and mission had apparently been detailed the preceding January. The Bureau would be supported by a technical secretariat. Both institutions were apparently provided for in statutes drawn up in early 1949 (Neumann, 1980, p. 2), but, as later variants until about 1959, were not generally published. The Bureau was to guide decision making regarding regional economic cooperation between Council Sessions and was thus thought of as a *quasi* permanent supervisory and policymaking body – perhaps even a regional planning institution to the extent that planning became the foremost preoccupation of CMEA cooperation soon thereafter.

The Bureau of the Council consisted officially of one (Lukin, 1974, p. 46) or two (Faddeev, 1974b, p. 35) delegates from each member and a small staff of advisers nominated by each member country. The confusion in the sources probably stems, as Hegemann (1980, p. 47) indicates, from the fact that one delegate was assigned to the Bureau proper to ensure liaison with the national planning offices whereas the other provided political and diplomatic liaison with the national governments and CPs. That is, the precursor of the Secretariat was not then thought of as an international civil service but as a group of specialists simply obligated to their country of origin. The Bureau was to be in session at least once per month (Hegemann, 1980, p. 58), but there is little evidence that this schedule was adhered to. It probably met fairly regularly the first year but thereafter increasingly deferred its responsibilities to other organs. The tasks entrusted to the Bureau chiefly included the preparation and implementation of projects, proposals, decisions and recommendations to be discussed at the plenary meetings of the Council. These were originally not confined to simple organizational matters. The Bureau's mandate was more purposeful. It initiated the preparation of detailed background materials and recommendations for higher-level negotiations on policy issues and especially for decisions to be scrutinized and endorsed by the Session and perhaps other top-level meetings of Party and government leaders (on which more below). In addition to preparing policy meetings, the Bureau also oversaw the activities of the specialists and subordinate staff in matters that had been delegated and mandated by the Council Session, and appointed the Secretary (Neumann, 1980, p. 2).

Incomplete evidence suggests that the Bureau and its technical staff were originally intended to fulfill the tasks eventually (in 1962) entrusted to the Executive Committee and the Secretariat (established in 1954), namely, the preparation and recommendation of tasks furthering economic integration (see chapter 7). Primarily, the Bureau was expected to take care of the following activities. First, as an executive arm of the Council, at whose request it prepared the Session, it directed the working apparatus, elaborated background materials for the Session, controlled the implementation and fulfillment of the Council's decisions and handled other such matters. Second, it was called upon to redraft proposals for questions that failed to be resolved, or that arose, during the full Session. Finally, it directed and supervised the specialized other organs of the Council, including the committee for the coordination of trade with capitalist countries and the first vestiges of a secretariat.

The forerunner of the present Secretariat was to consist of twenty-eight specialists and thirty-six auxiliary members (Čížkovský, 1966, p. 161; Čížkovský, 1971, p. 56).[2] How they would be able to settle the whole range of complex matters selected as their tasks (on which more below) is hard to fathom. Delegation of these wide-ranging tasks to such a small staff was baffling (Friss, 1974, pp. 2–3), all the more so because this staff would be subdivided into supervising three groups. One group would oversee individual economic branches (metallurgy, mining, machine building, energy, light industry, transportation and agriculture), another would handle single economic topics (e.g., the balancing of nonessential products, questions concerning finance and myriad aspects pertaining to foreign exchange, foreign trade, planning, statistics and legal affairs), and a third group would be responsible for specific aspects of bilateral consultations. This intended structure of the embryonic secretariat would imply that, on average, at most two specialists with a high degree of responsibility were to be placed in charge. Although there is unfortunately no hard evidence, I suspect that these specialists were to be chiefs of research and administration, with a subordinate staff located in the various member countries.

What is presented is a rather poor picture of what the CPEs then sought to set up by way of formal infrastructure for regional cooperation. However, more details are available concerning the principles of cooperation.

2.3 THE CRITICAL POINTS OF THE NEGOTIATIONS

The core issues of intragroup economic cooperation were not new. They had been the subject of bilateral trade negotiations and had also come to the fore at the political level, including within the context of the Cominform soon after its establishment in 1947. Even so, there is some evidence to buttress the proposition that the January 1949 conference was called to order without the founders having deliberated earnestly about the hows and whys of SEI. The participants in that conference apparently failed to fully endorse the Rumanian-Soviet proposal for the creation of the CMEA, or they decided first to consult with the top political leadership at home. As a result, various deliberations ensued between January 1949 and November 1950. Because the debate was not streamlined, these proposals and negotiations veered off into several, at times incompatible, directions. Some tangents stemmed from the fundamentally different interests of the relatively more developed CMEA members compared with those of the less-developed countries. The former tended to be more interested in fostering an integrated market with proper prices, exchange rates, multilateral settlement of accounts and other indirect instruments of coordinating economic decisions and their supporting institutions. The less-developed countries, for their part, were primarily concerned about industrialization, STC at minimal cost, protection of local markets, inflow of capital and related topics.

Although it is not easy to identify clearly what had happened, there is little doubt that the original tasks of the CMEA, aside from the purely organizational ones, referred to foreign trade, the coordination of production and the political aspects of regional cooperation (Kaplan, 1977, p. 16), including the coordination of activities to improve economic conditions for an ambient revolutionary situation in Europe and to structurally isolate the United States in (Western) Europe. As far as genuine integration is concerned, it may be instructive to allocate the topics pertinent to this inquiry to four categories: the organization of the Council and its subsidiaries; issues of coordinating national economic plans for the economy as a whole or for individual sectors; the ways in which countries could be interlinked through trade and payments, including the perennially knotty issues of proper prices and exchange rates; and gratuitous STC.

As clarified in section 2.2, the early deliberations agreed on the installation of the Council Session as the supreme organ, the Bureau of the Council, and the Bureau's working apparatus. As sources differ, whether a statute to that effect was accepted on 8 January 1949 is uncertain. But as the secretary with the longest tenure, Nikolaj V. Faddeev (1974b, p. 50), confirmed it and other recent observers point in the same direction, one may as well accept that some preliminary statutes were then adopted. This document set forth the purposes and organization of the Council in some fashion, including some of the features detailed in chapter 1.

From the CMEA's inception, the issues of accelerating growth in the member countries and eliminating differences in national levels of development played a critical role in the organization of regional economic cooperation. STC in its various dimensions was accorded a pivotal role in these endeavors to accelerate growth and economic diversity. Inside observers have confirmed that the less-developed CPEs, including notably the USSR, were keen on working out a framework for STC, even in preference to multilateral clearing and attendant forms of settlement for international transactions (Kaplan, 1977, p. 18). Especially important in this respect were the decisions of the second Council Session of August 1949, which agreed upon the modus of STC within the CMEA region.

A lengthy debate took place on the pros and cons of lending fraternal assistance in the form of STC. The countries that would be STC originators especially argued for making available blueprints at nominal cost only in the case of knowledge that had been fully amortized. The less-developed countries, however, favored free transfer of all technological achievements and their view won out until at least the late 1960s (Kaplan, 1977, pp. 86–7). As a result, blueprints of technological processes were to be made available for domestic utilization upon demand merely for the cost of reproducing the documents. Assistance in the form of temporary personnel transfer could also be requested at modest cost, essentially to provide subsistence to the engineers and scientists involved. On the other topics, however, the record is more convoluted, particularly for the economics of this exchange, or rather the lack thereof (see chapter 13).

2.4 PRINCIPLES AND PURPOSES OF CMEA COOPERATION

Though the full documents of the early meetings have not thus far surfaced, sufficient information is available to extract key pointers of the intended directions of cooperation. The minutes of the January and April 1949 meetings have been partly reproduced and interpreted in the literature. The following appear to have been the critical topics. First, consensus was reached about the construction of plans concerning reciprocal economic relations among members, as well as coordination of the national economic plans to foster production specialization and cooperation. More specifically, trade plans for important commodities were to be closely meshed. Second, plans designed to widen transportation and transit facilities were to be worked out jointly to facilitate other economic relations and keep pace with the rapid economic expansion and scope of industrialization the members coveted. Third, directions for extending mutual aid to offset or counteract the effects of Western discrimination and partial boycott were agreed upon in principle, if not in complete detail. Fourth, multilateral clearing, proper exchange rates and the steady improvement of regional settlements were considered crucial elements in fostering SEI on a sound economic basis. Fifth, the development of all-around STC was to be vigorously stimulated. Finally, control of the execution and fulfillment of the planned cooperation was to be entrusted to the Council's Bureau.

During the first official Council Session, the basic conditions and tasks of the CMEA were laid down around the following seven themes:

1. Aspects of enlarging the scope for mutual trade and how to quickly accelerate it.
2. Questions of trade with Western economies and coordination of foreign trade plans more generally.
3. The myriad aspects of instituting regional prices and multilateral clearing.
4. The coordination of economic plans, particularly production plans for important industrial products and primary goods in short supply, possibly including assistance in the construction of crucial enterprises, if necessary in the form of JSCs.
5. The further elaboration of solutions to key questions of the economic reconstruction of individual members.
6. Questions of technical aid, STC and standardization.
7. Issues related to economic relations with Yugoslavia, including the compression of CMEA's imports to indispensable strategic materials otherwise obtainable only in the West.

Most of the above issues bear close resemblance, even in some details, to the unsuccessful project of Polish-Czechoslovak cooperation that had been sporadically discussed since World War II and was then in advanced draft form (Spulber, 1957, pp. 427–8). This suggests that the plan for CMEA-wide cooperation was well under debate prior to the January 1949 conference or, at least, that the participants in that meeting were not completely ignorant of what may have been afoot. The fact that none of the fundamental issues appears to have been settled at this early date does not necessarily disprove the very earnest desire of at least some members to amalgamate Eastern Europe under the umbrella of a common, integrated economic policy.

As reported, the first Council Session had an astonishingly comprehensive agenda. Because of the many difficult problems at hand, it should not be surprising that apparently no solid agreements could be hammered out. But the second Session in Sofia (25–27 August 1949) endorsed a number of concrete solutions. The Sofia agenda contained, for instance, questions of foreign trade, pertaining in particular to CMEA relations but also to East-West interaction and, indeed, relations with Yugoslavia, the determination of CMEA trade prices and the introduction of multilateral clearing in 1950. The most promising forms of STC, which was to be free of charge and worked out in bilateral commissions, was also on the Sofia agenda, as were questions of normalization and standardization of production (including specialization in ball bearings), statistics and the like (Čížkovský, 1971, p. 56; Kaplan, 1977, p. 85).

Although the evidence is incomplete, we may infer that no acceptable solution was reached on most issues tabled under the first topic. It was perhaps easiest to reach consensus on the boycott of Yugoslavia. As far as the advancement of CMEA trade is concerned, there was extensive divisiveness on resource allocation. The intermingling of economic exchange with fraternal assistance was particularly confounding. Some members blatantly insisted that potential surplus countries use 'excess supplies' to cover deficits of other countries and forestall such imbalances in the future by creating long-term agreements on reciprocal deliveries of assorted quotas of major products. But agreement does appear to have been reached on a number of principles for the determination of trade prices within the group.

Furthermore, a 'first variant of multilateral clearing' had been thoroughly discussed. The meeting endorsed 'the principal positions, which were to form the fundamental basis of instituting multilateral clearing and guaranteeing its normal functioning' (Mazanov, 1970, p. 45), and only a few particulars of the multilateral clearing scheme remained for further deliberations. This would essentially entail submitting the proposed scheme for fine tuning at the next Session, suggesting that the countries involved unanimously accepted the principle of multilateral clearing as the core mechanism for settling trade and payments accounts. Unfortunately, as with so many of the documents of that period, no further details are available on how this multilateralization was expected to function.

The second Session laid down a number of principles that would govern the exchange of East-West trade (see Kaplan, 1977, pp. 85–6). Six of these principles are of sufficient importance to be listed individually. First, it was recommended that the members coordinate their own foreign policy *vis-à-vis* the Western economies in accordance with the particular foreign policy embraced by each of the countries involved. Second, the CPEs were asked to coordinate their export and import plans for products of central significance to CMEA trade. Third, it was decided to chiefly import noncompeting goods, including from the CMEA, and to focus exports on goods for which there was no shortage in the CMEA. At one point it was even argued that exports of strategic raw materials (including oil, coke, petroleum products, rolled-steel products, nonferrous metals and ores, manganese and so on) and heavy industrial equipment to the West should be eliminated or at best reduced to exchanges for products in critical short supply within the CMEA (Sláma, 1979, p. 26). Fourth, the CPEs were to coordinate their export and import price policies in relations with Western economies. As an important input into that process, fifth, they committed themselves to exchange information on economic negotiations and other consultations, including on BTPAs, with capitalist countries. Finally, joint efforts were formulated to counter Western discrimination and boycott. To render these precepts operational and implement them, a special commission of the Bureau on trade with capitalist countries was established. This organ was to control exports of critical goods (including wheat, oil and petroleum products, wood and lumber, iron and nonferrous metals, coke, coal and sugar) as well as some imports (e.g., textile raw materials such as wool, cotton and jute, as well as nonferrous metals, rubber and iron ore). Forty-eight categories of products were under the organ's scrutiny (Sláma, 1979, p. 26).

More information is available on the second and third points of the second Session's agenda as specific recommendations were adopted regarding gratuitous STC and the norming and standardization of production, trade and statistics to promote specialization (see below). Also, specific agreements were signed on specialization in ball bearings, the organization of railway freight shipment and other 'minor' issues (Lukin, 1974, pp. 47–8).

The question of multilateralizing trade and related settlements was again on the agenda of what Čížkovský (1971) refers to as the 'third session' of 10 January 1950. But it is a mystery to me what particular organ this refers to. Possibly it was a preparatory consultation of the Bureau for a Council Session to tackle the problems left unresolved in Sofia. The meeting may have been adjourned abruptly because no unanimous agreement could be reached on the questions of multilateralization and plan coordination. The apparent result of this meeting was, first, the acceptance of a number of the Bureau's recommended means by which mutual trade could be enlarged; the exchange of information regarding the practical realization of multilateral clearing for which the Bureau was requested to do more work on substantive issues; and, details regarding the coordination of trade with capitalist economies. In retrospect, this signaled the temporary end of the CMEA's activity, though a definite agreement on the more fundamental questions of integration through the coordination of national economic plans had not yet been worked out.

2.5 PLAN COORDINATION AND HARMONIZATION

Even in looking at all the details of the many tasks slated for the Bureau's attention, one should not forget, as M. Čížkovský (1970, p. 254) emphasized, that 'the prerequisites for organizing supranational unified planning were intentionally created with the decision to coordinate the plans, the main goal [being] the gradual planned elimination of all attributes of the national economies as autonomous economic units. Therefore, a supranational system should have resulted and, in consequence, the absoluteness of state sovereignty would be negated.' This is, of course, quite compatible with the attempted imposition of intra-CMEA unity in the late 1950s and early 1960s but an unexpected feature of the earlier activities. If correct, this notion infuses into the discussion quite a new element about the original intentions and decisions.

Some efforts may have been made to elaborate trade agreements based on the careful analysis of comparative costs and to institute multilateral exchange. But there is too little unalloyed evidence on the precise content of the earlier debates to suggest that such a relationship between the real and the monetary sides of intragroup trade was actually contemplated as the mainstay of CMEA transactions. In fact, it needs to be recalled that at least three members – Czechoslovakia, Hungary and the Soviet Union – had elaborated long-term plans of the classical Soviet-type (see Part III) that were in effect at the time of the CMEA's conception. Furthermore, all other members were frantically preparing the introduction of long-term socioeconomic development plans in late 1949 or early 1950. Their paramount purpose was to foster rapid industrialization in breadth largely through the control of detailed physical planning. The proposals favoring multilateral specialization along the lines of comparative costs, other indirect coordination mechanisms and the institutions required to support such decisions may have played more than an incidental role in the formulation of the broad outlines of the prospects for further developments. But they can hardly have been conceived as instruments for drawing up and coordinating the first plans. Too little is known about these earlier plans and how they were implemented in the early 1950s to unequivocally conclude that they were initially as rigid as the Soviet plans of the 1930s. The 1949–50 discussions probably gravitated mainly around the very important and involved problems of how to promote integration by means of plan coordination and mutual trade in spite of the Western boycott and strategic embargo, considerable differences in levels of development and other evident obstacles to synchronizing disparate economies.

Given that all economies had been brought under, or were about to be governed by, detailed central planning, it seems highly plausible that the discussions of 1949–50 centered more on how to attain some semblance of an integrated central plan from coordination of the national economic plans than on how to link the economies in the most effective manner. Even less thought appears to have been given to the question of how each member economy could draft efficient central plans. Although the evidence is unfortunately too inconclusive to support such logical inferences, any attempt to integrate the Eastern European economies through the coordination of central plans or by means of market-type relations would have required careful preparation for which the prevailing political, strategic and economic circumstances of the late 1940s and early 1950s were not propitious.

Nevertheless, the political leadership must have given some serious thought to the transition phase that would forcibly be required to move from postwar reconstruction and reconversion to strict central planning for the purpose of rapid industrialization. Other instruments and associated supporting institutions may also have been considered for facilitating the transition and expediting central planning nationally and especially on a regional scale. Particularly relevant to the discussion was the research on the goals and means of plan coordination, common planning and new trade and payments instruments tailored to the needs of economic interaction among planned economies, on which the Council's Bureau and various other research agencies were actively engaged until at least mid-1950. This work proceeded for about a year, beginning in early 1949, with as terms of reference the reduction of disparities in relative economic scarcities in the region – that is, economic integration as commonly understood (Ausch, 1972, p. 44; Faddeev, 1974b, pp. 130–1).

The complexity of formally inaugurating regional integration among countries that had engaged in only cursory economic interaction for over twenty-five years must have been daunting to even the most optimistic participant in the debates. Nonetheless, until circumstances forced them to abandon their ambitions, several members were determined to consolidate production, commerce and investment policies in the region. Under the impact of the rapidly deteriorating international political and military situation, however, and the lingering convulsions from the struggles for effective political control within each country and over the group as a whole, further work on the integration blueprint was discontinued. It was replaced largely by national development strategies and the 'embassy system' of intensive bilateral cooperation under the direct supervision of the USSR.

If my interpretation of the evidence thus far assembled is at all close to the truth, then many observers of the early CMEA scene may have erroneously equated its post-1950 immobility and passivity with the motives behind its creation – an unnecessarily misleading generalization because it reduces the motives underlying the Council's gestation to simple imitative fervor and dishonest power politics and because it ignores the, at times, fascinating sparring on how centralized economies could impart flexibility into their reciprocal economic collaboration while preserving the perceived advantages of national planning and the regional integration of these plans.

The formulation of a common economic plan for the harmonious development of the entire region was to be the prime task of this new institution (see chapter 1). Entailed in this strategic goal was the creation of broad-based regional complementarity in economic profiles, planning approaches and institutions fostered under the aegis of the Council. It was to help intertwine the members through the establishment of joint enterprises, particularly so as to boost their output of fuels, energy and basic raw materials in order to accelerate supplies of crucial inputs for industrialization. Through JSCs and the coordination of national plans, the Council was mandated to foster standardization and regional complementarities, presumably to capitalize on economies of scale. Also, the exchange of scientific and technical information and promotion of capital flows, including direct investments, were to be allotted an active role in achieving growth through swift industrialization. Initially, accommodation was to be sought for whatever goods and services the member countries had to offer to the rest of the region.

By the time the Council was set up, a considerable number of JSCs had been created, particularly in highly sensitive economic sectors (such as mining and processing of uranium ores) and in key sectors of the defeated countries (Bulgaria, the later GDR, Hungary and Rumania),[3] where JSCs were created by combining property formerly owned by the Axis powers, or their local sympathizers, and new national inputs. The confiscation was undertaken by the Soviet Union as part of the contribution of the defeated countries to the claimed war reparations on Germany and its former allies (Neumann, 1980, p. 177). New firms were also set up on the basis of equally shared participations. Because claims on Germany had been frustrated in the postwar squabbling among the former allies (see chapter 1), the USSR moved unilaterally to capture whatever it could get from the territories under its influence and control. Initially, this involved dismantling plant and equipment and physically relocating the material to Soviet territory. It was quickly realized, however, that this literal variant of technology transfer was counterproductive because, once in their new place, these assets retained only a small fraction of their original value. Dismantling was associated with considerable physical destruction or gutting of factories, problems of adapting existing technology to Soviet needs, inability to assimilate some of the technology altogether and other factors that determine the value of assets once they are committed.

There was also another important consideration. Dismantling of capital assets deprived the country of origin of the means to buttress reconstruction and reconversion. In some cases it even reduced the capacity to transfer future war reparations to the USSR. The Soviet Union could obtain comparable advantages by keeping the assets in place and counting the transfer of JSC profits and benefits associated with it against war reparation claims. Such standing involvement also enabled the USSR to play a pivotal role in the design of economic development programs, especially in new sectors. Additionally, the JSCs afforded the USSR an entry into actual economic activity, somewhat analogous to a Trojan horse with Soviet advisers and administrators. The evidence available for Yugoslavia is particularly illuminating in this respect.[4]

These JSCs were not precisely what was meant by the deliberations about founding joint companies when the CMEA was established. The discussions of 1949–50 sought to promote investment coordination – including through the transfer of long-term capital resources within the region – in part to avoid duplication of basic components of heavy industry, save on scarce capital resources and provide a major impetus to regional trade directly as well as indirectly. The direct benefits would have accrued in the form of the goods coming on stream via these joint ventures. Indirect benefits would have been reaped from ensuring proper inputs for these JSCs as well as counterflows to the procurement of new goods. At the same time, these JSCs should not be construed as embryonic mechanisms for fostering market-type relations among the CPEs chiefly through socialist transnationals. The elusive founding document is clear about the Council having been conceived as a supranational organ charged with enhancing regional economic interdependence through a common economic plan drawn up directly by the Council organs and indirectly through the instructions handed down by the Council Session and its Secretariat General to the national planning offices.

Nevertheless, the information about the written and other agreements arrived at in 1949 makes it incontrovertible that at that time the members did not intend to confine the CMEA's vocation simply to the physical coordination of national economic plans. Such plan coordination was stipulated as the Council's preeminent task only later, in 1954. Clearly, synchronizing national economic plans, given the ambitious development targets set nationally and amplified under impact of regionwide demands, would have figured prominently among the tasks of the organization in any case. But the debates organized around plan coordination during the first year or so of the CMEA's existence envisaged far more flexible cooperation than rigid plan harmonization. It called for combining comprehensive planning of the main macroeconomic aggregates with a host of other indirect coordination instruments to eliminate, during the transition phase toward a common policy, all attributes of economic sovereignty normally incumbent upon the national economies (Čížkovský, 1970, p. 254). These included, among others, the essentials of a monetary and financial cooperation mechanism appropriate to economic intercourse among sovereign states.

2.6 INDIRECT ECONOMIC COORDINATION

All CPEs involved in the initial debates evidently agreed to pool resources and cooperate actively in solidifying socialist cohesion by fostering the ISDL. But this transition phase would unfold with considerable flexibility. At the very least, plan coordination would be supplemented by multilateral clearing, proper exchange rates and adequate pricing. Already there was consensus on the elaboration of some kind of regional price system (Čížkovský, 1971, p. 5) according to a set of broad principles compatible with relations among CPEs (see chapters 3 and 15). For convenience, I shall henceforth refer to this as the transferable ruble price (TRP) system, although the transferable ruble (TR) came about only in 1964.

It is not clear to what extent regional pricing as such appeared as a self-contained item on the agenda of the high-level policy discussions that sought to shape SEI in the late 1940s. Was it treated as a separate policy objective or did it form an integral part of the multilateralization scheme that was then nearing preparation (Mazanov, 1970, p. 45)? Although the evidence is not very persuasive either way, the latter alternative probably comes closer to the truth. The multilateralization scheme was one of the key entries on the agenda of the first Council Session and absorbed considerable attention during the second in August 1949. Although the blueprint on multilateralizing intragroup exchanges had supposedly advanced far in the negotiations, the matter was referred back to the Bureau's secretariat. This was to require only some fine tuning, as it was firmly expected that the scheme would be formally agreed upon sometime in 1950 during the third Session (Mazanov, 1970, p. 45).

2.7 A RATIONALE FOR THE CMEA'S TEMPORARY DEMISE

The abrupt halt to the CMEA's official activity at the policymaking level in early 1950 occurred without the membership having concluded a definitive agreement on the more fundamental questions of integration on the basis of coordinated plans and their ramifications for planning, or on the organization of trade, pricing, balance of payments, commercial policy and related issues. Concerning this enigmatic third session, Čížkovský (1971, p. 56) adds that it 'was certainly not known [at the time] that such questions [plan coordination] would no longer be discussed, or that the activity of the CMEA would come to an all but complete standstill for the next three years.' Because the Bureau was a permanent organ in charge of preparing the plenary Session, it lost its official purpose in the early 1950s as no meetings that addressed substantive SEI issues were organized for a long time thereafter, and its already small staff was further curtailed (Lukin, 1974, p. 53). But this does not imply that the Bureau – as distinct from the Council Session – was dissolved or condemned to complete inactivity. It continued to be involved in finding solutions to facilitating trade relations among the CMEA members. In fact, Bureau officials (including the then Secretary Aleksandr I. Loščakov) were active in negotiating BTPAs, for example with Czechoslovakia (Kaplan, 1977, pp. 88–107). Hegemann (1980, p. 57) suggests that in 1951–3 the Bureau and its secretariat continued to work at a lively pace but that specifics of these endeavors were withheld from publication to prevent information being divulged 'to the enemy.'

In January 1950 it was by no means clear whether policymakers felt that further work on the more fundamental questions of plan coordination would be necessary. The Bureau thus continued to execute its mandate by developing a proposal on the principles and practice of plan coordination in preparation for the third plenary Session, which should originally have taken place sometime in November or December 1949. Following several postponements, it was finally scheduled for May 1950. As events unfolded, however, the third Session was in fact not called to order until 24–25 November 1950. To the surprise of the Bureau, the Session suddenly chose to limit further work to the practical questions of facilitating mutual trade relations in the immediate future. Most likely this decision materialized in consequence of the resolve of the CPE leaders, mainly under Soviet prodding, to quicken the pace of development, particularly in heavy industry and armaments. One of the key topics discussed at that time was the basis of price formation in intra-CMEA trade in view of the rapid inflation of prices of raw materials on world markets following the eruption of hostilities in Korea. It was at this Session that the CMEA members resolved to enact 'stop prices' (see chapter 15).

Near the time of the outbreak of the Korean War on 25 June 1950, without first informing other members, the Soviet Union abruptly ceased active participation in the CMEA's Bureau. The original functions of the Session and the Bureau were henceforth split up into those belonging to the USSR's sphere and those concerning other members (Čížkovský, 1970, p. 249; Čížkovský, 1971, pp. 60ff.). Thereafter, the Bureau and especially its supporting staff concentrated on isolated, relatively unimportant problems of economic collaboration among the smaller Eastern European members. By then the USSR had established its so-called embassy system of meddling in other countries' affairs directly and through bilateral consultations. In some cases, Soviet citizens, through direct placement or through their embassy affiliation, played an instrumental role in running the economy or even individual enterprises in Eastern Europe.

As a member of the CMEA Bureau at that time, S. Ausch (1972, p. 44) confirms this periodization and major shift in emphasis in CMEA discussions about economic cooperation.

> It may seem anachronistic to apply our *ex post* judgement to the period in question. It is, however, a fact that during the first months of CMEA's functioning, its working apparatus started its practical activity on the basis of principles much similar to what seems adequate in our days. Stalin, however, intervened and, by referring to the principle of national sovereignty . . . put an end to the activities of the CMEA apparatus in this field. He proposed a different solution, resting partly on autonomous national decisions and partly on bilateral agreements.

That is to say, sometime in mid-1950 Stalin's intervention disabled the CMEA's Bureau and relegated its subordinated staff of advisers and specialists to passivity and immobility. Prior to that momentous step, even under the deteriorating regional and international power relations, as Ausch (1972, p. 44) emphasizes, the common economic policy that was being formulated could have influenced industrial location in the individual members on the basis of more rational principles than it did later, when the system of direct plan instructions and their autonomous effects on the ISDL became predominant.

The virtual standstill in the CMEA's activities lasted from mid-1950 to mid-1954, but this does not mean that for all practical purposes the Bureau and its secretariat were dissolved. One commonly finds references to the Bureau's role in coordinating trade plans during that period. This seems to apply, however, to the coordination of a few selected, important trade products since the actual bilateral (and some trilateral[5]) trade and payments agreements were worked out during bilateral bargaining sessions by the national governments. The Bureau and its staff may still have supplied some input in terms of quantitative information, organizational facilities or methodological approaches that speeded up these negotiations, enhanced the smooth clearing of documents and facilitated intraregional transportation by standardizing rules of procedure. But its role in the actual process of decision making about foreign trade, let alone other matters, seems to have been marginal at best.

Today it seems wrong, however, to conclude that CMEA integration was expected to be fostered mainly by means of coordinating long-term plans, even if long-term planning was restricted to trade agreements that spanned a period of time longer than the annual planning cycle. Certainly these trade agreements helped, if only indirectly, to lay the foundations for some of the main branches of production of the CPEs. As such, they may have facilitated the coordination of the national economies to a certain degree. But it is doubtful whether this outcome had been earlier contemplated. The first long-term trade plans were hardly more than a practical device to tie the individual countries to the immediate interests of the USSR in its quest for supremacy and hegemony. In fact, long-term trade agreements between pairs of the smaller Eastern European countries first came about in 1952 (Lukin, 1974, p. 50). But even then they were not in the rigid and comprehensive form they assumed later.

My point of view may be reconciled with the more traditional interpretations of the CMEA's creation by distinguishing between the short- and long-term interests of the Soviet Union. Its short-term interests were undoubtedly vested, on the one hand, in economic reconstruction and reinforced industrialization at home and, on the other hand, in the neutralization of the smaller Eastern European countries into a strong ideological and military bloc to keep the West at a distance. Both the domestic and foreign objectives could be reached partly by relying on technological and other resources of Eastern Europe and by mobilizing the remaining resources for Soviet-type growth. When it became evident that no coordinated plan or looser regional policy serving the immediate Soviet interests could be devised, direct involvement in the fraternal economies better suited the USSR's needs.

The long-term interests of the USSR in the matter of economic cooperation were most likely vested, as they are now, in the integration of the entire socialist community into a strongly interdependent and dovetailed economic, strategic and political union. Particularly with reference to the situation in Europe, the long-term economic and other preoccupations of the USSR as a hegemonic and ideological mentor could be better served by a vibrant, economically developed Eastern Europe under the immediate influence of the USSR than by total control over countries that developed in virtual estrangement. Genuine economic development of Eastern Europe would have assisted regional collaboration, and *vice versa*. To reach such more genuine cooperation goals, Voznesenskij's alleged ideas about market-based coordination not only in relations among socialist countries but also within individual economies (see chapter 1) might have proved instrumental, and certainly of much longer-lasting value, than trade relations derived from autarkic economic policies and autonomous planning. This conjecture will be examined from different angles in the rest of this volume.

Seen against the background to the CMEA's establishment depicted in this chapter, it would seem fair to argue in favor of five basic intentions that may have been at the CMEA's roots. First, the CMEA was not established as a mere propaganda instrument or as the simple manifestation of sheer imitative fervor, chiefly to counter the divisiveness engendered by the Marshall Plan. Second, active discussions about the future course of real economic integration – that is, regional interaction based in part on the economic rationality of efficient resource allocation and helped along with indirect coordination instruments and their supporting institutions – lasted at least until mid-1950. Third, even though economywide planning of the Soviet variety was accorded a significant role, long-term trade agreements were not the only instrument under discussion in the genuine projects of integrating the CPEs. Fourth, although also intent on exercising economic control over Eastern Europe, the USSR permitted the Council's Bureau to handle selected practical projects, though not the more fundamental questions of long-term cooperation, throughout the period 1949–54 (Lukin, 1974, p. 53). Finally, the virtual standstill of the Council may have been the result of exogenous events such as the climate engendered by the cold war, the actual warfare in Korea and the imminent danger of a new, possibly final, global conflagration.

NOTES

1. For ease of reading, I shall reduce some of these historical dates and references in the text to a strict minimum. Appendix 2 gives full details of venues, dates and types of meetings.
2. There are many versions of the precise size of these organs. The numbers given here tend toward the high side compared with alternative ones; for example see Faddeev, 1974b, p. 35, and Lukin, 1974, p. 47.
3. It was also widespread in Yugoslavia, until the rupture of relations in 1948, and in Manchuria. But the JSCs in those areas fall outside the present discussion.
4. For useful eyewitness accounts, see Dedijer, 1971 and Djilas, 1963. The literature on the JSCs in the CMEA member countries is largely of Western origin and in many respects clouded by cold war precepts. For a good summary of the JSCs in Rumania, see Montias, 1967. Spulber, 1957 provides a more general account.
5. Tri- and even quadrilateral agreements usually involved one capitalist country as the swing partner. In most cases, Finland played that role in the late 1940s and early 1950s.

3 · ACTIVITIES IN THE 1950s

Although the role of the Council in the economic development of the European planned economies from its inception until the late 1950s cannot be accorded too much weight, it should not be ignored altogether. Important events did occur, though most of them contributed only to laying some of the foundation for the elaboration of the ISDL in the 1960s and SEI in more recent years. Their relevance to bolstering economic activity in the individual CPEs, or even directly in the creation of CPEs, the first broad industrialization wave, the New Course, the divisive developments of the mid-1950s and the second industrialization drive is much less easy to justify.

Describing the early role of the CMEA as being fundamentally passive is warranted as far as actual policymaking and developments at that time are concerned. But important shifts occurred in the policymakers' perception of the possible prospective directions of economic cooperation in Eastern Europe. It holds also for the major institutional changes and organizational innovations in the CMEA introduced mainly in the later 1950s. Likewise, important shifts manifested themselves in the range of types of production specialization and their depth in the production process. This was basically a new direction for CMEA cooperation; that is, away from autarky, or at least toward self-sufficiency if the cost proved at all affordable. Moreover, the members showed growing concern about how to impart greater flexibility and realism into the formulation and implementation of trade agreements, how to ease the pervasive stringency of bilateralism in negotiating BTPAs and what could be the first initiatives on the road to attaining greater flexibility in regional payments relations. Regarding the latter, some form of limited multilateralism in trade and payments was being debated. At the same time, serious consideration was being given to easing restrictions on intraregional economic exchanges, particularly in other than strict merchandise trade. The precise mechanisms and policies invoked form the subject proper of several chapters of Part III. What concerns us here, though, is the dating of these mechanisms and policies in the checkered growth of the Council and how their evolving nature fits into the postwar history of CMEA cooperation.

Section 3.1 sketches the historical backdrop to the economic and other changes in the region in the 1950s. The evolution of policymakers' perceptions of how a regional organization such as the CMEA could assist in fostering economic development occupies us in section 3.2. Institutional transformations are sketched in section 3.3. The first official charter is clarified next. The different ways in which these developments impinge upon the economic mechanisms for regional cooperation, as a prelude to the description and evaluation of these mechanisms in Part III, are pointed out in section 3.5. Though the strategy of the ISDL was in fact formulated in the 1950s, its real importance in bolstering or, as some observers believe, in retarding SEI was essentially a feature of the next decade and will be studied in detail in chapter 4.

3.1 HISTORICAL BACKDROP

The decade of the 1950s was exceptional in more than one respect. The first industrialization wave in Eastern Europe was inaugurated with a roar at the outset of the decade and set in even higher gear soon thereafter. The acceleration to a breakneck pace was urged upon Eastern Europe mainly by the USSR as it perceived the dire necessity of countering the Korean War, which was then believed to be the first skirmish of World War III. Yet, in a very short while, at the latest by mid-1953, the foundations of this expansionary policy were severely rocked. At the least, a tactical retreat was counseled in virtually all CPEs, and the acceleration of industrialization was reversed. The pace of industrialization in some countries was even brought to a near standstill. Even in those CPEs where rapid industrialization lasted into the mid-1950s, its character was modified in important respects and its pace decelerated markedly. This contributed to a palpable regionwide contraction in the buoyancy of economic activity.

Perhaps more typical than the synchronized deceleration in level of economic activity throughout Eastern Europe was that the paramount post-war policy goal of fostering industrialization in breadth (primarily by pursuing unbalanced sectoral expansion with a pronounced priority accorded to steady expansion of the heavy industrial branches at a very rapid pace) was abandoned shortly after Stalin died on 5 March 1953. Similarly seminal modifications occurred, especially about the place of centralized or collectivized agriculture in overall economic activity. The earlier drive to socialize that sector slowed down precipitously. In some countries, including Hungary and Poland, collectivization was temporarily reversed or its pursuit as a *sui generis* socialist economic policy was abandoned altogether. In the agricultural sector, a pronounced political and doctrinal retrenchment occurred largely in view of output considerations. The problems of ownership *per se*, the antagonism between private and collective property and the perceived need to communize agriculture at any cost clearly subsided.

One by one the CMEA members inaugurated what later became known as the New Course. This is shorthand for a sequence of shifts in policy precepts, growth objectives and especially policy-induced constraints on the distribution of economic resources. Other easements in the rigidity of the communist regimes could be included under that label as well. This appellation for the shift in economic policies originated under Stalin's successor, Georgij G. Malenkov. Indeed, Zbigniew Brzezinski (1967, p. 159) characterized this attempt as 'a new course in economics without basically altering the framework of essentially Stalinist politics.' Although this is an apt description, the New Course's intrinsic dynamism laid the foundation for the gradual evaporation of the very Stalinist policies that the leadership of several CPEs had sought to preserve.

The tactical retreat produced perhaps the most notable reverse in policy stances on income distribution in an effort to reduce the serious tensions that had built up during the rapid industrialization, political regimentation and collectivization drive of the preceding quinquennium. The shifting of income distribution in favor of final consumption and away from relentless accumulation of socialist property was the most direct beneficiary of the New Course. This major shift in investment policies, in fact, entailed a palpable mutation in development precepts, although this may not have been one of the objectives of the tactical retreat. Concurrently, political changes resulted from the natural death, forceful suppression or other transitions away from the Stalinist cliquishness that had been typical of the preceding five or so years throughout the area. This change had more than incidental implications for the formulation and implementation of economic policies. Popular pressure or political infighting at the highest levels of the Communist Party, government and administration in some cases accomplished similar results. Perhaps the most seminal transformation in intragroup affairs stemmed from the destalinization campaign launched by Nikita S. Chruščëv at the twentieth CP Congress in 1956, his Canossa as an attempt to bring Yugoslavia back into the socialist, if not Soviet, fold and the change in top-level personnel of Berija's security apparatus.

On the foreign economic front several seminal transformations also materialized. The potential contribution of foreign trade to sustained economic activity at a relatively high level was gradually recognized in a growing number of CPEs, particularly the more developed members. This shift in foreign trade policy called not only for intensifying the trade dependence of these economies but also for exploring markets other than those of the socialist countries, including markets for products that were not strictly among the 'selected' noncompeting imports and unnecessary exports at which earlier efforts had been aimed, with mixed success.

Perhaps more important were changes in foreign economic policy sentiment and regional economic relations. Suffice it to mention three. First, the notorious JSCs, with few exceptions (most notably in the mining of uranium ores in Czechoslovakia and the GDR), were abolished. As a result, the affected economic sectors could be more fully integrated in the home economies. Second, related to these companies, but encompassing a much wider area of the domestic economies (particularly in countries that had been occupied after World War II), was the gradual withdrawal of major segments of the Soviet advisory contingent in the planning and production sectors, not to mention defense, the security branches, in some cases politics and other areas. Finally, Eastern Europe's complaints about having been subjected to 'unequal exchange' (see Part III) by the USSR in the late 1940s and early 1950s were heard and heeded. At the very least, the most blatant instances of unadulterated price discrimination or even exploitation in favor of the Soviet Union were gradually reined in. The quintessential example of this new pro-region approach was provided by the revision of the price of Polish coal exported to the USSR.[1]

The extraordinary events in East Berlin (GDR) in 1953, Ostrava and Pilsen (Czechoslovakia) in 1952 and 1953, the Polish October in 1956 and the Hungarian October–November later that same year in many ways constituted the culmination of fundamental changes in economic and other policy stances that had been fermenting for several years, beginning shortly after Stalin's demise. Nonetheless, these particular manifestations of popular discontent provided a unique watershed in intra-CMEA economic and political relations. They not only left an indelible mark on the individual country concerned but, through their regional implications, also on the group as a whole.

The uprisings and political transitions of the mid-1950s in Eastern Europe in conjunction with the initial objectives of the New Course also affected the prospects for regional economic cooperation in more than one important way. The revival of the CMEA and the convening of a sequence of Council Sessions – starting in March 1954, barely a year after Stalin's death – signaled only the most overt manifestation of this mutation in the CMEA. Perhaps more important, when seen in their historical setting, were the Council meetings that led to various agreements on economic cooperation and production specialization (ECPS). Although these measures were essentially nullified by the political and economic events of the mid-1950s and the revisions in development plans for the second half of the 1950s that became necessary, the fact that they set new markers for SEI was important for subsequent developments. This applies especially to the various steps taken from about mid-1957 to impart the Council with a fresh breath as to its evolving goals, policymaking instruments, institutional setting and policy framework.

The transitions of the mid-1950s were critical for later developments in many respects, although their immediate impact on SEI was confined. Even the new policymakers installed after the eruption of popular discontent failed to see the near-disastrous socioeconomic and political developments of the mid-1950s as indelible signs of the need to engineer a permanent trans-formation in development ambitions. As a result, by 1957–8, virtually all CMEA member countries were about to embark on their second industrial-ization wave and, excepting notably Poland, the completion of collectiviza-tion in agriculture.

Though the emphasis was again on rapid expansion in breadth, particular-ly in industrial sectors to the relative neglect of agriculture, the policy focus was decidedly less one-sided than what had prevailed earlier in the decade. Both the purposes and character of the second industrialization wave were more carefully scrutinized. In agriculture, the vengeful way in which owner-ship relations had been manipulated earlier was considerably eased. Instead of accommodating ideological fervor at almost any cost in terms of human suffering and output forgone, agricultural production units were gradually based on sounder technological relations; concerns about encouraging out-put took some precedence over the ideology or political revenge that had earlier commanded prime attention in forcibly changing ownership relations.

The specialization agreements hammered out between 1954–6 for imple-mentation during the second half of the 1950s remained grounded in the wake of societal upheavals in some countries and, as noted, the venting of frustrations about Soviet exploitation. Nonetheless, the objectives embraced in the process resurfaced, albeit in a new cloak, during the CMEA debates of 1957–8. Though the second industrialization wave was conceived with slightly greater circumspection than was its predecessor, this drive quickly ran into various obstacles by the early 1960s. There were multiple reasons for this setback, including the limited size of the market in most countries, the excessive cost of duplication and import substitution for its own sake and the inefficiency of extensive production. These and related existential reflec-tions on the socialist development philosophy became basic inputs into two critical determinants of developments in the next decade, namely, the first wave of national economic reforms and the promulgation of the first SEI policy document.

3.2 EVOLUTION OF THE PURPOSES OF SEI

At the outset of the CMEA's existence (see chapter 2), several members had been critically concerned about the need to coordinate economywide and sectoral production and distribution plans. It was not the objective, how-ever, to completely lose the flexibility afforded by indirect coordination instruments and their supporting institutions. But comprehensive planning at the regional level, although gingerly endorsed, never matured into a firm policy. The problems that arose as a result of emerging bottlenecks during the latter phase of the first industrialization wave and especially as a result of the sudden shifts in the direction of economic policy and development goals during the New Course made it imperative to give priority to a comprehensive reexamination of regional economic cooperation endeavors, purposes and means.

Although the rapid and sizable gridlocks encountered during the first wave of industrialization had underscored the need for also changing gears in regional cooperation policies, by the mid-1950s the CMEA found itself still without even adequately defined operational purposes on which the majority of the members concurred. In fact, the bilateral cooperation efforts revolving around the USSR's foreign trade ministry completely usurped the purposes of whatever might have been scheduled, or even entertained conceptually, at the regional level. The USSR's involved embassy system of interacting separately with the CPEs immobilized the CMEA. It was a very effective expression of the USSR's initial intransigence with respect to SEI that, with few interruptions, remained the cornerstone of CMEA cooperation approximately until the mid-1980s. This was complemented, especially in the former enemy countries, by JSCs in critical areas of economic activity and the presence of Soviet advisers directly in planning centers, economic ministries and the enterprises that were the vanguard in enhancing the pace and scope of socialist industrialization. The other CPEs, supine as they were at the time to Soviet advice, influence and dominance, failed to check the USSR's encroachment on virtually all areas of regional contacts – by no means only the economic domain. Although the small CPEs organized their own efforts to ward off the worst implications of independent development, they in effect stifled whatever possibilities for intercountry cooperation could still be mustered (Brabant, 1976).

Instead of focusing on the essence of SEI, the Council's Bureau concentrated on aiding the clearing of bilateral trade, standardizing trade contracts and statistics, facilitating regional transportation, minor administrative tasks and a few areas in which stimulating regional cooperation and production specialization exhibited clear-cut universal advantages. These were obvious either because some countries continued to exploit their inherited comparative advantage (such as in the production of coal in Poland and petroleum in Rumania) or because the benefits of cooperation were so large that no careful quantitative computations were required to justify their emergence (as in the case of specializing in types of ball bearings or cooperating in the substitution of pipeline transportation for railroad or trucking haulage).

In light of the postwar changes in Eastern Europe, one may surmise that the bilateral type of cooperation embraced to facilitate trade could have been implemented in all major respects without the CMEA's existence. Because the Council did not undertake anything to support this odd system of economic relations, the regional organization for all practical purposes did not in fact exist until the second half of the 1950s, when it was revived and finally obtained a charter in which more details were specified about its principles, methods and goals. This new phase of the CMEA's history commenced as a result of the complex conflicts of interest aired during the New Course.

Following Stalin's death and the wrangling over his succession, fast industrialization *per se* as the goal of resource mobilization was temporarily abandoned in favor of a more balanced growth concept. This fundamental policy shift entailed serious conflicts, not only because of the transformed development ambitions of each country individually but precisely because the move caught planners and partners by surprise. Conflicts in regional trade intentions and possibilities were particularly pronounced. The sudden, in some cases dramatic, change in industrialization policies in 1953–4 diversified the aggregate demand for fuels, raw materials and foodstuffs and reduced the demand for manufactures, especially industrial machinery for investment purposes in vanguard sectors. It particularly upset the developed CPEs' trade prospects, which were predicated on exports of machines in exchange for primary products and foodstuffs. Orders placed in these countries for capital equipment, for example, were canceled as investment plans in the purchasing countries were drastically curtailed. The potential exporters of foodstuffs, fuels and industrial raw materials had to honor their new commitment to the improvement of domestic consumption levels and did not feel compelled to export to the fraternal countries to pay for imports that were no longer required.

The trade and other plans in place at that time could not be maintained as realistic policy goals – in any event they were not honored – as country after country revised its domestic development priorities in favor of correcting existing imbalances, including those in consumer markets. These unsynchronized actions had a cumulative impact on partner countries. Indeed, to the extent that these frustrated plans could not be alleviated through alternative trade channels, a negative trade multiplier manifested itself. Fortunately, by the mid-1950s the climate for trade and cooperation between Eastern and Western Europe had been favorably affected by the easing of the cold war. These trade channels not only demonstrated to the CPEs the importance of trade as such but also underlined the critical role of trade as a flexible escape valve.

Because it was difficult to ensure regional deliveries of goods required under the changed economic and political climate, a sharp redirection of trade was engineered. Such a diversion proved much easier for the net exporters of fuels, foodstuffs and industrial raw materials – all hard goods as these types of products were subsequently christened – than for the net exporters of machinery – chiefly soft goods. The inconsistency in trade intentions, and hence already strained external payments situation, was aggravated in the mid-1950s by the sale of the JSCs, especially in the case of the former enemy countries. Though they were chiefly net exporters of hard goods and had to effect these transfers in payment of the capital transfers from the sale of the JSCs, their demand for imports of new machinery had to be reduced commensurately.

Identifying precisely what are soft and what are hard goods is by no means an easy task. Because of the role of these categories in CMEA economic relations and disputes, it may be instructive to digress briefly on the issue here, although there will be an opportunity to return to it in Parts III and IV.

Hard goods in this context are essentially products that can be readily disposed of or obtained in world markets at prevailing world market prices (WMPs), particularly if TRPs and WMPs are compared at realistic exchange rates. It is not always necessary that the TRP evaluated at a realistic exchange rate is higher than the corresponding WMP for exports and the reverse for imports. This is so because in CMEA relations, TRPs are not really the terms at which alternatives are freely available to any taker (see chapter 15). Soft goods, by contrast, are products that can be sold in world markets, if at all in the short run, only at a marked discount. Sharp improvements in the quality and adjustments in the range of such products are required to attain world market levels and hence to be ensured of meriting WMPs, even in the long run. These characterizations of hard and soft goods will have to be modified as other aspects of CMEA cooperation are gradually brought into the analysis.

A more positive appreciation of the role of external trade in economic development emerged as a result of two main policy concerns. One derived from the long-run effects of import substitution in small economies. The other stemmed essentially from attempts to raise economic efficiency through so-called production intensification; that is, reaping a substantial share of growth from factor productivity gains rather than primarily from the injection of physical factor inputs. To maintain regional economic and political stability, mutual economic cooperation was looked upon more favorably as one pivotal channel for promoting the objectives of the New Course. But economic affairs were not the only force behind the renewed interest in the possibilities of placing intragroup economic collaboration onto a different plane and the first signs of the CMEA's renaissance.

Not the least important of the stimuli activating the CMEA came from outside the region when the Western European countries sharply eased their embargo restrictions on trade with CPEs. This does not mean that the contentious CoCom lists were immediately revised. On the contrary. Whereas the full lists remained firmly in place until later in the decade, trade relaxation occurred in two respects. On the one hand, the application of the lists was handled less rigidly than had been the case in earlier years. Perhaps more important, the sentiment against trade that the CPEs associated with the embargo and boycott underwent substantial modification. This opened up new channels for exports from Eastern Europe as well as for imports. This incremental East-West trade essentially diverted goods earmarked for CMEA markets – over and above those already required by the shifts in the level and composition of trade on account of overhauled short-term plans – in exchange for imports that were deemed to be essential. The result was a further exacerbation of the inconsistencies in short-term trade intentions throughout the CMEA.

Given the prevailing circumstances, the Council could do little in the short run to alleviate these structural conflicts. For one, it could not provide bridging finance to countries facing payments difficulties. Similarly, it had few means by which it could mobilize trade resources from within the group. These basic incompatibilities could be mitigated only through better integrating development plans for the second half of the 1950s and beyond. The latter escape from the bind, of course, fell within the competence of the national governments rather than the compass of operations of the CMEA as a regional organization.

After Stalin's death and the difficulties experienced with proceeding for an extended period of time along the improvisation path of the New Course, the CMEA members began to search systematically for ways to impart operational meaning to SEI. The decisions enacted during the New Course not only failed to be properly coordinated, they in fact violated major provisions of the bilateral agreements that had been worked out earlier. By early 1954, such a new mission for Eastern European economic cooperation was ostensibly found in an unambiguous commitment to the coordination of the national economic plans that the member countries had worked out by themselves – that is, without proper *ex ante* coordination at the regional level. At that stage, plan coordination was to be strictly reserved for dovetailing mainly intended trade flows. In other words, plan coordination in the mid-1950s meant little more than an attempt to harmonize trade intentions that followed from nationwide planning. In contrast, regional coordination consisted essentially of attempts to reconcile the demand for and supply of goods that countries intended to produce in excess of or in volumes falling short of domestic requirements, as conceived chiefly against the horizon of national resources and autonomous development objectives. The only exception was the firm commitments, largely for critical raw materials and foodstuffs, that countries had made in longer-term plans. But even those failed to be available in a synchronized form for the concurrent plan.

For all practical purposes, the members committed themselves to explore better ways and means of harmonizing *ex post* intentions; that is, the planned surpluses and deficits emerging from the national plans when the latter were already in a final draft phase or, in fact, finalized in a number of important respects. Though the conceptual differences between plan coordination and the fairly simple agreements on trade may suggest a major change in approach to SEI, the implications of the commitment made in 1954, namely, to pursue plan coordination, were far more modest. At best, some extra room for modifying planned trade intentions could be found by marginal shifts in planned trade, and hence domestic activity and consumption levels.

At the same time, though, the CPEs began to stress the potential advantages of specialization and cooperation in production and how such activities could be fostered through explicit agreements between two or more rather inward-orientated economies. The first of these ECPS agreements were signed in the mid-1950s, chiefly in connection with the development plans of the second half of the 1950s. As elaborated in section 3.1, the political and economic events in Eastern Europe in the mid-1950s, some part of which stemmed from the perceived unequal exchange (including through specialization), effectively nullified the bulk of these agreements, however. After the momentous Hungarian and Polish events of 1956, a new start with ECPS had become overdue. It was inaugurated in two dramatically different directions.

On the one hand, two or more countries, usually one combination at a time, found common ground in a few specific sectors of economic activity and thus resorted to genuine production specialization, even if based on very partial criteria of economic efficiency. The objectives were usually very pragmatic and anchored to the needs of the individual participants. Nothing much of this activity percolated through to the regionwide level, however, as the ambitious recommendations of the first newly created sectoral Standing Commissions succeeded in finding a weak response at best in the member countries. At this second level of CMEA events, the attention of policymakers focused on institution building, the debates on formulating a blueprint for regional economic cooperation, the endorsement of a charter for the CMEA and a number of related developments that set the stage for economic, commercial and financial relations among CPEs in subsequent years.

The first serious efforts directed at reviving the Council and at stimulating regional economic cooperation outside the confining straitjacket of BTPAs were made in the mid-1950s. Under the impact of the rapidly growing critical examination of traditional policies, the several meetings of the Council Session in the mid-1950s focused particularly on deepening ECPS, especially in branches in which the CPEs had been seeking similar, if not identical, output objectives. Production specialization in this context does not aim at redistribution of productive resources in response to shifts in relative product or factor prices. As examined in chapter 13, ECPS agreements entail the division of resources into areas that produce finished products about which some agreements on development, averting duplication, redistributing output plans or the allocation of new capacities are signed.

Preliminary agreements on specialization in key branches of machine building and metallurgy were reached in 1954 (Góra and Knyziak, 1974, p. 33), thus underscoring the swift post-Stalin change in regional cooperation. These largely political ECPS agreements were concerned basically with principles of deepening regional production cooperation. They were not derived from a fundamental search for a better allocation of resources in the region. It took the CPEs until mid-1956 before actual contracts were completed and endorsed at the May and June Council Session meetings. In the wake of the 1956 events, however, renegotiation of important provisions was deemed opportune, presumably also because the preliminary agreements did not qualify as a clear-cut set of guidelines to underpin solid decision making about production specialization and trade matters, even when confined to the planning framework. In spite of the renegotiations undertaken after the Hungarian and Polish calamities of late 1956, Eastern European evaluation of the implementation and effect of these contracts (and, incidentally, of later protocols as well) has not been favorable, as examined below and in chapter 13.

Under the impact of the New Course, the frustrated attempts to implement feasible specialization agreements, the explicit challenge to the USSR's supremacy over all communist states and the growing unification attempts in Western Europe, CPE leaders also sought to reinforce the Council's institutions and to codify principles of cooperation in a joint policy statement on the ISDL. This new realism was demonstrated when the members reportedly agreed to a fundamental shift in the original goals, mechanisms and principles of regional cooperation (Faddeev, 1974a, p. 59). The latter apparently transpired in 1954 into revised statutes (Čížkovský, 1970, p. 244), the content of which has never been disclosed in detail.

At the same time that these practical matters were being put to the test, and integrally woven around the debates concerning the matters introduced above, the CMEA members decided to elaborate a full-scale, comprehensive policy document on the goals, means and institutions for the effective enhancement of regional economic cohesion. Because the latter was endorsed only in the early 1960s and became the subject of a tangled, rancorous debate on a variety of economic and political issues in the first half of the 1960s, I shall discuss those matters in chapter 4. Suffice it to add to this soul-searching that for the first time an organ came into existence that eventually would come to play a critical role in the debates about the broad canvas of SEI. With the convening of the first economic summit proper in May 1958 (see chapter 7), the stage was fully set for involving the top political leadership of the CPEs more fully in the discussions of SEI.

3.3 INSTITUTIONAL TRANSFORMATIONS

The 1950s were the decade of important institutional transformations in the CMEA. That is not to say that the key organs that have emerged in more recent decades should not be accorded their proper place. Quite the contrary. The newer organs, however, could not have evolved without the experience gained in the various institutional structures first established in the 1950s. These include most notably the CMEA Secretariat (created in 1954); the Standing Commissions (first established in 1956) that superseded the temporary committees that emerged during the New Course; the Conference of Representatives of Member Countries (set up in 1954), which was eventually transformed into the Executive Committee; and a regional clearing institution temporarily attached to the foreign department of Gosbank and later to the USSR's foreign trade bank (*Vneštorgbank*). Other structures were also established and among these a number of common undertakings were launched. Some developed into the first common enterprises (especially *Haldex*), while others led to less formal interstate organizations and more technical cooperative ventures (such as the Organization for International Railway Cooperation, the Organization for Cooperation in Telecommunications and Posts and Danube Shipping). In addition, other ventures affected in particular specialized transportation undertakings (such as *Mir*). These largely informal affiliates of the CMEA are discussed in greater detail in chapter 8.

Especially notable in 1956 was the rapid profileration of the Standing Commissions. By the end of the year no fewer than twelve were in place. Further sectoral and general Standing Commissions were introduced or modified in subsequent years. By the end of the 1950s, seventeen commissions had already been established, two of which (agriculture and forestry) were combined in 1958 and another two (timber and cellulose, and geology) abolished in the same year; the one for geology was revived in July 1963. Of these, all but the Commissions entrusted with foreign trade and economic questions were sectoral ones (such as for chemical industry, machine building, light and food industry, which was split in July 1963, various energy sectors and the conventional metallurgical sectors).

Because these Commissions, unlike what their name suggests, are non-permanent organs (see chapter 7), the role of the Secretariat in serving the Commissions expanded considerably. The same applies to the coordinating functions of the Conference of Representatives of the CMEA countries, which began to play a critical role in the various phases of the ISDL by the end of the decade.

Apart from these purely institutional innovations, CMEA cooperation in the later 1950s was enhanced through a number of other steps. Suffice it to mention here the institutionalization of efforts to settle pricing and exchange rate matters, the elaboration of the first operative ECPS agreements with the cooperation of one official CMEA organ or another, the elaboration of a formal charter, the first vestiges of a capital market, talks about stepping over to more flexible BTPAs, perhaps even leading up to some kind of multilateralism in trade and payments and other measures. Because most of these issues impinge upon technical institutional or economic matters, the details are discussed in Parts II and III.

3.4 THE CMEA'S CHARTER

Until 1962 the CMEA does not seem to have had a commonly agreed (published!) policy on how the ISDL was to evolve. A weak first attempt emerged with the publication of the charter in 1959. Other statutes may have been drafted in 1949 and 1954, but they were never published and may have had only limited applicability. As a result, the only available documents from which one could infer official intentions prior to the Council's formal charter of 1959, which clarifies the legal organization of the CMEA, were the vaguely phrased founding communiqué and the equally abstruse communications of various meetings of the Session, the first full-fledged CMEA summit in 1958 and other meetings at party and governmental levels. Being formally without a clearly defined and agreed purpose, and without official statutes until 1959 – when the basic ideas behind the CMEA were recorded for the first time (Tokareva, 1967, pp. 45–54) – the CMEA as a regional institution was a unicum among international organizations (Szawlowski, 1963, p. 676).

The founding communiqué was not informative about the structure, purposes, principles and methods of the newly created organization, as documented in chapter 1. The common call for 'exchanging economic experience, extending technical aid to one another, and rendering mutual assistance with respect to raw materials, foodstuffs, machines, equipment, and so on' (Tokareva, 1967, p. 44) could be, and in fact was, interpreted according to whatever best suited the prevailing views on socialist international relations, national economic development and regional cooperation. More specific tasks failed to be agreed upon; at least they were not codified at that time. Consequently, the scope and content of socialist cooperation tended to be defined implicitly as a result of practical actions, or 'historical experience' as current phraseology puts it, taken largely outside the scope of the regional institution. But there may have been commonly agreed, but unpublished, statements about the more concrete goals, mechanisms and principles of regional economic cooperation (see chapters 1 and 2).

The official charter, which was first ratified in 1960, has been revised on several occasions to enable non-European CPEs to participate, to shift the policy goals from simple cooperation to integration and to enshrine new legal or other concepts. Nevertheless, the basic idea guiding the Council's mission remains:

> To promote, by uniting and coordinating the efforts of the [CPEs], the planned development of the national economy, the acceleration of economic and technical progress in these countries, the raising of the level of industrialization in the ... less developed countries, a continuous increase in labor productivity, and a steady improvement in the welfare of the peoples of the member countries. (Tokareva, 1967, pp. 45–6)

As a further specification of this general task, the members are expected to promote gradually 'the most rational use of their natural resources' and 'to accelerate the development of their productive capacities.' These goals are to be attained by means of coordination of national economic plans, comprehensive examination of economic and scientific-technical problems and implementation of common ventures in any project of more universal interest.

The charter is not entirely unambiguous as to whether common or national advantage should prevail in steering decision making. Certainly, the emphasis on full equality of rights, national sovereignty, national interest in carrying out common projects to mutual advantage and friendly assistance can be found as broad guidelines in most documents issuing from the CPEs. But this is usually not much more than paying lip service to the *de jure* organization of Eastern Europe. It is hardly always a reflection of actual political and economic realities. The charter's preamble states explicitly, however, that the signatory states are 'fully determined henceforth to develop all-around economic cooperation by consistently putting into practice the [ISDL], in the interest of building socialism and communism in these countries' (Tokareva, 1967, p. 45).

As an international organization motivated by these general objectives, the CMEA can hope to acquit itself of the concrete tasks at hand within fairly restrictive boundaries. These limits exist because the Council is not empowered to issue binding instructions on the substantive matters of plan coordination and production specialization. It was entitled to issue recommendations on matters of economic, scientific and technical cooperation, as well as decisions on organizational and procedural matters. Both can be adopted only with the consent of all interested countries, and each member is entitled to declare its interest, or lack thereof, in any matter considered by the Council (see chapter 7). In this connection, it should be recalled that the members also agreed to 'ensure the fulfillment of the recommendations' (Tokareva, 1967, p. 46) – a noble principle but hardly an operational modality of great practical importance.

Membership in the Council was to be restricted to 'other European countries' that 'share the purposes and principles of the Council and express their readiness to accept the obligations contained in the present Statutes.' For all practical purposes, then, the CMEA was conceived for the European CPEs. This remained official until 1962, when it proved expedient to admit Mongolia into the CMEA, and the relevant statutes were revised accordingly.

The charter lists the official organs as: the Council Session, the Conference of Representatives of the Countries in the Council, the Standing Commissions and the Secretariat. The purposes and tasks of each organ, and those added later, are detailed in chapter 7. The charter also specifies provisions for the participation of other countries in the CMEA, relations with international organizations, the financing of the Secretariat, working languages, ratification procedures and related organizational matters.

3.5 TOWARD A FIRST POLICY BLUEPRINT AND RELATED DEVELOPMENTS

As noted, the CPEs encountered a number of severe difficulties in the mid-1950s with specifying areas in which they could usefully seek to advance regional cooperation. Even greater obstacles were quickly faced as a result of inquiries into how best to harmonize regional cooperation with national policy objectives, instruments and related institutions. The unanticipated negative developments of the mid-1950s led to a search for new methods for invigorating economic cooperation. Although the institutional transformations undoubtedly helped, a commitment in principle to the goals and means of SEI was deemed useful to elevate concerns about SEI into the discourse about national and regional development strategies and economic mechanisms.

The debate evolved in two different directions. On the one hand, the members became seriously concerned about practical matters rather than merely seeking justification in socialist principles and precepts. These deliberations emanated in the formation of some bi- and multilateral organizations whose affiliation with the CMEA is not entirely clear (see chapter 8). It also engendered a keener interest in assisting with the domestic institutional, organizational and political changes (as discussed in the next chapter), to foster trade-promoting measures at the regional level. These included deliberations about the creation of multilateral clearing in the CMEA, which was first enshrined in the so-called Warsaw Agreement of June 1957. This led to minor institutional change in the sense that limited clearing at the CMEA level could henceforth be undertaken within the context of Soviet banks, as noted in section 3.3. But the leadership of national financial institutions and monetary policy had concerns that reached well beyond those that could be quickly accommodated within the narrow limits of the Warsaw Agreement. In fact, in the meeting of central bank presidents in Prague, May–June 1958, the groundwork was laid for a study of multilateral clearing proper and the introduction of an own currency for CMEA transactions. These deliberations eventually matured into the creation of a formal clearing bank (see chapter 8), the TR as clearing unit, the investment bank a decade later, measures to accommodate the clearing of so-called noncommercial transactions by way of special accounts and exchange rates and the establishment of effective exchange rates for certain types of transactions.

These meetings of technicians were in an important way mandated by the first full-fledged economic summit of the CMEA member countries held in Moscow (20–23 May 1958). This particular convention of top-level policymakers has rarely received its full due as its deliberations remained secret and the communiqué of the deliberations (see CMEA, 1979b, pp. 11–13) is exceedingly obscure. Nonetheless, this was the first time since the abortive attempts of the late 1940s that pinnacle decision makers became active in

CMEA affairs. The political summit held the preceding 14–16 November also in Moscow had laid the groundwork for this economic summit. However, the primary purposes of the 1957 meeting had been to examine the world political situation and the problems of the international communist movement (Neumann, 1980, p. 212) – both issues by themselves ranging beyond what could reasonably be tabled on economic matters. Although that meeting supposedly mandated guidelines on economic cooperation among the CPEs, this probably meant little more than a reaffirmation of general principles of international relations among sovereign states. The transformation of these general precepts into principles for regional economic behavior far transcended those that could be tackled in conjunction with a host of other matters in 1957 (Hoensch, 1977, pp. 149–51).

Though the November summit offered the first broad-based opportunity to reexamine the Eastern European convulsions of the mid-1950s, the economic summit presented the real occasion for coming to grips groupwide with a number of thorny economic complaints that had surfaced in the post-Stalin period. For the first time since the convulsions of 1956, CMEA issues were being considered at the policymaking apex. This presumably also reflected the felt need to reinvigorate the Council and thus facilitate more intensive trade ties within the central planning model than had earlier been possible.

Perhaps the most eventful aspect of this meeting was the coining of the ISDL notion together with suggestions on how to impart concrete meaning to this concept via coordination of economic plans, all-sided economic cooperation (including on information matters) and production specialization. All these were to assist in the elaboration of perspective development plans for the basic branches of the national economies. It also stressed the urgent need to place CMEA cooperation on a regional footing, particularly in machine building, for which the Standing Commissions were called upon to suggest areas for fruitful regionwide cooperation. The better utilization of scarce fuels and raw materials was also to be enhanced through joint efforts.

At the same time, the summit paid attention to the legal aspects of cooperation as well as to the institutional foundations. Other practical matters that were considered at that meeting, though they are not mentioned in the communiqué, include financial cooperation, the elaboration of multilateral clearing and improving regional pricing. Though so-called special purpose or target credits first emerged shortly before the full-fledged summit, they constituted an integral part of the proceedings.

As the name suggests, target credits are a form of capital transfer within the region that is associated with a commitment to lend resources from one country for well-defined expansion purposes in another country so as to enhance reciprocal trade. In practice, this implies that a country interested in obtaining incremental deliveries of scarce raw materials or fuels produced in another fraternal country would have to finance part of the investment needed to bring the required new capacity on line. Though first introduced as a way of assuaging the rancor about unequal economic relations in the mid-1950s, these special purpose credits were later targeted at expanding production in areas where CMEA cooperation had run into serious bottlenecks. Most of the funds committed during the first wave of so-called joint investments occurred from 1957 until about 1962. It involved chiefly transfers of capital resources in the form of tied loans from the more- to the less-developed CPEs. The sums involved were never spectacular, though they certainly were not trivial by previous Eastern European standards, as distinct from the role of the USSR in effecting capital transfers in the postwar period.

One of the most eventful Sessions occurred in 1958. When called to order it had as one major agenda item deliberation about a number of critical integration issues, most notably the endorsement of a set of uniform rules and regulations governing the setting of regional trade prices for regular transactions – that is, the TRP regime proper. The details of this agreement are analyzed in chapter 15. But the backdrop to the emergence of this so-called Bucharest agreement needs to be elaborated here.

The genesis of the peculiarities typical of the inflexible intra-CMEA trade model is rooted chiefly in the particular dislocations caused by World War II and its aftermath. The changeover from a war-economy footing to a peacetime civilian economy played an especially pivotal role in Eastern Europe, as it did in most other countries that participated in World War II. In some cases, this already confining environment was further exacerbated by major shifts in the political backdrop to the macroeconomic policy mechanisms, institutions and development objectives that were then being promulgated and eventually jelled into what has become known as the traditional CPE model. Most Western economies gradually sought to return to flexible market mechanisms in their external commerce. In contrast, the CPEs actively evolved their trade model and policy in line with the centralized control over economic affairs that they had chosen as their preferred means of accelerating economic growth and industrialization. Their becoming full-fledged CPEs had a special impact on the CMEA pricing mechanism, however.

From a practical point of view, the concrete development aims and organizational characteristics of the CPEs stand out. A significant inducement to a peculiar pricing debate was the general economic backwardness of most CPEs. Given the circumstances under which the postwar reconversion and reconstruction were accomplished, as well as the conditions that surfaced in conjunction with rapid industrialization, WMPs provided an interesting orientation for these countries (Grinev, 1984, p. 314). They represented indicators of labor productivity and quality of output that reflected conditions in advanced MEs. As such they posed a challenge for the CPEs to emulate such 'capitalist' achievements as quickly as possible.

One of the most essential characteristics of CPE planning has been an unambiguous preference for stability within the typical planning periodicity. This precept found a direct counterpart in external economic relations, including in securing guaranteed supplies at predictable prices to avoid balance-of-payments perturbations that would inevitably spill over into the domestic economy and disturb the planning framework. Although not altogether indispensable among the crucial policy instruments of the CPE, stable trade prices were deemed to be highly desirable for supporting detailed central planning. This was true especially in the countries that perforce depended on external commerce. As a result, price inflexibility emerged as an especially crucial feature in the context of the BTPAs that these economies resorted to while simultaneously diverting trade from outside markets to the region.

During the discussions preceding the creation of the Council in January 1949 and the high-level debates that took place until about mid-1950, the CPEs were also striving for multilateral clearing, proper exchange rates and adequate pricing in tune with demand and supply forces in world markets. As to the latter, there was already consensus on the elaboration of a 'regional price system' (Čížkovský, 1971, p. 5). It is not clear to what extent regional pricing as such appeared as a self-contained item on the agenda of the high-level discussions that sought to shape SEI in the late 1940s. This issue was probably bound up with the multilateralization scheme that was already in an advanced stage of negotiation (Mazanov, 1970, p. 45). Sometime in mid-1950 – remember the outbreak of the Korean War on 25 June 1950 – the issue of fluctuations in WMPs and how they would impact on TRPs became a priority item of high-level policy discussions. It figured prominently in the debates at the third Session in November 1950, when it was decided to adopt the so-called stop prices in regional trade. These eventually matured into the system known as socialist WMPs, or rather TRPs.

Although the many conceptual and practical questions of regional, and more importantly bilateral, pricing must have arisen on a number of occasions at the highest policymaking level, after the initial debates of 1949–50 they were not formally discussed in depth again in CMEA forums between November 1950 and the eighth Council Session in June 1957 (Faddeev, 1974b, p. 295). Agreement existed in principle that the CMEA should follow international price levels and modifications thereof revealed through the competitive operation of supply and demand. Only in such a way could the true international value of a commodity allegedly be ascertained (Hegemann, 1980, p. 123). At the same time, it was formally recommended that the anomalies of WMP formation as a result of caprice, speculation and discrimination by imperialist monopolies be removed from TRPs to the extent feasible.

These debates remained inconclusive in that a number of further studies were commissioned (Hegemann, 1980, p. 123) in time for analysis during the all-important ninth Session in June 1958 in Bucharest. Remember that the first full-scale summit had been held the preceding May! This conference decided that TRPs be fixed differently for future long-term trade agreements from those to be specified in agreements of a duration up to five years (Hegemann, 1980, p. 124). Whereas the ninth Session had recommended that prices through 1960 be based on average 1956–7 WMPs (Hegemann, 1980, p. 187), the five-year trade agreements then in place were generally kept intact but with *ad hoc* price adjustments.

Though perhaps less momentous in its implications for the conduct of trade and specialization in the CMEA, but certainly not negligible for these economies as a whole or for concerned individual CPEs, these countries adopted the first principles for more harmonized exchange rates (for details, see Part III). In 1956–7, however, the CMEA members agreed to search for a common way of encouraging noncommercial transactions among the CPEs, and, in fact included other non-CMEA countries. The basic purpose of these agreements, which were applied retroactively to 1 January 1956, was to obtain equivalent purchasing power of foreign exchange for noncommercial purposes by computing the value of binary baskets of goods and services typical for a diplomatic family expressed in prices of the two countries (see chapter 14).

At the same time that these practical matters were being tested, and integrally woven around the debates concerning the technical topics introduced above, the CMEA members elaborated a full-scale policy document on the goals, means and institutions for effective enhancement of regional economic cohesion. Because the latter was endorsed only in the early 1960s and became the subject of a rancorous debate early in the decade, I shall deal with it and related matters in chapter 4.

Suffice it to add here that for the first time an organ came into being that would in due course begin to play a critical role in the debates about the broad canvas of SEI. With the convening of the first true economic summit in May 1958, the stage was prepared for more fully involving the top political leadership of the CPEs in the discussions of regional economic cooperation. The role and place of this organ are discussed fully in chapter 7.

Because of the complex institutional and other aspects of regional pricing matters, exchange rate coordination or cooperation, multilateral settlement of accounts, the initial phases of a regional capital market and other cooperation problems examined in depth in the 1950s, this first decade of SEI provided important experiences. At the very least, such experience illustrated the real difficulties of organizing regional economic cooperation on other than simple ideological grounds. The practical problems encountered in the process and the various experiments tried in order to ease them in turn induced reflection and experimentation. As a whole, they amounted to a significant inspiration for the conceptualization and inauguration of new modes of cooperation in the 1960s.

NOTE

1. Whether this really amounted to discrimination in the strict sense is a different question altogether (see Brabant, 1987b, pp. 153–4). I shall return to it in Part IV, even though this book is not about contentious issues in Western analyses of CPEs.

4 · THE BASIC PRINCIPLES AND COOPERATION IN THE 1960s

The 1950s can be characterized as a period of political turmoil and conflict that led to seminal changes in the interactions of the European planned economies, the way these economies were steered, and the development objectives envisaged in the process, as well as the institutional reinforcement of the Council. Although very different in character and tenor, the next decade was beset by two eminently related developments. On the one hand, the CPEs reflected at great length upon the foundations of cooperation policies and on how best to organize them within the CMEA. This drive stemmed in large measure from concerns about solidifying the economic cohesion of the group, given the planning context of the member economies.

At about the same time, a comprehensive reexamination of the development precepts and the standard economic model of the national economy began to take shape and eventually entailed far-reaching transformations in institutions, policy instruments and macroeconomic policy objectives through the first wave of broad-based economic reforms. These affected especially the economic model but also the national and regional development strategy. Macroeconomic management of these economies, and the political leadership more generally, gradually became increasingly concerned about how to intensify the pace of economic growth through productivity gains, in part to satisfy social welfare commitments. The transition in political perceptions about social welfare issues stemmed from the realization that the call for postponement of consumption until future generations wears off quickly, especially when based chiefly on 'revolutionary' fervor.

Although they should have been intimately interconnected, these two features developed in tandem. In some instances, they were shaped largely by an adversarial relationship. The initial failure of reforms in CMEA policies and institutions led to some concessions in the policy autonomy enjoyed in the member economies, which, in turn, tended to be rapidly confronted with myriad problems related to implementing inconsistent reforms while simultaneously seeking to boost the pace of growth.

This chapter addresses the dilemmas between the course of national and regional reforms and between domestic resource mobilization and the increasingly more strident distributional demands that planners had to confront. Key developments during the decade are unfolded in section 4.1. The next section analyzes *Basic Principles*[1] as a policy statement without really isolating individual policies, instruments or institutions (which are dealt with specifically in Part III). Next I examine the institutional aspects of the evolution of cooperation in the 1960s. In the same context, I also assess the implications of both the reform wave and the relative attractiveness of East-West cooperation in seeking to bolster regional cohesion within the CMEA. Section 4.4 analyzes the implications of the effective unraveling of the domestic economic reforms and their replacement by a less-coherent economic mechanism and macroeconomic policies in search of viable initiatives. This provides the backdrop to the exploration of a new mode of cooperation and thus the transition to the 1970s, when regional economic integration in the cloak of SEI is formally recognized as *the* goal of the CMEA countries.

4.1 THE BACKDROP OF THE 1960s

The problems faced during most of the 1960s throughout Eastern Europe stemmed largely from the CPEs' inability to exploit the New Course as a logical transitional period toward an ambiguous alternative to the Stalinist economic model. As detailed in chapter 3, the CPEs embarked upon their second broad industrialization wave without really having resolved earlier national or regional obstacles. At the national level, one country after another reverted to largely autarkic industrialization at a forced pace in spite of the fact that national policy autonomy and self-sufficiency were clearly inadvisable objectives for the smaller countries. At the regional level, the countless practical and other aspects of the goals, means and institutions for enhancing regional economic cooperation, although debated at some length, remained unresolved during the New Course and its immediate aftermath. The CPEs, in fact, proceeded without having found plausible answers to the many questions involved with concretely formulating what kind of regional economic cooperation should be targeted and how to enhance it.

Admittedly, the second wave of industrialization was programmed more carefully than the voluntaristic excursions of the early 1950s. Nonetheless, its basic shortcomings, and in some cases systemic flaws, quickly surfaced in at least three respects: inadequate or even faulty resource mobilization and motivation, inability to sustain the pace of economic growth and limited capacity for mobilizing resources except simply by injecting new production factors into the material production process or by redistributing existing ones, chiefly from the rural sector to industry. After a brief interlude in the late 1950s, when performance appeared to resume at the earlier rapid pace, the more-developed CPEs especially were confronted with the drawbacks inherent in weak factor productivity growth. In some, including Czechoslovakia and the GDR, growth decelerated sharply and became even negative, at least for one year. Because the legitimacy of the political regimes in these countries significantly depends on delivering steady, even if modest, gains in per capita income levels, these countries needed ways of reinvigorating factor productivity growth given that resources for extensive development were decelerating, if growing positively at all.

In response, the CPEs began to experiment with an economic reorganization that surpassed the substitution of regional planning for the ministerial planning that the USSR had sought to enact in the late 1950s with the creation of the *sovnarchozy* everywhere and that Bulgaria and the GDR briefly emulated. Even the USSR began to look for alternative mechanisms as advocated at the time by Evsej Liberman and a few other economists who were permitted to vent novel ideas. A particularly conspicuous feature of the Eastern European economic reforms, in marked contrast to the policy concerns and activities of the Soviet Union, was the attention devoted to the foreign sector. CPE policymakers began to look upon external trade as a potentially substantial channel for growth through production specialization. This would not only permit scale economies but also the elaboration of dynamic comparative advantages that, so it was hoped, in time would secure a new foundation for sustainable economic development.

Of course, the interest of these countries in mobilizing modified, or even completely new, methods of engaging themselves more deeply in regular trade and economic cooperation channels had become particularly acute during the New Course. As examined in chapter 3, this shift in short-term economic policy entailed serious imbalances in intragroup trade, a diversion of commerce in favor of Western Europe and external payments pressures that could be mitigated in the short run only through emergency loans and economic assistance, in part from the Soviet Union. The rapid increase in interaction with the MEs demonstrated the potentially critical role of trade not only as an escape valve but also as a major contributor to productivity growth. In addition, six European market economies signed the Treaty of Rome in 1957 and began to implement it. This emerging customs union vividly demonstrated the potential of catering to foreign demand and of competition from foreign supply for the buoyancy and stabilization of economic growth. It also made it clear that in time Western market access for the CPEs would be impaired – or at least hindered – by the group preferences of the European Economic Community (EEC), the precursor of the European Communities (EC).

Paralleling the drive toward a gradual unification of markets, virtually all DMEs had succeeded through Marshall Plan aid, and the favorable climate for regional economic cooperation it engendered within the context of the European Payments Union (EPU), in gradually, but steadily, easing the formidable restrictions on the free flow of current account transactions. By

1958 the EPU had enabled most of its members to step over to currency convertibility for current account transactions; the Federal Republic of Germany
(FRG) abandoned the formidable exchange controls inherited from the
1930s in 1961.

As a result, considerable bandwagon pressures were exerted on the CPEs.
These tended to push for more satisfactory CMEA cooperation from three
directions: policymakers, particularly in the more advanced countries; the
need to foster greater economic cohesion within the group as seen largely
through Soviet eyes; and the requirements for sustaining economic growth
at a minimum pace even in the most-developed CPE. Against this background, the CMEA members negotiated *Basic Principles* as the first major
policy statement on regional economic cooperation.

Before clarifying the main features of this document, it will be useful to
sketch the major events of the decade from a CMEA-centered perspective.
There are basically four developments that need to be identified. First, the
negotiations about the first policy document on broad-based SEI, initiated
in the late 1950s for the reasons discussed in chapter 3, were concluded in
1961 and the document was promulgated in 1962. Second, soon thereafter
the document was disowned by several signatories. As a result, the CPEs
failed to implement the precepts on regional production specialization that
constituted the core of the doctrine on the ISDL as laid down in *Basic
Principles*. The germs of this unanticipated development might have been
manifest secretly before the conclusion of the deliberations. Third, the first
broad wave of national economic reforms swept like a brushfire through
Eastern Europe. In conjunction with the newly enlarged room for East-West
economic contacts, it deflected interest from grand CMEA cooperation
schemes. Finally, the Warsaw Pact's invasion of Czechoslovakia and its subsequent so-called normalization, including compromises on strengthening
regional economic cooperation, aborted the reform movements or at the
very least called for retrenchments in a number of important respects.

4.2 BASIC PRINCIPLES OF THE ISDL

For the first time in their postwar cooperation, in *Basic Principles* the CPEs
codified basic rules and regulations of intragroup cooperation as well as the
purposes to be promoted in this way. As noted, this first programmatic,
rather normative statement had long been under preparation. A number of
high-level meetings among CMEA policymakers, including at least two
economic summits (see chapter 7), had elaborated the basic philosophy and
approach underlying the ISDL. It is, then, paradoxical that by 1964 this
movement in favor of SEI was in shambles and led to an open and particularly
divisive controversy about the ISDL.

Whereas the sizable document is long-winded on declarations of the socialist principles on international economic and other relations among sovereign states (including respect for national independence, the inviolability of national sovereignty, strict equality, fraternal mutual assistance, mutual advantage and so on), it is skimpy on the concrete aspects of the ISDL. For the first time, though, the CPEs sought to identify the prospective bases for their economic cooperation. They also laid principal stress on a high degree of genuine coordination in national economic planning, the encouragement of production specialization and greater mobility of goods and production factors throughout the region.

The document strongly emphasizes the need for each CPE to map out development plans according to its own conditions. But it is firmly argued that this sovereign concern needs to be tempered by fully respecting the political and economic goals set by the leading Communist Parties and the needs and potentials of all socialist countries as a commonwealth.[2] It furthermore asserts that 'the new social system makes it possible to combine organically the development of [each CPE] with the development and consolidation of the world economic system of socialism as a whole,' and that 'the strengthening and widening economic ties among the [CPEs] will promote the realization of an objective tendency which was outlined by V. I. Lenin: The creation in the future of the world communist economy directed by the victorious masses of the proletariat according to one plan' (Tokareva, 1967, p. 24). This, in accompanying and subsequent analyses, clarifications and statements (particularly Chruščëv, 1962) was interpreted as a definitive signal to the effect that, in the very near future, regional economic cooperation would be directed under the aegis of a single, uniform economic plan. But this 'momentous decision' may have been inspired by substantially differing goals of the CPEs regarding the formulation and development purposes of SEI. In any case, the chief merit of this document does not lie in the articulation of the specific instruments for promoting regional economic advancement and for blending plans that are primarily nationally oriented.

Nonetheless, the objectives of the ISDL are much more clearly delineated in *Basic Principles* than in any other official policy statement up to that time. Perhaps the key stipulation is the following:

> The planned [ISDL] contributes to the maximum utilization of the advantages of the socialist world system, to the determination of correct proportions in the national economy of each country, to the rational location of production factors with respect to the socialist world system, to the effective utilization of labor and material resources, and to the strengthening of the defensive power of the socialist camp. The division of labor must guarantee each CPE a dependable market for the specialized products and the supply of the necessary raw materials, semifinished products, equipment, and other goods. (Tokareva, 1967, p. 25)

One can hardly interpret this statement otherwise than that the ISDL ought to be considering the best allocation of all available resources in the region so as to optimize regional, rather than national, socioeconomic tasks without, however, overlooking legitimate concerns about the strategic development interests of the separate CPEs. The tendency to create a self-sufficient economic system (that is, the 'economic complex' as it was then being referred to) in each CPE in breadth and in depth at the expense of regional specialization and the attempt to impose one-sided international specialization are recognized as counterproductive ambitions. These features apply not only to individual CPEs but, perhaps more importantly, also to the community as a whole.

International specialization according to genuine comparative advantage considerations is very much the theme underlying the document. To attain a more efficient and, in the end, optimal regional economy, measurably improving the synchronization of national plans as the basic instrument for enhancing socialist economic cooperation was deemed a priority. Bilateral and multilateral concordance of intentions should contribute to the formulation and implementation of the ISDL. But nowhere in the document is it stated how the CPEs are to assess comparative advantage as the economic basis for pursuing planned specialization. The close union of the CPEs within a single planning framework is considered a mandatory objective because of the 'objective laws of economic and political developments.' It will be a potent factor in encouraging 'the intensification of the production in all the countries of materials scarce in the socialist camp, taking into account natural and economic conditions' (Tokareva, 1967, p. 29). This tendency to restrict the horizon to the socialist region as a self-contained unit, rather than as one segment of international specialization, is also displayed in the emphasis placed in several passages on the institutionalization of regional mutilateralism and the gradual elaboration of an own price system, whose ties with WMPs would be much looser than those enshrined in the Bucharest principles (see chapters 3 and 15).

The fundamental objectives of the ISDL should be attained through plan coordination and eventually the construction of a single, consistent plan for the CMEA as a whole. This was to have been devised by a supranational planning authority invested with adequate decision-making room. Eliminating the problems of bilateralism and correcting inconsistent prices were explicitly mentioned as important tasks to be speedily resolved; multilateralism and appropriate scarcity prices in intragroup trade were to serve as the main catalysts for furthering CMEA specialization, particularly in the production sphere.

Although the document pays lip service to the national interest of each member, it was the call for the mutual solving of common problems, not only in trade and joint ventures but also in economic development in general, that was at the forefront of the discussion that was triggered off shortly after the document's endorsement in June 1962.

Perhaps it is unnecessary to explain here why virtually none of the above or other components of the program's intentions was carried out and why many of the proposals were slowly brought backstage, shelved and replaced by the incipient discussions about national economic reforms, the role of trade with nonmember economies in the intensive growth strategy to be elaborated and the initiation of discussion about a new policy blueprint targeted explicitly at the promulgation of SEI. Let it suffice to recall that *Basic Principles* does not specify how these largely political intentions were to be realized either in general or in detail. The document contains no methodology of plan co-ordination, production specialization, regional multilateralism or independent trade pricing, to name but a handful of the many crucial issues. Neither does it refer to any existing methods for ascertaining the proper functioning of these instruments and institutions. The document presumably subsumes that the Council and its members would start serious work on resolving the key components of the ISDL soon after the adoption of the program. But the emerging search for the most plausible alternative procedures of the ISDL was quietly replaced by more fundamental disagreements about the basic goals of SEI. In that light, *Basic Principles* presents a classic example of how a commonly endorsed, promising declaration on principles can exaggerate the purposefulness and ostensible policy coherence even of 'friendly nations.'

Whether or not the shortcomings of the ISDL approach resulted from intentional neglect by the political leadership will not be investigated here. The point is that although important, if vaguely formulated, goals were laid down in an accepted program for common action, nothing much was actually undertaken by the CPEs to promote regional specialization according to common advantages, however these should or could be defined. Research on the basic elements of cooperation was initiated but was often conveniently cloaked within national political options. Political deliberations on critical points of the program were pursued as well, but consensus proved elusive.

Instead of carrying out work on the basis of the program's provisions, a vituperative dispute erupted. Officially it concentrated on the inviolability of national sovereignty and the inalienable right of each CPE to select its own development path according to national advantage, or at least to what was perceived as the country's long-term interest. This debate was sparked by resolute opposition, notably from Rumania, to the gradual elaboration of a 'superplan' and the particular interpretation of the objectives and instruments of SEI as intimated in *Basic Principles*.

Though Rumania was then identified as the most vocal opponent to that kind of mandatory integration through planned production specialization, this distinction probably resulted from the country's traditional defensive stance *vis-à-vis* foreign encroachment. Its peculiar geopolitical position in the context of the Slavic majority in the CMEA and its own domestic political succession crisis following the death of Gheorghe Gheorghiu-Dej may have exacerbated matters. Rumania's main arguments were, however, more widely shared than the literature traditionally acknowledges. Many of the smaller developed CPEs were already searching for better ways to bolster factor productivity growth and attain more balanced regional economic cooperation than what had been typical for the 1950s. They saw, at best, limited salvation coming from transposing the problems of rigid physical planning to the regional plane. Placed in that perspective, then, there were several other countries (including Czechoslovakia, Hungary and Poland) that tacitly sided with the Rumanian position. This sentiment did not necessarily jell, however, because of a desire to pursue further rounding off of a national economic complex in each economy. Instead, it was felt, to be precise, that *Basic Principles* did not contain sufficient promise that the envisioned instruments and institutions, nor the policies they were to buttress, would promote any kind of regional economic cooperation that would support national development efforts.

Instead of taking *Basic Principles* as the fundamental cue for concrete national and regional policy actions, three main trends emerged after the document was endorsed. First, a wave of economic reforms was initiated, eventually encompassing the entire area, although the reforms exhibited diverse objectives and means and differed in how intently and quickly they should be pursued. Their objectives, regardless of the depth and intrinsic merits of the reform blueprints, were such that institutionalizing traditional regional central planning, as earlier pursued in each country, became increasingly unlikely and, for some, very undesirable. In Tibor Kiss's (1975, p. 747) words:

> The joint planning concept proved to be unrealistic, not only because it was cumbersome technically and methodologically, but also in terms of its economic and, last but not least, political implications. It did not reckon, namely, with the fact that an improvement in the multilateral system of harmonization . . . did not depend simply on improving methodology but hinges primarily on questions of self-interest. [It] disregarded actual production conditions [of the CPEs] and the objective necessity of maintaining economic independence.

Second, the mid-1960s provided a more congenial political and economic climate for an upswing of East-West cooperation and hence an inflow of new production methods. More opportunities existed for converting domestic products into foreign exchange and imports. Although political East-West détente was to assume its better-known dimensions only in the 1970s, commercial relations among the smaller European countries accelerated in the early 1960s, spurred in part by the negative impetus from the stillborn *Basic Principles* and moribund ISDL approach in the CMEA. Under these new conditions, each country pressed the issue of specialization according to more precisely defined criteria of economic choice and efficiency before making definitive long-term regional commitments.

Third, although true that the expansion of trade and development in the region slowed down, in hindsight it may be judged a fruitful period. The intense effort by nearly all CPEs, during a comparatively short period of time, of grappling with fundamental theoretical and practical problems of intrasocialist cooperation (price formation, labor and capital mobility, multilateralism, joint investments and so on) and its role in the intensification strategy then on their drawing boards set the stage for the policies that would take centerstage in the next two decades. These included soul-searching on the economics of SEI and the particular role to be played by a regional organization, issues that continue to influence the CMEA policy debate.

Despite joint planning having proved abortive at that stage, CMEA cooperation nevertheless advanced indirectly, chiefly because of efforts aimed at implementing specific cooperation projects of a modest, though not negligible, scale or at least fairly uncomplicated ventures. One can separate these efforts into two categories. The initial momentum engendered by the conceptualization of *Basic Principles* led to the creation of a number of organizations directed at regionwide cooperation (including the first regional bank, the TR as the CMEA's collective currency and a regional settlements mechanism for commercial, noncommercial and special cooperation transactions). Most achievements of the mid- and late 1960s, however, did not result from Council actions. They developed under pressure from the real needs of some CPEs singly or in combination.

4.3 INSTITUTION BUILDING

The major motivations behind codifying *Basic Principles* – that is, hopes for enhanced regional planning and plan coordination – could be realistically entertained as feasible policy objectives only if the decision-making organs within the CMEA would be invested with adequate authority and institutional support for fostering the ISDL. As Peter Wiles (1968, pp. 311–24) has emphasized on so many occasions, the proper framework for integrating CPEs should be central planning. That is, planning at the regional level should be directed at mobilizing all resources within the area. Certain side constraints may have to be imposed on the mobility of production factors, and indeed on the permissible distribution of value added within the region. This is required to ensure a modicum of socialist egalitarianism. Commitment to the gradual equalization of development levels throughout the community may usher in its own restrictions on resource allocation. Furthermore, constraints arise because of nonmaterial requirements, including education, medical care, the arts or social welfare. But the vast bulk should form components of one common pool mustered for a uniform course of action.

As indicated, it is unlikely that *Basic Principles* really reflected the ultimate desires of most top-level policymakers. Even under the most favorable of circumstances, countries could not realistically have foreseen delegating all at once the mobilization of their national resources to the regional authority. For a range of practical purposes, then, no regional institutional equivalent substituting fully for the national planning centers could have been entertained in the short-to-medium run; a complex transition phase would have had to be endured. This would have been constrained by minimum checks and balances to avert derailing the delegation of authority to the regional planning center into an undesirable, if not chaotic, situation. Furthermore, such a CMEA-wide planning center could not have been anticipated to be a fully autonomous organ. Because there is in fact no CMEA counterpart to the all-encompassing power of the national CPs, some consensus – say, through a council of ministers – would have had to emerge. For at least two decades after World War II the Soviet Union aspired to extending the authority of its own Communist Party to the whole region. Paradoxically, when this scenario could have been achieved quite easily under Stalin in the late 1940s, the USSR did not pursue it. Its ideological, strategic, political and moral strengths fell embarrassingly short of the required minimum for carrying this coveted status to fruition in the late 1950s and early 1960s.

In the absence of a solid authority over the CMEA region equivalent to the omnipresent CP in each member, as a palliative the Conference of Representatives of the countries in the Council was upgraded to a more powerful institutional lever. This provided the beginnings of the Executive Committee, which was slated to transform itself into a regional planning forum entrusted with cooperation matters between Council Sessions. Its proper place among the CMEA's pinnacle organs is discussed in chapter 7.

Numerous formal and informal organizations emerged in the 1960s. Their particulars are discussed in Part II. Suffice it to note among the formal levers the modifications in the Standing Commissions and the Secretariat. During the 1960s, the number of Standing Commissions rose considerably and their field of activity intensified, even though *Basic Principles* as such was no longer the guideline for SEI endeavors. Six new ones were added – a number that subsequently remained unchanged, save for a few deletions, additions or amalgamations in the mid-1970s and early 1980s, until the recent consolidation of these CMEA organs. Out of the six new commissions no fewer than four were concerned with economywide issues or areas of inquiry (including STC, standardization, statistics and currency and finance). Especially important in retrospect was the creation in December 1962 of the Standing Commission on Currency and Financial Questions (SCFQ), which was designed to play a critical role in facilitating the integration of the CPEs through plan coordination. Its mandate was ambitious from its inception (see chapter 7). In parallel with the modifications of the Standing Commissions, the Secretariat became fully realigned in order to better serve the Standing Commissions in particular and increasingly the emerging conferences and institutes (on which I provide more details also in Part II).

At the informal level of association with the CMEA, arguably the most important organ to appear in the 1960s was the first CMEA bank – the International Bank for Economic Cooperation (IBEC). Because it was put in charge of regulating the regional settlements of commercial and noncommercial transactions through the medium of a new international currency – the TR – several CPEs had placed very high hopes on the IBEC. All the more so because they had anticipated that some rapprochement would soon emerge between the real and the monetary sides of BTPAs and, indeed, that the rigidity and centrality of 'bilateralism' in these agreements would considerably ease. As such it was to lead to multilateral settlements and greater transparency in price negotiations, operational exchange rates and a wider range of transactions dealt with automatically and anonymously. Both qualifiers are critical for the emergence of effective multilateralism. Also, the price system for CMEA transactions underwent substantial modification and streamlining. For instance, a new reference base for TRPs was fixed in 1964 for implementation in 1965–7 (see chapter 15). The members mandated a comprehensive research effort to explore the possibilities and modalities of establishing an independent price system (IPS) for CMEA transactions – not just for merchandise trade proper.

At the time, the means to coordinate economic decisions of individual countries or their agents obtained much greater attention as well in the form of a streamlined system of pseudo exchange rates for segmented transactions. Rather than engage in the structural adjustments required to permit the unification of the exchange rates after some transition period, concerns about all kinds of foreign transactions and their potential contribution to growth and development, including in the consumer sphere, were such that policymakers continued to focus on the specific requirements of separate classes of foreign transactions, which are segregated simply because the various markets remain segmented. Especially important in terms of foreign transactions are the joint financing of investment projects, the settlement of noncommercial transactions, special arrangements for organized and unorganized tourist transactions and others detailed in Part III.

In addition, the informal institutional levels of CMEA cooperation were expanded in various directions. Particular importance was then attached to interstate agencies entrusted with specific tasks associated with the coordination of economic plans and scientific-technological research in one particular sector or another. Most conspicuously these include the coordination of small-tonnage chemical products (*Interchim*), metallurgy (*Intermetall*) and ball bearings (*Interpodszypnik*[3]). Undertakings aimed at rounding off the various transportation networks were also conspicuous. They received a significant impetus from the completion of the oil pipeline *Družba* and the addition of electrical networks into the integrated *Mir* power grid.

The joint financing of investment projects initiated in the late 1950s (see chapter 3) resumed, after a lull between 1963 and 1966, with new impetus.

Member countries desiring to expand their ensured imports of critical fuels and raw materials were once again expected to help finance this rise in production in the potential exporters through so-called joint investment participations. As during the first wave of these target or special-purpose credits, the major lenders were Czechoslovakia and the GDR. But in sharp contrast to the 1950s, the principal borrower was the Soviet Union, not the less-developed Eastern European CPEs. Because of the particular twist imparted by the Soviet Union's emergence as a substantial borrower, joint investment participation now solely meant joint financing of investment projects (see chapter 14).

Unlike during the first wave of target loans, donor countries became more concerned about the efficiency of such types of investment coordination. As a result, the first methodology – the so-called Berlin Method – for comparing alternative investment options was worked out, largely within the context of the SCFQ. The Berlin Method essentially aimed – and with some relatively minor modifications it still functions as such – at identifying similar types of investment contributions. Each such component is subsequently translated into a common denominator (usually the country where the project is sited and the TR) by means of exchange rates set specifically for each class of transactions. However confined this approach to rational economic decision making, at least it succeeded in placing the totality of these operations in a coherent framework and thus permitted economic computations and comparisons.

4.4   THE DOMESTIC ECONOMIC REFORM PROCESS AND ITS DEMISE

In some sense it is hard to assess whether the failure to implement *Basic Principles* contributed to the emerging economic reforms or whether these reforms were already at the root of the policy thinking that quickly superseded the document before it was actually endorsed. My own inclination is that the two were originally proceeding along different paths, although both had come about under impact, or as a result, of the negative phenomena that manifested themselves in the latter half of the 1950s (see chapter 3). But the two courses of action at some point interfered with each other. One may infer that the enactment of *Basic Principles* could have forestalled the need to explore new economic models in some of the CPEs. At the very least, it would have confined policy maneuverability in those countries that were envisioning reforms that reached well beyond the simple streamlining of planning, administration and entrepreneurial decision making, including in foreign trade. Conflict also emerged in the reverse direction. The more or less ambitious modifications of economic policies, institutions and instruments sought in virtually all CPEs would have inhibited the implementation of the first policy blueprint on planning regional economic relations for the simple reason that extensive economic development anchored to the central marshaling of economic resources through coercive means would have been impossible to adhere to in the more developed members of the group, including in particular Czechoslovakia, the GDR, Hungary and, increasingly, Poland. When the spirit of *Basic Principles* was officially put to rest around 1964, a new impetus to reforming the national economies was provided, if indirectly.

By the mid-1960s, all European CPEs, except perhaps Albania and to some extent Rumania, had embarked on streamlining their economic policy objectives and the means provided to their economic agents for discharging assigned tasks. Although this is not the proper place in which to reexamine the first broad wave of Eastern European economic reforms, it is useful to single out a few key pointers of what the majority of countries hoped to accomplish and by what means.

The most important goal of the reform, and which is again at the forefront of the present concerns of most CMEA members (see chapters 6 and 18), was to regain comparatively high, sustainable growth rates by substituting so-called intensive growth determinants for the extensive ones that had prevailed in development priorities since postwar reconstruction was nearly complete. Instead of fostering output growth by steadily injecting new factors into the production sphere and redistributing the existing capital and labor funds among sectors, the economic reforms aimed at bolstering macroeconomic performance mainly through total factor productivity growth. This concept does not, as is so often argued in the Eastern European specialized literature, simply mean an increase in average labor productivity or output per worker. Instead, it means that for any standard combination of production factors, output will be increasing over time. This gain may find its origin in the utilization of better-trained workers, new technology, novel combinations of factors, managerial innovations or other kinds of so-called X-efficiency.

Because it was felt that such a qualitatively different type of economic expansion could not adequately be ensured by detailed central planning, all the reforms sought to devolve decision making to some degree. This generally implied delegating authority over the utilization of production factors and intermediate inputs. In some cases, authority was extended to the procurement of all inputs as well as the disposition of output. Initially, this decentralization was seen as moving planning authority to intermediate agencies that would be entrusted with the supervision of territorial or output-related enterprises. But increasingly, and with urgency, the further delegation of authority to the entrepreneurial levels and, indeed, to individual firms dominated reform discussions and policies. That is, all economic reforms in the CPEs were characterized by a general trend toward curbing the wide range of authority vested in the central planning center and its associated ministerial bureaucracies and toward delegating their decision-making prerogatives and power partly to associations of economic agents or even to production firms themselves.

Second, such devolution could be properly enacted only if economic agents would be provided with proper guidance in terms of rules and regulations that would supplement or replace those associated with administrative coordination in the central planning framework. All economic reforms therefore sought to institute some measure of active macroeconomic policies in the financial, monetary and fiscal fields. The allocation of investment funds needed to be steered more completely through the banking sector, and profit needed to be used much more fully as a success criterion for producing firms and their associations. Naturally, prices being what they were in these economies, correcting the structure of wholesale and retail prices, streamlining wholesale and trade prices and introducing measures that would ensure some reasonable link between the two, at best on an intermittent basis, all figured highly on the agenda of policy ambitions.

Finally, virtually all reforms, excepting perhaps the Soviet Union's, recognized the possibilities inherent in more intensive trade ties, both within the region and with third partners, as a critical force in bolstering the pace of aggregate economic growth. Some type of foreign trade reform thus became integral to the overall reform approach. For example, measures were taken to give those who engaged in foreign trade some autonomy over what to trade and where; expanding the right to engage in foreign commerce to more specialized foreign trade organizations (FTOs) and even individual firms; fostering direct linkage of domestic wholesale with foreign trade prices, at least intermittently, including through more effective exchange rate policies; and creating opportunities for direct enterprise relations, especially in the form of East-West joint ventures. These were the most critical ingredients of the foreign trade reform and, in some cases, of the reform as a whole.

It is important to stress that the reforms in all CPEs, except the USSR, went further and were far more ambitious in the foreign trade sphere than in any of the domestic counterparts. The decentralization of foreign trade decision making in favor of a growing number of FTOs, and sometimes to individual enterprises, progressed further than devolution in the domestic enterprise sphere. In addition, policymakers were more concerned about improving the connection between external and domestic wholesale prices than about rectifying the policy-induced distortions in domestic retail prices. Wholesale prices in particular were henceforth intended to act as effective, if partial, decision-making signals, even though they were revised only periodically in most CPEs. The reforms in the foreign trade sector clearly intended that these activities provide a fillip to domestic growth by promoting specialization and trade, including within the CMEA arena.

As already mentioned, the reforms were essentially conceived independently at the national level, were generally unsynchronized – indeed, great diversity in approaches became evident fairly soon – and had virtually no direct impact on the CMEA organization or policies, which continued to smart from having failed to enact *Basic Principles* as the guideline for SEI. Nonetheless, the most ambitious reformers realized that it would be exceedingly difficult to enact piecemeal reforms on a country-by-country basis without factoring into the equation the implicit requirements for reorganizing CMEA relations. At the very least, the CMEA should not obstruct the most conservative reform. Furthermore, it was felt that the inhibitions for the most ambitious reform, which were engendered by having such an organization cater to economies at various stages of centralization and with differentiated development objectives, should be minimized to the extent that this was compatible with the regional status of the CMEA. In fact, it would have been desirable, then as now, to tailor changes in the CMEA to the most ambitious reforms while at the same time reducing repercussions on the most conservative members (see chapter 18). Nothing of the kind emerged, however, possibly because the wounds sustained during the miscarriage of *Basic Principles* were simply still too raw to permit genuine multilateral dialogue. That most reforms matured while being implemented and encountering initial difficulties, did not, of course, facilitate dispassionate deliberations within the CMEA.

One of the major reasons why the reform movement of the 1960s had only a marginal impact on the CMEA was the then rapidly improving climate for vigorous trade and economic cooperation between East and West, particularly among the smaller countries of Europe. For a time this channel obviated the need to adapt the CMEA economic structures to the fundamental requirements of the more ambitious economic reforms. Naturally, the circumstances of the Soviet economic reform, which was arguably the most conservative and had only minimal implications for that country's foreign economic relations, were key factors in the lethargy with which the CMEA organization continued to subsist and SEI of a sort proceeded.

An important factor, though not an overriding one, in fomenting economic reform is the degree to which the discussion can be confined to technical matters. But is it possible to introduce meaningful economic reforms that do not impact in some way areas of social intercourse other than the production sphere (e.g., politics, social organization, freedom of expression and cultural commitment)? A related question, though with very different roots, is to what degree it is realistic to anticipate beneficial growth effects from institutional and policy changes without also seeking a relaxation of restrictions in other spheres of social intercourse. It was a combination of the two that propelled Czechoslovakia and its Prague Spring into the forefront of international attention in 1968. The invasion into Czechoslovakia by Warsaw Pact forces (without Rumania), which commenced on 20 August 1968, was conceived as a way of bringing the country back into the socialist fold through forceful 'normalization.'[4] Its deleterious ramifications preoccupied regional policies for a number of years, and its stifling impact continues to be felt today, in spite of recent shifts in Soviet policies toward Eastern Europe and Gorbačëv's declaration on the need of each socialist country to map its own future.

It is no exaggeration to maintain that the forcibly interrupted reform, which was subsequently justified by the so-called Brežnev doctrine (which holds that socialist countries have an internationalist duty to safeguard communism in fraternal countries), proved to be a watershed in CMEA relations. As such it heavily circumscribed the arena for independent policy maneuvering. Regarding regional economic relations, the doctrine on limited sovereignty proved to be a milestone in CMEA cooperation for two reasons. For one, it signaled the beginning of the end of the reform movement in virtually all CPEs except Hungary, but even there reform ambitions were scaled down and temporarily shelved. Second, the 1968 events made it more imperative than ever to resolve the ways and means of fostering regional cooperation on the basis of the greatest common denominator of the requirements of the participating economies. It is against this backdrop that the search for a new cooperation model was introduced – the second major shift of the 1960s – and temporarily followed through by setting a comprehensive policy agenda for the next decade.

4.5 IN SEARCH OF A NEW COOPERATION MODUS

If the debates around *Basic Principles* had led to a number of disputes about the principles and role of regionalism in relations among ostensibly sovereign socialist countries, the discussions on how best to cope with the heavy-handed Kosygin–Brežnev treatment of Czechoslovakia and the other CMEA partners included major divergences about the purposes and means of SEI. As I shall demonstrate in chapter 5, the variety of issues tabled under this heading ranged from the bureaucratic, administrative approach to instituting a regionwide market open to competition by socialist enterprises, possibly from all the members. Clearly, this unwieldy spectrum of options was not apt to yield a concrete solution acceptable to most participants.

Second, though the economic reform movement was short-circuited, the underlying necessity of finding ways of bridging the transition from extensive to intensive growth was not obliterated by the invading forces. Quite the contrary: The postponement of even minimal adjustments in economic structures, institutions, policies and policy instruments only magnified the scope of the required remedial actions, thus rendering such actions all the more urgent. Though no master plan for CMEA reform could be initiated, cooperation tended to proceed pragmatically. This evolved at fairly low planning levels and economic activity in whatever forms could be accommodated. The most common format was within a bilateral focus on one sector or branch, or even at the plant level. The means used combined planning and market-type elements, again in a pragmatic manner.

At the same time, increasing the scope for East-West economic relations beyond the inroads made in the mid-1960s began to be explored. This emphasis on pursuing various possibilities of economic intercourse with market-oriented economies, particularly in Western Europe, was depicted in the Western literature of the time (with some exaggeration) as offering a clever substitute for domestic reforms. As subsequent developments in the 1970s clearly underlined, however, the substantial inflow of capital, technology, know-how and goods and services that took place in a number of CPEs was perhaps a necessary but certainly not a sufficient condition for shifting the production function of the typical CPE from an extensive to an intensive mode.

Third, apart from the external political and other pressures exerted on Eastern Europe, the unraveling of the economic reforms was largely due to internal inconsistencies of the reform projects as originally conceived, divisiveness in the political leadership of individual countries, inability to conceptualize a longer-term project that would support a temporary slowdown in the pace of output growth so as to accommodate structural change and adjustment and, indeed, opposition of entrenched Party, planning and ministerial vested interests to any change that might negatively affect their own position, no matter how much that was already confined.

Against this background, but particularly in an effort to assuage the wounds left by the Czechoslovak invasion, the twentieth anniversary of the CMEA in April 1969 was seized as an opportune moment for calling to order a new economic summit. Although the commemorative Session – the twenty-third 'special' one – had been slated to address the achievements of the CMEA in the preceding twenty years, it was attended by Party and government leaders from all member countries, hence the reason for its status as a 'special Session' (see chapter 7). Although commemoration did occur, this top-level summit in fact focused on the principles for developing a new integration strategy. As such, it set in motion soul-searching not only for a replacement of *Basic Principles* as such but also on whether the transition to SEI proper could be reconciled with market-type instruments and institutions. Because the program was endorsed in 1971 and the accompanying debates lasted well into the 1970s, I shall discuss these matters in chapter 5.

NOTES

1. The full title reads: *Basic Principles of the International Socialist Division of Labor*. It is reproduced in Russian in Tokareva, 1967, pp. 23–39 and in English in Butler, 1978, pp. 14–32.
2. Note that the document insists on laying down the ISDL for all socialist countries.

But only the then-CMEA members (i.e., those of interest here and Mongolia) signed the document.
3. This organization is usually referred to by its Polish name rather than its Russian acronym, OSPP, because the administrative headquarters is located in Warsaw.
4. Note that the Russian term *ozdorovlenie* (literally, to steer back to health), regarding the intended purposes of the invasion and its aftermath, is more accurate than 'normalization.'

5 · THE DOCTRINE OF ECONOMIC INTEGRATION IN THE 1970s

The invasion of Czechoslovakia, the wrenching normalization that followed and the long arm of the doctrine on limited sovereignty throughout Eastern Europe amounted, in retrospect, to a decisive turning point in CMEA developments. The normalization had two important consequences for Czechoslovakia: the gradual replacement of reformers and politicians of the Prague Spring, followed by the forcible subjugation of the new leadership into the straitjacket of nearly complete orthodoxy in most societal endeavors. The very concept of 'economic reform,' not just how it had been conceived there in 1967–8, was equated with a loosening of the grip of communist control over society, thus inviting calamity. In fact it was placed on the index of repugnant vocabulary and not even obliquely revised until early 1987. The aborted Prague Spring also signaled the impending demise of the first wave of wide-ranging experimentation with economywide reforms. Although repercussions of the invasion were not equally intense elsewhere in Eastern Europe, they had significant implications for virtually all CPEs. The efforts of the 1960s that were directed at bringing about decentralization and fostering factor productivity growth through indirect economic coordination mechanisms, incomplete as those attempts had remained, faltered. One country after another, with the exception of Hungary, dismantled major components of the reform, postponed implementation of certain parts of the blueprint that had been viewed as an evolving process and then eliminated them entirely, or otherwise retracted to more centralization and central planning by quantitative means. Even in Hungary the pace of reform decelerated until the turn of the decade, and some important components, including pricing and hardening budgetary constraints for economic agents, were temporarily reversed.

Two elements of the reforms remained in place, however, and they are important enough to warrant a separate treatment in section 5.1, if for no other reason than that they proved pivotal for SEI and the participation of the CPEs in subsequent years in global trade and financial networks. In that section I shall also sketch the backdrop to economic policymaking throughout the 1970s. Section 5.2 discusses the ambitious policy goals enshrined in the second official policy document on SEI. Next I summarize developments in the implementation of that programmatic document, including the shift in direction enacted in the mid-1970s. Section 5.4 details the blossoming of the planning approach in the second half of the decade, which was unexpected after the wrenching road the CPEs had traveled while hammering out the new policy blueprint on SEI. Section 5.5 outlines the most important developments in East-West economic relations. The chapter concludes with a discussion of the domestic and, especially, the external payments imbalances toward the end of the 1970s and the initial measures embraced to rectify them. Because these efforts on the whole failed to restructure the CPEs sufficiently so that they could withstand future payments pressures, external adjustment problems are discussed more fully in chapter 6.

5.1 THE END OF THE REFORMS AND THE BACKDROP TO THE 1970s

The collapse of the economic reform movement, as noted, had serious implications for policy design, the buoyancy of economic development *per se* and the enactment of changes in the structure of the CMEA economies. In order to appropriately identify what room for policy maneuvering existed and for exerting pressure in support of domestic, regional and other policy innovations compatible with the newly emerged political realities, it is important to recall two broad features of the process that generated the reversal of the economic reforms.

First, in spite of sharp retrenchments, central components of the envisaged economic reforms were maintained, even though most underwent noticeable modification. For example, the new economic mechanism (NEM) that Hungary introduced on 1 January 1968 was kept on course with two provisos. Efforts were made to ensure that some elements of the reform would be frozen indefinitely while others would proceed more slowly than originally intended. An equally important axiom of economic policy was that the reform not contaminate other spheres. In the early 1970s, in fact, the NEM approach was temporarily stalled and reversed. Because key ingredients of that reform revolved around the effective linking of the domestic economy with foreign economic activities, Hungary needed to push for progress with CMEA cooperation policies, mechanisms and institutions.

In fact, when the NEM was first introduced, Hungarian policymakers had hoped to synchronize it closely with the Czechoslovak reform initiated the previous year. This dovetailing was placed high on the policy agenda to ensure overt support for indirect economic coordination at least between the two neighbors who were then at the forefront of the reform debate. This interaction also aimed at exerting indirect pressure for proper adjustments in CMEA mechanisms and institutions. Though Czechoslovak support vanished by early 1969, Hungary's requirements for loosening up CMEA commercial and financial relations remained acute. In the end, however, they failed to be properly confronted. This policy dilemma had important consequences for Hungary as well as for CMEA cooperation.

Kept intact more extensively than other elements of the domestic reforms in most of Eastern Europe were modifications in the organization and economics of foreign economic relations. Although these sectors were also subjected to sharp retrenchments in some countries, several key components were maintained even in the staunchest antireform country. Thus, the institutional links provided by the large number of FTOs or producing enterprises trading on their own account, although curbed, generally remained intact. Leeway in independent decision making about what to trade, in what quantities and in which markets, although more strongly curtailed than the institutional setup, was nonetheless kept afloat. In some countries, in fact, a new wave of changes in the foreign trade sector briefly emerged. But much less remained of the commitment to effectively link domestic and foreign trade sectors, including through realistic exchange rates and further synchronization of trade, wholesale and retail prices. The relationship between the two domestic price tiers was especially allowed to loosen up.

In any event, reforms throughout the area in the foreign economic sectors were kept on track to a greater degree than was the case for the domestic components. The economics of entrepreneurial and other decision making, as distinct from the institutional aspects of the reforms, appears to be what suffered most in this process. Indirect coordination instruments and their supporting institutions were again being replaced by administrative methods and hierarchical interventions based more on planning expediency than on economic necessity. In other words, the entities that had obtained permission to autonomously engage in trade continued to conduct trade on their own account. However, their level of autonomy shrank, and the actual or anticipated economic, as distinct from institutional, linkup between foreign commerce and domestic suppliers, and indeed the whole economy, languished.

Second, the climate of retrenchment and the process of normalization in the arts, culture, politics and economics (stifling as they exceedingly were) did not suppress the original considerations that had urged policymakers to embark on a course of economic reform. Many reasons can be cited in evidence, but I shall restrict myself for the moment to the purely technical platform for economic experiments. The physical limitations on factor inputs required to ensure a steady and robust pace of economic growth remained unaffected by policy changes. The misallocation of resources resulting from nonscarcity pricing and administrative intervention was undeniable, even to the stodgiest *apparatčik*. In other words, the prevailing development conditions, particularly in Eastern Europe proper, were in desperate need of substantive remedial action.

Instead of redesigning the economic reforms comprehensively, conceptualizing timely policy decisions and formulating a transition phase that
could really be considered by policymakers, two events emerged that had
critical implications for the subsequent course of reform and regional economic cooperation. First, after a brief period during which the economic
reform blueprints faded away, leaders in nearly all countries, save Czechoslovakia, sought refuge in fostering active East-West economic and financial
relations. One critical component of that maneuver was the wholesale
importation of technology, which in some cases occurred on a massive scale.
This was perhaps most pronounced in the Polish import-led growth strategy
associated with Edward Gierek after he came to power in December 1970.
Such a substantial influx of technology required borrowing in financial
markets on an unprecedented scale. Initially it was hoped that this move
would encourage intensive growth without running the multiple economic
and other risks that tended to be endemic in reforms. But it was also
expected to be self-financing or self-liquidating. That is, policymakers
expected the inflow of technology to contribute immediately to an improvement in the quantitative, and particularly qualitative, aspects of their country's export offer and hence to the generation of sufficient foreign exchange
to service the convertible currency debt. At the time, the convertible currency debt was rising at an unheard-of pace. In some CPEs it was reaching
alarming dimensions given their inability to improve their competitive
position in world markets and to foster exports.

The second critical factor grew out of the concerted dismantling of the
economic reforms and the regimentation associated with the doctrine on
limited sovereignty. The purpose of this doctrine, of course, was to return
the Eastern European countries to the Soviet fold, including in trade and
finance. In the course of 1968, otherwise well-informed observers of the
CMEA cooperation scene (see especially Sorokin, 1968, 1969) launched
another trial balloon directed at the institutionalization of supranational
planning. But the 'scientific' suggestion that sought to resurrect Chruščëv's
ghost was shortly thereafter quietly disowned by those who had apparently
been behind the reopening of this sensitive topic. Indeed, the economic
reforms in most CPEs had progressed too far to permit complete resumption
of detailed central planning, which, in any case, was unacceptable to broad
layers of society and even to decision makers, including the most conservative
ones. Too many policymakers had experienced the drawbacks inherent in
traditional central planning mechanisms to support voluntarily their re-
enactment. A key vehicle had to be adopted at the regional level for streamlining the economic structures in line with the precepts that the individual
CPEs had been attempting to implant in their own economies, but it would
have to be innovated elsewhere than through central planning.

Under these circumstances, the CMEA celebrated its twentieth anniversary in early 1969. In an unusual summit meeting in April, which coincided

with the special twenty-third Council Session, it was formally decided to initiate economic integration in the CMEA and to elaborate a comprehensive policy document on the objectives, institutions and instruments of SEI and its conceptual framework. This decision formally sealed the fate of *Basic Principles*. The commemorative Session's recommendations formed the overall guidelines of a two years' search for a formal integration program that was officially endorsed in July 1971. It emanated from an unprecedented, comprehensive joint effort of all CPEs to address every aspect of genuine regional integration. The progress then being attained in Western Europe, particularly in the EEC, may have played a significant role in the conceptualization of the program. The document that emerged is variously referred to as *Complex*, *Comprehensive* or simply *Integration Program*;[1] in what follows I shall use the latter designation.

5.2 INTEGRATION PROGRAM AND SEI

Before clarifying the stipulations of *Integration Program*, a brief word is in order on the drift of the integration debate at the time of the elaboration and initial implementation of the economic reforms until early 1969, when it was decided to formulate a formal document on SEI. This debate may seem paradoxical given that, at least formally, the CPEs were committed to the ISDL as enshrined in *Basic Principles*. The paradox can be resolved within the situation sketched in section 5.1: that is, the need to bolster factor productivity growth through rapid trade expansion, even without domestic reforms being allowed to buttress economic 'intensification,' had to be factored into the growth equation in some way. Because of the constraints on East-West and East-South economic intercourse, some of the major reformers in Eastern Europe were agitating as well for reforms at the CMEA level, although the term reform was not then used in that context as it now is.

The proposals on the goals and methods of SEI in its generic context, rather than how it ensues from the program, were numerous and their portent differed widely. At one end of the spectrum were several Hungarian proposals that advocated market-based integration.[2] In some versions of this advocacy, even a full-fledged customs union was proposed. The farthest-reaching motions envisaged, among others, a common external tariff, transitorily differentiated internal tariffs for intragroup trade and the gradual unification and reduction of intraregional tariffs so as to bolster trade creation while checking trade diversion. But even in its minimalist version, SEI should at least comprise coordination of macroeconomic policies and the introduction of indirect instruments of economic control and guidance.

At the other end of the spectrum, a strong emphasis on some form of regional central planning could be easily recognized. The chief promoter of that position was the Soviet Union, although it had backtracked sharply from the approach advocated in *Basic Principles*. The disadvantages of now instituting traditional central planning at the regional level would, admittedly, be avoided, or at least mitigated, by supplementing central planning with substantial flexibility in decision making. Such flexibility was expected to be within reach by more appropriately utilizing instruments of coordinating economic decisions indirectly. Furthermore, regional central planning should be focused primarily on the basic tasks of long-term development and structural change rather than on details of day-to-day economic and trade cooperation.

Unfortunately, it quickly became apparent in the discussions that preceded the elaboration of *Integration Program* that the diversity of policy precepts among CMEA decision makers was still too deep-rooted, and perhaps fundamentally too irreconcilable, to permit a clear-cut new approach to SEI. This multiplicity of incompatible options was evident for the technically minded economist. It was equally apparent to the political leadership of the various CPEs. Unanimous agreement on such focal issues of economic policy as multilateralism, scarcity pricing, efficient international capital and labor mobility and convertibility were hence precluded. Under the circumstances, at best one could only hope for a vague phrasing of principles regarding the framework of prospective study and future deliberation on the concrete purposes, instruments, institutions and means of SEI. Not surprisingly, this statement on intentions rather than actual mechanisms builds precisely the core of *Integration Program*.

The program is an exceedingly long, carefully worded document that deals with virtually all aspects of regional integration and economic cooperation, the two not necessarily being separated. Yet it is not fully consistent and does not programmatically chart the policy goals and instruments of SEI. It minutely reaffirms the familiar principles and procedures of international socialist cooperation and provides a complex compendium of the spheres and topics at which common efforts ought to be directed. The program is inconsistent because essentially it amounts to little more than seventeen interim reports of Council and related organs, who in fact drafted them. No attempt was made to weave these propositions into anything remotely resembling a coherent, let alone comprehensive, concept of SEI and how it should or could be fostered. That is, the document presents an inevitable compromise that deferred major problems in the interest of temporarily securing a modestly satisfactory program of minimum measures that would be acceptable to all members.

Whereas previous CMEA policy statements referred vaguely to international specialization and economic cooperation as the goals of SEI, the new document is unambiguous in calling for full integration as defined here (see Introduction), though the exact meaning of SEI is not specified in the program. The CPEs gradually agreed to eliminate man-made obstacles to the free flow of goods, services and, to some extent, production factors, and to reduce the impediments stemming from 'natural' conditions by coordinating all relevant aspects of economic policy. In recognition thereof, the message in *Integration Program* may be viewed as one that endorses positive integration (see Brabant, 1980, p. 230); that is, a conscious effort to eliminate to the extent possible the root causes of differences in relative economic scarcities.

In spite of its fuzzy specification of the goals of SEI, the program contains two categories of noteworthy stipulations. First, it discloses a lengthy catalog of separate areas about which the members had reached agreement in principle to engage in common forecasting, to construct concrete projects and to elaborate specific agreements. These were to enhance cooperation particularly in mining, engineering, agriculture and transportation. Because of the nature of these stipulations, they are less important for the broad framework of integration, though their realization may impart considerable positive effects on the overall environment for SEI.

Second, the program stipulates a number of suggestions that address the future work of the CPEs and the Council on creating a meaningful mechanism of SEI. This has three broad dimensions encompassing the legal, economic and institutional-organizational facets of SEI. The elements of each of these components may need to be overhauled and, where necessary, partly or wholly replaced to facilitate ECPS agreements, plan coordination and STC. These features of the mechanism whereby SEI is to be fostered need to be discussed in more detail not only because the intensification of cooperation in general but also because implementation of the concrete steps already agreed upon depends on them.

The economic aspects of the integration mechanism are naturally most important for the purposes of this study. The program sets forth three principal types of instruments and associated institutional supports to be improved in the process of realizing SEI: policy consultations, the merging of economic plans and indirect coordination instruments and their infrastructure.

The program makes it clear that the CPEs agreed that the concordance of national economic plans should serve as the core of instruments for promoting economic collaboration because SEI is inherently a process 'regulated in a deliberate and planned way.' Plan coordination should encompass different efforts, including:

1. Forecasting future demand and supply as the basis for drawing up concrete plans.
2. Long-term perspective planning to determine main developments in key economic activities.
3. Reaching compromises on the basic aims of economic policies, not only at the highest policymaking levels but also through frequent and in-depth consultations on an array of national and international economic policies.

4. Improvement of the traditional methods of plan coordination by focusing more attention on coordinating even early drafts of national economic plans so that the synchronization of economic policies can be more fully extended to science, technology, production and investment.
5. Joint planning of selected economic branches on an optional basis, contrary to the obligation to participate in annual and medium-term plan coordination, which follows from the CMEA charter and resolutions adopted by the Council Session.

The other area of critical importance in defining the economic mechanism of SEI was presented in the form of how best to coordinate economic decisions indirectly. These instruments and institutional supports were slated as useful aids to underpin SEI in the draft phase of the plans and, indeed, had been intended to assist in the implementation of coordinated plans. But they were not even to be allotted the most important role in formulating plans or in setting up common projects. The sections of *Integration Program* covering monetary and financial instruments and their supporting institutions are not particularly noteworthy for their programmatic detail or for delineating in operational terms how, in the context of plan coordination, the CPEs expected them to function. A number of deadlines are specified for the examination of the bases of regional price formation and coordinating retail and wholesale prices with each other and with trade prices; how to enhance multilateralism; the possibilities of introducing nonquota trade; how best to improve the role of the TR so as to ensure its real transferability within the region and its convertibility into national currencies; what role exchange rates could play in the integration process and how to harmonize them by type of transaction and make them uniform in each CPE; and the desirable scope and forms of capital and labor mobility within the region.

An increasingly important role in coordinating the activities of sovereign states and avoiding or arbitrating conflicts is to be found in the creation of a legal framework capable of accommodating diverse integration processes. Greater compatibility among the different national legal provisions is needed. For that purpose, the program calls for drafting new legislation through international agreements and treaties designed to cope with the expected sharp expansion in the depth and range of economic, commercial and STC activities. This applies in particular to providing the proper framework for the operation of a variety of international economic organizations (IEOs) and, more generally, promoting capital and labor mobility within the region. Also, smoother and more comprehensive arbitration of disputes was to be achieved by streamlining existing provisions and, if necessary, replacing or supplementing them. This includes, among other provisions, the institutionalization of effective sanctions for noncompliance with contracted stipulations. Finally, effective protection of inventions, trademarks and samples was to be guaranteed. The program also specifies time frames within which these questions were to be addressed.

Finally, the importance of a proper organizational and institutional infrastructure to support SEI is emphasized. The program briefly mentions, and this is very important for future reference, the desirability of fostering more direct regional economic contacts among firms and other agents at the lower rungs of the planning hierarchies. But these are not anticipated to play any central role in plan coordination or in the formulation and implementation of concrete aspects of SEI. In fact, as usual in CMEA documents, the program remains notably silent – at least noncommittal and vague – regarding the domestic economic mechanisms of member economies. But some transition in trade relations is called for, most notably to foster greater multilateralism in part by rendering the BTPAs more flexible through a variety of measures such as nonquota trade, less strict annual balancing of accounts and greater capital mobility. Although the program emphasizes the streamlining of the institutional and organizational infrastructure, it is quite explicit about not introducing any new forms or institutions of regional cooperation during the validity of the program (between fifteen and twenty years). That is, the members were expected to foster SEI in all of the dimensions elaborated upon in the program within the existing institutions of the CPEs and with the methods then available in the CMEA organization.

From this brief summary of a very lengthy document, it should be clear that *Integration Program* specifies integration merely as a long-term aim to be promoted by policy instruments and supporting institutions whose precise type and role need to be more closely delineated in the near future. In other words, the successful implementation of the program revolved around the degree to which the CPEs would endow their existing institutions, instruments and policies with more substance and follow up on them through goal-oriented – even audacious – policy actions. Further study and deliberation would have been useful, but at some point the measures would have to be applied, possibly in the form of transitory adjustment policies and provisions as warranted by experience.

5.3 ON IMPLEMENTING THE PROGRAM

The process of giving operational meaning to the numerous tasks up for study and negotiation after the program's endorsement was characterized by three developments: institutional reinforcement of the cooperation mechanisms and policies in place; reconciliation of market-type instruments with the growing emphasis on plan coordination; and forging ahead with various new forms of plan coordination, some *ad hoc* and others in specification with the agreements enshrined obliquely in *Integration Program*.

First, in spite of the explicit proscription of institutional innovation –

arguably, as then hailed, the most significant event of the early 1970s – was the rapid creation of IEOs, particularly interstate economic organizations (see chapter 8). They were initially entrusted with coordinating the activities of the member organizations, as in the case of international economic organizations proper or of organizations resorting under the founding government agencies – as in the case of the interstate economic organizations – that would eventually engage in the coordination of production, trade and technical progress. But these organizations essentially failed to get off the ground for economic, institutional, financial, legal and other reasons examined in Part III. Meshing their activities with the planning tiers of the host country and effectively managing them for the benefit of all participants posed insuperable obstacles under the cooperation mechanism in place. Perhaps even more crucial was the ongoing effort to recentralize the domestic economic models.

As for institutional reinforcement, mention should also be made of the further streamlining of the CMEA organization through the creation of subcommittees in charge of well-defined critical tasks directly under the purview of the Executive Committee, research institutes, several new interstate Conferences and other more informal organizations (see chapter 7). Particular importance was attached to the creation of the International Investment Bank (IIB) and ways in which the bank could provide financial support for integration projects and assist implementation of coordinated investment decisions.

Second, the debates on the principles and methodology of plan coordination and joint planning and on harmonizing monetary and financial coordination instruments with planning activities ran a stimulating course roughly until the end of 1974. But debate on these two issues did not lead to generally acceptable solutions for any of the fundamental questions that *Integration Program* posed (Pécsi, 1977, pp. 30–9). Though the deadlines specified in the program were formally respected, it is doubtful that even the most fundamental issues labeled as such at the turn of the decade benefited from anything but a cursory examination. They certainly failed to facilitate substantively the enhancement of SEI. However, parallel with the more detailed examination of the principles and methods of SEI, practical matters of regional economic cooperation increasingly tended to be tackled within the traditional framework of plan coordination. This seminal shift in the debate materialized in 1974–5 after the world price inflation, the raw material shortage and after steep recession in the DMEs drastically curtailed the list of policy options available to most market-minded CPEs.

Third, by mid-decade the integration debate had shifted almost completely to the terms of reference of plan coordination, especially for fairly detailed projects about which specific ECPS agreements were then being developed. In this connection, two new and different planning instruments emerged in the second half of the 1970s: the Concerted Plan[3] and a sequence of Target

Programs,[4] both of which were associated with a new, multilateral wave of jointly financed investment projects and with detailed bilateral cooperation agreements elaborated through one form or another of coordinated planning. The latter especially were envisaged to fuse the region into a more coherent whole and thus provide a framework for and fillip to SEI efforts in the 1980s. But target programming was essentially a concept of SEI developed in the mid-1970s and therefore will be treated in the next section.

5.4 SETTING THE STAGE FOR COOPERATION IN THE MID-1970s

Beginning with 1974–5, integration discussions for the next decade exclusively focused on improving plan coordination, especially for detailed projects for which specific ECPS agreements were concluded. In this connection, two types of documents are of singular consequence for the evolving process of SEI. First, in 1975 the CPEs endorsed the first Concerted Plan. They have continued to do so at five-year intervals, and the Plan is currently in its third implementation phase. Second, the CPEs formulated five Target Programs with which to mold the course of SEI for the next decade or beyond;[5] the first three were adopted in 1978, the other two in 1979.

The Concerted Plan, worked out jointly for the first time in 1974–5 and since then every five years in parallel with the coordination of the national five-year socioeconomic development plans, is the CPEs' first concrete, common integration plan. The relevant parts of the Concerted Plan for the individual participants form an integral component of their concurrent national medium-term plans. Through the annual implementation plans, these provisions have the force of law in the participating countries that still have plan laws in which a section on integration measures is stipulated.

The Concerted Plan aims at very specific targets in a number of important economic activities. Broadly speaking, they can be divided into five classes. First, each plan enumerates material, financial and, in some instances, labor transfers for the jointly financed integration projects. These were first started in the mid-1970s[6] and have since been updated on a medium-term basis with new 'SEI projects,' which usually involve the pooling of financial and other resources. Second, numerous multilateral ECPS agreements, especially in the engineering and chemical sectors, are usually stipulated although concrete details are rarely disclosed. Third, several STC projects are outlined, particularly to improve and expand new sources of energy, fuels and essential raw materials. Fourth, a special section is devoted to the development of the peripheral CPEs, particularly Mongolia and more recently Cuba and Vietnam. Finally, consequences of common actions following from the Concerted Plan *vis-à-vis* third countries are drawn (Vorkauf, 1977, p. 12).

Because it is explicitly targeted at the piecemeal improvement of SEI, the

Concerted Plan is an important innovation. But its significance should not be overrated. As an adequately formulated long-term development strategy or even a commonly accepted body of sound ideas about the SEI path is missing, the gestation of the first Concerted Plan was difficult and its formulation as such 'can be counted as a success' (Nyers, 1977, p. 423). This acerbic qualification derived from the fact that the measures envisioned, if implemented, would have greatly alleviated the shortage of some goods on the CMEA market and improved production specialization in a few well-defined fields, although the preconditions for such steps were not yet firmly in place. The first Concerted Plan was promulgated chiefly as an interim solution, pending the approval of integrated long-term programs of common action. The coordination of jointly funded or realized investments to be stipulated in these programs would presumably be aimed at framing complementary structures rather than at isolated ventures (Biskup and Nosiadek, 1978, p. 10).

That the CMEA members elaborate a set of Target Programs was first suggested in 1975. They were to design a desirable and binding joint development path to be traveled in selected fields. Formulation of such strategies advanced full steam through much of the second half of the 1970s. These programs would be focused on selected activities with an initial time horizon of about ten years, but in some cases it could be extended to twenty. Target programming was designed to permit confrontation with a number of important aspects of plan coordination. Specifically, they were intended to enable the CPEs to coordinate policy intentions in areas that had traditionally been difficult to accommodate within the framework designed for the interlocking of annual and medium-term national economic plans, which by necessity are all-encompassing.

Initially, five areas of special significance for long-term growth and the maturing of SEI were identified and endorsed at the highest echelons. Actual formulation of the programs was entrusted to the CMEA organs and research institutes of the CPEs, and comprehensive drafts should have been available in mid-1977. The goals of target programming and the fields selected for intensive cooperation included:

1. Solving the problems of maintaining balance in energy, fuels and raw materials.
2. Enhancing specialization and eliminating duplication in engineering branches.
3. Improving balance in basic food supplies and increasing agricultural output.
4. Improving the supply and quality of industrial consumer goods.
5. Establishing a fully integrated transportation system for the region as a whole.

In these programs, demand and supply developments were to be jointly forecast, and investment intentions as well as anticipated trade flows were to be coordinated for greater efficiency in regionwide resource allocation (Kormnov, 1977a, 1977b).

Following the endorsement of these programs by the thirtieth Council Session in 1976, intensive preparatory work was carried out over the next five years. But it quickly became evident that specifying concrete integration tasks of such breadth and ensuring their operationality was a more arduous task than had originally been anticipated. Consequently, the thirty-first Council Session the following year recommended that attention first be directed at the programs dealing with energy, fuels and raw materials; foodstuffs and agriculture; and parts of machine building, particularly those supporting the other two programs. Furthermore, the scope of these projects, which were presented at the thirty-second Council Session in 1978 as well as the remaining ones in 1979, was far less comprehensive than what had originally been intended.

Though blueprints have never been released, scattered evidence suggests that the Target Programs focused especially on essential investment projects that would help ensure the partial autarky of the region (Chodow, 1976, p. 23). For that purpose, the CPEs concluded some important multilateral ECPS agreements, including one on electrical energy and the engineering required to link up the various energy systems of the CPEs. The original purpose of these endeavors was eventually to attain a unified power grid for all CMEA members except Albania, Cuba and Vietnam. Agreement was also reached on the construction of atomic power stations in the smaller CPEs as well as two units in the USSR to be hooked into the *Mir* integrated power network. Most of the agreements that were disclosed had 1990 as a time horizon, but the signatory countries expected to extend this time frame and merge a number of the agreements with new plans to be worked out by the year 2000.

Because these protocols need to be specified within the context of the traditional annual and medium-term plans of the CPEs, the Concerted Plan has become a recurrent planning instrument. It was originally intended as an explicit statement, recapitulation or reminder of some of the most critical features associated with the implementation of the Target Programs and the related bi- and multilateral specialization agreements (Vorkauf, 1977, p. 21), on which details are provided in chapter 13. Since then, the two have been divorced for reasons to be touched upon in chapter 6.

Do these new developments suggest that for all practical purposes *Integration Program* was abandoned as the central blueprint for common action? Although the course of SEI events since 1974 justifies an affirmative answer, unfortunately there is still too little information available on what the intentions of the CPEs really were in the late 1970s with respect to the future evolution of SEI to either confirm or deny the validity of the proposition. Because the Target Programs have never been published extensively, it is difficult to provide a coherent answer. Nonetheless, it bears stressing that *Integration Program* offers a rather broad framework. The Target Programs may therefore have been a further concretization of the general tasks outlined in *Integration Program*, as was claimed in the Eastern European literature. Although undoubtedly true that policy instruments other than plan coordination were deliberately downplayed in the discussions about how to enhance SEI, the enactment of Concerted Plans and Target Programs fits in rather well with the various specifications on plan coordination and joint planning in *Integration Program*. Of far greater interest, however, is a clarification of how the CPEs expected these new programs to contribute to the enhancement of SEI. This topic is considered in chapter 6.

5.5 EAST-WEST ECONOMIC RELATIONS

Pending the elaboration of an effective solution for the many issues associated with how to promote SEI, most CPEs sought to bolster their growth performance through more intensive East-West commercial and financial ties. Whether there was a generalized movement away from domestic reforms in favor of seeking capital inflows with which to procure technology from the West and thus prop up domestic performance is a thesis that at one point was widely subscribed to in the West. Perhaps it would be more accurate to say that a fairly rapid expansion of East-West economic contacts crystallized in the 1970s as a result of some fortuitous circumstances. The creation of massive amounts of petrodollars to be recycled through commercial banks rather than through official multilateral institutions certainly was one important factor.

The extension of détente, which had earlier begun between major Western and Eastern European countries, to the two superpowers and the amicable settlement of the German question also favored more intensive East-West relations. In lieu of a peace treaty for the continent, the *modus vivendi* reached first by the two Germanies themselves and then with Eastern Europe through West Germany's *Ostpolitik*, and finally through the Helsinki conference, gradually fostered an environment congenial to significant relaxation in East-West political tensions.

Furthermore, the rapid growth of transnational corporations, especially during the 1960s and early 1970s, and their search for new markets should not be ignored. The aftereffects of decolonization, which led to extending greater sovereignty over national resources at the expense of direct foreign investment, were making it more difficult to expand production operations. By then as well, East-West contacts, particularly on the part of key Eastern European countries, had progressed to such an extent that both financial and commercial facilitation of business had become routine. All these factors waxed the preconditions for an intensificaton of East-West trade ties in the 1970s. This, in fact, was limited to a few countries. In most instances, this spurt in commercial intercourse was more apparent in nominal than in real terms because of the rapidly rising dichotomy between TRPs and WMPs (see below). Primary beneficiaries of buoyant East-West economic relations were Poland, Rumania and the Soviet Union, each of which considerably extended their real dependence on the Western economies and did so at a pace faster than their commitment to CMEA trade markets, even when evaluated in real terms. Other CPEs did so as well, but largely in nominal terms.

Regardless of the philosophy underlying trade-through-borrowing or self-liquidating loans for technology imports, the fact is that the Eastern European countries (excepting Czechoslovakia) that sought to boost East-West ties succeeded in accelerating the pace of imports and some even raised their dependence on imports from key DMEs. But they failed miserably in balancing external accounts. Initially, the loans had been taken out to provide temporary financing. By the time the projects were to have come on line, however, either the surplus for exports was not available or not in the right amount, or the anticipated Western demand for these products was no longer accessible to the CPEs because of competition from newly industrializing developing countries (NICs). Thus, as goods could not be mobilized to raise sufficient convertible currency resources to square trade accounts, there was a steady increase in the CPEs' hard currency debt.

An important policy decision in the mid-1970s revolved around perceptions of the first oil-price crisis. Virtually without exception, the CPEs treated this event as a temporary aberration that could be ridden out through a combination of external borrowing, the trading and financing mechanisms available within the CMEA and their ability to cover the bulk of their procurements through BTPAs settled in TRs. These expectations in the end went unfulfilled. The shift in global energy markets contained a structural and a transitory component. The first entailed measurable changes that were exacerbated or alleviated by transitory fluctuations. The permanent component was also fed into the CMEA market, albeit with a considerable lag. Furthermore, in the mid-1970s conditions on the volume and prices of goods traded within the CMEA were suddenly changed to the detriment of importers of fuels and raw materials. This marked shift in the regional terms of trade continued through the end of the 1970s and well into the mid-1980s, when WMPs of fuels and raw materials had been on a steeply declining path for at least three years.

By the time it became clear that the global economic shocks of the mid-1970s were unlikely to be very soon reversed and that major changes in the pricing of goods within the CMEA – and in the trade and payments arrangements on which the CMEA had depended – could no longer be avoided, Eastern Europe especially found itself facing multiple imbalances. These setbacks stemmed in essence from the fact that absorption (total domestic demand) exceeded total supplies. This had to be corrected by compressing demand, including for imports, and bolstering supplies, particularly to markets abroad.

5.6 IMBALANCES AND THE NEED FOR ADJUSTMENT

The origin of the imbalances was domestic as well as external to the CPEs. Whereas the extent of external imbalances was more pronounced and acute for Eastern Europe proper than for the USSR, the latter was not altogether free of it. In fact, the Soviet Union suffered most notably from successive adverse performances in agriculture, even though 1978 yielded the largest crop on record. The Soviets also faced growing bottlenecks in transportation and communications, largely on account of faulty investment decisions, as well as frustrated consumer expectations. In Eastern Europe, especially, consumer expectations created havoc because, after the reversal of the reforms, policymakers had markedly raised expectations by policy commitments to various social welfare and housing programs adopted in the early 1970s. These domestic and external growth constraints were centerstage in the formulation of the new medium-term plans for 1981–5. The targets adopted for the first half of the 1980s were generally set well below the achievements of the late 1970s. This planned slowdown extended not only to current output levels in key sectors. It most notably encompassed the accumulation sphere, with investment levels forecast that, under the best of circumstances, would only slightly exceed levels achieved in the late 1970s. Consumption, on the other hand, was to be protected as much as possible. Similarly, on the output side production targets for sectors that were import intensive, particularly in the consumption of raw materials and fuels, and even those fairly intensive in domestically produced primary inputs, were slated to expand moderately at best.

The policy stances adopted in the late 1970s had a variety of causes, the most serious of which linger on in one form or another. While not all of them can be explored in depth here, it may be useful to highlight a few of the exogenous and endogenous elements that set the environment for policymaking. Among the structural issues, four stand out: faulty policy choices made early in the 1970s, including the import-led growth strategy then adopted by Poland and Rumania; inadequately anticipated shifts in the traditional SEI mechanisms, including TRP policies; failure to rationalize economic structures on a timely basis in line with transformations in real domestic and external growth opportunities; and the culmination of successive delays in transcending the deeply engrained extensive growth policies. A workable alternative to the postwar fervor associated with stabilization, reconstruction and broad and rapid socialist industrialization in line with the Soviet paradigm is yet to emerge.

Not all of the key factors underlying each of these structural deficiencies can be analyzed here (see Brabant, 1987a, pp. 92–105). I shall summarize the development constraints that are of a longer-term nature and *can*, therefore, be addressed in the plans, as distinct from transitory fluctuations in CMEA and global economic activity. Moreover, as noted, some of these factors are susceptible to appropriate domestic and regional policies. Others are by their nature largely exogenous. But it is useful to separate the constraints on primary and intermediate resource availability from those affecting the disposal of total products.

5.6.1 Domestic growth constraints

Fairly steady additions to the factor input stream have provided the alpha and omega of most of the postwar growth in CPEs. To the extent that these countries still possess underutilized production factors, they can continue to buttress such extensive development policies. But, in view of their domestic and external development constraints, simple resource mobilization for the modern industrial sector is no longer a viable option for most CPEs. It certainly is not a desirable option even for those still having an opportunity to pursue such a course.

The internal factors that since the early 1980s have complicated the resumption of sustained growth at the rate experienced during most of the postwar period can be separated conceptually into two distinct groups. On the one hand, the volume and distribution of primary production factors in the years ahead is bound to be more constrained than during the past decades no matter what policy configuration is resorted to. At the same time, though prevailing institutions and policy instruments determine feasible output combinations with given resource endowments, this 'environment' is not altogether immutable. Proper and timely policy measures can recast the development strictures embedded in factor availabilities, certainly in the medium run.

5.6.1.a Principal exogenous constraints

It may be useful to briefly touch upon the growth prospects emerging from the probable supply of labor, natural resources, land and capital. The labor force could conceivably be expanded by further absorbing women, pensioners or youngsters. Another option is to continue to relocate production factors to sectors that exhibit higher productivity. The available leeway is not extensive, however, and the effective labor force on balance has not in fact grown much. Higher educational requirements, concern about the welfare of infants and children, the demand for leisure, social pressures to lower the retirement age, low marginal productivity with an extended workweek (as experienced in Poland and Rumania), the high capital cost for infrastructure to support sectoral redistribution and the perceived need to strengthen defense all militate against any significant growth in effective working hours becoming available, particularly in the sphere of material production. Matters are not much better with other production factors. Except perhaps in the USSR, land in the CPEs is generally exhausted and in some cases already overworked. Furthermore, massive new resource discoveries are unpredictable and unlikely to materialize in Eastern Europe. Capital, of course, is the quintessential created factor of production whose determinants need to be explored in greater detail.

The prospective demand for capital resources in the decade ahead could be divided into six parts:

1. The restructuring of output profiles to strengthen the quality and range of competitive supplies.
2. The easing of capacity constraints in transportation, energy generation and raw material production.
3. Consumer-related services, including housing, education, social services and various types of product services.
4. Measures that enhance the well-being and long-term strength of a society, including through environmental protection and pollution control.
5. The implementation of programs that foster factor productivity gains.
6. The enhancement of SEI and technological progress.

The claims on resources to initiate projects for improving factor productivity had been growing steadily throughout the 1960s and 1970s and have not yet abated. This applies in particular to the need to improve the quality of output, and hence competitiveness in foreign markets. This rise in capital demand in the material sphere built up at a time of relatively slow output growth, which left little chance of raising aggregate savings. Moreover, it had to compete with an even more rapidly rising demand for capital resources, especially in infrastructure, transportation, communication, housing, sociocultural facilities and wider access to consumer services. Such so-called nonproductive investments may enhance labor morale and improve the productive environment. But these largely once-and-for-all benefits are unlikely to materialize overnight. The outlook at that time, therefore, was for a moderate recovery in the physical supply of capital funds that could be mobilized for productive purposes, certainly below the projected rates of total investment growth.

5.6.1.b Policy measures

The economic events of the late 1970s and early 1980s in such sectors as agriculture, transportation, trade, resource allocation, capital formation, energy and communication were partly unique and exogenous. Nonetheless, even constraints that could be treated as external in the short run are internal in a longer time perspective, at least to some degree. In other words, timely policy measures could have offset some of the adverse developments and might even have forestalled their emergence, as in the case of Poland, where the lingering struggle between private and socialized agriculture did not enhance either the country's domestic or external balances. Bold policy decisions that addressed inadequate support in sectors such as agriculture, transportation and communication would have mitigated the adverse implications for the economy as a whole. For energy in particular, adjustments initiated soon after the first energy crisis would in due course have geared output structures to less energy-intensive branches and would also have enforced energy conservation, thus easing demand for costly resources from abroad. In this respect, the decision of virtually all CPEs to treat the first oil shock as a temporary aberration, and thus to weather the storm through external borrowing, had very negative implications.

Other critical policy decisions should, of course, have been faced at the latest in the early 1970s, if only to have adequate lead time for preventing the emergence of bottlenecks. Most CPEs could have made progress by embracing proper adjustment policies affecting input as well as the process and output sides of the production process. Thus, the constraints on flexibility with investment policies largely derived from inadequacies in past capital formation. Hysteresis is a force that, perhaps paradoxically, is not very well heeded in most CPEs. However, it would be pointless to look at what went wrong in the past without exploring what could be done prospectively. But that I reserve for chapter 18.

5.6.2 External development conditions

Exogenous constraints are difficult to separate from those susceptible to proper policies. I shall, nonetheless, distinguish those factors that are predominantly given to most CPEs from those that *can* be influenced through appropriate policies.

5.6.2.a Exogenous constraints

In the late 1970s, domestic factor availability could conceivably have been expanded by attracting labor and capital from markets facing less-stringent supply conditions. Given the policy setting of the CPEs, however, the scope for a sharp boost in CMEA capital and labor mobility so as to equalize the region's relative factor scarcities remained highly confined by policy choice and institutional constraints (see Part III). The limits on resource inflows from outside were perhaps even tighter. Because of factor endowments, there are strong reasons for fostering capital movements from West to East and labor movements the other way around. Labor migration as a rule is proscribed (Brabant, 1987a, pp. 302–10). But global financial centers were and remain reluctant to 'invest' in the area unless major organizational and managerial changes are enacted. Direct foreign investment into the CMEA area could not be expected to make a quantum leap unless existing decision-making mechanisms were rendered compatible with those typical for market-type economies. Although this may inhibit equity participation on any significant scale, some obstacles could have been circumvented through the creation of various joint ventures, even though earlier experience had not been encouraging (see chapter 6).

5.6.2.b Policy-related constraints

Whereas factor mobility could not have provided the wherewithal for a more expansive source of growth under the prevailing institutional and other features of the CPEs, trading in goods and services is largely a function of appropriate policies. Here too the institutional and systemic issues that confined trade in the late 1970s need to be taken into account. Existing economic structures were not well geared for competing effectively in international markets. At best change could have been sought individually or in the groupwide context only gradually.

The decision-making processes and organizational features typical of these economies require that structural change in anticipation of or in response to shifts in real comparative costs must be planned; they cannot emerge spontaneously. This is one legacy of the long struggle between the market and plan in economic policies, to use once more these hackneyed opposites. Although some countries clearly still insist on 'planned commodity-money relations,' others may eventually sway opinion sufficiently to allow for indirect coordination instruments. A major dilemma arises here, for planned structural change can in the end only succeed if the detailed prerogatives vested in a small number of central planners are devolved. Some measure of economic sovereignty must be yielded in order to bolster participation in international commerce. Opening up such communication channels may entail other transitions that may still be perceived as inimical to the basics of a socialist society.

In addition to the overall external economic outlook, the conditions for CMEA cooperation in the medium run were becoming less flexible as a result of regional output constraints for basic materials and limitations on boosting export revenues from traditional manufactures – the backbone of the intra-CMEA commodity exchange pattern to date. Compared to the CMEA, world demand was even more exacting and subject to stiffer competition (Poznański, 1985, 1986a), particularly after the transformation in trade markets since the mid-1970s (see Brabant, 1987c, pp. 93–6). It is therefore more difficult to earn convertible currency than to raise an equivalent amount of TRs at prevailing exchange rates, even though the gap, at least for some CPEs, has narrowed considerably in recent years. Unless regional economic cooperation, including trading and financial mechanisms, are substantially modified, the already marked restrictions on attaining more suitable production methods, renewing capital assets and shifting economic structures and trade patterns will be compounded.

Against this backdrop, the medium-term plans for the early 1980s sought to slow growth largely through changes in the organization of the investment process and a reallocation of fixed assets. It was hoped that this would considerably moderate the demand for capital, accelerate the completion of ongoing projects still deemed to be worthwhile (especially in Poland) and speed up the highly selective projects to be commissioned in the early 1980s. Although this strategy looked coherent on the blackboard, it failed miserably in practice for reasons examined in chapter 6.

NOTES

1. The full title reads: *Comprehensive program for the further extension and improvement of cooperation and the development of economic integration by the CMEA member countries.*
2. Perhaps the most vocal proponent of this position was Béla Csikós-Nagy. For a useful summary of this position, see Csikós-Nagy, 1969, pp. 62ff. A supporting Czechoslovak view is in Petřivalský, 1969.
3. The full title reads: *Concerted plan of multilateral integration measures.*
4. The full title reads: *Long-term target programs of economic cooperation.*
5. None of these plans was ever published in detail. This is a summary based on the inventory provided in Brabant, 1981.
6. Agreement on most of these projects had already been reached earlier. Some projects were, in fact, under implementation when the first Concerted Plan was being elaborated.

6 · EXTERNAL ECONOMIC ADJUSTMENTS AND INTEGRATION IN THE 1980s

In many ways, the 1980s constituted a most unusual development phase for all European planned economies. Four sequences of events and their implications for SEI stand out: the emergency adjustment phase of the early 1980s and apparent abandonment of target programming as the focal strategy of the decade, the difficulties encountered in regaining a higher-level growth path because of persistent and large domestic and external development constraints, a new wave of economic reforms centered around the example of the Soviet Union and its new approach to CMEA cooperation and, finally, determined efforts to renovate SEI processes.

Many facets of the CPEs could be examined in the context of the externally induced adjustment efforts of the early 1980s. Section 6.1 looks at those that are most relevant in picturing the economic evolution of the CPEs individually and in their regional context. Particular attention needs to be devoted to the most critical reasons behind the external emergency adjustment efforts and why the measures embraced were largely adopted by each country in isolation rather than by a common approach to what in retrospect was, certainly for Eastern Europe, a shared phenomenon. The key overall features of national and regional development constraints that prevailed in the late 1970s have been addressed in chapter 5. Some of the unanticipated factors that aggravated this already complex situation in the 1980s are analyzed in section 6.2. The specificity in Eastern European developments of the second half of the 1980s is highlighted in section 6.3. How these issues were tackled at the highest policymaking level for the region as a whole is the subject of section 6.4. The documents of the 1980s' first summit are reviewed in section 6.5. The policy statement endorsed in late 1985 on fostering STC is explained in its proper setting in section 6.6. The key question is whether this document can be regarded at all as reflecting Gorbačëv's strategy for advancing SEI for the remainder of the century. I find it doubtful in view of the new wave of national, particularly Soviet, reform ambitions, concepts and measures (all briefly examined in section 6.7) that are likely henceforth to exert a measurable impact on SEI. The last section assesses the possible implications of recent developments for SEI in the future. But the details of how SEI might evolve, and the most plausible alternatives available given the constraints on policy maneuvering at this stage, are set forth in chapter 18.

6.1 GROWTH AND IMBALANCES IN THE 1980s

In many ways, the recent phase of Eastern European economic policies has been special because of the marked difficulties sustained in adhering to successive medium-term and many of the annual plans. This feature was very pronounced in 1981–5 because the CPEs were then engulfed in the global economic and financial crises. But neither has the second half of the 1980s progressed as smoothly as the CPEs had anticipated. Though these development obstacles were encountered in unequal degrees of depth and breadth in the various countries, common traits can be identified.

Although the five-year plans for the early 1980s had been formulated with an expectation of decelerated growth, the implementation phase was even more complex. The successive annual plans, particularly in 1981–3, attempted to factor the changed opportunities for economic buoyancy into the short-term development equation. Actual performance, however, particularly in the early years of the plan cycle, moderated to levels well below any of these medium-term or annual plan targets except in the GDR and USSR. In any event, growth in the early 1980s decelerated to its lowest pace since postwar reconstruction – with an unprecedented low for the group as a whole hit in 1982. Most Eastern European countries sustained several years of an absolute drop in per capita income levels; no country showed positive growth in each of the five years, even when such performance is measured by the official national accounting statistics, and the slowdown was pronounced throughout the so-called productive sphere.

The severity and nature of the deviations from plan targets especially in 1981–3 resulted in part from circumstances beyond the control of these countries. Unforeseen, mostly unforeseeable, external events had important implications for policy maneuvering and decision making. But some derailments could have been tackled more expeditiously and less painfully if proper coordination instruments and institutions had been in place. However, it would be a gross mistake to single out unforeseen adverse external events as the unique cause of the troubled plan cycle or even as its most important determinant. Some of the development problems ultimately stemmed from structural factors mentioned in chapter 5, while others came about because performance failed to meet planned levels in key sectors, which in turn compounded structural and systematic stresses. Finally, economic decisions were made in some countries that had marked repercussions on the concrete policy environment and economic buoyancy in other CMEA members. These included deliberately shunning the formulation of policy measures that would tackle the issues head-on; that is, putting in place adequate coordination instruments and supporting institutions. Instead of spurning the typical kind of CPE response, all countries resorted precisely to the *dirigiste* variants of central intervention policies that should have been avoided had they wished to make room for positive and sustainable structural changes.

The prevailing structural and policy-induced growth constraints (see chapter 5) were seriously aggravated by domestic developments. Among the many factors that could be cited, rising bottlenecks ensuing from the precarious situation in agriculture and in the energy and transportation infrastructure stand out. Problems in these sectors emanated in part from adverse weather patterns. Because of drought, inadequate or too-abundant precipitation at the wrong phase of the germination or growing cycle and other reasons, wide fluctuations occurred in agricultural yields.[1] Much the same comments can be made for transportation and distribution channels. Adverse weather, inadequate infrastructure and growing demands on services because of the greater distances involved in keeping user sectors supplied, particularly in the USSR, strained available resources. Energy, of course, has been the most critical sector even in countries that are net energy exporters. With few exceptions, including coal in Poland and some of the petroleum needs of Rumania, energy demand throughout Eastern Europe must be met through increasingly costly imports. Weather in some countries forced sharp cutbacks in sustainable electrical output levels or necessitated the substitution of thermal for hydroelectric power – an expensive proposition under the circumstances.

All of these unfavorable events put pressure on import demand, at given activity levels, and so policymakers frequently curtailed the buoyancy of user sectors to ease external payments pressures or tensions in domestic supplier or service sectors. Common emergency adjustment measures consisted of slashing domestic absorption through steep investment cutbacks while holding gains in personal consumption at very modest levels, boosting exports and redirecting demand toward domestic substitutes. Some countries also temporarily lifted the quantum of exports, though only briefly, chiefly in 1983–4. As noted, these policy shifts were primarily imposed by central administrative fiat rather than in response to careful economic scrutiny. By these means, external imbalances were temporarily redressed and tensions in domestic expansion eased – if at an anemic rate of aggregate growth – in all but Bulgaria (until 1985) and, for most of the period, the GDR for reasons specific to these countries.

Growth rates for 1981–5 for the group varied on average between a low of −0.8 percent for Poland and a high of 4.6 percent per year for the GDR. Compare this with an already disappointing performance in the preceding medium-term planning cycle, when the range extended from 1.2 percent in Poland to 7.3 percent for Rumania. As noted, per capita income growth was negative in 1981–2 in Czechoslovakia and Poland, and 1983 and 1985 in Hungary. The GDR maintained positive growth, though at a very low level, particularly in 1982. By their own measurements, Bulgaria and Rumania, though sustaining a sharp drop in the pace of growth, maintained sizable per capita output growth.

Perhaps the most palpable impact of forced adjustment has been some measure of 'decapitalization' – the erosion of the services from capital stock effectively available in the production process – in a number of CPEs, though to varying extents. Investment activity throughout Eastern Europe expanded slowly, if at all, in 1981–5; in several countries there was actually a pronounced contraction that affected construction and industry more than other sectors. The lackluster pace of capital formation came about as a result of several *ad hoc* policy decisions that magnified the apparent scale of decapitalization in the material sphere. Exacerbating the backlog demand for the renewal of economic structures and exerting a negative impact on medium-term growth prospects were a number of other factors, including: strictures placed on physically retiring obsolete plant and equipment; severe constraints on the level of investment activity because of no change in domestic aggregate savings behavior; sluggish progress in working off a still-expanding stock of ongoing investment projects, some of which may never reach the production stream; and, particularly, the substantial capital 'losses' deriving from cost shifts, including in trade.

Trade has been critically affected by forced adjustments, partly because of institutional and extraneous reasons (see chapter 5 and section 6.2 below). There were, however, also exogenous as well as endogenous shocks, largely as a consequence of past domestic policy decisions. Thus, Eastern Europe proper found itself locked into an increasingly 'automatic' output-related import pattern, while at the same time it lost ground in exports. The external pressures on necessary imports stemmed from the technology acquired from abroad during the preceding decade. Frequently these processes could be operated only if raw materials and intermediate goods continued to be procured from the countries originating the technology. The erosion of export markets resulted either from domestic supply difficulties, particularly in fuel and raw material sectors, or from an inability to adapt local manufacturing output to foreign demand. Not surprisingly, this constraint was much tighter in convertible currency relations than in CMEA trade. In other words, the experience with trade during the external adjustment phase of the early 1980s involved mostly import cuts. Some CPEs also lifted export quantum, as noted, but only for a brief time. The shift in resources toward tradables either did not materialize or it failed to yield a solid increment in convertible currency revenue. The export drive started to falter in late 1984 and, for most countries, had not recovered by mid-1988.

Among the unexpected external events in the early 1980s, four deserve to be identified:

1. The terms-of-trade slide for virtually all of Eastern Europe proper, which, because of the sheer magnitude of the most price-sensitive goods, was especially pronounced in CMEA relations.
2. Sluggish Western European demand for products from the CPEs, particularly during the economic recession in 1981–3.
3. The external payments crisis, which was aggravated by the Polish affair and the collapse of confidence in the financial standing of key debtors among DEs.
4. Largely endogenous supply constraints within the CMEA, chiefly on raw materials and fuels that could be obtained from the USSR at regular TRPs within the habitual TR payments mechanism (see chapter 15).

Finally, although not totally unexpected or truly exogenous in nature, some of the difficulties that were not properly discounted in the late 1970s derived from the lackluster progress made with the Target Programs (see chapter 5). Except for some elements of the fuel and raw material programs, few of the intentions of the late 1970s were kept afloat. Though a scant number of projects requiring joint financing in the proper sense had been adopted, in spite of what initially had been anticipated for target programming, even these modest resource commitments (about a third of what had been earmarked for the preceding five years) were deferred or the obligation was reneged upon altogether.

The depth and range of these unplanned growth constraints in the early 1980s have been critical in achieving attitudinal changes, particularly in Eastern Europe, regarding micro- and macroeconomic management. Stabilization policies are by their nature inimical to socialist growth ambitions. The recent adverse experiences have thus gradually swayed policy sentiment in favor of positive structural and institutional change, more realistic growth objectives and more flexible policy instruments. Even so, the prevailing environment in most CPEs is still not conducive to broad-based experimentation for fear of unleashing socially and politically undesirable, possibly disruptive, short-term effects. Regardless of the boldness of policy choices, the legacies from the past for factor supply and for flexibility in decision making offer an unpromising near-term outlook.

This needs to be counterbalanced, however, by discussing what amount of maneuverability may be attainable by modifying existing policy instruments and their supporting institutions. The recent bout of adjustment experiences has clearly underlined the limited reach of weak market-type signals in inducing structural modifications in the behavior of economic agents. After the reforms of the 1960s and 1970s, the instruments and institutions typical of the traditional CPE that were still at the disposal of central authorities in Eastern Europe were very useful in quickly reversing the worrisome external payments imbalances and in slashing domestic absorption to levels that for a short while could be sustained. Though these instruments and institutions were evidently accessible to a smaller degree and could only be activated by exerting greater caution (to avert dysfunctional social reaction), stabilization policies succeeded in reversing the deficit and in most cases servicing the debt in an orderly manner. But these goals could be accomplished only at a paltry pace of economic growth, capital formation and consumption. While ability and willingness of policymakers to intervene by *dirigiste* methods played a leading role in the CMEA area's resilience, they are not likely to be as helpful for overcoming the slow-growth syndrome of the 1980s.

6.2 A DIAGNOSIS OF DEVELOPMENT CONSTRAINTS

The key constraints on regaining a buoyant growth path have not changed dramatically from those that prevailed at the end of the last decade. Among the domestic exogenous conditions for accelerating economic development, prospective factor supply of labor, natural resources and land are all about as they were at the end of the 1970s. Demand and supply conditions for capital at this stage are even less propitious because of the decapitalization and weak investment of the early 1980s. On the supply side, prospects for boosting savings behavior are not very good. Some incremental leeway may be gained from the anticipated shifts in economic mechanisms. But their positive payoff will not be tangible until late in the 1990s. The outlook is therefore for a moderate recovery in the physical supply of capital funds that can be mobilized for productive purposes, which is certainly below the projected rates of total investment growth.

The greatest degree of flexibility in CPE policies still resides in foreign trade and payments. If ambitious economic reforms were to be embraced, eventually a much greater degree of domestic policy flexibility could be gained as well. But introducing comprehensive economic reforms is much harder than pushing resolutely for the promotion of trade and integration by whatever means suitable at the time. The success of external trade promotion hinges critically on domestic economic reform. As the NICs have demonstrated, such reform could be pursued gradually, perhaps with the trade sector as a priority area, without aiming at an immediate overhauling of society as a whole. As examined in chapter 5, there is little hope of redistributing factor supplies within the region or of rectifying it on balance by inflows of capital into and outflows of labor from the CMEA countries.

The limits on labor-resource outflows are essentially of the CPEs' own making. They keep insisting on the duty of the socialist state to guarantee a job to any able-bodied individual willing to work and, in fact, to secure lifetime employment regardless of individual performance or the market situation. In effect, then, labor emigration, or immigration as well, is usually proscribed or at least much inhibited by noneconomic factors (Brabant,

1987a, pp. 302–10). Changes may arise with the pursuit of the common market, but that goal is a distant one (see section 6.8). Capital inflow into Eastern Europe is not actively encouraged at this stage because policy-makers fear a recurrence of the dysfunctional constraints on their economic sovereignty, as experienced in the early 1980s. As the course of events of the past three years demonstrate, the CPEs are not completely averse to bor-rowing in financial markets to bridge setbacks in implementing contempla-ted development targets. Furthermore, global financial centers are reluctant to invest in the area unless major organizational and managerial changes are enacted. Though it has recently been provided for in the modified joint venture laws of several CPEs, direct foreign investment is unlikely to increase substantially unless decision-making mechanisms in these countries become more compatible with those typical of market-type economies. Although this may inhibit any significant equity participation, some obstacles could be circumvented through the creation of various joint ventures.

Eastern Europe's experience with joint venture provisions during the past fifteen years has not been very favorable for numerous reasons. As a result, the prevailing institutions and managerial regimentation of the CPEs effectively narrow the channel for inflows from third countries to loan capital. Borrowing abroad to overcome the present economic doldrums is unlikely to provide more than a temporary escape valve, however, unless economic mechanisms are sufficiently modified to bolster the export potential of the CPEs or make it attractive for foreigners to invest in the area. Even now every CPE is primarily motivated by concerns about capital inflows, access to foreign technology and managerial expertise and generat-ing additional convertible currency earnings. Potential Western partners, however, are looking for access to local and, if possible, CMEA markets and making use of relatively cheap labor. Under present circumstances, the CPEs clearly prefer so-called self-liquidating loans. Although this form of capital inflow can be integrated with conventional plans, it severely confines the scope for financial flows into Eastern Europe.

As with the possibilities embedded in changing domestic policies, policy instruments and supporting institutions, considerable mileage may be gained by instituting proper policies in the trade sector, both for integration within the CMEA and in East-West as well as East-South relations. Shifts in trade regimes, perhaps at a faster pace than domestic transitions, may also be useful. The longer-term opportunities possibly associated with such a changed policy attitude are evaluated in chapter 18. Suffice it here to draw attention to a few critical areas affecting the external sector.

Whereas factor mobility cannot be an expansive source of growth under the self-imposed institutional and other features of the CPEs, trading in goods and services is largely a function of appropriate policies. But here too the systemic and institutional features that confined trade in the early 1980s need to be recalled. Existing economic structures are not well geared to competing effectively in international markets, and change can be sought individually or in the groupwide context only gradually, as recent experience so forcefully underscores. Are the prospects for boosting merchandise trade better than those for factor mobility? On the strength of the resource endowment of CPEs, their comparative advantage will continue to move away from fuels, raw and other basic industrial materials, foodstuffs and standard, labor-intensive manufactures in favor of processed products of considerable technological maturity, although not quite at the cutting edge of the most advanced economies. Clearly, the industrial sophistication and innovative potential of these countries is far from identical. Structural change along the basic guidelines emanating from comparative-advantage indicators would therefore lead to diversified production patterns. A shift from the present to a more desirable composition of exports is promising, especially for the more developed CPEs, who have recently begun to place emphasis on integrating science and technology into the domestic and external economy (see section 6.6).

6.3 TOWARD A RENEWAL OF POLICIES AND INSTITUTIONS

The troublesome early 1980s particularly contributed to changing policy sentiment in a number of CPEs. Since mid-decade, policymakers have been insisting that a resumption of faster growth at a fairly steady pace critically depends on 'growth intensification.' This coveted growth strategy, based on reorienting economic policies so as to obtain output gains primarily from factor productivity, is by no means novel. It was debated at great length during the earlier part of the 1960s (see chapter 4). Though the content of the debate has not changed for twenty-five years, the determination with which a new strategy is now being explored is much more convincing than at any other time since the New Course. A number of key policymakers have strengthened their stance that such policies depend on devolving decision making to local planning agents. There is also a growing conviction that a shift in the direction of policies and in the management of these economies requires adequate material incentives to bolster centrally set guidelines. This is precisely the purpose of the second broad wave of economic reforms presently on the policy agenda. Furthermore, many leaders admit difficulty in envisioning how a strong and sustainable boost to factor productivity might be engineered on the basis of national productive and reproductive forces alone. As a result, trade in general and economic intercourse within the context of the primary intregrating region of these CPEs will have to be accorded special attention. This now includes a range of measures aimed at bolstering real SEI (see Part IV).

The striking fact that the economic crises of Eastern Europe evolved without measurable repercussions on the CMEA organization, on the collective development and integration policies enshrined in official documents, or on the exceedingly passive policy instruments and related institutions in place bears highlighting. This lack of response prevailed until late 1986, when the second economic summit of the 1980s gingerly forced through a number of changes in concept and approach that have been crystallizing ever since. Such nonresponse, until the changes now under way, is particularly surprising in light of the agitation for substantive changes that eventually culminated in the June 1984 economic summit (as detailed in Brabant, 1987d). Moreover, excepting the extraordinary case of Poland since 1981, even at the bilateral level – as distinct from multilateral collaboration within the formal framework of the CMEA as a regional economic institution – each CPE has largely had to fend for itself. In fact, unanticipated external constraints emanating from world markets in the early 1980s were sharply aggravated by simultaneous and subsequent CMEA developments, although these were not necessarily causally related. But the CMEA did next to nothing to ease the situation.

Seen against that backdrop, it is rather easy to understand the hopes of some CMEA participants to alleviate their development constraints through a reinforcement of integration. This was precisely the motive behind the protracted proposal for holding a new summit in the early 1980s, for developing a new cooperation program endorsed in 1985, for an unambiguous commitment to CMEA reforms advocated at the second summit of the 1980s and for translating the drift of that high-level meeting into operational details, particularly following the forty-third Council Session in 1987. In other words, since the early 1980s there has been nearly continuous debate on reforming the CMEA organization, policies and the policy instruments and institutions that regulate economic cooperation, including genuine SEI matters. Though originally these concerns may have been molded by the short-term and structural problems of individual members, as the situation evolved the entire edifice of SEI began to be questioned. This extended debate is now yielding to possibly far-reaching CMEA reforms that may set the stage for a different approach to SEI in the next decade (see chapter 18). For that reason, it will be instructive to sketch the evolution of the topics of the debate in sequence below in greater detail than was necessary for the earlier SEI policy stances.

6.4 ISSUES UP FOR A NEW CMEA ECONOMIC SUMMIT

The first high-level deliberations about SEI in fifteen years took place in Moscow on 12–14 June 1984. This summit held after several rounds of last-minute discussions among CPE leaders. Little of substance on the deliberations in Moscow leaked out; of several documents endorsed, only two were made public.[2] *Main Directions* merits the most attention in this context. But the strong commitment to furthering all-around economic cooperation expressed in *Preservation of Peace* should at least be mentioned. Before briefly highlighting the principal SEI tangents of *Main Directions*, it may be useful to rephrase the principal positions held by the various CPEs prior to the summit. These positions can be grouped into three stylized sets: policy options and instruments for coming to grips with the existing economic situation in individual CPEs; policy issues concerning and means available to foster target programming; and opening up the debates to discussions on the future of SEI, harmonization of economic policies, dovetailing of economic plans and the promulgation of new instruments whereby the goals of SEI, possibly redefined, might be vigorously pursued. A brief summary of these positions provides a broader canvas for assessing that meeting's achievements than what can be gleaned from the published documents.

6.4.1 Short-term considerations

How to manage the growing internal and external constraints on domestic policy flexibility in Eastern Europe since the second oil price shock in 1979–80 was perhaps the central topic for an economic summit. Clearly, the region's economic plight was perceived to depend in part on the resumption of import demand in Western Europe, which began its recovery from the protracted growth recession in 1983. But the external constraints posed by economic difficulties in the CMEA region and the internal problems of many CPEs are a different matter altogether.

The economic slide of a number of CPEs chiefly originated in the conflicts between efficiency and expediency built into their rigid central planning systems. Slow growth in agriculture and industry throughout the region in the late 1970s and early 1980s aggravated the constraints on policy flexibility embedded in stagnating or only slowly expanding factor supplies. These shortages have been exacerbated by the sluggish progress in factor productivity. In addition to internal bottlenecks, other issues that helped refocus the CPEs' goals with respect to an eventual economic summit included the situation in Poland and its side effects on CMEA partners, the embargo imposed by Washington, problems stemming from the indebtedness of several CPEs and the need for adjustment because of sharp shifts in fuel prices and absolute limits on the volumes procurable at the traditional TRPs.

Although all Eastern European countries faced short-term internal and external imbalances that needed priority consideration, only Rumania discussed them to the exclusion of other issues. The Rumanian policy stance in its most forthcoming version rested on the premise that without joint programs to surmount current difficulties in energy, raw materials and agriculture, long-term plans to deepen CMEA cohesion lack a solid foundation (Badrus, 1983, pp. 22–5). It was argued that synchronizing economic policies should at most be applied to already existing areas of convergence (including easing the fuel and raw material problems) and to fostering the equalization of development levels; only thereafter should it be aimed at other aspects of economic policy.

6.4.2 Fine tuning target programming

Reformulation of the goals of the Target Programs and reassessment of the means to implement them constituted another priority among the considerations that led up to the summit. Especially the advanced CPEs, with Czechoslovakia in the lead, pressed for an economic summit in order to grapple with questions of how best to map out the political and economic SEI strategy for the 1980s and beyond. A more realistic appreciation of prevailing internal and external development conditions could provide the basic cornerstone for steady economic growth of the community in the years ahead by safeguarding supplies of fuels, energy and metals; by processing and using these crucial inputs more efficiently; by securing sufficient supplies of foodstuffs and consumer goods; by promoting effective STC and ECPS especially in manufactures; and by providing transport services in support of CMEA trade, economic cooperation and the members' own development efforts. With the exception of the perceived need to bring the peripheral economies of Cuba, Mongolia and Vietnam more closely into the CMEA fold, the above points, argued chiefly by the Czechoslovaks, constitute a nearly point-by-point restatement of the goals that the Target Programs were to have addressed (Brabant, 1981, pp. 141ff.). A reexamination of the foundations of target programming, especially a realistic assessment of the objectives of SEI and of available resources and policy instruments, might therefore have been in the offing.[3]

6.4.3 Long-term strategy of economic integration

As Husák stressed (*Rudé Právo*, 7 April 1981, p. 3), the Czechoslovak position on target programming centered unambiguously on holding a 'strategic economic summit' to 'coordinate the group's economic policy.' However, it was not made clear what would come within the purview of either economic policy or strategy. But an expeditious meeting was requested so as to address the fundamental questions of the coordination of economic policies.

The Czechoslovaks as well as the Rumanians called for 'enhancing production cooperation' as the central agenda of the summit. It would be made contingent on coordinating economic policies, bringing closer together national economic mechanisms and effectively interlinking individual economic units of the CPEs. Even when thus phrased, production cooperation remained as vague as when the ECPS concept was first formulated in the mid-1950s. The principles for such a wide-ranging discussion had been adopted by the 1981 Session, and the CPEs had already explored the possibilities of implementing such an ambitious policy coordination in various documents. These would include main directions of the long-range socioeconomic policies of the CPEs; coordination of these policies; principal methods of intensifying SEI; the further economic development of Cuba, Mongolia and Vietnam; and an examination of the external relations of the CMEA community with other states and international economic institutions. The conceptual focus of the proposed meeting would 'offer an opportunity to adopt a position on practically every basic problem relevant to future socioeconomic developments in the CMEA community and to mutual cooperation in its member states' (Hamouz, 1982, p. 3).

Perhaps the most authoritative statement regarding the summit's goals was a Soviet Communist Party editorial in *Pravda* (15 October 1982, p. 1), which essentially argued four positions. First, the ordinary meshing of plans as hitherto practiced in the CMEA no longer sufficed to support production intensification. There was, therefore, an urgent need to complement it with harmonized macroeconomic policies. Second, the individual economic mechanisms, including planning, management and control systems, must be better tuned to each other in order to integrate overall policies. Third, direct links must be established between ministries engaged in cooperation, joint firms should be set up and investment strategies needed to be more closely coordinated. Finally, *Pravda* argued for strengthening the CMEA's technological and economic independence from DMEs.

The above pointers signaled that the summit would promulgate a new SEI document attuned to the prevailing economic circumstances. The precise contours of such a new program have never been clarified, although some clues have recently surfaced from the deliberations at the 1988 Session. The contemporaneous policy discussions of the mid-1980s suggest that a new strategy would seek to establish:

1. A more adequate pricing mechanism.
2. A greater role for monetary and financial instruments, including the TR.
3. More direct operational cooperation of firms across national borders and less attention to detailed specification of physical quantities and prices of most goods to be exchanged during the next planning period(s).
4. More comprehensive interlocking of those policy instruments that might bolster steady productivity growth.
5. More efficient utilization of primary and intermediate inputs.
6. Enhancement of specialization, especially in engineering, and upgrading the scientific-technical parameters of specialized products.
7. Fuller coordination of East-West trade, finance and technology policies.

How to effectively stimulate innovation and technical progress in production would in any case have figured prominently in the debates. Perhaps the prime obstacle to innovation and its prompt transmission into the production sphere emanates from the traditional planning and management systems of the CPEs. Because regional regimentation along the lines traditionally followed in the component economies would be stymied by the same influences that hinder production intensification, it is no surprise that the elaboration of proper support mechanisms for scientific-technical progress in production in combination with a more rational division of labor, especially in engineering, would be at the core of the envisaged summit.

6.5 THE DOCUMENTS OF THE SUMMIT AND THE LATTER'S AFTERMATH

While the broad range of issues listed above provided the backdrop to the summit's preparations, little is known about the actual negotiations. The thirty-seventh Council Session, when it was finally convened, finalized the preparation of the summit, including major portions of *Main Directions*. Although its context is opaque, the formulation of a new SEI program for the rest of the century was endorsed by N. Tichonov at that meeting (*Pravda*, 19 October 1983, pp. 1 and 4). Such a program would presumably draw primarily upon the perceived need 'to enhance the coordination of economic strategy' based on 'economic reforms that have been under way since the mid-1960s,' especially the components 'that have a direct impact on the development of mutual cooperation' (Bogomolov, 1983, pp. 79–80). But what precisely that might entail was not made explicit. There were some hints that a full-length SEI document that would chart the strategic goals and means of development had been under preparation, but insufficient progress had been made on it for it to be promulgated at the summit. *Main Directions* was being refined in late 1983 and early 1984, and Konstantin U. Černenko apparently agreed enough with its main thrust so that the summit could proceed.

Main Directions is a fairly long and carefully crafted statement. It clarifies that the summit 'concentrated attention on the solution of tasks stemming from internal and external conditions that have changed in recent years.' It endorses many positions that affect short- and long-term cooperation policies of the CMEA. The chief provisions can be summarized under the following headings: short-term national and regional economic problems, the long-term goals of SEI, measures to enhance the formulation and implementation of concrete SEI measures and other considerations. Items included under the heading of short-term economic issues are the potential expansion of trade beyond volumes agreed upon under the coordinated economic and trade plans for 1981–5, readiness to increase deliveries of energy and industrial raw materials in exchange for high-quality manufactures, and greater flexibility in the setting of TRPs, with the reference period to most WMPs being compressed for some goods, possibly starting with the next five-year plans.

As for the longer term, *Main Directions* identifies the most important tasks of the mid-1980s to be in the areas of domestic and regional economic policies and regional cooperation mechanisms. The most crucial component is probably the elevation of SEI to a new level by accelerating the transition to intensive growth so as to ensure structural change through the more rational use of resources within the region as a whole, including their proper location. Structural change, including at the CMEA level, should permit an export-oriented output structure that is simultaneously versatile, technically up-to-date, reliable and durable. Although policies that foster growth intensification must necessarily originate at the national level, further improvements in the coordination of all economic policies that, directly or indirectly, affect the economic interests of CMEA partners need to be undertaken, and new steps via coordination of selected sectors should be explored by interested CPEs. More regular summits, perhaps at five-year intervals, should help in these endeavors.

Regarding the mechanism of SEI, *Main Directions* underlines the primacy of plan coordination but also stresses that 'the task of organically combining ... plan activity with the active utilization of commodity-money relations retains its topicality.' Accordingly, there is room for improvement in the regional price mechanism and in the TR's functioning, but details need to be worked out. Plan coordination at the CMEA level needs to be improved, however, by focusing on essential regional tasks and by concluding it well before the national five-year plans are to be implemented. Mobilizing plan coordination to enhance production cooperation could be facilitated in more than one way by encouraging direct ties among economic agents, including through joint firms.

The prime sectors for further action are those earlier included in the Target Programs. STC more generally receives special emphasis in that the members committed themselves to elaborate a comprehensive program of scientific-technological progress until the year 2000 (see section 6.6). More rational utilization of scarce inputs and higher production and trade levels, possibly through joint investments and industrial reconversion, should enable the CPEs to collectively solve their fuel, raw material and foodstuff problems. Joint efforts in agroindustrial and fuel sectors receive special stress. But it is noted that due attention needs to be paid to feasible output levels and the necessity to exchange such 'hard' industrial inputs for manufactures in short supply (including food, up-to-date industrial consumer goods, selected construction materials and sophisticated engineering goods required by the net exporters of fuels and raw materials). Together with the gradual transition to intensive growth, *Main Directions* calls for measures to render CPE economic mechanisms more conducive to factor productivity growth and the ISDL. Emerging problems need to be tackled as soon as possible and the interest of economic agents strengthened, possibly with assistance from financial and monetary instruments.

Although they are carefully phrased and leave the door wide open for follow-up action, the published documents suggest that the summit accomplished far less than what the participants had anticipated. In addition to reaffirming the importance of buoyant East-West relations, three prominent decisions with respect to the CMEA were taken. Two have become well known. The first essentially concerns the future direction of the real terms of trade within the CMEA. This resolve emerged in response to the perceived need to 'harden' Eastern Europe's supply of mostly machinery and manufactured consumer goods, and to raise its exports of hard foodstuffs. Both were seen conditioning the maintenance of the export level of fuels and primary products (primarily super hard goods at that time), principally from the Soviet Union. Clearly, most of Eastern Europe found it nearly impossible to quickly harden export menus against which crucial industrial inputs would henceforth increasingly be traded. An up-to-date export pattern of high-quality goods can ensue only from a major modernization drive and change in managerial styles. Both require time even if the current leadership were inclined to act swiftly. Only a firm commitment to economic reform appears to have been reached in 1984. The other agreement is more systemic in nature; that is, to strengthen the bilateral approach to CMEA cooperation, possibly even reinforcing structural bilateral ties (see chapter 11). In other words, at least for the immediate future, the multilateral SEI approach envisioned in the early 1970s was abandoned in favor of wider exploration of bilateral ties. The strengthening of structural bilateralism called for in *Main Directions* and in some of the bilateral agreements thereafter signed with the USSR buttressed this ominous turn of events. The third crucial, published ingredient hammered out at the summit was the resolve to elaborate a new integration blueprint for the concertation of economic policies. This shift in emphasis on the goals and means of SEI was to be negotiated first around a broad-based document dealing with the advancement of scientific and technological progress by common means. It is this element of the summit that received considerable attention in the Eastern European media as signaling, once again, a qualitatively new step in the process of realizing SEI.

In addition to the two published documents and the one on STC promulgated a year later, the summit probably endorsed a number of other agreements on the strategy and mechanism of SEI and, more specifically, on the conduct of regular CMEA trade and payments relations. In all likelihood the latter included specifications on TRP matters (about which full consensus continued to elude the CMEA participants), the need to accelerate factor productivity growth and production specialization on the

CMEA scale, the development of direct interfirm relations, joint investments and the broad organization of CMEA economic relations. The post-summit literature occasionally hinted at the existence of such agreements, which, apparently, molded the subsequent SEI course at least until about late 1986.

6.6 SCIENTIFIC-TECHNOLOGICAL COOPERATION IN THE 1980s AND BEYOND

At their forty-first extraordinary Council Session held in Moscow on 17–18 December 1985, the CMEA members adopted a new policy blueprint that envisions measurably enhancing SEI in the years ahead. *Scientific-Technological Progress*[4] aims essentially at a further concertation of the economic policies adopted with considerable fanfare at the 1984 summit. But whether the program is actually the straightforward realization of the intramural decisions reached at that summit has been cast into doubt by Ceauşescu's emphasis, shortly after the document was approved, on the need to return to the 'provisions of the [summit] program we adopted' (*Scînteia*, 28 December 1985, p. 1). However that may be, in 1985–6 the CPEs elaborated implementation procedures for the program that could have had a measurable impact on the character, depth and speed of SEI processes, including East-West commerce. But this strategy gave rise to another one, which will be examined in section 6.8.

6.6.1 Key pointers on scientific-technological cooperation

The document is, as usual, expansive on general matters and intentions but inarticulate on what concretely needs to be done to accelerate technological progress in the CMEA. Members are called upon to work out a coordinated network of agreements and treaties about STC, ranging from pure development to practical application in the production process. These are gradually to be reflected in the respective annual and medium-term plans. But the program contains few pointers on the concrete measures to be enacted to initiate, guide and control the stated tasks. This is not terribly remarkable given that the document was meant to inspire SEI until about the turn of the century.

The program aims at the accelerated implementation of joint cooperation in five broad domains – namely, electronics, automation, nuclear energy, new materials and technologies and biotechnology – but the compass of some is so wide as to potentially impinge upon the entire production sphere in one way or another. The two areas mentioned last were deemed to be of sufficient weight to warrant the creation of two new Standing Commissions in early 1986 – the first new organs at that level since 1975 (see chapter 7).

These advances should permit an acceleration in the pace of productivity growth in the CMEA as a whole. The purpose of catching up with existing scientific and technological know-how is to accelerate factor productivity to more than double the present output per worker by the turn of the century. It also seeks to drastically reduce unit material content, particularly energy and critical raw materials.

Electronic development of the CPEs is to be achieved by supplying the entire production process with the most modern data-processing facilities as the cornerstone of a sustainable boost to factor productivity. But the goals also encompass a reduction in the material intensity of production, an acceleration of the pace of scientific-technical progress, sharp curtailment of research and development lags and qualitative changes in the nonmaterial sphere. The second area anticipates the complex automation of selected economic branches, chiefly by substituting capital for labor through robots, numerically controlled machinery and other sophisticated equipment. The chief goals of the nuclear energy component are to change the composition of the energy balance, ensure greater reliability in the supply of electricity and compress the consumption of organic energy carriers. A critical component of the acceleration of technological progress is the creation and manipulation of new materials and technologies. The goals envisioned are ambitious in depth and range, including rust-free and heat- and friction-resistant materials, new technologies to generate such products and other items. The biotechnology subprogram is initially directed at curing human ailments, enhancing the supply of foodstuffs, improving output of raw materials, bringing to fruition new types of renewable energy sources, improving the environment and curbing waste in production.

As for implementation modalities for these ambitious policy goals, the program calls for the usual concrete bi- and multilateral agreements to be formulated soon so that they can encompass the full cycle of 'science-technology-production-distribution.' Unlike in earlier attempts to bolster SEI, the program implores members 'to pay particular attention' to the appropriation of necessary human, material and financial resources so that these measures can be realized expeditiously within the standard coordination of medium-term and annual plans, including the respective Concerted Plan.

Existing scientific-technological research in the CPEs may have to be complemented with new bi- or even multilateral organizations set up specifically to tackle particular aspects of technological progress. Perhaps the key aim governing the elaboration of implementation provisions is the realization of effective direct relations among firms, associations and scientific-technical institutes. These are to be fostered not only in each CPE but also among the participants through conventional, though focused, bi- or multilateral protocols. Financing is to be arranged from regular budgetary appropriations as well as through loans from the two CMEA banks. Also, special funds may be set up for some future concrete agreements.

6.6.2 On implementing the program

The single most important question in late 1985 concerned the probability that the program would be implemented quickly and fully. As noted, one crucial determinant derived from the considerable restriction on policy maneuvering well into the near future. These were bound to limit the amount of funds that could be mobilized for the special components of the program. Not all provisions, of course, really required fundamental funding from the beginning. Indeed, more effective use of available resources, perhaps in combination with a slight acceleration in appropriations for the new ventures, could have measurably eased maneuverability. But the rapid realization of some of the program's provisions was also being hampered by two other long-standing factors. Some CPEs remained highly reluctant to subscribe wholeheartedly to the proposed implementation modalities, including the allocation of scarce capital to prespecified projects chiefly of interest in the short run to the Soviet Union (Širjaev, 1986, pp. 132ff.). The program's realization was also impaired by the inauspicious economic performance of 1986–7 compared with the five-year plan targets.

These factors appeared to be directly responsible for the unusual delay in holding the forty-second Council Session until November 1986 and for having this immediately followed by another summit, which had not been anticipated. The principal items on that Session's agenda, as well as on the 1987 one, were specification of a number of projects, especially those included within the programs for biotechnology and new materials and technologies; approval of several documents on the tasks, regulations and responsibilities of head organizations (see below); and drafting documents on direct enterprise relations and the program's implementation modalities, as well as on the legal, organizational-methodological and economic foundations of STC (Bakoveckij and Abolichina, 1986, p. 21).

Soon after the program's endorsement in late 1985, the CPEs initiated a series of studies and deliberations on how to proceed with the program's ninety-three separate research projects, which were to be fully finalized by the end of 1988. Most elements of these projects needed to be regulated by concrete agreements that could be signed as quickly as circumstances permitted (Syčёv, 1986a, pp. 47ff.). By and large these projects were conceived as comprehensive framework agreements for the specific topics subsequently to be addressed in bilateral protocols.

Available data suggest that framework agreements were negotiated rapidly. But nothing is known about the all-important bilateral implementation agreements other than those already in effect as of end-1985 and afterwards included in the program (see Širjaev, 1986; Syčёv, 1986b). It is precisely those concrete implementation agreements that specify resources to be earmarked for the project, the timetable for reciprocal deliveries and completion of the project, organizational aspects and all the other details required in the absence of a uniform legal and economic environment for SEI. These agreements were in jeopardy by the middle of 1986.

Originally, each broad project was slated to be supervised by a 'head organization' (*golovnaja organizacija*), which may or may not have called for new IEOs. The entire endeavor engaged seventeen CMEA organs under the overall coordination of the Committee for STC (see chapter 7). More than seven hundred CPE scientific organizations were mustered in direct support of the program. Each project, in fact, represented a number of smaller 'topics' or subprojects and, at a still more disaggregate level, an even larger number of 'themes' or 'targets' (Lér, 1986, p. 1), of which there were several thousands in the original plans.

Although the scientific-technological centers established in and among the various CPEs after *Integration Program* was endorsed in 1971 were called upon to play an important role in the implementation of *Scientific-Technological Progress*, the focal instances for initiating and managing STC are slated to differ considerably. The precise status of the head organizations in the planning, organization, currency and financial relations and legal provisions of the CMEA and the individual members were not clear in mid-1986. Some analyses (Zerev, 1987, pp. 25–6) contended that the modalities would be chiefly the regulations approved as far back as 1972 (see Brabant, 1988c, 1988d), which for the first time mentioned the 'head organization.' But in the past these modalities have never been very effective in spurring on STC.

Of special significance was the provision that each project should be headed by a Soviet entity specialized in the main subject matter and invested with extensive executive and managerial powers. Each would be placed in charge of working out the details of contractual arrangements that form the linchpin of the implementation modalities for the program (Syčëv, 1986c, p. 17). These contracts were to determine the relationship of the head organization with the constituent enterprises and other institutions throughout the CMEA region. Some observers stressed that the contracts would be 'instructed' to the counterpart organizations to forge direct and permanent intragroup links in research, development and production.

Although the creation of direct interfirm relations in the CMEA has been an essential topic of SEI debates in the 1980s, questions of how to realize this according to precepts on direct relations that not all CPEs agree upon have not yet been resolved. Judging by past experience, it is not a task that can soon be accomplished. Particularly important was the question of how such direct relations fit into central planning and how the MFT will be affected. According to Syčëv (1986c, p. 17), the 'centralized administration of foreign economic relations' is not to be disturbed. It is hard to see how this could be achieved without implementing wholesale trade reforms in the CPEs.

6.6.3 Implications of the program

How precisely the program would have affected the Council and the overall process of SEI cannot be determined unambiguously with the information at hand. As pointed out by Syčëv (1986c, p. 17), realization of the program would necessitate 'serious change in the structure of the CMEA, and in the style of methods of its activities.' By this he probably regurgitated Gorbačëv's scathing remarks (at the twenty-seventh Communist Party Congress in February 1986) condemning the 'armchair administration' typical of the CMEA organs. Inasmuch as the bases for generating technological progress and factor productivity were expected to be radically altered by the program's provisions, if successfully implemented, important consequences for traditional CMEA cooperation mechanisms were bound to ensue. For one, given that one of the fundamental aims was to create mutually compatible technologies throughout the CMEA area, anchoring SEI to the program would have generated numerous opportunities for trade and production specialization. It would also have enhanced space for East-West cooperation.

Even without the program, one could have anticipated far-reaching changes in the planning and organization of the CPEs. Thus, the USSR's abrupt decision in August 1986 to launch a foreign trade reform beginning in early 1987 and involving the devolution of authority to ministries and some large firms signaled a major departure from the way the Soviet foreign trade sector has traditionally been managed. There would be repercussions for the CMEA's organization, the goals of SEI and the means by which cooperation was to be forged.

6.7 IMPLEMENTING THE PROGRAM AND SEI POLICIES IN THE LATE 1980s

Key CMEA policymakers may have been dismayed by the slow progress made in 1986 with *Scientific-Technological Progress*. Their disappointment may have been due to the inherent nature of introducing novel ideas into CPEs, where bureaucratic inertia and top-heavy central planning structures are, by themselves, likely to initially stall any genuine efforts at bringing about changes in sclerotic structures and mountains of red tape. Perhaps more importantly, the program was not well prepared. It was ratified hastily just prior to the launching of the new five-year plans for 1986–90, which was too late for the CPEs that depend on national planning to incorporate the necessary changes and accordingly mobilize their resources. Not only that, the program's particular vagueness on the head organizations and the economics of interfirm relations more generally may have dissuaded some CPEs, including the GDR, from placing themselves in the vanguard of the search for a realistic solution. Finally, I doubt that all CPEs were suddenly bent on pursuing comprehensive policy coordination through direct enterprise relations.

As a result of this disappointing performance and the setbacks incurred with the new five-year plans, policymakers may have recognized the need for a new impetus. This may have been the principal reason behind the convening of a new economic summit only two years after the seminal one of 1984 and just days after the long-delayed annual Session. Curiously enough, at the time of this new summit in November 1986, reports on the deliberations were exceedingly brief and reticent. The communiqué of the two-day meeting (see *Izvestija*, 13 November 1986, p. 1) comprised seventeen lines of text other than the listing of participants! It did mention that the leaders had concerned themselves with the 'cardinal problems of development and improvement of cooperation' in the CMEA. This would be focused particularly on 'new, much more progressive forms of economic and [scientific-technological cooperation] in the interest of accelerating' socioeconomic progress. The rest of the communiqué acknowledges the achievements of the Reykjavik summit, the antinuclear stance of the CPEs and other topics.

With this cursory information, one could hardly read into the new summit more than that a meeting had failed to galvanize the obstacles to the realization of *Scientific-Technological Progress*. This impression was in fact reinforced with Syčëv's assessment (1987) of the achievements of the Session and the summit. Of course, the Soviet economic reform was then undergoing measurable change from the concepts that may have prevailed when the new leadership came to power. Its implications for CMEA cooperation would have to be clarified and evaluated.

This position was not really contested in subsequent events, at least not until the Central Committee Secretaries in charge of economic affairs (CCS), on which more in chapter 7, met in September 1987 in Sofia. Whatever ambiguity may have lingered in the minds of observers was removed when the forty-third Council Session was finally convened in October 1987 as an 'extraordinary' one (see chapter 7). From both meetings it transpired that in the course of the year, and perhaps even in 1986, heated discussions on the reorganization of the CMEA and the policies and instruments of SEI had taken place. Perhaps their importance can best be gauged by referring to the main achievements reported in connection with the forty-third and forty-fourth Sessions.

6.8 TOWARD ANOTHER COMMON MARKET?

The Prague Session in July 1988 signaled a seminal shift in the purposes and goals of SEI with the decision that from now on the CMEA would strive resolutely for the establishment of a unified or common market. This declaration of intent is only the latest addition to many recent calls for CMEA reform, which can be grouped under three main headings. First, a broad-based debate has erupted primarily around revamping the institutional setup of the CMEA by rationalizing the bureaucracy, streamlining the mechanisms through which issues get tabled and rendering the deliberative organs more effective. Second, the ultimate purposes of SEI and means (institutions, instruments, policy coordination and structural macroeconomic policies) to pursue it were to be comprehensively reexamined. Finally, the SEI mechanism in the strict sense was to be refocused, including in support of emerging reforms.

Disclosures about some of the intramural discussions have become perceptibly more interesting since mid-1987 and the important forty-third Session (Moscow, 13–14 October 1987), during which the seminal contribution of the November 1986 summit to polarizing the reform movement was finally revealed. Five groups of issues can be distinguished. First, the Moscow Session in 1987 agreed to streamline the CMEA organization by abolishing organs that have failed to consistently perform well, consolidating units that have duplicated one another, retrenchment of the civil service and generally gearing preoccupations entrusted to the CMEA less to the day-to-day planning of resource allocation than to the charting of the medium- to long-term strategic directions for structural change, similar to the intentions of Soviet *perestrojka*. Some organizational modifications were carried out in early 1988, particularly in the Committees, Standing Commissions and Conferences (see chapter 7). It was also decided to trim the CMEA civil service by six to seven hundred individuals, but I have no evidence that by early 1989 this decision had been implemented. There evidently remains considerable room for further retrenchment and coaxing the CMEA civil service into greater efficiency. Finally, a decision appears to have been made to eliminate a significant number of the IEOs (see chapter 8).

Second, there was widespread agreement in Moscow – although the assent in some cases was rather reluctant – to rechart assistance policies to Cuba, Mongolia and Vietnam. Past economic and technical development assistance efforts rendered to these countries were judged to have been less effective than desirable for donors as well as for recipients. Donors thus agreed to elaborate a coordinated multilateral approach and to enshrine it in a medium- to long-term coherent assistance program, thereby hoping to measurably improve the benefits accruing from these efforts.

Three separate drafts of comprehensive economic cooperation with each of the three CPEs were presented at the forty-fourth Session in Prague. Once fine tuned into a coherent stance on technical and economic assistance, it will become incorporated into the new SEI strategy (see below). The basic objective is to integrate these countries more fully into the CMEA edifice, including through concrete agreements on production cooperation and specialization, STC on more than a gratuitous basis and further commercialization of their economic interactions with the CMEA. Some forms of assistance to the non-European countries will continue to be provided by the developed membership on a gratuitous basis, however.

Third, there was virtually unanimous agreement to work out a new SEI strategy, tentatively entitled *Collective Concept of the [ISDL] for the Years 1991–2005*. An advanced draft was slated to be presented to the Prague CMEA Council Session. Its major objective would be to lay the foundations for a unified market and thus ensure the transition to a qualitatively new level of cooperation. In addition to reiterating well-tested forms of SEI and strengthening planning in medium- to long-term development, by putting in place proper instruments, the new program should foster economic efficiency and the role of economics in commodity and financial relations of all economic organizations involved in SEI. A draft was debated in Prague, although the 1–2 June 1988 CCS meeting in Budapest had strenuously objected to its excessive blandness and generality. It has, however, not yet been published.

The idea to create a unified CMEA market was first mooted by the Soviets in Moscow. At the Prague meeting, it was unanimously endorsed, except by Rumania, and placed at the core of the new ISDL concept. Its adoption on the eve of the fortieth anniversary of the CMEA may be symbolically significant. But the communiqué is very carefully worded and masks some of the more impassioned presentations, including Ryžkov's.[5] He noted that this market aims at:

> ensuring a high degree of uniformity of economic conditions, the relatively free movement of goods, services, manpower, and finances among our countries' economic organizations, and the unified macroeconomic regulation of economic processes – regulation based on a coordinated policy – are a matter for the remote future. But we must keep this prospect in mind even now. For us the unified market is not a fashionable slogan but an important guideline for the development of the integration process.

Directly related to the program, fourth, are major decisions revolving around the precise mechanism of SEI to be elaborated in conjunction with, and perhaps in support of, the ongoing reform process in critical CPEs. Gaining concurrence on this matter has been very convoluted. Although there was broad agreement in Moscow on the need to revisit certain elements of planning and monetary-financial cooperation, members were divided on a number of critical economic issues, including the introduction of a modified form of limited regional convertibility, multilateralism in trade and payments, determination of unified exchange rates, revision of the price-formation mechanism, the linking of domestic and trade prices and the role of capital movements within the CMEA. The Session also emphasized reinvigorating the implementation of the program on STC by measurably improving the economics of interfirm relations as well as the organizational prerequisites for fostering such relations. Stressed in particular was that such relations must be invested with economic guidelines and institutional supports to facilitate microeconomic decision making. Included are measures for the settlement of accounts for selected transactions, implying in fact some highly limited form of intraregional convertibility (see chapter 18). In addition, it was agreed to improve domestic and trade pricing, exchange rates, the credit mechanism of the IIB and trade and payments multilateralism through the IBEC.

The links of the reformed mechanism to this new integration program, as well as specifications on both, should have been the particular focus of the Prague Session. It emphasized the need to provide a support structure for more intensive forms of economic development and integration. For that, the role of the economic tools of management must be improved, the function of cooperation through the coordination of national economic plans must be modified and firms should now play a more significant role in the day-to-day pursuit of SEI. An essential role in enhancing interfirm relations based on economic incentives falls onto the TR and TRPs. These and other elements of the refurbished economic mechanism of SEI are to be firmly in place in time for the introduction of the next medium-term plans in 1991. An unusual item on the agenda was the creation of socialist multinationals centered around key national firms, but details are lacking.

Finally, the Moscow Session paid lip service to the necessity of achieving better results with the habitual coordination of economic plans and, indeed, of providing supports at the regional level for interfirm relations. Once again, this is nothing new. The speeches on behalf of the GDR and Rumania particularly stressed the paramount role of plan coordination to foster STC and to guarantee prompt deliveries of adequate volumes of critical fuels and raw materials. These policy stances contrast rather shrilly with the role accorded to these instruments by the commentators of the other CPEs. Enhancing the coordination of plans was also debated in Prague, but only marginally by the GDR and Rumania. A critical role is earmarked for production specialization, particularly in engineering, but not only through planning at the intergovernmental level.

Against this backdrop, expectations regarding the follow-up Council Session in 1989 are very high, particularly since the CPEs will be commemorating the fortieth anniversary of their organization. Not only must drafts on attitudes toward the developing-country CPEs and the new concept of long-term SEI be further refined, the CPEs have also committed themselves to further elaborating details on the new SEI mechanism (including prices, direct wholesale trade, exchange rates, convertibility and regional settlements) and its institutions (including the two banks), and perhaps also on the further streamlining of the organizational structure of the CMEA as such.

NOTES

1. For the USSR, for example, Padma Desai (1986, pp. 68ff.) found that during 1968–82 grain yields varied to a much greater extent than between 1955–67. Differences in weather patterns explained 52 percent of the variance of yields. The rest stemmed from variations in broadly defined inputs.
2. *Declaration of the main directions of further development and deepening of economic, scientific and technological cooperation of the CMEA member countries* (henceforth *Main Directions*) and *Declaration of the CMEA member countries on the preservation of peace and international economic cooperation* (henceforth *Preservation of Peace*). The latter is a major statement on international relations, especially between East and West, and will not be further discussed.
3. This position conflicts sharply with that held by those (e.g., Lavigne, 1983, 1984) who believe that the endorsed programs were being implemented as the final SEI strategy. For an alternative view, see Brabant, 1984b, 1984c.
4. The full title reads: *Comprehensive program to promote the scientific and technological progress of the member countries of the Council for Mutual Economic Assistance up to the year 2000*. It was published in all main CP newspapers of 19 December 1985.
5. The communiqué is in *Izvestija*, 8 July 1988, pp. 1 and 4, and the speech is reported in *Pravda*, 6 July 1988, p. 4.

PART II

THE INSTITUTIONS OF THE CMEA

In this part, I introduce the formal and other organs of the CMEA, how they relate to the various processes of SEI, with an emphasis on their contemporary configuration, and how they interact with the most critical organizational and institutional features of the members. It is of some importance to stress that the organs discussed here are chiefly those extant as of year-end 1987. With the broadly based economic reforms under way in various European planned economies and the already announced commitment to whittle the regional institutions down to size, the setup of the CMEA and its links with the CPEs are likely to undergo significant alteration during the remainder of the decade. Indeed, some excising of organs that duplicate each other or that have been ineffective in the past has already occurred (as of early 1988) and will be noted to the extent sources permit. But I cannot possibly delineate every change because of the lack of transparency in even the announced organizational changes.

Even if the full scope of the organizational changes were known, it would still be of more than marginal interest to have a solid overview of the various organizational and institutional aspects of economic cooperation among the CPEs within the framework that existed through 1987. There are at least three reasons for this. For one, it would be impossible to comprehend the past forty years of the CMEA's evolution without gaining an insight into the institutional aspects of SEI. It would also be difficult to place the current changes in their proper setting without taking into account the institutional legacies of existing organs. The experiences of nearly forty years of organized economic cooperation in the CMEA will be most valuable for understanding the ambitions and prospects of the newly created institutions, particularly their potential contribution to revitalizing SEI.

The generally recognized institutional hierarchy of the official CMEA organs is examined in chapter 7. Here I largely follow the institutional and organizational levels of the CMEA that are identified as such in the organization's charter. In addition, I discuss three other levels of critical importance to what the CMEA can accomplish, even though these formal and informal meetings do not strictly fall within the compass of the regional institution. I divide the official organs into various tiers of hierarchical supports that can be provided to the CPEs or SEI.

Chapter 8 does likewise for the regional organizations that are not formally part of the CMEA, some of which at best maintain very remote contacts with the official and other organs. But not all informal organizations can be detailed here. Following some categorization, I shall focus on those that maintain at least moderately close ties to the regional organization, that are entrusted with focal SEI tasks or whose operations depend critically on mechanisms of regional collaboration worked out in one of the formal CMEA levels.

Because I focus on the economics of integration policies, instruments and institutions in Parts III and IV, it is necessary to briefly clarify the foremost links between the CMEA organization and the hierarchy and administration of the members. I do so in chapter 9 by presenting a condensed, streamlined account of types of economic reforms, how they affect the foreign trade sector and their implications for SEI. But this is not the proper place to elaborate on the traditional and modified development strategies or economic models of the CPEs since World War II. Some generic comments, I hope, help to trace hindrances to SEI that stem from incongruities between regional and national institutions and policies.

7 · THE FORMAL CMEA INSTITUTIONS

In this chapter, I introduce the various official tiers of the CMEA as well as its most important, but unofficial, pinnacle organs, namely the summit, the CCS and the various national decision-making centers. The CMEA's primary organs consist of the Council Session, the Executive Committee and its subsidiary committees, the Secretariat and its departments, the Standing Commissions, the Institutes and the Conferences. In addition, a number of other bodies are usually discussed in connection with the CMEA's institutional structure, although their mutual links are formally somewhat tenuous. Their current position in the regional organization and SEI efforts are clarified in chapter 8.

Section 7.1 introduces several types of definitional, functional, advisory and hierarchical relationships among the CMEA organs. The pinnacle organs, which are outside the formal structure of the CMEA as an institution, are explained in section 7.2. This leads in section 7.3 to consideration of decision-making authority in the CMEA proper. Section 7.4 introduces the highest level of official CMEA organs. Important levers at the secretarial level are discussed in section 7.5, while section 7.6 details the most important coordinating tiers.

7.1 TYPES OF RELATIONSHIPS IN THE CMEA

It is instructive to distinguish among relationships that are predominantly of superiority or subordination, advisory, functional and typological. These various interactions are depicted in Figure 7.1, along with the CMEA's institutional levels. When the latter are generically specified, further details follow as the story unfolds. I distinguish among five types of relationships.

The first relationship is rather simple. A higher-level organ functionally directs a subordinate one, which in turn executes its instructions within set rules and regulations. For example, the Council Session is unquestionably superior to the Secretariat, which is its subordinate.

An advisory relationship is one in which a lower organ advises a higher one, or vice versa, without there being any strictly mandatory ties. Thus, the

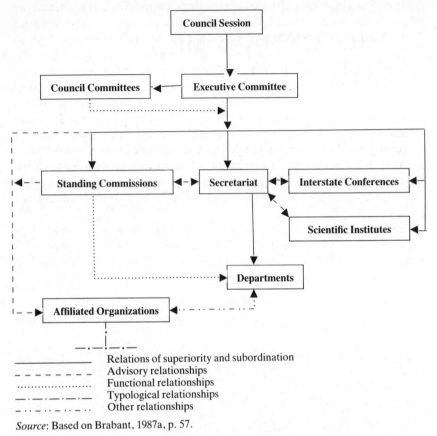

Relations of superiority and subordination
Advisory relationships
Functional relationships
Typological relationships
Other relationships

Source: Based on Brabant, 1987a, p. 57.

Figure 7.1 Formal hierarchical structure of the CMEA

scientific Institutes and interstate Conferences generally maintain advisory relationships with the Secretariat and their interactions are not characterized as either subordinate or superior. Usually, however, the Institutes and Conferences advise the Secretariat at the request of a higher organ.

A functional relationship embodies a certain degree of subordination, but one that is generally very weak. Thus, each Standing Commission is linked with at least one department of the Secretariat. The Standing Commission may at times 'instruct' or 'advise' the Secretariat counterparts into executing some task that falls within the parameters of policies agreed upon at a higher level of the CMEA hierarchy. It need not necessarily channel such a request through the formal chain of command, though officially these pass through the Executive Committee and possibly the Session to the Secretariat. Such an elaborate path is resorted to when the Commission fails to elicit the required response from the corresponding department of the Secretariat.

Typological relationships are exactly that. They refer to organizational links among units that share some similarities but are otherwise independent, usually also in the legal sense. These relationships are most prevalent, as depicted in Figure 7.1, among the so-called affiliated organizations of the CMEA. But they appear as well among the Institutes, the Conferences, the Secretariat departments, the special Committees and other CMEA organs at an equal level. They do, of course, interact. As a rule, however, within each category the linkages are of equal standing; none of the component organs is superior or inferior to another affiliated organ. The only exception concerns possible financial dependence. One or both of the CMEA banks, themselves IEOs, may lend to another IEO (including the IBEC to the IIB). From a purely financial viewpoint connected with the particular object for which a loan was extended, the IEO concerned is obligated toward, say, the IBEC.

Finally, a slot needs to be reserved for other relationships to ensure that all possible links are accounted for in the taxonomy. These are simply relations that, while not falling neatly into one of the above categories, are still relevant for CMEA cooperation.

7.2 THE PINNACLE ORGANS OF CMEA ACTIVITIES

Without a doubt, the most pivotal organs in charge of CMEA affairs are unofficial ones. They comprise foremost the summit meeting, but also the occasional meetings of the CCS, and indeed the various national governments, parliaments and other main bodies of the CPs. In the context of relations among the European planned economies this is not very surprising. From its inception, the CMEA as a regional organization was thought of more as a consultative organ entrusted primarily with secretarial functions than as an effective multilateral institution for the regulation of the constituent economies. As explained in Part I, this regulatory feature was not the one that had originally been envisaged, which was the likely form spelled out obliquely in the purported draft treaty of January 1949. The attempt to delegate effective control and influence over the national and international economic affairs of the member countries failed for a variety of reasons (see chapters 1 and 2). The well-known status of the CMEA as a weak consultative organ was fully entrenched at the latest by the end of 1950.

It also needs to be emphasized that the relative impotence of the official organs of the CMEA in charting pivotal integration strategies, spawning auxiliary institutions and providing effective SEI policy instruments is but one illustration of the marked disintegration of multilateral approaches to international affairs following World War II. The overpowering role of national governments in the form of summits, ministerial meetings and committees and parliamentary endorsements of recommendations handed down by official regional organs has risen rather than waned in recent years. They all illustrate that countries have been gradually stressing the role of their national sovereignty, paradoxically just as their autonomy over their own economic destiny has shrunk in the face of relentless integration of non-socialist trading and financial markets. Even for the CPEs, increased dependence on external trade and finance, especially with outside markets, has had a measurable impact on domestic policy flexibility.

In this section, I briefly survey the importance of the summit conference and the occasional CCS meeting because both have assumed in recent years a disproportionate influence over CMEA affairs in particular and SEI in general. The role of the national organs has, of course, been critical from the inception of the organization, particularly given the implications of clinging to nearly absolute sovereignty over affairs that normally fall within the purview of regional economic integration.

7.2.1 The economic summit

Holding summits has come to be favored by top-level policymakers, although the results achieved remain mostly intangible, if real at all. As George W. Ball (1976, p. 35) put it with reference to DMEs, a summit 'is comparable to an iceberg floating upside down, what one sees is a vast bulk, the substance is solely in the relatively tiny tip that is entirely submerged.' In contrast to the regular summits of leaders of DMEs and the wide publicity they engender, CPE policymakers meet infrequently and coverage of their deliberations is at best low-key, highly selective and only modestly informative. Nonetheless, there is little doubt that the most important CMEA organ is this unofficial occasional gathering of the political leadership, despite what is stated in the Council's charter.

The most critical problems of CMEA cooperation are generally discussed first within the framework of interparty relations, with the real core of decision making occurring during the occasional gathering of heads of party and state. This informal organ is known officially as the 'Conference of First Secretaries of Communist and Workers' Parties and of the Heads of Government of the CMEA Member Countries' – a cumbersome label that I shall condense to CCP. As a rule, all CP chiefs participate. On occasion, however, disagreements on fundamental issues prevent one or more leaders from attending the summit.

The national Communist Parties have played a leading role in CMEA affairs from the start of regional cooperation. But most of the political summits of the immediate postwar period, such as those reported in Part I, should be included here as well. However, in view of the impotence and near-dormant stage of the CMEA until about 1954, it can be argued that the weight of the CPs in charting CMEA cooperation began to be positively felt with the top-level meeting of May 1958, which was critically prepared by the

November 1957 political conclave (see chapter 3). May 1958 is conventionally taken as a watershed in the CPs' involvement in CMEA affairs because this meeting reached crucial decisions specifically related to the ISDL and the CMEA's role in it. The CCP has been convened infrequently since then. For reference the most important summit meetings on SEI are tabulated in Appendix 1.

Because of the informal nature of the CCP, debates cover a wide range and are not necessarily confined to SEI issues. The proceedings of these meetings are never divulged in full and so I can assess the CCP's contribution to SEI only on the basis of what is highly selective information. There is no doubt, however, that some sessions have been earmarked exclusively for the examination of the goals, instruments and problems of SEI. Furthermore, decisions reached there have been of seminal significance for the evolution of regional economic cooperation. In fact, fundamental decisions of the formal CMEA organs are usually formulated by the Council Session that is convened shortly after the meeting of the CCP (or when both coincide, as in the case of the twenty-third Session), for it is at that level that the directions and basic principles of the CMEA's activities are charted.

The most important of the early meetings of the CCP were the following: May 1958 on regional specialization and institutional reinforcement, June 1962 on the endorsement of *Basic Principles* and April 1969 on the explicit endorsement of SEI and authorization to draft *Integration Program*. Note that several other CCP meetings have been devoted substantially to economic issues not necessarily related to SEI. These include agriculture in 1960 and foreign economic policy in 1966 (see Kaser, 1967, p. 234; Schiavone, 1981, pp. 107–13). From then until June 1984, no full-scale SEI economic summit was held (Usenko, 1985b).

Although the decisions reached by the CCP are not formally binding for the CMEA organization and hence SEI, they are routinely confirmed by the appropriate bodies of the CMEA and have been peculiarly effective in invigorating the Council. In view of the 'role of these parties as the leading political force [of the CPE], the directives adopted by the [CCP] are in fact binding and the appropriate organs of the organization are only called upon to give them formal legal force' (Klepacki, 1975, p. 50). There is no doubt that the summit has had a marked impact on the Session, even in the early years of SEI (Savov, 1973). The reason for this is not very complex. Because of the supreme powers vested in the General or First Secretary of the Communist Party of each CPE, these summits can chart such authoritative political guidelines concerning directions and basic principles of CMEA activities. In that light, it is worthwhile to keep these infrequent deliberations, starting with the one in May 1958, quite separate from any other gathering of CMEA leaders, including the Council Session or even the meeting of the CCS – especially since the early 1980s when they began to be intimately involved in preparing top-level deliberations on CMEA affairs. Any of the latter can be deadlocked on the simple procedural ground that a delegation, even if headed by the Prime Minister because he is subordinate to the General or First Secretary of the CP, first has to clear substantive matters with the political leadership at home. Although true that each CPE's Politburo or even CC will usually have to endorse the agreements signed by their CP chief, normally that is nothing more than a formality.

The CCP has intervened in CMEA affairs only in special circumstances so as to formulate new SEI guidelines, but it has never concerned itself with the continuous steering of the Council. Nevertheless, recent years have again underscored that certain periods of stagnation or crisis in the operation of intergovernmental organizations, such as the CMEA, cannot always be remedied by resorting to ordinary procedures and instruments. Extraordinary actions seem to be required to reconfirm at the highest political echelon a firm commitment to the steady enhancement of economic or other forms of cooperation, which provides the impetus for follow-up action. That is probably the main justification for having recently convened two summits in just over two years (1984 and 1986).

In view of the achievements of earlier summits and their subsequent pivotal role in molding the course of SEI, the first full-scale CMEA summit in over fifteen years – June 1984 – should have been of more than passing interest. The personal imprints on SEI of the post-Brežnev leaderships in the USSR are obviously pertinent. More important perhaps are several fundamental economic issues that have swelled with increasing poignancy since the mid-1970s. These include the reshaping of economic structures of the CPEs individually and as a group, in part to cope with development problems that have evolved from a successive string of domestic and external circumstances (see chapters 6 and 18); the formulation of a less ambiguous integration strategy and the adoption of more flexible and active policy instruments to enhance SEI, including the more effective mobilization of the regional institutions to buttress intercountry cooperation; and the role of East-West trade and economic cooperation in intensive development policies. Regardless of what the June 1984 and November 1986 summits may have accomplished, the reshaping of the economic mechanisms of the CPEs remains crucial. In this connection, the most vital, though still ambiguous, link is the USSR's economic reform, including its policy stance on SEI. Without a firm commitment to reform and ensuring its steady implementation, it is difficult to get a handle on the CMEA's fundamental socioeconomic problems; much of the problem is due to the USSR's sheer economic and political preponderance in the area. Future CCP meetings may shed some light on the complex issues at stake.

7.2.2 The Central Committee Secretaries in charge of economic affairs

The party organ in charge of relations with the CPs of the fraternal countries has, of course, always had some responsibility for ensuring cooperation among CPEs. Until the early 1980s, this involvement rarely transcended the level of the habitual relations among fraternal parties. With the Soviet call in 1981 for convening the first economic summit since 1969 and the discord then prevailing among the members, the CCS was mobilized to prepare the ground.

Since the early 1980s (and similar to how summits among the industrial MEs are prepared), this Sherpa-like policy-smoothing organ has been left increasingly with the discretion of ironing out points of disagreement, setting the agenda, negotiating joint statements and finalizing documents. Where precisely the task of governmental organs begins and that of the political bodies ends is not clear. But there is no doubt that the boundary has been reset in recent years, with more and greater responsibilities being entrusted to special organs. In the case of CMEA matters, this task has largely fallen on the shoulders of the high-level CCS, which played a critical role in the preparation of the first economic summit since the momentous one that led to the enactment of SEI in 1969. CCS involvement was measurably intensified starting in late 1982. Since then, this organ has also been intensively preoccupied with the preparation of Council Sessions, the November 1986 summit and even some of the more critical Executive Committee meetings.

7.2.3 The national governments

Ever since the aborted founding treaty (see chapter 1), a fundamental precept of CMEA cooperation has been that supranationalism is anathema and can, therefore, not ever be considered. Although axiomatic from the very beginning of formalized CMEA cooperation in late 1950, evidently this guideline has not always been heeded by all parties. Nonetheless, particularly since the row over *Basic Principles* (see chapter 4), most participants in CMEA cooperation have felt impelled whenever appropriate – and even when not – to reemphasize that the organization is not at all supranational in nature, unlike some other integration schemes. The formal role accorded to the national governments and their respective parliamentary responsibilities therefore remains considerable. That these functions are, in practice, frequently usurped by CP preoccupations and precepts does not diminish the role of national interests as contrasted with community responsibilities.

7.3 SOVEREIGNTY AND DECISION MAKING IN THE CMEA

The sacrosanct role of the national governments, and particularly the individual CPs, in SEI is fundamental. It has been enshrined in every single document passed since the mid-1950s and needs to be recognized as such here as well. It derives from the CMEA charter's prescription that recommendations made within the CMEA organs are strictly subject to ratification by the member governments' proper parliamentary organs (art. IV, 1).

Decisions can be made only on organizational and procedural matters (art. IV, 2). All 'questions of economic and [scientific-technological cooperation]' (Tokareva, 1981, p. 18) are subject to recommendations. This prescription can, of course, be deleterious. When the aim is to foster regional interests, it is nearly always counter-productive. The fact that individual national governments could simply ignore to examine recommendations issued by the regular CMEA organs led in the late 1960s to a search for a more positive mechanism for ensuring minimum compliance with cooperation attempts. A first milestone was reached in 1967 with the declaration of the so-called interested-party principle. This is not, however, among the officially enshrined 'principles that govern economic cooperation' (Fiumel, 1984, p. 69) in the CMEA. Fiumel interprets it to mean a procedural principle that is directly related to decision making in the organization. However true this may be from a strictly legal standpoint, the principle sought to dilute the stultifying impact of the unanimity rule in the CMEA.

It should be stressed, however, if only to be complete, that unanimity in the CMEA context does not necessarily imply that voting is a regular phenomenon. Formal voting would, in fact, appear to be a rather rare occurrence there, as in most other intergovernmental organs. Instead, the CPEs generally aim at consensus building; that is, 'concerting the wills of the members' (Fiumel, 1984, p. 70) into a community view. All that the interested-party principle sought to accomplish was to harmonize the objectives and instruments of all those interested in the task at hand when the latter could not be attained for all members.

The interested-party provision, although not explicitly stated in the CMEA's charter, essentially amounts to affirming that if some CMEA members want to pursue a specific SEI endeavor in which others are not interested, they should not be bound by what other members decide to pursue (Kalbe, 1981, p. 257). As Kalbe puts it: 'The interestedness principle guarantees that the interests of the CMEA member countries are taken into account and dovetailed, and that no member without its permission becomes bound by CMEA decisions. This procedure clearly illustrates how CMEA cooperation reinforces the sovereignty of socialist countries.' There is, however, no agreement on what interestedness concretely may mean; it is not even mentioned in any generally accepted, and published, CMEA document. After laying down that 'recommendations and decisions shall be made only with the consent of the interested' (Tokareva, 1981, p. 18) members, the current charter stipulates only that 'nonparticipation . . . shall not affect the implementation by the interested countries of cooperation on these measures' (art. IV, 3).

As a result, this principle does not inhibit a country from declaring its interestedness simply to be in a position to oppose the integration intention, and possibly to subvert it from within the established regional channels (Fiumel, 1984, p. 72). Partly in recognition of this conundrum, various modifications of the interestedness principle have been entertained since then, with the most recent version postulating a more positive interpretation. While there continues to be legal ambiguity about the order of precedence between recommendation and interestedness, legally the former appears to embody it. If so, one may speak of positive and negative interestedness. The latter is precisely such a case of potential erosion of SEI initiatives from within (Fiumel, 1984, pp. 72–3). The former is clearly the only aim of SEI endeavors by interested partners, but that goal is hard to implement in the CMEA context.

Endeavors to modify the unanimity rule in CMEA affairs have been on the policy agenda for a long time, even though *Integration Program* especially underlined that the CMEA as an organ designed to galvanize the movement toward SEI would remain unchanged for the foreseeable future. This was especially prevalent after the calamitous changeover from the market outlook to the post-1974 emphasis on various types of plan co-operation and joint planning (see chapter 5). Rumors to the effect that major changes were forthcoming in the CMEA's charter, and in the procedures and methods of the various CMEA agencies, surfaced repeatedly in the discussions around several meetings of the Council Session held during the second half of the 1970s. Once again they allegedly led to major opposition on the part of Rumania, chiefly because the replacement of the sacrosanct unanimity principle with majority decision making was said to be the center-piece of the proposed revision. These rumors were particularly persistent at the time of the thirty-second Council Session in 1978, which supposedly debated a draft of possible changes for the charter and of modifications in procedures and methods that had been in preparation at least since 1975. That Session's communiqué (*Ėkonomičeskaja gazeta*, 1978: 28, p. 13) states that agreement had been reached on such a document,[1] which 'outlined concrete tasks of the CMEA bodies in enlarging [the scope of] systemic mutual consultations and the application of their results in the practice of cooperation' (Bagudin, Gavrilov and Šinkov, 1985, p. 12).

The precise bearing of this document, which was not released at the time and is not included in any of the official and quasi-official compendia of CMEA documents, has remained ambiguous.[2] L. Štrougal at the time endorsed the draft principles, but he called upon the Executive Committee to provide concrete follow-up.[3] On the basis of this and other evidence, I concluded (Brabant, 1980, pp. 216–8) that another failure had been registered. It seems that the Rumanians succeeded in enshrining in the document itself some of their reservations about joint 'undertakings' and 'concertations,' which were to be different from recommendations (see below), the role of the CMEA in international agreements, the delegation of functions to the CMEA and the softening of policy stances *vis-à-vis* third countries or other international organizations (Uschakow, 1983a, p. 175).

Even if such a document was approved, it could not have entailed a major change in CMEA cooperation. Countries not keenly motivated to participate in a particular project can still declare their interest and then stall implementation. Furthermore, the unanimity rule remains in effect officially as well as in practice in spite of a streamlining of the interestedness principle in the charter's revision – most recently in June 1979 (Vel'jaminov, 1986). In fact, the revised charter mentions only understandings (*dogovorënnost'*) in art. IV, 4; but the notion of concertations may have gained acceptance through other channels. Even if both are of equal standing in actual practice, note that understandings and concertations, as distinct from recommendations and decisions, are useful supplements to the CMEA's traditional decision-making instruments. But as the title of art. IV (recommendations and decisions) suggests, they are at best subordinate and certainly are not in addition to or modifications of the latter two, as suggested by Uschakow (1983b, p. 199). Furthermore, essentially they are stances taken by the individual members. As such, understandings and concertations are far from revolutionary. They hardly endow the Secretariat with much discretion for manipulating what should be vital SEI issues. But that is not to say that the Secretariat has no discretionary power at all (see section 7.5).

Because this document may still be on the CMEA debating table in one form or another, as perhaps alluded to in the demands for reforming the CMEA made at the forty-third Session, its spirit might be indicative of what the Soviet leaders are aiming at. This proposition can be supported by referring to the strong emphasis that is publicly placed on the need for members who are genuinely interested to forge ahead with SEI without being stymied by others, even if these others officially expressed interest in the project. If this assessment is correct, it may be appropriate to briefly examine the document's portent to see whether, if fully agreed upon and implemented, it might indeed amount to a quiet revolution, perhaps without this being adequately reflected in the organization's constitution as yet.

Essentially the document consists of two parts. First it presents a broad declaration on the shortcomings of the CMEA's organization, decision-making procedures and implementation modalities. The second part includes five substantive components: setting priorities; speeding up the examination of and decision making about questions submitted to CMEA organs; ascertaining the implementation of agreements and the protocols worked out on their basis; ensuring the general steering of the activities of the IEOs by the CMEA and increasing the effectiveness of its deliberations; and improving coordination among the CPEs and within the CMEA with respect to third countries and international organizations.

The document is a very broad statement on how to improve the role of the Secretariat and its subsidiary organs; how to delegate concrete responsibilities ensuing from agreed-upon programs to the various organs, especially the Council Committees, Standing Commissions and the IEOs, and to endow them with some authority over SEI; how these organs should better organize themselves so as to ensure swift implementation of decisions worked out by the legislative bodies; and how the functioning of these organs can raise their efficiency and effectiveness in advancing SEI. In not one instance did the members agree on concrete measures, including a timetable for follow-up suggestions; however, the document is strewn with shoulds and coulds. Furthermore, the Rumanian reservations that are enshrined in the document make it doubtful whether the CMEA's charter could have been affected by *Basic Directions*.

In this interpretation, the 1978 protocol pretty much amounts to another failed CMEA attempt to inspire an acceleration in SEI. The organization therefore continues to function broadly as it was created in early 1949, with, admittedly, a number of extensions in breadth and in depth, together with the organizational expansion of the official and other CMEA organs. But as experience has amply documented, so far the results have been disappointing. Thus, it seems advisable to maintain a healthy degree of skepticism about the transformations that may soon emanate from within the CMEA, even if Soviet reformers remain in the lead regarding change in the CPEs.

Unlike some observers of the CMEA scene, I feel that the practical bearing of interestedness is still far from resolved. The coexistence of positive and negative interestedness confounds concrete action. For as long as countries can declare themselves interested in a cooperation venture, there is nothing to prevent them from hollowing out its provisions from within and thereby stalling progress with SEI. The prospects of soon overcoming this fundamental drawback are not encouraging, as underlined by the emphasis that recent Sessions have placed on the issue of interestedness.

The problem of organizing multilateral cooperation in an environment dominated by bilateralism, as described in chapter 11, is of some interest here. When the main channels for promoting SEI are, for all practical purposes, available only to pairs of government negotiators, bilateralism severely constrains any meaningful regional economic cooperation. This question entails some controversy over how many 'interested parties' there should be to be able to speak meaningfully of a CMEA recommendation (Fiumel, 1984, p. 73) and the CMEA charter is silent on the issue.

In some of the specialized literature on the subject, it is argued that at least three members should be involved (CMEA, 1975b, p. 214). But this is disputed by legal scholars, who assert that it would be unacceptable to let the 'will' of an international organization consisting of at least ten members be set by only three. Fiumel (1984, p. 74) proposes that at least half of the members should concur on any issue. Given that the SEI *problématique* is different for the peripheral members than for the European group and that Rumania has frequently taken a particularly uncooperative stance on many SEI issues, this interpretation would leave an exceedingly narrow margin for disagreement.

7.4 THE OFFICIAL CMEA DECISION-MAKING LEVELS

The official CMEA decision-making levels are comprised of the Council Session, the Executive Committee and its subcommittees and some of the Standing Commissions. According to the charter, the CMEA's highest official organ is the Council Session, which is normally convened annually in June or early July. Participants in the Council Session are nominated *ad hoc* by each member, although, at least since 1970, each delegation is usually headed by the country's Prime Minister. Between these meetings, CMEA affairs are guided by the Executive Committee, which is composed of each member's Permanent Representative, who is generally a Deputy Prime Minister. The Session is normally attended by delegates from other socialist and fraternal DEs, as well as international organizations, as observers, associate members and cooperants (see Introduction). The level of each delegation's representation and its size depends on the country involved. Day-to-day affairs are entrusted to the Secretariat.

7.4.1 The Council Session

The Session is officially the supreme organ of the Council. By statute (since the changes introduced in the wake of the 1969 summit) this deliberative body normally meets once a year during the second quarter in one of the capitals of the member countries. Capitals rotate according to the Cyrillic alphabet of the Russian names of the European members. Occasionally, as in 1984, exceptions are made to accommodate non-European members. Until the delays sustained from 1983 on, target dates have been extended to early July only infrequently (see Appendix 2). An extraordinary or special meeting of the Council Session can be summoned only if at least one-third of the members consent. A special or extraordinary Session is normally held in Moscow. Although there is no standard terminology in the CPEs, the difference appears to be that a special Session is identified as one in which the Session coincides with the CCP, as in April 1969. An extraordinary Session is one convened out of sequence. By definition, it tackles 'special' matters, such as since 1970 the handling of summit meetings, or chooses to bypass consideration of the normal business of the regular Council Session and focus on 'extraordinary' questions. The latter explanation has been given only in connection with the forty-third Session, which, although meeting in Moscow in regular sequence, zeroed in on reforms of many aspects of the CMEA (see chapter 6).

The national delegations to this deliberative body are constituted on an *ad hoc* basis. Usually, however, each consists of the Permanent Representative in the CMEA, his deputies, high-level members of the national government and also, since the twenty-fourth Session in 1970, the Prime Minister, who officially heads the delegation. The exception to this rule occurred in June

1962 and April 1969 when the delegation was headed by the General or First Secretary of each CP because the Session and the CCP unambiguously coincided in 1969 and for all practical purposes in 1962. Another exception has frequently been provided by Cuba and Rumania, who have sent delegations at a lower level in the political hierarchy, presumably to manifest overt displeasure with some topic on which they disagreed with the majority of the CMEA. The Permanent Representative is in charge of relations between the Council and the members between the various meetings of the Council Session.

The principal function of the Session is examination of the fundamental problems of regional economic cooperation. It also directs the activities of the Secretariat and its subordinate organs. It may set up new official organs – as distinct from other, affiliated organizations (see chapter 8) – by unanimous decision. In accordance with the rules of procedure of the Council Session (Tokareva, 1976b, pp. 19–31) by statute the Session has very broad deliberative powers. It can make recommendations on matters of economic, scientific and technological cooperation as distinct from decisions on organizational and procedural issues. Interested members have sixty days after the Session's closure to consider these recommendations and must inform the Council's Secretary of the 'results of the consideration by the government or other competent agencies ... of the Session's recommendation.' Endorsing a recommendation entails an obligation to heed it. But such recommendations cannot be directly implemented as they constitute only the starting point in the process of plan coordination, with the emphasis being shifted to bilateral relations (Wasilkowski, 1971, p. 43). Once accepted, Council recommendations are usually implemented through bi- and multilateral treaties or other agreements on the rights and duties of the participants in the proposed measure.

The significance of the various Council Sessions has varied considerably according to attendant circumstances. The following meetings are currently regarded in the specialized literature as having been especially significant: the second (1949) on questions of trade agreements and free exchange of scientific-technical information; the fourth (1954) on problems of plan coordination and institutional reinforcement of the CMEA; the seventh (1956) on specialization, especially in machine building, chemical and metallurgical sectors; the ninth (1958) on principles of regional price formation, the further institutional strengthening of the Council and more topics of specialization; the sixteenth (1962) on institutional and programmatic changes connected with the acceptance of the document on the ISDL and the agreement to create a common bank; the twenty-third (1969) on principles of specialization and SEI; the twenty-fifth (1971) on the acceptance of *Integration Program*; the twenty-seventh (1973) on questions of plan coordination and the elaboration of multilateral specialization programs, which were actually endorsed during the twenty-ninth (1975); the thirtieth (1976) on drawing up Target Programs; the thirty-second (1978) and thirty-third (1979), which approved the Target Programs; the forty-first (1985), which endorsed *Scientific-Technological Progress*; and the forty-third (1987), which examined a wide range of changes in the CMEA organization and its policies, policy instruments and institutions that were further detailed at the forty-fourth (1988) meeting.

7.4.2 The Executive Committee

Created in 1962 to replace the Conference of Representatives of the CMEA Member Countries, the Executive Committee constitutes the CMEA's highest executive body. It was originally intended to mature into a planning center entrusted with regionwide responsibilities (see chapter 4). As a result of the controversy about *Basic Principles*, however, it never developed this supranational function. Instead, it has legally remained a consultative organ concerned with the broad guidelines of national and regional macroeconomic policies. It is a nonpermanent organ that is convoked regularly – at present at least quarterly – usually in Moscow, but that is not mandatory. It is composed of high-ranking officials, normally the Permanent Representatives. Its Bureau[4] (replaced in 1971 by the Planning Committee) was a working organ composed of the deputy chairmen of the planning offices on a level comparable to that of the Standing Commissions.

The Executive Committee's primary responsibility is the elaboration of policy recommendations and supervision of their implementation between Session meetings. Its functions also include supervising the work on plan coordination and STC and guiding the research and deliberations of the Standing Commissions and of the Secretariat, which it controls. It can reach decisions within its competence or on issues concerning its own organization and administration.

7.4.3 Council Committees

Since 1971 several Committees on fundamental general economic problems have been attached to the Executive Committee. These Committees are on a level well superior to that of the Standing Commissions. As a result, they have considerably strengthened the authority and importance of the Executive Committee. There are presently seven Committees entrusted with ensuring the comprehensive examination and multilateral settlement of major problems of SEI, especially in the fields of economic, scientific and technological cooperation. These are: the Committee for Cooperation in Planning (1971), the Committee for STC (1971), the Committee for Cooperation in Machine Building (1984), the Committee for Cooperation in the Agroindustrial Complex (1988), the Committee on Cooperation in

Foreign Economic Relations (1988), the Committee on Cooperation in Electronics (1988) and the Committee on Fuels and Geology (1988). The Committee for Cooperation in Material-Technical Supplies established in 1974 was abolished in early 1988. All are headquartered in Moscow, where the Committees normally but not always meet.

The Committees generally have much wider jurisdictions and greater prerogatives than those held by the Standing Commissions. This may have been symbolically underlined by the fact that all, except the one on material-technical supplies, were created from one or more Standing Commissions. Their importance lies in the influence they exert on the work of other CMEA entities in accordance with prescribed uniform principles and methods of instruction. More importantly, they are also empowered to set priorities and make appropriate assignments. The work of the Council's agencies must be molded according to these priorities. As such, these Committees constitute a higher-level echelon for dealing with critical components of national socio-economic plans; for elaborating mechanisms for attaining greater consistency in production and consumption, particularly of engineering products; and for furthering economic development through a more or less concerted effort to centralize and disseminate economic, scientific and technical information. As top planners and policymakers of the CPEs participate, these Committees deliberate about the most crucial facts and figures regarding the coordination of economic policies.

The Planning Committee, which grew out of the SCEP, has traditionally been the most important of all Committees, and arguably among all other official CMEA organs with the exception of the Session and the Executive Committee; indeed, the members are the chairmen of the all-powerful national central planning offices. In principle, therefore, this organ has direct access to top government and party leaders. Deputy chairmen of the national planning offices act as the permanent operating body of the Committee and form its Bureau. Were its recommendations not subject to approval by national government and party authorities, the Planning Committee would be in fact, if not in name, the CMEA's supranational planning office. Several CMEA members have coveted this status for almost two decades but have so far met stiff opposition from the others, especially Rumania. But, most emphatically I am not endorsing this organ as being a close substitute for supranational planning, as does Vladimir Sobell (1984, p. 17).

The Planning Committee's list of tasks is long and tedious (Bajbakov, 1976). Potentially it envelops all planning problems of concern to the national planning bureaus. However, practical work seems to be focused on more specific projects. In the late 1970s, for example, these included the preparation and control of the first Concerted Plan and the Target Programs. Of course, it also played a central role in the regular coordination of five-year plans and the concurrent trade agreements. The Planning Committee

was preoccupied in the early 1980s by adjustment efforts and the preparation of the summits and Council Sessions on reforming the CMEA from
within. Work on the SEI under CMEA reform appears to be the current
paramount issue of concern.

One of the more active Committees has been the one in charge of STC. It
too grew out of concerns about the modest success achieved under its
predecessor Standing Commission. It supervises numerous research and
cooperation centers located in the members. It is here that the actual
groundwork for the coordination and application of scientific and technical
work is concentrated. It has also been in charge of the Center for Scientific
and Technological Information, the Interstate Commission for Calculating
Techniques (both in Moscow) and the Council for Environmental Protection and Improvement (in Berlin). In addition to the coordination centers,
the Committee is also assured of the collaboration of scientific institutions
and other organizations participating in basic and applied research (Brabant,
1988c, 1988d; Kirillin, 1977, pp. 32–3). With the gradual emergence of a new
policy blueprint (*Scientific-Technological Progress*), the role of this organ
increased severalfold and in the early 1980s was preoccupied with the preparation of that document. Since then, putting teeth into the program – that
is, working out concrete provisions for selectively enhancing STC – has been
its prime task.

The Committee on Material-Technical Supplies was created in 1974 to
coordinate demand and supply, especially of scarce materials. It elaborated
measures to alleviate persistent disequilibriums, recycle secondary and waste
materials, computerize inventory control and foster better management and
organization of material and technical supplies (Dymšic, 1975). It did not
grow out of any specific prior CMEA organ. But some of the concerns of the
SCEP and probably some other related Standing Commissions must have
been at the root of the assignments carved out for this Committee. It was
abolished during the recent restructuring of CMEA organs.

The Committee for Cooperation in Machine Building, which replaced the
corresponding Standing Commission in 1984, is entrusted with the coordination of engineering sectors, forecasting demand and supply for machinery,
ensuring timely availability of such goods and the highest technical and
economic parameters and otherwise realizing the tasks ensuing from more
general CMEA policy documents. This Committee played a critical role in
the formulation of the corresponding Target Program and enhanced the
relevant implementation agreements (see chapter 12). Its central position in
ameliorating the foundations for the implementation of *Scientific-
Technological Progress* is beyond doubt.[5]

The Committee for Cooperation in the Sphere of the Agroindustrial
Complex is one of the first organs whose functions are to be enlarged (while
other entities are to be abolished) under the resolutions of the forty-third
Council Session. It probably supersedes at least the Standing Commission

on Agriculture and perhaps of Food Industry, as well as parts of Light Industry and Biotechnology. Its range of activities includes questions of cooperation in agriculture and forestry, the food industry and the use of biotechnology in these areas. Its main purpose is to promote further intensification and improved cooperation and the development of SEI in these areas to satisfy areawide food requirements. It does so by coordinating economic, scientific and technical policy for ways of collectively resolving the most important problems of collaboration within the agroindustrial complex. It is also slated to engage in traditional questions of long-term developments in agriculture, forestry and the food industry, including those revolving around science and technology. As such, it is to be entrusted with important problems of the entire cycle, from scientific research to the production and sale of output by those areas designated as under its responsibility.

The Committee for Cooperation in the Sphere of Foreign Economic Relations oversees tasks that were formerly assigned to the SCFT. It may even incorporate some functions previously handled by the SCFQ and perhaps even the Standing Commissions for Statistics and Standardization. The Committee is to focus attention primarily on major issues of multilateral activity concerning the interests of each side grouped in the CMEA. This embodies, first, perfecting the mechanism of economic cooperation in order to facilitate deepening and intensifying SEI. In addition to the tasks of the SCFT, its focus will be on TRP formation, direct enterprise relations and methods for raising the efficacy of IEOs.

The Committee on Electronics has probably taken over the tasks formerly within the domain of the Standing Commission for Radio Technology and Electronics. It may be conjectured, however, that its foremost assignment will be in automation, computerization, microelectronics and areas related to the particular tasks slated under those headings in *Scientific-Technological Progress.*

Finally, the Committee on Fuels and Geology, whose official name is still unclear, will be in charge of the entire solid and liquid fuel cycle as well as prospecting for fuels and other resources; but concrete details about this Committee are not available at this stage.

7.4.4 The Standing Commissions

The Standing Commissions are among the oldest of the CMEA institutions. They are organized by economic sector or by major areas of overall economic problems. Each has been paired since the early 1960s with a department of the Secretariat. If need arises, joint working groups of two or more Commissions are set up to examine issues that cross branch boundaries or to find solutions to common problems, although in recent years such issues have been more frequently addressed by the Executive Committee and its organs. Each Commission theoretically has its permanent head-quarters in one of the members and is chaired by the home country's minister or highest civil servant of the relevant sector. However, it can be convened in any member. The Commissions are in session at least twice each year, usually in Moscow as their secretariats were transferred to the corresponding departments of the Council's Secretariat in 1962. This move was made partly in anticipation of the imminent creation of a supranational planning agency at the Council level. Its actual work is carried out in the Secretariat's departments and in some national institutes and agencies.

As for other bodies, the Standing Commissions can only make recommendations. These have to be approved by the Executive Committee, presented to the formal Council Session for endorsement and then approved by the interested member governments. Each Commission usually comprises several sections, permanent and temporary working groups and scientific-technological centers. In addition, the Commissions maintain 'advisory' relationships with relevant affiliated agencies, even if these are legally autonomous institutions and, strictly speaking, not part of the CMEA (Brunner, 1976, p. 22). The Commissions existing at about year-end 1987 are listed in Figure 7.2, together with their location and the dates they were established. Only some of these organs survived the shake-up of early 1988, as shown in Figure 7.3. This restructuring is continuing and, as of late 1988, there is no sign where it may be heading.

The Standing Commissions, together with the Council Committees, are the real workers of the CMEA. They were first set up (see chapter 3) in 1956

Peaceful utilization of atomic energy (Moscow, 1960)
Ferrous metallurgy (Moscow, 1956)
Geology (Ulan Bator, 1963)[a]

Coal industry (Warsaw, 1956)
Light industry (Prague, 1958)[c]
Food industry (Sofia, 1963)[c]
Transportation (Warsaw, 1958)
Agriculture (Sofia, 1956)
Foreign trade (Moscow, 1956)
Civil aviation (Moscow, 1975)
New materials and technology (Moscow, 1986)
Biotechnology (Moscow, 1986)

Electrical energy (Moscow, 1956)

Nonferrous metallurgy (Budapest, 1956)
Post and telecommunications (Moscow, 1971)
Chemical industry (Berlin, 1956)[b]
Gas and oil (Bucharest, 1956)
Currency and finance (Moscow, 1962)
Standardization (Berlin, 1962)
Statistics (Moscow, 1962)
Construction (Berlin, 1958)
Public health (Moscow, 1975)
Radio technology and electronics (Budapest, 1963)

Notes: Within parentheses, the city indicates headquarters or main meeting place; date is that of founding.
(a) Created in 1956, abolished in 1958, and re-created in 1963.
(b) Includes the Commission for timber and cellulose, which was independent from 1956 to 1958.
(c) Created in 1958 as the Commission for food and light industries; the Commission for food processing was established separately in 1963.

Source: modified and updated from Brabant, 1980, p. 189.

Figure 7.2 The Standing Commissions of the CMEA at year-end 1987

to replace the *ad hoc* working parties and subdivisions of the Bureau and later of the Secretariat. Their number and field of authority have fluctuated widely, but they became relatively stable for the first time by the mid-1970s. Starting with twelve sectoral Commissions in 1956 (agriculture, chemical industry, coal, electrical energy, ferrous metallurgy, nonferrous metallurgy, foreign trade, engineering, forestry, oil and gas, timber and cellulose and geology), four more were added in 1958 (construction, economic questions, transportation and food and light industries). At the same time, three of those created in 1956 were abolished (timber and cellulose, forestry and geology). In 1960 the Commission for the peaceful utilization of atomic energy was founded. In 1962, four more were established (statistics, standardization, currency and finance and the coordination of scientific and technological research). The Commission for geology was revived (with headquarters relocated from Moscow to Ulan Bator), the food industry was separated from the Commission for food and light industries and a further Commission for radio technology and related electronics industries was created in 1963. Their number then remained unchanged in the wake of the serious dispute about *Basic Principles* and the ISDL.

In 1971 the Commission for post and telecommunications was established, while several others were abolished following the creation of the two Council Committees (the SCEP was superseded by the Planning Committee and that for STC by the corresponding Committee). Two new Commissions were created in 1975: civil aviation, which was detached from the transportation Commission, and public health, from STC. This remained the setup until 1984, when the machinery Commission was upgraded to a Committee

Council Session

Executive Committee

Planning	*Engineering*	*STC*	*Electronization*
Foreign economic relations		*Agrocomplex*	*Fuels and raw materials*

Secretariat

Standing Commissions

Electrical and nuclear energy		*Currency and finance*		*Metallurgy*
Statistics	*Chemical industry*	*Legal affairs*	*Environment*	*Light industry*
Transportation		*Standardization*	*Postal and telecommunications*	

Institutes

Economic problems   *Standardization*

Source: 'RVHP – nová struktura orgánů,' *Svět Hospodářství*, 1988: 106, p. 4. For other details, see Brabant, 1988g.

Figure 7.3 The CMEA organization in late 1988

attached to the Executive Committee. The number of Commissions rose once again in early 1986 with the addition of one for new materials and technologies and another for biotechnology, both closely identified with *Scientific-Technological Progress*. Two years later the third (on electrical and nuclear energy) and the fourth (on environmental protection) Commissions emerged as organizational outgrowths of the STC document. The Commission for electrical and nuclear energy absorbed the former Commissions on electrical energy and peaceful utilization of nuclear power. As of year-end 1987, there were probably twenty-three Standing Commissions.[6]

As a result of the restructuring of the CMEA that was endorsed by the two most recent Sessions, the number of Standing Commissions has shrunk significantly to only eleven, as illustrated in Figure 7.3. Some of these organs were created by amalgamating two or more Commissions or by upgrading one of the Conferences (e.g. on legal questions); at least two are genuinely new organs. Furthermore, there is evidence that the newly created Commissions, including those incorporating two or more formerly independent ones, are headquartered in Moscow, as are all of the new Committees.

Standing Commissions can be grouped into branch units and general economic organs. At least by year-end 1987, all of the general Commissions were located in Moscow except the one for standardization, which was in Berlin. Each of the branch Commissions is headquartered in one of the member countries, which is typically selected on the basis of the particular importance of the relevant economic sector(s) for that country. But all the important general Commissions and Committees, which really mold the framework and form the guidelines for overall economic cooperation within the CMEA, are concentrated in Moscow.

The geographic distribution of the Commission's organs is not a trivial matter as much of the range and quality of the work they perform depends on the initiative and imagination of the Commission's chairman and the senior officials or ministers of the industries who head the Commission's activities and set their work schedule. The role of a Commission in improving ECPS, hence SEI, becomes the more prominent the greater the number of experts involved, the more technical the nature of its assignments and the greater the initiative and clout of its chairman. The national delegations in the Standing Commissions are typically headed by the ministers of the respective field or at least by senior civil servants of the appropriate ministries or institutions.

Clearly, not all Commissions are equally important. Some are concerned essentially with the coordination of production intentions and STC. Others play a critical role in decision making about the macroeconomics and trade aspects of SEI. A third group provides secretarial functions. For the most important Commissions, their charter details their purposes and instruments. However, most Commissions follow the model rules that were first endorsed in July 1960 at the thirteenth Council Session and which have been periodically revised since (see Tokareva, 1976b, pp. 49–58; Butler, 1978, pp. 228–32). Because this section is concerned primarily with the critical organizational levers of SEI, I shall mention here only the real decision-making levers among the Commissions as of the end of 1987.[7] The role of the other Commissions will be taken up in subsequent sections.

7.4.4.a Currency and finance

The real locus of decision making about financial cooperation is, of course, vested with party and government policymakers. At the level of the national governments, the ministries of finance and foreign trade and the competent banks (either the central bank or the foreign trade bank, or both when available) are most influential in formulating and implementing financial policies. Proposals for innovations usually originate at the CPE level rather than in the official or affiliated Council organs. However, once such proposals are formally tabled at the regional level, top-level negotiations are prepared by one or more departments of the Council or those connected with it. Here, the SCFQ has played a vital role in the smooth functioning of the other organs and especially in the implementation of recommendations, whether official or unofficial in their origin.

The SCFQ was created in December 1962 at a time when some CPEs were earnestly seeking to modify their payments system by institutionalizing the regional capital market that had first tentatively emerged in the mid-1950s (see chapter 3). Although the SCFQ is unquestionably the center of discussions, coordination and recommendations on monetary problems, it is definitely not the only body concerned with such topics. Neither is it the instance of last resort as it is subject to the same statutory limitations typical of all CMEA Commissions.

The Commission's charter defines its authority as follows:

1. To ensure continuous improvement in the regional payments system for both commercial and noncommercial transactions.
2. To define principles on financing joint enterprises and other regional ventures.
3. To elaborate a methodology for determining the purchasing power of the national currencies and the TR.
4. To institute a common method of elaborating financial and balance-of-payments plans.
5. To reduce the differences in the foreign exchange regimes of the CPEs and improve the currency monopoly system.
6. To address the problems of cooperation between the financial and monetary organizations of the members.
7. To examine problems of multilateral cooperation between various banking and other financial institutions.
8. To ensure mutual collaboration between CMEA members on questions of financial relations with other countries.

9. To study international exchange and financial markets and make recommendations designed to minimize the monetary and foreign exchange risks to member countries.
10. To organize the exchange of information and experiences regarding all financial, banking and other questions of mutual interest to one or more members.

Apart from the elaboration of the bank charters and related documents, the SCFQ's most important work has concentrated on exchanging views and experiences, including the regulation of the acquisition and disposition of other currencies. In particular the SCFQ provides a forum where CPEs can compare the terms they have received in transactions with Western financial institutions and exchange experience with Western banks and international currency markets. Similarly, it has organized discussions on such subjects as the state of clearing imbalances in East-West trade and possible currency risks in the hopes of coordinating policies in these areas.

The Commission has also actively deliberated on questions of socialist currencies and operations in TR. One of its achievements was the agreement of 24 June 1963 that permitted private citizens of the CPEs who were traveling abroad to exchange the equivalent of up to ten rubles of their national currency (Garbuzov, 1973, p. 10); this limit was raised in 1973 to some thirty rubles (CMEA, 1974, p. 117). The Commission has also conducted studies on the exchange of national currency for tourists and an evaluation of contributions to joint ventures and enterprises. Other agreements have been reached that permit unlimited and unhindered conversion of wages, stipends and royalties between countries and for payments resulting from court decisions, alimony, inheritance, private remittances and similar flows.

The Commission organizes research into the financial problems of members. For example, it has investigated the compatibility of the national price systems to calculate reasonably equitable conversion coefficients. It has also shared research on the efficiency and profitability of foreign trade, the successive calculations of commercial and noncommercial exchange rates, the uniform computation of expenditures in domestic prices for joint construction projects, the daily operations of scientific and other international organizations and the immediate settlement of noncommercial payments. Proposals for changes in the IBEC's clearing system and IIB's credit system have been discussed by the Commission. When changes are introduced, it is the Commission rather than the relevant bank council that in effect makes the appropriate recommendations. The section of *Integration Program* on financial and monetary problems was worked out by the Commission. It continues to monitor these tasks, all of which are officially in its competence.

The relatively timid agreements reached during official meetings of the Commission should not make us overlook that even more important issues have been on its agenda nor that the Commission is likely to retain its crucial role in solving problems of monetary and financial cooperation. Because of its unstructured nature, the SCFQ provides a congenial atmosphere in which to air national points of view, to dispel impressions of supranationalism and to forestall the emergence of preemptive 'regional' decisions. This is particularly relevant because the members of the SCFQ are not international civil servants; they are top-level CPE decision makers, and money and finance directly or indirectly affect nearly all aspects of closer economic cooperation.

7.4.4.b Foreign trade

As noted earlier, since the CMEA's inception foreign trade has been central to the coordination of national economic plans. Foreign trade enabled members to seek greater stability and reliability than would have been possible through market-determined trade. Seen in that light, it is not surprising that one of the first Standing Commissions to be created was the Standing Commission on Foreign Trade (SCFT). Until its absorption into the new Committee on Foreign Economic Relations in early 1988, it had been one of the most active Commissions. It assumed a critical role in facilitating the exchange of goods and services for which the terms of reference were set at a different regional, bilateral or national decision-making level. The principal task of the SCFT was to ensure successful implementation of the planned expansion of goods and services exchanged among the CPEs. One goal of this endeavor was to enable the state monopoly of foreign trade and payments (MFT) to emulate in the international sphere the material-technical conditions for managing important tasks ensuing from mutual economic cooperation and intensified SEI.

Precisely because the SCFT was the only general economic Commission among the first twelve created in May 1956, its importance initially extended well beyond foreign trade in the strict sense. From its very first session in 1956 it conducted negotiations on creating an international bank. Other areas of interest from the very beginning have been establishing multilateral clearing in the CMEA, joint investment projects, a common settlements currency, questions of specialization and the principles of regional specialization and production cooperation. Other, rather general economic problems were entrusted to the SCEP when it was set up in June 1958. Most of the financial and monetary aspects of the tasks entrusted to the SCFT were diverted from it to the SCFQ in December 1962.

In other words, from the early 1960s until the end of 1987, the role and tasks of the SCFT were increasingly confined to trade questions in the strict sense. These included not only exchange of goods and services but also setting up the machinery to facilitate such exchange by streamlining documents, transportation, insurance, conditions of delivery, arbitration and so on. In that sense, the SCFT was like a CMEA chamber of commerce combined with an agency that smooths commercial exchanges. The SCFT naturally was involved in the annual and medium-term trade agreements, the elaboration of ECPS and STC agreements, trade aspects of Concerted Plans and Target Programs and other trade-related tangents of SEI.

7.5 THE SECRETARIAL LEVERS OF THE CMEA

Aside from the Secretariat, the other secretarial levers of the CMEA comprise essentially some of the Standing Commissions, the Institutes and most of the Conferences.

7.5.1 The Secretariat

The only permanent CMEA body is the Secretariat. In spite of what their name might suggest, the Standing Commissions do not have an independent permanent secretariat, research units or administrative staffs. Such is only the case for the Council's Secretariat, which has always been headed by a Soviet citizen: Aleksandr I. Loščakov (1949–50?), Aleksandr A. Pavlov (1950?–8),[8] Nikolaj V. Faddeev (1958–83) and Vjačeslav V. Syčëv (1983–present). Its headquarters is in Moscow in a futuristic skyscraper in the form of an open book along the Moskva river. The Secretary has several deputies in the upper echelon, in fact on the level of senior international civil servants, and oversees a professional staff recruited from the member countries. The Secretariat is divided into departments, generally corresponding to the Standing Commissions and several other staff agencies (Faddeev, 1974b, pp. 80–1), which undertake much of the preparatory work connected with policy recommendations and their implementation. These units are also responsible for background work needed by other CMEA organs for effectively examining problems within their purview.

According to the charter, the Secretariat is responsible for organizing and contributing to the meetings of other CMEA organs, particularly the Council Session. It also guides the implementation and execution of recommendations and decisions taken by itself and the other Council agencies. Officially, on the whole it has the same general functions as the administrative obligations entrusted to the secretariats of conventional international organizations (such as the Economic Commission for Europe in Geneva). More specifically, it is not empowered to enact and enforce recommendations to the member states on its own initiative. It merely prepares the recommendations and decisions of others and molds them into a practical form. Even with these limited objectives, the Secretariat may still play a crucial role in charting the course of SEI. This is so because the rules and regulations that guide a Secretary who has some initiative usually leave a lot of leeway for initiating and occasionally even autonomously undertaking actions.

7.5.2 Some of the Standing Commissions

Because one does not know what precisely is being accomplished at any given moment by any of the Commissions, it is difficult to separate the secretarial, coordinating and real branch-technical production-marketing functions of the remaining Commissions. Nonetheless, it seems fair to say that by their very nature the Commissions entrusted with standardization and statistics are primarily secretarial units. Their tasks essentially consist of collecting, organizing and disseminating quantitative and qualitative information throughout the CMEA; in addition, both Commissions devise methodologies for these informational activities. In some cases, recommendations by these Commissions may become mandatory for some aspect of CMEA cooperation, including trade matters.

7.5.3 Conferences

CPE officials in charge of specific economic, technological or scientific affairs often find that they share certain common preoccupations. Several interstate Conferences have been institutionalized to provide forums for discussing shared issues and exchanging experiences. They are not empowered to make recommendations as their functions are largely consultative, organizational or coordinating. At year-end 1987 seven Conferences were recognized as CMEA organs: Ministers of Domestic Trade (1986), Ministers of Labor Affairs (1974), Heads of Technological Inventions and Patents (1971), Price Office Chiefs (1973), Representatives of CMEA Members on Legal Questions (1969), Water Administration Heads (1962) and Representatives of Freight Transport and Shipping Organizations (1951), which supervises the Bureau for the Coordination of Ship Charters (1956). Only the latter may have survived the shakeup of early 1988. The Conference on legal questions was transformed into a full-fledged Standing Commission.

Conferences are organized as 'permanent' organs, presumably because they have a statute and are regularly convened, usually twice yearly. They are subordinate to and exist in an advisory capacity to the Executive Committee or its specialized Committees (Faddeev, 1974b, pp. 82–5). But many other meetings are also convened fairly regularly and in cooperation with or under the aegis of the CMEA, especially on theoretical or academic topics. Though Conferences are purely consultative, they have sometimes led to the creation of more formal CMEA institutions. For example, the occasional meetings of banking and financial experts in the late 1950s generated the IBEC and the SCFQ, and a conference on health led to the Standing Commission for health care in 1975.

Before their restructuring, the official Conferences fell into two groups: those that study special economic or other problems (such as prices and domestic trade) and those that supervise the operation of quasi-permanent tasks (such as the administration of shipping transportation). For example, the Conference of shipping directors, created by the Council's Bureau in October 1951 (Lukin, 1974, p. 399), coordinates the shipping activities of CPEs abroad, organizes common passenger and freight services and elaborates proposals on the unification of shipment conditions. These largely administrative tasks could just as well have been entrusted to the Standing Commissions, but the CPEs decided otherwise, probably for reasons similar to those behind the creation of IEOs (see chapter 8). One important inducement to this chronic aversion to delegating duties in general is that committal of authority to the formal CMEA echelons in itself implies the transfer of power from the national to the regional level. The relatively loose framework of a Conference, on the other hand, can satisfy the need for consultation and exchange of information without in any way implying a further commitment to the transfer of decision-making authority. Because formal channels of communication within the CMEA also appear to be top-heavy, inflexible and entrenched in the established bureaucracy, they are not positioned to effectively manage specialized issues when the need arises. In light of the importance of some topics, particularly pricing and legal affairs, it is surprising that the CPEs have not yet been willing to establish higher-level organs capable of handling these critical issues of SEI.

7.5.4 Institutes

The Institutes that fall under the CMEA umbrella and are not totally subordinate to the Standing Commissions or the Committees (as in the Dubna nuclear research facility) numbered three at the end of 1987. They are the Standardization Institute (Moscow, 1962), the International Institute for Economic Problems of the World Socialist System (Moscow, 1971) and the International Research Institute for Management Problems (Moscow, 1975). This third Institute was apparently eliminated in early 1988. The Institutes are concerned more with the theoretical, but possibly fundamental, problems of international cooperation than with the implementation of desirable or approved cooperation initiatives.

Standardization and unification of measurements, tolerances, profiles, complete products and the like can certainly facilitate the transfer across the region of commodities and services, and, to an even greater extent, components and parts. Since its founding in 1962, the Standardization Institute's mission has been to establish common scientific, technical and industrial standards especially for industry, agriculture and science. Its role, however, appears to have been more latent than active until, in the early 1970s, *Integration Program* called for greater standardization. Its authority has been immeasurably enhanced since ratification in 1974 of the protocol on technical standards. This document calls for compulsory adherence to CMEA technical standards as they are announced at regular intervals by the

Standardization Commission (Smith, 1977, p. 161). Members must instruct their industries, design centers and laboratories to adhere to common CMEA standards within a certain time frame following approval of the Commission's recommendations, which are normally prepared by the Standardization Institute.

The Institute for the study of CMEA economic problems has somewhat of a general research thrust in overseeing work on basic and other SEI topics. The role of prices in trade and specialization, for example, can be considered here against a much wider background than had been possible in the SCEP. Although its activities have definitely placed the problems of SEI in perspective, the Institute's influence on the decision-making process in the CMEA may not be large. But it probably does fulfill a perceptible role in preparing vast amounts of background information for more political and action-oriented debates at levels higher up. In that sense, it may have a very important function in enhancing the potential for capitalizing on the advantages of integration.

The Management Institute deals with the promotion of scientific management methods, which includes computer simulation of complex management processes, the prognosis of future developments in management and how the CMEA should be gradually prepared for this transition and, generally, with the theoretical analysis of 'philosophical, social, economic, legal, mathematical, and cybernetic management problems.'[9] Further details on its operations are lacking.

All Institutes are headquartered in Moscow and are staffed with specialists and academics recruited from the member countries. They are responsible notably for the coordination of research activities undertaken by academics and government specialists in the individual CPEs. In addition, these institutions frequently organize scientific and technical conferences within their respective fields of competence. In that sense, they should be considered as important coordinating organs in which comprehensive scientific-technical information is assembled. But these Institutes are by no means the real think tanks responsible for developing plausible alternative roads to SEI, options for solving fundamental economic and other problems pertaining to regional cooperation or for issues of how to integrate independent economies.

7.6 THE COORDINATING TIERS OF THE CMEA

The remaining Standing Commissions, some of the IEOs and the various, mostly *ad hoc*, bilateral and other intergovernmental or scientific commissions comprise the coordinating tiers of the CMEA. One could also include here some of the organizations mentioned in section 7.5, especially the Conferences and Institutes. The IEOs and related organs are examined in some detail in chapter 8.

Units entrusted with coordinating diverse branch-technical, transportation and other technical issues involved in fostering SEI must be numbered among the Standing Commissions with coordinating functions. By year-end 1987 there were no fewer than sixteen branch-technical units that essentially cover all standard economic branches of agriculture, industry and construction. Their tasks focus on assisting the coordination of production and consumption of goods belonging to one specific branch. Activities encompass specific details of designing and implementing standardization and cooperation in the given technical aspects of production, such as marketing, product development and organization. These include atomic energy, the food industry, agriculture, electrical energy, radio technology and electronics, ferrous metallurgy, nonferrous metallurgy, light industry, gas and oil, the coal industry and construction. In addition, some Commissions, especially in energy and health, have wider coordinating functions than the narrow branch-technical tasks incumbent upon other Commissions.

Of the Commissions concerned with transportation, before the reform there were three. The one devoted to transportation as a whole was established in 1958, when there were as yet no other such units concerned with these issues. Its focus has remained on finding solutions for problems not covered by the two specialized transportation Commissions – that is, those that manage civil aviation (which was reabsorbed into the overall Commission in early 1988) and post and telecommunications.

Finally there are some Commissions whose task is not specifically confined to one particular sector. They include the organs entrusted with new materials and technology, biotechnology, public health, geology and environmental protection – all were abolished in early 1988.

In some cases, these Commissions enjoyed close interaction with other CMEA bodies, including in particular other Commissions, but sometimes also with the Secretariat and with subcommittees of the Executive Committee. For example, in elaborating standards that are specific to one branch, close coordination of activities between the Standardization Commission and the branch-technical Commission was needed. This included complete delegation of assignments to work out standards to the branch-technical unit. Examining standards for application and recommending how they could be implemented usually remained the prerogative of the Standardization Commission, however. Likewise, the Transportation Commission could suggest the construction of new railroads, but such blueprints would have to be integrated with the freight requirements ensuing from other coordinating agencies, IEOs and others, as well as with the possibilities of obtaining financing for the project. The latter task has involved the SCFQ and has certainly called upon the managerial and financial resources available through the two banks.

NOTES

1. It is entitled: *Basic directions for the further improvement of the organization of multilateral cooperation of the CMEA member countries and the Council's operations.* I shall abbreviate it here to *Basic Directions*.
2. It was recently published (Uschakow, 1983a, pp. 164–80), but its provenance is unclear. Uschakow cites as his source a special CMEA publication that is not otherwise identified. The document is said to be appendix 7 of the protocol of the thirty-second Council Session. In another contribution (Uschakow, 1983b, p. 199), he has interpreted it as having entailed major changes in fact, as well as in articles IV, 3 and IV, 4 of the CMEA Charter. I find no such changes in the current charter (Tokareva, 1981, pp. 13–25).
3. See Bratislava's *Pravda*, 29 June 1978, p. 6. M. Mănescu, however, asserted at the end of the meeting that 'it is not necessary to modify CMEA's rules and its other basic normative documents' (*Agerpress*, 29 June 1978; Stancu, 1978, p. 26).
4. Set up in 1962, this was officially known as the Bureau of the Executive Committee for Integrated Planning Problems. It assumed considerable importance beginning late 1963.
5. For further details on the first three Committees, see the bylaws in Tokareva, 1976b, pp. 111–2. I am not aware whether the bylaws of this Committee have been assembled to date into one of the document collections.
6. Speculation exists that there is another Commission in charge of armaments (Kaser, 1967, p. 263). Given the usual dichotomy between civilian and defense sectors and the existence of the Warsaw Pact joint command, this would seem implausible.
7. Thus, the SCEP created in 1958 fulfilled a critical role in the elaboration of the ISDL approach. Because it was superseded by the Planning Committee in 1971, I shall not discuss it here.
8. I am inserting this question mark because the precise dates of tenure are not known. The first Secretary was reported negotiating with Czechoslovakia at least until October 1950 (Kaplan, 1977, pp. 103ff.). His successor was included as the Soviet delegate in the Bureau in early 1951 (Kaplan, 1977, p. 125).
9. This quotation is from one of the rare treatments of that organization in *DDR Aussenwirtschaft*, 1977:51, p. 1. Unfortunately, I have not seen any more-recent analysis of that organization. Though it still existed in 1987, some surveys of the CMEA's organization (as Organy, 1978) have long omitted this Institute. It is even reported to have had a branch laboratory in Sofia (see Beyer and Weidemann, 1987).

8 · THE AFFILIATED ORGANS OF THE CMEA

This chapter introduces the remaining institutions affiliated with the CMEA. Because of their close interaction with official organizations, some of them are genuinely linked to the CMEA and SEI. This is the case, for example, for the two banks and their cooperation, especially with the SCFQ. Other relationships are more tenuous, although, in most instances, their activities are in part a function of what the official CMEA organs are able to accomplish. Because a great number of such international economic and other organizations exist but there is no agreed-upon rule of categorizing them into homogeneous groups, there is no systematic way of proceeding with any discussion of them short of examining each separately, which would clearly be beyond the scope of this book. The current reorganization of the CMEA institutional structure is bound to reconceive, suppress, amalgamate or otherwise affect many of them in the next several years. Therefore I shall touch upon only the most important institutions and place them in pragmatic frame of reference.

Section 8.1 discusses the main issues involved in the emergence and role of these affiliated organs. The case for grouping them chiefly according to their bearing on SEI as defined here will also be argued. Given their importance in this respect the two banks will be introduced first in section 8.2. Next, I discuss the organizations that are involved in actual production and delivery of central transportation or other services, either as autonomous agents or as various kinds of joint ventures. Section 8.4 then divides certain most important IEOs according to their main tasks, which include the coordination of production decisions, the promotion of scientific-technological cooperation and ventures mainly involved with ECPS activities or direct enterprise relations. Section 8.5 discusses institutions engaged in other forms of coordination within the CMEA, but no attempt is made to fully address the plethora of miscellaneous forms of interchange. The last section briefly expands on whether some form of international economic organization might emerge as the wave of the future and what conditions must prevail for them to exert a stronger influence on the character of CMEA reforms. These reforms concern not only changes in the regional organization or in the principal modes through which countries interact at the CMEA level but also the means of effecting domestic economic reforms in the most important CMEA participants. But the specific issues that pertain to national and regional economic reforms are deferred to chapter 18.

8.1 A CLASSIFICATION OF AFFILIATED ORGANS

The number of CMEA organizations other than those classified as official organs in chapter 7 is quite large. They proliferated rapidly, particularly after the adoption of *Integration Program*. In fact, of the forty-eight IEOs reported at the end of 1974, no fewer than twenty-five were founded during the preceding four years, but primarily in 1972–4 (Zschiedrich, 1975, p. 1678). Of these, only twenty multilateral economic organizations existed just prior to the approval of *Integration Program*; their number has since more than doubled. Of the present two dozen or so bilateral organizations, by the same count only four were extant around 1970 (Vorotnikov and Lopuchova, 1985, p. 10). These data are, however, incomplete; certain affiliated organs that are only remotely related to CMEA activities proper are not included, and there is considerable uncertainty about how the addition was executed. This uncertainty results from the confusion that exists about which institutions should be considered as properly affiliated with the CMEA.

The juridical status of these organs may contribute to the ambiguity surrounding their affiliation with the CMEA, as may our poor knowledge of the purposes and operations of the vast bulk of them. Also, a number of joint undertakings were established before a specific CMEA code on IEOs evolved. Such ventures were usually based on the legal code on firms or commercial relations that was in effect prior to World War II and were, subsequently, difficult to classify according to the emerging terminology and jurisprudence on IEOs. Furthermore, not all of the organs mentioned in this chapter are concerned with regional economic affairs as a whole but refer primarily to well-tried bilateral undertakings. As noted in chapter 7, concern has been expressed in the specialized literature about when a particular venture can truly be labeled as a CMEA-affiliated organ. The legal profession would tend to exclude organizations that have a limited membership. In what follows, however, I shall even include some bilateral organs if their activities impinge on SEI.

Nevertheless, virtually all of these organizations were established in response to the need for member countries to move beyond the simple trade and cooperation modes then available at the intergovernmental level. We also know that the majority were set up with the immediate participation of CMEA bodies. Pursuant to recommendations of the Council Session and the Executive Committee, the official bodies have produced proposals and drafted legal and other documents to facilitate the establishment and regulation of the activities of, particularly, the IEOs. Finally, model legal, organizational and economic documents have been written that contain recommendations on the establishment and functioning of specialized multilateral organizations (Vorotnikov and Lopuchova, 1985, p. 8). I shall therefore interpret the notion of IEO somewhat broader than this is stated in *Integration Program* or in the legal documents worked out within the framework of the programmatic statement (Averkin, 1984; Tokareva, 1976a, 1980; Usenko, 1985a).

8.1.1 Nearly official differentiations

There is no generally agreed-upon methodology by which the IEOs can be categorized. One way of proceeding, which was the method chosen by *Integration Program*, is by distinguishing organizations based on their legal status. This approach tended to dominate subsequent CMEA discussions about the legal aspects of the SEI mechanism, which is sometimes referred to as the legal submechanism of integration placed at a level equal to the economic and organizational-institutional submechanisms. To the best of my knowledge, the differentiation then current is as depicted in the main categories of Figure 8.1. However, the most recent literature on reforming the SEI mechanism and the CMEA organization does not make it clear whether this terminology is still applicable.

The legal bases of generic IEOs worked out during the early 1970s yielded two separate classes. The interstate economic organization (*mežgosudarstvennaja ėkonomičeskaja organizacija*) was made separate from the international economic organization (*meždunarodnaja chozjajstvennaja organizacija*), which itself is further divided into two different forms – the joint enterprise and the international economic association or union (*meždunarodnaja chozjajstvennaja ob"edinenija*). By the mid-1970s a third subcategory of international economic organization was added: the international economic partnership (*meždunarodnoe chozjajstvennoe tovariščestvo*). The criteria utilized to allocate an IEO to one category rather than another are far from crystal clear, however.

In many cases, the legal features of these bodies may provide a clue.[1] Interstate economic organizations appear to be subject to public law and are generally financed from the budget of member states. International economic organizations have an independent financial status and are the subject of private or civil law; but these qualifications are not clear for the partnership or *tovariščestvo*, which also obtained an independent financial status. Partnerships can be created according to international law rather than either public or private law (Scheller, 1978, pp. 5–7), although either possibility is apparently permitted. In fact, a partnership may even exist without any legal status as it need not be accompanied by the formation

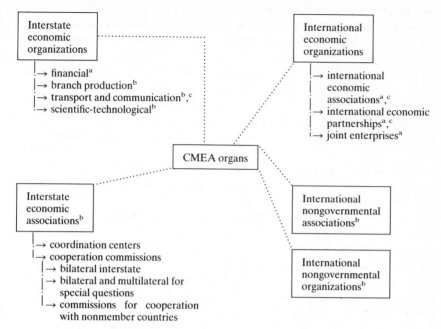

(a) economic accounting units; (b) budget units; (c) possibly temporary budget units.

Source: based on Brabant, 1980, pp. 189ff.; Brabant, 1987, pp. 57ff.; Tokareva, 1976a; and Vel'jaminov, 1977, to which the reader is referred for further details.

Figure 8.1 Various tiers of the CMEA affiliated organs

of a separate organ (Vorotnikov and Lopuchova, 1985, p. 16). To make matters even more intractable, recent classifications have co-opted some of the international economic associations established in the early 1970s, such as *Interètalonpribor*, into a partnership status without, it seems, changing the legal documents that were drawn up when they were first established!

Within the CMEA a model statute for these IEOs and common financial and managerial regulations (CMEA, 1975a) have been worked out, with the most recent set incorporating the above partition in a strictly legal sense. I am not aware, however, that these model provisions have ever officially been adopted or subsequently become constitutional doctrine of the CMEA, and hence an integral part of the SEI mechanism. In recent years, in fact, many Eastern European specialists have argued for a more differentiated approach, though these proposals tend to be tinted by the proponent's particular bent. Jurists center their efforts primarily on questions of membership, legal autonomy, CMEA affiliation and property relations. Much of their energy has been spent on deciding when an IEO is a proper CMEA organ and when not, and how the genuine types of IEOs fit into various national and regional integration channels. The issue remains unresolved. From a narrow juridical point of view (Caillot, 1971, p. 279), because its authority is restricted to the issuance of recommendations (see chapter 7), one may even question whether the Council itself is legally entitled to create autonomous organizations such as the IEOs.

The proper regulation in civil, public or international law of the precise status of each IEO is evidently pertinent to the smooth functioning of these units. But from an economic viewpoint, certainty about which institutions are and are not true CMEA organs according to their statutes is not very helpful. Their degree of involvement with official and unofficial integration activities seems a far more important criterion, especially as no IEO can be established without the participation, approval and supervision of the national governments. The emerging doctrine on direct interfirm relations, including CMEA joint ventures, may eventually change this fundamental precondition. But so far, direct enterprise relations have resulted in common organizations fostered with explicit governmental blessings. Most, if not all, IEOs have concluded formal agreements that regulate their participation with official CMEA hierarchical levels, usually through the offices of the Executive Committee. As a result, a clear-cut legal distinction between proper CMEA-affiliated IEOs and others is impossible as well as immaterial to the purposes at hand.

Economists, on the other hand, advocate a classification based primarily on two grounds. For those genuinely interested in advancing SEI, the most important focus has been on how IEOs blend in with methods of production integration. Economists concerned about planning usually place these organizations and their constituent firms and other bodies in the independent planning process of the centrally planned economies, especially the country where the IEO is located. But the profession is far from unanimous about how one should or could proceed in the most straightforward manner. Before I propose a pragmatic classification that may help to clarify the role of the IEOs in the economics of regional integration, I shall briefly examine the rationale for their proliferation. I hope to complement the arguments already advanced in chapter 7 regarding the multiplication of official CMEA organs that were not, however, primary actors in SEI *per se* prior to the recent shifts in administrative structures.

8.1.2 Rationale for the IEOs

It has never been very clear why a highly centralized organization such as a CPE, or the CMEA as its regional counterpart, would invest decentralized units with so much authority in a particular field of activity; this certainly seems to run counter to the logic of national central planning. Likewise, decentralization could undermine whatever vestiges of centralized decision making exist or are coveted at the regional level. Because of the predilection for comprehensive planning and central regimentation in the CMEA and its members – a sentiment that defeated the differentiated approach to SEI shortly after *Integration Program* was endorsed (see chapter 5) – the rapid mushrooming of IEOs in the early 1970s was an odd phenomenon. The micro- and macroeconomic policy considerations behind their emergence as such remain clouded.

Why indeed set up IEOs, especially in the loose form in which most were conceived, if the primary instruments relating to the SEI process are slated to be joint planning and plan coordination? Of the many possible answers, I find the following most convincing. First, from the organizational and managerial focus on executing assigned tasks, the creation of some form of decentralized organ may accelerate the introduction of well-defined integration measures on which there is no disagreement. An isolated venture is unlikely to be burdened with having to solve the world's problems or with taking care not to violate any of the supposedly essential precepts that are so prevalent in the CMEA's typical environment.

Second, decentralized IEOs may help in developing an operational format for matters to be settled at the 'willingness' stage or for delineating general principles at the highest policymaking level. At the high level at which such topics are ordinarily discussed, vital details are usually lacking. Enlarging the technical sophistication of the negotiating teams by co-opting various knowledgeable lower-level specialists or practitioners would prove cumbersome. In other words, just as the individual CPEs have felt a growing need to devolve decision making and coordinate economic activities through means other than physical planning, the CMEA organs themselves cannot possibly hope to cope with all details of SEI. IEOs are expected to broach possibilities for promoting regional collaboration that cannot even be explored or accurately gauged by the formal CMEA levels (Zschiedrich, 1975, p. 1682). They may also be entrusted with a particular set of issues that otherwise would preempt too much of the debates in established bodies.

Third, in spite of the official acceptance of the limited interestedness principle (see chapter 7), CPE policymakers are generally reluctant to create official organs in which some of the active European members are not willing, even *pro forma*, to participate (see Brabant, 1980, pp. 193 and 330). Because of their looser, less formal nature, an IEO with only partial participation of the CMEA members may therefore offer tactical advantages. Recognition of the special relationship of the non-European members, all of which can be categorized as true developing economies, makes it more acceptable to preclude their participation in official CMEA organizations and programs. Though this recognition has been emerging very slowly, it has gained currency in recent discussions about CMEA reforms (see Abolichina, Bakoveckij and Medvedev, 1987, p. 139).

Fourth, although IEOs are ostensibly independent institutions, the participating CPEs maintain a tight rein over their activities. Yet, because of their size and specific purpose 'international specialization and cooperation in certain relevant domains can be advanced much more quickly and effectively than is possible . . . within the framework of the Standing Commissions or permanent CMEA institutions'. This situation stems from 'a certain temporary contradiction between the stormy development of the factors of production and the rather strong resistance to change of the organized forms of the [ISDL]' (Proft, Liebsch and Werner, 1973, p. 141). In other words, it emanates from the inflexible bureaucratic organization of the CMEA.

Finally, IEOs were also originally depicted as being laboratories for SEI experiments (Kormnov, 1972, p. 314; Lehmann, 1973, p. 1318). In many ways they were viewed as successors of the 'spirit' of the former JSCs, possibly because of the lengthy and involved deliberations typical of the official CMEA organs. Major aspects of the economic, trade and financial problems of these common ventures cannot be given a comprehensive, general solution within the CMEA organizational framework. Their independent status does not, in any event, set a precedent for attitudes to the CMEA as such (Ptaszek, 1972, p. 5).

There are, then, in principle numerous explanations for the establishment of decentralized decision-making bodies within the CMEA. But neither their actual nor their potential role should be overemphasized. Clearly, an IEO often arose more as a demonstration of political commitment at a particular time than from a well-thought-out scheme through which certain aspects of SEI could be fostered. Precisely for this reason, as well as for others detailed in Parts III and IV, the explosive rise in their number ceased around the same time that a firm commitment to recentralization and plan coordination was hammered out. This occurred about a year after the first global oil shock – roughly by year-end 1974.

However expedient this trend toward establishing new institutions may ultimately prove to be, by the early 1970s some voices were already cautioning against an unchecked multiplication of isolated organizations, and hence a further devolution in formulating and implementing regional specialization (Alampiev, Bogomolov and Širjaev, 1971, pp. 82–3). Other voices, however, originally acclaimed IEOs as the basic, genuine 'long-lasting forms of intra-CMEA cooperation' (Morozov, 1974, p. 95). Whatever current official policy may amount to, until the debate on reorganizing the CMEA started in late 1986, there has been a remarkable lack of candor on the activities of IEOs. Nevertheless, it is indicative of the still-lingering ambivalence toward IEOs that few new ones have been set up in the past fifteen years, which contrasts markedly with the expansionist trend of the preceding decade, particularly the early 1970s.

8.1.3 A pragmatic classification

The legal tangle is confusing, and I must leave its resolution to those more acquainted with juridical matters. The economist interested in IEOs is likely to address three sets of problems that are only remotely related to legal issues. First, how do IEOs fit into the chain of command of largely autonomously planned economies? Second, what role is allotted to IEOs in the formulation of integration measures and, more importantly, how should they help implement these measures? Finally, to what extent, if any, have IEOs contributed to the enhancement of SEI and what is to be seen of their future role?

The detailed entries in the main categories of Figure 8.1 are designed to provide a comprehensive guide for placing individual IEOs, though not all of them can possibly be discussed here.[2] My largely functional classification is intended to encompass all governmental and nongovernmental institutions between two or more CPEs that were set up to promote SEI regardless of their legal affiliation with the CMEA. The various levels depicted in Figure 8.1 can be explained according to three criteria: the economic functions of IEOs, their financial autonomy, and the level of national participation in the IEO. I shall not elaborate on the third criterion here. Suffice it to note that not all members take part in all IEOs and that some organizations are composed of governmental institutions while in others the participants are individual firms from at least two countries.

Following the financial criterion, one should distinguish among autonomous units functioning on the basis of economic accounting, ventures financed permanently from the budgets of the participants and institutions financed temporarily from the national budgets but that are expected to become financially autonomous after some transition. Though several tiers are placed on self-accounting, most IEOs are full budgetary units (either on a recurrent or temporary basis) entrusted with coordination tasks rather than autonomous production ventures. From the very beginning of the proliferation of IEOs, Eastern European specialists have often advocated 'taking the necessary measures to let these organizations gradually finance themselves by retaining profits from their operations' (Constantinescu, 1973, p. 77). So far, however, this advice has not been heeded as the CPEs have largely failed to disengage their central planning organs from direct involvement in the IEOs. Even in those IEOs that have the self-financing principle enshrined in their charter, results have been disappointing (Fischer, 1978; Spiller, 1978; Válek, 1984), which is probably why the two recent Sessions have advocated abolishing inactive or nonproductive CMEA organs and transforming others into effective SEI agents, including placing them on a self-accounting and even self-financing basis.

According to their economic functions, it is useful to distinguish among common enterprises producing goods or services (such as *Haldex*); common ventures providing banking services (such as IBEC) or transportation services (such as *Mir*); joint organizations entrusted with the direct coordination of research and the preparation of technical, technological and scientific recommendations or specialization measures (such as *Interètalon-pribor*); units that coordinate production or that organize sales in addition to coordinating production (such as *Intermetall*) and possibly even research (such as *Interchim*); and other coordination units, particularly trade and cooperation commissions. Some of these IEOs will be briefly examined below, but I have no intention of discussing all aspects of even the most important ones.

8.2 FINANCIAL INSTITUTIONS

As elaborated briefly in chapter 9 and in greater detail in Part III, the domestic economic affairs of CPEs have traditionally been managed without relying extensively on money and finance. At best such instruments play only a marginal role in domestic economic decision making, the formulation and implementation of plans and in success indicators for measuring the performance of economic agents. Existing financial institutions and the monetary bodies that regulate them are exceedingly passive agents of the planning center. Finally, one can hardly properly speak of macroeconomic policy in the domains of money and finance. The passivity of monetary policy and the weak instruments available, as well as the incidental role of monetary and financial institutions, are a direct outcome of the aspiration of traditional CPEs to centralize decision-making power high on the planning hierarchy. Such a way of proceeding is possible for the bulk of transactions that are by definition domestic and hence subject to the full supervision, interference and control of top-level central decision makers in the government and the Party.

In external economic relations, however, monetary and financial relations have to be accommodated, which has had repercussions on policy, policy instruments and associated institutions, particularly as a supranational planning agency or an appropriate common plan at the CMEA level has not been available and CPEs are reluctant to engage in so-called nonequivalent exchange.[3] To meet these needs, two financial institutions on paper provide for the gradual emergence of a regional capital market (for details, see Brabant, 1977, pp. 103–244; Brabant, 1987a, pp. 269–356).

In 1964 the IBEC started operating as an organization eventually expected to assume duties similar to those once performed by the EPU in Western Europe. In addition, it was decided to create the TR as a special socialist currency unit. Its nominal value equals that of the Soviet internal ruble. But the TR is emitted only in response to payments imbalances in TR transactions with the CMEA region as a whole. With some exceptions, such as effecting transactions on regional loans or aid assistance in convertible currency, all CMEA commercial and noncommercial transactions were to be denominated in TR. At the outset the bank's goals were impressive. For instance, it was called upon to bring about the gradual multilateralization of intra-CMEA trade and payments. To permit the CPEs to reach that goal, the bank was to be active in eliminating the stifling system of BTPAs, which meant providing accounting and short-term bank loans to accommodate bilateral imbalances, bridging seasonal disequilibriums in trade and helping to cure structural balance-of-payments problems. The bank would also manage special funds for financing joint investment ventures that were soon expected to play a critical role in advancing the ISDL. Finally, the IBEC was to contribute to finding mechanisms for easing structural problems in trade and cooperation with third countries. It was to discharge itself of all of these and other functions through the emission of the TR and the management of balances denominated in that unit.

There is little doubt that in a narrow, technical bookkeeping sense IBEC has played a significant role in providing CPEs with accommodating loans in TRs. It has also been instrumental in channeling capital funds acquired in Western money markets to its members. But as to its main function – substituting regional multilateralism for bilateralism and gradually bridging the formidable gaps between intra- and extra-CMEA commerce, among others, with the aid of the TR – the bank has been a dismal failure (see Part III). Suffice it to say that the bank's failure is largely due to the fact that the TR has essentially remained a pure accounting unit. It certainly plays no role at all in the integration process (Brabant, 1977, pp. 108–16; Brabant, 1987a, pp. 278–85). This situation is unlikely to change as long as the CPEs refuse to make fundamental reforms in their planning systems; the bank by itself cannot be expected to become an active participant in the process of SEI.

The second critical CMEA financial institution is the International Investment Bank, which started operations in January 1971 with the overt goal of partially financing investment projects conceived within the SEI specialization strategy. Although the IIB's structure as a financial organization is sounder than the IBEC's, by itself it cannot perform wonders in promoting CMEA-wide coordinated investment policies. The rationale for this conjecture is basically the same as the reasons that explain IBEC's lack of vigor. Each CPE continues to be free to decide whether to curtail or to imitate production processes such as those financed by the IIB. In fact, the bank itself can only propose at best joint projects for funding and execution as the funds at its disposal are a small fraction of total CMEA investments. Because the bank's funds are in principle tied to specific projects for five to fifteen years, its actual role in the coordination of investment strategies through its own financial resources remains marginal in terms of the overall coordination of investment activities. That is not to say that the bank could only become instrumental if it was designated as the primary coordinator of investment projects. An effective role in supervising just a small proportion of the key projects related to SEI endeavors would be all that is required to set in motion the process of molding major components of investment activity. But even that has not yet been condoned, except perhaps for one or two transportation and resource-related projects that member countries felt compelled to finance jointly.

Nevertheless, it is useful to mention several noteworthy elements of the founding and operation of the IIB. First, the bank has a substantial subscribed capital (over 1,021 million TRs), of which 30 percent can be called up in gold or convertible currencies. Second, the bank was the first affiliated organ to formally disregard the unanimity rule[4] by allowing majority voting, albeit with a three-fourths majority, on important operational questions. Third, the bank has clearly delineated guidelines regarding projects to be supported, although the criteria for project selection and evaluation are not precisely defined. Until broadly based domestic reforms anchored in one way or another to indirect economic coordination are introduced, no effective rules and regulations could possibly be devised. As a financial institution, the bank is entitled to charge commercial interest rates and to augment its own resources (capital and retained profits) by floating bonds on nonsocialist markets, though it has not yet done so. It could also borrow in the member economies. However, because the Eastern European currencies are not convertible, such ventures could only succeed if tied in with specific projects that are coordinated from the start, possibly with IIB guidance.

IIB's role in furthering regional specialization should be seen primarily within the context of its ability to channel funds borrowed in global money markets into CMEA projects. Loans denominated in TRs have usually remained unconsummated because of problems in acquiring appropriate goods and services outside regular BTPAs. As explained elsewhere (Brabant, 1977, pp. 232–41), most of the disbursed commitments – as distinct from nominal loans – have been financed from outside funds. But it would not be necessary to endow the bank with large homegrown capital funds for it to succeed in playing a positive role in the process of fostering SEI. It could do so through comparatively small funds targeted at critical cooperation projects. It could also positively influence SEI by indirect means. Thus, although its own or borrowed funds are too limited to enforce the coordination of members' investment projects and policies, successful financing of a jointly coordinated venture, such as the Orenburg gas-condensate plant and the associated *Sojuz* pipeline, may demonstrate to all interested CPEs that closer cooperation in highly selected areas is beneficial to them all. This in turn may eventually prod the members to relax several other obstacles that are currently severely hemming in SEI (see especially Part IV).

8.3 PRODUCING AFFILIATED ORGANIZATIONS

Organizations involved in actual production can assume various legal forms, including IEOs and joint enterprises. But there are also a number of branch-technical and scientific-technological organizations that belong in this group. Some are formal entities while others are *ad hoc* specialized forums for tackling specific issues at the bilateral or multilateral level. I shall briefly discuss each type of formal IEO in sequence without being exhaustive.

8.3.1 Joint enterprises

In principle, a very promising type of IEO is the common enterprise. The creation of common enterprises can be a powerful institutional lever in enhancing SEI. Such an enterprise has an own capital fund, an independent status (naturally within the overall policy objectives of the participating CPEs, especially the host country), is managed on the basis of profitability criteria and has the task of alleviating the shortage of high-demand commodities. *Haldex*, the first such enterprise,[5] was created in 1959 with Hungarian and Polish contributions of capital fund, technology and specialized machines and at the time was greeted as an important pilot venture that would soon be followed by many more. Lacking any better mechanism, it was essentially set up within the provisions of the Polish enterprise law of the interwar period.

The Hungarians and Poles were pioneers, but not because they wanted to create a joint enterprise. Rather, existing conditions for CMEA cooperation did not provide any elegant way around the official Sofia doctrine of free exchange of scientific and technical know-how (see chapter 2), and Hungary was very reluctant to adhere to the Sofia rule in this instance. It was, indeed, looking for a way to capitalize on its technological advantage in extracting coal and construction materials from slag heaps. In addition, Hungary was a leader in conceptual innovation in CMEA economic affairs.

Despite the complicated accounting system agreed upon to maintain 'equality of partnership' and economic analysis manageable for both partners – for instance, sixty-two *ad hoc* exchange rates had to be worked out! – by the early 1960s the Hungarians were bent on emulating their first venture, especially with Czechoslovakia and the USSR. Subsequent efforts in that direction foundered, among other reasons because of 'the extremely complicated system of accounting required under the [prevailing] internal and external mechanism' (Ausch, 1972, p. 210). Or, as in the case of relations with Czechoslovakia, they only bore fruit more than two decades later with the creation of *Haldex-Ostrava*.[6] Likewise, in the mid-1960s Czechoslovakia and Poland were actively negotiating the creation of a joint enterprise for the production of tractors and other agricultural equipment, but it proved impossible to arrive at a commonly acceptable format (Čížkovský, 1968, pp. 292–3).

Approximately a dozen joint enterprises are now extant, although most were created in the 1980s. Unfortunately, the nomenclature in vogue in the specialized Eastern European literature is ambiguous about which IEOs should be considered a proper joint enterprise in the legal sense. I shall draw attention here to a few prominent features of these organs and then identify some of the more important joint ventures.

Apart from the fact that most joint ventures were created only recently, it should be stressed that, with the exception of *Interlichter* (for which there are at least four member countries[7]) and a few recently created ventures under the direct enterprise label, these projects are all bilateral undertakings. Furthermore, with the exception of *Przyjaźń-Freundschaft*, all are concerned with activities other than manufacturing. Cooperation in the extraction of raw materials or in transportation activities is the primary objective. Most joint ventures were created in the early 1980s to alleviate certain constraints on the supply of raw materials and basic services within the CMEA. Unfortunately, many interesting details about the functioning and operations of these ventures remain unknown. Because of their youth and inexperience, as one CMEA source (Vorotnikov and Lopuchova, 1985, p. 19) identifies it: 'They are accumulating experience, improving the mechanism of their operation, and looking for ways to reach optimal decisions that reconcile common interests with the interests of each participant in an organization.'

Przyjaźń-Freundschaft (1972) is a joint GDR-Polish venture in Zawiercie (Poland) that manufactures cotton fibers. To extract and enrich copper and molybdenum deposits in Mongolia, the Soviet Union and Mongolia founded *Ėrdėnėt* in 1973. That same year, they also created *Mongolsovcvetmet* to organize geological prospecting in Mongolia, to enrich ferrous ores and to gradually enhance Mongolia's ferrous metallurgy. More recently, both Bulgaria (*Mongolbolgarmetall*) and Czechoslovakia (*Mongolčechoslovak-metall*) have established similar bilateral ventures with Mongolia for extracting and enriching ores. Furthermore, there is a joint Ulan Bator railroad transportation organization between Mongolia and the Soviet Union. The Bulgarian-Hungarian firm *Intransmaš*, which deals with the development and production of intrafirm transportation equipment, should be mentioned (see Válek, 1984, pp. 24–5), though it is frequently omitted from enumerations of joint ventures. There is also one enterprise in foreign trade and technical assistance, and *Dunai*, a joint Bulgarian-Rumanian venture for economic cooperation and trade.

There is little doubt that some of these joint ventures have effectively enhanced SEI on the limited scale for which they were created. As with so many of the present IEOs, most were established because of a real need to circumvent certain restrictions on trade and cooperation within the CMEA.

From the frustrated initial debates about SEI in 1949–50 until the recent turmoil about direct interfirm relations and economic reforms, it seems that the CPEs never intended to enhance SEI mainly by establishing jointly owned – whatever its legal implications – independent enterprises that would become the mainstay of company cooperation in Eastern Europe. Ideological, organizational, administrative, legal and economic, as well as other, obstacles have all contributed to the hesitancy toward joint ventures. Thus, such ventures have remained the exception rather than the rule for enhancing certain types of SEI efforts. But the emerging wave of direct enterprise relations and joint ventures in the CMEA may change this outlook in the future.

8.3.2 International economic associations

Between 1972 and 1974, nine legally independent international economic associations were created. They include the multilateral associations for the coordination of research, production and sales of nuclear machine construction (*Interatominstrument*), textile machinery (*Intertekstil'maš*), atomic power stations (*Interatomènergo*), artificial fibers (*Interchimvolokno*), measurement equipment (*Interètalonpribor*) and electrical installations (*Interènergoremont*).[8] Also, two bilateral associations were established at that time between the GDR and the Soviet Union for photographic materials (*Assofoto*) and household chemicals (*Domochim*). The GDR-Polish venture *Interport* was created in 1973 to facilitate port activities in the Baltic. More have been added since (Válek, 1979a, 1979b; Vorotnikov and Lopuchova, 1985, pp. 14ff.). Most notably these include the Czechoslovak-Soviet association *Robot* created in 1985 under the auspices *avant la lettre* of *Scientific-Technological Progress*. But the new ones belong more to the branch-technical organizations (see below).

8.3.3 International economic partnerships

As noted, the precise place of international partnerships in SEI is not clear. One indication of this uncertainty is that some of the agreements that establish these 'organs' foresee that, as experience is accumulated, the participants may transform the joint activity into a more formal kind of IEO. If the precise place of these units remains cloudy neither is it clear which entities belong to this group. According to recent classification practices (see Vorotnikov and Lopuchova, 1985, pp. 15–16), the following bilateral and multilateral partnerships, including those without a formal juridical or organizational structure, are to be included.

Among the multilateral organizations, the most important are *Interètalonpribor* (1972) for the development of experimental and standard measuring equipment; *Interèlektrotest* (1973) for cooperation in large-capacity and high-voltage experimental laboratories; *Medunion* (1966) for cooperation in supplying complete equipment for medical projects, usually to DEs; *Intervodoočistka* (1977) for cooperation in all phases of sewage purification and water-treatment techniques and equipment; and *Inter-nefteprodukt* (1978) for cooperation in small-tonnage petroleum products, additives and catalysts.

There are, of course, also many bilateral organizations. These include the joint Hungarian-Polish organization *Interkomponent* (1973) for coordinating the production and development of and fostering cooperation in electronic components; the Bulgarian-Soviet organ *Elektroinstrument* (1975) for the organization of scientific, technical and production cooperation in hand-held electrical power tools; the Bulgarian-Soviet transport organization *Dunajtrans* (1976) and freight-forwarding organ *Intermorput* (1979); and the Czechoslovak-Polish freight-forwarding organization *Spedrapid* (1946), which is perhaps the CMEA's oldest extant IEO.

As already noted, some of these institutions are bilateral ventures. This applies to the majority of the joint enterprises and to all that are actually engaged in material production as distinguished from services. Others involve most, if not all, CPEs. They are separate from the joint enterprises in that international economic associations are actually cartel-like institutions with the participating enterprises from two or more CPEs keeping their own separate identity; the association in the partnership is even less formal. Except for *Interatominstrument*, all are involved either in some kind of plan coordination or in the advancement of STC. They develop proposals and draft agreements on specialization, joint production, STC and mutual supplies by developing proposals on joint economic activities and by sponsoring conferences of various kinds. In addition, *Interatominstrument* also engages in economic activities, including the technical servicing of instruments and nuclear technology as well as contract work in nuclear-power technology.

8.3.4 Branch-technical and transportation organizations

From the viewpoint of facilitating cooperation under existing conditions, the transportation and branch-technical units are perhaps the most significant IEOs and presently number more than two dozen. Critical transportation organizations include the unified power grid *Mir* (1962), the common railroad wagon pool (1964), the joint container pool (1976), the coordination of port activities *Interport* (1973), the coordination of ocean and river shipment *Interlichter* (1978) and the network of oil and gas pipelines, which includes *Družba* (1958), *Bratstvo* (1974), *Sojuz* (1975), *Progress* (1986) and their extensions.

Of the branch-technical IEOs, perhaps the most prominent are the ball-bearings organization *Interpodszypnik*[9] (1965); the coordination of surplus rolled-steel products and excess rolling capacities *Intermetall* (1964); the specialization of low-output, high-value chemicals *Interchim* (1969); the coordination of agricultural, especially horticultural, machinery *Agromaš* (1964); the coordination of electrotechnical equipment *Interėlektro* (1973); the oil and gas exploration venture *Petrobaltik* (1975); and the units concerned with internal transportation equipment *Intransmaš* (1964).

8.4 MAIN COORDINATING UNITS

Given the importance of integrating economic policies among countries that purport to merge their economies through conscious decisions at the highest levels of policy formulation and implementation, it should not be surprising that plan coordination *per se* is an important function at every tier of the CMEA and proceeds at many levels. The four most critical ones to be considered are production activities, scientific-technological processes, production specialization and direct enterprise relations.

8.4.1 Units involved in the coordination of production

Coordination of production processes across the region, or the main components thereof, is perhaps the most important SEI activity. It should not be surprising to learn that all affiliated organs of the CMEA, as well as most agencies discussed in chapter 7, are inherently intimately involved in the coordination of some development, production, implementation or distribution activities. The principal mission of a few, however, is to coordinate production decisions to the exclusion of actual manufacturing, marketing and product development activities that by themselves constitute a meaningful component of the operations of some CMEA affiliated organizations. Because of the importance of coordination *per se*, I shall discuss those organs separately.

Among the crucial economic organizations belonging to this group, several should be remembered: the ball-bearings organization *Interpodszypnik*, the metallurgical coordinating center *Intermetall*, the low-volume chemical organization *Interchim*, the horticultural planting organization *Agromaš* and the development and joint production of within-factory transportation equipment *Intransmaš*. These are, of course, some of the branch-technical agencies mentioned in section 8.3 under the heading of units affiliated with production. Their coordination of production activities may, but need not, include possibilities of reallocating national output goals to take advantage of scale economies, to redistribute capacity utilization or to otherwise affect the concrete setting of output targets by considering the present and prospective requirements of one or more foreign partners.

8.4.2 Units involved in STC

Given the emphasis on scientific-technological exchange back to the beginning of the CMEA in 1949, most specialized organizations, in one way or another, are directly involved in STC. During the first two decades of CMEA cooperation, STC was largely confined to the exchange of technological blueprints and assistance in transferring that knowledge by temporarily assigning technicians and engineers abroad. The Sofia Principle (e.g., the nearly gratuitous exchange of blueprints), discussed in chapter 2, was kept intact. From the late 1960s on, it had become acceptable to engage in such exchanges on a commercial basis if the partners could reach an appropriate agreement. Needless to say, the countries receiving this form of economic assistance have never been keen on voluntarily agreeing to such commercialization (see chapter 13).

Increasingly, however, it is being realized that an institutionalized framework of cooperation could smooth the obstacles embedded in adhering to the Sofia Principle when the economic task is explicitly identified with 'growth intensification' or with sustaining the pace of productivity growth through steady technological progress. Explicit adoption of a strategy for such cooperation was culminated in December 1985 under the heading of *Scientific-Technological Progress*. Since then, members have been concerned about the elaboration of an appropriate institutional infrastructure for promoting such a linking of scientific research to prototype development, technological innovation, the transmission of knowledge into the production process and, indeed, commercializing such activities into the final distribution sphere. Much remains to be done, though, as will be explained in chapters 13 and 17.

8.4.3 Units involved in production specialization

Beyond all doubt should be the centrality of fostering SEI directly in the production process rather than indirectly through the interaction and signals of demand and supply in market relations. Every formal and informal CMEA organ at some level is concerned with production specialization. The level of cooperation discussed here refers to a number of entities that must be mentioned so as to clarify the analysis of production specialization and its role in the CMEA, especially as this is presented in chapter 13.

Production specialization essentially evolves at four levels: the redistribution of existing production capacities, the transfer of production facilities across geographic boundaries, commitments to avoid further duplication of production activities and the joint development of new products. Depending on the kind of activity foreseen, one form or another has been stressed to the exclusion of others. The first three, of course, have been most practiced in activities for which wide industrialization was expansively pursued during the two waves of industrialization. These include ferrous and nonferrous metallurgy, some basic engineering branches and the chemical industry.

8.4.4 Direct enterprise relations and SEI

As analyzed in chapter 6, in the mid-1980s the CPEs began to emphasize the importance of fostering SEI through direct decisions involving producing and consuming units. As it has proved extraordinarily difficult to launch genuine wholesale trading outside of the traditional material-technical supply system in any of the CPEs, or as a substitute for its peculiar bargaining variant in Hungary, where precisely the debate on direct enterprise relations may be going is anyone's guess. Thus far there seems to be sufficient pressure for pursuing such types of cooperation not only through legal means – that is, making it possible for enterprises to engage in direct contracts – but also for providing essential economic instruments so that partners can more fully exploit their shared interests. In my view, however, this drive has a chance to succeed only if it finds a clear counterpart in the domestic economies through comprehensive national economic reforms before it is tried at the CMEA level.

8.5 OTHER INTRA-CMEA ORGANIZATIONS

There are several affiliated organs detailed in Figure 8.1 that I have not yet discussed. Among the interstate economic associations, these include a number of coordinating centers and cooperation commissions all organized at the official or governmental levels. There are also international non-governmental bodies that play some role, even if only indirectly, in galvanizing the SEI process or CMEA cooperation more generally.

As is evident from the notes in Figure 8.1, all of the organizations are budgetary units, they are generally not formally attached to any of the CMEA tiers and most of them are organized bilaterally, except some scientific and technical organizations that comprise the bulk of the non-governmental entities. Perhaps of most direct relevance to fostering CMEA cooperation are the interstate coordination centers and cooperation commissions, some of whose tasks are purely ceremonial or diplomatic; many, however, over the years have facilitated the exchange of information and provided for unhurried, nonbinding deliberations about many aspects of SEI and bilateral economic cooperation. As such, they form an integral part of the infrastructure of bilateralism and structural bilateralism (see chapter 11).

8.6 THE ROLE OF THE AFFILIATED ORGANIZATIONS IN SEI

To properly evaluate the role of the affiliated organizations in the process of CMEA cooperation, we must distinguish between the experiences gained prior to the mid-1980s and those that may soon surface as a result of national and regional economic reforms.

8.6.1 Organized economic cooperation in the past

Given the number of legal and economic problems (see Parts III and IV), the activities of the affiliated organizations, particularly the IEOs, have been severely confined primarily to the exchange of information, research, development and production coordination. In some cases, even such tasks as these have had to be scaled down and the actual operations of the venture postponed until important financial and managerial issues can be settled. The initial activities of these organizations often remained severely compressed until, it was hoped, more comprehensive planning could be worked out (Lehmann, 1977, p. 22). With the surging of the wave that established so many IEOs in the 1970s, it had been anticipated that the most vexing obstacles to their proper functioning could soon be removed, thus enabling the CPEs to take their proper place in the process of SEI. It was hoped that this might even start with the next medium-term plans.

Until the drift toward comprehensive reforms in key CMEA members became evident and contributed to the agitation later in the 1980s for reforming the CMEA both from above and within, the outlook for joint ventures in SEI did not appear to be bright (Válek, 1978). Though the obstacles inherent in the socialist IEOs are of a different order of magnitude from those that have held back the expansion of joint ventures involving firms from Western economies, there are still several common traits that could usefully be itemized.

8.6.2 Direct enterprise relations, affiliated IEOs and the future of integration

With the recent changes in attitude on the part of key CPEs regarding direct interenterprise relations, the outlook of joint ventures may brighten measurably in the future. This is likely to be particularly pronounced when the genuinely new programs contained within *Scientific-Technological Progress* are implemented. Of course, this is subject to these CPEs remaining interested in promoting new areas for intensive economic cooperation. Before that is likely to happen, however, the presently existing affiliates are bound to be 'remodeled' themselves. Some are already slated to be abolished, if only because it has proved so difficult to foster cooperation through them. Others will probably be restructured so as to change not only the concrete membership of the organizations but also the rules agreed on for formulating the purposes, instruments and institutional setup of these areas of cooperation (see chapter 6). Others are likely to be created in order to ensure that the genuinely new ventures are stipulated in, or are elaborated within, the context of *Scientific-Technological Progress*. More on these and related issues in chapter 18.

NOTES

1. Note that in some, largely unofficial, translations from Eastern Europe, what I call here international economic association is referred to as international economic amalgamation; the notion international economic partnership is translated as international economic association. Until clear legal terminology emerges, I shall adhere to my own translations.
2. A survey of the IEOs with membership and main tasks is provided, among others, in Apró, 1969; Caillot, 1971; Konstantinov, 1977; Lavigne, 1973; Menžinskij, 1971; Szawlowski, 1976; Tokareva, 1976a; Válek, 1979a, 1979b, 1984; and Vel'jaminov, 1977. But none is really complete.
3. This is an exceedingly complex category. It usually denotes that the amounts of value (normally expressed in terms of standard labor units expended in equilibrium) exchanged in one balanced transaction are not equal. In the international context, it means that one country is exchanging a smaller (or larger) amount of socially necessary labor than what it obtains in return (see Brabant, 1987b, pp. 15–27). I shall briefly return to the issues involved in chapters 9, 11, and especially 15.
4. To the best of my knowledge, there is apparently only one other IEO, namely *Interatominstrument*, that has such a provision enshrined in its statute.
5. Recall from chapters 1 and 2 that a number of joint ventures had been anticipated at the CMEA's inception. The first concrete project between the GDR and Rumania was sufficiently advanced to draft a founding protocol in September 1952, but it was never implemented (see Neumann, 1980, p. 169).
6. The first enterprise is now frequently referred to as *Haldex-Katowice*, but I am not aware that this reflects a change in legal status.
7. That is, Bulgaria, Czechoslovakia, Hungary and the Soviet Union. Its main occupation is to facilitate the transshipment from Danubian and Mekong Delta river transport to, mainly Indian, ocean transportation by using standardized barges that can be loaded directly onto mother ships. Its services are not limited to those four members, however.
8. The latter two were apparently reclassified in the early 1980s to the simpler partnership category (see section 8.1).
9. This is the Polish acronym; the Russian reference is usually the abbreviation OSPP.

9 · THE CMEA AND THE COMPONENT ECONOMIES

Since the middle of this decade, most of the European planned economies have announced their intention to introduce minor and major changes into their economic policies and systems. In some countries, policymakers have already embarked on far-reaching modifications. Others are still conceptualizing not only the purposes to be served by these incompletely defined changes but also designing the architectural nuts and bolts of the transition phase toward that modified economic environment. Note, however, that some countries, including the GDR and Rumania, have not yet even announced an intention to seek similar modifications. In fact, both countries have expressed more than one sign of displeasure with Soviet *perestrojka* and that for them there is no need for further reform.

Almost in spite of present policy commitments, transformations are bound to emerge even in the most reform-aversive countries. The modified mechanisms for reaching economic decisions, and especially their implementation, cannot but affect their external sector. Adjustments within the framework of SEI may be required. Because of the importance of CMEA relations, changes in SEI will reverberate on all member economies, including those that are currently most reluctant to pursue autonomous reforms. The implications of this second broad policy reform are drawn in chapter 18.

This chapter places this sweeping new wave of economic reforms in perspective and explores the organizational and institutional links between individual CPEs and the CMEA. Because of the current diversity of reform concepts, section 9.1 defines prime notions of reform, economic model and economic mechanism in a generic CPE. Any discussion of changes in economic mechanisms or reforms greatly depends on the historical circumstances within which the CPEs arose (see Part I) and the particular ideology embraced in the process, especially as it concerns indirect coordination instruments. Section 9.2 therefore examines critical aspects of the law of value. Its repercussions on the traditional and modified CPE are studied in section 9.3. Given that the current cycle of broad-based economic restructuring is not without precedent, section 9.4 summarizes the experience with economic reforms since the mid-1960s. The next section explores the external impacts of the economic reforms. Section 9.6 examines the broad links of the reforming CPE with the CMEA and how they may evolve. The details of the organization of foreign trade in CPEs and implications for CMEA cooperation are the subject of chapter 11, however.

9.1 KEY CONCEPTS OF ECONOMIC RESTRUCTURING

Because of the societal organization of the CPEs and the prevailing precepts on socioeconomic policies, any reform becomes a complex social phenomenon that affects all dimensions of society. Rarely are a reform's principal features restricted to economics. Modifications sought in economic behavior spill over into social attitudes and actions in many spheres. The intricate interrelations of the social and economic policy fabric of these countries are very important. These links are particularly visible in areas such as employment, the price system, wage regulations and income provisions. In fact, every reform introduced since the establishment of the traditional CPE has arisen, to a larger or smaller extent, in response to acute social concerns. These may have ensued simply from the need to accord a greater role to economic accounting as a technical tool in improving resource allocation, but even such limited reforms affect social precepts. Similarly, economic reforms contain a political dimension and may be sought as one way of modifying the political sphere. Still to be drawn up, however, are comprehensivve blueprints that encompass all of these aspects in a single, coherent framework. While these systemwide sociopolitical ramifications of economic reforms are important for understanding the dynamics of a socialist society, this chapter focuses on the economic aspects of reform.

In its most general connotation, an economic reform is a process for enhancing the way in which resources are allocated so as to satisfy present and future needs, private as well as social, better than before the reform. As such, its features may range from the philosophy of development policies to economic institutions and technical guidelines for economic behavior. It may be useful, even if only for heuristic purposes, to separate the postulated development strategy from the economic model. Both ultimately derive from the metaeconomics of Marxist-Leninist precepts on the historical road to development. These ideological beliefs include the doctrine on economic laws (Brabant, 1987b, pp. 15–6), which essentially postulates that socialist society is consciously organized, exhibits no antagonistic conflicts, controls itself primarily through the central regulation and administration of the allocation of the means of production, which are socially owned, and thus generates the fastest transition to the communist welfare state – the ultimate destination of the inexorable process of historical development toward full communism.

The core of socialist development doctrine is that the custodians of society dispense with the negative aspects of some laws of capitalism, such as exploitation and imperialism, and that man can and should master these phenomena of human nature in full awareness and in better understanding of his own behavior and seminal role in historical development. The initial development strategy adopted by socialist policymakers aims to carry out these doctrinaire precepts, as well as other objectives, through full employment, a rapid pace of socioeconomic growth, extensive industrialization as the foundation for steady economic development and a substantial degree of domestic policy autonomy. The stress placed in particular on steady economic development and domestic autonomy differentiates socialist policies from the development process in DEs. But there are other differences as well between alternative roads to industrialization (see sections 9.3 and 9.4). Pronounced priority is accorded to selected industrial branches, and policymakers mobilize resources chiefly for rapid and broad industrialization. Such objectives can be pursued with alternative policy instruments and institutions. For the traditional CPE, however, this process involves the creation of large-scale enterprises capable of capturing economies of scale and utilizing modern production technologies for the introduction of new products. It deliberately disregards static economic scarcities, whether domestic or external, in reaching macroeconomic decisions about accumulation and investment. Such decisions are, at best, usually accorded a secondary place in policy formulation and implementation modalities. Furthermore, implementation is done through central planning rather than through real indicators of micro- and macroeconomic scarcities and their associated policy institutions. In large measure the rationalizations of this policy choice hark back to the doctrine of the labor theory of value and its ramifications in the socialist economy (section 9.2).

A particular economic model, or organization, consequently, was embraced to further rapid growth. This model consisted of:

1. Central planning of most economic decisions and strict regulation of the role of economic agents.
2. Nearly exhaustive nationalization of all production factors, capital, natural resources and, usually, land, but with variations among the countries.
3. Strict regulation of labor allocation.
4. Collectivization of agriculture combined with state agricultural enterprises.
5. A pronounced disregard of indirect coordination instruments and associated policies and institutions in favor of directive planning of resource allocation in considerable physical detail.
6. Managerial autonomy strictly circumscribed by central planning and controls exerted by local party and, in most countries, trade union interest groups.

7. The channeling of economic decisions through a complex administrative hierarchy, where matters are handled bureaucratically in spite of the fact that some personal initiative is condoned at all levels of production and consumption, which inhibits proper coordination with overall or enterprise plans.
8. Rigid separation of the domestic economy from foreign economic influences.

Economic reforms include measures that modify one or more aspects of this economic model. A reform may also be pursued in conjunction with, or in response to, a shift in emphasis on development priorities, which may encompass a reexamination of the entire socialist development strategy. Because changes in the economic model must germinate within existing instruments and institutions, economic reform is an evolving process, even if introduced as a rounded blueprint. Gradual maturation is required to formulate and anchor the necessary laws and regulations and to elicit at least minimal attitudinal change in economic actors, who may respond to appropriate material and other incentives that will allow their activities to be coordinated at the macroeconomic level. Thus, the transition from a pervasive, highly centralized physical planning system to one based on economic accounting – including by economic agents – requires incisive adjustments in monetary policies, in the financial infrastructure (including the role of the central budget and the banking sector) and in the behavior of enterprises. All of these shifts are to be enacted through formal laws that may engender new managerial styles, shifts in worker attitudes and changes in household and managerial behavior that cannot be achieved overnight.

The original economic model of the CPE may be defined as the combination of institutions, rules of behavior and policy instruments that help to implement planned economic development with emphasis on broad industrialization. It may be useful here to digress briefly on 'rationality', for its configuration in alternative social settings accounts for one of the most conspicuous substantive differences between a CPE and an ME, as well as between evolving CPE types. Divergences can arise for systemic, institutional and policy reasons. Rationality in price formation, price structures and the general role of prices in resource allocation is especially important. Barring unintentional planning errors, prices, for instance, have not been administered arbitrarily in the sense that they were selected randomly. Quite the contrary. Fiat prices have functioned as an integral part of the logic of the development objectives adopted by socialist planners and their political and administrative mentors. As such, centrally administered prices in a CPE have had a rationality of their own that differs palpably from that of the stylized market-type economy. Price rationality in a CPE must therefore be appraised against the background of the economic aims, development conditions, social priorities, economic mechanisms or other features that typify a standard Western economy. However, this does not mean that all current price relations in a CPE should automatically be declared rational. Rather it suggests that it could be totally irrational to transplant the price structures and mechanisms of an economic system whose policy aims and development conditions differ markedly from socialist ambitions. It also suggests that the 'environment' should be fully heeded when evaluating how good the price systems are or in what ways they could be modified to better promote *prevailing* development objectives.

The concept of rationality and how it has been enforced has gone through frequent major and minor revisions. The most recent format is a move toward the market-orientation sought by several CPEs. In this context the concept of economic mechanism *per se* has come into its own. Economic mechanism is similar to what used to be referred to in the mainstream specialized literature on CPEs as the economic model, but it reaches beyond that in at least two respects. First, an anticipated change in economic mechanism invariably entails the creation of new institutions and policy instruments and is usually also characterized by broad-based follow-up efforts to complement or even replace those that already exist. Furthermore, an economic mechanism typically incorporates active macroeconomic policies (including monetary, financial, fiscal, trade, price and income spheres) that traditional central planning sought to allot a neutral role. As such, an economic mechanism may be defined as a model that helps allocate resources through indirect coordination via guidance from macroeconomic policies that themselves depend on medium- to long-term structural transformations that are planned macroeconomically at the highest policy-making level. Such macroeconomic planning usually gives greater import-ance to foreign economic cooperation than is the case within the traditional economic environment. Although trade policies adopted at that level attempt to foster decentralized decision making by FTOs, economic reform does not usually foresee the wholesale introduction of foreign competition.

A word here is necessary about 'protectionism' in the CPE context. It is particularly appropriate to question whether the evolution from a strictly centralized to a more liberal environment changes a CPE's protectionist stance. The link between domestic and foreign trade prices in capitalist economies is often considered a key parameter in measuring the degree of protection. Because I devote considerable attention to price formation in the CPEs and in CMEA relations, it is legitimate to ask whether one can properly speak of protection in the case of the CPEs and the CMEA as a regional grouping. The question is interesting because the CPEs, individual-ly as well as a group, are frequently accused in international forums of being 'overly protective.' But that terminology often results from careless transposition of the term protectionism from the capitalist to the socialist context (see Caffet and Lavigne, 1985, pp. 288ff.).

The systemic, structural isolation of these economies individually and within the region relative to third-country markets, which is a result of pursuing policies for the whole economy through central planning, enables them to avoid formulating and imposing explicit commercial policies. Because the normal operation of its institutions and policy instruments evolves without recourse to any coherent, separate commercial policy, it is difficult to speak of protectionism in the CPE context without clarifying what precisely is meant by it. External financial difficulties – when a country needs to restrict imports because it lacks suitable exports and will thus 'protect' domestic absorption and output levels – might be an exception.

Nevertheless, in what follows I shall adhere to the convention that describes a CPE as being endowed with a substantial 'protective environment.' But here a trade regime that proscribes spontaneous access to domestic markets by outsiders is especially being referred to. If the CPE implements reforms so that prices are invoked to discriminate between domestic and external markets, the concept protective environment should suggest a trade regime that prohibits spontaneous access to markets to exploit price differentials.

9.2 THE LABOR THEORY OF VALUE AND CPE POLICY INSTRUMENTS

Price and value are central concepts in the economic theory of socialism and the ideology that underpins the Marxist-Leninist framework for the analysis of development processes. The rudiments of the classical labor theory of value provide an essential backdrop for the proper placement of debates on domestic and regional price gestation under socialist conditions, including deliberations about alternatives to TRP formation (see chapters 4 and 15).

Marx's labor theory of value is an intricate edifice. It can only be understood in its sociophilosophical context, particularly the doctrine on 'commodity production' (see Haffner, 1968, pp. 20ff.). A commodity is a useful good created by independent producers through the use of labor so that it can be exchanged for other goods or money. Commodity production is ordinarily a consequence of the division of labor, but the reverse is not necessarily true. Issuing as it does from a labor process, a commodity is circumscribed by certain socioeconomic preconditions. It can only exist when partners are independent, autonomous participants in an exchange economy. Because of its essential connotation as labor's contribution in the production process, commodity production in Marx's framework excludes all other goods (such as natural resources, land and capital) in determining a commodity's value. Goods or services flowing from nonlabor resources may, of course, have a price.

By being tradable in an exchange economy, a commodity possesses the dual features of having use value as well as exchange value. The quantitative relationship at which different goods are traded or exchanged against each other is what defines exchange value. By its very nature, it is coincidental, purely relative and conditioned by time and place. In a sense, we are talking about the externalization of a commodity, the outward form of the social relations among independent commodity owners, or the phenomenal incarnation behind which hides value as the true motivating force in societal relationships. As the material embodiment of exchange value, use value emanates only from the consumption of goods. But it is held to be an objective and quantifiable performance indicator. In other words, as materialized abstract labor, 'value' differs from use value as well as from exchange value. Because use value is the result of concrete labor processes (Ehlert, Joswig, Luchterhand and Stiemerling, 1984, p. 987) and thus not a social category, it falls outside the usual purview of political economy (Sweezy, 1968, p. 26). This is, then, diametrically opposite to standard Western utility theory.

The measurement and precise magnitude of value should be kept separate from the concept of value as such. Value is simply the label ascertaining that a commodity embodies abstract human labor. When it takes on the form of an object it becomes the equivalent of a commodity. As a result, market categories such as interest rates, prices, rents, exchange rates and wages are not the fundamental factors that impart value. Instead, they are its reification or material manifestation, which forms the core of Marx's doctrine of commodity fetishism.

In bridging the gap between the abstract 'economy producing goods' and a precise determination of their embodied value, a yardstick for measuring them is required. For this, the amount of labor expended reduced to simple labor is essential for ascertaining the relationship between the magnitude of value, exchange value and price. This measure of value coincides with the socially necessary labor outlay and, hence, buttresses the thesis that value is solely resultant of labor. It is the amount of standardized labor required to produce a commodity when the economy as a whole is in equilibrium (see below). All other factors that may enter the production process are deemed immaterial in determining value.

Exchange value is the form under which value emanates in social relations and manifests itself in actual trade. In particular, the relationship between exchange value and the measure of value provides the link between the real world and abstraction. The actual determination of value is a function of whether all output can be sold on the market. In other words, in order to be labeled a commodity, that product, given its qualitative features, must have a demand in the marketplace and the intensity of that demand must be sufficiently large to warrant the scale of production actually set by producers. Marx's principal preoccupations were that aggregate value coincides with the aggregate of all priced goods, that both value and priced goods should be distributed among sectors, production factors and economic agents, and that a relationship must exist between values and prices at these various levels. Of particular importance was Marx's contention that 'exploiting' capitalists withhold surplus value from labor – the sole creator of value – because wages are inferior to value. But market forces reallocate the overall surplus value among sectors until the rate of profit (defined below) equalizes. As a result, the mutual relationships between production and exchange find their reflection in the operation of the law of value. In the final analysis, conditions of production retain uncontested superiority and primacy over those influencing market exchange.

Marx's questions regarding price theory, then, vary distinctly from those of standard microeconomic analyses. One basic motive of Western economic theory is to clarify the role of prices in guiding the allocation and distribution of resources. Instead of trying to identify price determinants, Marx's price theory begins with the proposition that demand and supply are already in long-run equilibrium. Value is, therefore, primarily a theoretical concept for analyzing the production and distribution of goods in a given economy; that is, a particular set of social relationships. But it does have practical implications, such as 'the regulation of working time and the distribution of social labor among various groups of production, and finally the accounting that encompasses all this' (Matlin, 1985, p. 76).

The most direct relevance of value for the corresponding market price is through the value measure, whose fluctuations are mirrored in the production price. In addition to prime cost, which is the sum of fixed and variable outlays, Marx's price, as it manifests itself in the marketplace, also contains surplus value. Though the rate of surplus value in the determination of value in equilibrium tends to be uniform, from the standpoint of prices it is variable. This is a consequence of the fact, says Marx, that in equilibrium a uniform rate of profit must prevail. Matters are different for value. A uniform rate of surplus value is supposedly added to socially necessary labor outlays. In Marx's framework, the rate of surplus value is the proportion of total surplus value to the sum total of live labor. Profit, on the other hand, is the proportion of aggregate surplus value to the sum of embodied and live labor. Because the ratio of constant (or embodied) to variable (or live) capital – the so-called organic composition of capital – differs among sectors, a uniform rate of profit in equilibrium cannot generally exist concurrently with a uniform rate of surplus value. The calculus of value and price, and the transformation of one into the other, therefore, are specific Marxian problems because he accepted a fairly stable deviation of price from the underlying value; however, he maintained that this difference would not affect the underlying value (Frenzel, 1966, p. 75). This conundrum has had critical implications for rationalizing price policy and price setting in the evolution of the CPEs.

Whether the law of value as applied to capitalist production relations remains relevant to the socialist economy has been an emotional topic, particularly in the USSR. Marx's law of value basically required investigating the rules that govern the allocation of labor to different production endeavors in a society of commodity producers (Sweezy, 1968, p. 34). In a socialist economy, the theory of planning should be as preeminent as the theory of value is in a capitalist economy. But policymakers in the CPEs were hard-pressed to advocate appropriate pricing policies solely on the basis of the planning principle. As one outgrowth of this controversy, for decades the 'validity' of the law of value in a CPE was denied because the 'planning principle' could not tolerate spontaneity, private ownership, market exchange or any redistribution of labor. This attitude was subsequently modified when Stalin (1953), *ex cathedra*, affirmed the law's validity in a CPE, though in a limited and transformed manner. Such phenomena as the denial of commodity and money status to transactions within the state sector led to the creation of a peculiar price system in all CPEs. Simply put, relations among state units should have a price tag purely for accounting reasons. Prices were to play a modest role in transactions between the state (socialized) sector and nonstate (nonsocialized) entities, which includes commercial relations.

In the isolated CPE, the operation of the law of value may be denied or restricted because of the planning principle (Mitrofanova and Starikova, 1980, p. 165). But any actual price system is inseparably bound to other features of economic planning and macroeconomic management (Popov, 1968a, p. 67). Domestic prices are normally set not only to reflect underlying values – that is, socially necessary labor expenditures – they are also a means of distributing and redistributing the social product among production and user sectors.

9.3 PRICING IN EASTERN EUROPE

Because prices are so important for effective decision making on economic policies and their implementation, it is instructive to examine more closely the bases of socialist pricing. A CPE's price system and pricing policies are more convoluted and complex, and certainly more controversial, than are those of Western economies. This is so because, fundamentally, pricing is not only a matter of economics but eminently one of ideology, politics and social objectives (Bautina, 1968a). Superimposing these dogmatic precepts upon unwieldy economic, financial and trading systems has had ramifications that have only complicated matters (see Brabant, 1987b). Here I shall point out the primary facets of the pricing debates, particularly emphasising their crystallization in the late 1980s. This analysis will be critical for the evaluation in chapter 18 of the directions taken in transforming regional pricing to buttress realistic reforms.

As they are derived from the ideologically all-important value category, prices cannot be dissociated from labor outlays. The central importance of

Marx's value category in theories of national and regional price formation is uncontested; whether it is also paramount in pricing policies (Zolotarëv, 1970, p. 191) is a different matter (Matlin, 1985). Socialist policymakers are impelled to deliberately deflect prices from their underlying values in order to simultaneously reach competing social targets. These deviations have crucial ramifications for a spectrum of domestic socioeconomic decisions, including those relating to external relations. Furthermore, because of the authority vested in each country's pricing center, policies are often formulated from more general political considerations that only incidentally take into account ideology and social objectives. In addition, actual prices must be deliberately deflected from the prices that would be compatible with their true reference values because the proper allocation of resources according to economywide priorities is only one policy goal.

9.3.1 Price policies in the traditional CPE

Against the above backdrop on price policies, one should rationalize, first, the emergence of a relatively autonomous two- or three-tier system of producer (or wholesale) and consumer (or retail) prices, the separate steering of both price regimes, and, then, the insulation of domestic prices from values transmitted through foreign trade. Prices of producer and consumer goods, as well as of agricultural procurements, form the familiar trireme of socialist price policies. There are, of course, other prices – such as for handicrafts and goods sold in free peasant markets – as well as related scarcity indicators, such as interest and exchange rates. I lump all of these elements together because none has ever adequately reflected prevailing scarcities.

Prices of producer goods are based on some past average-cost figures that are usually justified by reference to the Marxian category of socially necessary labor expenditures. In the environment of a CPE, this structural adjustment process is controlled by plan iterations that in principle are designed to yield an efficient solution. Wholesale prices of consumer goods are typically established before turnover taxes are imposed or subsidies are granted. Most economies have gradually moved toward imposing these charges on producer prices, however. In the case of consumer goods, the industry price normally coincides with the producer or ex-factory price. Otherwise the industry price is derived from the sums of the producer price, which itself is defined as the aggregate of the average branch cost of labor and capital as well as a profit markup, and turnover taxes or subsidies, relative to total output. Wholesale and retail prices are usually separated by turnover taxes, budget subsidies and trade markups or discounts (including normal transportation, insurance and handling charges). Of course, product quality and modernity are also considered when each country sets the actual price, which further compounds the tenuous relationship between retail and wholesale prices. In the worst case, no readily discernible parametric relationship any longer exists between the two price levels and their dynamics over time. Finally, the retail price equals the wholesale price plus a retail margin, which also includes a profit markup. Note that prices of agricultural products and foodstuffs more generally may be set differently, depending on how agriculture is organized, the specific goals the government intends to pursue with its agricultural procurement prices and the planning center's influence over free peasant markets.

The disparity between the prices paid by the state to the producer and prices paid by the consumer for retail goods and services is considerable. It derives not only from commercial margins and the government's fiscal needs; the two price systems are in fact largely independent of each other. This divorce is maintained because the price regimes are modified according to criteria deemed suitable for reaching specific objectives either in the social or planning sphere. As a matter of socialist policy, prices of consumer goods are normally fixed so that a reasonable balance is struck between supply and demand; feedbacks from prices have, therefore, invariably been left at the discretion and ingenuity of production managers. Once set, prices remain in force for quite a while, usually at least one medium-term plan period. Prices are overhauled only at great intervals and normally do not encompass all possible goods. Even on the free market, particularly in peasant outlets, prices can only marginally influence production. As a result, such prices may fluctuate considerably due to seasonal variations and state supply policies.

Because wholesale and consumer prices, in principle, derive their quintessential traits from the centralized calculation of average production costs, how these costs are set, particularly for 'primary' products, has a crucial bearing on how 'informative' administrative prices can actually be. The basic approach in setting wholesale prices is to distribute overall branch costs of live and embodied labor plus some standard markups over total branch output. According to Marxian value theory, this redistribution should be undertaken so as to ensure equilibrium, thus putting socialist planners in a perfect position to emulate value prices. Within the context of a CPE, value prices are, theoretically, set so that the total surplus value generated suffices to fund the aggregate reproduction process. But this is not necessarily the sole preoccupation of planners.

A defect of traditional wholesale pricing in CPEs has been the relative disregard, initially largely for dogmatic reasons, of an appropriate scarcity cost of land, nonreproducible natural resources and capital. Similarly, the true domestic cost of imported intermediate goods is rarely fully assessed when computing domestic prices. This misconception of the composition of costs leads, in an economic sense, in particular to a significant downward bias in the wholesale prices of commodities with very little transformation. The chronic undervaluation of goods that have a large natural resource content is characteristic for a whole range of scarce industrial primary products, fuels and agricultural products (Petrakov, 1986, p. 10).

Because average production costs are inferior to marginal costs with an upward sloping supply curve for the branch as a whole, the pricing rule in a CPE suggests that there are always firms that lose money and others that gain. This calls for the continual redistribution of value added within each production sector. But it is not a convincing justification for the broad redistribution of value added among sectors that is achieved by manipulating prices and price determinants. Neither can it explain why price levels and relative prices are manipulated so that adequate means to finance capital accumulation can be generated.

9.3.2. International trade and the labor theory of value

Matters are different for rationalizing the international relations of the CPEs. Particularly within the sphere of their intragroup relations, the objective necessity of the law of value is said to ensue from the existence of socialist property and the autonomous material interests of commodity producers, both here seen within the context of the individual socialist country. A CPE's specific interests as commodity producer derive from the precept that each country wants to minimize that part of its national income 'expended' as an input into the procurement of necessary imports as 'output' from abroad (Bautina, 1968a, p. 70). As a result, the basic determinant of international value is not the level of socially necessary labor expended in the producing country, just as labor actually expended in an exchange economy may differ from what is socially necessary. International value is the magnitude of labor necessary at the international level to generate equilibrium between aggregate demand and supply of two or more countries, which, of course, includes balanced exchange for any well-determined product (Gräbig, Brendel and Dubrowsky, 1975, pp. 30–1). The main function of TRPs is, therefore, the 'accounting of international socially necessary labor expenditures for the production of goods' (Popov, 1968a, p. 69). But TRPs have other tasks (see chapter 15).

9.3.3. Factoring trade prices into the traditional CPE model

On a national scale, a state may successfully cripple the allocative function of the price mechanism. If external economic processes are allowed to supplement domestic availabilities, however, it is not clear how such alternative opportunities, which are inherently difficult to control, can be merged with the rigidly centralized domestic economy. This is not a trivial matter, particularly in Eastern Europe, because extensive use of foreign trade was imposed on an otherwise autarkic domestic policy, even though few instruments were available for rationally evaluating such developments.

Because CPE planners desire a high degree of domestic policy autonomy, the relationship between domestic and external prices is crucial. This should be remembered as well when discussing the serious problems associated with the dichotomy between TRPs in the CMEA and WMPs. In line with the precepts of an autonomous system of centralized planning and administration, for more than two decades the link between trade and domestic prices was initially severed through the MFT and its so-called price-equalization mechanism (see chapter 11). This divorce of domestic prices from changes in real export returns and import costs ensured considerable policy autonomy but could hardly foster a rational allocation of resources.

9.4 CENTRAL PLANNING AND THE EVOLUTION OF THE ECONOMIC MODEL

Since the mid-1950s, a nearly constant modification, which may assume major or minor dimensions, has been going on regarding the economic model of the traditional CPE. Minor alterations are usually introduced to fine tune certain production, distribution, consumption, income or trade regulators without substantively changing the basic features of the model. Major changes signal economic reform. Nonetheless, it would be an oversimplification to speak of the first or second wave of economic reform or to associate a reform with any particular date without making it obvious what precisely is meant. To do so, I first clarify key characteristics of the traditional CPE that have not already been examined. I then consider three generic reforms.

9.4.1 The centralized economic model

The centralized economic model is dominated by a hierarchical system of planning and management. Decision-making authority is vested at the center of national power to ensure a particularly close interrelationship between political and economic functions. The physical details of producing and distributing critical goods and services are delineated by the planning center, which itself or through its agencies assigns producers a mandatory plan on inputs, outputs, pricing, wages, capital allocation and other variables. Planning by central fiat is intended to formulate instructions that leave no alternative as to their execution. Questions concerning what is to be produced, how production is to be organized, what inputs are to be used and so on are, in principle, settled by the plan's specifications and not by entrepreneurial foresight, risk taking or creativity. Moreover, initiative and leadership, if present, are not to diminish the priority of physical yardsticks set by central decision makers.

Of course, the real world of production and consumption differs substantially from this ideal paradigm. For example, conscious human activity cannot be reduced to the simple act of pulling a lever because the planning center cannot possibly tend to every minute detail of the economy. Even if this were possible at the early stages of socialist planning, the appropriate functioning of an increasingly complex economy via coordinated directives and regulators demands that modifications be introduced. These will usually be required early in the creation of a CPE because of the various uncertainties in economic decisions that must be faced. Uncertainties derive from the existing or rapidly growing complexity of steering an economy, the difficulty of accurately forecasting complex economic interactions and the unpredictability of activities such as trade and agriculture. Such perplexity has to be eventually resolved either by introducing a flexible type of planning (such as continuous planning) or by *ad hoc* solutions formulated by the ultimate economic agents. Because the lower tiers of the planning hierarchy may harbor preferences (such as private income considerations or the promotion of local activities) other than those of the central policymakers, their decision-making sphere coincides with the center's only by fluke. Usually, therefore, the plan must eventually be supplemented with criteria that will properly guide economic agents.

From the beginning of socialist economic organization, it has been accepted as axiomatic that socialism implies the effective control of the economy, in particular of productive resources, by society in pursuit of its objectives by appropriate policy instruments and associated institutions, and, second, the planned steering of economic life by the state. Without this being necessarily well articulated, the accepted premise of traditional planning has been that tools of indirect regulation are not dependable. Resource allocation in a CPE therefore proceeds largely by other signals, some of which may be concealed as a result of the discretionary economic authority of the political leadership.

Socialist price policies offer an illustration of how value criteria are subordinated to physical targets (see section 9.3). Price theory and the alleged fundamental principles underlying fiat prices in the classical CPE are not conducive to rational resource allocation. But even these eclectic guidelines were often casually treated because a price center cannot be fully informed about everything, such as sectoral production costs, the desire for price stability to facilitate plan implementation and gratify consumers, the intermingling of sociopolitical preferences[1] with technical economic matters and the poor feedback from markets that results in ossification of prices at 'historical' levels.

The deliberate choice to underplay value planning through the price mechanism was carried over to nearly all familiar instruments and institutions of economic policy that exist in market-type economies. These were not to interfere with the realization of the plan's decreed priority goals, although to some extent they did. The CPE's fiscal policy is almost exclusively concerned with indirect taxation (that is, turnover taxes) to ensure equilibrium between demand and supply of consumer goods. This stance is facilitated by individual incomes being essentially limited to labor revenue, which itself is centrally controlled. Based overwhelmingly on the real bills doctrine, which posits that credit should reflect real flows – in which sense it becomes 'productive' and hence conclusive to monetary equilibrium – monetary policy has, at best, been passive. Credit policy is geared toward facilitating interfirm transactions. Capital investments, which are usually financed through the budget, are undertaken with only minimal regard for macroeconomic efficiency, and no scarcity levies are applied. The credit institutions are expected to simply finance the investment targets set by the center. A more active monetary policy to equate income with the planned value of consumer goods is sporadically instituted to counter open or repressed inflation.

At the macroeconomic level, this model operates with a monobanking system. Money plays a passive role, particularly in the production sphere. Funds are simply made available to implement the allocation of resources previously earmarked in physical terms. Household financial assets are generally limited to cash, savings deposits and occasionally government or enterprise bonds. Government bonds are especially disposed of with only minimal regard for consumer sovereignty. Financial assets of enterprises are normally limited to bank deposits. Fiscal policies are subordinated to the general aims of the plans and social precepts on income differentiation, profits and price regulations. Most enterprise profits and losses are ventilated through the central budget. Managerial and worker incentives are largely nonmonetary.

Foreign trade does not play an important role in either the determination of the development strategy or in its implementation. An integral element of the CPE model is the nearly complete disjunction of the domestic economy from external influences, especially in the microeconomic sphere (see chapter 11). Interaction with other economies is compressed to the minimum still compatible with the overall development goals, especially rapid industrialization. To the extent that trade cannot be forgone, the traditional CPE insulates its own processes from direct interaction with agents abroad. It attempts to minimize indirect influences as well. Actual trade events impact on the local economy, but usually not through price pressures, because of domestic price autonomy. But there may be macroeconomic impacts (see section 9.5). Planners attempt to neutralize these perturbations by sterilizing trade results, varying budgetary expenditures or plan adjustments.

Although a state may successfully cripple the price mechanism on a national scale, how inherently uncontrollable foreign trade opportunities can be integrated with rigidly centralized internal economic relations is unclear if external processes are allowed to supplement domestic availabilities. This becomes particularly important once the potential for extracting the traditional sector's surplus dries up and policy options in the CPEs begin to parallel those in their Western counterparts. In particular, the CPEs stand to benefit, including politically, from improved efficiency in allocation and from reduced imbalances, which would make it possible to relax the state's coercive redistribution.

As experience has shown, the centralized economic model was well suited for carrying out a consistent, rapid and radical transformation of a relatively backward economy into an industrial society. It allowed accelerated economic growth and transformation of major segments of the economic structure. Standards of living were markedly improved by overcoming various growth bottlenecks, such as an unstable regional or global economic environment, initial domestic strife over sociopolitical organization, inexperienced management, a labor force unaccustomed to industrial production and a burdensome agrarian overpopulation. But the centralized model is less suited for ensuring steady growth in a moderately to highly diversified industrial economy that can ensure output increments by means other than adding primary production factors to the production process.

9.4.2 Selectively decentralized economic model

Most policymakers realize fairly quickly that an extensive growth strategy must eventually be replaced by one that emphasizes factor productivity gains. However, designing the proper model for managing not only the phase of intensive growth but also, especially, for facilitating the smooth transition to that new model is a more arduous assignment. Various attempts were first launched in the late 1950s and throughout the early 1960s. Though these national attempts were anything but uniform, the experiences can be summarized for expository purposes under the second form of the economic model.

The selectively decentralized model exhibits various transformations in the policy instruments and in some of the supporting institutions of the centralized economic model. But the basic precepts that anchored the regulation of economic development in the model are kept intact. This is particularly so for the broad goals of extensive economic growth. Reforms therefore focused almost exclusively on a more pragmatic division of administrative and economic duties between the center and local planning tiers. An enterprise policy was sought that could facilitate local decision making on the basis of cost-benefit analyses and in recognition of market preferences, especially toward external trade and foreign economic cooperation.

Central planning and its administrative machinery are normally retained, though some decision making may be delegated to enterprise associations in a given branch or to regional planning bodies, and in some instances extends even to individual enterprises, which now allows them to influence the central plan's formulation or implementation. The number of directive indicators becomes significantly reduced. Gross output norms are replaced by other control levers, such as sales, net output, profits and net export revenues. Material incentives are attached to other plan indicators. Sometimes these are even formally attached to the actual values of the indicated success indicators through norms on the permitted level of incentives associated with their magnitude. Success indicators are set annually through an exceedingly complex administrative decision process. Because of the lack of a flexible price system (see below), the actual accounting indicators of economic performance cannot reliably reflect the true scarcity magnitudes of the variables being quantified.

During the 1960s, almost without exception enterprises were absorbed into or brought under the authority of much larger economic associations. Devolution emerged in the sense that ministries or central administrators no longer vied to unilaterally determine enterprise policy. The associations were given the responsibility of guarding the 'social interest' of the firm. But the separate units obtained greater latitude in formulating appropriate enterprise policies. The tasks of the associations consisted not only of promulgating measures attaining centrally prescribed targets but also of working out, at lower planning levels, some of the norms previously prescribed by the center.

The logical outcome of the most determined reform would have been the transformation of central planning into a system capable of guiding qualitative and quantitative macroeconomic policies and controlling microeconomic decision making. Such a transformation would maintain congruity between the precepts underlying the central plan and the motivation of agents entrusted with day-to-day local planning and decision making. There might have been some continuing need for the associations, but their role in formulating enterprise policy and appraising its performance would ultimately shrink to purely administrative intermediation between the center and the autonomous economic agents. Also, by disengaging itself from the detailed chores of instructing production units, the planning board was henceforth expected to formulate better strategies for the CPE's future. Enterprise activity would be based on selective indirect coordination instruments developed within the framework of medium- to long-term socioeconomic development priorities.

One of the prime elements in enhancing coordination between the center and local executors is the improvement of relative prices (including interest rates, exchange rates, rents and capital levies), which has been sought since the mid-1960s. The goal has been to establish links between the various domestic price tiers as well as between trade and domestic wholesale prices. But a price overhaul is by no means the exclusive focus in adjusting the coordination instruments. Extensive use of selective price, fiscal, credit and income policies that will induce enterprises and households to cooperate with overall plan objectives was also to be fostered, although in this model authorities cling to direct control over other economic processes. Most forms of nonprice resource allocation, some of which are concealed, may be intended as transitory elements, but subsequent events suggest otherwise. Furthermore, even after the transition period, the preferences of the ruling elites continue to be given disproportionate weight.

For example, credit and interest rate policies in the selectively decentralized model are intended to guide the allocation of capital funds. Instead of gratis budgetary appropriations, a greater role is reserved for banks. Firms can procure from these banks loans to finance improvements in production capacity and consumers can obtain funds for the purchase of durable goods. Bank financing remains closely supervised by the central authorities, however. The interest rate policy associated with this devolvement of financial policies was to guarantee greater economic rationality in the allocation of investment funds. Key investment decisions, however, such as the establishment and financing of new factories, were to remain the prerogative of the central authorities. None of the reforms envisioned autonomous financial markets in which local or foreign agents could mobilize voluntary savings.

Firms obtained more authority, though not the exclusive right, to determine premiums, basic salary scales, personnel policies and so on to foster productivity. Exclusive authority could not be delegated to them because the objective of full employment and other socialist aims remained vital elements of overall policies. Instead of many detailed prescriptions relating to employment and wages, temporarily a trend emerged to confine controls to just a few norms and indirect regulators.

Perhaps the most pivotal of the instruments to be enhanced when planners devolve decision making to lower tiers is the setting of prices, as understood here. Establishing wholesale and retail prices that are indicative of prevailing scarcities (relative to both domestic and worldwide indicators) may act as the fulcrum for reforming the entire CPE economic mechanism, but few economies foresaw this transformation. One should therefore consider separately the liberalization of the price regime, the information content of fiat prices and the connection between domestic and trade prices.

Liberalization of the price regime means that prices are reset approximately in line with relative production costs, even if this is done only to reduce the need for subsidies and to attain desired levels of profitability for different branches of the economy. However, by itself comprehensive price revision is not likely to move prices closer to underlying costs unless a more appropriate computation of average production costs is first specified. Even if properly recomputed at a certain point in time, planners must keep prices in line with real or perceived scarcities on a timely basis, at least intermittently. By proceeding in this way, shifts in domestic production conditions or in world markets will be reflected in price adaptations, although these definitely do not instantaneously materialize. But the lag should be brief; otherwise the information value of prices for proper resource allocation evaporates.

Regardless of the chief goal of the price reform, actual calculations can be executed in various ways. Even in the most conservative CPE, the spirit of reform has achieved revision of administratively set prices on a periodic basis. Fluctuations in domestic as well as foreign supply and demand are now taken into account. Greater flexibility in administrative price formation has been sought so that prices will continue to convey meaningful information to those who must execute the plan. Either more frequent recalibrations of centrally set prices are made or more authority over price formation is delegated to the lower planning tiers, though numerous ideological and political shackles are usually attached.

A related issue is the degree to which centrally set or market-type prices can act as guidelines for the decision making of enterprises. It may well be that enterprises have no direct control over price formation, although they are expected to react to the parameters issued by the central pricing authority. These centrally set prices may or may not reflect somewhat better the true scarcities of capital, land, natural resources and foreign currency at the time of their introduction. In few countries do prices provide feedback on the status of product markets to central policymakers. In some countries, enterprises or their associations have the ability to occasionally revise prices in response to changes in costs. Firms could influence costs directly through a more careful selection of inputs and suppliers, by producing according to market demand and, in some cases, by using their authority over price formation. Profits were to become more meaningful in order to, especially, determine premiums and social advantages to workers, provide for self-financing and, more generally, guide entrepreneurial behavior. In all CPEs, however, including those in which price adjustments are now a *quasi* continuous process rather than a one-time major undertaking, price movements are permitted only within preset narrow margins.

As to the information content of prices, all CPEs have gradually allowed prices, even if set by central fiat, to play a more active role in regulating production and distribution processes. Although prices never fully reflected objective economic relations, they were moved closer to actual production costs and in some cases were even enabled to react to changes in supply and demand. Elsewhere, however, most prices continue to be primarily parameters that transmit orders from the center to the lower planning units as well as to the units for accounting and control. Limited authority to set prices has sometimes even been extended to the enterprises or their associations.

In certain countries, fiat prices for selected products can fluctuate depending on supply and demand, possibly within preset boundaries. Three generic price types exist: those administratively set, as in the classical CPE, those determined by markets (although they are subject to informal controls) and prices that are above a certain floor, below a certain ceiling or that range between a floor and a ceiling. Countries that allow such partial flexibility normally commit themselves to more frequent periodic price adjustments. Centrally controlled prices should, as a category, shrink as the 'from-to' group and, to a lesser extent, fully fluctuating prices gain a greater prominence. But this planned evolution is only rarely adhered to for many reasons. Athough retail prices are also modified, pricing authorities continue to adjust them to ensure equilibrium in consumer markets and to hold inflationary pressures in check. The process is not without administrative arbitrariness, however.

Though prices in most reformed CPEs, therefore, continue to play much the same roles as they did previously, the static as well as dynamic connection between domestic and trade prices remains crucial for proper decision making in trade-dependent economies. The majority of CPEs have set pseudo exchange rates and have gradually accorded more importance to real foreign trade opportunities when prices are centrally recomputed. Few countries, however, have allowed trade results to directly influence domestic prices, even if their economic agents have been granted latitude in generating individual product prices.[2]

A sharp distinction should be drawn between using trade results in domestic resource allocation and in profit calculations. For domestic allocation, trade figures have been introduced in an attempt to motivate producers or traders to promote selected export and import contracts. But, as enterprises are not necessarily entitled to pass on real costs, their decisions on matters not covered by the plan are reached based on what appears to be profitable from the microeconomic point of view. Although foreign trade prices have exerted a growing influence on domestic prices, the price system in most CPEs has largely remained inflexible, more so for consumer than for producer prices. For consumers, various subsidies and taxes buffer the domestic price system against socially undesirable changes in the cost of living. Although setting prices administratively ensures a high degree of stability, the rigidity inherent in the practice conflicts sharply with the desire of many high-level planners to utilize prices as one of their primary allocation levers.

It was hoped that the reforms would elevate the ability of foreign trade to buttress domestic growth. Multiple opportunities in both the domestic and foreign trade sectors challenged the CPEs into exploring ways in which they could stimulate more efficient trade relations without completely abandoning their autonomous economic policies. This change involved decision-making mechanisms as well as the organization of trade (see chapter 11).

9.4.3 Modified centralized economic model

In all but Hungary, the reforms initiated in most CPEs in the early 1960s came to an abrupt halt by the early 1970s. Even the NEM's pace slowed markedly or was temporarily reversed, though key components of the NEM as blocked out in 1968 remained on the drawing board until the mid-1980s. Sociopolitical concerns caused some derailments while other reforms faltered because the anticipated stimulus to factor productivity growth did not materialize. To rectify the situation, most countries reverted to central allocation of resources, reduced the autonomy of enterprises, curbed the flexibility of decision-making instruments and sanctioned other retreats from partial reforms.

The label modified centralized model refers in particular to the fact that essential aspects of the MFT's transformation in the 1960s are retained and, in many respects, strengthened. Change in enterprise organization and in planning and control methods gradually continued in the foreign trade sector, although setbacks were encountered here as well, in marked contrast to the abrogation of reforms elsewhere. Such changes are the logical consequence of the need to tackle multiple opportunities in foreign trade when autarky and industrialization as overriding policy objectives recede. Major and minor aspects of this modified centralized model are frequently revised, primarily because of emerging domestic and external imbalances. In this, payments problems with DMEs play an especially important role in searching for an appropriate positive adjustment strategy (see chapter 6).

Though recentralization was, to some extent, embraced because of disappointment with partial decentralization, there is no return to a strictly centralized planning system because the original motives for the reforms did not evaporate as they were abandoned, downsized or curbed. The need to boost factor productivity, provide sufficient resources for consumption and finance accumulation in order to stimulate factor productivity remains particularly important. The modified centralized economy explores means other than indirect economic coordination to attain these goals. Two are important. First, many CPE policymakers viewed the crystallization of political détente as a signal for them to import technology, if necessary through capital borrowed in DMEs. The second path taken by some CPEs harks back to the question of how to reconcile output maximization with certain rules and regulations on input minimization when the existing coordination mechanism is incomplete. All European CPEs tried various experiments that made intermediate economic units responsible for their own decisions.

The all-embracing control hierarchy of the centralized model, though re-shaped, is maintained in all its essential respects. The shift from sectoral planning to the creation of large units with economic accounting responsi-bilities in the 1960s and 1970s (in Czechoslovakia, the GDR and Poland), or the fusion in the 1980s of economic agents engaged in related activities (as in Czechoslovakia and the GDR), did not affect the principle that all eco-nomic units are administratively subordinated to the center and form integral parts of one comprehensive hierarchy. The only exceptions occurred in Czechoslovakia in 1967–8 and Hungary since 1968. Medium-level control agencies were either abolished or transformed into the central management of nationwide enterprises. The remaining firms were formally released from subordination to the state administration. Strict plan targets and physical norms were replaced by a general qualitative requirement to satisfy domestic demand, meet obligations contracted abroad and achieve satisfactory export performance in Western countries. Centralized resource allocation was to be complemented, but not generally replaced, by market-type transactions in the means of production, which have remained highly monopolized and strongly controlled by the state. Though still under political control, frequent price revisions and changes in enterprise profit tax rates were to be enacted to reflect modifications in macroeconomic policies and the gradual movement toward genuine microeconomic decentralization. Excepting the GDR,[3] where the experiment went the furthest, the partially recentralized model is replete with hedges because the experimental stage has not yet been abandoned or because policymakers have resumed the on-off partial reform cycle typical of the late 1950s.

At the level of intra-CMEA cooperation, the era of the modified centralized economic model is directly related to the difficulties encountered with effectively linking the member economies together on the basis of *Integration Program* as a loose policy blueprint and SEI as the ill-defined strategy for progress. Various experiments were also tried at that level, including through Concerted Plans and the Target Programs. Ultimately, however, what could materialize at the CMEA level reflected the conservative attitude toward reforms on the part of Soviet policymakers and the CPEs' growing concerns about managing various unanticipated domestic and external constraints on short-term policy flexibility.

9.4.4 The decentralized economic mechanism

Pivotal to the decentralized mechanism is effective decentralization and coordination of decisions through indirect policy instruments and their supporting institutions rather than the simple devolution of administrative authority that was typical of previous reforms. As noted, establishment of such a mechanism is normally associated with other societal transformations that together could be labeled as radical restructuring, but these will not be considered here.

The goal of economic decentralization is to curb administrative guidance in determining output, resource allocation and the distribution of incomes; eventually it should be abolished. Entrepreneurial activity is coordinated through market-type economic links rather than through vertical chains of administrative command. Supply and demand can influence more flexible domestic prices that are related to WMPs, thus guiding decisions on inputs and outputs. Profits become the appropriate measure of a firm's contribution to the economy as a whole and the basis on which personnel are rewarded. The state's control extends to three spheres. Most nonmaterial sectors and their infrastructure remain by necessity the responsibility of central authorities. Central planning of the material sphere becomes more focused on structural decisions and on medium- to long-run economic strategies. But a coherent macroeconomic policy needs to emerge in order to regulate income distribution, saving and investment behavior, monetary policy and the financial sphere, fiscal policy, wage and price behavior and so on.

Among the instruments of a decentralized economic mechanism, the following are the most critical. Rather than losing in importance, the role of planning for structural decisions is reinforced. The material-technical supply system is decentralized, with economic agents obtaining responsibility for deciding by themselves the disposition of outputs and some inputs. Moreover, these agents are expected to react to changes in indirect economic parameters, which include prices, exchange and interest rates and larger differentials in wage schedules. Furthermore, enterprise behavior is evaluated largely on the basis of net performance indicators, with profits as the paramount criterion of success. Subsidies for wholesale and retail prices or for ailing enterprises are gradually to be compressed and abolished. Enterprises that cannot be salvaged should be discontinued, which requires a government policy on bankruptcy. Finally, the decentralized economic mechanism necessitates changes in and additions to the traditional economic institutions of these countries. Transformation in planning requires that the role of ministries and associations in the day-to-day affairs of the economic agents under their jurisdiction be downplayed. Also, implementing a credible monetary policy involves the monobank becoming a bank of issue and lender of last resort in charge of monetary policy. At the same time, the monobanking system is to be dismantled and replaced by a network of institutions that cater competitively to the financial requirements of economic agents.

In the foreign trade sphere, FTOs are transformed into effective self-accounting trading enterprises or their tasks are assigned to individual producers. The decentralized economic mechanism may change the character of cooperative organizations, including in agriculture. Invariably, this mechanism imparts an important role to small-scale private or cooperative enterprises, particularly in service sectors. Finally, the new mechanism may promote new forms of ownership, not only by encouraging small-scale private enterprises but also by attracting capital from abroad through joint ventures or the creation of special economic zones.

9.5 THE FOREIGN TRADE SECTOR OF THE CPE

As already indicated, trade has played an ambivalent role in the development strategy and economic models of the CPEs. Although the role of trade has waxed and waned with the buoyancy and vitality of economic reform, and indeed with the environment for international cooperation, two types of foreign trade strategy and organization are present that must be distinguished in order to clarify in section 9.6 the fundamental properties of the link between the CPE and the CMEA. Other aspects will be explored in chapter 11.

In the traditional CPE, selection of trade institutions and mechanisms resulted from the failure in the late 1940s to adopt a regional economic policy. Instead of anchoring economic development to an internally consistent, comprehensive regional program, each country sought to isolate its national economy from the rest of the world. By doing so, it shielded itself from foreign events and reduced its interaction with other economies – including other CPEs – to the minimum still compatible with rapid and broad industrialization. Foreign trade is not allocated any central role, in such an environment, partly because of the intrinsic features of detailed central planning. This isolation also derives from the circumstances under which that economic organization was ushered into Eastern Europe (Brabant, 1987a, pp. 35ff.). Comparative advantage considerations, whether static or dynamic, were downplayed in implementing the chosen strategy.

Organizationally speaking, the complete disjunction between the domestic economy and economic activities abroad forms an integral component of the traditional model. This is accomplished by the 'nationalization' of the foreign trade and foreign exchange systems (Grote, 1981; Konstantinov, 1984). Foreign trade resorts under the Ministry of Foreign Trade, which in principle is in charge of the MFT. Though the state monopoly manages all foreign economic transactions, it usually delegates the authority to engage in trading to a few individual FTOs, which are as a rule organized by broad economic sectors, separately for exports or imports or for both activities simultaneously. Assignments may even be based on trade-partner grouping, such as socialist and others.

Trade chiefly serves as a means of fulfilling overall development goals and is therefore entrusted to the MFT. The level of trade, as well as its commodity composition and geographic distribution, results primarily from the home economy's need for noncompeting imports, export commitments and the relative surpluses and shortages revealed in the process of balancing the economy; some may have been consciously planned to comply with BTPA commitments. Comparisons of prevailing prices as basic inputs into trade decisions are rarely undertaken because the price-equalization mechanism siphons off (covers) apparent trade profits (losses). Of course, this near-irrelevance of prices applies also to the official exchange rate (see chapter 11).

To the extent that trade cannot be forgone, CPEs insulate domestic processes from direct interaction with agents abroad. In reality, this is accomplished by keeping domestic agents away from their foreign counterparts, with the FTOs acting as buffers. Indirect influences are minimized as well. Actual trade events can influence the domestic economy, though not usually through price pressures, because domestic prices are set autonomously. The nominal gains and losses from trade are simply absorbed by fiscal means. But there are macroeconomic impacts. A disturbance from planned import cost and export return, if accommodated, affects the disposable budget, and ultimately consumer income, as well as the foreign exchange situation (see Brabant, 1987a, pp. 110ff.). Planners attempt to neutralize the impact of this perturbation by sterilizing trade results that deviate from anticipated magnitudes. Alternatively, they offset trade gains or losses by manipulating other budgetary expenditures, or they postpone adjustments until the next plan enables policymakers to schedule a reversal that will replenish foreign exchange reserves or enable the country to service any foreign debt incurred in the process of weathering the disturbance.

Because of concerns about increasing factor productivity, economic reform, particularly in the smaller trade-dependent economies, sought to accomplish this task by prioritizing trade expansion. Precisely because of their dependence on intragroup markets, a more trade-intensive growth strategy will mature only if CMEA partners can accommodate such shifts or if outside channels can be explored more intensively. As the cold war and Soviet predilections regarding regional cohesion discouraged the exploration of outside channels, since the mid-1950s a more pronounced positive attitude has emerged toward regional economic cooperation. The dual nature of the reforms has affected the strategy as well as the model of the traditional CPE's trade, perhaps to a larger extent than has been true for the more domestically oriented elements. The previous sharp separation of the trade and domestic sectors thus became increasingly difficult to justify at a time when most CPEs sought to give highest priority to expanding the exports of manufactured products. Prolonging the disjunction between trade and production also became increasingly wasteful with the greater dependence on trade. There was hence a general trend toward reinforcing the organizational ties between trade and production and strengthening the role of trade prices in domestic price reforms.

Thus, in the partially decentralized framework many enterprises are free to engage in trade directly, and the link between domestic and trade prices is not entirely severed. Rather, the creation of new surrogates for exchange rates that affect at least the accounting of firms engaged in foreign transactions strengthens the linkage. At the policy level, this stance is affected by two important events. First, efforts are explored to bolster SEI and regional interaction. An all-out drive is then launched to upgrade production capabilities by importing whole technological processes, especially from Western Europe.

The role of trade in development as manifested in micro- and macroeconomic decision making undergoes changes when the partially decentralized model is replaced by the partially recentralized one. But the changes are generally more a matter of degree than of substance. The same applies when full decentralization is pursued as a firm policy aim that assigns the external sector different roles in economic development and in entrepreneurial behavior. But the shift, once again, is one of degree not substance. Decentralization in the foreign trade sector can proceed the furthest in an environment that has become more receptive to indirect economic coordination.

Foreign trade reforms generally affect four areas: price formation, price levels and relative prices, possibly including more effective ties between domestic and external markets by utilizing surrogate exchange rates; the central regulation of trade largely on a macroeconomic basis; the specific operation of the MFT, which finds itself simultaneously strengthened and weakened; and the promulgation of links with foreign enterprises through various industrial cooperation endeavors, including joint ventures. Although all of these measures are loosely connected in partial reforms, innovations in the trade sector, as detailed in chapter 11, are made compatible with each other and with internal changes in the comprehensive reforms.

9.6 ECONOMIC REFORM AND THE CMEA

Economic cooperation within the CMEA has been regulated mainly through detailed BTPAs that are rarely negotiated within the framework of an accepted CMEA-wide policy. Nonetheless, lack of a central planning agency at the CMEA level while important component economies cling to centralized management detracts from CMEA cooperation mechanisms. This model emerged largely from the expressed needs of the participants rather than from a comprehensive approach to what is required to cater effectively to the collective demands of regional economic integration. Formal multilateral settlements of bilateral payments imbalances through the TR as accounting unit are part of this model, but bilateral accounting of real trade flows is kept intact. The model includes the creation of TR settlements and short-term credit at the IBEC, but the *caesura* between money and commodity transactions is maintained. Coordination of investment intentions and the promotion of joint investment financing through the IIB is carried out. The model also includes the establishment of TRPs in CMEA trade that are autonomous and stable through the plan period, although, in fact, they are set bilaterally, almost on an *ad hoc* basis. A multiple exchange rate regime has been elaborated for various types of transactions that are at best poorly interlinked, and regional economic organizations, chiefly to facilitate the coordination of decisions in production, science and technological progress, have been established. As it has matured to date, the CMEA mechanism does not, however, embody a clear-cut set of macroeconomic policies for the region as a whole.

It is essential to realize that none of the above links has ever operated automatically. Because the role of the BTPAs is so central (see chapter 12), not just for ordinary commerce but even for implementing multilateral trade and cooperation agreements, such as in Target Programs, SEI can only be fostered within the frameworks provided by concrete bilateral intergovernmental arrangements. That is not to deny that individual enterprises can sometimes cooperate with each other without the direct intermediation of the MFT. But these activities develop only when the MFT explicitly arranges for them to emerge and flourish. In other words, the linkup between the CMEA as a regional organization and the institutions of the member economies operates in an exceedingly indirect manner. The CMEA organs simply aided the member economies, if they so wished, in formulating and realizing BTPAs that would have been negotiated in any event.

The above proposition can be illustrated by the ineffectiveness of the IBEC in fostering multilateral trade and payments agreements (MPTAs), on which more in chapter 14. Because commodity streams drive monetary flows in the CMEA – not the other way around – and because the IBEC has never been assured of participating in the negotiation of the BTPAs, the bank has remained very passive. Essentially, it handles the accounting operations associated with regional economic transactions. But it plays no role whatsoever in actual negotiations. This state of affairs was, of course, known at the outset, and so the bank was initially to take part in trade negotiations at two levels. In preliminary negotiations it was to help clear intended flows that the CPEs could not accommodate in their BTPAs. But if the parties themselves cannot reach a workable agreement, how much more difficult must it be for the bank to try to superimpose itself upon the negotiating process! It would also later get involved to help offset bilateral imbalances incurred either because of partial noncompliance with the provisions of the BTPA or because one member voluntarily expanded its deliveries beyond volumes contracted in the balanced BTPA. At best it could hope to accomplish this by establishing multiangular trade flows. But the other feature of the trading regime of the CPEs, namely the discordance in bilateral TRPs, must have rendered this task nearly impossible. Under the circumstances, the bank's formal intermediation failed to assist in clearing trade flows that were impossible under the habitual trading schemes of the CPEs, let alone assist in improving the conditions for trade through its lending and clearing policies.

NOTES

1. Thus, consumer price stability has been a solid constant of the credo of socialist policymakers for years, and consumers have been reluctant to tolerate any retail price change. In fact, Soviet renditions of Marxist economic theory during the early phases of revolutionary industrialization posited that prices should steadily decline because socially necessary labor inputs shrink due to technical progress, the growth of labor productivity and rising efficiency in the exploitation of the other means of production (see Miastkowski, 1980, pp. 896–7). In the initial euphoria of socialist construction, it was even argued that this tendency should also emerge in CMEA pricing (see Kohlmey, 1955, pp. 267–8).
2. For a summary of the various forms of the relationship between internal and external prices at the height of the reforms of the 1960s, see Mitrofanova, 1973, pp. 90ff.; Mitrofanova, 1974, pp. 41ff.; UN, 1968, pp. 43ff.; UN, 1973, p. 36.
3. This began in 1978 in a major way with the introduction of the *Kombinate* as the basic units of production. The law that mandated such a reform was not enacted until November 1979, however.

PART III

THE GOALS AND INSTRUMENTS OF SEI

Part III addresses the broad goals and the principal instruments of socialist economic integration (SEI), especially as these are currently evolving. Chapter 10 examines presently prevailing integration goals and offers a broad perspective on the means policymakers hope to utilize for advancing the process of SEI in the years ahead. The main purpose here, unlike in Part I, is to summarize the chief SEI objectives that now prevail. Flashbacks to the preceding decades are also provided in order to trace the origin of what now appears to be crystallizing. This broader approach will also prepare the ground for a rounded discussion in chapter 18 of the changes in SEI policies, institutions and instruments that may appear in connection with the economic reforms going on at national levels as well as within the regional organization. The main channels through which SEI can be actively promoted under prevailing and prospective circumstances will also be highlighted, though emphasis will be placed on prevailing currents because I prefer to minimize speculation on what might eventually materialize in Eastern Europe.

The remaining five chapters of Part III are concerned with the instruments available to the CMEA members for fostering integration. These may be grouped under three headings, namely the organizational, planning and indirect coordination components. The planning and indirect coordination components are assigned here essentially the place that *Integration Program* originally reserved for them, at least in some of the interpretations of that blueprint (see chapter 5). By organizational components I mean something different from the institutional setup of the CMEA, the member economies or the infrastructure for economic relations with third countries, socialist as well as others. It is not possible to neatly separate the particular features of the institutional aspects of SEI from the organizational instruments, just as it is not always possible to divorce planning from the indirect coordination instruments, or to rigorously distinguish between the institutional and policy supports associated with indirect coordination instruments. However, most of the existing institutions offer clear implications for how SEI instruments operate. To a large extent, they set the environment within which the real instruments of SEI can settle and the way in which they can assist the integration processes in the area.

Because the organizational implications and features that affect the SEI instruments are so important, I address them first in chapter 11, after an examination of the purposes of SEI. Chapter 12 is devoted to the planning instruments of SEI. Because of its singular importance in advancing SEI, the entire array of issues related to ECPS and STC agreements is discussed separately from the other planning instruments of SEI in chapter 13. The remaining two chapters concern the indirect coordination instruments of furthering SEI and their supporting institutions (chapter 14) and price formation in the CMEA as perhaps the most critical of the indirect coordination instruments (chapter 15).

10 · THE GOALS AND MEANS OF SEI

The evolution of the official goals of SEI since the Council's creation in 1949 has been detailed in Part I. The main purpose of this chapter is to emphasize the presently prevailing purposes of integration that are being stressed at this juncture and the channels for facilitating their implementation.

A good place to start is with the wrenching soul-searching that policymakers engaged in during the preparation of the June 1984 economic summit. Certain of its manifold aspects have already been discussed in chapters 6 and 7, but others need further elaboration. This discussion inevitably touches upon the major instruments and institutions that have been placed at the disposal of economic agents and technical policymakers, as distinct from the political levels at which decisions on principles are usually entertained. The details thereof, however, are examined in the subsequent five chapters. This is not to deny the supreme role of each country's Communist Party, but I have already covered its paramount position in chapter 7.

In section 10.1 integration in the CMEA is differentiated from what its principal objectives and means are in MEs. I shall refer here mainly to the traditional paradigm and the contrast offered by the integration scheme of the European MEs and the one ostensibly coveted by the centrally planned economies. Section 10.2 illustrates the concept of production specialization as seen since the endorsement of *Basic Principles*, with the main focus on Soviet policies regarding production specialization. Section 10.3 clarifies the various ways through which Eastern European policymakers hope to foster one set of goals rather than another, again with the details being deferred for later review. Some of the precepts held by Eastern European leaders compared to those championed by the USSR are also outlined here. The traditional planning instruments available to foster production specialization are juxtaposed in section 10.4 with other forms of coordinating economic decisions so as to clarify the so-called mechanism of SEI. The key components thereof will be examined in subsequent chapters.

10.1 MARKET AND PRODUCTION INTEGRATION

It should be clear by now that the CMEA aims at enhancing the integration of the CPEs in the production sphere directly rather than through market interaction. Markets inherently foster indirect coordination of the economic decisions of economic agents whose behavior is shaped by the different 'national' entities with which they are associated and by the macroeconomic policies set by national leaders. This effort to bolster coordination may be very passive. For instance, the simple removal of tariffs calls for adjustments in the behavior of economic agents because the effective market has now been enlarged. This process may proceed without any coordination other than what had been practiced before the removal of duties. But it may also be active, as when policymakers deliberately aim at removing other obstacles to the fuller integration of economic agents in this larger market.

As a result of removing impediments that interfere with the smooth conduct of trade and other forms of international economic relations among the participants, policymakers in MEs countries hope to bolster competition in product and factor markets and, in the process, exploit economies of scale to improve factor productivity. Production specialization sets the same overall goals; that is, the smooth conduct of economic relations among the integrating partners. However, this objective is sought primarily by directly coordinating production decisions rather than indirectly through the interactions of demand and supply in competitive markets. The precise shape of the production integration envisioned by the CPEs is the principal topic of Part III.

The contrast between market and production integration is primarily one of emphasis and philosophy rather than an issue derived from fundamental differences in the economic problem as it confronts policymakers in CPEs compared to the way in which markets try to resolve issues. The basic economic task is to fully satisfy the nearly inexhaustible wants of present and future consumers with limited resources. There is nothing particularly special in the nature of resource availability when comparing market and planned economies. Similarly, the wants of consumers in both systems run rather parallel. What is different in the two kinds of societies is the emphasis accorded private preferences contrasted with statewide priorities. The expected behavior of economic agents also sharply differs. While the fundamental economic paradigm is shared by both systems, how their economic organizations tackle the issues and the weights given in ascertaining real economic scarcities can vary remarkably.

Seen against the backdrop of the economic problem *per se*, the core objective of integration in Western and Eastern economies must be much the same. That task is twofold – namely, lessening absolute scarcities and narrowing disparities in relative scarcities by exploiting the economies of scale embedded in dissimilar factor endowments and possibly production processes. But there may be a number of variables, both regarding the objectives and how economists in the two systems try to reach those objectives.

What precisely is the purpose of SEI? No outside observer of the CMEA scene can divine precisely what CPE policymakers may concretely covet as the ultimate goals of their integration endeavors. Mobilizing a group of countries into regional economic cohesion may serve diverse goals, some of which may be purely political, perhaps even just an exercise in exerting individual power over the group. Also, military and strategic considerations may come into play, as might sociocultural ambitions. But surely at some stage of the integration debate, economic tasks must be given considerable weight in choosing the procedures adopted. When economics plays some role, it may be useful to begin with a purely technical or existential observation. Economics is *in se* concerned with economizing scarce means so as to satisfy preferences to the best of agents' and policymakers' ability to manage diverse events. In itself, this basic proposition does not change, no matter in what particular ideology, organization, property relations or other features of the environment it is placed. The precise solution adopted will inevitably be an explicit function of these metaeconomic features. In certain situations, sociopolitical preferences may even overrule economic logic when the goal is satisfying ideologic or political preferences. Soviet collectivization (Conquest, 1986)[1] illustrates this point. Even if integration is pursued for other than economic reasons, costs and benefits will be involved that must be made explicit so that policymakers can be given as accurate a range of decision-making options as circumstances afford. This consideration lies at the heart of Part IV.

Most definitions of economic integration in one way or another stress at least three features. Integration involves a conscious effort by at least two countries to remove barriers to cross-border economic interaction, including trade. Also, by removing obstacles to the equalization of relative scarcities, such countries seek a higher economic optimum, possibly at the expense of other nations. Finally, integration is, essentially, a process that may be finite or practically without a time boundary. It is finite if the members set themselves to accomplishing a concrete goal, such as removing tariff barriers. If they opt for other, more qualitative goals, however, such as those held by EC members who want a fully integrated (Western?) European market, further progress can always be achieved. The integration process is thus without a foreseeable boundary. It would terminate if the participants fully decided to fuse. In that case, integration as a policy issue becomes part of the discourse of regional economics. But this does not remove the inherent logic of integration.

It may be instructive here to briefly clarify a recent view on the issue of integration through the market or through the plan that has been widely propounded, most effectively by Vladimir Sobell (1984). In his approach, the ultimate purpose of integration can be formulated as either of two alternatives: maximizing productive efficiency or using it to equalize levels of development. In the Sobellian world, maximum efficiency is held to be the fundamental goal of an international trade system (ITS), whereas for equalizing development levels Sobell coins the term international protection system, which I modify to an international protection organization (IPO).[2] This format for trading allegedly emerged as a result of a deliberate choice by CPE leaders to protect their self-chosen differentiation from the comparative advantage precepts prevailing elsewhere in the world. Sobell (1984, pp. 6–7) defines the IPO as '. . . an international system of commodity exchange whose purpose is not the maximisation of the benefits of comparative advantage, but the protection and expansion of production, the regulation of which is not by prices reflecting relative scarcities but by bilateral and multilateral intergovernmental agreements reflecting political aspirations.'

While trade effects are very important in an ITS environment, in an IPO the success of integration is a function of the extent to which the mutual exchange of resources ensures steady output expansion. Trade flows within this IPO 'cannot be regarded as trade in the conventional sense but as internal supplies taking place within a virtually closed, self-contained production system, such as a large vertically structured corporation or within the USSR itself between regions' (p. 7). In fact, Sobell's approach is very eclectic. Thus, he sees the CMEA resource flows determined primarily by ideological and technological factors rather than by comparative advantage indicators. Nonetheless, he ardently affirms that 'there has developed a degree of convergence of interests and solidarity which might be interpreted as Comecon-specific inducements to industrial co-operation and specialisation' (p. 25).

The volume, structure and distribution of such commodity flows are perceived to be regulated by individual production unit managers on the basis of ECPS agreements. These are hammered out at bargaining sessions in which production units try to maximize the subsidy they obtain and in which the primary loss-making unit – the USSR – strives to minimize the subsidy it involuntarily extends. Sobell sees the proliferation of ECPS agreements as 'the collective response to alleviate the disadvantages associated with participation in the [CMEA]' (p. 248). The CMEA is accordingly defined as an institution whose main purpose is the international management of the burden of inefficient production. The alleged spreading of the burden of the Soviet subsidy and reduction of the losses incurred from the exchange of hard for soft goods are viewed as the main propellants of industrial cooperation and production specialization.

The primary justification for labeling the CMEA an IPO is supposedly that CMEA cooperation has been used as 'a vehicle for the promotion of Soviet-type industrialisation' (p. 6) or as a potentially 'impressive transnational production system' (p. 21). This position is most odd, to say the least, because at the height of Soviet-type industrialization during the early 1950s the CMEA hardly functioned, and there were no attempts to foster anything even resembling the weakest kind of SEI. In fact, as sketched in Part I, for a long time the Soviet Union was only marginally concerned about how to enforce SEI, although it evidently did not completely ignore integration issues during some phases of postwar developments. Given its preponderant weight in CMEA economic cooperation, the USSR could have imposed on Eastern Europe nearly any type of SEI.

10.2 BROAD RANGE OF PURPOSES

As far as the economics of SEI is concerned, the policy goals of SEI have crystallized only gradually and have undergone several metamorphoses of varying dimensions. At the outset in 1949, the chief economic objective may have been to effectively intermesh the economies so as to overcome economic backwardness, a burdensome agrarian overpopulation, and the legacies of World War II and to address major shifts in ideology and societal organization, a radically different philosophy of development and numerous political transformations. These initial objectives were toned down in the founding communiqué. Extending mutual economic assistance for repelling attempts to interfere with SEI from outside the group became the objective instead. The means then utilized to enact this goal consisted chiefly of instituting ways to facilitate the 'necessary' trade of the CMEA members, primarily from within the region. During rapid industrialization in the early 1950s, SEI also proceeded on the basis of exchanging scientific-technical information, primarily from the more-developed CPEs (especially Czechoslovakia and to a lesser extent the GDR) to the less-developed CMEA members (including Albania, Bulgaria, Rumania and the Soviet Union). Finally, the Council Bureau and the Soviet embassy system of interacting separately with each CMEA partner, if we include this under the heading of (genuine) integration, afforded other kinds of exchange. Perhaps the most important exchange occurred by imposing upon the newly won partners the 'ideal' socialist economic strategy to be pursued and the economic institutions and policy instruments for facilitating the development objectives and metaeconomic goals, which were largely sociopolitical and ideological.

It is important, however, to distinguish, at least for heuristic purposes, between the largely implicit policy objectives in the interaction of the CPEs under Soviet leadership – if perhaps not outright tutelage – in the early 1950s from more recent attempts to explicitly specify the goals of regional cooperation and the structures established to realize them. Since the late 1950s, the CMEA members have made several attempts to adopt explicit goals for regional cooperation and to incorporate as best as circumstances permit the instruments and institutions through which they should be addressed. Three such phases should be distinguished.

Basic Principles was the culmination of a lengthy process by which the CMEA members had been trying to formulate not only operational criteria for regional economic cooperation but also agreements on how best to achieve them. In a way, the goal adopted, perhaps after some inconsequential modification, was simply the projection of national planning onto the regional level. Although such an ultimate purpose may have fitted well with Lenin's vision about the creation of a unified plan for all communist countries, the aims of *Basic Principles* were more modest; that is, the construction of a unified plan for all CMEA countries based on national economic plans. The regional plan would not, of course, have permitted the same degree of freedom in redistributing resources as had been true for each country alone. Not only would local and regional interest groups have to be contended with – indeed, rewarded in some fashion as in each national plan – the CMEA plan would also be constrained by explicit national economic objectives and the need to gradually but steadily equalize levels of development throughout the group. Economic considerations would be integral to the planning process but subjected to the dictates of the 'law of planning' (see chapter 4). Regional planning instruments would of necessity have to be reinforced. At the same time, regional exchange was to be facilitated through the multilateral settlement of accounts and creation of regional enterprises, including one or more financial institutions.

The second critical attempt to arrive at explicit SEI goals and means was divulged in *Integration Program*. Like its predecessor, this program for the 1970s in a way presented the culmination of an intensive search for some method for simultaneously resolving the perceived needs of members of a tightly knit integrating community and the desire to mutate certain of its fundamental traits that no longer proved helpful to the new goals. This inherent conflict was magnified by the diverging needs for national reforms and the apprehension about explicitly changing key characteristics of the community as a whole.

Integration Program is not as explicit on the goals and means of SEI as one might have wished. Nonetheless, the document ensures us that by the early 1970s the CPEs were moving closer to making greater use of economics as a technical means. Pursuing this goal, however, continued to be subject, at least somewhat, to reconciling economic logic with sociopolitical and ideological precepts of regional economic relations among socialist countries. In other words, with a little goodwill, one can read into *Integration Program* that the CPEs were henceforth aiming at narrowing prevailing disparities in relative scarcities as a precondition for attaining an interrelated set of economic and other objectives. The means to do so were not as clearly stated as had been the case with *Basic Principles*. In fact, though *Integration*

Program hints at an integration mechanism, it does not picture one even in its essential dimensions (see chapter 5). Nonetheless, the document contains useful ingredients that may help to pinpoint the kind of SEI mechanism the members were perhaps then looking for. I shall discuss below, in section 10.4, the major building blocks of what might be considered to be the critical components of a mechanism.

The third broad attempt to define the mechanism of SEI coincides with the emerging external adjustment difficulties of most CMEA members in the early and mid-1980s. This attempt is definitely associated with the two recent economic summits, with efforts to endorse and implement *Scientific-Technological Progress* and with the search for ways to blend domestic economic reforms and support them on the basis of a solid integration foothold.

Whereas the aim was originally to buttress the third official document with operational criteria for decision making, the most recent CMEA policy discussions make it appear that an entirely new program is being worked out, namely the *Collective Concept of the ISDL*. Allegedly, its main purpose is to set the foundation for the creation of a common market. Planning instruments will be utilized to chart medium- to long-term strategies. But the operative policy instruments and institutions will be those identified here as assisting with the indirect coordination of policy decisions.

From an economic point of view, the leaders of a regional economic union should vie with each other to minimize the cost of protection associated with union formation – given preferences about the extent and comprehensiveness of the insulating cordon – and seek an equitable distribution rule. Making these components more explicit has been, in my view, a major preoccupation of the reform attempts as amply emphasized in recent discussions at the highest policymaking levels. Indeed, this has been pivotal to the debate on commodity-money relations and the crystallization of an SEI mechanism. In spite of protracted evaluation of alternative means by which SEI might be enhanced, no uniform, cohesive or clearly paramount position has yet evolved. Instead, a serious clash of concepts stemming chiefly from a profound diversity of strategic aims has emerged. The dispute about introducing a market-based mechanism, rather than planning, on an international scale has more dimensions than those readily apparent from the somewhat tautological juxtaposition. It is increasingly acknowledged in the literature and political debates that efficient planning cannot exist without correct market-type indicators.

10.3 PAST ACHIEVEMENTS AND THE SEI MECHANISM

Because of political, ideological and hegemonic overtones, the purposes and means of SEI have historical as well as conceptual dimensions. Conceptually, the mechanism of SEI can be usefully viewed alongside the protracted controversy about possibilities for combining the virtues of the market with the advantages of the plan in promoting regional economic cooperation. Because I primarily need the mechanism as a framework for the discussion in the remainder of Part III, I shall first investigate whether it is necessary to identify a mechanism, because that depends on what the CPEs have been able to achieve in terms of SEI.

As to its historical dimension, perceptions depend on the analyst's view of what the CMEA has thus far achieved and how it has been accomplished. The literature can be divided into four broad categories. One widely held view, especially by Western observers, argues that nothing of note has been realized. As this refutes or ignores any solid results from forty years of close economic cooperation, it is obviously useless to inquire about the underlying economic mechanism because none needs to be postulated.

The second group admits, at most, that Eastern Europe's principal interest in SEI lies in having a relatively reliable, advantageous mechanism of commodity exchange available. Within that framework, the acquisition of primary industrial goods – particularly fuels but also valuable raw materials – from the USSR on favorable terms becomes the backbone of economic collaboration in the CMEA. The terms of trade are generally advantageous for Eastern Europe because the USSR principally imports manufactured goods that, at given CMEA prices, cannot be diverted to third partners without pronounced terms-of-trade losses being incurred, at least in the short to medium run. Note that Western and some Eastern analysts have been careless about the treatment of quantities and prices. Because the majority of their products have a positive price, the CPEs must in principle be able to divert trade to outside economies, even if at a sharp cost. These products may well be below standards prevailing in the most developed market economies, but they can hardly be invariably inferior to the technological standards current somewhere in the nonsocialist world.

Although this second view contains at least a grain of truth, essentially it posits as the SEI mechanism the involuntary, unidirectional redistribution of value added within the integrating group so as to attain some elusive, perhaps even eclectic, policy goal(s). The corollary of this thesis presumably is that once a binding limit is set to this exchange, the very foundation of SEI sags, and may even collapse. Such rationalizing implies that the term integration is not readily justified for CMEA collaboration and that, therefore, there is a small canvas on which a solid SEI mechanism might emerge.

Contrary to the first view, as well as considerably different from the second, is the claim that SEI has been quite successful and that further progress is guaranteed to emanate from the intact policies and instruments. Even in most of their details, such assertions founder on the glaring reality of widespread dissatisfaction so far (see Part IV) with the results of SEI.

These proponents include not only uninformed or inadequately briefed observers; serious economists, from East and West alike, have also endeavored to bolster their claims by reference to quantitative success indicators.

Between the first and the third views lies a more nuanced interpretation that affirms that progress with SEI has been positive but that there remains large room for further improvement and hence marked integration effects. These gains may be captured through trade expansion, greater standardization, higher levels of economic efficiency or more robust growth, or as other improvements in micro- and macroeconomic performance. It is difficult to synthesize this multiple outcome into a single aggregate success indicator, such as gains in trade, growth or efficiency. This is because of the disequilibrium in these economies, which is not directly addressed when the CPEs formulate integration policies. In fact, it may well not be an explicit objective of the SEI drive; otherwise it would be platitudinous to advocate some variant of the thesis that greater efficiency can be obtained with less trade (on which more below). Typical for this group of observers, with whom I associate myself, is the presumption that these, potentially vast, integration gains can be reaped only if more flexible forms of economic cooperation are gradually resorted to. These comprise policies that are specifically designed to steer the economies individually and as a group by macroeconomic means while simultaneously enacting shifts in the organization, institutional setting and policy instruments that determine the environment within which agents are expected to rationally operate. There are different ways in which these tasks could be accomplished (Brabant, 1987a, pp. 399–417). One useful mode would be by anchoring indirect coordination instruments within a constitutional framework.[3]

10.4 ON THE MECHANISM OF SEI

An important attribute of integration concerns the policy means by which the process is to be fostered. These means may vary greatly in composition between the market and plan extremes, to revert back again to these clichés. In a market environment, integration is in principle fostered primarily by removing obstacles that inhibit the smooth functioning of the market. In the plan context, however, integration is enhanced through direct intergovernmental agreements on what particular aspects of the integration process need to be addressed, in what degree of detail and against which time horizon. Usually the object of planned integration is, by definition, the integration of some aspects of production and consumption planning rather than the creation of uniform markets, even if conceptually adapted to the CPE world.

Production specialization is not usually a familiar concept to the student raised in the Western economic tradition. To be clear, then, the mechanism of the SEI must be elucidated because it has acquired a special meaning, particularly since *Integration Program*, even though it first appeared during the economic reforms of the 1960s. Its principal features, although not always transparent and variously emphasized by different authors, generally mirror those of the members' economic model, as briefly caricatured in chapter 9.

The mechanism of SEI is a complex topic, and it is often unclear what is precisely meant by it. Basically, it stands on three pillars: the legal, economic and institutional-organizational aspects of SEI. The legal issues, though important and sometimes critical to the realization of purely economic aims, fall outside the purview of this study. Organizational aspects were discussed in Part II in connection with the regional institutions. Other organizational features will be analyzed in chapter 11. Because opportunities for intensifying cooperation and enhancing the implementation of agreements already reached, in principle, at the level of political command depend on the proper economic stimulation, here I shall focus on the economic means by which the CPEs hope to foster SEI processes.

I define the economic mechanism of SEI as the set of interrelated measures comprising policy instruments, institutions and guidelines or rules on micro- and macroeconomic behavior and policies that have been mobilized to attain regional development goals that are congruent with the policies and institutions of the economies involved. As such, the mechanism resembles the economic model of the members, though there are also differences. The most important subsystems of the traditional CPE economic mechanism comprise centralized allocation of resources; directive central planning of the activities of economic agents, particularly in the production sphere, through mandatory plan indicators and associated gauges for measuring and rewarding plan fulfillment; centralized redistribution of income; administrative setting of material and other incentives; and other subsystems (see chapter 9). Gradually, a system of vested interests has emerged at various producer and consumer levels and this has molded the behavior of economic agents such that it does not generally conform to the exigencies of an intensive development pattern (Pilat and Dăianu, 1984, p. 254). These elements of the domestic economic mechanism of the CPEs are unambiguous. Those to be included in the SEI mechanism are not. Little controversy arises in connection with the listing of elements. It is when one tries to assess their relative importance in encouraging regional cooperation that serious conceptual and practical problems crop up.

Unfortunately, there is no standard source on what one should understand as *the* SEI mechanism. Even *Integration Program* is not a rounded discourse on the coveted integration mechanism, although it sets forth interesting views on essential components of such an ideal integration model and the submechanisms that will eventually need elaboration and endorsement. But here I shall delve only into the economic components.

The program essentially proposes three types of economic instruments and institutions to be perfected in the process of SEI: policy consultations, integrating economic plans and indirect coordination of economic decisions. The first two are naturally closely intertwined in that plan coordination is generally pursued by government agencies fairly high in the planning hierarchy, where political precepts, including on economic matters, routinely come into play. For now I am keeping them separate, but in chapter 12 I consider them together under the rubric plan coordination. Being by their very nature CPEs, the CMEA members must reserve an important role for planning, and not only to formulate the implementation modalities of a jointly conceived SEI strategy. Planning is also essential in the actual implementation of jointly formulated cooperation endeavors. Currently, planning mechanisms are quite differentiated and range from simple *ex ante* trade agreements to complex joint plans. Most of this activity concerns plan coordination. But there is a rapidly growing component that can be identified as a higher stage of economic planning, including joint planning. The importance of joint planning has been raised severalfold since the mid-1970s, provided one does not needlessly confine its connotation to the drafting of an all-encompassing joint plan, something that is not soon likely to materialize.

Given the circumstances under which *Integration Program* was conceived and drafted, it could treat the involute issues of plan coordination and joint planning at a more general level. An operational program for closer planning cooperation was to be worked out during 1971 and then steadily improved upon as new problems arose and further experience was gained. With the exception of the coordination of medium- and long-term plans, which, as a matter of principle, should become routine, the program left common forecasting, joint planning and the exchange of experiences to the discretion of interested members. Synchronizing medium- and long-term plans was to become more important, however, because governments agreed to submit draft plans to the other CPEs and to the Council organs. These preliminary plans on investment and distribution strategies were slated as the starting point for detailed discussions on the most advantageous prospects of each CPE and the community as a whole. But it was made clear that no member can be compelled to scratch a particular project if it is deemed 'untouchable,' even if realization of it endangers regional cooperation objectives and interferes with the interests of other Council members. A conspicuous place in plan coordination is reserved for the promotion of STC.

Second, plan coordination is not to be pursued in a vacuum. It must shape high-level policy decisions into operational plan tasks with the assistance of other policy instruments. An important role in SEI was allocated to frequent bi- and multilateral consultations on a vast array of national and international economic policies. Instead of being placed in a proper institutional framework, frequent policy consultations were to be conducted at the governmental and planning levels as well as by all those responsible for drafting and implementing plans. The levels, forms and procedures of these consultations, as well as the topics to be discussed, were to be decided by interested members who, in principle, commit themselves to certain common targets but reserve the right to determine what concretely needs to be done in each case, which includes the option of opting out. Perhaps this explains why one searches the document in vain for specification of the broad institutional infrastructure that will support CMEA plan coordination.

Third, *Integration Program* devotes considerable attention to the indirect means of coordinating economic decisions. These instruments (for example, exchange, wage and interest rates, credits of various maturities and prices) and their associated institutional props (including multilateralism, common banks, transferability and factor mobility) are expected to bolster integration in the draft phase of the plans and to then assist in the implementation of coordinated plans. Such monetary and financial market-type instruments are not expected to be allotted a significant role at the stage of plan formulation or while common projects are being set up; this is preempted for planning and plan coordination. Though the crucial role of instruments of indirect coordination and their associated institutions is acknowledged, these decision-making levers are not to be the ones that will determine common tasks. They may, however, help in the concrete formulation and implementation of SEI. Comparative advantage indicators will be utilized, but within the framework of common and coordinated planning. Recent debates on reforming the CMEA suggest that the CPEs may soon usher in important shifts in the range of indirect coordination policies, instruments and institutions and their role in fostering SEI.

In fact, for our purposes it is instructive to distinguish five interrelated components of the economic mechanism:

1. Economic policy consultations.
2. Synchronization of sectoral and overall economic plans and joint planning.
3. Trading price systems and how they interact with each other and with domestic price systems.
4. Financial and monetary cooperation systems, including interstate credit mechanisms.
5. Matters concerning STC.

I am separating the price system from the broader aspects of monetary and financial cooperation because TRPs continue to play such a critical role in the gestation of SEI, even under directive central planning. This focal concern would not diminish even if the other, more market-oriented, aspects of financial and monetary cooperation were to recede.

10.4.1 The planning mechanism

From the early 1970s until very recently, there was little dissent at official policymaking levels about the importance of integrating national economic plans. As the chief subset of instruments to promote SEI, plan integration is inherently a process 'regulated in a deliberate and planned way,' as *Integration Program* does not fail to stress. Normally, national central planning boards have been responsible for coordinating activities in 'broad cooperation' with Council organs. Plan coordination involves deepening common efforts in five directions simultaneously. First, the members resolved to jointly forecast future demand and supply levels as the foundation for developing concrete plans. Those forecasts would reconcile the levels that planners might hope to achieve with the need to meet consumer demands. Second, the CPEs decided to pursue long-term perspective planning in the form of Target Programs in order to regulate the chief determinants of primary economic activities. Third, plan coordination also anticipates compromises on the basic aims of national economic policies. Such compromise should be worked out at the highest policymaking levels as well as through frequent and intensive consultations on numerous national and regional economic policies. Fourth, traditional methods of coordinating medium-term plans need to be improved so that the compass of coordination can be shifted at the earliest draft stages away from the trade sphere toward production and investment strategies. The areas envisaged include STC, production specialization in accordance with regional market forces, the joint construction of investment projects and the scope and timing of reciprocal commodity exchange. Finally, plan coordination is also sought on a voluntary basis in the form of joint planning of selected economic branches or specific production types.

However vaguely defined in *Integration Program*, joint planning is a distinct category inasmuch as it could become an embryonic form of regionwide planning, with the special feature that it is still currently facultative, which is a sharp contrast with the obligatory nature of annual and medium-term plan coordination. Properly speaking, joint planning should be understood as consisting of three parts. First, a coherent complex of linked documents exists, some of which may have been jointly prepared, that covers the kind and volume of work done, the resources required to implement the agreement, the participation of individual countries, the concrete economic and administrative agents responsible for individual plans of the projects agreed upon and the technical and economic terms of cooperation. The second component envelops a set of legally binding agreements concerning the results of integrated work programs and which covers the tasks of CMEA bodies, IEOs or individual countries. Finally, special parts of the national medium-term and annual socioeconomic plans reflect each country's duty to execute the tasks of joint planning (see Kerner and Trubač, 1975, pp. 103–12). A particularly conspicuous place in plan harmonization is reserved for the promotion of STC, which comprises research, development, production specialization and perhaps even joint marketing and distribution activities, with assistance provided by planning and indirect coordination instruments. An STC mechanism is considered essential for fostering technical progress and intensifying production in each country and in the region as a whole.

10.4.2 Instruments of indirect economic coordination

Since the mid-1950s, policymakers have sporadically concerned themselves with the instruments and institutions that help to coordinate economic decisions indirectly. *Integration Program* also highlights these means and acknowledges their crucial role in fostering SEI from the draft phase through the implementation of coordinated plans. Such means were not, however, to be given primacy in the formulation of plans or in the establishment of common projects; these were preempted for planning and plan coordination. But even in the 1950s they were seen as useful for assisting with the concrete formulation and implementation of common and coordinated plans. They are bound to be even more esteemed in the era of generalized *perestrojka*.

There is an entire array of indirect instruments of economic coordination as well as a variety of institutional supports. The most important are those pertaining to price, monetary and credit systems (Špaček, 1981, p. 15).

10.4.2.a The collective currency

As the preeminent socialist currency, the TR was gradually to have been transformed into a real international currency, at least for intragroup relations. This goal was to be promoted by improving those economic and organizational conditions that circumscribe the TR. Modifications were to evolve slowly in order for the CPEs to squarely face up to the tasks arising at each stage of SEI. In particular, the CPEs' hopes were high for ensuring the transferability of the TR and establishing realistic, stable exchange rates. The fundamental prerequisite for this is proper pricing. Only by tackling the price system can conditions be sufficiently improved so that the TR can become a real currency unit capable of supporting trade as well as specialization, STC and joint investment. However, decisions need not always be based solely on rational economic criteria.

On numerous occasions the CMEA members have agreed to enact measures that would change the TR into something more useful than a simple regional accounting unit. They also want to enhance its role so that it can eventually join other international currencies in global markets and more adequately reflect the position of the CMEA in the world economy. Foremost among the preliminary steps will be elaborating the conditions under which nonmembers can participate in the system of multilateral settlements in TR.

10.4.2.b CMEA price mechanisms

For many years now, CMEA members have studied the feasibility of gradually reducing the substantial differences between retail and wholesale prices, of improving TRP formation and of enhancing the links between domestic and trade prices. At the same time, they have emphasized the importance of adhering to the principle of fixing contract prices on the basis of past WMPs, albeit with modifications of the criteria by which prices are adjusted. Determination of adequate relative TRPs is a paramount precondition for promoting efficiency in each member economy and hence SEI.

10.4.2.c National, regional and other exchange rates

Provided the CPEs really intend to transform the TR into an international currency, or even only a regional medium of exchange, they need to set realistic exchange rates for their own currencies and the TR. This is especially important for making the CMEA settlements system truly fungible within the region and attractive to other countries without jeopardizing the stability of national and regional economic policies. For the TR to properly function as an international currency, it must have 'real' purchasing power for all potential holders. This can be accomplished only if the participants unanimously agree on the mechanism that sets and maintains a realistic exchange rate – hence realistic TRPs. But such a critical parameter cannot emerge from free market forces or from unplanned competitive pressures exerted by real demand and supply forces of the member countries.

The exchange rate issue is seen primarily within the context of intragroup transactions. The present system of multiple rates inhibits even the expedient merging of the partial plans all members have fully agreed upon. Each country must set its own exchange rates for commercial, as distinct from so-called noncommercial, transactions at an economically meaningful level. Their various rates should also be reduced to a single common denominator through actions on the domestic price front. First focus should be placed on wholesale prices and later on a better integration of retail with wholesale prices. These actions would permit the creation of an interrelated set of exchange rates for commercial transactions that fall under SEI decisions. The same should be pursued for nonmerchandise exchange. A uniform exchange rate can then be declared at least *vis-à-vis* the TR and, at a later stage, also for convertible currencies. Whether these rates should eventually be set in response to actual or simulated market forces with frequent fluctuations depends on the underlying exchange regime that the CPEs are willing to support. It is a particularly important function of the degree to which each country links domestic with foreign trade prices. In other words, the desired degree of domestic price autonomy is central.

10.4.2.d Interest rates

The forward price of goods and services is a potentially critical determinant of many features underlying any type of regional economic integration. But this depends on a realistic time preference. Such a proper trade-off enables decision makers to allocate resources intertemporally as well as spatially. Moreover, such comparisons are critical for establishing an effective capital market, institutionalizing a smoothly functioning system of multilateral settlements and instituting other aspects of regional economic cooperation.

10.4.2.e Wage rates and related parameters

If regional mobility of workers is to be effectively secured, not only must an infrastructure be provided that will foster such movement but workers must also be free to do so voluntarily through material and other incentives tailored to the principal goals of SEI. For this to actually happen, the CPEs must cooperate in formulating wage and wage-related income and welfare policies, especially if unplanned migration is to be discouraged by economic rather than political means.

10.4.3 Institutional supports for indirect instruments

Intensifying CMEA cooperation critically depends on having in place an appropriate organizational and institutional infrastructure. In the context of indirect economic cooperation, I shall refer to the creation of direct ties among economic agents, the multilateralization of regional trade and payments, convertibility, the conditions for an effective capital market, labor mobility and so on.

10.4.3.a Decentralized decision making

Although the issue of allowing firms to interact across national borders has been repeatedly debated since the mid-1960s, direct regional economic relations, as distinct from informal contacts at the lower rungs of the planning hierarchies, are not expected to play a central role in plan coordination or in the formulation and implementation of concrete aspects of SEI. Because this so depends on the domestic organization of the CPEs, the CMEA, as a regional institution, can do little to foster direct contacts beyond involving major firms and their associations in the early stages of discussions about STC and ECPS agreements. As *Integration Program* affirms, each country organizes its economy according to its own conditions by taking 'steps to create within the framework of national economic planning and management systems the requisite economic, organizational and legal conditions for the successful realization' (Tokareva, 1972, p. 100) of the program.

10.4.3.b Multilateralization of trade and payments

Changes in the trade sector, especially the transition to multilateralism, have been promised for many years. These were to be effected in many ways, including a search for greater flexibility in BTPAs and permitting nonquota trade, less rigorous annual balancing and greater capital mobility. At various times members agreed to sharply improve traditional principles, methods and tasks of economic cooperation and to explore new possibilities within the existing CMEA framework. Because little transpired from these efforts until the ongoing reform, SEI has had to be fostered within the existing national institutions and through the methods available within the CMEA organization.

Multilateralism is largely contingent on the TR's role. Without making excess TR earnings interchangeable, regional bilateralism will likely remain; there is even less hope that MEs will embrace the TR as a medium of exchange. Without eliminating bilateralism in a constructive way, the CPEs cannot realistically expect that the TR will eventually support other SEI goals (such as improving TRPs and establishing a capital market). Therefore, it is expedient to separate multilateralism from the more restricted task of the TR's transferability and its eventual convertibility. Enhancing the TR primarily depends on creating stable multilateral trade and accumulating reserves that will permit multilateral settlements.

10.4.3.c Convertibility

Conceptually, convertibility of the national currencies and the TR should not be confused with transferability or multilateralism, although all three are intimately related. Whether the aim of the CPEs is to render their currencies and the TR fully convertible or whether foreign exchange will be subject to differentiated limitations is crucial to future relations of the CPEs with each other and with third countries. Though officials have discussed convertibility for the TR as well as for domestic currencies for nearly two decades, it remains fundamentally unclear what particular type of convertibility is being envisioned and how realistic such a policy goal might be. *Integration Program* affirmed that the member countries would study and prepare for the implementation of regional convertibility; the conditions and procedures for introducing it, and in what forms, were to be jointly worked out according to what is suitable for each CPE. Although the official stipulations are consistent with various modalities, the CPEs are certainly not aiming at full convertibility, nor are they intending to abolish or significantly weaken the currency monopoly.

The recently introduced agreements on instituting, beginning in 1989, some limited form of regional convertibility among certain CPEs works precisely in the direction that *Integration Program* may have already intended since 1971. All that policymakers hope to accomplish is to facilitate settlement of preselected transactions among firms by guaranteeing anonymity and automatic settlement via the TR accounting system at the IBEC.

10.4.3.d Capital mobility
It is useful to distinguish between credits and direct investments because they have different effects and implications. Credits are critical for ensuring that the two CMEA banks function properly and especially strengthen the banks' ability to contribute to enhancing integration. In other words, the role of settlements and short-term credits (in the case of the IBEC) and of investment credits (in the case of the IIB) depends on how the banks are allowed to operate within the context of trade and payments arrangements that are reached on quite a different level.

Related issues pertain to investment itself, whether it is undertaken through national planning, direct interfirm contracts or joint economic organizations. An entire array of planning, management and control issues could be discussed, but this is not the proper place in which to do so. The CPEs should develop appropriate economic, legal and organizational prerequisites so that these agreements are compatible with internal planning and regional plan coordination.

10.4.3.e Labor mobility
In a world with free movement of capital and labor, as well as goods, the gradual leveling of relative scarcities can be expected to proceed the fastest and farthest. So far the CPEs have severely restricted labor mobility because of various economic, ideological, political and other noneconomic considerations. The prevailing impediments should be seen chiefly against the background of the isolation and decision-making autonomy coveted by each CPE.

Now that the core planning and market-type instruments and institutions of SEI have been sketched, I can clarify how they have functioned and interacted with their national counterparts, and whether they have functioned well or poorly. The first set of issues, which covers the organizational and planning sides of the mechanism, is addressed in the next three chapters. In the subsequent two chapters the monetary-financial aspects are discussed. The second set of issues is explored in detail in Part IV.

NOTES

1. I do not deny that collectivization may also have had important economic tangents, including the transfer of the surplus to finance industrial expansion. This thesis has, however, been contested by Michael Ellman (1975, 1978) on the

grounds that, over the long haul, agriculture received more investment resources than the surplus it delivered to the state.

2. Though this terminology is not free of ideology, I retain it here to explain Sobell's thesis. I shall revert to the more familiar extremes of integration through the market or through production in subsequent sections.

3. For details, particularly in the case of Poland, see the useful elaborations in Kowalik, 1986. I have used this framework to argue the case for CMEA reform as well (Brabant, 1987e, 1987f, 1987g).

11 · ORGANIZATIONAL INSTRUMENTS

Because economic activity in centrally planned economies is highly regimented, many organizational instruments are associated with SEI. These comprise planning instruments, institutional and other requirements for indirectly coordinating economic decisions, various institutions of the member countries and the regional organization as a whole and the national and regional infrastructure of the CPEs and the CMEA. The most important institutional aspects of the CPEs as they have evolved, as well as of the CMEA organization itself, were explained in Part II. Because the process of SEI depends on more than the actual organization chosen to carry out the coordination of the MFT, FTOs, price equalization, BTPAs and other features of the foreign trade and payments regimes of the CPEs, the foreign trade sector must be examined in greater detail.

The organizational aspects of SEI are many. In this chapter I underline five broad topics that relate to the critical elements of regional economic organization. First, I elaborate further on the organization of trade in CPEs and pay particular attention to the MFT, the FTOs, the price-equalization mechanism, the currency monopoly and segmented currency markets. In section 11.2 I briefly discuss the organization of planning, including the technique of material balances, macro- and microeconomic planning in physical detail, the extensive subordination of the financial infrastructure to real targets and other issues. Particularly important for gauging the role of the CMEA are bilateralism and structural bilateralism, which are examined in sections 11.4 and 11.5 following an analysis of the nature of BTPAs in section 11.3. Many of these elements exhibit tangents that pertain to broader issues of foreign policy, including hegemony and superpower ambitions. Because such societywide policy issues cannot be completely divorced from purely organizational questions, I shall touch upon them if and when they help to explain the emergence of trade regimes. The last section looks at the organizational components of the SEI mechanism, particularly at the organs (including the Planning Committee, SCFT, SCEP and SCFQ) that assist in coordinating policies.

11.1 THE ORGANIZATION OF FOREIGN TRADE

One of the most critical components of the traditional economic model of the CPE is the nearly complete disjunction of domestic from external economic activities. External trade and payments in the typical CPE, as with most other economic activities, fall under central policy control and resort *de facto* under the central plan, which includes plan formulation and implementation as well as the planning process. As noted in chapter 9, this came about through the nationalization of foreign trade and the creation of the MFT as two of the most significant policy decisions that were implemented soon after the countries shifted to socialist-type development. The separation of markets even extends to intragroup relations, although in and of itself this may stifle SEI. But I shall not dwell on the possible rationales for ushering in such a nearly complete *caesura* between domestic and external markets in plan formulation and implementation.

The MFT simply means that the right to engage in any foreign transaction belongs exclusively to the state even if the state opts not to exercise this right directly. External trade and payments are under the strict control of numerous central government agencies that belong to two institutional hierarchies (Grote, 1981; Konstantinov, 1984) which themselves are subordinate to the Planning Commission and the chief policymakers. The first, captured under the label trade monopoly, is concerned with real flows of goods and services. It consists of the Ministry of Foreign Trade, FTOs and firms authorized to trade on their own account, the customs administration, the chamber of commerce, trade research institutions and various ancillary entities. The second is the exchange, foreign currency or valuta monopoly, which is concerned with all the monetary aspects of foreign economic relations. The valuta monopoly is usually entrusted to the Ministry of Finance but also encompasses the National Bank, the Foreign Trade Bank or its equivalent (where established), financial research organs and institutes and foreign currency shops. It issues permits that entitle domestic trading or producing firms to acquire foreign exchange. From those domestic agents the valuta monopoly purchases all foreign exchange obtained, including that from private transactions.

The MFT empowers the state to undertake external market relations, to procure goods sold abroad and to dispose of foreign goods according to national economic needs as perceived by macroeconomic policymakers. Given this concentration of power, even technical trade decisions may be subject to the primacy of politics – for example, commercial diplomacy. The MFT definitely tries to protect the economy against undesirable fluctuations abroad. Naturally, the state itself does not conduct trade operations, nor does itself formulate all trade decisions. The MFT really means that authorization to engage in foreign transactions can be granted only by the Ministry of Foreign Trade within the policy guidelines of the plan and the targets therein expressed. Actual transactions are normally entrusted to FTOs and, since the reforms of the 1960s, to individual enterprises or their associations.

Authority to engage in trade usually implies the right to acquire foreign exchange. Therefore, the Ministry of Foreign Trade must synchronize its decisions with the positions of those in charge of foreign exchange matters. The Ministry evaluates whether or not a proposed transaction is required for performing the tasks stipulated in the plan. Until recently these authorizations were issued by or under close supervision of central authorities. The basic issues concerning the level, commodity composition and geographic distribution of trade were resolved while the overall central plan was being formulated and implemented. Details of these operations with broadly defined trading zones (see below) were delegated to FTOs. The implications of this type of decision making and organization will first be explored with reference to the stylized model of the CPE and will subsequently be expanded by including specific features of the CPEs.

The MFT is designed to neutralize all influences from abroad, whether beneficial or disruptive. In fact, it ensures that autonomously set trade targets (quantities as well as prices) are strictly implemented, circumstances permitting. Unlike in MEs, therefore, trade does not emanate from market relations. This deliberate avoidance of short-term market opportunities may be understandable given the prevalence of taut planning, which inhibits acting upon trade opportunities as they arise. The traditional CPE often operates within a narrow margin of flexibility in terms of foreign exchange reserves, exportable commodities not earmarked in the plan or access to foreign loans. This ignoring of comparative advantage extends to annual and medium-term plans, which are often drafted with only cursory attention to external trade. Even adverse trade results do not necessarily induce changes in trade positions in the course of the current planning period. But they may impact on the subsequent plan, provided that current disturbances can be bridged through loans, foreign exchange reserves, extra exports and other such measures.

This practically complete disjunction between trade and the domestic economy extends in particular to the transmission of price signals. The key instrument that separates domestic and foreign trade activities is the so-called price-equalization mechanism. This simply means that the FTO buys or sells domestically at the centrally set fiat prices but sells and purchases abroad at the 'prevailing' foreign trade prices (which mostly applies to trade with the West since negotiated TRPs govern relations within the CMEA). Many noncompeting imports do not have a domestic fiat price and so a price is computed in line with the domestic price regime.

Differences between foreign prices normalized by the official or the commercial exchange rates and the corresponding domestic prices are offset through a budget account kept at the central bank. Because exchange rates are usually overvalued in terms of convertible currencies, and hence WMPs (see chapter 15), exports must usually be subsidized and imports taxed so as to bridge the price gap. But there are no fixed price rules for the bulk of traded goods and services; the substantial domestic price autonomy sought by CPEs prohibits this. Under those distorted relative prices and the separation of domestic from foreign producers and consumers, there is little leeway available for making decisions on the basis of differences between domestic and foreign trade prices. Thus, there is a tendency to confine trade to imports implied by plan targets. The insulation of the domestic economy against actual or potential influences from abroad strictly holds in the microeconomic sphere. As long as that impact is not too large, neutralizing foreign fluctuations is also characteristic of macroeconomic decision making, which can proceed without heeding real profits and losses until a foreign exchange crisis erupts. Crises may stem from depleted foreign exchange reserves, inability to raise revenue through incremental exports, vanishing access to further foreign credits or from other factors.

The official exchange rate is not an important parameter in allocating resources. Trade decisions usually result from economic and other forces. Planning of the level and composition of trade, as of other economic activities, is largely intermeshed with the overall system of material balances. Whether to import or to produce a product locally is a question typically answered by assessing domestic availability of inputs and the need to pay for imports. The central planner, therefore, exhibits only marginal interest in reaping the potential benefits of export-led growth or in minimizing the real economic cost of the preferred import substitution. The technique of material balances might help to ensure equality between physical demand and supply, but it is not conducive to efficiently exploiting trade opportunities.

The MFT is in charge of implementing the trade plan(s), such as they are set. It attempts to do so by determining the geographic distribution of trade, partly in accordance with the commodity composition of potential exports and imports as prescribed on the basis of the domestic imbalances included in the overall socioeconomic plan. But it must also ensure that economic units do not ignore the important foreign policy role that can be ascribed to external trade and payments. Although, in principle, the MFT is asked to acquire the targeted imports with a minimum of export outlays (and thus square accounts), the degree to which it can patiently select among alternative markets is subject to limitations arising, among others, from bilateralism, currency convertibility, embargoes and trade controls.

The rigid separation between the domestic economy and foreign trade has been modified to some extent in all CPEs since the late 1950s. Though a closer interrelationship has existed since then between domestic and trade prices, the connection has remained weak even under the best circumstances. In fact, many CPEs still insist on delinking domestic and trade prices in the hope of preserving domestic price autonomy especially of competing imports

(Forner, 1987, p. 1479). To the extent that stable trade prices cannot normally be ensured by only one partner, the CPEs neutralize, as much as possible, short-term fluctuations in trade prices through the price-equalization mechanism and regulate external trade chiefly through BTPAs. Reforms of the trade sector, therefore, do not necessarily seek to abolish the MFT.

11.2 PLANNING, BTPAs AND THE DOMESTIC ORGANIZATION OF TRADE

One of the principal factors restricting a CPE's choice of alternative trade partners stems from the organization of external trade and payments, which has been appended to detailed central planning of the domestic economy. Without state control over external transactions, it would have been more difficult to sustain policy autonomy through far-reaching central planning and hierarchical control of domestic production, trade and money. The particular form in which this state control is expressed in practical matters depends on the specific configuration of domestic planning. That is, the issue of the overall role of trade in development as an economic problem may be quite different from how it is resolved under various concrete economic models. I shall therefore first look at the problem in its own right and then sketch how it has been managed in the classical and the partially reformed CPE.

11.2.1 Trade and economic planning

The similarity of the economic paradigm in CPEs and MEs (see chapter 10) also holds in the foreign sector, despite overall policy prescriptions that impose constraints on the conduct of trade. The trade theory of the ideal CPE should closely parallel the conventional discourse. Difficulties arise when we attempt to rationalize actual trade behavior. Admittedly, a real market-type economy also fails to behave exactly as economic theory prescribes. Unlike CPEs, however, trade decisions in such an economy are more easily rationalized in terms of standard theory. But this parallelism loses much of its poignancy when the instruments and information available to economic agents in the two kinds of societies are confronted.

The CPE's lack of adequate and ample value criteria for making choices poses formidable problems in reaching efficient trade decisions. Furthermore, trade as such creates dilemmas for central planning because it depends on demand and supply forces that cannot be controlled by a single national planning center. This conflicts with the desire to generate rapid and stable economic development by concentrating resources in pacemaking sectors. Import substitution, the planner's perceived requirement of stability and the felt need to protect the domestic economy against foreign disturbances generally compress trade below levels warranted by considerations of efficiency. Overenthusiastic compliance with the requirements of socialist organization ultimately calls for rigid trade controls under the aegis of the MFT.

As trade cannot be altogether dispensed with, it remains a sector that eludes the complete control of one planning center and can hardly be managed in quantitative terms. Nevertheless, to gain greater stability in domestic economic activity, the CPEs have traditionally also tried to accurately forecast trade flows. But not all activities and fluctuations abroad are predictable. Born out of necessity in the immediate postwar economic, political and strategic constellation of forces, detailed *ex ante* BTPAs at relatively stable, if artificial, TRPs suited the administrative planning system fairly well. In addition, they facilitated implementing political aspirations that would have been risky in a multilateral trade network. In other words, the perceived need to control trade as if it were a domestic economic sector imposes a passivity hitherto allotted to exports. This follows in particular from the fact that the plan demands that more attention be devoted to fulfilling the minimum imports required to offset shortfalls in material balances. As a result, socialist policymakers attach great importance to trade planning as a basic tool for attenuating the degree of uncertainty inherent in forecasting and engaging in foreign commerce.

The trade-reducing effect of the planning institutions is by no means the only or principal explanation behind the CPE's relative disregard for trade. As noted, trade and other economic interactions between nations is intricately bonded with their overall foreign policy. The traumatic experience of postrevolutionary Soviet Russia, which was faced with threats from all countries as well as with the profoundly insular and nationalistic mentality of its leadership in the 1930s, dictated a trade strategy that was, in fact, not a strategy at all but an attempt to eventually cut ties with the rest of the world. These formative experiences with socialist trade policies imparted autarkic features to the development strategy imposed on Eastern Europe. Though not all import-substitution endeavors succeeded, this permeation of concerns about safeguarding national security and promoting autonomous development is crucial for understanding the CPE's trade policies.

11.2.2 Trade organization in the classical CPE

The primary tool used in the traditional CPE to select the level and commodity composition of trade, particularly of imports, is physical product balances. These so-called material balances form the principal CPE planning instrument. They are drawn up so that demand and supply of key products and services are equated. Demand needs result both from the preferences of political leaders and from constraints emanating from production possibilities, consumption needs and trade opportunities. On the other hand, supply from domestic and foreign sources is stipulated with greater autonomy, at least as far as the domestic components and the *ex ante* selection of imports are concerned. The stipulated level and composition of trade largely result from the need for noncompeting imports, export commitments and the relative shortages and surpluses revealed in the process of balancing the economy. The geographic distribution of trade is, in principle, selected so that surpluses flow to the markets yielding the largest effective return and shortages are met by importing at the lowest possible cost. However, several exogenous constraints stemming from economic and other conditions typical of CPEs curtail the number of feasible alternatives that can be explored. The likelihood that the distribution of trade can be optimal is, under the circumstances, exceedingly remote.

Ideally, trade contracts concluded as an integral part of the general economic plan should lead to the indirect coordination, but not optimization, of various national plans by merging individual components of the CPE's trade needs. This desire to ensure more stability in trade through formal agreements is, as noted, already an important restriction on the distribution of trade. Economic and political circumstances chosen partly by the CPE itself and partly imposed by whatever concrete geopolitical realities then exist further compress the degree to which markets that yield the highest export return or entail the lowest import expenditure can be chosen.

The principal internal factor limiting a CPE's market choice is the administrative system of planning with material balances, which ignores or is unable to assimilate real relative prices and even precludes the creation of market-clearing prices. This planning instrument's main effect in terms of determining the level and composition of trade consists of ignoring relative production costs, alternative production processes and trade programs and the interdependencies between trade and investment. Apart from its failure to encourage optimal choice, a possibly more significant factor is its inflexible nature (Montias, 1959, pp. 242–51).

Socialist growth strategy also consciously disregards alternative development paths that require substantial trade participation. Also not to be overlooked is that the ideology dominant in the CPEs and its conflicts with other policies may preclude trade with certain countries despite their obvious economic potential.[1] These obstacles are probably more important in generating the distribution of trade than, say, differentiated tariff or exchange rate policies, which do play some role in distributing the trade earmarked for nonsocialist countries as a whole or to their principal components.

As experience was gained with socialist administration and as the economy reached a higher level of complexity, decision makers began to explore ways of taking advantage of external trade as a focal contributor to buoyant economic activity. Trade matters are usually at the center of concerns that lead up to economic reforms.

11.2.3 Trade and economic reforms

Because the level and composition of imports are largely predicated on the economic strategy pursued, research on those CPEs that embark on partial devolution has primarily been concerned with export efficiency. This has been reflected in the modification of organizational links, institutions and policy instruments affecting trade during the reform process. Note, however, that the more general problem of how to minimize the domestic and foreign cost of exports for a given import bill cannot be unambiguously solved, especially as prices based on average production costs do not express true scarcities; they may be very misleading if used in determining the composition of exports. Also, CPEs are not completely free to select the most advantageous trade channels; this difficulty stems from bilateral trade policies, specific preferences for domestic development, currency inconvertibility, non-scarcity TRPs and the fiat type of clearing imports and exports in CMEA markets.

In view of these and other matters, trade reforms can assume different shapes, but not all elements can be examined here. I shall only touch upon the four critical areas affected by reforms and shall not even try to clarify which CPE accomplished what particular reform in any of the three components enumerated above.

11.2.3.a Prices and exchange rates

A crucial first step both in domestic price reform and in the trading system is forging a meaningful link between internal and external prices. As far as the exchange rate goes, policymakers generally seek relationships specific to certain segments of foreign transactions. Because of the dichotomy between TRPs and East-West prices (EWPs), or even WMPs, this segmentation is usually applied separately to convertible currency and TR trading areas. As a rule, the official exchange rate becomes a mere accounting unit, particularly for foreign trade statistics. Most countries derive various conversion co-efficients from comparisons between actual domestic and foreign trade prices for prespecified bundles of goods and services. These prices may reflect those observed in world markets, those actually attained in trade, or found in magnitudes that planners feel should be within reach of the FTOs.

The role of trade prices and conversion coefficients in domestic price formation differs considerably among CPEs and depends on the specific reference time period. In the more comprehensive reforms, actual trade prices are allowed to influence major decisions by firms or their associations as well as the calculation of domestic prices. Usually the reform also anticipates establishing a multiple-column tariff system that, in some cases, functions as a regulator of the relationship between domestic and trade prices.

One should not, however, exaggerate this price nexus. In most reforms, firms are not entitled to pass on their additional import cost to domestic consumers or to more fully exploit their profit margin by boosting exports beyond planned levels. This is so because domestic price flexibility remains problematic in all CPEs. Most price reforms have endeavored to narrow, at least intermittently, the gap between domestic prices and real trade costs and to some extent harmonize domestic and trade prices. But palpable buffers between trade and domestic prices via target taxes and subsidies remain. Precisely because price differences are too big to be bridged quickly and policymakers are reluctant to connect the domestic economy with countries abroad, social interests have to be safeguarded through instruments other than perfect taxes and subsidies.

11.2.3.b The regulation of trade

All CPEs seek to extend decentralized decision making to trade and allow individual economic agents to interact with foreign partners within prescribed boundaries. This devolution has gone the farthest for prespecified import and export volumes. However, material balancing and central supply allocations continue to confine entrepreneurs' initiative in trade matters. Nevertheless, an important change can be observed in the administrative linkup of trade with production or user. Foreign trade specialists in ministries, branch associations or individual firms are expected to participate both in developing plans and in providing efficiency calculations on alternative processes. This entails a sharp reduction in the number of material balances denominated in physical units. Though foreign trade instructions continue to be mandatory, more targets are now being formulated in terms of value indicators. Also, fewer specific restrictions are being seen on the composition of exports or imports, partners to be broached and target prices for planned transactions.

The existence of two broad trade markets, namely CMEA and other partners, poses formidable problems. The CMEA's perpetuation of BTPAs, with all their deleterious ramifications for price formation and balancing requirements, entails knotty problems, especially for CPEs that expect lower tiers of the planning hierarchy to formulate their own decisions. Numerous arrangements between artificial TRPs and EWPs on the one hand and domestic wholesale and retail prices on the other have had to be worked out and manipulated in accordance with shifts in demand and supply. Periodically they have had to be updated.

11.2.3.c The role of the foreign trade monopoly

In addition to the proliferation of FTOs, perhaps one of the most visible signs of foreign trade reform is the granting of foreign trading rights to selected firms or associations. This has been particularly pronounced in important manufacturing sectors because of planners' interest in increasing exports of manufactures. This by itself suggests the easing of the MFT under impact of the reform. But it should not be forgotten that the MFT is also strengthened in more than one respect. As noted, the MFT is simultaneously eased and centralized. It is relaxed in the sense that other ministries, associations of firms and selected individual firms obtain greater autonomy to engage in trade directly, or at least to influence that trade. New incentives are devised to encourage foreign trade and especially to promote export efficiency. The transmission of actual foreign trade prices into the domestic price structure via modified exchange rates or their surrogates is also actively promoted, though in some cases only intermittently. At the same time, the MFT is reinforced in many ways. This is reflected most notably in liberating the MFT from the chores of day-to-day planning and trading activities. The macroeconomic steering of foreign trade and payments by direct and indirect instruments as well as potentially far-reaching qualitative controls on trade and foreign exchange strategies now receive prime attention.

11.2.3.d Other institutional innovations
The potential for trade and cooperation with Western economies has played a critical-enough role in the formulation and implementation of the reforms that some CPEs have now created the legal framework for direct relations among firms. These can assume several forms and need not be restricted to Western agents as partners. Initially, CPEs primarily sought to bolster industrial cooperation and joint ventures with DMEs. But they increasingly realize that other forms of cooperation may be more profitable, including in science, technology, product development and the design of production processes. The search for joint East-West ventures found little reflection in CMEA relations until the early 1980s, when countries began to stress direct interfirm relations. Such transnational socialist ventures in production and marketing may soon become more visible.

To increase the possibilities for interplay, many CPEs have sought to abolish BTPAs with nonsocialist partners, or at least to somewhat curtail their negative features, such as by placing clearing arrangements on a convertible currency basis. In addition, some CPEs have sought to overcome ideological and political obstacles by joining international financial – including the IMF, the International Bank for Reconstruction and Development (World Bank) and the Bank for International Settlements (BIS) – and trading organizations, including the General Agreement on Tariffs and Trade (GATT). Some countries have even signed association or cooperation agreements with important trading blocs, including the EC, and have generally improved the facilities for accommodating rapidly expanding interbloc trade and payments flows.

11.3 BILATERAL TRADE AND PAYMENTS AGREEMENTS

To reduce the uncertainty associated with trade within the context of facilitating plan implementation, information about the trade intentions of potential partners needs to be acquired. This knowledge can be obtained in several ways, but one of the most expedient is by concluding formal trade and payments agreements as integral complements of the macroeconomic plan. Economies willing and able to enter into such firm commitments are naturally those with a similar proclivity for forecasting and controlling trade, especially the other CPEs. Such relations could have been regulated through general trade agreements, but the format of BTPAs was chosen, for reasons to be explored here. This preferred format complicated attaining the desired trade and payments agreements with MEs. The reason for this is rather simple. Governments in MEs entering into trade and payments agreements have no power to guarantee their implementation even if detailed targets are stipulated. At best, they can try to foster trade with CPEs indirectly, especially by relaxing 'extraeconomic' regulations, because state trading is usually small and differently organized than it is in CPEs. Western leaders can, for instance, open up their borders to exports and imports of particular products and can encourage contacts between private traders and CPE trade organizations. Firm promises to buy and sell can be made only in relations between CPEs and individual firms, but such agreements differ substantially from the BTPA under review here. As to the payments aspects of such agreements, governments in MEs can do more, for example, by accommodating clearing currencies, providing credits and so on. Yet, owing to comprehensive central planning, payment means in whatever form are only incidental in eliciting market response in CPEs. What drives international transactions is the agreement on the exchange of commodities for which payments must be arranged.

It is pertinent to include in this analysis relations between CMEA members and other socialist countries. I shall not go into great detail, however, because of the comparatively small share of trade with these countries (particularly since the early 1960s), because of the arguments given in the introduction regarding the role of some of these countries in the CMEA, and because the two main partners (China and Yugoslavia) trade with CMEA members in convertible currency. The comments below on the importance of trade contracts apply, therefore, mainly to trade with other CMEA members.

The heavy reliance on intra-CMEA trade through formal and comprehensive BTPAs is an especially important complement of the socialist domestic planning mechanism because doing so buys stability in internal and external activities, though perhaps at the cost of flexibility in trade. Although CPEs could have acquired greater trade stability by concluding *ex ante* agreements with all partners at the same time, they have not done so for a number of reasons. For instance, it is easier to reach an understanding between two partners than to settle all exchanges through multilateral negotiations. Also, in its relations with CPEs, the USSR has generally favored bilateral over multilateral agreements. Negotiating separately with each CPE has better suited the USSR's political supremacy and hegemony over Eastern Europe, particularly during the first decade after World War II. Third, the nature of domestic physical planning targets provides a rationale for the choice of bilateral agreements. The CPEs' commitment to bilateralism essentially stems from this model's congruence with national planning as both are controlled by central planners. In multilateral trading each country's trade balance could be adversely affected by the terms of settlement in its trading partners' commerce with each other. Also, the planners' deliberate disregard of real scarcity indicators makes it difficult to offset bilateral balances through multilateral agreements.

A typical trade agreement for current transactions between any two CPEs contains two-way targets for the trade level, the projected composition of exports and imports by main commodity groups and an itemization of approximately four-fifths of what will be delivered and at what prices during a given trade period. Although the specification of the anticipated trade flows has no doubt become less rigid than it was in the early 1950s, all main goods are in principle still stipulated in the BTPA. Within the agreed targets for turnover and commodity groups that are not preempted by specific commodity flows (such as fuels), individual ministries can settle further details during the period the agreement is active. This means, for instance, that in principle a planned export target cannot be exceeded unless the parties concurrently agree overtly or tacitly upon supplementary import flows.

With this in mind, it seems fair to say that BTPAs are concluded as a useful device for mitigating the uncertainty of foreign economic relations, as a way of attenuating fluctuations in international reserves and, in some instances, dispensing with reserves altogether, as a convenient means of accommodating ostensible administrative needs, and for other reasons. Seen in this light, it is easier to understand the transformation of the classical CPE's trade sector into an organizational framework that mirrors and complements domestic central planning. So far so good. But is the particular type of bilateralism employed by the CPEs only a convenient organizational tool or is intra-CMEA bilateralism far more complex?

The conclusion of BTPAs by pairs of governments is a normal phenomenon in the trade relations of many countries. Such contracts serve several interrelated purposes. First, it is hoped that a larger volume and more appropriate composition of reciprocal trade will ensue compared with what would have resulted from simply instituting comprehensive exchange controls. Agreements usually promote an immediate stimulus to trade, thereby facilitating, for example, economic reconstruction and consolidation. These are the circumstances under which the adoption of bilateralism has become generally accepted even in DMEs. Its worth lies not in its drawbacks when compared to multilateralism, which is not usually a realistic option under the circumstances, but in making trade possible and at a higher level than would otherwise be feasible. Thus, following World War II, the Western European economies turned to bilateralism and the financing of trade with inconvertible currencies primarily because it was difficult to acquire sufficient hard currency reserves given the general state of disequilibrium and that policy-makers were reluctant to deflate economic activity. In addition, BTPAs provided for financing trade with short-term credits, which would not have been forthcoming had trade been conducted with convertible currencies. This widely prevailing concern about the financing of foreign trade (Mikesell, 1954, p. 436) also lurked behind the Eastern European BTPAs. As the economies returned to more normal conditions, the agreements were primarily used to stabilize trade at a desirable level and thus permit uninterrupted production and avoid inadvertent relocations. Of course, in CPE trade there are other economic and weighty political factors behind BTPAs.

Bilateral bargaining in intra-CMEA trade has utilized several instruments and *quid pro quos* that have allowed the CPEs to ensure bilateral balance (Brabant, 1973, pp. 100–3). It is now a moot question whether these instruments have emerged as a result of a careful evaluation of the welfare and trade implications of bilateral trade policies or whether the reverse is true, although, in my view, the former presents the more persuasive line of reasoning. Bilateralism has been maintained because of the experiences of these countries in the period between the two wars, the need for trade controls under central planning, the USSR's championing of the bilateral approach and the obstacles to multilateral trade negotiations for countries with inconvertible currencies that also lack firm criteria for measuring their own success in technical economic terms. The gradual evolution of the present system of CMEA bilateralism is altogether a different matter, however.

11.4 BILATERALISM

Bilateralism may be variously defined (Brabant, 1973, pp. 66–9). Here I take it to mean a foreign trade policy designed to equate intended exports and imports between two countries in such a way that unplanned transactions are avoided or, at least, that actual transactions do not need to be compensated for by unanticipated capital movements. A preliminary note: there is nothing inherently sinister or even significant in seeking an exact balance of payments between two countries, even if this continues for years. The peculiarity of bilateralism lies in endeavoring to achieve such balance at the possible expense of alternative trading partners. The result of this trade strategy is entirely predictable; reciprocal turnover is typically compressed below levels that prevail in a multilateral environment because trade tends to be restricted to the export capacity of the weakest partner, after allowing for price and income effects that necessarily accompany the process of curbing absolute trade. But note that under the particular postwar environment the focus of bilateral clearing schemes was not on trade denial but on how to attain an orderly exchange in a distorted trade world.

Bilateralism is only one form of general exchange control. Typically, it is resorted to when countries face severe payments problems for which the more subtle forms of trade intervention and regulation (including discriminatory tariffs and general commodity quotas) no longer suffice for attaining overall foreign economic policy objectives. In other words, a bilateral trade policy is usually embraced in an effort to manage the multifarious trade and exchange controls created by acute disequilibriums in an important component of the world economy. Though a symptom as well as a result of serious economic disarray, it is an unsatisfactory solution for those difficulties. But it may permit mechanisms for alleviating the strictures of rigid bilateralism to be identified. For instance, parties may work seriously at developing mutually satisfactory BTPAs without infusing other policy goals into the negotiations.

Instead of managing foreign trade at the macroeconomic level by indirect means, bilateralism is *in se* a conscious policy designed to maintain nearly complete control over the foreign exchange market. Difficulties in analyzing bilateralism in the real world arise because of the diverse forms in which it has appeared, the amazing variety of motives behind its emergence and the complex network of measures embraced to implement such a trade policy, including home currency inconvertibility. Indeed, in the context of MEs bilateralism is usually treated as one particular, somewhat peculiar, form of preferential trading (Caves, 1974, pp. 32–9) – in other words, a special type of trade discrimination. The circumstances accompanying or generating CMEA bilateralism embody many complex phenomena that involve considerably more than simple organizational convenience or the express desire to discriminate. The same applies to the instruments through which bilateralism is usually implemented. Hypothetically, BTPAs could be reconciled with a multilateral trading world whose short-run flexibility is circumscribed. In the case at hand, this would include the institutional and organizational needs issuing from the particular configuration of central planning. Until broad-based, meaningful CMEA reforms are inaugurated, bilateralism is inextricably expressed through BTPAs. One would be hard pressed to imagine BTPAs that do not reflect bilateralism in one way or another. In other words, although bilateralism is primarily a trade policy and BTPAs the quintessence of a particular trade model, neither can be discussed in isolation.

BTPAs provide for financing current trade between two countries in the form of clearing credits with a fixed ceiling and time frame. These funds are freely available for one country to use in making payments for goods and services from the other. Thus, one component of bilateralism focuses on the financial aspects of trade, especially when endeavoring to economize on scarce foreign exchange reserves. Whereas fully unregulated, free trade cannot be permitted under bilateralism, the licensing schemes that guide real export and import flows, or currency allocation schemes that accompany the special exchange controls, are administered by each country separately. Rarely are trade flows accommodated under clearing arrangements completely planned in advance; shifts occur in response to movements in the respective bilateral debit and credit positions. In the arrangements instituted by the CPEs, however, the BTPAs are generally trade quota contracts that allow export and import licenses to be issued for specific types and quantities of goods and services that both parties have agreed upon in advance.

Although bilateralism emerges primarily because of problems in foreign exchange markets, eventually every exchange-control system loses the rationale originally inspired primarily by financial considerations. Among the interferences to trade, protectionism, autarchy and, in some cases, totalitarian control will gradually assume ascendancy over the original aims, thus furthering ulterior goals, not necessarily economic in nature, that may have been at the root of the introduction of bilateralism in the first place. This ascendancy, as experience proves, can persist for a long time. Partners may find such a trade policy stifling if they do not coordinate their trade behavior or if noneconomic motives prevail in selecting trade. Precisely in order to contain the potential trade-reducing effects of bilateralized trade, partners bent on maintaining intensive exchange usually adopt, without completely revoking other features of bilateralism, various refinements and *ad hoc* instruments that codetermine the outcome of negotiations and implementation of the BTPAs. It is this adaptation to individual needs that creates the amazing variety of specific bilateral trade policies and institutions, thus seriously complicating generalizations.

11.5 STRUCTURAL BILATERALISM

Whenever bargaining and expediency in implementing bilateralism allow disparate relative prices in BTPAs to emerge, the role of prices in formulating trade decisions becomes precarious. Yet, countries that adhere to bilateralism must choose by way of prices and other yardsticks. Structural bilateralism as one of these criteria is one possible outcome of bilateralism, which means that some partners may deem it advantageous to 'force' the composition of trade away from what would prevail under multilateralism or overall bilateralism chiefly in lieu of price adjustments. This enables partners to promote commodities not otherwise exported, it permits a more extensive exploitation of arbitrage and it may improve the gains to be reaped from bilateralized trade. That is, it is an extension of bilateralism to clear some trade, particularly under conditions when the regular features of bilateralism – even when augmented with refinements and *ad hoc* policy instruments – no longer suffice to make traded goods interchangeable and policymakers are inclined to remove such goods from the particular bilateral commercial exchange circuit.

Eastern European leaders have displayed a chronic obsession with the composition of trade in general and that of individual bilateral flows in particular (see Brabant, 1973, pp. 126–39). Although desirable details are still lacking, the level and composition of trade achieved with the aid of BTPAs are not commensurate with the economic profile of the participants. Certain exports may have emerged partly as a result of an honest effort to promote economic development through regional trade, though this is not necessarily the best course economically speaking. Nevertheless, by far the larger proportion of such exchanges seems to have emerged because some CPEs have deliberately distorted their export capacity by means other than those inherent in general bilateralism, even when modified.

Structural bilateralism may be defined as an *ex ante* trade policy that aims at attaining overall bilateral equilibrium by reducing trade imbalances in selected commodity groups and in some bilateral relations in support of an autonomous domestic development pattern. As in the case of bilateralism, it is difficult to separate BTPAs as an expression of a commercial policy from them as a trading tool that is congenial to detailed traditional planning. As this policy variant introduces new constraints on the distribution of trade, and most likely on its level and composition as well, I shall treat the subject here. How it has entangled CMEA relations over the years cannot be studied in detail (see Brabant, 1973, pp. 118–55). But it may be useful to discuss the reasons for the emergence of such a policy, the specific features of its application and its most important implications.

Compared with bilateralism, structural bilateralism leads to the further segmentation of trade markets into noncommunicating units (Alampiev, Bogomolov and Širjaev, 1971, pp. 72–3). Goods will no longer flow to partners with whom a bilateral balance as such exists; they will be diverted to where a contracted balance for the relevant commodity group has not yet been exhausted and to markets in which structural bilateralism is less rigidly enforced, if it is enforced at all. The consequences for intragroup trade become complex. Given the problems in clearly distinguishing between the causes and effects of this trade policy, they cannot be pinpointed or exactly quantified. As noted for overall bilateralism, the reasons for embracing special constraints on commodity group balances are usually reinforced when this policy is introduced.

The implications of structural bilateralism may be quite nefarious. Apart from compressing trade to levels below those afforded under general bilateralism, structural bilateralism in a regional integration effort markedly narrows the possibilities for fruitful cooperation. In the CMEA context this is most pronounced for ECPS and STC agreements (see chapter 17). Even without further political and other complications, that this trade policy comes about for lack of flexible prices renders it even more difficult to connect the domestic economy with foreign sectors. It certainly complicates the computation of more effective domestic prices, regardless of what policy-makers may want to accomplish with such prices. These encumbrances of CMEA trading markets carry over to the East-West sphere because technically sound economic comparisons are virtually impossible.

The gradual complication of CMEA relations as a result of restraining intersectoral exchange has doubtless contributed to the malaise in regional trade and cooperation of the mid-1960s and to an exploration for alternative means of promoting SEI. To that extent, structural bilateralism may have had a salutary effect on the design of future economic policies. Indeed, it played an important and constructive role in the formulation of reforms. But structural bilateralism still prevails in CMEA cooperation and continues to hamper SEI.

11.6 ORGANIZATIONAL LINKS IN THE CMEA

Shielding national economies from foreign influences would normally have made a regional organization superfluous. There are two possible exceptions. Such an organization could have played a major role had it been given plenipotentiary powers to help enforce this market segmentation yet minimize the implicit cost. It could also have been assigned a leading role in coordinating economic decisions if it had possessed sufficient powers to help overcome the fragmentation of the regional market. Direct assistance could have been provided through central planning at the regional level, including through BTPAs and multilateral trade and payments agreements (MTPAs). Help could also have been indirect; that is, by ensuring the smooth functioning of an economic mechanism that enhances the proper indirect coordination of decisions at the CMEA level. All of these forms affect macro- and microeconomic policy, direct or indirect policy instruments and various institutions of central planning or of implementing macroeconomic policies in a more indirect way. Most of these elements are examined in other chapters of Part III. Here I am concerned with the broad organizational implications.

As shown in Part I, the direct organizational ranking of the CMEA organs was, paradoxically, largest when the organization was weakest. This prevailed after the fateful decision sometime in 1950 to abandon the search for a proper SEI mechanism (see chapter 2). Since then, the CMEA has facilitated intragroup exchanges largely by assisting in smoothing the administrative and other infrastructures of commerce. The first one has taken the form of trade and payments documentation, establishing clearing agencies and later the common banks (see Part II), regulating conditions for delivery of goods and services, endorsing model ECPS and STC agreements and model rules for various joint ventures, providing technical assistance with standards and standardizing nomenclatures, as discussed later in Part III.

It is to be highlighted here, though, that the only time any attempt was made to invest the CMEA with far-reaching planning powers since economic cooperation through inauguration of the Soviet embassy system was when *Basic Principles* was endorsed. Emulating Soviet-type planning institutions at the regional level failed, and no consistent alternative was implemented in its place. Rather than aim at a clear-cut coordination mechanism, some elements of planning and of indirect coordination were instituted. The first was assigned essentially to the Planning Committee, although its ultimate powers in regulating or controlling the regional, let alone the national, allocation of resources is highly confined. More indirect coordination efforts were assigned to the SCEP, SCFT and SCFQ, although their mission has always been dubious as they replicate at the regional level a weak substitute for the domestic organization of the monetary and financial sectors. The creation of several new subcommittees of the Executive Committee in early 1988 may provide the necessary fillip for placing indirect coordination mechanisms and institutions on a more solid footing than has so far been the case.

In both areas of cooperation endeavors, organizational links are encountered that I have so far touched upon only *en marge*. Regarding the planning instruments, there are obvious domestic and CMEA institutional links, which are discussed in the next two chapters because they can be better explained within the context of the planning approach to SEI; similarly for indirect economic coordination endeavors. By their very definition they include institutional and organizational features (including multilateralism, convertibility and transferability) that were addressed here only in passing. It is easier to examine these organizational and institutional features in the context of indirect economic coordination as such as a means of invigorating SEI, as discussed in chapters 14 and 15.

NOTE

1. For example, one of the most conspicuous areas where the CPEs have deliberately ignored sharing in the benefits of trade is with the NICs. Such trade has sometimes remained low because of delicate foreign policy problems (as with the Republic of China (Taiwan), Hong Kong and Korea). Only recently, in the search for a renewal of the CPE model have some policymakers addressed, among other things, this potential for useful interaction.

12 · THE PLANNING INSTRUMENTS OF SEI

As argued in Part I, from the beginning of the CMEA, the member economies have explored alternative mechanisms for effectively interlinking their economies. This eventually came to be viewed as attainable chiefly by intermeshing detailed national plans. With hindsight: 'Development according to plan as a general form of economic relations and a method of social production is objectively inherent in socialism. It is therefore natural that the development of mutual cooperation among [the CPEs] is organized on the basis of planning' (Bagudin, Gavrilov and Šinkov, 1985, p. 7). But this decision, if such it was, failed to be implemented immediately. As a result of the inactivity of the CMEA during 1950–3 and the obstacles being faced in implementing the New Course in an orderly fashion, considerable shifts in policy stances and palpable vacillations in preferences regarding national autarky and regional economic cooperation manifested themselves. At the fourth Council Session, at least the most important partners straightforwardly identified the promotion of economic cooperation on the basis of coordinated plans as the overt goal of SEI.

In 1954–6 efforts were launched to translate this aspiration into an effective policy directed at guaranteeing a rapid pace of economic expansion at the regional level, with some regard for efficiency and equity, but these efforts foundered. The absence of a unified central planning agency with plenipotentiary powers equivalent to those of the national planning centers undoubtedly contributed to the failure to erect a truly effective regional economic policy. An additional cause was the operational ambiguity of what plan coordination was to accomplish in the absence of a single central planning agency.

Section 12.1 outlines my approach to understanding the various aspects of plan harmonization, but agreement is lacking in the profession on these or related topics. BTPAs elaborated until the late 1950s involved little genuine economywide coordination. As detailed in section 12.2, essentially the aim was to reconcile, in a bilateral sequence, trade intentions embedded in economywide plans that could no longer be substantively modified. Moving from pure trade agreements to intermeshing *ex ante* plan intentions either partially or comprehensively has always been the ambition of plan coordination. Much of this activity results from concrete ECPS and STC agreements. Because STC agreements are such important instruments of planned integration, I shall discuss them separately in chapter 13 and limit discourse here to the other planning instruments. Section 12.3 sketches the process through which plans are coordinated. Because the two components concerned with Concerted Plans and Target Programs have become the mainstay of intentions regarding plan coordination since the mid-1970s, these topics are discussed in sections 12.4 and 12.5. This naturally leads to an exploration in section 12.6 of what scope is available for coordinating economic policies. The emerging forms of joint planning form the subject of section 12.7. The overall experience with plan coordination and how that fits into the advantages and drawbacks of SEI are detailed in Part IV.

12.1 ON THE TERMINOLOGY OF PLAN COORDINATION

Because of the nature of economic policy in CPEs, it may seem trite to emphasize that plan coordination is the primary vehicle for enhancing SEI; but I do not think so given the imprecise terminology used in the CMEA literature. A pragmatic clarification of this weasel word is useful.

Economies can be interlinked voluntarily by economic agents whose decisions are guided through indirect coordination instruments, such as broadly defined prices. Synchronizing key macroeconomic policy decisions may prove useful in improving stability and buoyancy in economic activity levels. However, these may also be advanced through *ex ante* coordination. If pursued through indirect coordination instruments, this approach is still market-type integration. If concordance is sought on the basis of draft national plans, one enters the realm of plan coordination proper. Note that this does not necessarily preclude the utilization of market-type instruments while blending decisions during the preparatory planning stages or in later implementing the plans.

For instance, single BTPAs may be concluded as a way of securing, or perhaps reserving, markets specifically for the exports that the plan earmarks and of identifying sources from which imports can be procured to fill any shortages implied in the plan. At this stage of the planning ladder, one is faced with the most elementary form of plan coordination. If BTPAs are worked out on the basis of preliminary decisions that can still be modified, then higher levels of plan coordination are called for. I use this qualifier intentionally to suggest that such variants of plan coordination may afford a higher level of economic efficiency compared with what is feasible under ordinary BTPAs. The elimination of some previously operative constraints on feasible production levels and desirable absorption targets, *ceteris paribus*, is bound to positively affect efficiency.

Ex ante coordination of plan intentions may take many forms. It may involve negotiating BTPAs that include exchanges emerging from the synchronization of production processes, which is essentially production specialization as discussed in chapter 13. It may also comprise the iterative elaboration of BTPAs that emanate from the reciprocal merging of some plan intentions; here, the fewer and less detailed the commitments made by policymakers, the greater the flexibility. The degree of detail of policy commitment is likely to be most pronounced with joint planning. As the term suggests, however, this is not necessarily equivalent to supranational planning, a notion that has been branded as anathema in CMEA debates since the early 1950s. As it has been explicitly precluded from the discourse on SEI since the late 1960s, I shall not further explore that topic here.

Essentially, joint planning is regional planning conducted by two or more national planning agencies that may or may not wish to reconcile national preferences. Usually a joint assessment is made of future demand levels and structures and of available resources and production levels. It may also call for fitting together regional demand and supply, which may require several iterations of sustainable demand or supply levels, or both, by combining a redeployment of resources with a reevaluation of the preference structures in at least one country. Such mutual adjustments may refer to one broad area of economic activity and involve production specialization or could encompass the economy as a whole, though that has not been the case so far.

Joint planning may include the dovetailing of economic policies if that planning is applied to the economy as a whole, or at least to its major components. Thus, structural economic policies could be coordinated at the regional level. This would be one form of joint planning. Otherwise it essentially refers to policy consultations of various degrees of commitment, detail and comprehensiveness. In most cases, any union of economic policies involves plan coordination at the level of political commitment. This concept of policy consultation is at odds with the prescriptions of *Integration Program*, which posited joint planning as one of the three subcomponents of the economic mechanism of SEI, in addition to the intermeshing of national economic plans and the utilization of indirect coordination instruments.

Finally, there are different ways to coordinate plans in the strict sense. A plan may range beyond the precisely gauged *ex ante* implications of demand and supply for reciprocal trade to include nontraded goods, services and items that may eventually become tradables. At its most elementary level, plan coordination here, at least to some extent, denotes the possible rearrangement of demand and supply of traded goods and services. In other words, I do not include under the label plan coordination the repercussions for domestic planning of BTPAs based solely on intended exports and imports when they cannot be fully satisfied. The most involved type of plan coordination in the present terminology is joint planning of the national economies as a whole. This may still be a coveted policy objective, although the new Soviet leadership seems to be slowly, but steadily, relinquishing such ambition for the CMEA as a whole. Whether this redirection of traditional Soviet precepts regarding the CMEA will last long is a different matter, however. But joint planning continues to be remote from the day-to-day CMEA plan coordination purposes and means as traditionally practiced. As argued in section 12.7, this may soon change as the importance being attached to plan coordination, joint planning and indirect coordination gets translated into concrete activities.

12.2 REGIONAL TRADE AND BTPAs

In the typology chosen here, a BTPA is an instrument of trade policy that is activated during the ultimate or penultimate phase of the national planning process (see chapter 11). BTPAs attempt to reconcile reciprocal demands for imports and supplies of exports that emanate from the national planning processes, which themselves evolved into independently formulated blueprints. Clearly, if all intended trade is to be conducted in this fashion, perhaps by a factor of two the number of constraints exceeds the number of parameters that must be determined to clear all planned flows; a reconciliation procedure is therefore needed.

BTPAs are not only a mechanism through which some elementary form of plan coordination is sought. Their origin can be found in the bilateral trading world of the postwar period, and their rationale rests on the perceived need to secure stability in the CPEs, as underlined in chapter 11. As such, BTPAs are integral to how external trade and payments are organized in CPEs. They have been appended to the model underlying the organization of detailed central planning, including the MFT as one instrument for fostering socialization of economic activity. Without such state control over external transactions, comprehensive planning and management of domestic production, trade and money would be impossible. The particular form in which this state control becomes expressed derives from the traditional guideline for planners to devote more attention to fulfilling the import plan, as formulated on the basis of minimum requirements and the disequilibriums of material balances, than to optimizing trade. As a result, socialist policymakers value the planning of trade as a basic tool for attenuating the uncertainty inherent in forecasting and engaging in foreign commerce.

As explained in chapters 9 and 11, trade poses intricate practical obstacles for comprehensive central planning, even when such planning focuses on rapid and stable economic growth primarily in pacemaking sectors and when the CPE chooses not to extensively rely on trade. Furthermore, compliance with the metaeconomics of socialist economic organization mandates rigid trade controls under the aegis of the MFT. To reduce the uncertainty of foreign trade, and thus to facilitate the implementation of domestic growth targets, CPEs endeavor to accurately ascertain the trade intentions of potential partners. This knowledge can be acquired in several ways. The most expedient means is by concluding formal trade and payments agreements, which in their entirety complement the national economic plans. But not all economies are in a position to make such firm commitments. Those most likely to do so are the other CPEs, all of which share a proclivity for forecasting and controlling their external trade to the extent feasible (see Brabant, 1980, p. 124).

In the context of market-type economies, BTPAs usually provide for financing current trade between two countries in the form of clearing credits, which one country can use for paying for goods and services from the other. Bilateralism, therefore, is normally concerned with the financial aspects of trade, especially as this represents an endeavor to economize on scarce foreign exchange reserves. But the licensing procedures that guide real export and import flows, or the currency allocation schemes that accompany the special exchange controls, are administered by each country separately. Trade flows accommodated under clearing arrangements are rarely completely planned in advance, and their shifts are responses to movements in the bilateral debit and credit positions of each country. The arrangements instituted by the CPEs for executing BTPAs, however, usually take the form of comprehensive trade quota contracts that provide for issuing export and import licences for specific types and quantities of goods and services that both parties agree upon in advance.

The conclusion of BTPAs by pairs of governments is a normal phenomenon in the mutual trade relations of the CPEs, who initially embraced BTPAs as a network of trade instruments that permitted a certain level of trade to be cleared rather than as a means of harmonizing the CPEs' economic structures. But BTPAs need not be limited to that endeavor. It would be possible to enter into negotiations with 'desirable' partners and conduct BTPAs as an integral part of the planning process. Coordination could be started either with BTPAs or by specifying a first round of desirable gross output targets or net final user levels, as in a stylized input-output framework. If the process begins on the trade side, a considerable number of iterations may be needed to identify desirable net final user levels because trade represents a comparatively small component of aggregate economic activity in several CPEs. But if countries approach the coordination of their economies from the side of planning for domestic production and utilization, while making certain plausible assumptions on obtainable competitive imports and exports (see Brabant, 1980, pp. 111–4), the discourse shifts to some form of actual plan coordination. This topic will be covered in subsequent sections.

A typical trade agreement for current transactions, as distinct from medium- to long-term BTPAs, contains a target for exports and imports, the projected composition of trade by main commodity groups and a detailed listing of approximately four-fifths of what will be delivered and, in most cases, at what prices during a given transaction period. Although the specification of anticipated bilateral trade flows is now probably less rigid than it was in the early 1950s, all main goods continue in principle to be stipulated in the trade agreement. Within the agreed targets for turnover and commodity groups, excluding the detailed commodity flows, individual ministries, enterprise associations or even individual firms can settle further details while the agreement is in force.

Ideally, trade contracts concluded as an integral part of the general economic plan should, by merging individual components of the CPE's trade needs, lead to the indirect coordination of the various national plans. There are several ways to alleviate this overconstrained decision-making space. First, countries know that they have a comparative advantage in some goods *vis-à-vis* the region as a whole. For example, Poland does not need to produce lengthy calculations to ascertain that, at least with respect to the CMEA region, it has a comparative advantage in hard coal. But the precise extent to which advantages should be pushed may be determined through fairly detailed and comprehensive calculations. Second, not all of the CPEs' intended trade has been earmarked for BTPAs that are concluded with CMEA partners exclusively. Thus, trade with MEs can offer an exceedingly useful escape valve. Finally, by forgoing trade in order to preserve a high degree of self-sufficiency and domestic policy autonomy, as during the early 1950s, the CPEs can preclude irreconcilable trade intentions. But there is a cost to such activities.

12.3 ON PLAN COORDINATION

When domestic planning proceeds with minimal regard for the trade intentions of potential partners, the number of constraints generally exceeds the number of parameters to be determined. The severity of the constraints under which BTPAs are ordinarily hammered out can be eased by coordinating targets in some form. This may exert beneficial effects in terms of heightened efficiency. The synchronization of targets does not have to take the form of detailed quantitative concertation. Provided that coordination instruments and institutions are in place, qualitative coordination by itself could have a positive impact on economic efficiency at various stages of the planning process. This may occur at the microeconomic level for one specific product or for a range of products (for instance, ball bearings). It may also be more ambitious and include, as mentioned, various forms of production specialization, harmonizing specific policies in the short to medium run or simple consultations about preliminary production, consumption and trade intentions.

As should now be obvious, the CPEs have engaged in some kind of plan coordination since the late 1940s. It is paradoxical, though, that perhaps the closest the CPEs ever came to integrating economywide policies was during the early 1950s. The Soviet embassy system of 'supervising' economic planning and performance of the Eastern European CPEs provided the perfect, if one-sided, link through which potentially divergent concepts were forced into a tight uniform format (Širjaev, 1987c, pp. 786–7). Party discipline and obeisance to Soviet dictates, including in economic affairs, further narrowed maneuverability for individual countries. I am not suggesting that the Eastern European leadership should be allowed into history scot-free when it comes to placing blame for inefficient economic structures and low productivity levels. In fact, each CPE's leadership must bear a large share of the responsibility for economic mismanagement that is often ascribed to Soviet dictates or meddling. While the Soviet Union bears responsibility for initially having insisted on the transfer of an inappropriate development strategy and model to Eastern Europe, not all the blame for the economic backwardness and inefficiency of the CPEs can be unloaded onto the USSR. Submission to Soviet directives was especially prevalent. The primary instrument available for aligning some aspects of national economic plans was the omnipresent BTPA. However, given the trade embargo and the CPEs' predilection for saving on convertible currency requirements, efforts to reconcile planned trade volumes with greater consideration than simply offsetting independently conceived plan targets were eventually limited to a few items that presented severe bottlenecks.

Since 1954, plan coordination as the explicit objective of SEI has progressed through successively more ambitious reformulations as new goals have been tested. It found its most comprehensive, if most ambiguous, formulation in *Integration Program*. Three phases of proper plan coordination can be usefully distinguished. Iteratively linking trade intentions with domestic planning is the lowest phase, but this usually occurs only during the final stages of formulating domestic economywide plans. Trade intentions therefore cannot be properly integrated consistently. Plan coordination may proceed to the stage of plan drafts, an objective that has apparently been implemented since the early 1970s. However, given the turmoil in world markets since that time, followed by major shifts in CMEA economic relations and severe economic retrenchment in most CPEs, the extent claimed for this coordination must be taken with a grain of salt. A final form of plan coordination involves consolidating economic policies in one concrete domain or another, with the highest stage involving the merging of overall development goals and instruments of two or more countries.

Plan coordination must transform the consensus reached at high-level policy consultations into operational tasks with the assistance of other policy instruments. This is the second cornerstone of the economic mechanism. Frequent bi- and multilateral policy consultations on a multitude of issues should lead to joint economic initiatives and should also facilitate embodying concrete steps into national plans, which was one explicit goal of *Integration Program*. But the compass, level, forms and procedures of these consultations were to be decided by interested members. Note that the realization of concrete measures would inevitably be subject to national policymaking, if only because of the nature of Council recommendations (see chapter 7).

There are two special configurations of plan coordination that must now be addressed in some detail; namely, the Concerted Plan and the Target Program, both of which were introduced in the 1970s (see chapter 5). If properly executed, these instruments offer great possibilities for synchronizing overall or sectoral economic policies. They may also incorporate opportunities for joint planning. For that reason, I shall treat them in separate sections.

12.4 ON THE CONCERTED PLAN

The Concerted Plan, which was first adopted for the second half of the 1970s, emerged as the first concrete manifestation of the increasing tilt toward fostering SEI through plan coordination. In principle, it could be a form of joint planning because the Concerted Plan supposedly issues from integrating economic policies in a few selected domains. It inherently embodies an expression of intentions derived from SEI policies in diverse activities.

Thus far the Concerted Plan has been a catalog of selected policy measures aimed at specific targets in a number of diverse economic activities. Unlike other instances of plan coordination, the Concerted Plan is designed to have a direct counterpart in the national economic plans and is therefore usually synchronized with the concurrent five-year socioeconomic development plans. But this fact is rarely detailed in published plan reports. In other words, relevant parts of the Concerted Plan's provisions for individual participants form an integral component of the concurrent national medium-term plan. Therefore, they have the force of law in those countries that still pass plan laws through the annual implementation plans, which include a special section on integration measures. That component as well is rarely specified in the published versions.

Unfortunately, no single Concerted Plan has so far been published, even in the form of an informative summary, let alone in all its formal details. Broadly speaking, a Concerted Plan encompasses five classes of SEI endeavors. Its most spectacular part, according to most Eastern and Western commentators, concerns the specifications of jointly financed investment projects. Because this usually involves the pooling of financial and other resources, the Concerted Plan does delineate the concrete material, financial and, in some instances, labor transfers required for implementing projects. Second, many multilateral specialization and cooperation agreements, especially in chemical and engineering endeavors, are concretely stipulated, though without their specifics being disclosed. From the available information, those measures may take one of two forms. Either they broadly catalog specialization measures already agreed upon through bi- and multilateral agreements, or they record basic top-level policy commitments that need to be elaborated upon by formulating solid implementation agreements during the course of the Concerted Plan's reference period. Third, several scientific and technological cooperation projects are included, especially for improving and expanding new sources of energy, fuels and essential raw materials. Fourth, a special section is always devoted to means for enhancing the development of non-European CMEA members, generally with a particular focus on Mongolia. Finally, consequences of shared actions *vis-à-vis* third countries that result from the Concerted Plan are also drawn (Vorkauf, 1977, p. 12). Though the first Concerted Plan was hastily drawn up in a vacuum, it should properly be placed in the context of agreed cooperation policies, particularly the Target Programs.

12.5 ON TARGET PROGRAMMING

The adoption of target programming as a pivotal activity for enhancing SEI may be viewed as the temporary conclusion of the long and complex conceptual debate of the early 1970s about the proper goals, instruments and methods of SEI (see chapter 5). That the programs were constructed on the initiative of the Soviet Union (Kormnov, 1977b, p. 86) underlines this point. Whether they indeed provide 'a new important step in the process of improving the economic mechanism of [SEI]' (Širjaev, 1977, p. 68) has never been validated.

12.5.1 Target programming as a planning concept

What is target programming? Essentially it is a detailed outline of common intentions regarding the prospective output and capacity increments required to ensure commonly agreed final consumption levels of selected products. The ensuing trade volumes among the CPEs, and even with other countries, committed to target programming are a consequence of a deliberate joint choice of production and consumption objectives, not an issue in itself. To facilitate the attainment of these target increments, the program specifies the policy instruments to be activated through negotiated bi- and multilateral cooperation agreements, which in turn are to be merged with the conventional national plans. It is not a mandatory planning document or a detailed blueprint of ways, means and practical measures for the joint solution of any particular developmental problem. In other words, target programming represents an earnest and voluntary systematic mobilization of the resources necessary to resolve a major integration task by utilizing the well-tried methods of economic cooperation of the postwar period. In and of itself it is not capable of surmounting the inhibitions to SEI embodied in the traditional cooperation mechanisms, nor does it replace customary planning methods. But it does attempt to alleviate the first and enrich the second of these factors by taking direct action in production and/ or consumption.

Although not a genuinely new approach to responding in a programmatic way to structural change, CMEA-wide target programming may nevertheless represent an innovation. This qualifier is especially justified because through target programming the CPEs mean to move well beyond the simple declaration of intentions while maintaining the traditional methods of short- and medium-term plan coordination. In that light, the approach to SEI advocated since the mid-1970s has been appropriately characterized as enveloping 'a system of measures for the planned solution of the most important selected problems in the realm of material output, coordinated in terms of resources, deadlines, and participants' (Georgiev, 1978, p. 26).

To intensify common efforts, plan coordination should proceed simultaneously in several directions. This follows perhaps most immediately from jointly forecasting future demand and supply, particularly when placed in the context of long-term planning – ten to twenty years – that aims at charting a shared development perspective for key economic activities. Target programming also enhances plan coordination because it can make headway only if it measurably improves the traditional methods of coordinating medium-term plans and shifts the focus of coordination away from the trade sphere toward production and investment activities, which encompass STC, ECPS, jointly financed investment projects, perhaps some genuine joint investment undertakings and so on. Finally, target programming affects plan coordination because it may elicit truly joint planning of selected branches or specific production processes.

Perhaps the most novel aspect of target programming is the stage at which joint actions are formally examined. Instead of harmonizing goals and means during the final phase of national plan drafts, Target Programs are to be formulated during the earliest planning stages, when there are still opportunities for appropriating resources and enacting reciprocal adjustments on the basis of final consumption targets (Kormnov, 1977b, p. 93). In principle, these are to be projected via so-called economically justified requirements (EJRs), on which more below, of the CMEA region as a whole. They would definitely not be constructed as the simple aggregate of individual CPE submissions (Engert, 1978, p. 27). Output targets were then to be set in line with the material and other resources that interested CPEs could and would mobilize for joint projects.

To the extent that the CPEs succeed in drafting Target Programs when the future allocation of resources is still relatively unencumbered by preemptive national decisions, this SEI approach could constitute 'a means toward the elaboration of a uniform common strategy aimed at the solution of well-specified problems of common interest' (Engert, 1978, p. 26). In most cases, this way of tackling shared problems envelops a structural or industrial policy. Successful target programming is evidently contingent on solving many conceptual and practical problems. Institutional, organizational, economic, legal and other basic aspects of SEI affect the stage at which goals can be jointly selected; they also critically determine the mechanics of plan formulation, implementation and control.

12.5.2 Target programming and SEI

The need to elaborate common action programs for selected economic sectors was first publicly advocated by the USSR at the 1975 Session, although the topic had apparently already been approached as far back as the momentous 1969 Session. Because of ambivalence about fostering SEI through market and planning instruments, this project could not realistically be discussed until the removal of that divisive issue. As cornerstones for promoting SEI, in 1975 four broad development domains were identified: agriculture and food processing, durable consumer goods, machine building and energy, fuels and industrial raw materials. At the 1976 Session it was formally decided to construct these four programs as well as a fifth, which would encompass the entire transportation complex. This particular segment was added because of the outdated transportation capital stock and inadequate infrastructure that was increasingly hampering delivery of planned transportation services. That Session also specified the overall nature and the chief directions of target programming (Szita, 1976, p. 1018).

Organizationally, the task of coordinating the work was entrusted to the Planning Committee, which took longer than originally planned with the preparation of framework agreements. Partly this delay stemmed from the sheer complexity and magnitude of the tasks as well as from the fact that 'people tend to set aside the difficult and demanding questions' and 'deal with new matters, where the necessary experience is only now being acquired' (Štrougal, 1977, p. 77). Therefore, in 1977 it was resolved to first concentrate on readying three programs (agriculture and food processing; energy, fuels and raw materials; and that part of the engineering program that supports the other two programs) in time for the 1978 Session and to defer debate on the other programs to the 1979 Session. This timetable was formally kept. According to Ju. Pekšev (1978a, p. 3), the endorsed programs 'embody the basic principles that determine the cooperation strategy of the [CPEs] for satisfying their [EJRs], and consist of concrete measures worked out on their basis.' However, because none of the programs has ever been released, it is difficult to ascertain to what degree of detail the programs were then worked out.

12.5.3 The goals of target programming

Among the overall goals of target programming, the following are crucial:

1. Fully meeting requirements for selected products in the region.
2. Concentrating resources on key components of SEI.
3. Balancing requirements against the resources that the CPEs are prepared to mobilize.
4. Specifying all parameters for the solution of the selected topics, including time frames, implementation methods and resource and product apportionment.
5. A high degree of concentration to exploit scale economies by utilizing up-to-date technology.
6. Effective transmission of basic knowledge into production with minimum delays (Engert, 1978, p. 27).

Other relatively new elements introduced by target programming included the construction of EJRs, consumer norms, security of supply and self-sufficiency. Though the EJR concept is reminiscent of socially necessary labor cost, it is much broader in content because it refers more to the satisfaction of final demand than to attuning production costs to world standards *per se*. In satisfying reasonable final demand levels, particular emphasis is placed on improving economic efficiency through various cost-reducing measures, including structural change, relocation of economic activities and branch process substitution.

If EJRs are closely connected with traditional 'norms' in Soviet-type planning, the second unusual emphasis in target programming is on consumer norms. But what conceptual role consumer norms have in SEI has never been clarified. In the late 1970s it was mentioned that agreement on the methodology and results of demand projections would be crucial if final consumption was to be satisfied. For foodstuffs and manufactured consumer goods, especially basic goods, the CPEs wanted to specify norms that, combined with demographic projections, would yield target consumption levels for the next decade that would help to balance partial consumer markets. Two approaches appear to have been explored. For foodstuffs, an attempt was made to specify standard diet requirements and desirable regional self-reliance indicators. In addition, demand studies were to be undertaken in order to anticipate likely shifts in consumption patterns that might occur in response to changes in personal incomes and habits, which would affect the structure and level of demand at given income levels. From budget studies and cross-section analyses of household expenditures, the CPEs hoped to identify basic pointers for setting proper production levels.

Security of supply to buttress steady growth has been a basic goal of CMEA cooperation since the Council's inception. Several components of the Target Programs were slated to be anchored to more stringent targets, with regional self-sufficiency as an overt objective (Chodow, 1976, p. 23; Weiss, 1978, p. 932). This may have called for (possibly palpable) changes in the pattern of East-West trade. Cost considerations as such appear to have had a subsidiary role in the selection of specific subprogram goals, a circumstance that has been explicitly acknowledged (Bíró, 1978, p. 1203). Self-sufficiency in basic foodstuffs and relative independence of machinery and technology imports from outside the region were definitely on the policy agenda.

As a policy objective, conceptually EJR is closely attuned to regional self-sufficiency. A political compromise on the desirable degree of regional self-reliance was under study, at least regarding primary input needs. Combined with the goal of security of supply, such a decision could have important implications for the production and trade of the CPEs.

Although the overall directives for pursuing SEI through target programming may help to strengthen regional cohesion in the CMEA, these directives are excessively general and too vague to be helpful in preparing concrete projects. In addition to the overall guidelines, each program also has a separate set of objectives that bear directly on the strategic development of the sector(s) covered, and concrete goals are specified for each subprogram. In the case of agriculture and food processing, the program maps out the road to regional autarky for selected products. Whenever possible and economically warranted, the CPEs aim at 'completely satisfying [their] needs for high-quality foodstuffs,' including grains, meats and other basic farm products (Pekšev, 1979a, p. 3). For some products, particularly semiluxury goods, the goal may actually be to enhance exports from the region. The program contains targets for consumption, capacity increases and technologies to be explored for many products. Where mechanization in agriculture, automation in food processing and improvements in agricultural equipment are involved, the program interacts with the engineering program. It also hooks up with the program on energy, fuels and raw materials, for example, so as to secure a sufficient supply of fertilizer.

The program on manufactured consumer goods seeks to maximize satisfaction of basic consumer needs through specialization, the restructuring of production processes and improving the supply of material inputs. This is to be carried out in accordance with consumer norms for basic goods projected regionally and nationally up to 1990. The program also anticipates substantially improving the quality, availability, reliability and range of supply of durable consumer goods and timely servicing of those products.

By far the most important program is the one on energy, fuels and industrial raw materials. Its prominence has resulted not only from the then-imminent second energy crisis in the CMEA but also because the security of supply of primary industrial inputs continues to be a cornerstone of CMEA cooperation and, at least in the eyes of some observers, constitutes the only *raison d'être* for SEI.[1] Although this extreme position is contestable (Brabant, 1980, pp. 277–9), it is beyond doubt that by enhancing SEI the small CPEs hope to secure firm commitments on exchanging primary industrial inputs for manufactures.

The objectives of the primary input program are formulated around the perceived need to ensure substantial regional self-reliance. The CPEs are called upon, among other tasks, to more intensively utilize their own natural resources, reduce the specific consumption of primary inputs, stimulate regional output by pooling funds, accelerate technological innovation in the production of secondary materials, shift energy consumption toward use of solid fuels and nuclear energy and locate new production facilities through-out the region, particularly by more completely prospecting the peripheral CPEs. This places substantial claims on engineering.

The mechanical engineering program anticipates gradually equipping and reequipping selected branches through mechanization and automation, computer technology, automated control systems, specialization and cooperation in production, plan coordination and joint research and development. Its primary tasks are those resulting from the other programs, but it is also looking at structural change in the engineering sector itself so that the CMEA's requirements for capital goods can be ensured through improvements in the structure of production, including the better location of facilities, regional specialization in parts and components and standardiza-tion.

Finally, the transportation program focuses on the 'fullest, prompt, and efficient satisfaction of the rapidly growing needs of [CPEs] for all types of transportation' (Petrova, 1979, p. 5) through qualitative and quantitative improvements in the infrastructure, servicing and production of transporta-tion equipment. More concrete goals are implicit in the sequential signing of specific agreements that are components of an overall master program whose priorities include the creation of an up-to-date transportation network and a supporting mechanical engineering sector.

12.5.4 The relationship between target programming and planning

From the best evidence available, the Target Programs appeared to embody merely a set of intentions and preliminary commitments regarding the overall framework within which legally binding trade and financial protocols were to be negotiated. Therefore, it will be instructive to examine the sequential relationship between planning and target programming to enhance our understanding of the substance of target programming and hence the type of commitment assumed by the participants. This systematic exposition may also prove helpful because no comprehensive elaboration of methods, procedures and guidelines for drafting, ratifying and implementing the programs has ever been published.

The first step in program formulation is the selection of the time frame within which the policymaking bodies of the CPEs and the CMEA's pinnacle organs agree to bolster common activities. Against a working horizon of 1990 (possibly 1995 or even 2000), the CPEs resolved to meet their final needs for selected goods and services by steadily expanding the regional supply of primary materials, production technologies, infrastructure and production factors. At this stage, target programming amounts to little more than a set of common principles for strengthening certain aspects of SEI as a matter of policy priority. To translate these overall desires into operational tasks with concrete supply and demand targets, the following approach is followed (Georgiev, 1978, p. 27).

The Planning Committee is formally entrusted with minutely examining the guidelines developed by the policymaking bodies. It can muster expert help from individual CPEs, *ad hoc* multinational working groups or the formal and informal CMEA organs, including other Committees under the CMEA Executive Committee (Kormnov, 1977b, p. 93; Pekšev, 1978b, p. 96). In its capacity as overall coordinator, the Planning Committee normally appoints one member as chairman of a special working group that will make a *tour d'horizon* of the alternative specifications of a particular program in light of member interests.

To assess cooperation possibilities, each working group then mobilizes various subgroups, CMEA official and affiliated organs and collaborative study groups, each of which addresses a specific subcomponent of the broad tasks on which most CPEs agree, in principle, to intensify collaboration. The working group sorts through the findings of these subgroups and submits a draft Target Program to the Planning Committee, where it is evaluated on its merits, including how well it meshes with other Target Programs. This Committee, perhaps after some further deliberation, prepares a final draft for party and government leaders, and, finally, for the CMEA Council Session, which formally approves the documents.

Once accepted, the stage is set for deliberations on the specific output, specialization, trade, resource transfer and implementation modalities. Each topic included in a program is negotiated separately. Successful negotiations are concluded by a formal bi- or multilateral intergovernmental agreement (the so-called implementation agreement), which imposes legal obligations on the participants. Once these agreements are in place, reciprocal obligations are disaggregated into medium-term targets, which in turn form the backbone of a Concerted Plan that parallels the national five-year plans. Coordination at that stage naturally also encompasses the regular areas of annual and medium-term plan development. Specific targets for the annual plans, which are the real operative instruments of short-term economic policy in the CPEs, are set based on the annual trade and cooperation agreements (the so-called final agreements), which contain the timed flow of goods and services in detail.

The importance of the timely transformation of Target Programs into realistic plan targets should be underlined. Experience has demonstrated that overt political and moral commitments are too vague to ensure the smooth implementation of understandings reached at the highest party and government echelons. Timely drafting of the implementation agreements, and hence determination of the precise legal obligations emanating from the programs, enables the CPEs to draw up the Concerted Plan and coordinate the national medium-term plans without having to rush against fixed deadlines.

12.5.5 On the construction of a Target Program

It is unclear whether the CPEs elaborated common procedures for formulating, ratifying and implementing the Target Programs that were endorsed in the second half of the 1970s. Therefore, it is a matter of speculation precisely how these agreements are drawn up and fit into the planning framework of the members. The following is a useful phasing of program construction, although it does not identify every intricacy of the steps involved, nor is the implied time sequence applicable in all instances.

Basically, there are eight formulation stages:

1. Selection of common goals and their sequential priorities.
2. Projection of the region's future needs.
3. Designation of time frames for the various tasks.
4. Assessment of resource requirements and ensuring that available resources are not overcommitted.
5. Determination of target production levels for each phase.
6. Selection of the forms and methods for solving set tasks and determination of which organizational tier (national, regional and so on) will oversee their implementation.
7. Agreement on reciprocal trade flows, possibly allowing for cooperation with third countries.
8. Setting the economic conditions for implementation (including price-formation rules, currency regimes and capital and labor transfers).

Once past these hurdles, the program is structured into four parts (Mirov and Dimov, 1977, pp. 32–3): the target block with the overall goals of the program; the structural block with the concrete measures to be embraced; the resource block, in which the material, financial and labor requirements are identified; and, fourth, the planning block, which comprises indicators that link the program with the national medium-term plans by way of preliminary targets for the Concerted Plan. However, this sequence is sometimes bypassed because of existing agreements that are simply co-opted (CMEA, 1977a) and because several of the endorsed programs were accepted before completion of the last two stages – possibly, as in one case, because of considerable controversy during the negotiations.

12.5.6 The compass and economics of target programming

The foregoing suggests that, at least for two reasons, target programming cannot be equated with planning. First, it does not specify legal obligations or operational targets for the national planning tiers. Furthermore, no attempt is made to balance all aspects of demand and supply of the selected sectors. These features are rooted in the fact that, even under a policy designed to bolster SEI, traditional central planning remains a prerogative of sovereign state decision making (see chapter 7).

Needless to say, the economics of target programming falls within the compass of the SEI mechanism. As detailed in Part IV, the absence of an operational integration mechanism and the failure to plan jointly for integration have prevented substantive SEI progress, not only with the Target Programs. But the shaky foundations of the economic mechanisms have, almost from the very beginning, doomed the efforts of target programming. This is surprising because, by the mid-1970s, the CPEs had accumulated sufficient experience with technical economic hindrances to SEI. Certainly, commitments were made to tackle 'all' economic issues, but little effort was devoted to overcoming fundamental deficiencies in the CMEA's monetary and financial systems (Dimov, 1978, p. 5).

Perhaps the most surprising element in the weak economic basis of target programming was the embedded claims on financial, labor and material resources, which were variously estimated for the 1980s at between TR 66 and 90 billion.[2] Doubtless, the bulk of these claims would not require cross-border transfers. Nonetheless, despite the fact that the economics of target programming could be largely internalized through the habitual national planning apparatus, the inherent desirability of placing such ventures on solid economic foundations was not removed. This was especially necessary because some CPEs were then placing great emphasis on stepping up factor productivity growth.

12.5.7 Target programming and SEI in the 1980s

For a short while after the Council Sessions of the mid-1970s, the tenor of the discussions (Mirov and Dimov, 1977, p. 32; Pekšev, 1978a, p. 3; Pekšev, 1978b, p. 95) suggested that the programs would be very comprehensive, contain details on economic penalties and incentives and specify the parameters of production tasks as well as the economics of effective cooperation, including credit and price questions. Accordingly, framework programs should have been formulated so that systematic implementation of their provisions would only have been a matter of organizational accommodation. As such, they would have entailed *de facto* economywide plan coordination. In other words, the original objective of the programs was steeped in the mechanistic view of clocklike central regulation of economic processes.

Although the programs initially held vast aims, shared interests extended only to the most vital aspects of the fuel and raw material sectors, including the related engineering requirements. As a result, the original scope of target programming was markedly scaled down during the process of preparing the five programs. Under the impact of rapidly swelling external adjustment requirements and the need to manage considerable domestic disequilibriums, one country after another, particularly in Eastern Europe proper, deviated from its medium-term plan and hence from the agreements reached at the CMEA level through target programming, including the associated second Concerted Plan. But I do not want to suggest that nothing of the original blueprints was carried out. In the fuel, energy and raw material branches, some countries certainly forged ahead, but at a reduced pace and toward lesser goals. I am skeptical, however, about suggestions that by mid-1985, much later than originally forecast, 'the elaboration of measures for [the Target Programs] has been practically completed and more than 200 agreements on economic, scientific, and technological cooperation have been signed' (Bagudin, Gavrilov and Šinkov, 1985, p. 18).

Why discuss target programming at such length when the programs established in the 1970s for all practical purposes foundered and could not possibly be revived? The answer lies in the fact that at least some of the original components were economically justified in terms of a structural policy approach to SEI. As such, target programming *in se* remains a critical planning tool, one that may help the CPEs individually or collectively tackle what I have identified in chapter 6 as a positive structural adjustment policy. If properly conceived and implemented, it need not contradict the economic reforms based on indirect coordination that I advocate in chapter 18. A thorough reevaluation of target programming is also in order because the issues that were to be addressed in the later 1970s are exactly those highlighted in *Scientific-Technological Progress*, albeit with minor variations. Finally, if the currently envisioned reforms soon work out as intended, national planning agencies should find themselves better positioned for pondering the advantages and drawbacks of target programming.

12.6 COORDINATION OF ECONOMIC POLICIES

The policy coordination instrument of SEI has various connotations, which can range from a simple discussion on intentions by high-level policymakers to a blending of objectives and resources for a particular endeavor, including the economy as a whole, though that is likely to remain an ideal. Precisely because of the concept's fuzziness and that policy coordination in the CMEA for many years was really not voluntary, some observers (see Bagudin, Gavrilov and Šinkov, 1985) treat policy coordination very casually. They give the impression that it has always been a major SEI activity.

What is at stake, especially when one peers into the future possibilities of SEI, is something quite different, however. Essentially, coordinating economic policies requires the collective mapping out of solutions to major economic problems of common interest to the majority of CPEs. It therefore involves identifying medium- to long-term directions for economic development and cooperation and the 'joint planning of direct interaction in science, technology, material production, and capital construction' (Bagudin, Gavrilov and Šinkov, 1985, p. 13), though I find that requirement beyond present CMEA capabilities. Clearly, meetings at the highest governmental and Communist Party level – including formal economic summits, intergovernmental meetings, occasional inter-party meetings, Council Sessions and other regional contacts – coordinate policies (see Part II). Making real headway will depend on the degree to which sovereign economic leaders will be prepared to articulate their visions of future structural developments, how they hope to accomplish them and how these conceptions can be modified to mitigate conflicts of interest.

12.7 JOINT PLANNING

As noted in section 12.1, joint planning is a particular form of integrating economic policies that could have been attained through a CMEA planning agency, which was seriously contemplated in the early 1960s when *Basic Principles* was endorsed. Nothing came of this vision at that time (see chapter 4). Nonetheless, since then joint planning has been mentioned in SEI debates as an option members can increasingly and voluntarily use. As Csaba (1983, pp. 107–8) underlined, joint planning 'can only be employed if, in connection with developing some concrete production activities, the interests of several countries coincide to such an extent . . . that the elaboration of a uniform development program, efficient from the viewpoint of *every participant*, is realistic.' As one Eastern European specialist put it, 'joint planning differs from the coordination of plans mainly by its facultative character' (Wasilkowski, 1971, p. 47). The obligation to participate in plan coordination, however, derives from CMEA statutes and resolutions that the CPEs have explicitly endorsed.

Joint planning will usually encompass some of the other forms of plan coordination examined in this chapter. In particular, it requires joint forecasting of demand and supply; agreement on standardizing production technologies, possibly after appropriating minimum capital and labor resources; negotiating concrete multi- and especially bilateral implementation agreements; and making links with annual and medium-term plans as well as with the relevant Concerted Plans and Target Programs. Whether it is still realistic to seriously entertain any kind of joint planning other than the common charting of medium- to long-term structural policies is doubtful. I shall explain this position in chapter 18.

NOTES

1. This position has been defended by many commentators on East-West trade, especially Korbonski, 1976, pp. 586ff.; Lavigne, 1983, 1984; and Montias, 1974, pp. 676ff.
2. There are many different sources. Ivanov, 1979, p. 28, projects TR 70 to 90 billion; Petrova, 1979, p. 5, states eight to ten times the expenditures earmarked under the first Concerted Plan, or TR 72 to 90 billion; Šarenkov and Djakin, 1979, p. 9, and Semënov, 1978, p. 104, estimate TR 80 to 90 billion; and Ju. S. Širjaev in *Die Presse*, 10 March 1979, suggested TR 66 to 86 billion.

13 · PRODUCTION SPECIALIZATION, TECHNOLOGY COOPERATION AND SEI

This chapter examines the traditional efforts employed by European planned economies to enhance SEI directly through production specialization and STC, as distinct from market-oriented approaches. Three interrelated topics are broached under this heading: ECPS agreements in the strict sense, production cooperation and STC agreements. Fundamentally, ECPS agreements are treaties in which at least one country agrees to specialize in manufacturing a specific product or range of products for the purpose of satisfying its own needs as well as those of its cooperating partners. In turn, partners promise to buy the product(s) under treaty and thus not build up a capacity of their own that would substitute for CMEA imports or perhaps even compete with the specializing country. As such, ECPS agreements are designed to exploit economies of scale and accelerate technological advances by concentrating resources according to mutually acceptable criteria. And as such they are closely interrelated with cooperation agreements.

Cooperation agreements involve economic agents from at least two CPEs that commit themselves to jointly produce one or more products. Agents obligate themselves to supply parts and components for production of the product(s) under investigation, possibly by a single other partner. Such agreements may involve joint development work, sharing existing designs, pooling sales and/or service networks, supplying parts and so on. In other words, cooperation agreements focus on direct interfirm relations whereas ECPS agreements concentrate on joint procurement of certain goods. Nonetheless, the two types of agreements are often intermingled and difficult to separate. For that reason, I shall discuss ECPS and cooperation agreements under one rubric, namely ECPS efforts. I am earmarking most of this chapter to that bewildering issue because the literature on the experiences with ECPS agreements within the CMEA, as intimated in chapter 10, is rife with conflicting arguments and views on the purposes and accomplishments of that type of policy instrument in SEI. These contradictory appraisals prevail not only in the Western literature but also in many Eastern European analyses, increasingly in conjunction with plans for national and regional economic reform.

As indicated, STC agreements are closely intertwined with the other two types of agreements, which may constitute one component of STC efforts, especially if STC comprises the entire cycle from research and development to production and sales. For practical purposes, however, and for reasons to be explained as I proceed, I shall keep STC and ECPS protocols and experiences separate.

Section 13.1 presents the framework that exists for fostering production specialization in the CMEA, basically within the microeconomic context, although its role in implementing economywide programs is also addressed. How to appraise the CMEA's legion of bi- and multilateral agreements within a context of rationality appropriate to CPEs forms the subject of section 13.2. Section 13.3 addresses the issue of STC. How one can ascertain the progress achieved with ECPS and STC within the integration structure that the CPEs have blueprinted in their main policy documents forms the subject of section 13.4. In the final section, I illustrate the pitfalls of taking at face value the ubiquitous specialization indicators presented in the Eastern European literature, as well as in some recent Western research. I also outline ways in which an independent measure of the trade and production effects of ECPS and STC agreements might be constructed. Actual magnitudes or tentative results of these more desirable, yet partial, empirical assessments of integration effects are analyzed in Part IV.

13.1 THE NATURE OF PRODUCTION SPECIALIZATION

To properly sketch how integration effects could be measured, the dimensions of the process by which this policy is fostered need to be recalled. This is required not only to properly interpret the quantitative and qualitative results occasionally reported as illustrations of the beneficial effects of specialization but also to evaluate ECPS and STC agreements for their own sake or in conjunction with more general efforts designed to bolster SEI.

13.1.1 Specialization in the context of MEs

When MEs specialize in response to the further opening up of their economy to global competition, it is usually because of factor movements induced by shifts in effective demand and supply forces for one or more products on a 'global' basis. That is, pre-union trade prices are modified, either because costs change or because tariffs and related transaction costs incurred in assessing markets are compressed through the scale economies of specialization. These shifts warrant adjustments in demand and supply that in turn call for modifications in factor use and output patterns. Factor immobility is usually assumed, but that is only a convenient assumption for specifying measurements rather than a condition for exploiting further comparative advantages. Therefore, production specialization in MEs is a means for capitalizing on changes in market forces. In the CPE context, however, specialization is a direct object of decisions regarding the supply of certain goods and services within the context of the needs and resources of at least two countries. Whether unionwide demand is also anticipated depends on the circumstances under which the specialization protocols are signed and implemented.

When economies that decide to integrate are in equilibrium, it is fairly easy to ascertain whether, if one or more decision parameters are changed, production specialization should be fostered and in which direction. For example, because the effective world terms of trade change when tariffs are removed, new opportunities to shift domestic consumption and production arise. Production will expand in goods for which the country has a comparative advantage and will contract for other goods. Consumption of the product that becomes relatively cheaper is encouraged at the expense of other goods unless all goods are subject to a uniform tariff that is now cut across the board. With factor immobility, trade is bound to expand and will do so more in favor of partners for whom tariffs have been reduced, possibly to the detriment of third countries.

If factor mobility occurs *solely* in response to differences in relative factor rewards, those scarcest will tend to be augmented while the most abundant factors will move abroad. Depending on the magnitude and direction of these factor shifts, union formation may immediately effect a rise, a contraction or no change in the pre-union trade level. In the immediate future, union formation with factor mobility is likely to have a negative trade effect because factor mobility is being substituted for the mobility of goods and services. But this substitution does, of course, entail positive integration effects regardless of whether the impact on trade registers a minus or a plus sign.

However, results conjectured in a static world should not be generalized to all circumstances. In a dynamic frame of reference, even with the initial movement of production factors, positive trade effects are bound to eventually register, provided that factor mobility is not too extreme (that is, tending to exhaust the scarcest production factors). But that process may take a long time.

13.1.2 Specialization in the CPE context

The above stylized facts of production specialization in the context of MEs do not necessarily apply to CPEs. For one reason, these countries do not make decisions utilizing indirect coordination instruments as the primary levers with which to steer the desired integration format. Perhaps more important, generally these economies are in macroeconomic disequilibrium.[1] A decision to expand output of some goods at the expense of others is not typically based on comparative advantage indicators. CPEs set prices (that is, all parameters that define scarcities) intermittently by central fiat, including on strictly administrative grounds, rather than by reflection of demand and supply forces on a fairly continuous basis. In fact, the CPE may specialize in the wrong direction. If it is on the right course, it rarely expands to the level where the comparative advantage could be fully exploited.

13.1.3 Alternative views on specialization in the CPE framework

Of course, the above elaborations hold only if ECPS agreements are signed with the intention of enhancing SEI. Though such an assumption may be self-evident, in the CMEA context it has turned out not to be so. Commentators on production specialization have held divergent views on the CPEs' interest in furthering integration. The reader may refer back to chapter 3 for a refresher on the ups and downs of the first ECPS agreements that were signed in the mid- and late 1950s and how they failed to be implemented. The recurrence of the ECPS theme in subsequent SEI documents suffices to illustrate that specialization has still failed to make the intended headway.

Paralleling the four views on the mechanism of SEI elaborated in chapter 10, four attitudes regarding ECPS agreements also flourish. Because the first argues that the CMEA is primarily concerned about matters other than enhancing economic progress and welfare, presumably ECPS agreements would be interpreted as being primarily for show. The second view, which is anchored to the basic exchange of assured volumes of fuels and raw materials against uncompetitive, if perhaps not entirely shoddy, manufactures, tends to take a similar position: Eastern Europe agrees to endorse ECPS agreements but these are not taken very seriously when development paths are designed and priorities are set. This discrepancy between the written word, intentions and actual deeds lasts for as long as the partner delivering the hard goods fails to enforce greater cohesion through its command over traded goods.

However, the two remaining positions are critical. One derives from the broader views of SEI represented most cogently in the Western literature by Vladimir Sobell (1984). The other has a range of adherents. Sobell, as noted in chapter 10, argues that SEI has been quite successful and that further progress will emanate from the policies and instruments available, which are anchored to what he calls the IPO, as distinct from the ITS, which he considers the foundation of Western-style integration. Finally, a category of views exists that acknowledges that progress with SEI through production specialization has been undeniably positive, but that there remains considerable room for further improvement and hence marked integration and trade effects. This group typically projects economic integration as a process concerned with enhancing efficiency. Sobell's perception, however, varies not only with the alleged purposes of SEI but also with concerns about the means utilized to implement these endeavors and how best to measure integration results.

Sobell sees the ultimate purpose of SEI as the equalization of levels of development of different countries through the protection provided by the CPEs' self-chosen differentiation from economic structures that would have emanated from comparative advantage precepts prevailing elsewhere. This protection enables production to expand not on the basis of 'prices reflecting relative scarcities but by bilateral and multilateral intergovernmental agreements reflecting political aspirations' (pp. 6–7). Under such arrangements, the success of integration is a function of the extent to which the mutual exchange of resources ensures steady expansion of output. Sobell argues that trade flows 'cannot be regarded as trade in the conventional sense but as internal supplies taking place within a virtually closed, self-contained production system, such as a large vertically structured corporation or within the USSR itself between regions' (p. 7).

The volume, structure and distribution of such commodity flows are perceived to be regulated by individual production unit managers who operate on the basis of ECPS agreements reached through bargaining sessions that are focused on the regional distribution of value added in the form of implicit subsidies. As such, Sobell considers the essence of the proliferation of ECPS agreements to be 'the collective response to alleviate the disadvantages associated with participation in the [CMEA]' (p. 248). Thus, he sees the flow of resources within the CMEA as determined primarily by ideological and technological factors rather than by comparative advantage. He argues that ECPS agreements are negotiated not because the specializing country volunteers to supply certain goods to the nonspecializing country but 'to organise production of such products with a view of satisfying, partly or fully, the needs of the non-specialising country (enterprise); the conditions of supply are, in the context of an agreement, of secondary importance and may be agreed upon in parallel with the production agreement or in a supplementary agreement' (p. 12). Therefore, specialization as such is only an instrument for obtaining access to certain goods and services, not a means for enhancing domestic economic efficiency and welfare levels.

As to effects, Sobell argues that 'there can be no doubt that [SEI] has had a profound impact' (p. 3) on the CPEs, but that this emerges clearly only when the countries' own success criteria are scrutinized. Accordingly, measuring integration effects requires either quantifying the extent to which SEI has contributed to the equalization of development levels or the amount by which it has enriched members of the group. He is skeptical about the wisdom of attempting to quantify the visible impact of SEI in terms of trade increments.

In principle, I do not object to this multilayer approach to measurement issues, provided it is consistently adhered to. I find it odd, though, that Sobell passes overall judgment on the benefits and drawbacks of SEI chiefly by referring to and describing various microeconomic aspects of resource mobilization through ECPS. It is, of course, correct to argue that 'an attempt at precise quantification of the cumulative impact of [ECPS] would have to resolve several formidable methodological problems' (p. 15). Precisely because he assumes that the CPEs do not consider economic benefits as the main purpose of SEI, he advocates an alternative approach, namely the extent to which the mutual exchange of resources within the CMEA ensures steady expansion of production because it is allegedly free of ideology and consonant with the criteria applied by CPE governments themselves. Foreign trade plans, BTPAs and ECPS protocols are thus a necessary, though not a sufficient, prerequisite for maximizing stability in a relatively self-contained system.

13.2 SPECIAL FEATURES OF ECPS AGREEMENTS

In addition to the prevailing economic disequilibrium, the measurement of SEI effects is complicated by other unusual characteristics of ECPS agreements. The objectives, complexity and time horizon of ECPS agreements must be kept in mind when appraising what precisely the CPEs hope to achieve.

13.2.1 On the goals of specialization agreements

ECPS agreements can, inherently, have at least four distinct objectives, although these are not necessarily mutually independent: relocating production facilities, redistributing existing production capacity, avoiding duplication of identical production processes and creating new production capacity. Essentially, an agreement to relocate capacity seeks to transfer production across national frontiers. This may or may not imply an allocation favoring the country with the lowest production costs for a given product. The discontinuation of the production of certain locomotives in Czechoslovakia and the transfer of that technology to Bulgaria is an example. If the process is profitable in the recipient country in the real sense, as distinct from results assessed at fiat prices, such specialization is presumably useful. However, the sign and size of its trade effects are difficult to predict as they depend on several national features that enter into such an agreement. The key parameters concern who was trading locomotives with whom and at what cost prior to the ECPS agreement. Assuming that Czechoslovakia had been producing for only its home market, such specialization may entail less trade (if Bulgaria had been importing the locomotives), no trade effects (if Bulgaria had not previously imported the product), trade expansion (Czechoslovakia and perhaps other CMEA partners now import from Bulgaria), trade diversion (Bulgaria substitutes for imports from third countries) and other effects. Any one of these alternatives, or a combination thereof, is plausible and none can be preferred over another until the details of the agreement and its implementation become known. Only then can the potential effects be disentangled by designing controlled experiments that may be capable of measuring the trade and possibly other effects of the ECPS agreement.

A second type of agreement aims at redistributing production capacity to take advantage of economies of scale, particularly for products with many variants for which the retooling of existing output capacity is uncomplicated and for which resources for a less-diverse output range can be appropriated without requiring anything but the resource mobility internal to existing firms. An example would be ball bearings. Instead of each country producing thousands of varieties, the union agrees to maintain total production in tonnage at approximately existing levels but to redistribute the components over the union, thus fostering scale economies. The agreement may also be structured so that incremental capacity is preallocated to accelerate the exploitation of scale economies, but that variant more appropriately belongs with a third alternative, which will be described below. Incidentally, reapportioning existing capacity for a product that is technologically similar to another has been an objective of SEI from the very start (see chapter 3), including for ball bearings.

Because the ECPS agreement is explicitly designed to substitute for domestic production through CMEA imports and boost exports of specialized items, trade creation must occur. Trade diversion may also be involved if part of the pre-ECPS consumption of ball bearings was acquired from outside the union. However, that effect could be strictly incidental to the ECPS protocol or it may be a subsidiary objective. Again, a detailed analysis of the ECPS agreement should clarify issues and hence permit the design of measurement experiments.

A third type of agreement seeks to avoid production duplication. In its simplest form it may validate existing production structures and capacities while simultaneously forestalling further capacity duplication along the lines foreseen in the ECPS agreement in the future appropriation of resources. Such an agreement can yield only marginal positive trade and integration effects. When the agreement specifies that new capacity be geared to incremental demand of the signatory countries as a unit, positive trade effects will appear only when that incremental capacity becomes available.

An alternative purpose might be to discontinue certain capacities in some countries while concurrently shifting production to the lowest-cost site. Incremental demand will be served directly from new capacity in the specializing country. In time, however, the economic and technological obsolescence of the 'confirmed' production structures will also be met through specialization as the prevailing total demand is gradually catered to. Again, *a priori*, the sign and size of the trade and integration effects are unclear. A careful study of the specifications of the ECPS agreement in question, in conjunction with follow-up actions that include possible modifications of or additions to the original ECPS agreement, is therefore required.

Finally, the agreement may anticipate the creation of new product lines in a variety of configurations. Partners may introduce a product jointly or substitute for imports from third countries through the *ex ante* division of labor. This may be associated with the, usually temporary, migration of capital and labor, but such factor mobility is not necessary and tends to be unusual in the CMEA. Agreement to create new capacity by joint efforts so as to effectively meet the incremental demand of the union as a whole might also be coupled with the destruction or modification of existing production capacity. Depending on the provisions of the agreement, within-group trade may increase, remain unaffected or even contract, and the ECPS protocol may or may not involve trade diversion, possibly from other CPEs.

13.2.2 The time horizon of specialization agreements

As already indicated, the time element is critical in evaluating the contribution of ECPS agreements to trade and the enhancement of SEI at any given point or even over time. It is often omitted from accounts of the effects of union formation. This is regrettable because adjustments in economic structures and demand take time, not only in CPEs. However, it is more critical in CPEs for the following reason. Even under the most favorable circumstances, when the signatories wholeheartedly agree, in principle, to foster positive production specialization in a product line and act upon their resolve, the effects on trade, efficiency and availability of goods for consumption will not become tangible until these measures can be woven into the planning process and actually implemented. In most instances this process requires at least several years. Under certain conditions, execution of ECPS provisions may have to be deferred until the next medium-term plan can be launched because resource reserves are lacking or countries are unable to switch resources already appropriated.

13.2.3 Complexity of the agreement

An important parameter of the scope and speed with which ECPS agreements can be implemented is the complexity of the objective being sought. Thus, the more complicated the product or process, including the particular specialization configuration desired, the longer it takes to implement the ECPS provisions, even without other obstacles interfering. Furthermore, the more complex and time-consuming the task, the greater the chance that corrections will be sought at some stage, either to ensure that the program is kept on course or to mitigate the repercussions of noncompliance. Both factors are probably more important when the agreement targets an existing product or technology, thus involving structural change through positive adjustment policies, than when it focuses on development of a new technology for which resources can be appropriated. The problems are probably most acute when existing production facilities are to be decommissioned in favor of new, specialized processes for the CMEA as a whole, but when the products are intrinsically identical for planning purposes.

13.3 SCIENTIFIC-TECHNOLOGICAL COOPERATION

From the beginning of CMEA cooperation, a principal objective has been to promote the exchange of scientific-technological information. Joint innovation through basic research and laboratory testing, even as a policy precept, materialized only much later. How such exchange or development of basic knowledge should be organized, appropriate ways to bear the true costs of such cooperation, and how best to capitalize on and distribute the benefits of STC are basic questions that should prominently appear on the agenda of decision makers. At times such questions have been the focal point of policy discussions and the object of acrimonious exchanges within the CMEA, and inability to satisfactorily resolve them has hindered the promulgation of a steady course toward the effective realization of STC as a springboard for advancing SEI.

13.3.1 STC after World War II

This soul-searching has a rather long history. It was very much in evidence after World War II in connection with the implementation of the reparations that the Soviet Union felt were due it by the former Axis powers and their allies (see chapter 2) and during the integration debates of 1949 and 1950. A critical decision – known as the Sofia Principle – was handed down at the second Council Session. Accordingly, CMEA members pledged a near-gratuitous exchange of scientific and technical knowledge and agreed to make specialized human capital available almost on demand. In effect, this arrangement secured the type of STC that would hold centerstage in the CMEA for the next two decades.

As a result of these twin developments, the basic economic questions on STC mentioned above subsequently receded, or at least were rarely raised at the policymaking level. Nevertheless, under the cover of bilateralism, and with the Sofia Principle as ultimate guarantor, these fundamental questions simmered underneath the lid of 'unequal' STC based primarily on the exchange of existing scientific and technical information. The joint fostering of a continuous regeneration of the stock of such information, directly through plan integration or indirectly through proper economic coordination instruments and their supporting institutions, has occurred more recently. Its basic rationale has long been recognized – at least in policy declarations and programs, particularly in Eastern Europe.

The pure economics of SEI hardly occupied centerstage in considerations about revamping and evolving the CMEA until discussions about *Integration Program* jelled in the late 1960s. Perhaps an exception should be made for the envigorating debates from the CMEA's foundation until mid-1950 (see chapter 2). Nonetheless, after these were forcibly terminated, genuine regional economic integration failed to regain a significant role in CMEA policy discussions until the late 1960s at the earliest (see chapter 4).

13.3.2 On the Sofia Principle

At the start of CMEA cooperation (see chapter 2), a protracted debate took place on the pros and cons of lending fraternal assistance by transferring scientific-technological knowledge across the region at a nominal charge. Some countries, particularly those that would be 'exporting', argued in favor of selling blueprints at nominal cost, but only for technology that had been fully amortized. In other words, the less-developed countries would be able to gratuitously obtain documentation for outdated, perhaps even old-fashioned, production processes that might still be of interest to them. In turn, they favored the free transfer of technological achievements regardless of the degree of recoupment of outlays in the country of origin. In the end, the receiving countries won the day. This precept continued to be the guiding beacon of STC in the CMEA – in some instances even the cement of Soviet-type industrialization – until the late 1960s (Kaplan, 1977, pp. 86–7).

The Sofia Principle holds that blueprints of technological processes are available upon demand at the cost of reproducing and shipping the documents. If blueprints do not exist, the country requesting the transfer may also be charged for the labor incurred in customizing and preparing the documents. It was also resolved to encourage the exchange of engineers, scientists and other specialists, most of whom would be compensated by their home country; if this was not possible, the host country would reimburse these personnel for their subsistence in local currency. Concerning the exchange of documents relating to inventions and technological processes, it was stipulated that this information could only be used for production destined for domestic utilization, even if it had been considerably transformed (Neumann, 1980, pp. 182–3).[2] That is, the recipient could dispose freely of the documentation, in either its original or transformed form, only within its own borders and only for meeting domestic requirements. On the other topics, especially the economics of this exchange (see chapter 17), the record is more convoluted.

When it was decided in August 1949 to reduce the economic aspects of STC to the simple marginal cost of preparing, duplicating and expediting documents or of temporarily delegating skilled personnel, the economics of STC vanished, as it were, with the stroke of a pen. In principle, any CPE could request blueprints of any other member's technical knowledge for merely a token cost. Likewise, any CPE could ask that specialists be temporarily delegated to set up a particular production facility, process, technology or similar endeavor at the simple cost of reimbursement of travel and local expenditures.

If the recipient wanted to start exporting goods and services produced on the basis of such free documentation, it was expected to obtain prior concurrence from the original donor. The purpose of this measure was to prevent the recipient country from undercutting the donor's market, whether inside the CMEA or elsewhere. This principle was hard to police, however, even when its focus was narrowed to simply acquiring a straightforward production technology for a particular product. For example, Bulgaria may have produced locomotives on the basis of blueprints received from Czechoslovakia and eventually may have wanted to export these, possibly and perhaps inadvertently, in competition with CMEA partners. How much more difficult must the policing have been in the case of complex technologies or fundamental scientific and technological knowledge that would eventually become part of a truly homegrown production technique!

13.3.3 Toward commercializing STC

The drawbacks of the decade-long free exchange of STC prompted a growing sentiment on the part of the more developed CPEs to withhold newer findings and to insist upon research and development costs being shared by those actually or potentially interested in exploiting the knowledge acquired in the process. This sentiment crystallized in part from perceptions that profit was being forgone as a result of free exchange. In addition, as the more developed CPEs began in the early 1960s to participate in global trade in patents and licenses, the losses being incurred by continuing with their technological generosity quickly became highlighted. For reasons examined elsewhere (Brabant, 1988c, 1988d), it took nearly another decade, until the thirtieth meeting of the Executive Committee in July 1967, before the formal principle was slightly relaxed, at least officially. The practice of recognizing *ad hoc* forms of compensation had already much earlier started on a significant scale (Gatzka, 1985, pp. 46–7; Monkiewicz, 1975, p. 91). Such exceptions to the Sofia Principle had already been instituted under various guises, including in the context of *Haldex* (Brabant, 1988c).

After several Executive Committee meetings, particularly in 1967, it was concluded that the preservation of the Sofia Principle might discourage research and constitute a drag on development efforts in the more developed CMEA countries. To mitigate this adverse feature, it was recommended that payments to the donor could be justified in the case of costly projects and when the recipient stood to make substantial financial gains. These principles were later further elaborated, most notably at the forty-eighth session of the Executive Committee in July 1970. They were subsequently embodied in *Integration Program* as:

The transfer of results of scientific-technical research shall be passed on in accordance with arrangements made between interested countries. Depending on the level and value of the results of scientific-technical research, they may be passed on free of charge as well as for a financial compensation in accordance with agreements reached, bearing in mind that for such transfers it is necessary to consider the national interests of every individual country and the common interests of all CMEA member countries. (Tokareva, 1972, p. 50)

This recognition of the problem was sufficient to set in motion a search for a firmer legal basis of STC, a task that was entrusted to a working party of the newly created Conference for Legal Questions (first convened in 1969). In turn, these deliberations resulted in a formal document that was endorsed by the Executive Committee on 26 October 1972.[3] In essence, this document stipulates (CMEA, 1977b, pp. 377–81) that the transmission of the best inventions from the more developed CPEs be effected under conditions similar to those prevailing in world markets. However, assimilated and amortized technologies can be handed over without payment to the least developed CPEs, especially to Mongolia.[4]

The gist of the decision was to split STC into two components. On one side were the results of research that could lead to inventions protected by patents and other kinds of proprietary rights. This type of STC should primarily be regulated by issuing licenses in which details of the use of the license, including a price relative to some overall value, is stipulated. The second group would, in particular, refer to technical documentation, information on management and so on, which would be transmitted gratuitously, as in the past, but with the proviso that the recipient not transfer that information in any form to a third party without the explicit consent of the donor.

Yet even the recognition, as expressed later in *Integration Program*, that STC must be arranged on an *ad hoc* basis in bilateral relations and must reflect the interests not only of the individual partners but also of the entire community failed to solve the economics of STC. It merely shifted the emphasis of the root problem to that of appropriate payment. The real problem, then, has been how to determine the terms of the transfers and how to transform such transactions into effective determinants of STC. Complicating the situation is that, well into the 1970s, none of the CPEs (except Czechoslovakia) had domestic prices for licenses as a license was not considered a commodity. In the traditional CPE, inventions and scientific-technological knowledge are treated as state property available for commercialization and exploitation by national enterprises without any particular payment. The originator of the invention is normally compensated by means of a certificate of authorship or some nominal prize unrelated to the economic value of the invention.

New methods were thus called for. The problems encountered in the process are actually rooted in the economic accounting typical of CPEs, which is addressed in the next two chapters. The issue of pricing technology in the

CPEs, in part as an incentive to innovation, continues to be debated. Though technology is no longer absolutely free, the quandary of how to price 'nonmaterial goods' continues to complicate matters. Patents and inventions are now explicitly recognized as having at least use value. Inventors themselves, however, only marginally share in the fruits of their labor – a paradox of sorts that can only be explained within the context of the orthodox interpretation of the labor theory of value.

To the best of my knowledge, the regulations promulgated in 1972 and provisionally adopted by the Executive Committee are by and large still valid. The document ratified at that time, but apparently not by all members, has meanwhile been revised, most recently in 1985 at the 116th session of the Executive Committee (Matějka, 1985a, p. 13) and in January 1986 (Rüster, 1987), though only inconsequentially as far as the topic here is concerned. In fact, a recent treatment of the legal regulation of STC refers *only* to the 1972 version (Bikovski, 1988, p. 40).

A major dilemma emanating from the traditional accounting framework of CPEs, once it was recognized that compulsory free exchange should be abolished, was how appropriate payment could be determined and effected. The first vexatious problem is inherent in how to determine a proper charge for technological information and research. This has also been a complex issue in global trade because there are no competitive markets for such information, even when it is transformed into patents and licenses. In any case, the latest scientific-technological information is rarely traded competitively. It is difficult to be marketed without divulging information to such an extent that a potential purchaser can undertake production independently; also, it takes time and effort to obtain patents and licenses. As a result, the cutting edge of technology tends to be internalized in firms and traded internationally within the context of transnational corporations. This has enabled these firms not only to protect their special knowledge but also to reap the resulting profits on a near-global basis.

If pricing technology is a thorny issue in global trade, it is compounded in the CMEA by the usual difficulties of irrational prices and exchange rates, not to mention bilateralism and currency inconvertibility. And, of course, there are still no socialist transnationals in the proper sense of that term, although recent policy statements may alter that situation (see chapter 6). For quite a while an attempt was made to define charges for STC along the lines officially endorsed under the guise of the Bucharest principles (see chapter 15) for the formation of TRPs. Locating accurate WMP references for well-defined goods is so difficult, however, that it is nearly impossible to identify proper, equitable compensation for patents, inventions and related types of STC. The second bothersome aspect – that is, how to effect payments for STC and blend them with other external transactions – derives from the absence of multilateralism, intransferability of claims and from lack of convertible currency and goods for the bulk of intra-CMEA exchanges.

13.4 ON MEASURING THE EFFECTS OF ECPS AND STC
     AGREEMENTS

In a mature market context, as argued in section 13.1, specialization usually generates trade, provided it proceeds without entailing an unusually large movement of production factors across boundaries. As noted, if such mobility is allowed, specialization may actually entail less trade, especially in the short run. In the CMEA, however, factor movements are not usually tolerated (see chapter 14). If production specialization within the CMEA region were to proceed as in MEs, the trade effects should be positive. Possibly they could be very significant if, in conjunction with specialization, the CPEs agreed upon the gradual, if perhaps partial, elimination of shortages. Nonetheless, as noted in section 13.1, the normal trade effect of an ECPS agreement may be positive, zero or negative. In principle, this mix of outcomes is possible because ECPS agreements are implemented under conditions of economic disequilibrium; thus, it may pay to specialize by destroying productive capacity or forgoing traditional trade lines in favor of other partners. For instance, one partner might bribe another into aborting a planned capacity or limiting its scope to domestic needs so that the first partner can avoid being undercut in international or even regional trade. Under those circumstances, it is not clear how the magnitude of specialization effects can be gauged. It would certainly be a mistake to restrict the area of inquiry to whatever particular project is at hand. What appears to be required is an investigation into the effects of individual ECPS agreements for the economy as a whole.

Unlike ECPS protocols that may or may not be implemented, STC is known to have involved the transfer of blueprints and, temporarily, skilled workers and scientists. How valuable was this gratuitous STC? An answer is difficult to come by. For one, most empirical information is confined to the number of complete blueprints (perhaps up to fifty thousand from 1949 to the end of 1967) exchanged or the number of technicians and scientists (about thirty thousand for the same period) who participated in STC (Lavigne, 1976). But even these data are shaky. Because details regarding coverage are usually lacking, every study on STC has come up with its own, at times very different, data. To cite but one, Stepanenko (1985, p. 33) reports that from 1948 until 1981 the USSR gave the CMEA members, as well as Yugoslavia, nearly forty-four thousand complete scientific-technical documentations and received about half as many in return. He also reports that the number of Soviet specialists delegated to these countries during that period amounted to some twenty-two thousand.

Whatever the precise numbers may be, to put a dollar-and-cents magnitude on the economic value of this exchange, one would have to impute a price that was not actually paid. Moreover, such a shadow price would have to refer to 'world values' to permit translation into dollar terms. Even should this ambitious target be abandoned, a proper valuation would at least require translating the assistance into a uniform currency unit, which itself is difficult to achieve for reasons explained in chapter 16. Although STC may at first appear to be advantageous, this is not necessarily so. The country that transferred the information free of charge under the Sofia Principle was almost certainly a loser, as detailed in chapter 17. But, in the medium to long run, even the recipient probably failed to gain from the free transfer.

Therefore, it may be simplest to say that, during the 1950s and most of the 1960s, there was a generous transfer on a considerable scale of technical knowledge within the socialist community, and that this was particularly pronounced during the two industrialization waves of the 1950s. The direction was specifically from the more-developed to the less-developed CPEs, who were able to embark on their own development path without having to defray the cost of acquiring, and at times assimilating, foreign technology. Furthermore, this large-scale STC exerted considerable influence over the development pattern pursued by the less-developed CPEs. The Sofia Principle was, therefore, critical in accelerating the rate of technological progress in the CMEA and bridging the technological gap between the individual members. All the more significant is that this STC chiefly occurred when the export embargo maintained by most DMEs on the transfer of know-how to CPEs was at its rigid peak.

13.5 EASTERN EUROPEAN MEASUREMENTS OF ECPS EFFECTS

Eastern European efforts to measure SEI effects have rarely been based on well-founded analyses derived from their own theory, or rather competing theories, of production specialization. Though bits and pieces of measurement pervade the specialized literature, there are serious problems in making proper use of them. I shall discuss these matters in turn.

13.5.1 Types of measurement

The empirical information about ECPS agreements that can be pieced together essentially falls into two categories. One is highly descriptive and may include discrete details about the purposes and accomplishments of the signed agreements. Most of this information is highly product-specific. Sobell (1984) has explored this source sector by sector to the fullest microeconomic detail possible given the general lack of comprehensive information even about the agreements as such, let alone their implementation.

The second category is more directly comparable to what one would normally construct for MEs. It usually refers to the value or share of exported or imported goods in the production or consumption in the aggregate, per sector or per product category subject to one or more ECPS agreements. The information available falls into two types. Several CPEs now publish details of the absolute value of their specialized products exported or imported over time. Though not always explicitly stated, I suspect that these indicators generally exclusively refer to intragroup trade. For example, since the late 1970s, Bulgaria regularly furnishes detailed data about its specialized exports of engineering goods[5] but not about other types of specialized products. Because the listings of branches and subbranches for specialized products are organized so that they can be compared with total or CMEA exports in at least some categories, one can easily compute specialization indexes as the share of specialized exports to total regional exports (see below). The second group of data is similar to that for Bulgaria, but its scope and nature differs slightly. These data refer, first of all, to the CMEA region as a whole or to individual countries or sectors on a standardized basis.[6] So far I have not seen the degree of branch detail in data covering the entire CMEA that could be considered comparable to Bulgaria's data for exports of specialized machinery and equipment. Furthermore, this regionwide information is usually made available not only for total trade but also for major trade categories, particularly machinery and equipment and chemicals.[7] Finally, most evidence is typically presented in the form of shares in regional exports, imports or trade turnover as a whole or in a particular category that has been the subject of one or more ECPS agreements.

13.5.2 Interpreting the evidence

Given the way in which these specialization indicators tend to be constructed, numerous interpretation problems arise. The traditional Eastern European practice is to label specialized products as any product about which an ECPS agreement has been signed. As a result, there may be a rapid increase in the quantified specialization indicator without any discernible trade effect or real specialization at all or for quite some time. Whether these magnitudes reflect arrangements that in turn regulate the production, consumption or distribution of certain products, and to what extent, must be verified on the basis of the details of the agreements. Because this information is rarely published, the outside observer is severely handicapped.[8]

Such difficulties may be variously illustrated. The simplest starting point may be to assess the impact of an ECPS agreement that has been signed but not implemented for products that are already traded. While the share of apparent specialization in regional trade immediately rises, aside from the simple signing of the agreement, nothing at all has enhanced specialization in production, consumption or trade. The situation is considerably more complex when it is known that an agreement is being implemented. Here the time dimension is critical, although it can only be adequately gauged if the details of the implementation modalities and procedures are known. Furthermore, though the envisioned product category may be very specific, the trade nomenclature may be sufficiently coarse to include other goods; thus, the measure overstates even further the possible trade effects of the agreement. Moreover, at some point an ECPS agreement may no longer be relevant for the products being produced, possibly because of earlier specialization to suppress duplicate capacity or introduce new products. Yet, even products not specifically addressed in a new ECPS agreement continue to be included in the measurement.

Apart from these conceptual and implementation issues, there is another practical problem to be faced: namely, that the so-called specialization coefficients apparently have been computed according to quite different definitions. This was particularly the case with early estimates referring to the 1960s and the first part of the 1970s (Brabant, 1974b, pp. 279ff.). The evidence from more recent publications, including the supposedly recomputed data for the benchmarks of the 1960s and early 1970s, has tended to be more uniform following the CMEA's efforts to standardize methodology and measurements (Lukin, 1981). The CMEA Secretariat's own publications about SEI are also now providing more uniform data.

If details of the methods used in compiling the indicators were fully known, a range of other skeptical arguments regarding the information value of these specialization indexes could be formulated. Even so, placed against the backdrop painted above, the conclusion is inescapable that these so-called standardized specialization indicators are inferior measures of CMEA production specialization, if only because they overstate the extent actually achieved.

13.5.3 An illustration of specialization indexes

The above propositions may be illustrated both for the Bulgarian and the more general CMEA indicators. Although in theory it is possible that Bulgaria's export specialization data reflect genuine production specialization, I doubt this to be the case because of the CPEs' peculiarities and the nature of ECPS agreements. This proposition can be illustrated by perusing the summary of the available data provided in Table 13.1. Bulgaria's exports of specialized products, although sharply contracting in 1986, have accordingly grown spectacularly, by more than 16-fold between 1970 and 1986 – or at a compound growth rate of 19 percent per year. Interpreting these data is a different matter. Among the individual product groups identified, and when placed in the context of Bulgarian economic development since the early 1970s, electrotechnical and electronic equipment have evidently shown the most rapid growth, presumably primarily as a result of ECPS agreements. For the remaining product categories, the picture is clearly mixed. Because of the nature of the agreements about within-factory transportation, forklifts and some horticultural equipment, the indicators for the sector hoisting and moving equipment may reflect genuine production specialization. The

Table 13.1 Bulgaria's exports of machinery,[a] 1970–86
(in million leva at current prices and percentages)

	1970	1975	1980	1985	1986
Total	679.4	1847.4	3948.7	7342.9	7719.8
CMEA exports[b]	623.8	1579.1	3308.8	6635.3	6897.7
Specialization[c]	224.0	827.4	1789.7	3679.3	3610.1
Share of specialization	35.9	52.4	54.1	55.5	52.3
Energy and electrotechnical equipment					
Total	110.7	168.6	335.3	563.7	620.2
Specialized	0.6	32.6	129.3	338.8	246.5
Percent	0.5	19.3	38.6	60.1	39.7
Hoisting and moving equipment					
Total	179.4	393.7	824.7	1370.2	1361.3
Specialized	146.6	274.4	666.6	881.0	883.4
Percent	81.7	69.7	80.8	64.3	64.9
Food and light industrial equipment					
Total	22.4	51.3	96.8	212.0	203.5
Specialized	0.5	19.2	42.7	92.9	67.1
Percent	2.2	37.4	44.1	43.8	33.0
Tractors and agricultural equipment					
Total	95.6	159.7	231.6	268.4	273.0
Specialized	49.4	64.5	86.5	209.2	54.4
Percent	51.7	40.4	37.4	77.9	19.9
Computing and organizational equipment					
Total	27.7	329.3	698.5	2069.7	2471.1
Specialized	1.4	265.1	441.3	1324.7	1511.8
Percent	5.0	80.5	63.2	64.0	61.2

(a) Category ETN 1.
(b) Own estimates.
(c) Defined as products about which CMEA-wide or bilateral specialization agreements are in effect. In theory they could contain goods exported outside the CMEA, but I do not believe this to be the case.

Source: *BT*, 1985, and 1986, pp. 24, 26, 35.

remaining goods probably fall in the mixed categories; that is, some products exported have originated as a result of ECPS agreements, but the larger part of the indicator stems from 'validation' of existing production and trade patterns.

Similar problems are evident for the more comprehensive CMEA indicators. According to a recent CMEA estimate (Božkov, 1987, p. 104), the share of specialized products in intra-CMEA trade rose from 18 percent in 1980 to 21 in 1984 and 21.6 in 1985. The corresponding data for engineering goods are likely to be even more revealing because it is for this sector that greater than four-fifths[9] of all ECPS protocols at the bi- and multilateral

Table 13.2 Share of specialized machinery in CMEA exports of machinery (ETN 1)
(Percentages)

	1965	1966	1967	1968	1971	1973	1975	(1975)	1977
Bulgaria	39.1	37.2	41.0	39.6	...	37.3	35.7	...	36.7
Czechoslovakia	15.7	15.1	18.7	19.0	6.1	11.4	16.0	(14.6)	29.5
GDR	25.3	26.2	25.9	...	...	18.9	25.9	...	40.9
Hungary	8.6	12.1	15.2	14.2	...	14.0	22.5	(23.6)	43.5
Poland	11.3	5.1	29.8	29.9	...	15.7	18.3	...	26.0
Rumania	...	26.0	...	...	...	8.5	36.2	...	44.1
Soviet Union	5.5	23.9	36.5	...	...	18.9	16.7	...	23.6

	(1977)	1978	1980	1981	(1981)	1982	1983	1984	1985
Bulgaria	...	42.4	(54.1)	52.1	...	...	...	...	57.6
Czechoslovakia	(34.7)	30.0	27.8	33.4	(31.2)	34.2	35.6	46.0	48.2
GDR	...	43.8	40.0	41.0	...	...	...	53.5	51.2
Hungary	(41.1)	50.6	(47.2)	43.8	...	...	...	...	44.8
Poland	(24.3)	26.7	(27.6)	27.1	...	...	...	...	18.7
Rumania	...	38.4	21.2	35.6	...	...	...	46.3	51.3
Soviet Union	(23.7)	23.3	(25.0)	20.5	...	...	...	...	20.1

Notes:
1965, 1968: Želev, 1971, p. 111; 1966: Constantincescu, 1969b, p. 75; Constantincescu, 1969a, p. 66; Faddeev, 1969, p. 128; 1967: Mirošničenko, 1970, p. 107; Šalamanov, 1971, p. 22; Faddeev, 1969, p. 128; 1971: Novák, 1984, p. 7; 1973: Božkov and Dulovec, 1985, p. 72; Kuznecova, 1981, p. 47; 1975: Kowałewski, 1980a, p. 18; Kuznecova, 1981, p. 47; Novák, 1984, p. 7; (1975): Dulovec, 1983, p. 18; Kowałewski, 1980a, p. 18; 1977: Božkov and Dulovec, 1985, p. 72; Kuznecova, 1981, p. 47; (1977): Kowałewski, 1980a, p. 18; Kowałewski, 1980b, p. 48; 1978: Kuznecova, 1981, p. 47; 1980, 1981: Božkov amd Dulovec. 1985. p. 72 and bracketed data estimated from Božkov, 1987, p. 106; (1981), 1982: Novák, 1984, p. 7; 1983: Dulovec, 1983, p. 18; 1984: Božkov, 1987, p. 106; 1985: Panjuškin, 1987, p. 50.

level have been negotiated. The aim, particularly, was to reduce exceedingly wasteful duplication in economic structures that had been nurtured by socialist industrialization strategies and CMEA bilateralism. Trade effects should therefore have been unambiguously positive for the whole sector as well as for broad categories. This holds even though some countries ceased to export certain products. Similar measures should prevail for the chemical sector, which accounts for most of the remaining specialization.[10] A more recent measure (Nosiadek, 1988, p. 3) indicates that the share of specialized products in regional exports of manufactured goods rose from 18.3 percent in 1980 to 22.9 percent in 1987, with the most spectacular progress (more than 26 points) recorded by Rumania (!), followed by Czechoslovakia (15), the GDR (10) and Hungary (8). The USSR's share stagnated, however, and Poland's contracted by 3 points. Unfortunately, these data do not mesh with the more standard measures reported in Table 13.2 for machinery (ETN 1).

Accordingly, machinery specialization has risen rapidly in countries such as Czechoslovakia, the GDR, Hungary and even Rumania (note that the indicators for years prior to 1971 are evidently inconsistent with later data). These are paradoxical results. For example, trade in machinery products suffered during the economic adjustment phase of the early 1980s. Yet, the reported export shares of Czechoslovakia's, the GDR's and Rumania's specialized machinery purportedly rose at least 15 points between 1980 and 1985.[11] According to Božkov (1987, p. 105), the value of specialized machinery and chemicals in CMEA trade rose, on the average, 13.5 and 17.5 percent annually between 1980 and 1985. Could these changes and those reported by Nosiadek have been due to genuine production specialization? Some share of this gain may have originated from that source, but the factual evidence is too weak to allow me to venture a quantitative guess based on firm theoretical and empirical foundations. A more plausible explanation for the bulk of the expansion is the following. A large number of ECPS protocols were negotiated in connection with the Target Programs and bilateral cooperation agreements signed with the Soviet Union in the early 1980s. These agreements must have imparted an upward bias to the habitual specialization indexes. Given the economic disarray in the early 1980s in Eastern Europe, the contention that genuine production specialization accelerated at a pace even remotely resembling that suggested in Table 13.2 is improbable. In fact, given the setbacks in the implementation of the annual and medium-term plans for 1981–5, it is doubtful that production specialization accelerated at all during that period. Perhaps widespread substitution of specialized products for machinery products traded earlier occurred, but even that development is difficult to reconcile with the parameters of the unusually adverse economic and integration environment of the first half of the 1980s.

13.5.4 On alternative specialization measures

Because the official and other Eastern European specialization indicators are ambiguous, hard stipulations of the agreements are absent and gaps exist in our knowledge about the concrete implementation of such ECPS protocols; little solid information is available in which to assess the degree of CMEA specialization. With some work, however, the researcher can construct partial information that may help illuminate and evaluate quantitative aspects of various SEI efforts. I suggest three complementary measures.

13.5.4.a A traditional measure of integration effects
In my estimate, an informative tool for evaluating the influence of ECPS agreements is to study the evolution of the ratio of exports to production or imports to consumption, or both; these measures should preferably be specified by different partner groupings and commodity groups. The logic is as follows. If one or more CPEs intensify specialization with respect to the group or the world, aggregate trade and occasionally broad categories of

trade with some partners must logically rise faster than domestic production, consumption or total trade if the product is acquired from third countries as well. This result need not be valid for each isolated agreement. Because of the implications of the ECPS agreements, the more time that elapses between the signing of the protocol and the measurement date, even in the case of most ECPS agreements that initially erode commerce, trade must eventually expand.[12] If one knows that the majority of agreements refer to, say, machinery, then the import dependence of apparent domestic consumption of these products with respect to partner trade or, depending on the direction of trade, the corresponding export-dependence index should be rising over time. The more disaggregated the measurement, the more likely it is that the export- and import-dependence indexes will not move in tandem; but at least one of them should exhibit a strong trend over time.

Provided comparable data on production, exports and imports are available for several years, constructing ratios of exports to production and ratios of imports to apparent consumption (or production minus exports plus imports) is a straightforward matter. If measured by broad categories of goods and by meaningful trade partner groupings, the impact of ECPS agreements can be evaluated indirectly. Unfortunately, this procedure is exceedingly cumbersome to apply to the CPEs. There are many reasons for this, but two that are critical suffice to illustrate the point. First, production and/or trade data are not available in sufficient detail and are altogether lacking for many sectors. Second, the absence of compatible price systems in which the available production and trade data (including CMEA and East-West trade data) are expressed causes formidable problems. The results of an exercise based on Hungarian output and trade data revalued at comparable trade unit values as well as in comparable domestic wholesale prices will be discussed in Part IV.

13.5.4.b A more limited indicator

Measuring export and import dependence as sketched is exceedingly costly. For this and other reasons, it would be useful to construct a less ambitious indicator to intermittently evaluate the impact of specialization on economic performance and trade. I shall look briefly at two such indicators: the import dependence of machinery investments and the comparative development of such indexes over time.

Bulgaria, Hungary, Poland and Rumania all report comparable data in domestic currency units for total *ex post* investment demand and its import component, at least for some period of time. From this, export- and import-dependence indicators for machinery goods can be constructed on the assumption that domestic production minus exports equals domestic consumption minus imports in the statistical accounting framework used by the CPEs concerned. Such indicators can be disaggregated further into trade with CMEA and other countries. For Hungary, domestic values of imports from socialist and other countries are available. For the other countries, an assumption needs to be made regarding the relationship between, say, TRPs and EWPs.[13] The results obtained are discussed in Part IV along with the other measures of specialization.

13.5.4.c Elasticities and differential impacts of domestic or external shocks
The data that can be gathered for the exercise just discussed may be transformed into import elasticities of the apparent demand for investment goods. The argument is as follows. If one believes that the CPEs have implemented ECPS agreements for a wide range of machinery products, the following propositions should be verified. First, import substitution, which was one of the chief features of industrialization in the 1950s, should show evidence of declining in recent years. Second, because these agreements are primarily implemented with CMEA partners, the gap between the elasticities for domestic supply and CMEA imports should be smaller than with other imports. Finally, the discontinuities in elasticities for imports from CMEA and other partners should increase over time. Whether these propositions can be verified will be taken up in Part IV.[14]

These are rather simple, perhaps even naive, ways of trying to comprehend measurement issues. However imperfect, these measures are capable of yielding some useful, if tentative, clues on selected issues of CMEA cooperation, as will be demonstrated in chapter 16. The arguments about ECPS can be extended to several other instruments that are utilized by CPEs to reach their own integration objectives. Neither these objectives nor the instruments employed in the process, or even the institutions that help to pursue them, are necessarily identical with those of MEs. However, the ultimate underlying purpose of both coincides; that is, the exploitation of trade and economies of scale to bolster factor productivity growth. If this argument is accepted, diverse alternative measurement methods are at hand to broadly verify the trade impacts of SEI.

NOTES

1. I realize that serious controversy exists in the literature about the nature and extent of disequilibrium in CPEs. The extremes of the position are presented by János Kornai, who strongly argues that macroeconomic disequilibriums are endemic to CPEs, and Richard Portes, who denies that persistent shortages in CPEs are possible. For a more nuanced view with pertinent interpretations of these views, see Nuti, 1987b, and Brabant, 1988a.
2. But this condition was frequently violated. The ambiguity was not resolved, at least formally, until the sixty-second session of the Executive Committee in 1973 (CMEA, 1979a, pp. 75–6; Neumann, 1980, p. 183).
3. The full title reads: *Organizacionno-metodičeskie, èkonomičeskie i pravovye osnovy naučno-techničeskogo sotrudničestva stran-členov SĖV i dejatel'nosti organov SĖV v ètoj oblasti*. It is reproduced in CMEA, 1977b, pp. 328–86.

4. This rule about development assistance has since been extended to Cuba and Vietnam (see Matějka, 1985b, pp. 30ff).
5. The most useful details are available in the foreign trade yearbook (*BT*). The general statistical yearbook (*BY*) contains only an abbreviated, quite aggregate rendition. Although not labeled as such, these data refer only to trade with CMEA partners. That is, if Bulgaria also exports specialized forklifts to other economies, these values are not included in the estimates.
6. The Standing Commission for Statistical Questions has developed principles for the computation of these indexes (see, for example, Lukin, 1981, p. 40). I do not know, however, whether the standards used in the national publications reflect regional recommendations. Judging by the convergence in the data reported in various regional and national publications in recent years, I suspect that this guide was not generally utilized until the mid-1970s.
7. That is, ETN 1 and ETN 3 (without rubber), respectively, in the standard CMEA trade nomenclature or *Edinaja tovarnaja nomenklatura*.
8. Keith Crane and his associates have recently made a valiant attempt to compile an exhaustive list of specialization agreements (Rand, 1986). In spite of its 970 pages, the manuscript evidently fails to provide a complete set of ECPS agreements. Furthermore, owing to the pedantic way in which most such agreements are treated in the specialized CMEA literature, the details about many of those listed are insufficient for providing even minimum information.
9. According to Božkov (1987, p. 105), 84.6 percent of the value of specialized trade in 1980 and 82.5 percent in 1985.
10. As a share of specialized trade, it amounted to 10.5 percent in 1980 and 12.2 percent in 1985 (Božkov, 1987, p. 105).
11. The data for Rumania in 1980 and 1985 are implausible. The magnitudes reported in Božkov, 1987 (p. 106) lead to a very improbable estimate (61.5 percent in 1985).
12. In the meantime, additional ECPS agreements may have been signed, possibly in response to the negative effects initially resulting from the first. I would be prepared to aggregate all such sequential effects and view them as the outcome of the ECPS agreement first to encourage structural adjustment and later to foster real production specialization.
13. For Poland and Rumania, the cross-rates derived from internal or commercial exchange rates (see Brabant, 1987a, pp. 202–14) can be applied; after some modification they may also illuminate the transformation for Bulgaria.
14. The measurements of such elasticities should be undertaken only after normalization. That is, I first estimate a logarithmic time trend and measure the percentage deviations from the estimated trend in demand for machinery investments, obviously *ex post* as these are the only data available. I do likewise for domestic supply, as well as for total, CMEA and other imports. Percentage deviations from trend in various sources of supply are then regressed against the corresponding demand variable.

14 · INDIRECT ECONOMIC COORDINATION

The last set of SEI instruments, institutions and pertinent short-term macroeconomic policies are those concerned with indirect economic coordination. Those in the monetary and financial sphere are particularly pertinent. In this connection, it is useful to extend the discussion beyond indirect coordination *per se* so as to situate and analyze the potential role of macroeconomic policies in general in selecting the boundaries, rules and parameters that guide indirect economic coordination.

This chapter examines the three enumerated components, with particular attention to those elements that may become critical in enhancing direct cross-border interfirm relations. The more holistic macroeconomic policies that determine indirect economic coordination will be discussed in chapter 18 in connection with feasible and desirable national and regional reforms. I will cover here the formation of and policies underlying TRPs as well as the relationship of TRPs with domestic and East-West prices, but only briefly because that complex set of issues is addressed in chapter 15. Also studied in this chapter are foreign exchange policies in the context of markets that are split regionally, by commodity groups and by domestic party; the TR and its position in SEI; regional credits with a short-, medium- and long-term horizon, including capital movements designed to enhance the joint financing of investment projects that purport to buttress SEI now and even more so in the future; interest rate policies; and bi- and multilateral settlements for commercial and other transactions.

Section 14.1 sets forth at some length my understanding of the meaning of a monetary-financial mechanism. I do so because this mechanism will be at the core of likely reforms of the role of monetary and financial institutions, policy instruments and cooperation as detailed in Part IV. The macroeconomic policies that steer indirect economic coordination are clarified in section 14.2. The monetary and financial instruments of SEI are dealt with next. The corresponding key institutional and organizational features are discussed in sections 14.4 and 14.5. The final section amplifies the links between regional and domestic monetary and financial matters that were touched upon in chapter 9.

14.1 ON THE CONCEPT OF A MONETARY-FINANCIAL MECHANISM

The monetary-financial mechanism of SEI is an awkward term that is rooted in the complex Marxist-Leninist perspective of what motivates individual agents to engage in economic activities that yield value added. Especially relevant are the ideologic assumptions on how economic agents respond to certain policy and other precepts; in other words, how producer and consumer behavior is molded by centrally set guidelines. It denotes, of course, a subcomponent of the economic mechanism of SEI (see chapter 10).

The recent elevation of the notion 'monetary-financial SEI mechanism' out of the ideological realm of the Marxist concept of commodity-money relations appears to reflect a recognition of the fact that, within regional trade, commodity-money relations should play an essential role. Proper commodity-money relations may not only facilitate the proper conduct of regular trade and payments, they also enhance the pace, depth and scope of CMEA cooperation and the feasible pace of growth of its constituent economies. In what follows, this component comprises the policies, institutions and policy instruments through which the economic activities of the CMEA members, which themselves are in principle guided by firmly agreed-upon behavioral rules, are coordinated through the intermediation of 'money.' I use this term guardedly, if expressly, in a rather broad sense because most CMEA economic transactions are, in essence, nonmonetized. They tend to emerge (see chapters 11 and 13) within BTPAs and ECPS protocols that focus more on the physical quantities to be reciprocally delivered than on the intrinsic value of the transactions.

It is no easy task to summarize what precisely may already be in place concerning the monetary-financial mechanism of the CMEA; space does not allow a lengthy discourse (see Brabant, 1977, 1987a). Instead, my purpose here is to highlight the most important characteristics of the various elements of that mechanism in order to set the stage for an overall assessment of SEI and the feasibility of meaningful economic reforms.

The monetary-financial mechanism of SEI comprises a range of cooperation issues and institutions. The TR stands centerstage as the monetary unit of account. Because the TR is issued by the IBEC and is considered to be (or perhaps capable of becoming?) the key unit for joint capital formation and joint investment cooperation within the context of IIB activities, or at least under its guidance and inspiration, these two institutions are central. But other CMEA payment and credit flows must also be identified; their streamlining is essential to reforming the CMEA. A discussion of the mechanisms by which payments on both current and capital accounts are effected should be included in the analysis. That is, the CMEA settlements mechanism as well as the scope for capital mobility need to be highlighted.

It may be useful to separate the issues of commercial settlements regulated within the context of BTPAs from so-called noncommercial transactions; that is, all those that do not constitute merchandise (including payment flows for tourism; transfers of royalties, student stipends, honoraria, awards and gifts; transmissions of unrequited transfers; and transactions that facilitate local disbursements by diplomatic, consular or trading agents). Furthermore, the degree to which the CMEA members' national currencies are convertible into goods and other currencies ought to be touched upon because there is considerable confusion in the literature about convertibility in Eastern Europe. The needless complications include when convertibility could realistically be anticipated, whether it should even be considered in a generalized form in the short to medium run, in which spheres it already applies and to what degree and related questions.

Perhaps an unusual element of a monetary-financial mechanism is the terms at which goods and factor services are exchanged in the CMEA – that is, pricing in its most general setting. Proper pricing is critical for obtaining the desired productivity from economic reforms, particularly through the links yet to be forged between domestic and trade prices. The role of prices has been at the center of recent discussions about the monetary-financial mechanism of SEI (Leznik, 1987; Petrakov, 1987). Against this backdrop, I devote all of chapter 15 to TRPs. Here I touch upon this complex and murky area of Eastern European economic cooperation merely to place it precisely where it belongs in the arsenal of SEI instruments.

Put briefly, it is no exaggeration to characterize the monetary-financial mechanism of the CMEA as exceedingly primitive and passive. This is because the existing economic mechanism as a whole in the CMEA is rather simple. It is geared more to the reciprocal exchange of physical goods and tangible services than to the enhancement of SEI through the indirect coordination of economic decisions, including in the context of national, concerted or joint planning. In what follows, I shall concentrate on the nature and role of the TR, the typical foreign exchange mechanism, the trade and payments mechanisms that have provided the backbone of CMEA cooperation since World War II, the nature and role of factor mobility in the CMEA, the extent and importance of bilateralism insofar as commodity transactions are concerned and the key features of pricing.

Monetary policies, institutions and policy instruments at the regional level are virtually nonexistent. In a nutshell, the CMEA has:

1. The TR as a common unit of account.
2. Strict control over the emission of that 'currency' – if one wishes to call it that – in accordance with export imbalances that are either bilaterally agreed upon or that result from over- or nonfulfillment of a balanced BTPA.
3. Two banks that were initially conceived as a counterpart of the Fund and World Bank but that are actually highly passive, functioning more

as accountants of measures agreed upon at political and administrative levels than as units entrusted with meaningful SEI tasks.
4. An embryonic, primitive type of capital market and universal prohibi-
tion of voluntary labor mobility.[1]
5. Dual and separate exchange rate and price regimes.
6. A vaguely specified set of rules for the formation of TRPs that are
easily manipulated to whatever suits bilateral balancing requirements.

A sharp improvement in at least these aspects of the CMEA's monetary-
financial mechanism will be critical for formulating and implementing
positive adjustment policies within individual countries and the region as a
whole, for regaining higher growth levels and for fostering SEI as a means of
enhancing economic growth. The need for such changes should become
obvious from the discussions in this and subsequent chapters.

14.2 MONETARY AND FINANCIAL POLICIES IN THE CMEA

Regulating the money supply is a critical element of macroeconomic policies
in DMEs that hope to provide sufficient funds for financing steady economic
expansion while keeping inflationary pressures in check. The regulation of
financial institutions, broadly understood, forms an integral part of a
monetary policy that is yet to mature. What I have in mind is not the legal
ability of any one institution to engage in, say, commercial or investment
banking. Instead, what matters is the way in which macroeconomic policies
provide the framework and rules for and the regulation of financial
intermediation, including linking savers with investors. Macroeconomic
policy with respect to the external sector includes rules and regulations for
balance-of-payments adjustments; determination of the exchange rate;
commercial policy, including tariff and nontariff barriers, rules of origin,
preferential treatment and adherence to regional or international trading
rules; the foreign exchange regime more generally, or government policy
regarding the acquisition and disposition of foreign exchange, which usually
distinguishes between current and capital account transactions; the regulation of foreign agents operating in the domestic economy; and other
features.

Depending on the desired kind of regional unification, MEs generally
evolve toward a common or regional policy on tariffs and other obstacles to
trade, as in the case of the free trade area (common internal tariffs) or
customs union (common internal and external tariffs), or on the harmonization of trade and some other macroeconomic policies, as with economic
unions or common markets. In addition to region formation, policy
coordination may be essential for assuming obligations entered into under
international agreements. Examples are tariffs under GATT rules,
foreign exchange and balance-of-payments policies under the IMF regime

or others pertaining to the World Bank or Bank for International Settlements (BIS).

From the earlier analysis of the model of the centrally planned economies and the evolution of the CMEA, it can be proposed that few counterparts to the above exist in either the domestic or, *a fortiori*, the regional policies of the CPEs. Had the regional organization evolved as the greatest common denominator of the policies pursued by the members, integrating macroeconomic policies in the monetary and financial spheres would not have been necessary as all requirements would have been met through detailed regional planning.

The key to describing the macroeconomic policies of the CPEs is that what is not explicitly legitimized as an appendix to detailed physical planning is forbidden or is not allowed to exist. Thus, as each CPE arrogates to the sphere of state decision making the right to steer foreign economic transactions solely according to state interests, a severe damper has been placed on developing a positive foreign exchange regime nationally, which thus detracts from regional concordance. Likewise, because capital and labor resources in CPEs do not respond to the utilization of money balances, scarce room exists for formulating and implementing a positive financial policy centered on fostering efficient intermediation between savers and investors. Because this situation is so prevalent in the member countries, developing any such policy at the regional level is hardly possible.

14.3 MONETARY AND FINANCIAL INSTRUMENTS

Although a multitude of monetary and financial instruments could be discussed here, I shall focus on the nature and role of the TR, the foreign exchange mechanism typical of the CPEs, the trade and payments mechanisms that have been the backbone of CMEA economic cooperation, the nature and role of CMEA capital mobility (but the two banks are discussed in section 14.4), key features of the TRP mechanism (on this, more in chapter 15) and the overriding role of bilateralism in determining the scope of the monetization of CMEA commercial relations. The purpose of this examination is to evaluate in what ways these elements of the monetary-financial mechanism hamper or support the ongoing reform processes.

14.3.1 The common currency and monetary control

Ordinarily the TR is given short shrift by Western observers as well as by many Eastern European commentators. Such peremptory rejection of the TR's monetary status is deserved because it is not really a currency in the economic sense, as distinct from its legal status. But the TR is not without interest; officially it is the only truly international, or 'ideal' (see Brabant,

1987a, pp. 257–9 and 278–9), monetary unit in the world in comparatively wide use. It does not depend on any one or a combination of national currencies, and its emission is not controlled by national monetary authorities.

Concerns about multilateralizing trade and payments within the CMEA as a way of stimulating SEI as envisaged in *Basic Principles* were prominent when the TR was instituted (see chapter 8). It was created as an abstract unit, initially set equal to the Soviet *valuta* or external ruble with an identical gold content. Its creation is not dependent on the monetary policies of any one or any combination of member countries. Instead, it ensues directly from the ability and willingness of individual CPEs to export more to the region than they import. TR balances are thus created that illustrate what is sometimes identified as the degree of multilateralism in the CMEA (on which more below). They are, however, primarily indicative of the extent to which countries will forgo or cannot enforce immediate bilateral balancing as a means of stimulating regional economic cooperation.

Before the advent of *glasnost'* in mainstream economic affairs, including in Bulgaria and the Soviet Union, many commentators on these and other CPEs emphasized that the TR fulfills all the major functions of world money: a measure of value, a means of payment, an instrument of exchange and an asset for the purpose of accumulation. This characterization of the TR has been sporadically debated with various degrees of solid economic argument, ideological *obiter dicta* and overriding foreign policy considerations. From a technical economic point of view, it would be more accurate to say that there is nothing inherent in the TR that would inhibit it from exerting world-money functions. But the mechanism through which the TR has actually been emitted since its inception considerably weakens its ability to discharge those functions to any meaningful extent.

A few pointed comments must suffice. The TR cannot be considered a means of payment because countries usually proscribe the exchange of goods and services when this is not explicitly provided for in the context of a BTPA (see chapter 11), though this does not necessarily mean that absolutely no transactions take place in the CMEA that are not the explicit subject of a BTPA. Nor does the statement imply that CPE enterprises or trading units themselves must ascertain whether there is room in the relevant BTPA for the particular kind of exchange anticipated. This point, raised among others by Fedorowicz (1978), although true, does not detract from the fact that the TR remains notional for all macroeconomic decision makers, as well as for most economic agents, primarily because most trade decisions are usually made at high rungs of the governmental or Party hierarchy. Nevertheless, this and related characteristics of the CPE trade and payments regime signal that there are many circumstances that negate using the TR as international, or even as regional, money acceptable on demand. That is, willing holders of that currency generally do not know when and under what conditions they can liquidate their money balances. Involuntary holders of TR balances grant transaction credit, chiefly but not exclusively for trade. They may hope to utilize some of these resources for purchases coming under the provisions of the next BTPA, but there is no guarantee that such an agreement can be negotiated or, if officially formulated, that it can be implemented.

Holders of TR balances are very restricted in what they can purchase with it now or in future BTPAs and are uncertain about the expected value of such imbalances. For these reasons, the accumulation, or store of value, role of the TR is highly confined. True enough, the CPEs have accumulated sizable balances at the IBEC and have committed a nontrivial amount of capital resources to activities sponsored in some degree by the IIB and to other jointly financed investment projects (see section 14.4), but generally these forms of cooperation have come about only *after* the members conclude a sequence of BTPAs either in general or, more commonly, as agreements that specifically relate to the particular project under discussion.

The role of the TR in measuring values, and hence in providing a medium of exchange, is also a highly convoluted topic. Obviously, goods and services exchanged within the CMEA are denominated in TRs. For some goods, however, these magnitudes are derived solely from WMPs observed during previous years. For other goods, TRPs are essentially negotiated bilaterally, and any currency unit could then be the unit of account, or they somehow derive from the exporter's prevailing domestic prices (see chapter 15).

Thus, even under the best of circumstances the TR cannot play an independent role as a fiduciary intermediary, and its ability to be the so-called socialist international money is dubious. There is no TR policy that could legitimately be imposed upon the CMEA region with the expectation that it would affect regional merchandise, labor and capital flows. It could not even influence relations with third partners, in spite of various efforts made to extend its regime outside the region (see Brabant, 1978). Because money is associated with some kind of automatism and TR imbalances do not lead to adjustments other than a possible reconsideration of intended future trade flows, one has to stretch the notion that the TR is socialist international money, in the economic sense, as distinct from its legal standing (see section 14.4).

14.3.2 Credits and the emergence of the CMEA capital market

At various times during the postwar period, most CPEs have embraced measures to encourage the transfer of wealth from one country to another – that is, to provide for some sort of capital mobility. But such transference has never been allowed to emerge spontaneously as it would contradict the built-in anticapitalist bias of the CPE. But planned capital flows are entirely possible and do occur on a fairly regular basis. In this connection, it is useful to distinguish among government credits, special-purpose or target credits, institutionalized forms of investment coordination, investment loans and financial flows in conducting regular trade.

Government-to-government loans are inherently bilateral and, under most circumstances, highly politicized. They played a major role, *inter alia*, in the postwar political and economic transformations of the Eastern European regimes (see chapters 1 and 2) and in alleviating the sociopolitical and economic crises of the mid-1950s (see chapter 3). They also contributed to resolving other destabilizing events, such as the major adjustment in the way in which CMEA reference WMPs are calculated, and, beginning in 1975 (see chapter 15), in computing reference TRPs for transactions for which no WMPs can be identified; as well as the Czechoslovak and Polish crises of 1968 and 1981.

Two particular kinds of capital transactions should be highlighted separately: the short- to medium-term credits granted by the IBEC and the medium- to long-term loans issued by the IIB. The first is potentially critical to the smooth settlement of current trade transactions, and the second might eventually assume a central role in restructuring the CMEA and SEI as such.

14.3.3 Investment coordination and capital movements

For a number of reasons, the CPEs have never favored direct foreign investment as a potentially important buttress to economic development. This aloofness toward foreign capital prevailed particularly in the early years of the CPEs and lasted well into the 1960s. While it primarily referred to direct foreign investment from private, corporate or official investors from MEs, it also inhibited direct investment across national frontiers, including the group of CPEs that makes up the CMEA. This reluctance to allow foreign, including fraternal, partners to participate in the domestic economy did not lessen the attractiveness of obtaining access to the usufruct of such productive resources. At the start of CMEA cooperation, trade and government-to-government credits were frequently granted, or simply condoned, as a way of facilitating socialist construction, particularly in the least-developed CMEA members. Bulgaria has perhaps been the greatest beneficiary thereof. But these *ad hoc* capital movements not only inhibited development, they also contradicted intentions of enhancing the ISDL and SEI, particularly after the New Course of the mid-1950s (see chapter 3). By 1957, a new form of capital movement had come into being, the so-called special-purpose or target credits.

Special-purpose credits, as the designation suggests, are capital movements geared toward a particular purpose or specific target project. Essentially, because they are earmarked for a specific purpose and repaid by the exports of goods produced with the project, they are tied project loans. There have been two phases of these capital movements (see chapters 3 and

4). Between 1957–62, especially Czechoslovakia and the GDR extended sizable loans for ventures to be constructed primarily in other Eastern European partners. This kind of financial cooperation saw a resurgence in the later 1960s when both countries again significantly 'invested' capital abroad, but this time chiefly in Soviet projects.

These capital contributions were generally *sui generis*, principally motivated by the desire of some importers to raise their assured quota of critical primary goods and fuels normally procured from other CMEA partners, who were, by definition, unwilling to commit their own scarce domestic resources to expanding some desired production or, in most cases, mining facility. The real economic parameters of the transactions involved in these loans were generally rather difficult to assess. Aside from uncertainty about future TRPs, favorable treatment regarding available quantum or in the form of a concessionary price of other goods, low interest rates, tied sales and help and other modifiers all greatly complicated any quantitative assessment, as well as a qualitative evaluation, of the explicit and implicit benefits and costs of such project loans (see Brabant, 1971; Brabant, 1987a, pp. 323–8).

In discussing capital mobility, particularly as it relates to so-called joint investments, it is worth stressing that what in fact takes place is the *joint financing* of investments. I consider this designation to be a far more accurate description of what really occurs in the CMEA than the label joint investment. The latter differs in many respects from the 'joint financing' of a capital-construction project for the following reasons. Joint financing means that the act of cooperating is by definition temporary and that the project remains the property of the host country – that is, where the project is sited. It also implies, generally speaking, no more than simply contributing the means by which a particular project is to be 'financed,'[2] as distinct from the joint design, construction, management and exploitation of the project. Perhaps most important, 'investors' receive a fixed return, as a rule a low simple interest rate of between 2 to 5 percent but usually toward the lower end, and so they really do not directly profit from the project. In fact, the IIB was created specifically to remedy these drawbacks and thus ensure that jointly financed projects would yield maximum benefits in terms of accelerating SEI processes.

14.3.4 Price regimes

CPEs have traditionally opted for a high degree of domestic economic autonomy, particularly in price determination, and have conducted their foreign economic relations largely through BTPAs; where that was not possible, such as in relations with DMEs, they have endeavored to embrace a trading framework that resembles a BTPA as closely as possible. As noted, the *caesura* of domestic wholesale and retail prices from each other and from external prices still flourishes even in the modified CPE, though with respect to trade prices, the dichotomy is less pronounced for wholesale than for retail prices. Moreover, TRPs follow their own logic and are only *grosso modo*, and coarsely at that, related to WMPs or, more to the point, to EWPs because these are the actual opportunity-cost indicators for CPEs. This warrants a brief digression.

What is the real opportunity cost of transacting at TRPs? Should one look primarily at so-called WMPs observed in trade among MEs, or should one find some inspiration in EWPs; that is, actual prices observed in trade between DMEs and CPEs? Of course, the proposition makes sense only if one is really convinced that one should look for an extraneous price system (see chapter 15). It is now true that EWPs are influenced by various noncompetitive factors, including discrimination against CPE exports by DMEs, products that do not appeal to Western tastes, the lack of a CPE infrastructure within the Western nations to offer adequate servicing of products and so on (see Marer, 1984, pp. 176ff.). But unless the CPEs can overcome these obstacles, and prices obtained in exports to the West will become equal to those obtained for comparable products by Western competitors, which may eventually be feasible, actually observed EWPs constitute the opportunity cost for comparatively small trade diversions. With large diversions, the implicit small-country assumption – that is, that trade can be rechanneled to other partners without affecting prices and the terms of trade – needs to be revised. In an ideological perspective, it may be true that TRPs should be patterned on WMPs, but that necessarily leads to profitable arbitrage because EWPs are bound to diverge from WMPs.

Essentially, the TRP regime consists of multiple price layers, with reference prices derived from average past WMPs, contract prices negotiated bilaterally and transaction prices being finally invoiced (see chapter 15). In principle, these prices are derived on the basis of a common set of price-formation rules that were formally endorsed in Bucharest in 1958. Since 1976, these prices have supposedly been patterned after a five-year moving average of WMPs observed before the implementation year and which have been converted in each of the reference years at the official convertible currency exchange rates of the TR set by the IBEC. The relationship between TRPs and EWPs or WMPs is far more streamlined for raw materials and fuels than for processed manufactures and foodstuffs (Brabant, 1987b, pp. 196–207). It is also closer for products traded under regular BTPAs than for those transacted outside the planned volumes, for the joint financing of investment purposes or for specialization agreements. But they do not reflect scarcity relations in any meaningful way.

14.3.5 Exchange rate regime

Because CPEs have, in part, maintained their considerable domestic economic autonomy through strictly regulated trade, the role of exchange rates in the formation of prices has been sharply proscribed (see chapter 11). Precisely because the classical CPE desires extensive domestic decision-making autonomy and seeks to attain it by divorcing domestic from external markets, the exchange rate becomes a pure accounting unit. Even in the modified CPE, the exchange rate's role in price formation has been sharply curtailed. Furthermore, these countries generally possess no uniform exchange regime. Certainly, to the extent that their interest in exploiting foreign economic relations has risen, it has become desirable to introduce a positive foreign exchange policy, which could have entailed implementing a more positive foreign exchange regime applicable to all, or at least major, transactions abroad.

However, instead of explicitly pursuing such a goal with determination, policymakers have tenaciously clung to their domestic decision-making autonomy. As a result, the modifying CPE has segregated foreign transactions into noncommunicating layers, each of which is regulated, if at all, by target surrogates for effective exchange rates. Consequently, for most members' CMEA transactions one can distinguish among official, commercial, noncommercial, tourist, black market, special store, joint investment and other exchange rates or their surrogates (Brabant, 1987a, pp. 207–21). Some of these are interlinked under highly confined conditions. Thus, in some countries tourist exchange rates for convertible currency holders are set in relation to the commercial or official exchange rate. But for most categories, *ad hoc* policies are pursued that are not always, or even primarily, based on economic considerations. Hungary and, to some extent, Poland are exceptions when it comes to convertible currency transactions for which exchange rate uniformity ostensibly prevails. But their official commercial rate is not the real one at which all foreign exchange is firmly bought and sold, and it is certainly not a rate at which domestic and trade prices are actively linked – owing to pervasive subsidies and taxes, most of which are *ad hoc*.

14.3.6 Interest rate policies

Interest rates are a very special category in Marxist economics, not only in the scholastic approach to it. These concerns are perhaps inspired by ethical and religious, or possibly other, motives but rarely by economic considerations – that is, the efficient intertemporal allocation of scarce capital resources. The reticence with which appropriate and flexible interest rate policies have been pursued domestically has been magnified at the regional level. Since the foundation of the two banks, interest rates for regional capital transactions have presumably been determined by these banks' policies and will hence be addressed in section 14.4.

It suffices to note here that the interest rate has traditionally been a parameter with a marginal role, if that, in the intertemporal allocation of capital resources both domestically and regionally. Thus, the precise rate of interest fixed in loan agreements is almost incidental to the rationale of the agreement or to the profitability of the capital transaction for lender and borrower alike. For one thing, interest rates tend to be exceedingly low compared to those in effect in international capital markets and those warranted by the apparent marginal capital productivity of either lending or borrowing CPE. Orthodox Marxist dogma was what initially prompted the injunction against compounding interest. However, as the nominal rate does not really matter, its compounding is a secondary concern, at best. Third, because rates were low, the borrower's differentiation of rates according to maturity and risk rarely influenced attempts to set the precise rate.

14.4 THE PREVAILING MONETARY AND FINANCIAL INSTITUTIONS

In this section, I outline the particular place of the two monetary institutions of the CMEA, the IBEC and the IIB, though no attempt is made to comprehensively evaluate their operations and role in CMEA cooperation.

14.4.1 The settlements bank and multilateralization of trade

The IBEC was originally entrusted with effecting TR settlements on a multilateral basis by issuing accounting and various kinds of short-term loans. Until 1970, there were five such types of short-term credit: for seasonal, extra-plan, trade expansion, balance-of-payments and joint investment transactions. Because this compartmentalization proved unworkable, the variants were consolidated into a single type in 1970 (see Brabant, 1977, pp. 125–6). Since then, the IBEC has issued two kinds of loans, the revolving settlements credit and the short- to medium-term credit with a maturity up to three years, all associated with an interest rate increasing with maturity. Through such lending, the IBEC was to generalize the *ex post* type of settlement of imbalances under well-specified conditions provided for in the Warsaw Agreement of 1957, which had attempted to offset *ex post* imbalances of exacting specificity (Brabant, 1977, pp. 77–88). Unlike the limited scope envisioned in the Warsaw agreement, the IBEC was to make it possible to effectuate multilateral settlements both in the *ex ante* sense – that is, during the elaboration of BTPAs – and in the *ex post* sense – that is, arranging for partners to reciprocally offset bilateral imbalances sustained as a consequence either of having violated some part of the BTPA or of having exceeded agreed trade values in an unbalanced manner.

Although the bank was put in charge of settlements, it was not allowed any meaningful, that is, active role in negotiating the all-important BTPAs (see chapter 9). As a result, it could not even discharge itself of its constitutional role and has thus remained purely a bookkeeping agency. Likewise, the bank's loan policy is commercially meaningless; it amounts either to simple bookkeeping or to a reconfirmation of loans agreed upon in the appropriate BTPA. While it is true that this system has enabled countries to incur imbalances at any given moment without being compelled to mobilize their own or borrowed convertible currency reserves, it should be recalled that before the IBEC's creation no such funds were used either.

The bank can, and indeed does, impose some interest rate on imbalances and accords progressive rates on deposits of various terms. Likewise, it has formulated a nominally independent loan policy with a string of maturities. Under the circumstances, however, neither has been of more than formal significance. Interest rates have remained exceedingly low – less than 5 percent for even the longest maturity (three years). They have also remained remarkably stable (see Brabant, 1987a, pp. 291–2). Interest balances are owed to (or form claims on) the bank and not to (or on) identifiable individual holders, who can, therefore, rarely effect payments, except for reverse interest flows, because such payments can materialize only for settlement of goods and services specified in one or another BTPA; and there is no BTPA on interest rates, of course. True, an *ex ante* balanced BTPA could be partially executed by the partner who has a credit balance on its interest account at the IBEC. On a net basis, it would thus reduce its claims on the bank. In fact, however, it will be called to terms by the partner who failed to obtain the contracted imports, regardless of whether he is a net interest debtor at the IBEC.

In other words, the bank is a highly technical institution that has sharply reduced delays in processing payments transactions and has kept member banks regularly informed of their various accounts. Also, by now it is sufficiently acquainted with the problems of intra-CMEA trade so that it could institute a more active kind of multilateralism with the assistance of the TR, national or reserve currencies or any new CMEA medium of exchange that may be in the offing. For that to succeed, however, the members must empower it to assume those functions – that is, to synchronize the trade and payments regimes. The bank has probably also garnered sufficient experience to activate the TR and its associated settlements mechanism; to formulate appropriate monetary, lending, interest and reserve policies; and, indeed, to serve as an embryonic regional bank of issue. But without significantly downgrading BTPAs, and especially their degree of bilateralism, there is scant hope for the bank to emerge from its straitjacket (see Brabant, 1987a, pp. 299–300).

14.4.2 Investment coordination through the IIB

The difficulties encountered with medium- to long-term capital movements discussed in section 14.3 and the debates about the elaboration of *Integration*

Program, on which work was then rapidly progressing, led the CMEA members to establish a special institution to facilitate joint investment projects and coordinate investment activity so as to enhance SEI. In fact, the creation of the IIB did not really spur on regional capital mobility as such, though at the time many Eastern European observers portrayed this as an important feature. Instead, the institution was mandated to organize the process of negotiating 'the financing of temporary investment participations' of the CPEs.

Perhaps the most elementary stumbling block for the IIB in fulfilling its mission has been the lack of multilateralism and transferability within the CMEA. Unless two or more members agree explicitly outside the IIB framework to jointly finance a given project and are prepared to appropriate the necessary resources, the IIB can do little through its own lending policy to expedite the enhancement of SEI. That is, an unsecured IIB loan is just like any other capital flow not explicitly tied in with commitments to deliver real goods; hence, it is difficult to mobilize. The same obstacles that inhibit the IIB from playing a more positive role beset other forms of CMEA credit. Ultimately, then, in the economic sense it is difficult to separate a TR loan granted by the IIB from an intergovernmental loan to finance a joint investment project. Precisely, this is because the IIB's constitution integrally exhibits the manifold inadequacies characteristic of the CMEA capital market.

In fact, the IIB was particularly created to ensure that the selected integration projects would be of the highest technological and economic quality, to oversee the construction and management of such ventures, to monitor the continued efficient operation of jointly financed ventures at least until the loan would be repaid and, thus, to ensure that jointly financed projects would yield the highest benefit in terms of accelerating the process of SEI. Whether the bank has been successful in discharging these constitutional tasks is doubtful. Doing so would have required members to relinquish some of their national sovereignty in the appropriation and allocation of capital funds – an unlikely eventuality. The bank apparently has not even been capable of performing a midwifery role in the process of interstate capital and investment relations, except for certain highly spectacular ventures such as the construction of the *Sojuz* gas pipeline and condensate plant in Orenburg.

14.5 THE ORGANIZATIONAL ASPECTS OF INDIRECT COORDINATION

In this section, I examine the trade and payments regime, the issue of multilateralizing regional transactions, making room for transferability of imbalances, factor mobility and the possibilities and desirability of advancing to convertibility.

14.5.1 The trade and payments regime

As analyzed in chapters 9 and 11, perhaps the most critical component of the trade and payments mechanisms in the CMEA is the existence of the MFT in each member country. The presence of the MFT implies that commercial transactions abroad and indeed the commercial policy of the CPEs are, as a matter of course, strictly the province of the nation's Ministry of Foreign trade. Likewise, foreign exchange transactions are the exclusive preserve of the Ministry of Finance, which may delegate some responsibilities to the foreign trade bank.

In the classical CPE, the price-equalization mechanism guarantees that a lofty degree of domestic price autonomy can be preserved. The normal implication of operating with an overvalued exchange rate is that taxes on imports and subsidies on exports are called for. But other combinations of price differences are entirely possible because the outcome essentially depends on how arbitrarily administrative prices are set (see Brabant, 1977, pp. 248–52). Imbalances between trade taxes and subsidies are typically offset against the government budget. In the case of a net increase in 'earnings from foreign trade' beyond what was budgeted, the MFT is able to sterilize such revenues. In the reverse situation, in time there may be a sufficient-enough drain on government outlays away from what had originally been planned, as in the late 1970s and early 1980s, to indirectly induce some sort of macroeconomic adjustment.

The MFT implements its foreign trade and currency strategy largely within the context of bilateralism, particularly in relations with other CPEs. Not only do these countries regularly work out BTPAs, they generally do so at special prices. In fact, BTPAs are negotiated for various kinds of foreign transactions, the most important of which are merchandise transactions on regular accounts, noncommercial transactions and transactions on special accounts – such as for joint investment financing or for the repayment of such loans – or transactions undertaken to enhance production specialization. Within a highly refined set of BTPAs, neither relative prices nor exchange rates matter, except within the specific context of each BTPA at any given moment. I shall return to the exchange rate issue below.

14.5.2 Multilateralism

Multilateralism can only proceed with the automatic, anonymous clearing of transactions that have been previously agreed upon. The success of multilateralism, then, depends on the simultaneous negotiation with all partners of MTPAs that have a high probability of being executed. The agreement may be tacit, as under full convertibility when no limits are placed on the amount and kind of currency that can be exchanged for goods or another currency. An MTPA must at least be involved. Because each participant's *ex ante* imbalances can only be identified with respect to the group as a whole, TRP uniformity is a prime criterion for such a sequence of MTPAs to succeed. The negotiation of MTPAs could proceed either simultaneously or iteratively. Clearly, an iterative process was one of the possibilities held in abeyance when the IBEC was mandated to ensure CMEA multilateral settlements (see chapter 9), but it has apparently never been implemented. I do not even know if it has ever been explicitly considered in actual negotiations. One exception perhaps now on the drawing boards is the recent explorations of how best to foster direct enterprise relations given that regionwide transferability or convertibility cannot be achieved in the near future.

14.5.3 Transferability

Transferability is closely related to the concept of multilateralism discussed earlier, and it is an integral part of multilateralism, though the reverse does not hold. Though the TR is nominally transferable,[3] particularly for merchandise transactions, its translation is highly confined in the context of BTPAs (see chapter 11). However, there are instances in which TR balances on one account can be transferred to another, but this is normally restricted to a preset bilateral relationship. Thus, in principle, balances on noncommercial or tourist accounts can be translated automatically into commercial TR equivalents without reference to the specific bilateral relation (Vostavek, 1987). This is executed via the so-called ruble-linking coefficient, which is actually an internal exchange rate of domestic rubles per TR. This coefficient approximately relates the purchasing power of CPE domestic currencies as measured by a standardized basket of goods and services with weights roughly applicable to local spending by a diplomatic family and the corresponding TRPs or, in the case of most services, surrogates thereof (see Brabant, 1987a, pp. 214–7). In practice, however, the disparate price regimes for the various categories of transactions, even when in principle closely related (for details, see Brabant, 1987a, pp. 217–8), preclude multilateral transferability. But bilateral transfers are practiced on a regular basis by some pairs of CPEs.

14.5.4 Convertibility

Because Eastern European currencies are by definition inconvertible, it may seem odd to suggest convertibility as one component of the existing monetary-financial mechanism. I am doing so to clarify what precisely may be meant by convertibility. Indeed, there is a choice among convertibility of goods or purely financial transactions, for all kinds of merchandise and/or financial transactions or only for some types of interchange, for all holders of the currency or only for some balances and other criteria that may be usefully invoked in considering the situation of CPEs (see Brabant, 1987a, pp. 366–9).

Although there is a high degree of inconvertibility in the CMEA region, a limited form occurs in some transactions. Pertinent examples are the limited convertibility of CPE currencies for tourist purposes as well as for other noncommercial transactions. Admittedly, this is a highly confined form of convertibility of the national currencies against each other and of the national currencies into the TR. Making it more automatic and extending it to other transactions (see Brabant, 1987e) are two tasks that prominently figure in suggested ways for improving the CMEA's monetary-financial mechanism (see chapter 18). They also present instances in which quick gains could be reaped for the benefit of the respective citizenry.

14.5.5 Labor mobility

The motivation of people to cross national frontiers can hardly be reduced to simple material rewards and related benefits. Hence, as an issue, labor mobility fits awkwardly into the central theme of this chapter. Nonetheless, the lure of differential material and other benefits accruing to the would-be emigrant for free spending, perhaps within certain regulated boundaries, could figure prominently in the decision to relocate from one CPE to another. But the regional movement of people in Eastern Europe is narrowly circumscribed. To the extent that labor mobility is tolerated, the conditions that permit it are usually strictly laid down in specific bilateral protocols and are normally congruent with the national labor code of the country of emigration (see Brabant, 1987a, pp. 302–5). The many issues associated with the convertibility of labor rewards are normally handled on an *ad hoc* basis.

When assessed on strictly economic grounds, the ability of people to cross borders is just as important as the movement of capital. As the example of the EC has clearly demonstrated, a liberal regional labor code rarely entails a sharp rise in labor mobility because linguistic, cultural, historical, family and other inhibitions are present that discourage lengthy sojourns abroad. In the CPEs, however, labor mobility is usually proscribed for ideological, political, social and economic reasons. Labor mobility is not expected to help narrow differences in relative economic scarcities in any major way. This is an unfortunate, chiefly political and ideological, stance, as will be argued below.

14.6 REGIONAL MONETARY AND FINANCIAL LINKS

Given that real merchandise flows constitute the principal economic relations among CPEs, the possibilities for establishing monetary and financial links between the CMEA organs, whether official or affiliated, and the relevant national institutions are rather confined. Essentially, they occur on two different levels. One way is by the now-familiar interaction through the two CMEA banks. Regular TR trade flows, but not necessarily other flows – including those conducted in convertible currency and those used to offset imbalances on noncommercial accounts – somehow find their way into the IBEC's accounting facilities. All capital transactions on TR accounts in which the IIB may be an intermediary are channeled through the IBEC's accounting mechanism. This is so because the vast majority of these transactions, especially those denominated in TR, are effected in real goods and must therefore be settled through the IBEC and its formal links with the IIB. Though policy issues may occasionally be raised at those levels, the two banks are, generally speaking, technical institutions whose role in formulating trade and cooperation policies remains mundane even under the best circumstances.

The policy coordination that is achieved particularly through the deliberations of the SCFQ, possibly in cooperation with the Planning Committee, is perhaps more important. The SCFQ's principal tasks and its place in SEI were examined in chapter 7. From the point of view of monetary and financial coordination and links between the CMEA and the members, recall that it is at this level that urgent policy matters regarding indirect economic coordination are raised, discussed and possibly resolved.

Not surprisingly, the role of the SCFQ is the greatest when conflict accompanies the intersecting material interests of the CPEs and simple bilateral protocols are no longer adequate either for fostering SEI in one domain or another or for attaining the minimum desirable degree of equivalence. This extends naturally to the regime that affects several types of exchange rates, including for tourism, other kinds of noncommercial transactions, the uniform denomination of capital assets in the creation of common IEOs and subsequently ensuring satisfactory bookkeeping in those organizations. As a proactive body, chiefly in creating conditions for third countries to participate in the TR payments regime of the IBEC, the SCFQ has so far been rather unsuccessful.

The financial links between the CMEA and the member economies are, perhaps paradoxically, most intimate when it comes to transferring funds borrowed from international money markets to one of the CMEA members. Though an independent policy cannot have been expected to emerge in those matters at the CMEA level, it is nevertheless true that some harmonization of national and regional objectives and tasks must occur at the regional level if the regional banking institutions are to function credibly in Western money markets. The same is true regarding the formulation of convertible currency policies more generally, including the IBEC's and to a lesser extent the IIB's participation in Western-led money lending, chiefly to DEs.

The instruments of indirect economic coordination and their associated institutions in the CMEA, as analyzed, are obviously primitive. The policies governing their management are even less developed. There is absolutely no fiscal policy to speak of. Given the disarray of national fiscal policies, it would likely require an exorbitant amount of time to influence absorption at the regional level through fiscal means. There is an embryonic form of monetary policy, but even that is heavily circumscribed by individual national interests, even more so, by each member's incomplete extant monetary policy.

Although this summary of the discussion may appear pessimistic, the outlook is not uniformly bleak. As argued in the case of the IBEC, the CMEA has mechanisms in place that could prove constructive in enhancing SEI through indirect coordination, provided certain criteria are fulfilled. One glaring defect of the role of the IBEC in the past has been its alienation from trade negotiations. To the extent that these will increasingly result from interfirm relations, the focus of the debate on activating and complementing existing mechanisms should shift more toward identifying what the countries hope to accomplish domestically as well as regionally and which elements of the monetary-financial mechanism now act as brakes. The present TRP regime appears to be one of the most significant drawbacks, as will be examined in the next chapter.

NOTES

1. Since the early 1980s, Hungary has allowed its citizens to be employed abroad under some conditions regarding repatriation of savings and social security contributions. Although this law applies generally, it has not eased the built-in constraints on intra-CMEA labor movements.
2. I am using this as a shorthand to signal that goods and services transferred in payment of the investment contribution are not necessarily directly related to the material needs of the project in question.
3. In a rather unusual admission, A. Zverev (1987, p. 21) recently characterized the TR as 'for the time being not yet transferable in the true sense of the word.'

15 · REGIONAL PRICING AND COOPERATION

To the student raised in the Western economics tradition, the centrality of prices in resource allocation is self-evident. Therefore it may seem trite to emphasize the role of pricing in proper planning of the European planned economies individually and as a group. Paradoxically this is not so. These countries have always in their domestic and regional price policies superimposed a special dogmatic value scheme upon unwieldy economic, financial and trading systems. As a result, pricing as a general policy issue presents an exceedingly complex agenda for CPEs, with a host of political, ideological, technical and institutional ramifications. Space allows me to delve only into some important facets of the regional pricing debates and practices (for others, see Brabant, 1987b), with particular emphasis on their relevance to pricing issues in the late 1980s. This analysis is critical for the proper evaluation later in chapter 18 of the near- to medium-term directions of transforming regional pricing into an instrument that provides a major support for – and impetus to – realistic domestic and regional reforms.

Though I do not wish to open Pandora's TRP box, section 15.1 nudges the lid ajar for a few introductory amplifications on the earlier discussion in chapter 9 of the background to pricing in the individual CPE. Without this further elaboration it would be difficult to place the debates on TRP formation and related matters in their proper systemic and political perspectives. Section 15.2 sketches the TRP issues in their generic context. Note that I am using the TRP acronym here as a convenient shorthand because the TR was only created in 1964. How the options were treated after World War II until the Bucharest price-formation principles forms the subject of the next section. The same is done in section 15.5 for these principles. Both analyses must be placed in the context of the function of trade prices in CPEs to understand, in theory and practice, why CPEs desired to delineate a set of firm principles for TRP formation. This forms the subject of section 15.4. How practice has diverged from theoretical assumptions and agreements on ostensible principles of TRP formation is the subject of section 15.6. The most cogent rationalizations of these divergences are succinctly captured in section 15.7. Issues raised by the unsatisfactory state of pricing in the CMEA and how countries might achieve a feasible reform, while insulating the CMEA market from the daily fluctuations of world markets, is described in section 15.8. That section also sets the stage for linking in chapter 18 these propositions normatively with feasible reforms.

15.1 VALUE THEORY AND SOCIALIST INTERNATIONAL PRICES

The bare bones of the classical labor theory of value, which occupies a central place in the economic theory of socialism as well as in the entire ideological edifice that underpins the economics and politics of development in the Marxist-Leninist framework, is also germane to the regional pricing debate, as was emphasized in chapter 9. Some additional remarks are now required to illuminate the theory of TRP formation and various complications that arise in applying it.

As argued, in the isolated CPE the operation of the law of value may be denied or strongly restricted because of the planning principle (Mitrofanova and Starikova, 1980, p. 165). When the focus of policy rationalization shifts from the domestic economy to the conditions governing the international, including mutual, relations of CPEs, matters change. Especially in intragroup relations, the objective necessity of the law of value supposedly ensues from the existence of socialist property and the material interests of autonomous commodity producers, both seen within the context of an individual country, whose specific interests as commodity producer derive from the precept that each CPE intensely wants to minimize national income 'expended' through exports to procure needed imports (Bautina, 1968a, p. 70).

Recall from chapter 9 that the labor theory of value for the open economy determines international value on the basis of the amount of labor required at the international level to balance aggregate levels of demand and supply. Therefore, the main function of TRPs is said to be the 'accounting of international socially necessary labor expenditures for the production of goods' (Popov, 1968a, p. 69). The functions of TRPs also include assisting in supporting structural shifts in social production to promote 'progressive' branches, ensuring balance between demand and supply in the aggregate and in individual markets, enhancing the development of economic cooperation, and fostering the rational ISDL (Bautina, 1968a, p. 71).

Two features of the 'operationality' of the law of value at the international level – namely the principles of mutual advantage and equivalent exchange – deserve brief explanation because they are so central in SEI debates. Mutual advantage means that all participants in international trade accrue economic and other benefits otherwise not attainable (Mitrofanova and

Starikova, 1980, p. 167). It is generally determined by the savings of socially necessary labor at the national level and the resulting positive increments in utility. The amount of savings need not be identical between partners as goods and services are exchanged according to the principle of equivalent exchange. The assessment of advantages, in contrast, is based on the social, rather than private, gains of each participant in isolation (Gräbig, Brendel and Dubrowsky, 1975, p. 37).

A confusing, but important, other principle concerns the equivalence of exchange values. In the Marxian frame of analysis, equivalent exchange with reference to international trade simply means that commodities are reciprocally exchanged at prices that reflect socially necessary labor expenditures measured at the level of *all* participants. In other words, 'average units of universal labor,' as Marx labeled it, is what counts in ascertaining whether or not one is dealing with equivalent exchange at the international level. Equivalence of value, therefore, refers to international value, which is considered to be 'modified value' (Bogomolov, 1973, p. 35). Unequal exchange occurs when price permanently deviates from its corresponding international value (Bautina, 1973, p. 191) after allowing for the usual factors (Kiss, 1971, p. 209) that explain the divergence between price and value (see chapter 9). But this is perfectly compatible with inequality of national labor values exchanged in the international market, which is often treated as the necessary concomitant of the operation of the law of value (Bogomolov, 1973, p. 35). Would not such a thesis imply that, as the embodiment of competitive producers, countries try to equalize their 'international rate of profit' on traded goods and services? Orthodox Marxist analyses would confirm this because a 'temporary' imbalance exists between demand and supply as perceived by the international 'market' of labor value. In other words, 'national value is related to international value in the same way that individual value is related to social value within a country' (Pechlivanov, 1981, p. 9). But some specialists strongly contest applying this notion to value and price categories, particularly at the regional level. Thus, Bautina (1968b, p. 46) argues that labor value in international markets is not manifested in the form of production prices. Therefore, there is no tendency to even out different national profit rates into a uniform average world profit rate. This presumably stems from numerous 'separators' among various national markets.

Regarding intra-CMEA trade, then, equivalence should mean that the CPEs trade at prices that reflect the socially necessary labor expenditures warranted at the international level. Socialist WMPs may thus at any one time mirror the temporary discrepancies between value and price inherent in transforming one into the other. From this follows the perceived need to utilize 'competitive' WMPs in CMEA trade because the objectivity of the law of value holds these international prices as the locus around which national values fluctuate (Bautina, 1968a, pp. 67–9). Given that equivalence is only part of the doctrine on mutual advantage, 'modified original values' (Bogomolov, 1973, p. 35) may emerge without violating the principle of mutual advantage. Socialist regional and domestic market relations are thus assumed to be inherently different.

As detailed in chapter 11, all CPEs continue to hinder the direct linkup between domestic and trade prices. Moreover, concrete domestic prices are routinely set according to specific criteria that suit economic policy in an individual country at a particular point in time. Even if only for ideological reasons, this would tend to disqualify domestic prices from being used in international trade. There are other socioeconomic factors as well. Particularly pertinent is that the redistribution of value added that is encouraged under the typical CPE price regime is considered counterproductive at the international level; unplanned transfers constitute a 'loss' of national wealth and thus signal 'unequal exchange.' Yet, the CPEs face the problem that they do not want to emulate pricing forces characteristic of international trading markets.

In fact, the situation is much more complex because the CPEs have been deeply committed to one another, if not for economic reasons then at least by a sense of geopolitical and ideological cohesion. Recognizing that the existing domestic price mechanism could not foster 'equivalent exchange' and desiring to perpetuate these differentials (if only to safeguard domestic price autonomy), an alternative solution had to be devised. Both ideological and practical convenience argued for emulating WMPs, one practical reason being that the CPEs never totally severed their ties with MEs. As a result, they could always ponder alternative outlets and sources of supply based on their economic merits. Intrasocialist trade should, therefore, be effected at relative prices that all partners could accept in their trade with 'outside' transactors. Under the circumstances, expediency – certainly not efficiency – dictated that TRPs show some relationship with WMPs.

15.2 REGIONAL TRADE PRICING

For several reasons, it is important to clarify the motives behind the evolution in theory and practice of TRP formation. Actual pricing behavior crystallized in reaction to the concrete circumstances of the postwar period, including the genesis of the peculiarly inflexible trade model then selected (Grinev, 1984, p. 314). In some cases, this already confining environment was further exacerbated by major shifts in the political backdrop to macroeconomic policy mechanisms, institutions and development objectives. Under the circumstances, actual pricing behavior was influenced by numerous factors, including several that were only remotely related to economic principles *per se*. Also, for some transactions pricing principles were gradually adopted that subsequently became enshrined in some way in the so-called Bucharest pricing rules. Moreover, until about 1958, the principles and practices of pricing intragroup trade exerted a formative influence on subsequent pricing behavior. Finally, in becoming full-fledged CPEs, these countries had a special impact on the TRP mechanism. For one, they sought practical guidance from an awkward theoretical framework of analysis. Given that context, three principal reasons may offer insight into the CPEs' fascination with WMPs for their intragroup trade, in spite of recurrent complaints that these prices are decidedly not 'the ideal instrument for stimulating interstate economic cooperation in the world socialist system' (Tarnovskij and Mitrofanova, 1968, pp. 62–3). First, the CPEs trade with MEs at current WMPs; but for some products, they influence the formation of individual WMPs. Second, how international 'values' in the world socialist economic system are formulated is subject to specific features for different goods, which requires an in-depth scientific analysis (which is not yet available) of theoretical and methodological questions of how best to fine tune intragroup price formation. Finally, the methods for setting international values in accordance with the Marxian framework are not sufficiently reliable.

The key issues at stake in external pricing parallel those of domestic pricing. Ideology, politics and expediency have been crucial determinants of the TRP system. Economic agents have had to forge ahead with trade and pricing in spite of the serious dichotomy between theory and practice, endless debates on the proper basis for TRP formation and recriminations about various aspects of TRPs aired at the highest policymaking level. As a result, the voluminous, controversial literature about TRPs and the world socialist system has, at best, made but a dent in the evolution of TRP principles that are grounded in actual trading in a highly constrained environment. Only gradually were efforts made to align prices more closely to the WMPs of main markets, but the gap has not even 'temporarily been fully bridged' (Meister, 1975, p. 15).

From a more practical angle, the concrete development aims and features of the management models of the CPEs stand out. Not the least of the inducements to peculiar pricing was the general economic backwardness of most CPEs. Given the circumstances under which postwar reconversion and reconstruction were accomplished, the conditions that subsequently surfaced and the rapid industrialization in the region, WMPs provided an interesting 'orientation' (Grinev, 1984, p. 314). They represented indicators of 'labor productivity' demonstrably feasible within DMEs, which challenged the CPEs to emulate them soonest.

The policy of stabilizing domestic prices for long periods of time found a direct counterpart in external economic relations. Stable trade prices were supportive of central planning, especially in CPEs that perforce depended on external commerce. Price inflexibility became an especially crucial feature of the typical BTPAs these economies concluded. Whereas certain characteristics of the domestic pricing systems were to be emulated in external commerce, the two systems could not be synchronized due to varying price levels, structure and policies. For that reason, during the discussions preceding the creation of the Council in January 1949 and the high-level debates that took place until mid-1950 (see chapter 2), the CPEs sought to ease the transition phase toward full plan coordination, which would include adequate prices and elaborating a 'regional price system' (Čížkovský, 1971, p. 55).

Sometime in mid-1950 in conjunction with the price push engendered by the Korean War, the issue of WMP fluctuations and their repercussions on TRPs became a priority item of high-level policy discussions, although it had already been under review. Well before the sharp price drift in world markets appeared, the CPEs agreed to temporarily keep existing bilateral trade prices intact, regardless of actual WMP fluctuations (Hegemann, 1980, p. 60). Because palpable price movements were dislocating the global economy, 'stop' TRPs were adopted at the third Session in November 1950 (Huber, 1974a, p. 9); these eventually matured into the system of so-called socialist WMPs, or TRPs. Intensive negotiations on trade agreements, including actual TRPs, also took place and greatly influenced setting TRP rules (Kaplan, 1977, p. 27). Trade agreements worked out with the USSR as the center of CMEA activities were paramount for subsequent pricing practices.

To minimize the confusion that surrounds the theory and practice of TRPs, it is useful to segregate base, reference, contract and transaction prices as four alternative TRP concepts. Of course, they are not necessarily manifested for each product and in each trade relationship at any given time. The base price is the actual WMP that the CPEs select as the starting point for the computation of a reference price; it may be set bilaterally or multilaterally, or partners may conduct *ad hoc* negotiations about the valid price base. The reference price is the average WMP of some earlier period and relevant market(s) as per the parameters agreed upon bilaterally or, in some cases, even multilaterally. The contract price is what is agreed upon in the process of negotiating the actual annual or multiannual (usually, the quinquennial) BTPAs. The reference price may be instrumental in reaching agreement on the contract price, but it need not be. Even if there is a direct functional relationship, the contract price normally diverges from the reference price adjusted for 'quality' variations because of the 'half-freight' rule (on which more below) as well as other, possibly systemic, factors. There may also be noneconomic influences that help illuminate the observed differences in price levels. Finally, the transaction price is the one at which actual trade occurs. This may, but need not, coincide with the contract price. For example, negotiators may postpone fixing contract prices until delivery is made, thus yielding identical contract and transaction prices. The transaction price is rarely the same as the reference price and definitely does not coincide, save by fluke, with any base price.

15.3 CMEA PRICES PRIOR TO THE BUCHAREST RULES

The nature, validity and applicability of early TRPs can best be underscored by distinguishing four separate regimes. Note that neither this subdivision nor the exact periodization specified below is standard.[1]

15.3.1 Current world trade prices, 1945–8

Prior to the CMEA's creation, as a point of departure the CPEs sought to anchor their physically detailed annual BTPAs to current WMPs. However, formal principles about how trade prices for CPEs should or could be determined were lacking (Tarnovskij and Mitrofanova, 1968, p. 49). In some cases an effort was made to pattern TRPs after prices prevailing in main world markets, usually at the time the trade contract was signed. However, given the convoluted political, ideological and economic situation in 1945–8, adherence to a uniform set of price-setting principles in Eastern Europe was not a major preoccupation of interstate economic relations. Rules tended to be rationalized after the fact, including those relating to noneconomic price determinants. Nevertheless, the CPEs earnestly attempted to approximate WMPs at fairly realistic exchange rates. Major exceptions were deliveries accounted for under reparation obligations, transactions within the context of the JSCs and certain inequitable prices (such as for Polish coal).

15.3.2 Lagged average WMPs, 1949–50

By the start of 1949, all CPEs had reached formal trade agreements with the USSR, and several other reciprocal arrangements had been hammered out that typically specified TRPs at the time the trade protocol was negotiated – that is, the year preceding actual transactions. But in some relations the reference WMP for 1949 was not always 1948. In some cases with the 1949 trade agreements, a two-year period of *ex ante* annually fixed trade prices set in. Concluding BTPAs for the next entire calendar year on the basis of average WMPs of the year preceding transactions was certainly general practice for the 1950 agreements (Grinev, 1984, p. 314). The agreements being implemented in 1949, however, had largely been conceived within the context of the prices that prevailed in whatever markets could be identified (Basiuk, 1974, p. 151).

Though a trend to standardize pricing practices along with other principles for clearing trade emerged, the disarray continued to be pervasive and included distortions stemming from transactions conducted for reparation purposes, JSC deliveries and related rationalizations for price divergences. These were substantial in various relations of a given exporter and *a fortiori* among other bilateral relationships. Because coherence in price levels, policies and structures failed to emerge, the Council Sessions through late 1950 (Brabant, 1974a, pp. 200–4; Brabant, 1979, pp. 250–3) sought to establish generally applicable principles, including the validity of average WMPs, price stability, reciprocal advantage and price uniformity. Whether it was formally decided to enshrine such abstract pricing principles in trade agreements or whether these came about as a practical point of reference for ensuring implementation of the overall trade agreements is a matter that remains murky. Generally speaking, in spite of (or perhaps because of) the abstract pricing criteria written into BTPAs, informal pricing continued to prevail, if only to permit the clearing of desired trade quantities in a prespecified commodity composition.

Although the principles apparently endorsed in 1949–50 have remained deliberately vague, three additional features of TRPs at that early stage are worth recalling. Once any pair of partners selected a contract price for a particular product, it remained valid for the duration of the agreement. Also, proper reference WMPs, suitably identified 'from-to' and averaged over an agreed reference period, would be considered as only the *starting* point for bilateral price negotiations. Finally, it was explicitly recognized that the CPEs could enhance the clearing of their reciprocal trade by adopting modified WMPs.

15.3.3 Stop prices until 1953

The price drift engendered by the Korean War considerably complicated prevailing commercial arrangements. Among other, largely systemic factors (Brabant, 1987b, pp. 66–71), this unease forced the CPEs to declare stop prices in the summer of 1950 (Hegemann, 1980, p. 59), an action that was confirmed in November. It is unclear, however, which body first promulgated the ruling. Stop pricing proved congenial to the physical planning framework, including in trade, then strictly enforced in all CPEs. In other words, these countries elected to hold TRPs at average pre-boom levels, generally 1949 and the first half of 1950, and to implement existing multiannual trade agreements at unchanged prices so as to guarantee continuity and stability in their trade relations at a difficult juncture of their reciprocal economic cooperation (Hegemann, 1980, p. 60).

15.3.4 A transition in trade pricing, 1954–8

As the years went by, new products gradually emerged in CMEA trade and were factored into the TRP system according to current WMPs (Grinev, 1984, p. 314). But other considerations were also pertinent. These included the increased potential for trade with the DMEs and the possibilities for profitable arbitrage it created, Stalin's death in March 1953 and the convoluted Eastern European political situation of the mid-1950s and, third, the emergence of the New Course in many CPEs and the concomitant emphasis on better husbanding of scarce resources, including through trade. As a result, the price freeze, which in retrospect is officially held to have lasted until the end of 1957, was actually far from absolute. Modifications of stop prices had been sought as early as 1952 (Mervart, 1963, p. 17; Savov, 1977, p. 85), allegedly to align TRPs with prices in world markets. But for most goods, the moratorium on price flexibility lasted at least until late 1953, when the last agreements with the Stalin Administration expired or were revised. Thereafter the freeze was frequently disregarded, especially for critical products whose WMP had considerably changed, thus opening the door to profitable agreements.

Bilateral price adjustments were undertaken so as to eliminate the most glaring inequities without jeopardizing bilateral balancing. As price changes were generally limited, their overall impact on the terms of trade and bilateral balances of payments remained fairly small. There are two subperiods here. First, as a result of *ad hoc* bilateral negotiations in 1954–6 over marginal price adaptations, TRPs that varied from the 1949–50 averages were progressively adopted, but without this being coordinated within the CMEA. As a result, more inconsistencies in TRPs appeared (Mervart, 1963, p. 18) and discouraged regional economic cooperation. Bilateralism caused some price divergences, but others occurred because no regionwide agreement on proper procedures to justify price adjustments existed. Nevertheless, even during 1954–6, few changes emerged in absolute TRP levels or in the broad structure of relative TRPs. This was due to the absence of a built-in mechanism to manage the economic adjustments imposed by major shifts in the terms of trade or in the regional balance of payments. In addition, it was facilitated by the fortuitous circumstance that no large changes in WMPs appeared until the Suez crisis. Therefore, changes in TRPs could be confined to piecemeal trade-offs. In some cases, quantum adjustments through trade diversion to Western Europe provided the only means of coping with sticky prices.

The second subperiod, during which numerous special price adjustments were made, lasted from early 1957 until late 1958. Mainly because of the political dispersion of the mid-1950s, the CPEs requested a full-scale review of reference prices for the 1957 BTPAs. This task was entrusted to a group of experts attached to the newly created SCFT. As the annual price revisions unfolded, the CPEs found it expedient to refer back to some common principles to buttress their reciprocal TRPs. This was presented as an especially important item on the agenda of the June 1957 Council Session in connection with the discussions about revising the then-valid medium-term trade agreements (1956–60) for the remainder of the 1950s (Faddeev, 1974b, p. 195; Hegemann, 1980, pp. 120–3). Actual contract and transaction prices would, of course, continue to be set bilaterally, in some cases with reference to averages of recent WMPs; but this was not applied to all CPEs or to all commodities. Also, to the degree that changes were sought, in all likelihood the approach was far from standard (Tarnovskij and Mitrofanova, 1968, p. 135).

CMEA members wanted to avoid importing into their price system the 'speculative bubble' that resulted from the Suez crisis. Revisions were applied selectively in view of the complexity of price negotiations and substantial inertia on the part of negotiators. After duly allowing for variations in product quality and transportation costs, serious efforts were made to achieve greater price uniformity. Similar provisions applied to the 1958 trade protocols. Therefore, TRPs for the 1958 agreements were to refer to 1957 WMPs, though this principle was not widely heeded.

15.4 ON THE ROLE AND FUNCTION OF TRADE PRICES

Because the theory of domestic and trade prices in Eastern Europe has rarely been justified from the standpoint of the functions and role of prices, it is not clear how authors from CPEs view the determination of trade prices in a stylized framework. Matters are quite different when it comes to price policies, especially domestic pricing.

At some point in the discussions of the early Bucharest formula it was hoped that firm TRP principles would exert a positive influence on the development of labor productivity throughout the CMEA (Gräbig, Brendel and Dubrowsky, 1975, pp. 76ff.). For this to materialize, however, TRPs should accurately reflect relative scarcities. Only then can they steer economic agents toward consumption and production decisions that stem from rational choices at the micro- and macroeconomic levels. This is particularly appropriate in policy discussions about ECPS and how to place national and regional capital accumulation processes on a firmer economic footing (Ljutov, 1973, p. 51). To foster those goals, it is argued that TRPs must become a yardstick for measuring international comparisons, a means for stimulating economizing nationally and regionally, an accounting medium for ascertaining mutual advantage and effecting the clearing of regional economic transactions and an instrument for redistributing incomes by providing reciprocal economic assistance (Huber, 1974b, p. 515). I hardly need to add that these functions nearly coincide with those ascribed to domestic prices.

As a yardstick, prices should reflect the real cost of production so as to promote rational decisions about fully exploring comparative advantages and hence determining the level, commodity composition and geographic direction of trade. In particular, prices must give sufficiently objective information for evaluating the effectiveness of cooperation in production, science and technology, thus making it possible to adopt correct decisions at all levels of management (Neustadt, 1982, p. 65). Planned development in this connection limits the spontaneity of the theory of comparative costs as evaluated at competitive international prices (Csikós-Nagy, 1975, p. 334), but it does not altogether invalidate it. That also should be the basis of the ISDL. Additionally, prices should provide the correct orientation for decisions about national and regional macroeconomic structural changes (Csikós-Nagy, 1973, p. 180).

Prices must be attractive enough to encourage individual countries to produce particular goods according to regional preferences or national interests. In other words, prices should influence decision making about the proper substitution of imports for domestic products, possibly by concurrently lifting export levels of other goods. That function is crucial in reaching satisfactory decisions about regional cooperation in production and specialization, the planning of economic structures, the proper location of production facilities and how these activities are to be implemented.

Prices must also be an accounting tool if settlements of intragroup transactions are to be conducted smoothly. In a properly integrated economic region that possesses adequate indirect coordination instruments, this function normally derives directly from the first one. However, this is not necessarily true in the CMEA context. Prices are also to be a critical accounting tool in shoring up self-financing and autonomous economic management goals, even when domestic and external prices are kept apart through various buffers.

As an instrument for redistributing incomes, TRPs should be set according to the explicit preferences of the participants. That is, the divergence of a product's price from its underlying value in order to permit a country to explicitly transfer part of its own value added to other partners as a form of development assistance should not be a casual consequence of TRP rules.

Given how TRPs are set and their sharp separation from domestic prices and WMPs, to what extent do they embody the characteristics necessary to perform the above functions? It is clear that during the first dozen years or so of CMEA cooperation, TRPs inadequately met the measurement tasks. The production stimulus of TRPs was frequently exerted for the wrong goods, especially finished manufactures, and hence may have contributed to promoting the wrong economic structures. Actual TRPs for identical products were too diverse to permit smooth bilateral, let alone multilateral, settlements. And, the redistribution of national incomes within the group was often involuntary because CPEs only imperfectly control price-formation processes – a host of noneconomic determinants influence the level and structure of actual transaction prices.

15.5 THE BUCHAREST PRICE-FORMATION PRINCIPLES

One of the most often cited CMEA meetings is the ninth Council Session held in 1958. Its main accomplishment, apart from continuing to reexamine

ECPS agreements and creating new Standing Commissions (see chapter 3), consisted of endorsing a number of documents concerning the basic principles for determining TRPs. The twofold purpose was to eliminate pricing deemed inconsistent with trade among equal partners and to correct pricing practices that obstructed multisided regional specialization. Because these documents have never been published, even in an abbreviated form, their precise content and the extent of the decisions reached in Bucharest have remained enigmatic. Much conjecture and common sense is required to divine the probable Bucharest pricing principles from occasional disclosures about price practices that are made in the Eastern European specialized literature.

15.5.1 Backdrop to the Bucharest meeting

The ninth Council Session took place after seminal socioeconomic transformations in the smaller CPEs (see chapter 3). Of particular relevance were the rancorous allegations in the mid-1950s about unequal exchange during the Stalin era, the need for some price flexibility to contain the scope of profitable arbitrage with DMEs (Basiuk, 1974, pp. 158ff.) and the generalized concern about fostering a more flexible economic model capable of accommodating trade, the ISDL and production specialization as means for promoting mutually satisfactory economic relations. Newly constructed TRPs were to become a crucial determinant of SEI as envisaged during the elaboration of *Basic Principles*.

Secondary sources suggest that in Bucharest the CMEA members codified principles that rationalized practices in vogue since the late 1940s. But the literature is bewildering about the broad principles on which the CPEs agreed and even more enigmatic concerning the concrete details hammered out in Bucharest. What is at issue here is not the precise contours of key parameters of the pricing rules. A pronounced lack of clarity exists about the principles endorsed in Bucharest and how the CPEs expected to apply them.

Near unanimity prevails about the acceptance, for the time being, of some 'competitive WMPs' that would be stable, uniform and mutually advantageous. Stability was not to be equated with absolute immobility, however. Price adjustments were to be permitted when economically justified, even if made after the conclusion of price and volume agreements. The bilateral determination of actual contract and transaction prices was also formally retained. Participants would periodically search for a mutually acceptable new reference base, application period or both by multilateral agreement; neither was to be rigidly fixed. In 1958 members only agreed upon a reference base for the immediate future, possibly up to 1960 (Hegemann, 1980, p. 187), pending study of the desirability and feasibility of evolving an IPS mechanism for the CMEA, a task first entrusted to the SCFT and subsequently transferred to the newly created SCEP.

Greater ambiguity surrounds the determination of reference prices for products with a 'complex character.' This lack of clarity presumably makes it possible to consider quality differences as well as to legitimize deliberate modifications of properly set reference prices and thus to mitigate the effects on the commodity structure of trade and BTPAs of changes in the price base. It also allows members to set stimulatory, preliminary, relational and incentive prices; to price goods traded above planned magnitudes; and to ensure 'reasonable' effects on the bilateral balance of payments.

Though the Bucharest principles were thought of as a strictly temporary expedient of an exploratory character, a major change in the interpretation, though not the precise principles, of the Bucharest price guidelines did not come about until January 1975. Instead of keeping average WMPs for reference purposes unchanged for a number of years, starting with 1976 reference and contract prices could be recomputed annually on the basis of WMPs of the preceding five years. For 1975, average WMPs of the preceding three years were to be used for reference purposes. The modification introduced in January 1975 (the so-called Moscow principle to some observers) is not a major shift away from the Bucharest rules (see Brabant, 1987b, pp. 92–3) because it simply involved applying one of the technical Bucharest principles; that is, the ability to revise TRPs when the underlying reference WMPs substantially change. In spite of numerous objections, this formula was reconfirmed for the duration of the medium-term trade agreements of the 1980s. Ongoing discussions about CMEA reforms may soon lead to greater flexibility in the selection of reference prices (see chapter 18). To comprehend the economics of CMEA trading, then, it is crucial to understand the theory and practice of the Bucharest pricing principles.

15.5.2 On the Bucharest principles

The Bucharest principles can be usefully discussed in terms of three sets of overlapping guidelines: basic rules for price setting in the CMEA, modifications of key recommendations justified by the need to foster CMEA cooperation and special exceptions from the principal rules. But it is ambiguous whether these guidelines were endorsed in Bucharest. The first set includes five fundamental pricing principles: WMPs of main world markets form the base of the system, these prices are transformed into reference prices, such reference prices are to remain stable for moderate to long periods of time, they should exhibit a high degree of uniformity, and reference prices should permit the proper distribution of advantages accruing from saved transportation charges.

WMPs are held to be adequate indicators of actual values of goods and services on the strength of the central theoretical and methodological principle of TRP policies; that is, the redistribution of national income through domestic pricing is undesirable in international transactions.

Domestic prices tend to violate the doctrine of 'equivalent exchange,' as explained in section 15.1. Socialist economists believe that international value reflects socially necessary labor cost and that WMPs fluctuate around international value (Bautina, 1972, p. 143). By eliminating the 'distorting' elements from observed WMPs, 'it is usually possible to crystallize the objective essence of this category so that it becomes practically possible to utilize [WMPs] as the basis for contract prices' (Mitrofanova, 1977, p. 117). In other words, properly defined competitive WMPs over some reference period are taken to reflect true labor values, just as equilibrium production prices reflect underlying labor values in Marx's frame of reference (*pace* proper transformation).

International value is approximated by averaging WMPs, which supposedly eliminates short-term perturbations stemming from conjunctural, cyclical and speculative fluctuations fundamentally unrelated to 'true' labor values. If world markets are not truly competitive, weighted average WMPs should be purged of monopolistic influences, exploitative features, distorting taxes and subsidies and related factors. In some cases, only the direction and proportion of price changes should be taken into account because prevailing WMPs may be '20 percent or more of what is a more objective price base' (Tarnovskij and Mitrofanova, 1968, p. 82).

More concretely, WMPs are understood to be prices of main world markets or of main producers. This implies that CPEs confine their selection of references to a few markets or leading manufacturers from whom they would import if the CMEA did not exist (Faude, Grote and Luft, 1976, p. 201) because prices there emerge regularly in convertible currency for large transactions conducted by independent operators (Tarnovskij and Mitrofanova, 1968, p. 83). Such prices can be documented for many primary goods on the basis of commodity market quotations, auction prices, price catalogs of major representative producers, actual prices in CMEA trade, EWPs and similar evidence.

A third fundamental axiom is that WMPs must be averaged over some period of time and remain valid 'as far as possible for the entire course of long-term agreements, but at least for one year' (Černianský, 1963, p. 157). This was resorted to because 'price stability increases the probability of implementing the national plan and thus makes the realization of definite macroeconomic state preferences possible' (Kamecki, 1966, p. 22).

Although the negotiators in Bucharest expected to build averages over a three- to five-year period (Mervart, 1963, p. 22), in 1958 it was decided as an interim solution to set prices for the renegotiated three-year trade agreements (1958–60) on the basis of average 1957 prices (Zolotarëv, 1970, p. 186). A few exceptions were granted to eliminate the unusual fluctuations in the prices of some goods during the first quarter of 1957 that stemmed from the Suez conflict (Tarnovskij and Mitrofanova, 1968, p. 135). Thereafter the CPEs hoped to finalize an appropriate multiyear period. This interim measure was advocated by the SCFT because negotiators failed to reach consensus on how to swiftly implement the recommendations of the May 1958 economic summit. The one-year reference period was kept through 1960 and subsequently extended to 1964.

To understand the more recent evolution of TRP recommendations, recall that no specific time frame, aside from the initial one-year period, for the averaging was accepted in Bucharest. It was not until late 1964 that the Executive Committee finally recommended that new reference prices be introduced gradually in 1965, at least for the most important products. These were definitely to be in place in 1966 for the duration of the then-valid five-year plans (1966–70). The primary reference would be to 1960–4 WMPs, though for some products the base was extended up to eight years while for others it was truncated to as few as two years. The five-year reference base, with one exception (1975), has remained a premier operative guideline up until today. The base can be shifted only upon recommendation of the CMEA's Executive Committee. This requires a unanimous multilateral agreement as the Bucharest principles do not incorporate provisions for automatic adjustments according to standardized criteria.

Neither did the CPEs endorse a target period for which averaged WMPs would serve as reference for TRPs. At Bucharest the CPEs only resolved to apply the rules for the remainder of the 1950s, primarily because they anticipated a swift transition to an IPS. As a result, the application period valid at any point in time is normally settled in the same multilateral agreement as the one on the price reference. Since the mid-1960s, the application period derives from synchronized medium-term BTPAs based on stable reference and contract prices. To the extent possible, stable transaction prices should also be encouraged, but with some exceptions (Tarnovskij and Mitrofanova, 1968, pp. 154–87) allowed for price revisions in case of major changes in WMPs, the 'contemporary' pricing of new products or other unanticipated changes.

Although not explicitly stated in the Bucharest price clauses, in practice stability was understood to imply relatively small changes in prices from one reference base to another. If major changes were required, the terms-of-trade effect (Basiuk, Jaroszyńska and Krawczyk, 1975, p. 96) and adjustment of individual product prices were to be absorbed over a transition period of at least two years. Thus, the 1964 agreement was introduced over two two-year periods to spread the terms-of-trade effect over 1966–7 for Bulgaria, Hungary and Mongolia; for the others the effects were absorbed in 1965–6 (Popov, 1968b, p. 132). In practice, price stability became such a fetish that, until the mid-1970s, the level and broad structure of TRPs were largely still as implied by the stop prices of the early 1950s. In any case, in time the range of products for which new prices were negotiated remained small (see Ausch, 1972, p. 94; Rutkowski, 1977, p. 4). Even after the 1975 reinterpretation, with the evident exception of energy products, few systematic price revisions were undertaken and these fell within a narrow band (Klawe, 1976, p. 95).

The fourth principle calls for price uniformity, after factoring in quality variations and transportation costs. For this reason all CPEs need to agree *ex ante* on unique reference prices that, after proper weighting and averaging, form the basis of trade negotiations and BTPAs. Because this has not happened, actual TRPs as well as contract and reference prices diverge in each pair of CMEA relations. This circumstance has perhaps generated the knottiest cooperation obstacles in the CMEA.

The fifth principle is arguably the most obscure – at least the most esoteric. It states that TRPs are to be set f.o.b. border of the country of delivery plus half of the transportation charge that an importer would have to bear if a similar commodity had to be acquired from its most likely alternative supplier minus the actual freight cost involved. This principle referred in particular to bulk and heavy goods (Ausch, 1972, pp. 82–3; Brabant, 1987b, pp. 191–3; Popov, 1968b, p. 131). In 1958 it was decided to draw this markup from lists of posted international freight charges (Koz'menko, 1986, p. 25). Contractual supplements are levied irrespective of factual transportation costs within countries, however (Konovalova, 1968, pp. 135ff.; Mitrofanova, 1978, p. 96; Šanina, 1973).

This particular charge is usually justified because the precise location of a CMEA importer may be a source of benefit or loss in terms of all the factors that make up the difference between f.o.b.- and c.i.f.-based prices (Teichmanowa, 1976, p. 37). This factor, which may be equated with a differential rent (Koz'menko, 1986, p. 25), should be equally shared. It is customarily seen as a markup. Kohlmey (1974, p. 71) reports that it could also be negative should CPEs incur transportation disadvantages in importing from the CMEA. Clearly, however, there are limits to this cost sharing, as in the case of Cuba.

Even if all costs were equally distributed so as to maintain international solidarity and equivalent exchange, the freight principle lacks firm economic justification. In fact, international solidarity could have been promoted more productively by using these phantom charges as a funnel through which to fund a CMEA capital reserve (see Brabant, 1987b, pp. 101–2) for joint investment projects specified for enhancing SEI.

The second set of price principles contains modifiers of reference prices because averaged WMPs, after allowing for the freight adjustment, are not rigidly transmitted into the TRP formula. Basic modifiers ensue from considerations about mutual advantage, economically warranted deflections from WMPs and the bilateral setting of contract and transaction prices. Reference WMPs should be mutually advantageous on the seemingly logical principle that the benefits, relative to international value, emanating from the socialist world market should be shared equally by both parties. Advantage was held to be crucial so that the set TRPs would contribute to the planned development of all participating CPEs and stimulate their mutual trade turnover (Kohlmey, 1974, p. 71). This has been a particularly important determinant of an emerging own price system for many manufactured goods (Tarnovskij and Mitrofanova, 1968, p. 172).

Although striving for price stability, the CPEs also want to keep abreast of 'secular changes' in WMPs, as distinct from temporary perturbations; hence the principle of reciprocal advantage (Tarnovskij and Mitrofanova, 1968, pp. 167–87). Contract TRPs can be changed by mutual consent but only if it is economically justifiable (Černiodský, 1963, p. 158). Accordingly, if fundamental shifts are perceived in reference WMPs during the implementation of the medium-term BTPA, another reference price could be set bilaterally. Simply to preserve price uniformity, this would presumably have become applicable to all potential CMEA partners. Regardless of the uniform principles that may prevail in the construction of reference WMPs, the CPEs agreed to determine contract and transaction prices bilaterally. Reference prices were to be adjusted for quality differences between the actual commodity traded and the reference good agreed upon, as well as the transportation charge.

But other considerations could and did come into play, and these form the third set of principles. As noted, it is not clear to what extent these other principles were formally included in the Bucharest deliberations. Because some of them had at one point been major determinants of trade price policies in the postwar period, at the very least they must have been touched upon in Bucharest. First, new products, however defined, introduced after the conclusion of the BTPAs were to be transacted at 'relational' prices, which requires adjusting the original contract price by a coefficient relating the original to the new reference prices. This principle was already well entrenched in CMEA practice at least since the early 1950s.

Second, partners may see advantages in encouraging mutual trade and therefore set incentive prices for commodities they cannot or will not acquire from third markets (Pechlivanov, Krůstev and Christov, 1978, pp. 138ff.). Setting incentive prices requires special deliberations by those parties interested in stimulating the production and trade of the concerned products (Savov and Veličkov, 1966, pp. 14ff.). It is not obvious, however, how exporters are to be weaned of this, presumably temporary, protection.

A related principle concerns the need to set incentive prices for products with a pronounced seasonal character, presumably to avoid arbitrage driving them off the CMEA market. Accordingly, for most agricultural goods seasonal product prices were to be established with reference to appropriate variations in WMPs.

Three other principles that may have been debated need to be addressed. First, prices could be set in a 'complex' way; that is, to include economic and other factors not necessarily pertaining to the transaction in question (see Brabant, 1984c; Brabant, 1987b, pp. 103–5; Popov, 1969, p. 147). Second, for above-plan deliveries, current WMPs would be emulated. Whether these transactions would also require convertible currency payments was not even considered at the time. But this variation on price movements has been an important qualifier of TRPs, especially since the early 1970s. Third, whenever negotiators failed to specify a particular reference WMP, rules were devised for setting preliminary prices, pending the resolution of the matter by an organ entrusted with arbitrating pricing disputes. But such a trade court or related arbitration organ has never been created (Brabant, 1987b, pp. 111–2).

15.5.3 Practical application of the Bucharest principles

It is important to remember that the Bucharest principles apply solely to regular commercial transactions resorting under the TR clearing regime. That is, the Bucharest rules may not be valid for above-plan deliveries, for trade denominated in convertible currency, for specialization and special cooperation transactions and they do not, of course, apply to any transaction not directly related to actual merchandise trade.

Because WMPs come in all kinds of currency units, when and how these different values are to be converted into a common measure must be specified. The logic of the Bucharest principles would suggest conversion at average annual exchange rates. This practice (reported only in Špaček, 1984, p. 439; Špaček, 1985, p. 1) was apparently recommended by the SCFQ, possibly in late 1978 (Konstantinov, 1982, p. 128) after the Soviet Union started to compute the convertible currency exchange rates of the *valuta* ruble in terms of a currency basket with weights applicable to Soviet foreign exchange transactions. At the same time, the logic of the Bucharest principles demands that WMPs be converted into TR for each observation year before reference prices are established. Unfortunately, there has never been a definitive statement to that effect.

15.5.4 The conundrum of pricing practices

The principles discussed above are generally quite straightforward. Some make good sense within the context of chiefly physical planning of nearly all economic activities. However, it is in interpreting and even more so in applying these murky principles that formidable problems arise. What tends to result is a peculiarly complex *quasi* general-equilibrium model in which individual products are identified by producer, importer, transaction time, type of product contract, degree of hardness of traded goods and other attributes, all of which makes for a kaleidoscopic environment. Precisely because these unwieldy prices do not indicate the terms at which alternatives are really being offered *ex ante*, the TRP system itself has been the root cause of the failure of any automatic type of multilateral clearing across partners or time to become a potentially useful regulator of SEI (see chapter 17).

Even if the TRP category is properly identified, how to reconcile price stability with competitiveness and avoid frequent multilateral agreements on reference WMPs has posed a major dilemma in the CMEA; it is also a central cause for the elusiveness of price uniformity. Although price uniformity is often heralded as a fundamental characteristic of TRPs, in contrast to the alleged discriminatory treatment received by CPEs and DEs alike in world trade, opinions on the degree to which it is achieved vary enormously. In this connection, recall that the CPEs do not negotiate on the basis of standardized reference price lists; rather, they haggle according to their bilateral interests.

How divergent are bilateral prices? Within the context of the search for an IPS, a number of interrelated investigations were conducted to estimate the degree of price divergence. One view argued that there was substantial uniformity, with deviations perhaps ranging between 7 and 10 percent (Tarnovskij and Mitrofanova, 1968, pp. 164–6; Mitrofanova, 1978, p. 170). Others disagreed on the grounds that the principle of economically justified adjustments had been interpreted very liberally, perhaps because at this stage of CMEA relations they offered 'one of the necessary forms to change production structures and turnover proportions according to CMEA precepts and, it goes without saying, all on the basis of methods developed with reference to equivalence' (Bautina, 1968a, p. 70). However, the refutations of such claims, as stated in Uspenskij and Ždanov, 1987, pp. 21–8, are more persuasive, as set forth below.

15.6 APPLYING THE PRINCIPLES – CONCEPTUAL ISSUES

The abstract TRP principles generate complex conceptual questions that in particular attempt to clarify the empirical dimensions of the enigma. In addition to severely restricted evidence on TRP practices, remember that in commercial practice the application of vague principles may itself cause confusion. Recall that the CMEA is only an interstate agency that lacks supranational power (see chapter 7). Hence, the Council may initiate recommendations on commercial principles and practices, such as TRPs, but it cannot bind the members. For example, multiple base and reference WMPs may be calculated at the regional, national and decentralized decision-making levels. While basic WMPs have probably at most played a guiding role, reference WMPs continue to serve as one of the take-off points for concrete trade negotiations.

Second, given the circumstantial evidence and the available CMEA agreements on similar issues, the pricing documents probably contain broad recommendations and general intentions rather than strict, fully delineated rules and regulations that can be applied without being stymied by conceptual obstacles. If the signatories of these agreements ever sincerely anticipated them to be of practical use, the exceedingly open-ended, at times even deliberately obscure, wording of the TRP principles has allowed ample scope for bargaining skills to become a critical determinant of transaction prices in BTPAs.

Third, if the principles themselves are exceedingly vague, reliable and hard information on actual pricing practices is even more disjointed, and very rare. There are plausible reasons for this. For one, commercial practice is generally confidential, and in the CMEA context doubtlessly it is also treated as a political secret. From a strictly empirical point of view, trade statistics and related sources of information do not generally afford an opportunity to check pricing practices according to *a priori* models. Writers on pricing matters are usually far removed from high-level ministerial negotiations about TRPs and even those set by FTOs. Even had these commentators been fully briefed on the vexing price policies, would the evidence have surfaced?

Finally, although the atmosphere in which the pricing principles were endorsed may have imbued negotiators with the spirit of an SEI world yet to be molded in *Basic Principles*, several important components of the trade regime then in place have meanwhile not changed. Here it is crucial to recall that a double inconsistency exists between the theoretical and the practical parameters of this peculiar TRP system. On the one hand, uniform trade prices for a circuit of CPEs are *in se* incompatible with bilateralism, and *a fortiori* with structural bilateralism, whenever the latter's balancing constraints are operative. Given the considerable opportunity for arbitrage embedded in the typical trade model, full TRP autonomy cannot long be sustained. As a result, price uniformity on the basis of principles that fail to reflect actual decision-making parameters cannot be indefinitely supported because of its, possibly prohibitive, costs.

15.6.1 The Bucharest principles and trade conduct

How trade negotiations actually proceed is unknown. The specialized literature, which is generally unsystematic and sometimes purely anecdotal, stresses intensive bargaining on contract and transaction prices. This affords a key explanation for the considerable divergence between TRPs and some concept of WMPs, even for readily identifiable products that fall under regular trade agreements. Negotiators apparently do refer to averages of some WMPs, but it is not clear how markets are selected and, with few exceptions (such as petroleum), whether all negotiations revolve around identical markets. Matters are even less structured when it comes to eliminating what are judged to be undue conjunctural fluctuations, the monopolistic setting of WMPs (including for many minerals and metals) and the effect of output and price 'controls' on WMPs of some goods (including many agricultural products). Finally, there is hard evidence that the 'half-freight' principle (on which more below) has been an important, if highly capricious and volatile, codeterminant of TRPs for certain commodities. Rarely can the bogus freight charge be defined unequivocally, but it constitutes one of the special tactical weapons in bilateral negotiations (Ausch and Bartha, 1969, pp. 112–3).

A detailed examination of Eastern European commentaries (see Brabant, 1987b, pp. 118–42) underscores two theses. First, there is a broad spectrum of opinion on the origin of TRPs or what it should be. Furthermore, there is ample evidence that a deep chasm exists between theory and practice. This may sound surprising, and only dialectics may point to a solution (D'jačenko, 1968b; D'jačenko, 1969, p. 18). Whatever the metaphysical link applied, TRPs have *de facto* influenced not only trade but also the pace and direction of economic development (see chapter 17). As the rationales for price guidance advocated in the literature diverge so extraordinarily, it will be useful to clarify here why the Bucharest principles have been modified. These rationales can be divided into two groups. First, there are those that eschew WMPs even if such indicators could have been identified and CPEs had really wanted to apply them. Then there is the systemic disregarding of WMPs for reasons that help elucidate why it may not always be feasible to imitate WMPs.

15.6.2 Trade negotiations and WMPs

Assuming that WMPs could be computed and CPEs intended to utilize them as basic inputs into the construction of TRPs, the following reasons may offer insight into why the two would, by necessity, have to diverge in practice. First, the trading system of the CPEs is such that the key behavioral properties of the MFT's attitude toward individual trade prices are crucial. The MFT is inherently primarily interested in executing the central plan directives, namely, acquiring the most-needed imports in exchange for the least-needed domestic products. It is generally guided by the broad results of trade rather than by economic parameters applicable to individual goods (Ausch and Bartha, 1969, p. 112). Mutually advantageous prices are negotiated in concert to minimize variations in the overall terms of trade – and hence the bilateral and regional payments balances – and the terms of trade per broad commodity group, especially since the mid-1950s.

Second, the art of documenting WMPs and the obstacles that inevitably emerge in the process are such that the easier the comparison with WMPs, the smaller in principle the divergence between TRPs and WMPs. But WMPs have not always been used as the effective terms of exchange. Even in the case of primary goods traded in commodity exchanges, WMPs may not constitute the factual basis of TRPs; but they do provide a handy check on their variations. In other words, it has inevitably been more difficult to let TRPs deviate from WMPs when alternative opportunities are readily available, even though the CPEs do not forcibly seek them through arbitrage.

Third, it is much harder to establish average WMPs for manufactures than for primary industrial goods and foodstuffs. Thus it should not be surprising to learn that for 'advanced' goods WMPs were systematically ignored. Although the obstacles encountered in fixing such prices would have deterred anyone, other reasons can be cited for departing from the Bucharest principles. For example, manufactured goods are only a modest share in the exports of all CPEs, except Czechoslovakia and the GDR, in the 1950s. Knowledge of concrete WMPs was inadequate because of the trade embargo and the cold war. The transaction costs incurred in circumventing these obstacles have been heavy. And, the impediments that DMEs put in the way of trading with CPEs were such that exports tended to be absorbed only at some discount. Further reasons for the differences between EWPs and WMPs are examined below. As an alternative to WMPs, then, a 'mechanism of special bilateral clearing' (Ausch and Bartha, 1969, pp. 115–7) for manufactures came into existence. Because of the MFT's lack of interest in individual TRPs and knowledge of details on WMPs as reference points, 'domestic prices of the individual countries bec[a]me the basis and the economic contents of the formation of "[WMPs]" for finished products' (Ausch and Bartha, 1969, p. 116).

Because WMP is ambiguous as a concept and often difficult to concretely document, it might, fourth, be thought that EWPs could offer a useful surrogate, though possibly only after some additional transformations to reflect the special features of East-West commerce. These peculiarities of East-West trade may be grouped into three categories (Brabant, 1987b, pp. 122–7). First, political animosities exacerbate the hindrances to smooth trade and thus raise the cost of circumventing the obstacles. Second, most CPEs do not enjoy most-favored nation (MFN) status and are often treated at the fringes of commercial policy. And third, a variety of problems encountered by the CPEs in simply mastering dependable marketing skills for interacting with Western economies often explains why CPE products trade at a discount.

Fifth, once divergences are permitted it is difficult to repeal the practice, especially if the MFT lacks interest in individual prices. The reform movement may have somewhat changed this inertia, but greater attention to individual prices is effective only in trade among countries inclined to more fully exploit trade opportunities. This excluded the USSR until the measures launched in early 1987, which may enforce greater price awareness.

Finally, trade must be conducted on a regular basis. This means that the time required to arrive at agreed prices that conform with the principles often exceeds the time available. Further, susceptibility to individual price variations and the primary concern for quality being what they are in the CPEs, agreed prices diverge because of the nature of the negotiating process.

Thus, participants cannot escape the impact of WMP fluctuations that occur when TRPs are being negotiated. In that sense it is not surprising that Ausch and Bartha (1969, p. 115) found a significant correlation between the time TRPs were set and price fluctuations both in DMEs and recently concluded BTPAs.

15.6.3   Major determinants of actual TRPs

Although the CPEs may aspire toward TRPs derived from reference WMPs, this generally cannot be a rigid rule because of the existence of so many factors that impinge upon the determination of actual TRPs. Four of these need to be considered. First, CPE management systems and their peculiar development strategy go a long way toward explaining the difference between internal and external prices. The central planner is usually not keen on ascertaining proper prices because planning does not proceed on the basis of comparative advantage indicators.[2]

Second, *ex ante* BTPAs enabled the CPEs to achieve greater realism in the national planning process and to ensure the dependability of central planning. Perhaps more important was that it also provided them as a group with the means to ward off temporary disturbances in world markets better than each member could have done alone, and it allowed them to take into account microeconomic as well as economywide considerations and to pursue a variety of noneconomic goals. In principle, comprehensive trade agreements could have provided the necessary infrastructure for the coordination of economic policies (see chapter 12) if other, including noneconomic, constraints had not inhibited their emergence.

Third, the single most important determinant of TRPs is undoubtedly bilateralism as it has been practiced in Eastern Europe for nearly forty years. The broad TRP-formation principles are too vague for selecting concrete prices. By definition, negotiations of BTPAs resemble a monopoly-monopsony situation. The indeterminacy of the outcome is tempered by two sets of factors. Because CPEs seek imports for plan fulfillment, concessions in the form of clearing or swing credits, capital transactions, reexports and the like usually emerge during negotiations. Also, opportunities for arbitrage with nonsocialist markets that vary among partners as well as over time narrow the range of indeterminacy.

Fourth, the greater the negotiators' determination to reduce the terms on which alternatives are offered to explicit monetary values (for given flexibility with third partners), the more prices satisfy *a priori* notions of effectiveness. This environment permits the selection of a range of TRPs situated between actual WMPs and some variant of the domestic prices of the exporter, depending on the type of product and the state of the markets in which these goods are normally traded. Because price bargaining has traditionally been conducted at a relatively high rung of the planning hierarchy, negotiators are inevitably motivated by overall trade benefits in preference to commodity-by-commodity trade gains. Oftentimes, national assessments are made and these local evaluations thus influence actual regional prices (Kraus, 1985, p. 10). Such trends are especially likely to emerge in the case of specialized or nontraditional manufactures for which it is always hard to construct acceptable WMPs in bilateral, let alone region-wide, relations.

15.6.4 Toward a regional price system?

Although the CPEs officially profess to adhere to one set of principles anchored to WMPs, this claim often amounts to little more than paying lip service to the ideology of 'equivalent exchange,' which paradoxically enough, calls for, and in fact mandates, a gamut of 'condoned' price adjust-ments that reflect the *de facto* state of the market. These implicitly con-tribute to the establishment of a significant degree of regional price autonomy (Faude, Grote and Luft, 1984, pp. 197–8); but others see it as the outcome of a consciously designed policy (Kunz, 1982, pp. 142–6). Thus, over the years comparatively stable price relations have emerged for many processed goods, especially subassemblies, parts, components and products tailored to CMEA demand that have no readily identifiable counterpart in world trade.

Following these propositions, the TRP determinants can be divided into those that are inherent in traded goods and the specific organizational arrangements under which goods are transacted. Regarding traded goods, it may be useful to distinguish among homogeneous goods, including most fuels and raw materials; finished products from processing industries; inter-mediate processed products, including subassemblies, parts and compon-ents; individualized finished products; and services, including wage products. Only for the first group can WMPs be unambiguously identified. For the second group, reference prices are largely shaped by the particular interests of the trading partners and tend to move in line with the exporter's home prices (Tarnovskij and Mitrofanova, 1968, p. 196), which may be tailored in some cases to the price catalogs of a few major DME firms (Knyziak, 1974, pp. 180–1). For all other groups, the domestic prices of the exporter and proper exchange rates or surrogates must influence the determination of reference prices.

In addition to the type of traded good, different trading regimes need to be separated. Especially regarding the evolution of TRPs since the early 1970s, the following hierarchy may illuminate matters: currency of account-ing or actual settlement (TR or convertible currency), type of trade agree-ment (regular, supplementary and *ad hoc*), type of transaction (regular exchange, specialization and joint investment) and market tension.

The most fundamental distinction may be the currency of payment, closely followed by type of trade agreement. Because convertible currency transactions already embody a higher degree of hardness than TR-priced goods, they usually entail markedly different prices from comparable TRPs, regardless of whether or not they are included in regular or special agreements. Similar provisions apply to trade resulting from specialization agreements or jointly financed investment projects. For hard goods, the TRP is likely to closely approach the current WMP obtainable by the exporter. WMPs may be averaged for deliveries planned in the context of either regular or, more likely, supplementary agreements. *Ad hoc* transactions in turn may involve incentive prices to reflect the true marginal cost of ensuring delivery over some mutually agreed period of time.

Matters differ considerably for the bulk of trade conducted in TR. Regular trade protocols attempt to adhere to the Bucharest price principles for goods that have a more or less identifiable WMP. In the case of most engineering products and for many durable consumer goods, the problem of finding a proper reference WMP is probably resolved bilaterally. Once the base price is agreed upon and averaged over some period of time, the resulting reference price helps set the corresponding TRP. TRP transactions generated from supplementary or *ad hoc* agreements are more likely to be cleared at whatever price the situation can bear. TRPs are likely to be attuned more to current WMPs – and in some cases current domestic production costs of exporters – than to reference WMPs as per the Bucharest guidelines. This situation is even more prevalent for specialized products or the exchange of goods emanating from jointly financed TR investment ventures. Some guidance in prescribing the negotiating range may come from current WMPs or price relations, but the actual terms at which these goods move basically emanate from bilateral trade negotiations. The production and market balance situation of the participating CPEs is bound to play an important role.

Although the CPEs have unquestionably tried in earnest to observe some level of reference price uniformity, the nature of the bilateral trading process is such that it yields individualized contract and, even more so, bilaterally differentiated transaction prices. The greater the 'distance' between domestic producer (or user) and the foreign user (or producer), and the stricter the enforcement of the MFT through government means, *ceteris paribus*, the greater the disparity in individual prices and the harder it is to identify determinants of individual trade prices. Because the particular type of CMEA bilateralism provides only marginal allowance for price flexibility, the actual scarcity of individual goods in foreign commerce has increasingly been expressed through nonprice commercial conditions, which include special purpose credits, *ex post* capital flows to regularize bilateral trade imbalances, reexports, convertible currency payments, combined or tied-in sales of hard and soft goods and conditional specialization agreements. Especially important has been the emergence of a panoply of hard and soft goods. Consequently, a particular type of structural or commodity bilateralism has arisen that continues to be a crucial determinant of the CMEA trade model because the price mechanism cannot, or is not allowed to, perform its allocatory function under overall bilateral constraints.

15.7 MODELING PRICE BEHAVIOR – THE LITERATURE

By now sufficient evidence is available to affirm that prices in intra-CMEA trade are not uniform, that they differ markedly from those observed in trade with other countries and that they bear only a tenuous relationship with domestic prices in any of the CPEs. At the very least, this situation is paradoxical when placed against the backdrop of the time and effort devoted to the gradual elaboration of common TRP principles and their alleged implementation since the mid-1960s. The heterogeneity of TRPs and their systematic divergence from reference prices stem somewhat from conceptual problems about the proper interpretation and application of vague principles that have mutated over time. The primary culprit, however, is the environment within which these pricing rules must be applied, if they were intended as rules in the first place.

In recent years, support has increased for the thesis that neither EWPs nor WMPs are basic inputs into the pricing of a widening range of CMEA products, though both continue to act as important control levers over the level and variation of TRPs. Inasmuch as these topics pertain to empirical advantages and disadvantages of the relationships between CMEA and world prices, they are analyzed in chapter 17. Here I shall examine various inquiries into the alleged principles that may have guided the formation of TRPs.

Unfortunately, the literature on certain empirical features of TRP behavior is full of hybrids. With few exceptions, research on TRPs has rarely entertained explicit hypotheses about the relationship between some definition of TRPs and WMPs. In the Western literature, focus has mainly been on such topics as exploitation, the opportunity cost of CMEA trading, price divergence, price discrimination and implicit subsidies in CMEA trade. These politically sensitive hypotheses may or may not be germane to a dispassionate economic discourse about TRPs. To the extent that they are relevant, most investigations have concluded that, if anything, price uniformity and mutual advantage have never been attained and that TRPs have diverged from relative EWPs and WMPs in important respects. Most CPE commentators have retorted that such price differentials stem only from variations in the quality and makeup of products and from the implications of the rule to divide 'saved' transportation costs.

For obvious reasons, published investigations undertaken by CPE economists of the relationship between TRPs and some concept of WMPs have appeared only sporadically. Furthermore, their methodological approaches and results have rarely been disclosed. Published findings are *usually* so terse that even ascertaining the approximate methodology and data explored in deriving the advocated position is often impossible. Moreover, a published position is typically quite inarticulate and often, therefore, lacks operationality. This observation is particularly germane to a large group of studies that hope to exploit quantitative evidence to substantiate claims about the allegedly very tangible advantages of trading with the CMEA. Ascertaining the veracity of these advertisements is especially difficult. Replication of their methods is hardly ever possible because either the raw data are not accessible or the methodology introduced is too equivocal.

Western empirical research on TRP issues since the mid-1950s can be sorted into five categories: price discrimination, customs union effects (which was an explicit outgrowth of the critique of the discrimination hypotheses), opportunity cost analyses, implicit trade subsidies and direct tests of the Bucharest principles.[3] Except for the last group of studies, this research has posited the simple hypothesis that divergence between WMPs, however defined, and TRPs cannot be avoided because of the pronounced inequality inherent in relations between the USSR and Eastern Europe. The logic of this approach is grounded in political analyses of relations among states that are obviously unequal, rhetoric notwithstanding, for geopolitical and strategic reasons. Therefore, the research has been motivated chiefly by two considerations. First, an attempt has been made to quantitatively measure the divergence between some WMPs and prevailing TRPs – actually unit values in most cases. Second, these empirical results have subsequently been placed in a theoretical or conceptual framework that reflects the precepts or presumptions held by those authors responsible for the research, and sometimes their sponsors, about countries belonging to an organization such as the CMEA.

Eastern European research fits into a few of the above categories, but not all. Published empirical inquiries into TRPs are essentially of two types. In preparing background information for comparatively high-level policy deliberations, CPE economists have tried to animate discussions on economic policies and guide them in one direction in preference to another. The arguments advanced are usually situated between the need to heed relative scarcities on the world market and the recognition that CMEA preferences inherently diverge from those reigning outside the group. The second tier of studies has tracked relationships among domestic wholesale prices, TRPs and some measure of WMPs. Though the research must be voluminous by now, relatively few studies have actually been published. As noted, these analyses vary from Western research in a number of respects. The differences range from approach, methodology and conceptual framework to published results. If divulged at all, published results are not easily interpreted unambiguously for two reasons. Results are presented in a fudged way and the underlying methodology and data sources remain obscure. Though specialists may conjecture about the nature of these research strategies, such reading behind the published word at best constitutes an educated guess. Nonetheless, the majority of these studies can be grouped with the fourth and fifth categories of their Western counterparts. But recall that Eastern European verbal critiques of virtually all Western investigations have been legion and are sometimes based on solid evidence and principles.

Motivation for the discrimination hypothesis (see Mendershausen, 1959, 1960) can be found in the precepts of the cold war in the 1950s. This formative political, ideological and economic environment logically posited that the USSR intended to exploit its allies because of its size, geopolitical dominance, strategic supremacy *vis-à-vis* the CMEA group as a whole and its presumed calling as the *primus inter pares* of the world communist movement. Although now generally accepted in Eastern Europe that un-justifiable price inequalities existed at least until the mid-1950s, the thesis of pervasive, generalized discrimination advanced in the West has always been soundly rejected by all CPE authors both at home and even more so when sojourning in another CMEA partner. Defectors, exiled politicians and other, not necessarily impartial, observers of CPEs, however, unambig-uously champion the thesis.

As a direct outgrowth of the controversies spawned by the interpretations of the findings released by the discrimination studies, the customs union hypo-thesis was advanced (see Brada, 1985; Holzman, 1962, 1965, 1986a, 1986b). It sought to interpret TRP behavior within the context of the regulations and rules of a customs union, free trade area or common market adopted by two or more market-type economies. In essence, it was argued that such a union has preferences that yield different prices from those obtained in trade with third countries. If the union favors trade in goods in which an internal producer has a comparative disadvantage, the union price exceeds the comparable WMP and *vice versa*. The problem with such an analysis is that it ignores agreed-upon pricing rules and posits an agreement on union preferences for which there is, in the case of the CPEs, simply no evidence.

Few formal CPE studies exist on this subject, although many of them do, of course, have ties with the standard Western treatment of customs unions. Though this approach is not widely adopted in the CPEs, informed econo-mists and high-level policymakers have increasingly been stressing the reality of CMEA-wide preferences. They also stress that preferences should somehow be reflected explicitly in the terms of exchange, possibly in the form of 'regional price differentials' as a more desirable alternative to commercial practices that are nonparametric and often lack transparency (Grinberg and Ljubskij, 1985; Rácz, 1986, p. 25). These hark back to the discussions of the mid-1960s concerning the creation of a CMEA customs union (see Csikós-Nagy, 1969).

Studies focusing on the opportunity cost of being a CMEA member approach the subject either in a static or a dynamic framework. Placing the opportunity cost hypothesis in a dynamic framework, one strand of analyses (Marer, 1968a, 1968b, 1972) conjectures that one or more CPEs could have emulated the development path of a comparable DME. As such, the CPE could have obtained the same export and import unit values as those observed for the comparator DME, who is posited as the *alter ego* of the CPE had the CPE not been forced into the CMEA straitjacket. The results obtained were ambiguous and difficult to interpret, in no small part because the opportunity cost of trading with the CMEA could not convincingly be identified in terms of differences with another country's trade prices. This particular approach is, of course, *ipso facto* rejected by CPE commentators. But in recent years a growing number of studies assert that CMEA conformity has been costly in terms of resource misallocation (see Brabant, 1987a, pp. 407–15). A more considerate, flexible Soviet approach toward other CPEs would have engendered a more appropriate allocation of resources. This is judged to offer a *prima facie* case for price subsidies or other unilateral, unrequited transfers from the USSR to Eastern Europe that could rectify these deformations.

One could also ask about the static opportunity cost; that is, the benefits forgone by deliberately not trading with the outside world even when partners do not have a true comparative advantage in the goods that were or could now be obtained elsewhere. Both Eastern and Western economists have adopted this approach. Western observers (especially Dietz, 1986; Poznański, 1986b) have done so with special reference to price subsidization, which offers a richer framework of analysis than do inquiries into static opportunity costs.

The basic motive for gauging the existence and extent of implicit subsidies is similar to that underlying investigations into the static opportunity cost. Instead of placing the analyses within the context of regional market formation, however, advocates (Marrese and Vaňous, 1983a, 1986) adopt a peculiar framework that revolves around the so-called unconventional gains from trade (Marrese and Vaňous, 1983b; Marrese, 1986) acquired in exchange for price subsidies. That subsidies and taxes are implicit in the divergence between WMPs and TRPs cannot, of course, be denied by any objective analyst. But the underlying conceptual framework and many of the interpretations of the results are generally roundly rejected by CPE authors (Köves, 1984); they are also seriously contested by many Western specialists (Marer, 1984).

Lastly, other studies attempt to clarify the relationship between the TRP for one or more individual goods, or broad commodity groups, and the corresponding WMP or EWP. Alternative formulations depend on relations between prices and pertinent price indexes for a class of goods, or relationships between alternative price indexes for individual or broad classes of goods. Essentially, the goal is to empirically verify whether the CPEs have, in practice, lived up to the Bucharest pricing principles (see Brabant, 1987b, pp. 183–213). Some studies have emphasized the relationship between price levels at official exchange rates. Others argue for focusing primarily on the verification of the transmission of broad changes in levels of the adopted concept of WMP (Ausch, 1972, pp. 76–110; Ausch and Bartha, 1969; Brabant, 1987b, pp. 173–8; Hewett, 1971, 1974). Certain Eastern European analyses of individual commodity pricing behavior (Mitrofanova, 1973, 1974, 1977, 1978) have advanced hypotheses on the relationship between the two sets of prices that must also be taken into account here, although their approaches differ in many respects.

15.8 CMEA INTEGRATION AND REGIONAL PRICING

A properly functioning price system is one of the most critical elements of economic decision making when there is no alternative to coordinating economywide decisions. National and regional central planning could have accomplished this task had it grown into the omniscient mechanism that early CPE planners envisioned. At the regional level, a smoothly functioning price mechanism is essential when no central plan exists and the component economies are not eager to redistribute national value added in an uncontrolled manner. The TRP mechanism has had unquestionable advantages but many micro- and macroeconomic drawbacks as well (see Part IV). The first may have outweighed the latter at the time of rapid industrialization and reconversion. Since then, there seems to be rare unanimity among CMEA economists that the reverse balance has been hampering SEI. Since the mid-1950s, there have been two intensive phases of the search for an acceptable alternative to the historically evolved price-formation principles. One was the movement that started in earnest with the endorsement of the ISDL, *Basic Principles* and the Bucharest pricing rules. This was followed, particularly in the 1960s, by the search for an IPS. The attempt faltered not because it did not make sense to evolve toward such a price regime under any circumstance. Rather, it failed because many CPEs were then determined to reform their domestic economies and hence infuse SEI with new elements that could not be subsumed under the specific terms of reference of the IPS.

The second major attempt at studying alternatives to the received price-formation principles and practices was launched in connection with *Integration Program*. The purpose was to generate a pricing system that would support the more general indirect economic coordination efforts then being launched by several Eastern European CPEs. The investigations of alternatives were conducted at a time when controversy about fostering SEI through plan coordination rather than through the market reigned (see chapter 5). Since the change in the price reference basis introduced in 1975, the issue of proper trade pricing and TRP reform has consistently been on the agenda of top-level policy discussions, including the recent economic summits (see chapter 6). It is one of the most critical elements of the ongoing debates on reforming the CMEA from within (see chapter 18).

NOTES

1. But there is considerable agreement in Pěnkava (1975, p. 652) and Zápotocký (1980, p. 254) on the periodization justified in Brabant (1987b, pp. 63–112).
2. The point is well illustrated by Kaplan (1979) when he quotes criticisms of CMEA partners, especially by the USSR, of Czechoslovak plans in the early 1950s.
3. A broader summary of the debate with empirical evidence and references is presented in Brabant (1987b, pp. 144–82).

PART IV

SEI ACHIEVEMENTS AND ECONOMIC RESTRUCTURING

In this final part, I look at three sets of interrelated issues. First, I review the qualitative and quantitative evidence of the successes and failures of CMEA economic cooperation. Next I single out areas in which improvement is definitely feasible and desirable but whose realization requires such incisive institutional and policy changes over a protracted period of time that the transition phase becomes *the* paramount ingredient of the reform. Finally, I identify the presently available potential for making significant progress with SEI in light of economic reforms as these are now crystallizing. Even in their purely national cloak, reforms cannot but affect the SEI mechanism. There are also feasible measures that can be enacted at the regional level by those who are insisting on reconstruction.

Even with these explicit limitations, each of these topics itself could easily warrant a full-length study because the issues at stake are so complex and controversial. Furthermore, there is still ample room for improvement in the conceptual and empirical ways of measuring integration effects, not only in the CMEA. As the complexity of economic reform will undoubtedly generate several weighty tomes in the years to come, I feel justified in here simplifying these specialist issues.

Chapter 16 summarizes the theory of integration effects and discusses some of the evidence for SEI. Given that the CMEA has, for four decades now, been progressing by leaps and bounds, one would expect to have a plethora of empirical investigations into the advantages and drawbacks of SEI on which to rely. Although numerous general studies have been launched over the years, few have attempted to quantify the conjectures or unsupported statements made in qualitative analyses of SEI. This requires some explanation that applies to integration movements more generally.

By definition, integration effects are the outcome of attempts to harmonize decisions in two or more economies. Therefore, as a result of studying the effects of that movement, one should be able to identify the benefits and drawbacks of integration. I shall save this examination for chapter 17 because of the many consequences of integration that cannot be measured. In addition, CMEA leaders envision integration effects that are positive as seen in light of *their* policy preferences. But not all of these perceived advantages or drawbacks can be reconciled with stylized analyses of integration. Also, the logic must be good for spurning agreed CMEA programs and institutions; decisions to do so derive from political obstacles, the nationalistic tendencies of most Eastern European decision makers, the built-in autarkic features of CPEs and other such familiar themes. Although by no means negligible, such explanations cannot rationalize all setbacks, which to a great extent often derive from the CPEs belonging to an integrating region that proceeds by way of the habitual instruments of planning and physical controls.

Finally, chapter 18 examines how likely it is that the prevailing SEI mechanism may soon be reconstructed from within the CMEA. Two encouraging developments warrant such a broad reexamination of the very foundations of SEI. One follows from ongoing changes in some CPEs' economic mechanisms, a few of which are ambitious. The second set derives in part from the implications of the national reforms and the autonomous change in SEI policy stances recently displayed by key policymakers. Both indicate that considerable scope exists for examining alternative SEI modes, possibly among a subset of members. Clearly, it is beyond the boundary of this study to examine in detail each of these options. But the major structural pillars of plausible alternatives need to be sketched and appraised, however roughly.

16 · THE RESULTS OF SEI – AN ASSESSMENT

Because CMEA observers fail to agree on either the details of integration in Eastern Europe or on how SEI fits into the development processes of the component economies, considerable ambiguity surrounds what should be measured as SEI effects and how to execute such measurements. Before investigating the realism and magnitude of some of the reported results, it is instructive to identify what could realistically be expected from SEI. As already shown in chapter 13, considerable controversy exists in the literature not only about the nature of ECPS and STC agreements but even more about their effects on the pace and character of growth and trade in the CPEs. However, these are by no means the sole mode of cooperation envisaged by the members and certainly not the ultimate objective of SEI.

This chapter, then, has two objectives: first, to clarify the effects of integration in general and of SEI in particular, and then to examine the more cogent measurements of SEI effects found in the specialized literature. Unfortunately, Eastern European analysts have largely refrained from exploring[1] feasible quantitative research on the achievements of SEI. Certainly, there is a great variety of almost journalistic appraisals of the advantages of an individual project, such as the transportation charges saved by substituting crude oil shipments through a common pipeline for railway or truck haulage, but exceedingly little of interest has surfaced by way of aggregate measurements. In fact, the late Lev Lukin (1981, p. 40), at the time a key insider of CMEA affairs, suggested as recently as 1981 that 'no attempt has been made so far to produce' any measurement of the effects of production specialization. His statement may contain some hyperbole, but it is indicative of the primitive state of Eastern European empirical SEI investigations.

This dismal record of Eastern European assessments of the benefits and costs of SEI is largely the result of the dearth of quantitative information in CPEs more generally. It should not be surprising, then, to learn that Western research on measuring SEI effects has also not produced much. In fact, the literature about the static and dynamic benefits of integration – the drawbacks are rarely examined – is not particularly noteworthy for having validated the invariable enthusiasm with which policymakers promote regional integration. If the assessment of benefits and costs of regional integration in general has been far from encouraging, the timid attempts devoted to CMEA integration have been even less impressive.

Section 16.1 sets forth the standard customs union typology of integration effects. Whether it is proper to view the CMEA as a customs union and whether the effects measured in that format can be attributed to SEI are issues discussed in section 16.2. Some of the conceptual and other obstacles to Eastern European measurements of trade effects are addressed in section 16.3. Section 16.4 illustrates alternative measurements of SEI trade effects. The implications of STC as perceived by standard economic analysis are briefly reviewed in section 16.5. As analyzed, the TRP system has at least implicit consequences for protection; how to rationalize them is discussed in section 16.6. A major component of CMEA cooperation has been STC, and its effects are touched upon in section 16.7. Selected results are introduced to illustrate points made in chapter 13.

16.1 ON THE TYPOLOGY OF THE EFFECTS OF UNION FORMATION

One could legitimately assess the benefits and drawbacks of regional integration in many different ways. This multiplicity of defensible approaches holds even if the inquiry's purpose is confined to the strict economics of regional integration as objectively as rational discourse permits, although this is not invariant to the basic underlying philosphy. Particularly with respect to SEI, what may be identified as an economic advantage at one point by an integrating partner may be a disadvantage for another or may be transformed into a perceived disadvantage by the same partner at a different time, or both. This dualism need not result exclusively from the meta-economics of SEI. Thus, perhaps due to policymakers' perverse preferences, some countries may oppose SEI regardless of the welfare, trade, production and consumption results. To make headway, it is simply not possible to investigate all potential avenues. I shall therefore develop my own way of looking at SEI results. This can be justified by summarizing the general theory of the effects of union formation.

16.1.1 On the benefits of union formation

Standard trade theory makes it clear that regional economic integration is a second-best commercial policy choice. If opening up domestic markets to international competition by removing tariffs or eliminating other trade obstacles is deemed useful, doing so with respect to only one group of countries is, on the face of it, an exceedingly shortsighted policy decision.

Provided that a clear-cut choice is available between discriminatory and unilateral tariff reductions, the latter is invariably the superior option. Rarely, however, can commercial policy be formulated within maneuvering room wide enough to allow an unambiguous choice between discriminatory and unilateral tariff reductions. Furthermore, concerns about world welfare hardly ever dominate the national policy agenda, which is the only one that matters in an environment with sovereign states. This is so even if union-forming countries first aim primarily at lowering tariffs, or their close substitute, in integrating regions with other arrangements for the implementation of regional preferences. As such, a commercial policy that leads to economic union is perceived as beneficial in some sense. At the very least, it enables participants to capture the incremental gains from union formation and distribute them cooperatively, which is difficult to achieve in a global setting.

But a logical case for customs union formation can also be made on the basis of a recognition of constraints on government policy, even if the maneuvering room is, in principle, the global framework of trade theory. As Jones (1979) has elegantly summarized it, the first-best choice between union formation and unilateral tariff reduction is rarely free or costless, if only because of the time required to adjust. Social and private valuation of the costs and benefits of domestic production may also diverge. In other words, attempts to rationalize union formation by recognizing the existence of constraints on domestic policies might strengthen the case for clarifying CMEA matters by delving more into the customs union theory.

16.1.2 Types of unions

The particular effects envisioned and their magnitude are a function of the type of integration being entertained. Thus, a free trade area will gradually eliminate tariffs within the union but maintain differentiated national tariffs for third partners. A customs union will in addition adopt a common external tariff. The tariff wall that applies to third countries may be higher or lower than any of the national external tariffs under a free trade area. A common market permits factor mobility as well as free trade within the union. Some of this trade may substitute for merchandise flows in the sense that relative differences in factor endowments, which are the main inducement to trade, will shrink when international factor mobility occurs, thus reducing the scope for trade at any given moment relative to what might materialize in a free trade area or a customs union. Fourth, countries may also envision the construction of a full-fledged economic union, which has all the attributes of a common market. In addition, it seeks to harmonize monetary and fiscal policies throughout the union. The final stage of integration is one in which there is full political integration; that is, where the issues of national sovereignty, chiefly as expressed through the rule of a national government, are no longer pertinent.[2]

16.1.3 The effects of union formation

If economic integration means the gradual narrowing of differences in relative economic scarcities between two or more economies, as defined in the Introduction, one may conceptually distinguish between static and dynamic benefits. Static benefits accrue from reallocating domestic production factors in response to shifts in the relative prices of products and the supply of primary production factors caused by regional integration. Dynamic effects result from the modification of growth processes in the economies participating in integration. Union formation may provide opportunities for pursuing completely different growth processes than what the members could have aimed at in isolation.

Generally speaking, there are five groups of effects of a free trade area or a customs union. Production efficiency will be raised as a result of specialization. Higher output levels for some products are attainable by further exploiting economies of scale. Also, participants strengthen their international bargaining position both individually and as a group, which in turn may yield better terms of trade. Increased competition may lead to further gains in production efficiency. Finally, technological progress, which is bound to assume a different character from what would have occurred for participants in isolation, changes the volume and quality of production factors. Political agreement beyond the measures leading to economic union may yield further gains from factor mobility, macroeconomic policy coordination and the harmonization of development objectives.

Each of the four types of economic union identified above has distinct economic effects. Perhaps these can best be illustrated by starting from the well-known implications of forming a customs union. The key change is the reduction of tariffs within the union. The primary effect of a tariff change will be on trade flows, with unit cost remaining unchanged. But a reduction in tariffs is likely to have an impact on the current account. To maintain the *status quo ante*, the exchange rate may have to be adjusted, which in turn has implications for the trade-off between domestic production and trade as well as for consumption from domestic supply or from imports.

The implications of the impacts of tariff changes on trade, the exchange rate and demand are also likely to be manifest in production, even when unit costs remain unchanged. But this feature is anticipated to be short-lived due to the economies stemming from longer production runs, manufacturing progress and feedback of these cost reductions on trade, the exchange rate and demand. However, as this feedback will probably be dampened over time, there will be a return to equilibrium at a higher welfare level for all participants.

16.1.4 Stylized trade effects

Increased merchandise trade is not, of course, the ultimate economic goal of union formation; rather, it is raising welfare levels beyond what is otherwise

Table 16.1 Trade effects of integration

	Domestic	Partner	Rest
Trade creation			
double trade creation	–	+	+
internal trade creation	–	+	0
external trade creation	–	0	+
Trade diversion			
external trade diversion	0	+	–
internal trade diversion	0	–	+
Trade destruction or erosion			
double trade erosion	+	–	–
internal trade erosion	+	–	0
external trade erosion	+	0	–

attainable. But welfare is hard to measure. Perhaps an effort could be made to assess the contribution of trade to aggregate value added as an approximation (see Marques-Méndes, 1987[3]), but even such a measure, provided it can be executed at all, is unlikely to be more than a proxy of true welfare levels. There are three reasons for this. At best, national accounts are a crude measure of welfare. Integration is unlikely to be limited to merchandise trade. And, postulating what would have happened without integration is difficult. Furthermore, each of the integration effects can be evaluated according to its impact on one of the member countries, the other union members, third countries or the world as a whole. Given that the only argument in favor of a partial union would be that there are severe constraints on a unilateral reduction in tariffs, the particular point of view taken is not necessarily irrelevant to judging the benefits and drawbacks of union formation. Perhaps the better-known differentiation is the one that has been made for trade effects. Nonetheless, as argued in chapter 13, changes in trade level, composition and direction may provide *prima facie* evidence of the welfare effects of union formation. Therefore, it is useful to briefly examine them.

Eliminating customs duties among integrating partners, at given production and consumption patterns, will increase the share of imports from the preferential partners because this substitutes either for imports from third countries or for domestic production. The various combinations of the sign of the effects on domestic supplies, supplies from partners and supplies from outside the integrating region are illustrated in Table 16.1. When domestic supplies are being replaced by imports, one speaks of trade creation. In the reverse situation, where domestic supplies substitute for imports, one speaks of trade diversion. Trade creation may be internal, external or general. Internal trade creation is a reallocation of resources that results in greater trade with union members. External trade creation is the same measured for nonmembers. Similarly, trade diversion may be internal, external or general. Internal trade diversion means the replacement of union trade by trade with third countries. External trade diversion is the reverse; that is, the substitution of union trade for trade with third partners. When trade diversion applies to both internal and external partners, one usually speaks of trade destruction or erosion because it refers to a situation in which regional partners cannot substitute for former imports from third countries, which may seem an oddity of sorts. Note, however, that Holzman (1985, 1987) has argued for viewing the CMEA as a trade destroying customs union! Trade erosion may occur with respect to members or to outsiders, which corresponds to internal or external trade erosion.

Note that trade creation or diversion rarely occurs without some contrary movement. Thus, one of the great concerns about customs unions has been the possibility of internal trade creation in combination with external trade diversion, which is worrisome for global welfare because union leads to a replacement of more efficient suppliers by union members which do not have a genuine advantage,[4] and thus to lower global welfare.

Trade affects domestic, partner and possibly third country welfare levels through changed consumer and producer surpluses and redistributed tariff revenues. These elements are readily explained in any standard textbook and do not need to be explicitly restated here. Of course, one should take into account that tariff reductions have direct and indirect income effects for consumers, domestic producers and government revenues and will thus generate secondary shifts. When the small-country assumption does not hold, in addition there are price and terms-of-trade effects, which in turn may produce shifts in demand and supply schedules.

Post-union adjustments of demand and supply will inevitably occur when the integration effects are examined in the case of expanding or contracting economies. These yield the dynamic effects of integration that may be disaggregated into, first, an increase in factor inputs leading to more rapid growth of output, and, second, a gain in factor productivity with constant factor supplies (Brada and Méndez, 1988).[5] Furthermore, integration of countries that are experiencing growth will generally have ambiguous effects on income and welfare for the union as a whole. In the interest of its viability, if one country gains from growth, then some form of income redistribution will become necessary. As argued in chapter 18, such a compensatory transaction may also be required simply to make the union viable by finding an acceptable trade-off between costs and benefits.

16.1.5 Union formation and its benefits

The benefits of regional integration essentially derive from the members becoming part of a larger market. By definition, a larger market offers economies of scale that may be quite palpable, particularly for small countries or for economies whose resource endowment is highly skewed. Realization of these benefits may take some time, however, especially when the economies embarking on integration find themselves in serious disequilibrium (Padoa-Schioppa *et al.*, 1987). But there is no doubt that integration will eventually require concentrating production in the goods for which countries have or establish a comparative advantage *vis-à-vis* the region as a whole, though not necessarily with respect to the entire world. In turn, increased specialization calls for a larger part of domestic production being marketed within the region rather than in the isolated producing country. This combination of production and trade permits the realization of a higher level of consumption, and hence welfare, than would be possible if the country had opted for continued protection.

16.2 THE CMEA AS A CUSTOMS UNION

The benefits of integration specified in the received customs union theory do not necessarily apply to planned economies. For one, these results are phrased in terms of comparative statics, virtually assuming away the transition period between a change in the tariff and demand and supply adjustments. Moreover, this return to equilibrium is presumed to follow after a small perturbation of the preunion state. These assumptions do not generally hold for CPEs.

16.2.1 Is the CMEA a customs union?

Whether the CMEA is equivalent to a customs union is an issue over which the literature has long agonized. It is important to note that the CPEs have never set constructing a customs union as a goal for themselves. In fact, creating a 'unified' or 'common' CMEA market has only been proposed since the forty-third Council Session, and no strong preferences have yet been specified (see chapter 6). Nonetheless, many of the CMEA's economic activities can be interpreted as being equivalent to a peculiar customs union. Franklyn Holzman has been the chief champion of this approach. Initially, he (1962, 1965) viewed it as reflecting tacit agreement on discriminating against imports from third partners and arranging for the distribution of the gains and costs. But this is largely a convenient reading into CMEA matters (see Brabant, 1987b, pp. 154–62). More recently, Holzman (1985, 1986a, 1986b, 1987) has refined his views by postulating that the price divergences between TRPs and EWPs can be interpreted as stemming from implicit preferences for products from within the CMEA. Because their trade is controlled through the MFT, CPEs do not need to set explicit tariff barriers, such as a common external tariff. Others (Broner, 1975, 1976; Pelzman, 1976a, 1976b, 1977) have argued that, analytically speaking, the actual differences between CPE internal and trade prices can be treated as implicit tariffs and subsidies designed to promote planners' socioeconomic objectives and to discriminate *de facto* between CMEA and other regions.

There are, however, substantive differences between tariffs in market and centrally planned systems. In CPEs, for many reasons, implicit tariffs are not *ad valorem*. They are defined as the difference between internal and external prices. They are known only *ex post*. The size of the tariff also varies with shifts in domestic prices, which are enacted administratively and not necessarily in response to real economic forces. No common external tariff is used, and, because TRPs vary from domestic prices, implicit tariffs within the union are not altogether removed. In an operational sense, then, such tariffs cannot be utilized for studying integration effects for CPEs, nor, for that matter, do differences between internal and external prices yield reliable yardsticks about the level of protection maintained while these economies pursue autonomous domestic price policies and the MFT precludes effective competition from abroad.

While many operational obstacles exist to viewing SEI trade effects as stemming from changes in customs union preferences, perhaps the most important is that the CMEA members have never explicitly agreed on what their reciprocal preferences are or should be. Weak evidence can perhaps be inferred from the pronounced preferences for price stability and predictability that are emphasized in the Bucharest principles. Furthermore, the CPEs rarely refer to preferences for CMEA trading relative to domestic prices, which is an almost essential ingredient of any customs union approach. If this continues, some explicit preference intermediating between TRPs and the corresponding WMPs or EWPs would be needed in the form of a stable supplement to import prices from outside the group.[6]

16.2.2 The benefits of SEI

Seen against the above backdrop, the stylized results of regional economic integration are not necessarily applicable or easily interpreted in the case of the CMEA. Trade creation, diversion and erosion are ordinarily defined with respect to shifts in trade levels, composition and the geographic distribution resulting from price changes. In the CPE, however, domestic prices do not perform the allocatory role attributed to prices in MEs, and they are out of sync with actual trade prices. Not to be omitted from the picture is that a CPE works with at least two domestic and two external price systems that are poorly integrated, if related at all. Perhaps more important is that the conventional customs union effects are defined for economies that before the union were in equilibrium and that do not obstruct adjustments in demand and supply to restore balance after tariff changes. Finally, the transition period is presumed to be brief so that no forces other than tariffs affect trade.

Integration is unlikely to mature in countries that, before union formation, are in obvious domestic and external imbalance without major modifications being made in demand and supply. The effects can be quite different from the textbook case (see section 16.1) if the union is formed while also rectifying imbalances in the context of a larger market. Nonetheless, the sign and size of the results considerably depend on the time horizon that one might usefully envisage.

In addition to the standard production, consumption and trade effects, the contribution of union formation to raising the efficiency of resource allocation in the participating countries may also be investigated. As noted in chapter 13, trade shrinkage, for example, may signal a beneficial effect of SEI if it results from the elimination of less efficient production undertakings.

16.2.3 Measuring integration effects

Of course, specifying conceptual issues is very different from measuring their magnitude. Given the definition of integration embraced here, the benefits of union formation must be assessed as the gains accruing over and above what would have obtained without integration. As this counterfactual world cannot be measured, it is thus not possible to assess the precise benefits. A pseudo analogue may be sought by examining the preferences of similar countries that have not embraced integration. Alternatively, one must specify a hypothetical world of what would have prevailed without the union. Such an *anti-monde* might be assembled by extrapolating previous trends or concurrent behavior in other countries on the assumption that that is what would have prevailed in the union-forming countries had the decision to enter the union not been made. But matters are far more complex.

Although changes in tariffs may exert straightforward static effects on trading patterns, these effects are observed in the dynamic context of evolving trade, payments and economic activity (Mayes, 1982). That evolution must also be explained if one is to measure integration effects. Ignoring these realities by simply exploring the differences between actual behavior and some hypothetical *anti-monde* is bound to result in biases because all residual changes in behavior are imputed to integration, not just those that can be directly explained by it.[7] Even if the customs union effects in CPEs were to be estimated by utilizing implicit duties, severe conceptual problems surface. For example, as the CPEs are generally in persistent disequilibrium, including in trade, their trade prior to the decision to seek SEI was probably suboptimal. This not only implies less trade than desirable on the basis of comparative cost considerations, it also entails trade in goods that would not have materialized under competitive conditions. Also, SEI only marginally resembles market integration, where prices act as a key in resource allocation, including a narrowing in relative scarcities. As a result, it is uncertain if SEI will change the members' static trade conditions, as distinct from the future implications of production specialization, which is the principal vehicle for enhancing greater regional interdependence in Eastern Europe. In particular, changes in the level, commodity composition or geographic distribution of trade cannot be solely imputed to relative price changes. In any case, given TRP-setting techniques, it is unclear whether SEI entails shifts in trade prices and if these are initially reduced relative to prices faced in trade with nonmembers. Furthermore, as domestic prices in CPEs do not clear markets and trade decisions are not based solely on comparative advantage indicators, integration may or may not stimulate regional trade, perhaps through trade diversion.

16.2.4 Customs union theory and SEI effects

Because direct measurement of the benefits of union formation, even among market-type economies, is not possible, most researchers have adopted an indirect approach. They have centered on trade while assuming that integration decisions affect the external sector. External commerce normally helps to bridge differences in relative scarcities, especially when it is reasonable to hypothesize factor immobility. Clearly, foreign trade as such is not necessarily the direct goal of integration policies. But frequently it is its most visible result and, in most measurements to date, the most conspicuous medium through which the participants hope to narrow their disparities and further their more general sociopolitical objectives. As a result, most studies have been cast around the price effect of tariff changes. In fact, one recent review of SEI suggested that, in general, the integration process could not possibly be considered complete while relative prices in the component economies, after adjustment for transportation costs, continue to differ (Marer and Montias, 1981, p. 134). But one need not go that far. Even in an integrated economy such as the United States, one is hard-pressed to buttress the thesis of uniform relative prices throughout the country. Perhaps it would be more relevant to suggest that relative prices should not differ by more than what is normally warranted by differentials stemming from other parameters of time and place.

Should the CPEs embrace a customs union, the resulting trade effects are certain to be the joint outcome of the effects of the agreed specialization and adjustment measures that move the members' economic structure toward greater equilibrium. It is conceivable that the measured effects could be disappointing, yielding considerable trade erosion or even internal trade diversion, both of which would run counter to the expected advantages of union formation. But in the CMEA context they may emerge, and in some cases they would be judged as being beneficial. It is difficult to separate out those effects that can be specified analytically as pertaining to the results of SEI so that the trade gains, as distinct from the negative implications of trade diversion, or erosion in the case of the CPEs, can be properly identified.

CPEs cannot phase their integration process in accordance with efforts to harmonize tariffs because, simply, they do not seek to regulate foreign trade through such conventional commercial policy instruments. Nonetheless, prices and tariffs provide a useful starting point because they are measurable in money; other restrictions that foster scarcity differentials when lifted or eased as a result of integration cannot as subtly and rigorously be analyzed. Furthermore, because tariffs are more susceptible than are other trade restrictions to concerted international action, the most interesting element of integration from both the analytical and policy viewpoints is the revision of customs duties, including the replacement of other trade restrictions by explicit *ad valorem* duties. Provided one adopts an explicit assumption on how the level, commodity composition and geographic distribution of trade would have developed without union formation, estimating the size and sign of trade effects stemming from integration is, at least conceptually, quite straightforward.

16.3 TRADITIONAL EASTERN EUROPEAN MEASUREMENTS

Most Eastern European observers usually take the demonstration of a high degree of apparent unity in sociopolitical and economic affairs in conjunction with some observations about regional trade dependence as sufficient evidence for the success of SEI. However, not all CPE economists content themselves so easily. Indeed, a score of scholars has harshly criticized the sluggish pace of SEI, the lack of enthusiasm or political will about modernizing the SEI mechanism and the conservative policies that determine the latitude for cooperation with the existing policy instruments and supporting institutions. Regardless of the writer's political bent, however, the paucity of published empirical inquiries into the matter is remarkable; studies that disclose comprehensive details about data sources and methodology are even rarer.

In contrast to the dearth of empirical information about the results of SEI, or even the diffident academic attempts to wrangle with such difficult measurement issues, pronouncements of possible indicators of SEI effects abound. In one comprehensive theoretical survey, Kalčev (1983, pp. 9–10) distinguished among hard quantitative indicators, measurements with a more qualitative character, and joint efforts to streamline economic mechanisms, as well as among macroeconomic, political, social and other SEI consequences. I could select other Eastern European proposals, but Kalčev's is illustrative of the recent literature. Typically, among the twelve indicators of empirical measurements advocated, at least seven depend directly on some measure of specialized exports and imports, as defined in chapter 13. The remaining five measure various kinds of joint activities, particularly their trade consequences. Of course, no effort is made to implement any of these suggestions. Among the measurements with a qualitative character, the author distinguishes between various aspects of the efficiency of resource use for exports and savings through imports and a set of measures that relate export and import prices for various integration projects relative to other export and import prices. Needless to say, these suggestions are also not implemented.

Eastern European scholars have rarely attempted to quantify in a synthetic measure the trade effects of SEI; at least, few such investigations have been published. Most of the available empirical studies have been constructed around, first, savings in outlays resulting from a single cooperation venture, such as the cutback in transportation charges afforded by substituting pipeline shipment for truck haulage; analyses of the level, commodity composition and geographic distribution of trade that purport to show a different, more advantageous, level, commodity composition and geographic direction than what would have prevailed without the union; and, finally, around various measures of the effects of ECPS and STC agreements (see chapter 13).

As argued on several occasions, integration is intimately connected with trade. This is particularly the case when the union is formed between countries that inhibit factor movements. With this as perhaps a vague rationalization, numerous books and articles on SEI published in the CPEs have approached the statistical measurement of the effects of SEI by focusing narrowly on trade. Indeed, the CPE literature is replete with citations of gains in the absolute volume of trade, of changes in the share of trade turnover accounted for by CMEA partners, of the number of signed bilateral and multilateral trade agreements, the number of ECPS protocols, the share of trade attributable to ECPS agreements, the shifts in the commodity composition of regional trade and of others as indicators of SEI effects. As already argued, if such measures are applied to static conditions of efficiency, under some conditions they could provide at least limited information on integration results. As they stand, however, particularly when seen in the context of growth of the CPEs and their unpredictable equilibrium, trade measures are poor indicators of SEI achievements.

Over the years, observers from the CMEA countries have attached particular importance to trade dynamics. Inevitably reference is to the high growth rate of intraregional trade, the large share of regional to total trade and the 'progressive' commodity composition of trade, which is due to the large share of finished goods. This usually leads to optimistic conclusions because, if for no other reason, since the early postwar years the CPEs have by choice, as well as because of constraints imposed by the cold war, transacted the bulk of their trade among themselves. That these shares have increased as well as contracted at certain times has caused some concern. Although one must be skeptical about identifying SEI progress with an increasing regional share in overall trade, data corrected for price movements and the gap between TRPs and EWPs demonstrate that the CPEs clear a

Table 16.2 Share of intrasocialist trade, 1970–85
(in percent of current and constant trade values)

		1970	1975	1980	1985
Bulgaria					
Exports	Nominal	79.3	80.0	70.8	77.0
	Real	79.3	83.2	78.1	77.3
Imports	Nominal	76.2	72.3	78.9	77.0
	Real	76.2	77.4	81.3	72.1
Czechoslovakia					
Exports	Nominal	70.6	71.5	69.6	77.0
	Real	70.6	72.8	73.1	74.8
Imports	Nominal	69.4	69.8	70.2	80.7
	Real	69.4	73.8	72.3	75.4
German Democratic Republic					
Exports	Nominal	73.9	73.2	69.5	65.0
	Real	73.9	78.5	77.0	66.1
Imports	Nominal	69.4	66.6	63.7	67.2
	Real	69.4	73.3	69.2	61.9
Hungary					
Exports	Nominal	65.6	72.2	55.1	58.6
	Real	65.6	72.8	71.7	74.5
Imports	Nominal	64.5	65.7	50.6	54.4
	Real	64.5	70.0	67.2	67.2
Poland					
Exports	Nominal	63.9	59.9	55.9	54.8
	Real	63.9	65.5	61.9	70.6
Imports	Nominal	68.6	45.8	55.6	60.7
	Real	68.6	52.9	61.1	72.2
Rumania					
Exports	Nominal	58.1	46.0	44.7	42.2
	Real	58.1	53.3	55.7	52.9
Imports	Nominal	53.9	43.5	37.8	50.2
	Real	53.9	53.3	52.2	65.6

Sources: All nominal values are as documented in official national statistics. Real values are my estimates based on price indexes chiefly derived from Hungarian and Polish information on price developments in trade with socialist, or ruble, and nonsocialist, or dollar, trade (which are not identical) by separate commodity groups (either the nine SITC categories 0 through 8 or the augmented – that is, fuels separated from other industrial raw materials – nine ETN categories of the CMEA trade nomenclature). The price indexes do, of course, take into account differential exchange rate movements, including shifts in exchange regimes.

substantial part of their trade within the group. Considerable shifts have occurred over time both in nominal and real terms. Because I only have nominal and real trade data available for socialist and other Eastern European countries since 1970, Table 16.2 compares selected data on that different definition. These clearly illustrate the unusual integration behavior of Poland and Rumania in the 1970s and Bulgaria late in the decade, when it was grappling with an acute deficit on its convertible currency account.

These movements cannot be attributed solely to price variations. Another important feature is that remarkable differences exist in the commodity composition of trade with Eastern Europe compared to commerce with Western countries. Whereas fuels, raw materials, semiprocessed goods and foodstuffs dominate in exports to the West, in relations with CMEA partners most exports consist of machinery and consumer goods. For imports, greater similarity is found, although the share of foodstuffs, fuels and raw materials imported from outside the group is substantial. This is unlike the commodity composition of Soviet trade. Finally, it is worth noting that, except in the early 1950s and 1980s, the elasticities of exports and imports with respect to aggregate output have exceeded unity.

The above features of the CPEs' trade have been valued in and of themselves as useful consequences of integration by all participants, at least at some stage of their cooperation. The explicit preference to rely extensively on CMEA trade is partially a function of the economic conditions and institutional arrangements characteristic of the region. One can therefore presume some positive impact of SEI endeavors on trade. The CMEA partners, particularly the Soviet Union, have unquestionably provided useful markets for obtaining necessary imports and disposing of domestic output. From an economic point of view, however, such a high degree of regional trade dependence cannot, in itself, be taken as an indicator of the advanced stage of SEI, although it does support the thesis of an advanced stage of regional trade dependence (possibly with political and other ramifications implied by this trade dependence). Whether these are advantages from a strictly economic point of view will be taken up in chapter 17.

As argued in chapter 13, the degree of regional specialization is potentially a more useful concept in that it bears directly on the definition of SEI embraced here. Unfortunately, the measurements available fall short of the minimum required to derive useful inferences from such statistics. Though not devoid of some interest, such data are of little help in quantitatively assessing the trade effects of SEI measures, let alone their welfare implications. I have illustrated this proposition for the so-called specialization indexes in chapter 13. Similar comments apply to listings of ECPS and STC agreements or their numerical representation in total trade, per sector, per partner, by number of participants or variations on those themes.[8]

Partial indicators of SEI effects abound. For numerous infrastructural projects and various jointly financed investment projects undertaken in the CMEA, some estimate has been provided of cost savings with respect to this or that project. The better-known one is for transportation infrastructure. Truck or rail haulage of bulk raw materials such as gas and petroleum is unquestionably more expensive than transport through pipelines, though the CPEs' administrative prices may not reflect this in all its nuances. Similarly, integrating the various power grids benefits everyone, especially if proper managerial and investment arrangements are made so that drawdowns are primarily 'expected' through specific agreements and that the remainder amounts to marginal and brief drawdowns that even out temporary differentials between supply and demand at national levels. Owing to the distorted domestic and trade prices of the CPEs, it may be difficult to unambiguously express such advantages in dollars and cents. Even if measurements are available, it is difficult to place them in context and, even harder, to aggregate them into a synthetic indicator of the trade effects of SEI.

16.4 ALTERNATIVE MEASUREMENTS OF SEI TRADE EFFECTS

Essentially, there are two alternatives: the customs union effects and the trade results of ECPS and STC agreements.

16.4.1 Customs union trade effects for CPEs

Despite considerable conceptual and practical obstacles, several analytic studies have been inspired by Western customs union theory and the empirical investigations based on it; that is, they are anchored to residual imputation techniques. In spite of the drawbacks of thus measuring customs union effects, including because distinctly different effects are lumped together that may not be related to tariff-like rescheduling (Brabant, 1980, p. 255), most estimates of the trade effects of SEI rely on some variant of residual imputation of shifts in trade levels, the geographic distribution of trade or on the observed expenditure shares of apparent consumption between a base year and one or more hypothetical predictions derived from the *anti-monde* specified. Such shifts are subsequently examined and interpreted in the light of known integration decisions or other special measures that bear on trade participation and the distribution of trade. All these investigations have been conducted with reference either to ECPS agreements or to inquiries based on the so-called gravity model of trade. They are examined below.

16.4.2 Trade effects of ECPS agreements

To the extent that precise information is available on the implementation of ECPS agreements, it should be fairly simple to quantify the resulting trade effects. However, specialization enacted in the CMEA region so far does not seem to have greatly influenced domestic and trade prices, which continue to be governed by nonscarcity considerations, because the effects of scale economies on real costs are largely ignored when TRPs are formed. Furthermore, as noted in chapter 13, obtaining pertinent information on ECPS protocols so as to estimate trade effects is virtually impossible (see Crane and Skoller, 1988).

Specialization in finished industrial goods has been the subject of a number of inquiries, but few were specified as clearly as the one pioneered by John M. Montias (1968, pp. 135–40). His inquiry focused on the degree to which a CPE depends on alternative sources of supply and whether there is a noticeable change in the impact of deviations from normal domestic demand (in this case, machinery and equipment for investment purposes) on deviations from normal domestic, partner or third country supplies. For Rumania, he found that the CMEA supply of investment goods, though more responsive than domestic supplies, was, by the mid-1960s, much more embedded in the domestic consumption of such goods than procurements from outside the region. This suggests that the 'ultimate condition' for full integration in market-type economies – namely, equality of relative prices – is far from being met in the CMEA. Nonetheless, the CMEA supply of engineering goods appeared to be better integrated in Rumania's demand than what is procured from world markets. Similar experiments applied to a larger time period, and other CPEs yield disturbing generalizations of Montias's findings. Given the potential importance of ECPS protocols in SEI, I shall defer discussion of these issues to section 16.7.

16.4.3 Less formal trade effects

Most empirical investigations into the integration of CPEs have emphasized that overall trade participation among CPEs is below that of MEs of comparable size and level of development. Furthermore, there is little evidence that the CPEs have a pronounced preference for intragroup trade as opposed to trade with outside partners. The first type of inquiry has usually been associated with autarky. Apparently this systemic feature has not been alleviated by the CPEs being integrated in the CMEA. In some cases this conjecture is not explicitly tested but is derived from the fact that the estimated degree to which the CPEs fail to trade as intensively as comparable market-type economies does not appear to shrink noticeably once major integration decisions can be identified. This has been contested by several Western authors, most notably by Adam Broner (1975, 1976) and Joseph Pelzman (1976a, 1976b, 1977). Their investigations hinge, however, on several implicit assumptions that are not very realistic (see Brabant, 1980, pp. 261–70).

The second type of inquiry is explicitly directed at detecting deviations from 'normal' levels of bilateral trade, usually through some variant of the gravity model. Such inquiries associate bilateral trade levels (total or by commodity groups) with levels of a combination of demand and supply factors of the countries involved as well as with special features of some bilateral relations. Thus, in addition to population and national income size, these models usually specify some variables of regional preferences, geographic or psychological distance and political allegiance. If the regional or political allegiance variable is significant, one speaks of a regional preference. There is no doubt that, as with the EC, positive regional preferences for the CMEA can be shown and that these have increased over time (Brada and Méndez, 1988; Hewett, 1976; Pelzman, 1977). However, in no single case has a Western or Eastern investigator carefully traced the logic of the gravity equation over time so that one could speak of truly regional preference as a result of identifiable integration decisions.

16.5 IMPLICIT SUBSIDIES AND CMEA DEVELOPMENT ASSISTANCE

Forming a union usually entails more than simply reaping the welfare impacts of reducing union tariffs and harmonizing external tariffs. In all common markets, policymakers explicitly adopt some objectives on solidarity for 'equally paced' development, which justifies a redistribution of the benefits of union formation. This may take several forms, including lump-sum subsidies, price supports, regional investment assistance and development assistance more generally. All of these and others also occur in the CMEA. Perhaps the most conspicuous instrument through which this has been enacted has been by adopting an own pricing system.

Pricing evokes many ideological, political and other connotations (see chapter 15). Although these metaeconomic issues are important in any regional integration scheme, it could be useful to tackle the pricing issue primarily from the viewpoint of techniques *before* other issues are allowed to encroach on economic decision making. How it could fit into the need for structural adjustments in the 1980s and beyond and what its precise place might be in the ongoing reform movement are questions I address in chapter 18. But a brief recapitulation of the major rationalizations of the TRP regime, its possible positive and negative consequences – themselves examined in more detail in chapter 17 – for SEI and earlier reform efforts (for a summary, see Brabant, 1987b, pp. 220–44) may provide a sobering reminder of what can be achieved without a major political impetus to reform. In this subsection I shall look only at the effects of the TRP system on CMEA trade.

As indicated in chapter 15, TRPs are a strange instrument of integration. There is little doubt that relative TRPs diverge from corresponding WMPs. That is, there is an implicit opportunity cost and benefit of trading with the CMEA, if only because of price divergences. The opportunity cost debate has been waged ever since the USSR published the first CMEA trade statistics containing values and quantities in 1957. The debate goes back to the discrimination or exploitation hypothesis that began to be seriously debated in economic and statistical terms with the work of Horst Mendershausen in the late 1950s, although Holzman (1987, pp. 22–3) recently furnished evidence that he had undertaken similar calculations somewhat earlier. An alternative interpretation of price differences then arose, namely that they stem from the customs union effect, and that these differences are similar to those obtained by market-type economies that integrate. This subsequently led to investigations of the effects of the Bucharest principles on the divergence between TRPs and WMPs. Finally, the debate was most comprehensively carried forward in the thesis of implicit trade subsidies to Eastern Europe by the Soviet Union. In what follows, I shall indicate the main results and the salient interpretations advocated by the principal participants in the debates.

16.5.1 Discrimination

The purpose of the investigation into price discrimination was to assess the magnitude of the divergence between Soviet unit values obtained in exports and imports with Eastern European partners and the corresponding unit values obtained with Western partners. Mendershausen subsequently aggregated these specific commodity price divergences with various sample weights and concluded that the West paid between 7 and 16 percent less for Soviet exports than did Eastern Europe, whereas the Soviet Union paid 13 to 22 percent more to Western economies than to Eastern Europe for imports of comparable products. These divergences were interpreted as evidence of Soviet price discrimination against Eastern Europe.

Later, Holzman extended these exercises to other CPE data (especially Bulgaria and Poland, which had then just begun to publish comprehensive trade statistics). He found that not only did the Soviet Union discriminate against Eastern Europe but that Eastern Europe also apparently discriminated against the Soviet Union. This entailed an elaboration of absolute versus relative discrimination and, indeed, led Holzman to formulate his alternative explanation for these paradoxical results.

16.5.2 The customs union effect

As elaborated in section 16.2, the customs union approach to CMEA cooperation efforts essentially argues that union members may express their preferences through a variety of tariff and other indicators, all of which filter down into the alternative terms on which goods are exchanged with the region compared to trade with third countries. In other words, for many reasons, union members may be prepared to pay extra for goods procured from within the region. The issue that should be addressed, then, is not whether there is a legitimate difference between TRPs and WMPs but whether that variance reflects regional preferences that members wish to uphold voluntarily.

If regional preferences are expressed through resources that members are willing to commit to regional cohesion, the issue should be assessing these preferences, establishing the cost members are willing to bear and devising the most equitable rule for distributing that cost among members. Those issues are slightly different from the trade effects as well as from the advantages and drawbacks of SEI (see chapter 17), including through TRP differentiation. They are therefore examined in chapter 18.

16.5.3 Opportunity cost debate

A country's opportunity cost of trading with the CMEA at TRPs is what it could have obtained for exports and would have paid for imports had these transactions been effected with partners other than the CMEA. Considerable misunderstanding exists on what constitutes the opportunity cost of trading with the CMEA. It has been specified in three distinct ways: by utilizing prices or unit values observed in transactions among MEs, or so-called WMPs; by imputing price quotations in commodity exchanges and catalogs of leading firms in MEs, or so-called competitive WMPs; and by assuming that observed EWPs, or unit values computed from trade returns, would hold even should the CPE divert all of its regional exports and imports to the West.

Analyses of the explicit opportunity cost of TRPs have been couched in dynamic or static perspectives (see chapter 15). In fact, the two types of inquiries just discussed are variants of the opportunity cost debate, but the interpretation and motivation of the research differ considerably from those subsumed under a technical investigation of opportunity costs. Seen in a dynamic perspective, the issue was whether without integration within the CMEA a member could have followed a development path similar to that of a comparable market-type economy, whose trade prices are taken as the opportunity cost and benefit of TRPs. Quantification efforts led to the assessment that an Eastern European CPE (chiefly Hungary) obtained poorer terms of trade with the USSR than it would have obtained had it followed Austria's development path. As a result, SEI posed a palpable cost for Hungary and, presumably, a sizable advantage to the Soviet Union. But this result was not invariant to the measurement period, with 1955–7 yielding favorable terms of trade (on the order of 17 percent), while the reverse prevailed in 1958–64 (approximately 11 percent).

Essentially, static opportunity cost studies analyze the export return forgone or the import cost not paid in comparison with actual trade returns. They generally assume that in some cases the CPEs could obtain prevailing WMPs or EWPs for any amount of trade diversion chosen. In that sense, the static opportunity cost approach differs only in its interpretation from the thesis about implicit trade subsidies.

An important assumption of all opportunity cost investigations posits that the CPEs operate as small economies and, hence, that the alternative terms available are those observed in East-West trade or, in some cases, in

West-West trade. Some investigators, particularly Poznański (1986b) and Marrese and Vaňous (1983a, 1983b, 1986), have adjusted these alternative terms of trade for presumed differences in quality, most notably in the case of machinery products. However, no investigator appears to have taken into account that Western demand for goods from the CPEs and that the supply of Western goods to the CPEs must exhibit some price elasticity, and hence that prices cannot be held to be fixed. The small-country assumption is particularly unrealistic when it is invoked over time, as if neither the CPE in question nor the new trading markets would adjust as a result of the CPE's trade diversion. At the very least this ignores the time element required for reciprocal adaptations of supply and demand, and thus shifts in market-clearing prices.

16.5.4 Opportunity cost and price subsidies

The implicit subsidy debate also falls within the class of static opportunity cost analyses, but the motivation for doing the analysis and the rationalization of the findings are quite distinct from the inquiries summarized above. The thesis itself is very simple. Basically, it hinges on the incontrovertible fact that a systematic difference between TRPs and EWPs exists that can possibly be attributed to the domestic and foreign political objectives of the CMEA member 'granting' the subsidy – in this case the Soviet Union.

There is, of course, no point in denying that there are sizable differences, owing to the adopted intragroup pricing rules, between TRPs and WMPs. But I find it hard to accept the notion that these price differences can be primarily attributed to specific, explicit subsidies granted by one country to another as a payoff for the security that some Eastern European CPEs presumably provide to the USSR. I shall explain my position on that issue more coherently in chapter 17.

16.5.5 Toward an own price system

At least since the late 1950s the CPEs have aspired to establishing an own price system tailored to the demand and supply conditions and policy objectives within the region (see chapter 15). This may sound paradoxical given the Bucharest pricing principles and their ideological justification. However, the logic of the Bucharest principles as well as the practices that can be identified from existing trade and payments regimes are such that one would anticipate an own pricing system with links to WMPs or EWPs that are tight for some commodities (primarily fuels and raw materials), less tight for others (foodstuffs and intermediate industrial products) and nonexistent for still others (particularly for finished machinery, services and customized products, including those transacted on the basis of ECPS agreements). Though not all useful hypotheses can, for lack of data, be tested empirically,

I have explored several of the propositions (Brabant, 1987b, pp. 183–213) and found evidence of an emerging TRP system whose links to EWPs and WMPs become looser the more processed the products investigated.

In East and West alike, the outcome of the pricing investigations has been that some CPEs will occasionally derive an advantage from the TRP formation principles, relative to what could have been obtained in alternative markets, and at other times will derive a disadvantage. Because of the peculiar composition of Soviet trade set beside that typical for Eastern Europe, when raw material and fuel prices escalate in world markets, the advantage has tended to be Eastern Europe's; at other times, such as before the mid-1960s, the USSR definitely benefited from averaged prices (see Brabant, 1984b, 1984c).

16.6 THE CONTRIBUTION OF STC TO INTEGRATION

From the inception of Eastern European economic cooperation after World War II, one of the principal purposes of fostering closer interstate interaction has been the promotion of STC. When CMEA cooperation began, a drawn-out debate took place on the pros and cons of fraternal assistance in the form of STC at a nominal charge regardless of the recoupment of outlays in the country of origin. Eventually this was adopted as the Sofia Principle. This precept continued to be the guiding beacon of STC in the CMEA until at least the late 1960s (Kaplan, 1977, pp. 86–7); in some instances it amounted to the cement of Soviet-type industrialization. Later, the commercialization of STC slowly began. What economic effects were anticipated and to what extent have they materialized?

In effect, the Sofia Principle reduced the economic aspects of STC to the marginal cost of reproducing and exchanging pertinent information or of providing subsistence for personnel temporarily delegated abroad. Thus, the economics of STC, as it were, vanished with the stroke of a pen. How valuable was this gratuitous exchange of thousands of technological blueprints, scientists and engineers (see chapter 13)? Assigning an economic value to this exchange is not an easy task. It requires imputing a price that was not actually paid. Another question concerns whose price is to be imputed? Should the administrative price in the donor or in the recipient be considered? Or rather, should a scarcity value be calculated, perhaps by looking for some WMP?

Seen in that light, it is small wonder that there is a considerable range of estimates of the imputed value of documents and technical assistance. Estimates vary between $10 and $25 billion for the net transfer of STC from the USSR to other socialist countries (particularly Albania, Bulgaria, Poland and Rumania in Eastern Europe and China and Mongolia among the Asian

CPEs) before the gratuitous exchange gradually ceased, beginning in the late 1960s.[9] Even less is known about the concrete composition of these transfers and what exactly the recipients did with them. Thus, Bulgaria may have requested documentation for relatively simple mechanical lathes from, say, the Soviet Union. The transfer occurred and was duly factored into the numerical and imputed values of transfers. But if Bulgaria eventually decided not to implement the design, the value of the transfer would at best have been zero. Even if the transferred STC was actually implemented in the production process, it is not certain that the estimates provided by Eastern European researchers for the Soviet evaluation of its net transfer even come close to the benefits the recipients derived. Because such price heterogeneity flourishes and the imputation itself is a hazardous undertaking, I am not aware of any concrete, plausible estimate having been made either in the East or the West. Precisely because of the wide range and the uncertainty of imputing values, for the purpose of analysis one should remain skeptical about the accuracy of estimates and the information that might be derived in the process. As noted in chapter 13, under the circumstances it may be simplest to acknowledge that, during the 1950s and most of the 1960s, a generous transfer of technological knowledge occurred within the socialist community and that it exerted considerable influence over the pattern and direction of the area's industrialization.

Similar observations apply to the STC transferred at some positive charge since the end of the 1960s inasmuch as a genuine market for trading science and technology is lacking and, in any case, domestic and trade pricing exhibit considerable disarray. Also, efforts have been made to fund joint research and development projects, but the methods embraced have remained primitive. Thus, the results obtained are not really commercialized in the proper sense of that term; they tend to be available at little or no charge to those who participated in the jointly funded project. Though licenses may be issued to third parties, the market for trading them in the CMEA has remained primitive, and so the effects of STC have not been as positive as they could have been nor as positive as the members have recently hoped to eventually obtain. This entails advantages and drawbacks that go beyond the existence of a union (see chapter 17).

16.7 PRODUCTION SPECIALIZATION AND CMEA DEPENDENCE

Chapter 13 discussed several ways in which alternative measures of CMEA specialization could be constructed that would presumably impart more tangible information than what can be extracted from the specialization indexes. Here I shall discuss a few results of the export- and import-dependence data that I have constructed, the import dependence of investments in machinery and equipment and the degree to which the latter data suggest greater synchronization of CMEA trade over time as well as when compared with trade with other countries.

16.7.1 Import- and export-dependence indicators

An up-to-date estimate of trade dependence as defined in chapter 13 is very time-consuming.[10] The following are the results of an earlier study (Brabant, 1979b). First, comparing the mid-1970s with the early 1960s, Hungary had undeniably raised its dependence on foreign markets. This was done at a rapid pace in the 1960s but had markedly slowed by the early 1970s, when trade dependence appeared to be stagnating. In addition, by the mid-1970s Hungary had become more dependent on CMEA partners than on the rest of the world. This rise in export dependence mostly stemmed from raw materials, consumer goods and foodstuffs, particularly with CMEA partners. Import dependence, on the other hand, rose rapidly for fuels, manufactured consumer goods and, to a lesser extent, machinery products. Finally, I found evidence of trade diversion in favor of the CMEA area, except for foodstuffs, but it was not sufficiently large to swamp the trade-creation effect. These results were hard to reconcile with the ECPS and STC agreements then in place. For CMEA trade, much less ambiguous evidence of the positive effects in engineering and chemical activities should have emerged from the exercise. Whether similar results will be obtained from the experiment under way, which is larger in scope and more accurate as it is based on domestic wholesale prices rather than unit value weights, remains to be seen.

16.7.2 Import dependence for machinery investments

Recall that this measure is defined as the ratio of imported machinery, possibly from alternative external sources, to total investments in machinery and equipment. It can easily be constructed for Bulgaria, Hungary, Poland (until 1983) and Rumania (until 1985), all of whom report comparable data in domestic currency units for total *ex post* machinery investment demand and its import component. These data can be further disaggregated into trade with, for example, the CMEA and other partners. But assumptions are necessary on the relationship between trade and domestic prices for investment goods for all countries but Hungary, which details its data by socialist, or ruble, and nonsocialist, or dollar, partners.

These data exhibit several paradoxical features of the economic policies these four countries pursue. First, evidently the least-developed member of the group (Rumania) has the highest level of relative autarky in the domestic consumption of machinery products for investment purposes. The import share peaked around 30 percent in 1965 and has since been halved. The same

Table 16.3 Estimated quadratic trends

	time	t	time^2	t	R^2	DW	SE
Bulgaria (1953–86)							
Total	0.185	16.10	−0.002	−7.42	0.977	0.883	0.159
Domestic	0.164	17.27	−0.001	−4.92	0.988	0.683	0.132
Imports	0.205	11.23	−0.003	−6.75	0.927	0.764	0.254
Socialist	0.187	11.30	−0.003	−6.67	0.930	0.817	0.230
Other	0.327	9.11	−0.006	−5.74	0.880	0.835	0.498
Czechoslovakia (1948–86)							
Total	0.144	23.00	−0.002	−10.06	0.988	0.677	0.107
Domestic	0.131	20.02	−0.001	−8.48	0.984	0.720	0.112
Imports	0.221	36.89	−0.003	−18.83	0.994	0.960	0.103
Socialist	0.312	14.99	−0.005	−9.19	0.949	0.473	0.357
Other	0.138	4.51	−0.001	−1.12	0.838	0.286	0.525
German Democratic Republic (1950–86)							
Total	0.194	32.79	−0.003	−19.05	0.991	1.379	0.093
Domestic	0.182	30.67	−0.003	−18.30	0.989	1.369	0.094
Imports	0.267	19.61	−0.004	−11.24	0.975	1.572	0.216
Socialist	0.272	16.95	−0.004	−9.84	0.966	1.470	0.254
Other	0.264	14.19	−0.004	−7.91	0.956	1.027	0.294
Hungary (1950–86)							
Total	0.193	10.93	−0.002	−5.04	0.947	0.638	0.279
Domestic	0.129	9.15	−0.001	−2.94	0.949	0.636	0.222
Imports	0.346	14.68	−0.005	−8.76	0.952	0.685	0.373
Socialist	0.349	14.30	−0.006	−9.21	0.940	0.742	0.385
Other	0.362	11.99	−0.005	−6.34	0.944	0.420	0.478
Poland (1961–86)							
Total	0.135	6.01	−0.001	−1.20x	0.941	0.534	0.206
Domestic	0.085	4.76	−0.001	−1.25x	0.961	1.070	0.164
Imports	0.225	5.78	−0.004	−3.08	0.850	0.370	0.358
Socialist	0.159	7.30	−0.002	−2.86	0.935	0.491	0.201
Other	0.324	4.87	−0.007	−3.05	0.738	0.386	0.612
Rumania (1953–85)							
Total	0.164	15.02	−0.001	−3.74	0.984	0.370	0.166
Domestic	0.171	19.98	−0.001	−4.88	0.991	0.528	0.130
Imports	0.168	7.13	−0.002	−2.54*	0.914	0.301	0.357
Socialist	0.099	4.00	0.000	0.03x	0.886	0.330	0.375
Other	0.342	7.05	−0.005	−4.03	0.838	0.351	0.735

Note: Sources and methods are described in Brabant, 1988b, pp. 308–13.

x = relevant at 95% t-value.

* = not relevant at 90% t-value.

applies to Bulgaria, whose import share reached 65 percent in 1965 and then declined to 38 percent in 1985 – still more than twice the ratio for Rumania. The reverse is true for the most-developed member of the group. Hungary expanded its share to about 55 percent in 1980, but this has shrunk slightly since then. Similar trends prevail for Poland, whose share peaked at 50 percent in 1975; owing to adjustment efforts, it has since sharply contracted. For Czechoslovakia and the GDR no comparable data are available. However, I have made use of whatever could be assembled to illustrate some of the points below.[11]

I utilized these data to estimate two quadratic time trends for investments in machinery and equipment and its apparent origins; one takes advantage of the entire data set and the other is applied to identical time periods because, notably for Poland, the series only starts in 1960. The results, some of which are shown in Table 16.3, reveal that the coefficients for time squared are negative or insignificant for all equations. But the size of the time coefficient for imports is larger than that for domestic supplies only in the cases of Czechoslovakia, the GDR, Hungary and, marginally, Poland. There is strong evidence, however, that the reverse prevails for Bulgaria and Rumania. These quantifications confirm that the less-developed CPEs tend to pursue an import-substitution policy that has been intensified over time, as buttressed by the more negative coefficients for time squared for the shorter than for the longer period. The reverse holds for the more-developed members. These magnitudes and their sign offer *prima facie* evidence that the industrialization policies of these countries have not been well integrated in the sense that regional or worldwide specialization has not been a motor force of development. This has especially been true for the least-developed members of the group.

16.7.3 Elasticities and dependence

The data indicate the presence of considerable instability in investment in machinery and equipment and not only for the import component. It is also reflected in total domestic investment activity. However, the two are not necessarily synchronized. To the extent that the CPEs have increasingly harmonized ECPS with their relatively insulated domestic economic policies, a notable increase in the stability of CMEA imports relative to domestic supplies, away from imports from the rest of the world, should be evident. Such estimates have also been prepared, and some are shown in Table 16.4.[12]

For the long period measured, the elasticities for domestic supplies are inferior to those of CMEA imports, which in turn are smaller than the elasticities for imports from the rest of the world, except in the case of Czechoslovakia, the GDR and Rumania. For the shorter period, however, the thesis is true only for Bulgaria. Furthermore, except for Rumania, there is a sharp contraction in the elasticity for domestic supplies. The estimated CMEA import elasticities show a decline for Czechoslovakia and the GDR, near stability for Hungary but an increase for Bulgaria and Rumania. But the gap between domestic and CMEA import elasticities failed to shrink in any country; perverse results are evident for CMEA versus other import elasticities, particularly for all but Bulgaria. These data confirm earlier findings about the growing or declining import-dependence ratios in the countries for which data are available. By relating the above information to relative dependence on the CMEA and other countries, striking results are

Table 16.4 Estimated impact elasticities

		b	t	R^2	DW	SE
Bulgaria						
1953–86	D	0.377	2.99	0.186	0.576	0.113
	S	1.322	12.59	0.820	0.787	0.094
	O	2.941	6.82	0.553	1.056	0.387
1961–86	D	0.130	1.08x	0.005	1.105	0.067
	S	1.420	11.27	0.828	1.225	0.071
	O	3.660	5.41	0.501	0.968	0.379
Czechoslovakia						
1948–86	D	1.028	37.39	0.973	0.768	0.018
	S	1.094	2.57*	0.100	0.289	0.274
	O	0.765	0.91x	0.059	0.233	0.543
1961–86	D	0.981	33.62	0.977	1.376	0.013
	S	1.056	6.95	0.644	1.053	0.066
	O	0.656	2.46*	0.160	1.268	0.116
German Democratic Republic						
1950–86	D	0.947	16.99	0.886	1.477	0.031
	S	1.790	3.73	0.250	1.789	0.265
	O	1.531	2.90	0.152	1.140	0.291
1961–86	D	0.852	15.25	0.899	1.352	0.013
	S	1,654	7.00	0.678	1.331	0.056
	O	0.698	0.69x	0.034	1.084	0.240
Hungary						
1950–86	D	0.743	22.39	0.930	0.777	0.051
	S	1.390	6.55	0.519	0.434	0.328
	O	1.731	6.58	0.516	0.718	0.407
1961–86	D	0.723	15.79	0.905	1.616	0.032
	S	1.418	13.49	0.873	1.304	0.073
	O	0.788	4.96	0.473	1.144	0.110
Poland						
1961–86	D	0.628	8.02	0.707	1.194	0.078
	S	0.791	6.95	0.642	0.986	0.113
	O	2.983	8.16	0.696	1.154	0.362
Rumania						
1950–85	D	0.675	9.81	0.724	0.510	0.067
	S	2.278	14.59	0.851	0.998	0.152
	O	1.710	1.70+	0.018	0.656	0.979
1961–85	D	0.859	15.04	0.900	1.146	0.037
	S	2.679	13.10	0.869	1.494	0.134
	O	0.113	0.33x	0.005	1.141	0.222

Note: A description of sources and methods is available in Brabant, 1988b, pp. 308–13.
x = relevant at 95% t-value
* = not relevant at 90% t-value

obtained. In fact, the indicators of whether the CMEA market has become a more stable source of supply for machinery investment are inconclusive or just plainly contradictory.

16.7.4 Export and import dependence for commodities

In a recent empirical study, Crane and Skoller (1988) report on a broad-based investigation into the possible effects of ECPS agreements. Their intention is similar to the one outlined in chapter 13, where I conjectured that ECPS agreements should lead to an increase in aggregate trade or, at least, to trade dependence of the product categories for which most of these agreements have been signed. This proposition should hold even more strongly for the individual products that are the subject of these agreements. In other words, Crane and Skoller suggest that, if ECPS agreements hold, the share of exports in production of the specializing country and the share of imports in apparent domestic consumption of the partner country should rise. To distinguish this from the normal increase in trade shares that may take place for reasons other than an ECPS agreement, they specifically test for evidence of a shift in the slope of the time trend following the signing of an ECPS agreement.

The rather simple model posited that the univariate transformation of the percentage of output exported to the partner is a function of time and a multiplicative dummy variable set equal to zero before the signing of an agreement and to time once the agreement is signed. The dummy variable was probably imposed on the assumption that the more time that passes after the signing of an agreement the more unlikely it is that a weak or no increase can be attributed to the ECPS agreement. It would have been interesting, however, to refine the test for a simple one-time shift in the slope of the regression curve, which they decided to drop 'to reduce possible multicollinearity' (p. 43), as no *a priori* reason exists for imposing a tightening time constraint on the implementation of an ECPS agreement once it is established.

This model was applied to 103 commodities, with measurements being conducted in physical units – certainly an advantage over the aggregate estimations reported earlier in which price dichotomies proved to be a serious obstacle to implementation. Of the total number of commodities studied, the authors found evidence of a significant rise in integration after the signing of an ECPS agreement only for 11 products. But contrary evidence – a significant decline in the trade share – was found for 32. The test was considered significant at the rather generous 10 percent two-tailed level of acceptance.[13] For the other commodities, uncertainty was even much greater. The investigators therefore concluded that, 'using these results, it is very difficult to argue that specialization agreements have significantly contributed to economic integration in CMEA' (Crane and Skoller, 1988, p. 45).

Note that the authors did not entertain the possibility that an ECPS agreement may explicitly have been designed to confirm existing industrial structures or to undertake domestic expansion unrelated to any trade intentions. Neither did they speculate on problems that might arise from the coarse trade categories they were forced to work with. The agreement might conceivably have focused on only one component of the category. Also, rationalizations following the signing of an ECPS agreement may have called for an initial contraction of trade. Finally, the authors did not consider that ECPS agreements might have been implemented in order to destroy unprofitable trade lines. Therefore, an immediate positive effect of the ECPS agreement on export- and import-dependence measures would not have been anticipated.

The evidence of the trade effects of SEI presented in this chapter is not very encouraging. Certainly, STC and ECPS agreements appear to have had some effect on trade, but the estimated magnitudes are fairly small. In other words, the results are ambiguous and fall far short of confirming steady progress with specialization within the CMEA region as a result of embracing integration policies. Of course, this weak evidence immediately begs the question of why the CPEs have tried to fuse themselves, at least in political rhetoric, over the past forty years. The answer could be a cynical one, referring once again to the preponderant political, ideological and strategic weight of the USSR within the CMEA. But one could look at it from a different angle, namely from the preferences of CPE policymakers themselves. I shall now turn to the perceived advantages and drawbacks of SEI, most of which cannot be adequately measured.

NOTES

1. Of course, it is entirely possible that such measurements are deemed too sensitive to be publicly aired. Knowledgeable observers have informally told me that measurements have remained rather simple. The many problems of empirical investigations in the context have so far not been sufficiently addressed.
2. This does not require absolute uniformity throughout the union. Regional differentiation will simply substitute for international differences.
3. This critique of the traditional approach to measuring integration effects argues that a more fruitful approach would be through the foreign trade multiplier, postulating export growth as the major component of autonomous demand and thus addressing the dynamic effects. Though perhaps useful in the capitalist context, the rigid separation of foreign from domestic markets in CPEs inhibits the transposition of the argument.
4. Though this has been a concern from the first coining of the notions of trade creation and diversion by J. Viner in the late 1940s, the evidence is weak that trade diversion has been substantial enough to offset the gains obtained through trade creation. For a recent comprehensive measurement for the EC, see Jacquemin and Sapir (1988).
5. The investment and factor productivity effects found from union formation

tended to be very small, 'of minor consequence to countries contemplating participation in such schemes' (p. 167). This conclusion is heavily contested in analyses of the dynamic effects anticipated from the creation of a genuine uniform market by '1992' in the EC (see Padoa-Schioppa *et al.*, 1987).

6. Brada (1985) and Desai (1986) have recently also couched their explanation for TRP-EWP differences in terms of the customs union approach by postulating that factor endowments in the CMEA differ from those prevailing elsewhere and, with factor immobility, justify divergent prices. The price gap can then be attributed to union preferences. But this is not the most expeditious way of looking at CMEA developments (see Brabant, 1987b, pp. 160–1).

7. This has been the case for inferences on SEI effects. For a detailed discussion of the results and their shortcomings, see Brabant, 1980, pp. 261–7.

8. Illustrative details of such measures are compiled through the early 1980s in Sobell, 1984.

9. Lavigne, 1976, provides an overview of the various data available by the mid-1970s. Because their range is so wide and our ability to verify them is virtually nonexistent, I shall not further discuss the absolute value of STC.

10. I had wanted to report on an exercise for Hungary that has been under way for some time, but definitive results are not yet available. Essentially, the investigation is a refinement of the study of the level and evolution of Hungarian trade dependence reported in Brabant, 1979b, pp. 225–35.

11. Czechoslovakia and the GDR report investments in machinery and equipment in constant prices; their imports (total and by geographical groups) can be estimated in comparable prices. This enables the computation of time trends for total investment and imported supplies. Note that these data are not even approximately in 'similar' prices. Though this should only affect the intercept, some of the results are odd, possibly because of the mixture of data.

12. Again, for periods through 1970 the results are in Brabant, 1974b. More recent estimates for the period through 1985 are in Brabant, 1988b, pp. 310–1. All equations for the data through 1986 were reestimated for our purposes here.

13. Inasmuch as one is testing for a rise in the share following identification of the existence of an ECPS agreement, the proper test should be one-tailed.

17 · ON THE ADVANTAGES AND DRAWBACKS OF SEI

At least since *Integration Program*, as reiterated in every CMEA document endorsed more recently, the Eastern European economies have stressed the paramount importance of raising 'consumer levels of living,' including through SEI. Rather than being identified with consumer surpluses or welfare gains, as they would in analyses of market-type integration schemes, the CPEs formulated this objective in terms of rapid and stable growth in aggregate output, uses and factor productivity, in part through the security of supply and export markets afforded by ECPS, STC or similar agreements. These modes need to be evaluated in the CPEs' own framework.

Interpreting the trade effects discussed in chapter 16 as reflecting greater efficiency and welfare levels than would have been feasible with tariff walls or their equivalent in each country in isolation proved to be difficult. This is particularly true when trying to evaluate the effects of the TRP system, of far-reaching STC and of a peculiar system of ECPS agreements. Nonetheless, significant advantages of SEI do accrue to CPEs. Every available indicator, however, points to a vast potential for expanding these benefits – not just the trade effects of SEI – by establishing proper institutions, instruments and macroeconomic policies.

Section 17.1 discusses the metaphysics of what is and is not an advantage – this is not an easy question to answer, but simply postulating some arbitrary markers will prove useful in making some headway. These markers are set in section 17.2 with reference to growth and the stability of belonging to the CMEA. The overall benefits and costs of national and regional autonomy are treated in section 17.3. Drawbacks associated with domestic policy autonomy as buttressed by the CMEA and market segmentation *inter alia* with an own price system are taken up in the next section. The benefits of TRP autonomy for some CPEs have a counterpart in the costs of, mainly, the Soviet subsidy. How this might be viewed by Soviet or other observers is considered in section 17.5 in conjunction with a more general evaluation of the TRP system, including key issues of implicit subsidies and development assistance. The costs and benefits of STC are next briefly discussed. The marketability of specialized and other products forms the subject of section

17.7. In the final section, I examine critical aspects of simply having to formulate decisions within a context of pronounced domestic and external market dichotomies.

17.1 ON THE BENEFITS AND DRAWBACKS OF INTEGRATION

The repercussions on production, consumption and trade need to be looked at comprehensively because what economic integration is all about is gaining economies of scale, accelerating productivity gains, obtaining aggregate economic growth at a faster pace, generating larger consumer surpluses and other such policy objectives. The means through which these goals are pursued by planned and market economies can be quite diverse. But the ultimate result, just as with the economic paradigm in its technical setting, should be gains in welfare levels as perceived from a social and/or private standpoint. Though some SEI welfare gains can be depicted within the context of the stylized customs union model, this is an exceedingly narrow way of appraising SEI. In addition, in contrast to the stylized economic rationale, the CPEs perceive other effects in terms of their economics and related aspects of socialist planning. One may disagree with some of these claims as they are often based on other than verifiable, let alone quantifiable, facts and figures. This is just to underline the conundrum of how best to reconcile claims based on different preference schedules, such as those implicit in the behavior of CPE policymakers and those considered standard in Western trade theory.

But there are also genuine drawbacks to being an integrated CMEA member, something the CPEs themselves have increasingly acknowledged, and which is even being assumed by those who reject other drawbacks identified by Western observers. The rationale is not unlike the reasons that make some of the claimed benefits of SEI look illogical to the Western economist trained in standard trade theory. The drawbacks perceived by Eastern European observers may be especially pronounced in the non-economic sphere, in the sense that the establishment of the CMEA group enforced an even greater degree of regional cohesion and hence loss of sovereignty in all but economic matters. Such drawbacks are likely to emerge in circumstances in which the metaeconomic aspects of integration policies constrain culture, politics, defensive capabilities and other aspects of societal life. However, these items will not be discussed because there are ample economic issues to consider.

As indicated in chapter 16, the costs and benefits of integration as assessed at a given moment of time are interrelated. Such views are likely to diverge among commentators, even when the claims are presented along with quantitative and other explanations. Even any single observer's perceptions of the benefits and drawbacks of SEI are bound to change over time. Thus, when centralized economic administration was upheld as *the* key to development and industrialization, accessing trade outlets in countries with a similar need for regulating and controlling the foreign trade sector was legitimately perceived as advantageous. The magnitude of the advantage shrinks when priorities shift and policymakers attempt to streamline central regulation (see chapter 9). Some of these factors were noted in their historical (see Part I) or systemic (see Part II) contexts. In what follows, I focus on the critical advantages and drawbacks of SEI primarily with the hindsight of prevailing development priorities.

I realize the considerable problems of implementing this agenda, which necessitates a less-than-rigorous analysis of SEI. This is required especially for accepting the paradox that what may be an advantage from one angle can easily be turned into a drawback when the focus of study is slightly redirected. Realizing this regrettable fluidity is one thing; remedying it is quite another task. I can do so only partially because of the paucity of previous research on the impact of SEI on aggregate categories, including production, consumption and trade in a static as well as a dynamic framework. I do not mean by this to denigrate integration among the CPEs in comparison with better-known attempts to harmonize some set of economic decisions. Given the extraordinary circumstances under which the CMEA edifice was erected and the major determinants of its evolution, at best one hopes to gain insight piecemeal into the results of SEI.

17.2 GROWTH AND STABILITY OF BELONGING TO THE CMEA

As noted, perhaps one of the most surprising features of the CPEs has been their substantial degree of autonomy in domestic policymaking, which is particularly paradoxical given the ambition of some leaders to foster integration. This conflict in policy ambitions has historical, political, ideological and other tangents (see Part I) that help to clarify the initial desires to foster domestic policy autonomy. But these do not explain why all CPEs have upheld domestic autonomy as a supreme goal of economic administration. It is probably impossible to unambiguously opt for or against such domestic autonomy being an advantage of SEI. That cooperation in the CMEA framework has contributed to strengthening the degree of national and regional policy autonomy seems beyond doubt, even though most CPEs have become dependent, most notably, on CMEA supplies of fuels and raw materials. The proper comparison is not what has happened over time but the degree of policy autonomy that could have been maintained without CMEA cooperation. Preserving policy autonomy would have been much more difficult had each CPE been forced to fend for itself in competitive markets, although it would probably be impossible to measure this in any satisfactory way. But it seems self-evident that some CPEs, for example, would have failed to expand their infant industry into the backbone of economic activity. It may be true that a considerable part of that newly created industry is not very competitive by world standards, but that is a different matter whose policy concern has been surfacing only in the past decade or so.

Do CPEs still aspire to pervasive policy autonomy? Especially since the recent revival of interest in placing SEI on a firmer economic footing, most CPEs appear receptive to yielding part of their domestic policy autonomy, which is certainly no longer considered as a *sui generis* advantage of SEI by those in the vanguard of the reform movement. However, even these CPEs are concerned that the loss in autonomy that would be required to enhance SEI may have adverse repercussions on economic stability and growth. Perhaps the only way to make headway on this issue is to examine to what extent SEI has contributed to maintaining fairly rapid and stable growth, which is an objective that has always been invoked as a key ingredient of the desire for domestic policy autonomy.

17.2.1 Regional cohesion, market size and development horizon

In principle, one cannot deny the benefits of producing for a larger market or of formulating consumption decisions against an offer curve that is more flexible than the national one. Thus, questions concerning the advantages and drawbacks of integration derive from the ways in which economic goals can be pursued while yielding other sociopolitical benefits. That is, the gains of working for a larger market are a direct function of the institutions and instruments available for pursuing regional cohesion. Could CPEs derive benefits from coordinating policies, harmonizing investment intentions and generally formulating decisions against the opportunities provided by a market larger than their own national one? In principle, the answer should be a decisive affirmative. As noted though, realization of the benefits directly depends on the institutions and instruments through which such policies can be integrated. The paramount instrument wielded over the years has been some form of plan coordination, especially in trade matters. Without the political will to integrate and establish a regional planning agency, the degree of interdependence possible through existing instruments and institutions is limited even under the most favorable circumstances.

From the inception of SEI, the CPEs have stressed the advantages accruing from facilitating the clearing of trade that would have been more difficult to effect had they integrated themselves more fully with the global economy. This is not to argue against the benefits of competing in world markets. But competing within the adverse political environment engendered by the cold war and some of its unstable successor regimes while simultaneously pursuing rapid economic growth through industrialization might have proven self-defeating. For one thing, trading with Western

Table 17.1 Growth characteristics of CPEs and DMEs, 1960–87

	Lowest	Highest	Average	Deviation
Aggregate growth				
Belgium	−1.5	7.0	3.43	2.31
Denmark	−1.8	10.0	3.20	2.58
France	0.2	7.4	3.96	2.11
Germany (Fed. Rep.)	−1.6	7.6	3.22	2.31
Ireland	−6.4	11.5	4.00	3.48
Italy	−3.6	8.1	3.43	2.75
Luxemburg	−5.4	10.1	2.96	3.37
The Netherlands	−1.4	8.7	3.38	2.50
United Kingdom	−1.5	8.8	2.33	2.18
All nine	−1.3	6.2	3.40	1.80
Bulgaria	1.8	11.1	6.54	2.14
Czechoslovakia	−2.2	9.2	4.04	2.62
German Democratic Republic	1.6	6.5	4.55	1.06
Hungary	−1.4	9.6	4.26	2.89
Poland	−12.0	10.8	4.45	5.22
Rumania	2.2	13.5	7.92	2.99
All six	−1.9	8.6	5.01	2.54
Without Poland	2.3	7.9	5.26	1.63
Soviet Union	2.2	9.3	5.48	2.11
All seven	1.7	8.7	5.33	2.00
Industrial growth				
Belgium	−6.5	11.6	4.50	3.92
Denmark	−8.0	12.8	3.17	4.47
France	−2.1	9.4	4.04	3.26
Germany (Fed. Rep.)	−5.2	12.2	3.16	4.48
Ireland	−6.3	12.4	5.38	4.34
Italy	−11.3	12.6	4.53	5.30
Luxemburg	−18.6	11.1	2.54	7.00
The Netherlands	−18.3	39.7	3.50	10.12
United Kingdom	−15.9	17.0	1.26	6.46
All nine	−6.8	9.0	3.75	3.62
Bulgaria	3.2	14.6	8.23	3.28
Czechoslovakia	−0.6	11.7	5.28	2.56
German Democratic Republic	3.1	7.8	5.54	1.23
Hungary	−1.6	11.9	5.00	2.83
Poland	−10.8	11.4	6.49	4.68
Rumania	1.1	16.0	10.32	4.00
All six	−0.6	10.6	6.47	2.62
Without Poland	2.3	10.6	6.48	2.05
Soviet Union	2.9	10.1	6.49	2.22
All seven	2.3	9.8	6.48	2.25
Agricultural growth				
Belgium	−16.8	12.8	1.25	6.41
Denmark	−25.7	30.3	1.88	11.57
France	−7.2	11.6	1.70	5.04
Germany (Fed. Rep.)	−10.0	17.9	1.45	6.29
Ireland	−15.3	15.8	2.43	7.32
Italy	−7.3	8.8	1.49	4.15
Luxemburg	−13.6	22.0	0.74	9.87
The Netherlands	−18.3	39.7	3.50	10.12
United Kingdom	−8.4	17.4	2.42	6.37
All nine	−6.0	9.6	1.93	3.98
Bulgaria	−12.2	14.3	2.29	6.01
Czechoslovakia	−7.0	11.3	2.03	4.12
German Democratic Republic	−13.8	10.0	2.07	5.16
Hungary	−6.1	10.9	2.01	4.58
Poland	−10.7	10.4	1.92	4.77
Rumania	−8.3	18.9	4.03	6.55
All six	−4.1	8.1	2.27	2.94
Without Poland	−3.5	9.8	2.49	3.01
Soviet Union	−7.5	16.1	2.36	5.45
All seven	−3.6	11.9	2.30	3.90

Source: Data for DMEs are for the period 1960–85 and are drawn from a special data base on national account statistics with 1980 constant prices and dollar exchange rates. Data for CPEs are based on NMP national data aggregated with 1981 CMEA weights. The reported lowest and highest data are average annual growth rates. The average is measured between endpoints. Deviation is a simple standard deviation.

economies would have required sizable transaction balances in convertible currency. It would also have entailed greater uncertainty and fluctuations in trade, including as a result of price movements, than would trading under CMEA coordination and thus may have significantly perturbed the CPEs. By allowing the clearing of transactions at stable prices with automatic swing credits, the TRP regime has undoubtedly facilitated intragroup commerce. By its nature, however, the TRP regime has bestowed advantages, in terms of opportunity costs, on some countries and sizable disadvantages on others. This has proved to be a two-edged sword. Even a clear short-term TRP advantage has been associated with serious disadvantages in a more comprehensive, long-term perspective, if only because it has failed to provide the correct decision-making signals (see section 17.5).

17.2.2 Stability and growth

Has growth in the CPEs been more stable than it would have been without the union? This is a very difficult question because it requires postulating an *anti-monde*, which I shall not do here. It may be useful, however, to compare the CPEs' growth stability with that of selected other countries. For the purposes at hand, Western Europe will provide a useful comparison.

The variables illustrated in Table 17.1 may suffice to underline the points I wish to make regarding the stability of overall growth as well as stability in industrial and agricultural activities. Provided the data are equally accurate in reflecting the picture of all countries and over time, there seems little doubt that, though the range of aggregate growth has been slightly narrower and the average substantially higher in CPEs than in DMEs, the standard deviation for the two groups is very similar. In fact, it is slightly larger for the CPEs, but that may primarily stem from Poland's erratic growth in the past decade. Without Poland, there is a substantial reduction in the range, a higher average and a somewhat smaller standard deviation for the CPEs compared with selected market-type economies. Matters are quite different for industrial expansion, for which the range is much wider in DMEs and the average is about half of that in CPEs. Not surprisingly, a more stable industrial growth pattern is evident in CPEs. For agriculture, the range is roughly the same – the average slightly higher and the standard deviation about the same. But that is largely due to the erratic Soviet performance. For Eastern Europe proper, the range and variability is much smaller and the average slightly higher than in the chosen Western European economies.

With due respect for the difficulty of comparing these data, some of which are derived from different conceptual magnitudes, Eastern Europe should be given the benefit of the doubt on stability and growth performance. To the extent that Eastern Europe, particularly, could have sustained this pattern only by procuring fuels and raw materials from within the CMEA under rather favorable conditions, these may be partly attributed as advantages of SEI.

17.2.3 Trade facilitation

Bilateralism and structural bilateralism have provided stability and reliability in CMEA trade that would have been much more difficult to realize in a global trade environment. The exporters of so-called soft goods have especially profited from this situation. This gain may be phrased in terms of price differentials, but I find this too limited an assessment. Without the ability to trade soft goods with the CMEA in exchange for necessary inputs that for most of the postwar period have been hard to superhard goods, the less-developed CPEs especially would simply not have been able to cling to the preferred domestic industrialization path for as long as they have. Given that structural bilateral constraints (see chapter 11) have tended to be applied chiefly on the margin rather than to trade as a whole, this opportunity has been particularly valuable. Only since the early 1980s has the disadvantage of structural bilateral constraints multiplied as a result of, especially, the Soviet Union insisting on better terms of trade in its BTPA negotiations. This extension of structural bounds beyond the 'ratchet' effects of trade expansion has been enforced through quantity constraints on the export of hard goods, demands for raising the quality of the goods obtained in return (possibly through embodied convertible currency imports), lowered prices for imports and higher prices for exports either explicitly or implicitly by trading such goods only for convertible currency rather than TR and through other forms.

Facilitating trade by establishing a moderately efficient physical and administrative infrastructure has undoubtedly provided economic advantages, although it may have made countries more vulnerable to policy actions by others. The first advantage should be clear. Streamlining administrative structures yields benefits if only because international commerce is not simply an extension of domestic trade. Apart from linguistic differences and customs formalities, conditions of sale, packaging, payment and regulation are not usually homogeneous among countries. Standardized conditions of delivery are essential to the smooth conduct of trade and were one of the first administrative achievements of CMEA cooperation (see chapter 3).

One can only speculate whether or not the CPEs' trade would have expanded more or less rapidly had CMEA cohesion of some form not been imposed on the region. Without it, trade expansion and economic development would certainly have been very different from what actually came to the fore. It may have been more efficient or may simply have contracted to a level that would have generated dysfunctional effects. Unfortunately, there is no easy way to picture this counterfactual trading world with any degree of precision.

17.2.4 Facilitation of noncommercial transactions

In considering regional relations, noncommercial transactions should be mentioned, if only marginally. Such interaction has undoubtedly remained underdeveloped when measured by conditions that are now largely standard among industrial countries. Yet, seen in the traditional framework of inconvertibility typical of the CPEs, facilitating tourism, the transfer of stipends and unrequited transactions, coordinating foreign exchange regulations and other measures of interdependence should not be dismissed, though much more could have been accomplished in these areas. A mountain of work lies ahead if in the foreseeable future the CMEA is to earn anything close to the designation 'unified market.'

17.3 ADVANTAGES AND DISADVANTAGES OF POLICY AUTONOMY

Why are countries that form a union willing to remove some interferences with trade and not others? That is, why do they opt for a second-best solution? This familiar paradox can be explained only because countries do perceive benefits even though it also entails a cost in terms of renounced efficiency compared to unfettered integration into the world economy. Constraints on macroeconomic policy may be so severe and the costs of transition to global integration so extensive that it would not be helpful to compare union results with what would be feasible with nondiscriminatory tariff reductions without taking other realities into account. This is particularly applicable to the CMEA as the regional organization and to the planning horizon of the CPEs. Even so, members must decide how much of the cost of protecting the union they can afford and how to apportion that cost. In the capitalist context, the extent and incidence of protection can usually be assessed, however incompletely, by looking at differential tariffs, discriminatory nontariff restrictions and other actions that lead to unequal access to markets. For CPEs the situation is quite different as it is not readily apparent how the extent and incidence of protection could be ascertained.

As discussed in chapter 9, 'protection' in CPEs is an ill-defined concept as countries have no need to embrace explicit commercial policies. Unlike in a Western economy, where access to local markets is equal unless explicitly inhibited, in a CPE access to markets is forbidden unless explicitly permitted through various nonprice mechanisms. Because of the great amount of domestic policy autonomy desired, regional policies must be reconciled with domestic priorities. Therefore, the cost of protection cannot legitimately be attributed solely to SEI. It may be difficult to ascertain the part that does stem from SEI, and the mechanisms to apportion this cost may be elusive. Yet, the allocation of resources in the CPEs certainly falls short of what could be accomplished under less-constrained decision-making criteria. Making such costs more explicit, translating them as much as feasible into *ad valorem* values and devising an equitable distribution rule are some of the key issues that have recently been raised in connection with revamping integration objectives and reconstructing the associated policies, instruments and institutions that support SEI. When one looks statically at what could be achieved in another constellation of policies and institutions, the drawbacks of integration are likely to differ from those that could be formulated from a dynamic perspective.

17.3.1   Static costs of autonomy

Two kinds of drawbacks need to be distinguished: those emanating from differential desires for autonomy and those attributable to the complications of ensuring a certain degree of autonomy through regional integration policies and institutions. Thus, if these policies or institutions extend the degree of autonomy desired by some members to others, the perceived need for emulating domestic autonomy in CMEA relations is a drawback of SEI for those countries that would have adopted a less-confining level of policy autonomy. Similarly, the model of integration chosen may be so costly in terms of the resources required to ensure autonomy that a static drawback of integration arises. In fact, there may be a third dimension; namely, what could have been achieved by the union-forming members individually or as a group had they chosen a different model, perhaps one patterned after attempts by DMEs to bolster efficiency. As discussed earlier, this is related to the differential degree of autonomy desired by policymakers. However, I feel that this is not really a legitimate drawback unless some of the integrating countries are forced into the straitjacket of an integration scheme that exhibits such asymmetric policy autonomy or policy dominance by one member over another that the scheme inflicts costs.

Western observers and disgruntled Eastern European policymakers frequently adopt this third dimension. That is, the low levels of economic efficiency and productivity in Eastern European countries are attributed to their having been 'forced' to integrate themselves into the CMEA. Undoubtedly some truth exists in the contention that the basic model and strategy of socialist development were imposed by the USSR from without. But two points should not be forgotten. Until recently the Soviet Union has not pressed hard for greater integration within the CMEA, which it could have accomplished given its clout in Eastern Europe's trade. At best, the USSR can be faulted for having so long ignored its buying power, for the Eastern Europeans must have benefited from this relationship, at least in the restricted sense in which I have posed the paradigm. Related to this feature is the rationale for why CPEs presently cannot compete with these products in world markets. This backwardness largely derives from the shortsightedness or incompetence of local leaders rather than from the allegedly overbearing Soviet precepts on what Eastern Europe should produce and consume, and how to accomplish such tasks.

Such advantages and drawbacks can be expressed in terms similar to price differentials in union-forming MEs. This at least holds for goods that are actually traded. The disadvantages that ensue from the substantial *caesura* between domestic and external markets, including through different price systems, could also be measured if domestic data on real scarcities could be approximated. Unfortunately this is not possible with the information at hand. Nonetheless, it would be instructive to ascertain the opportunity costs and benefits of CMEA trading. This technique has provided the essential backbone of all the price inquiries reported on in chapter 16 as union effects. Interpreting the results empirically and rationalizing them within a certain view of SEI are contentious issues, however.

In my view, the other two types of drawbacks are more important, or at least more amenable to economic discourse. The first, inefficiency deriving from the way the union is formed, can be easily shown – though not measured – in the case of the CMEA. It is largely caused by the absence of institutions, instruments and policies at the union level that are comparable to these features in each of the member countries. All other things being equal, had central planning been implanted at the regional level, certain cumbersome and inefficient trading and cooperation practices could have easily been eliminated. Also quite important, as I showed in Part I, is that from the inception of the CMEA the members have had different opinions on the purposes and means of SEI. Those whose preferences have found a paler reflection in what has actually materialized may thus consider CMEA membership a drawback that offsets some of the benefits. This factor is likely to figure more prominently when the costs of policy autonomy are viewed in a dynamic perspective.

17.3.2 Dynamic drawbacks from policy autonomy

In a dynamic framework, the drawbacks of policy autonomy engendered by CMEA integration fall into two categories. The first arises from the inability of some countries to move to a different level of policy autonomy, which would require implementing some economic reform. However, the CMEA system as such may be so confining that it inhibits economic change and technological progress even without the participants modifying their precepts on the desired degree of policy autonomy. In parallel with the third static drawback, a dynamic one could also be specified: active opposition by one or more integrating partners to changes coveted by other members.

Most Western observers, disgruntled Eastern European insiders and a score of critical Eastern European commentators have stressed this third factor in the form of the Soviet Union actively inhibiting economic change in the region. There is a grain of truth in this argument for a few years of the postwar period (see Part I). But it cannot hold for the entire past forty years and is not true for those CPEs that have recently tried to modify their economy. Soviet dictates may be pervasive when it comes to undermining sacrosanct precepts of communist rule, such as the vanguard position of the

Communist Party or centralized control over the economy, but, with the noted exceptions, the shortcomings in past reforms were not usually of the Soviet Union's making. They stemmed instead from two broad factors. Virtually all reforms have exhibited hesitancy, inconsistency and timidity (Kowalik, 1986), which was partially due to the active opposition by important wings in the Communist Party, much of the ministerial bureaucracy, the enterprise sphere and labor to reforms that would not – and could not – quickly pay off.

In my view, the other two kinds of obstacles are more critical drawbacks of CMEA integration than the pervasive dominance of Soviet predilections regarding permissible economic reforms. It is difficult to decide unambiguously which of the two is the more important. All that is clear is that any one trade-dependent CPE embarking on domestic reform is likely to encounter the rigidities that emanate from the way in which trade and payment relations are organized in the CMEA. As the growth record since the early 1970s has demonstrated, the command economy system individually and in the CMEA concert is not conducive to pursuing technological progress, growth intensification or factor productivity gains.

17.3.3 Policy autonomy and rectifying existing drawbacks

One may ruminate about the level of efficiency or the pace of growth that could have been attained had more consistent policies been adopted. But such contemplation does not afford a handle on those areas in which improvements may be prospectively sought. I do not pretend to be in a position to identify all elements that should be specified, but the following strike me as the major negative elements of regional and domestic policy autonomy: market segmentation, discrimination among groups of alternative foreign markets, inflexible trading and payments schemes, price subsidies and top-heavy institutions to foster regional economic cooperation. Some of these elements will be discussed in the following sections.

17.4 MARKET SEGMENTATION AND ITS DRAWBACKS

The CMEA's existence may have aggravated the drawbacks of domestic policy autonomy through market segmentation because of the critical role allotted to BTPAs, the national MFT and the absence of real scarcity indicators in CMEA trade and payments. The divorce of markets weakens the potential allocatory role of prices. Policymakers may wish to establish buffers against inducements to change called for by sudden price fluctuations. The variety of reasons includes legitimate economic ones such as conflicts with other policy objectives, possibly price stability and employment. In principle, coordinating adjustments with domestic development priorities could be enhanced through the planning process. This failed to be acted upon, however. Because market dichotomy separates producers and foreign markets, the incentive to raise exports and curtail imports subsequent to shifts in terms of trade has been exerted, if at all, through the planning bureaucracy. Domestic producers have remained uninformed of, and moreover disinterested in, shifts in scarcity relations in international markets and have thus not been provided with proper decision-making signals. The ministerial planning tiers and their counterparts in various CMEA organs have rarely been motivated to search for more profitable export and import patterns. In part this is because they have been ignorant of the real comparative advantages of domestic producers and, moreover, uninterested in exploiting them. As a consequence of this market intermediation being absent, domestic structures quickly evolved that were far removed from what socialist policymakers really desired for insulating their local markets against foreign economic developments.

This situation was considerably aggravated by the further segmentation of foreign markets into CMEA and other potential trade partners through mechanisms that were destined to make the assessment of real foreign opportunities and costs more complicated. Inasmuch as the CMEA trading world has not been organized on the basis of scarcity indicators, CPEs yet desire to stay abreast of the real costs and benefits of their economic operations; a proper balance must be maintained between insulation and staying attuned to the magnitude and speed of changes in relative economic scarcities in world markets. Although this concern has been an underlying preoccupation of economic policies in many CMEA members since the late 1950s, to date – even after more than thirty years of experimentation – no satisfactory solution has been reached. Over the years, several CPEs have tried to bridge the gap between domestic and TR prices on the one hand and domestic and world prices on the other through various formal and informal exchange rates (see Brabant, 1987a, pp. 196–235).

Market segmentation has permitted CPEs to preserve a substantial degree of consumer price stability, which for many years was a solid constant of the credo of socialist policymakers. Recently, however, more flexible price policies have had to be instituted to ensure better consumer market balances. Whether this trend should be continued or whether planners should revert to the doctrinal purity of constant or even declining prices (see chapter 9) is a question associated with very explosive social issues in most CPEs. A troublesome by-product of this policy practice and ideological exhortation for so many years, at least until the mid-1970s, has been the reluctance of consumers to tolerate any type of retail price change, even when initially fully offset by compensatory income allowances. Illustrating this proposition are the sequence of societal upheavals over intended price changes that buffeted Poland before the declaration of martial law in December 1981 and the elaborate, time-consuming and often tedious preparations of the population by government, Party and trade union officials in the case of Hungary.

Inasmuch as the price system is the key ingredient of the policy measures and economic incentives that may enhance the rational use of resources, trade and domestic prices should be closely interlinked. Social priorities may call for shielding consumer prices somewhat more than wholesale prices, but the respective nexus should not altogether be ruptured. The desirability of price stability has an unquestionable trade-off in terms of feasible levels of economic efficiency. The more efficiency becomes the explicit focus of economic policies, the higher the social cost of upholding price stability as a policy objective and instrument. At least since the mid-1970s, concern has been growing about the precise trade-off of price stability. In fact, an increasing number of CPEs have expressed doubts about the wisdom of maintaining at any cost the postwar price system. Only Hungary in the late 1970s took the logical first step of linking domestic and trade prices directly, though this policy aim was subsequently severely pounded by untoward domestic, CMEA and global disturbances that were perceived to justify placing new buffers between domestic and trade prices. The CPE price mechanisms, therefore, remain as convoluted as they have been over the past four decades. But major changes may be in the offing (see chapter 18).

17.5 TRADE PRICING IN THE CMEA

Most CPE policymakers stress the advantage of planning with fixed prices. This is also the case for TRPs 'based' on average WMPs because they are predictable once the broad pricing rules are agreed upon, they exhibit fewer fluctuations than WMPs and, by ostensibly removing monopolistic and other distorting influences, they are deemed to be more equitable. These issues differ from those listed under the heading of implicit subsidies (see chapter 16). Here the broader aspects of the TRP regime are examined as most of its advantages and drawbacks ensue from the particular preference scale revealed by CPEs. Some benefits and drawbacks are shared by all, at least at some point in time. Most aspects of the TRP regime, however, amount to advantages for some CPEs that have drawbacks for partner countries. These can be apportioned in ignoring arbitrage and involuntary subsidies, shortcomings in selecting TRPs, faults in applying the principles, inability to guide proper adjustment and placing brakes on reforms. A discussion of whether or not it is desirable to maintain the TRP regime concludes this section.

17.5.1 The principles of TRPs

There are few issues on which CMEA economists have maintained greater unanimity than on the drawbacks of the traditional TRP principles. I shall not describe the ideological foundations of the propositions on the efficiency of WMPs. Clearly, if WMPs are indicative of an efficient way of economizing, average past efficient prices cannot be, unless relative WMPs remain unchanged. Because transaction prices differ from WMPs, all observers agree that the bilateral setting of TRPs inhibits trade, specialization, multilateralism and the intensification of SEI. Patterning TRPs after some measure of WMPs may be expedient, but it fails to reflect true scarcities in the CMEA region and thus cannot properly guide integration decisions, no matter how these are formulated and implemented. Regardless of the origin of TRPs, they neither express the proper comparative advantage of the CPEs nor reflect regionwide economic scarcities. Abstracting for the moment from the fact that the CPEs form an integral part of the global economy and thus cannot fully divorce themselves from global economic scarcities, it is useful to briefly consider the CMEA in isolation and the fact that TRPs negotiated around average past WMPs cannot reflect the social, economic, technological and physical-geographic conditions typical of the CMEA. Not only that, but, to the extent that WMPs are not really competitive prices but are instead dominated by the market power of large firms in DMEs, TRPs usher into the CMEA the question of exploitation of the poor by the rich. Although this attitude has softened somewhat to allow greater scope for the doctrine of comparative advantage, the theses on unequal exchange are still formidable (see Grote and Kühn, 1986, pp. 1141–2).

17.5.2 The implementation of TRP principles

Transaction TRPs have highly diverse origins and have increasingly been determined by some domestic producer prices. From a technical economic standpoint, TRPs fail to provide the information required for reaching economic decisions according to what is justifiable on the basis of some criterion of rationality appropriate to the CPE environment. The crucial CMEA problem is that TRPs do not reflect relative scarcities, are highly heterogeneous, cannot generally be adjusted in order to better mirror market conditions, cannot be integrated into a uniform 'price list' for the region as a whole, do not really encourage adjustment in either demand or supply and certainly fail to foster regional specialization.

The drawbacks of TRPs largely result from superimposing a set of arcane principles upon bilateralism. As such, TRPs embody a disparate set of bilateral pricing practices that are shrouded in mystery and, by implication, create confusion and tensions in CMEA relations. If these tendencies are visible at the level at which bilateral negotiations take place, they are infinitely more complex for individual firms. The principles themselves are too general to quickly yield satisfactory uniform prices throughout the group. This price heterogeneity is also due to the fact that the link between bilateralism and TRPs is reciprocal. Bilateralism leads to heterogeneous prices that do not fully reflect economic scarcities, which in turn foster structural bilateralism – hence, further distortions in TRPs. These causes and consequences of general and structural bilateralism tend to reinforce the CPEs' already highly restrictive trade model. In one way or another, such trade controls become expressed as nonprice regulators that may add new dimensions to the existing brand of structural bilateralism. Because decision making takes place on the national level, *ex ante* imbalances between demand and supply must be corrected through numerous nonprice adjustment measures, trade denial or trade diversion to Western markets. Often TRPs cannot be adjusted to induce shifts in demand and supply, even if one is willing to confine attention to the periodicity of planning and hence the inevitable leads and lags.

The general contours of these imperfections, however, would not have changed much had the CPEs adopted uniform prices on the basis of the Bucharest formula, as suitably reinterpreted in 1975 and instilled with more realism in response to the real trade criteria in the CMEA region. TRPs are particularly troublesome for those CPEs bent on investing the lower planning organs, and even individual agents, with decision-making authority and on more comprehensively exploiting the advantages that can be reaped from international trade. Finally, the eclectic way in which trade prices are set, even if they were standardized for all, inhibits the development of higher forms of integration. It also compresses the range within which profitable trade opportunities in the strict sense can, even under the most favorable circumstances, be explored. TRPs are especially difficult to apply in an economically meaningful sense when the CPEs attempt to improve the conditions for capital and labor mobility within the region (Grebennikov and Jakovlev, 1985, p. 82).

17.5.3 Arbitrage

Because the CPEs never totally severed relations with other economies, arbitrage transactions enabled them, if desired, to evaluate alternatives on their merits. Therefore, intragroup trade could be effected at relative prices that all partners did or could face in their trade with outside transactors. Under the circumstances expediency – certainly not efficiency – dictated that their TRPs should bear some relation with WMPs and, in fact, should not be too far removed from WMPs. If TRPs could realistically be taken to reflect the terms on which alternatives are effectively offered in the CMEA, the most rational decision of the smaller countries would be to engage in pure arbitrage. This admittedly unrealistic option does suggest directions for the analysis of a variety of incentives for taking advantage of partial arbitrage. Individual agents are constantly confronted with opportunities to do so. This is necessarily a short-term activity that may sharply impair harmonious relations within the integrating region.

17.5.4 Price subsidies

As argued in chapter 16, price subsidies in the CMEA are a two-edged sword. For those benefiting from them, subsidies constitute a possibly palpable advantage of being integrated in the CMEA. For those incurring an opportunity cost, they may constitute a real drawback. Because most price subsidies in the CMEA have emanated from the lagging and averaging of CMEA fuel prices and the Soviet Union is the principal net exporter of fuels, TRP subsidies are inevitably associated with Soviet attitudes toward such implicit assistance.

17.5.5 The lack of a nexus between domestic and trade prices

Even if the adopted terms were efficient, at best they would permit the realization of only part of the potential trade benefits because the domestic economy would not directly be urged to specialize or pursue technological progress. Indirect effects, however, could emerge from the influence of the MFT on the decisions of domestic planners. Yet even that is complicated by the dichotomies between TRPs, WMPs, EWPs and the domestic prices of any CPE and their varying determinants, depending on the type of products traded and the environment in which commerce takes place (see chapter 15). At best these alternative 'markets' are very loosely connected; so, imbalances in one market cannot be rectified in time by correcting imbalances in another market.

Price heterogeneity not only hampers effective decision making, it also prolongs and exacerbates this separation. Thus, TRP heterogeneity has been directly responsible for the failure of any attempt to institute multilateralism in the CMEA (see Brabant, 1977, pp. 66–102; Brabant, 1987b, pp. 217–44). It also aggravates the already complex task of instituting an effective exchange rate system, even one tailored only to partial commercial and noncommercial markets.

The traditional price policy the CPE pursues has several consequences for domestic growth, though not necessarily in the short run. If no meaningful link between domestic and trade prices exists, the decision maker has no clue as to how best to decide upon the extent and pattern of trade, let alone in which direction efficient long-term domestic developments should be pursued in order to maximize the benefits of external trade opportunities. In fact, the situation is even more complex because the CPEs have been deeply committed to one another, if not for economic reasons then at least by a sense of geopolitical and ideological cohesion. Because external economic relations are divorced from domestic economic developments, the price mechanism as such cannot function properly. Moreover, as the price systems of individual CPEs differ, tacit or overt desires to perpetuate these differences prevent the price system from guiding or even from managing trade as such.

The issue of proper price policies does not derive solely from how to price domestic activities and how to regulate the link between trade and domestic prices through the MFT and price equalization. Regardless of the key objectives of domestic policies, in the event of unexpected price movements in world markets, two separate issues arise. Concerning domestic prices, a proper response to sizable, sustained movements in WMPs includes a thorough reevaluation of the room that is available for improving own allocation mechanisms, including adapting domestic prices and allocative policies so as to better reflect international economic scarcities. At some point, the CPEs need to relinquish some of their considerable price autonomy. But evidently they do not need to directly imitate WMPs. For one thing, the preference of CPE managers for greater stability than what typically prevails in world markets is very real. A second reason is that these countries cherish different social priorities from those held by most MEs and these social goals are partly implemented through the deflection of prices from relative real scarcities.

17.5.6 TRP autonomy and domestic economic reforms

Whenever policymakers hope to decentralize decision making and link domestic with foreign economic decisions, the dichotomies perpetuated through the TRP system become a palpable obstacle to utilizing the CMEA and its trading opportunities in support of domestic reform. However formal this may be, economic reforms attempt to mobilize microeconomic knowledge through managerial decisions that are guided by criteria set by central policymakers. If these criteria are not clear or coordinated, for example through mutually adjustable prices, firms cannot be expected to engage in profitable trading activities. The desired degree of autonomy in TRPs is thus important.

Irrespective of whether TRPs are anchored to WMPs, EWPs or domestic prices, price stability may be highly desirable in planning trade and in assisting with the orderly implementation of the domestic annual and medium-term plan targets. It is, however, detrimental from a number of viewpoints, most of which have already been stated. In addition, it deters technical progress or any joint efforts designed to accelerate it. Averaging over a five-year period and then keeping these reference prices intact for another five years or so (as was done until 1974) or even only for one year (as has been the principle since 1976) is not apt to convey even the right direction of price changes to those called upon, explicitly or implicitly, to respond to relative price signals. Over the past two decades, the pace of technical progress in the world has been so swift that for many manufactured goods from the fastest-moving sectors, such as electronics and informatics, going back to the past implies reverting to an altogether different product generation.

There are various ways of coping with this situation. One is to preserve the averaging over the medium term by using WMPs from one or two years and 'inferring' relational prices for the other years (see Šamraj, 1981a, p. 35; Šamraj, 1981b, p. 31). This may provide a modicum of consistency in the price-formation principles, but it is not capable of meeting the chief objection, which is that TRPs invariably trail the pace of technological progress by several years. This is not a desirable feature, particularly if the CPEs intend to accelerate the pace of innovation within the CMEA region. It should be recalled that the CPEs have, both in their 1984 economic summit documents (see Brabant, 1986) and the recently endorsed *Scientific-Technological Progress*, claimed that this is their explicit policy objective in matters of trade, integration and more general economic development for the rest of the century.

17.6 SCIENTIFIC-TECHNOLOGICAL COOPERATION

The specifics of STC since the Sofia Principle was inaugurated in 1949 were covered in chapter 13. The advantages and drawbacks of the free exchange remain opaque. Therefore, it may be most simple to retain that, during the 1950s and most of the 1960s, particularly during the two industrial leaps forward, a generous transfer of scientific and technological knowledge occurred within the socialist community. The direction was specifically from the more-developed to the less-developed CPEs, who were thus able to embark on their own development path without having to be concerned about how they would defray the cost of acquiring, and at times assimilating, foreign technology. Furthermore, this large-scale STC exerted considerable influence over the development pattern pursued by the less-developed CMEA members. The Sofia Principle was, therefore, critical in accelerating the rate of technological progress in the CMEA and in bridging the gap between the individual members in that respect. This particular aspect of STC was all the more significant because these transactions chiefly occurred when the export embargo maintained by most DMEs on the transfer of know-how to CPEs was at its rigid peak. From an economic point of view, such generous assistance policies for the sake of socialist internationalism were quite misguided, however beneficial they may have been in the short run when focusing narrowly on the cost of technology *per se*. As noted, the free dissemination of technology in its widest sense, apart from its unquestionable benefits, has severe disadvantages. I shall distinguish here among five, but others could also be discussed.

First, the economic incentive for the donors – usually the more-advanced partners in these exchanges – to gratuitously provide the fruits of their research outlays, which are costly to them, diminishes. However, this concern may not loom high in negotiations concerning STC for which the costs have already been borne, if perhaps not yet fully recouped. But it is bound to influence policy thinking on prospective research and development and how best to capitalize on it.

At the same time, the recipients – usually the less-developed partners – are not motivated to earmark resources to their own research and development when they can obtain its results free of charge, though this may be less of a handicap at the earlier stages of the transfer of information. The drawback of this transmission is bound to become greater, however, by the cost of assimilating ever more complex technology without having a homegrown base. Therefore, there seems to be a *prima facie* case for distinguishing among development assistance at highly concessionary terms, the trading of scientific and technological findings and the joint fostering of research and development from basic research to production and marketing. Such findings are tradable 'products' no less real than physical goods and services whose output needs to be encouraged by economic stimuli.

Third, gratuitous exchange undercuts the donor's export markets not only in the recipient CPE but subsequently in other parts of the region as well. Furthermore, as most of this aid-on-request was rarely motivated by genuine economic considerations, the exchange was not necessarily in the direction of markets where other production factors were available in such a composition that the recipient country could produce the product in an economically justified way. That is, the total return on the investment per dollar or ruble may have been inferior than if a proper price had been charged to guide the allocation of other resources in accordance with their contemporaneous and prospective availability.

Fourth, once policymakers of the principal donor countries become fully aware of the benefits forgone and the costs incurred in this free exchange of STC, they may attempt to withhold the most up-to-date information, which they can do simply by refusing to respond to a request by the potential recipient. The information blackout can also be sustained by shielding one's own technological accomplishments – not too difficult in the context of the closed, at times even paranoid, society fostered in the traditional CPE. Such dissimulation may steer structural change in the recipient countries in the 'wrong' direction. In some cases, it led partners interested in an economic exchange to deliberate about alternative, sometimes very complex and ingenious, forms of STC in order to circumvent the gratuity rule and to reduce the inhibition to share new technology. The quintessential example here is *Haldex*, for which Hungarian technological knowledge constituted the primary capital contribution in the joint Hungarian-Polish enterprise (see Brabant, 1977, pp. 285–9; Brabant, 1988c, 1988d).

Fifth, and perhaps most detrimental, free exchange inhibited the steady progress with scientific and technological knowledge even in the more advanced countries, and it certainly did little to enable the less fortunate CPEs to carve out some proper markets for themselves. Admittedly, the

Sofia Principle itself cannot be blamed for all the shortcomings with technological progress in the traditional CPE. Those systemic drawbacks should definitely not be invoked in buttressing the 'paradigm of the exchange of inefficiency' (Sobell, 1986, p. 136) within the CMEA region. This may be an attractive notion as it permits capturing in a compact, perhaps superficially appealing, way some of the problems faced by the CPEs. But it is simply not acceptable unless the following proposition can be refuted or the next one proved. Inasmuch as the technology acquired through STC in the CMEA was superior to that already in place and available at virtually no cost, the inefficiency paradigm, as already intimated, can be upheld only if the return on the investment from the no-cost STC in the end remained inferior to what could have been obtained from investing in an alternative technology, possibly one acquired at a high cost from DMEs. I am not sure *a priori* whether the balance of the proposition would have been in favor of the alternative technology, as Sobell implicitly affirms without any reservation. Even if it were to support his thesis, two questions remain. Would such transfer have been possible given the Western embargo? And, would the CPE in question have been able to obtain appropriate and timely financing? I have no strong evidence to provide a satisfactory answer to either question. But I suspect that at the time the cost of acquiring Western technology may have been exorbitant, at least in the short to medium run.

Whatever argument one might wish to advocate, I readily admit that gratis STC was far from costless in the medium to long run from the point of view of the group as a whole and even occasionally from the perspective of individual participants. It most certainly failed to exert pressure for altering the already lethargic process of indigenous innovation embedded in the traditional CPE model as a result of effective foreign competition.

These and related drawbacks of the decade-long free exchange of STC generated a growing sentiment on the part of the more-developed CPEs toward withholding newer findings and insisting upon developmental costs being shared by those actually or potentially interested in exploiting the knowledge acquired in the process. This attitude crystallized in part from the perceived profit forgone as a result of free exchange. But also, beginning in the early 1960s, as the more-developed CPEs gradually began to participate in global trade in patents and licenses, the losses entailed by prolonging their technological 'generosity' were quickly highlighted. For reasons examined by Brabant (1988c), it took nearly another decade – until the thirtieth meeting of the Executive Committee in July 1967 – before the formal principle was, at least officially, slightly relaxed. Indeed, the practice of recognizing *ad hoc* forms of compensation had already started much earlier on more than a trivial scale (Gatzka, 1985, pp. 46–7; Monkiewicz, 1975, p. 91). The Executive Committee's ruling of 1967, as well as subsequent elaborations, permitted payments to the country of origin in the case of costly projects and when the recipient stood to make substantial financial gains. But that, of course, called for a more vigorous place for money and finance in the CMEA.

Once it was recognized that the compulsory free exchange should be abandoned, one of the key problems emanating from this accounting framework revolved around pricing, how to determine appropriate payment and in what ways this transfer was to be effected. As noted, the pricing problem continues to be the central conundrum in CMEA relations, and this is particularly true for STC. Even the commodity character of scientific-technological knowledge is something about which controversy continues in more than one respect.[1] It harks back to the epistemology of commodity in the Marxian framework as suitably interpreted by Soviet practitioners, especially until the late 1950s. The accounting problem is inherent in determining how to charge for technological information and research. Within the CMEA framework, it is greatly compounded by the usual difficulties relating to irrational prices and exchange rates, not to mention bilateralism and currency inconvertibility. The attempt to define charges that are proper and congruent with the habitual Bucharest principles has foundered because it is nearly impossible to identify 'proper' compensation for patents, inventions and related types of STC. The third bothersome aspect, how to effect payments for STC and blend them with other external transactions, derives from the absence of multilateralism, the intransferability of claims and, indeed, from currency and goods inconvertibility for the bulk of CMEA exchanges.

17.7 SPECIALIZATION AND MARKETING PRODUCTION

As outlined in chapter 13, production cooperation and specialization in the CMEA proceeds through specific ECPS and similar agreements. Most of these protocols are worked out at a high planning level, with the economic agents ultimately addressed being involved only peripherally. Decisions reached at the summit political level or in high-level interministerial committees are generally drawn up against the backdrop of less-than-complete information or even without the technical and economic details that are available to firms. Furthermore, as a rule they fail to provide the minimum economic incentives required to persuade or induce economic agents to restructure and balance out the necessary adjustments. It is primarily for that reason that specialization has usually been resorted to in an effort to avoid further duplication of capacity, to redistribute existing capacity or to introduce products that would be too costly if developed by one country alone. If economic agents themselves were allowed to make comprehensive explorations within overall guidelines set by macroeconomic policy in line with the precepts of central decision makers, specialization as traditionally aimed at in the CMEA could be given a real stimulus. In the process, the scope and depth of SEI could be measurably enhanced through ECPS agreements.

These observations can be supported by looking at the peculiar features of TRPs in the process of hammering out specialization agreements. Given that TRPs are not uniform and do not even approximately reflect real economic scarcities, decisions based on them may be highly misleading. This can be quite costly from the viewpoint of fostering regional economic cooperation. To pursue production specialization, a decision to proceed must be taken either on the flimsiest kind of evidence or on the basis of detailed examinations of very concrete production and marketing processes. Not only is this a costly and time-consuming operation, it is also one that discourages and impedes venturesomeness and initiative, including technological innovation. Such drawbacks become particularly pronounced during the formulation and implementation of economic reforms, as will be examined in the next section.

Even if agreements reached at the usual high rung of the planning hierarchy had been fully implemented as envisaged when negotiated, they would still have fallen far short of providing partner countries with the amount of assured supplies that can usually be obtained from processes coming within the compass of domestic planning controls. This is particularly the case for what has been the most dynamic segment of international trade in recent decades: trade in parts, assemblies and components. Enhancing such flows has been one of the ostensible goals of ECPS agreements at least since the early 1970s. Nonetheless, among existing ECPS agreements and even among those signed but not yet implemented, a serious bias toward final goods can be detected. This particular predilection is the result of national resistance to becoming more dependent on foreign markets as well as the other way around. Because production, not just the satisfaction of final demand, is crucially a function of obtaining parts, assemblies and components on time and of the requisite quality, countries are even more reluctant to become dependent on a CMEA partner for these than they are in the case of final goods. Turning to another CPE for supplies is bound to be fraught with uncertainties because a manager holds no control – legally or otherwise – over the supply of the parts, assemblies and components on which his domestic performance critically depends.

National reluctance to become dependent on foreign supplies or foreign demand for a large part of production, which itself may consist of foreign supplies, depends importantly on the lack of incentives to deliver their committed goods, of the quality specified and on schedule. In all CPEs bonuses depend on meeting sales, cost reduction, profit and related targets. These can all more easily be met by concentrating on the domestic market than by going for exports. Moreover, if export targets are trampled upon, there is usually little repercussion in terms of the bonus structure embedded in the domestic planning situation. The same reluctance appears even while implementing the agreement unless it is associated with the appropriation of resources not otherwise committed. Managers of existing firms are loath to dismantle the production of goods – including parts, assemblies and components – for which production lines have already been set up, the labor force trained and the sources of material-technical supply established. This peculiar aspect of adhering in practice to agreements hammered out by ministerial bureaucrats is but one extension of the more general aversion to innovation and change, however minuscule, exhibited by CPE managers. This does not necessarily stem from the innate conservatism of firms or local planners, though that as well as ignorance may play a role. Perhaps more important is the inadequate incentive system. Now, what is lacking with respect to domestic policy intentions is but one aspect of the key elements missing from the foundations required to foster regional competition in its widest sense.

17.8 ECONOMIC REFORM IN THE CONTEXT OF MARKET DICHOTOMIES

One drawback of becoming integrated into an economic environment dominated by traditional CPE features has become particularly clear to countries that aim at comprehensive economic reform. The conflict is simply this. The reforming CPE depends for at least half – in some cases up to four-fifths – of its external commerce on the CMEA, primarily the Soviet Union. At the same time, it predicates its reform ambitions to a substantial degree on the acceleration of external commerce – notably including with CMEA partners. Yet, the pivot of the economic reform itself revolves around managerial decentralization and coordinating independent microeconomic decisions through the various indirect instruments and institutions summarized in Part III. The conflict quickly materializes and calls for special measures to buffer the domestic economy against the dysfunctional features emanating from trading with the CMEA. This is especially complicated when the pivotal CMEA partner – the Soviet Union – is not interested in seeking broad-based reforms anchored to the devolution of decision making. This was the condition that prevailed until the second half of the 1980s.

In fact, the functional separation of domestic decision making from trading with CPE partners implies that the critical components of the reform can only be implemented toward one part of the trading world – that is, most of the capitalist countries. As for CPE partners, business as usual prevails. This is difficult to reconcile with the envisioned devolution of decision making. Overcoming this obstacle would entail the simulation of efficient decision making by central planners or ministries, which is something they increasingly failed to do well before the reform. It was for that particular reason, as well as for others, that the reform was embraced in the first place. In other words, this has constituted an especially cumbersome vicious circle that only now may have a chance of being broken if CPE leaders, even without Rumania, are genuinely seeking to enhance a unified CMEA 'market.'

In this context, critically important is the real conundrum engendered by the sharp dichotomies between TRPs and EWPs. Apart from assessing their formidable statistical problems, these divergences impair the formulation of more effective decision making by economic agents who face multiple relative prices that are only poorly interrelated. The situation may be variously remedied. One answer could be to identify goods and services traded by the CPE with both areas or in terms of the goods that it has not explicitly proscribed from being traded with both areas. A more general solution could aim at taking advantage of a comprehensive reallocation of resources in favor of the trade sector. Two separate issues arise in this connection. First, given the dichotomy between TRPs and EWPs, how can socialist managers hope to instill greater realism in domestic price formation without first bridging the gap in trade prices? Second, because most CMEA members have complained about the unsuitability of the TRP system for SEI, could not the need to formulate positive adjustment policies in several of the smaller countries be seized upon as a unique opportunity for revising the present TRP system and putting regional cooperation on a more solid footing, at least from the economic point of view? This issue is taken up in chapter 18.

The defects of the CMEA as an economic decision-making zone and as an outlet for the more buoyant trade envisioned by reformers are not limited to the existence of BTPAs that call for settlements mainly in TR and at odd TRPs, when compared with the emulation of WMP tendencies in the domestic economy. Fundamentally, they inhibit formulating efficient decisions, unless these are guided mainly by the reforming CPE's perception of WMPs and the willingness of governmental organs to buffer the implicit losses and gains in CMEA trade for the sake of proceeding with the reform while simultaneously minimizing disruptive impacts on relations with fraternal countries.

NOTE

1. For pertinent details, see Dietzel, 1988; Engel, 1988; Schelling, 1988; Schneider, 1984. Rusmich (1988, p. 56) recently called for doing away with 'prices that are not prices and money that is not money', as one way of ridding the CPEs of the noncommodity or anticommodity theory of the socialist economy.

18 · REFORM OF THE CMEA AND SEI

National economic and related reforms as well as shifts in the SEI mechanisms have been under serious review since the mid-1980s. In addition to SEI being at the forefront of discussions at the CMEA level, national policymakers, including in the USSR, have exhibited genuine concern about changing ways of pursuing SEI. Because this debate has not yet been settled and ample room for serious reflection remains, a realistic alternative mode of CMEA cooperation can be anchored to the drawing up of, what I call, a constitutional framework for SEI. I conceptualize such a framework largely within the context of, especially, Hungarian and Polish (see Kowalik, 1986) views on desirable economic reforms for which one can now also muster support from ongoing discussions, most notably in the USSR.

This chapter does not present a fleshed-out blueprint for an alternative form of SEI. It principally focuses on the lessons that could be usefully drawn from the recent economic experiences of the European planned economies, the ferment about economic reforms or changes in economic mechanisms, the shifting stances on the most desirable policy measures to foster 'economic intensification' nationally and regionally and how to proceed from the current situation to a more desirable alternative. I shall proceed largely by reinterpreting the current debate about direct interfirm relations and the joint enactment of a positive structural adjustment policy as posited in CMEA debates since the early 1980s. Such a policy must be tailored to the institutional and other requirements of the region, the aspirations of policymakers – particularly regarding the desirable levels of interaction with global trade and financial networks – and the preferred degree of combining relative domestic policy autonomy with CMEA-wide 'security of supply' considerations.

Section 18.1 presents a brief sequence of crucial, partly coincidental, factors that may lead to the eventual endorsement of a constitutional framework in the CMEA as an essential ingredient in accommodating more buoyant growth policies. This is meant as a guide through the multitude of CMEA characteristics that must be taken into account, but which cannot be fully integrated here, to properly evaluate the proposal advanced in the final section. The next section diagnoses the developmental problems that inhibit a swift resumption of growth through familiar instruments, institutions and policies. Section 18.3 illustrates the gradually shifting stances concerning the proper economic policies to be adopted for weathering the storms of the early 1980s and fostering long-term economic growth. In connection with long-term growth, section 18.4 considers the alternative development paths available to CPEs, and section 18.5 examines the emerging reforms in key countries. Because these incipient reforms are still incompletely defined, I next outline major features of a constitutional framework for promoting SEI and reinvigorating the antiquated CMEA institutions, policies and cooperation mechanisms. In the final section, I evaluate what chance the course advocated here has of materializing any time soon.

18.1 THE MAJOR DETERMINANTS OF CHANGE

Instead of projecting the lessons of the past onto a broad canvas of postwar economic policies (see Part I), here I identify key pointers for change in the CMEA from the sequence of unsettling economic experiences, particularly of the early 1980s, and the uncertain outlook for more buoyant economic activity in the years ahead. This uncertainty follows in good measure from the strongly defensive nature of the economic policies embraced during the early 1980s to manage unforeseen events in the CMEA as well as from the largely fortuitous global developments in international capital markets, the multilateral trade framework and international price adjustments. Section 18.2 briefly reviews the major growth and trade prospects of the entire region.[1]

As discussed in chapter 6, the emergency adjustment measures embraced in the first half of the 1980s helped reduce external constraints principally by slashing investments, curbing consumption growth and suppressing imports from DMEs. This cannot be a long-term development strategy because it does not permit steady growth. Defensive, reactive adjustment undercuts the efforts of the CPEs to legitimize their overall sociopolitical precepts through comparatively stable annual rises in *per capita* incomes – something that most CPEs have had difficulty sustaining since the late 1970s. As a result, a positive structural adjustment policy needs to be developed; that is, a package of proactive development objectives and policy initiatives that tackle institutional as well as behavioral features so as to quickly regain a higher-level growth path without creating chronic domestic or any external imbalances.

Clearly, there are several ways in which the CPEs could redirect their growth efforts. Greater integration in global trade and financial networks by vigorously exploiting their true static and dynamic comparative advantages provides one avenue and would place the CPEs in a better strategic position in the global economy. Another mode primarily calls for bolstering regional economic cohesion and the security of supply and demand as well as protecting the region against untoward outside events. Finally, in principle, the countries could turn inward – that is, look for ways to substitute for imports at the national level. Although I do not view this as a credible option, various CPE policymakers early in the 1980s did seriously contemplate it as a plausible escape from the prevailing economic stringencies; some, including Rumania, have actually been pursuing such policies simply to eliminate at any cost the foreign debt.

The third principal development is the change in Soviet leadership and the greater attention being devoted to economics as a decision-making technique. Gorbačëv's strong emphasis on the need to improve domestic productive efficiency is certain to generate direct and indirect ripple effects for the main partner countries. Direct effects emerge in view of the alleged cost of Soviet participation in the CMEA and the foreign trade impacts of economic reform. Indirect repercussions ensue from the *de facto* preeminent role of the USSR in Eastern Europe. Thus, economic reform in the major CMEA actor will, of necessity, elicit some fine tuning of economic mechanisms in partner countries. This is especially important at a time when, independently of Soviet changes, several CPEs have been significantly experimenting with new ways and means of reinvigorating their economic performance.

Finally, it is striking that the recent economic crises of Eastern Europe evolved, at least until late 1987, without measurable repercussions on the CMEA organization, the collective development and integration policies enshrined in official documents or on the exceedingly passive policy instruments and related existing monetary and other institutions. This passivity has been especially surprising given the agitation for substantive changes that eventually prompted the economic summits and subsequent top-level meetings (see chapter 6). Moreover, except for the extraordinary case of Poland since 1981, even at the bilateral level, as distinct from multilateral collaboration within the formal regional institutional framework, each CPE has largely had to fend for itself. In fact, unanticipated external constraints emanating from world markets in the early 1980s were sharply aggravated by simultaneous and subsequent CMEA developments, although these were not necessarily causally related. The passivity of the CMEA setup is likely to change under the impact of ongoing transitions in domestic policies, institutions and policy instruments in several countries, particularly now that the USSR is a major contestant in comprehensively exploring the envisioned institutional modifications. It would be most extraordinary if these transformations failed to mandate palpable adjustments in CMEA policies, institutions and organizational behavior.

18.2 GROWTH PROSPECTS AND PREVAILING IMBALANCES

Although the severity of development obstacles during the medium-term and annual plans of the 1980s varied widely among countries, certain common traits can be identified. The problems resulted in part from unanticipated domestic and external events in these countries, which largely remained beyond their control. Some problems could have been avoided or their impacts eased had proper and more timely adjustment policies been embraced, especially in the late 1970s. Others, however, primarily emerged as a consequence of national and international policies over which the CPEs individually or as a group had little influence.

Although not all factors can be explored in depth here, it might be useful to highlight a few of the domestic, external, exogenous and endogenous elements that influenced developments in the 1980s. Among the structural issues, four stand out: faulty policy choices made a decade or so earlier; inadequately anticipated shifts in the traditional CMEA cooperation mechanisms; failure to rationalize economic structures on a timely basis in line with transformations in domestic and external growth opportunities; and the culmination of successive delays in implementing effective measures to move away from engrained policies that favored extensive growth. Many of these components linger on and cast a pall over prospects for accelerating performance in the years ahead; this in spite of the fact that the depth and range of unplanned external and domestic growth constraints encountered in the early 1980s have been pivotal in changing attitudes toward managing a CPE.

Instead of enumerating all factors, I shall summarize those constraints that are of a longer-term nature and *can*, therefore, be addressed in development plans, as distinct from fluctuating CMEA and global economic factors. Some can be influenced through appropriate domestic and regional policies. Others, however, by their nature are largely exogenous, at least for the isolated CPE. In considering these multifaceted influences on development prospects, it may be useful to separate primary resource availability from intermediate resources, and indeed from the disposal of total product.

18.2.1 Domestic growth constraints

Fairly steady additions to the factor input stream have been the principal element in most of Eastern Europe's postwar growth. To the extent that the CPEs still possess underutilized production factors, they can continue to prop up such extensive development policies. But simple resource mobilization for the modern industrial sector is no longer a viable option for most countries in light of their domestic and external development constraints. It is not even a desirable one for countries that still have the option of pursuing such a course for a while longer.

The internal factors that complicate the resumption of sustained growth at the rate experienced during most of the postwar period can be separated into two distinct groups. On the one hand, the future volume and distribution of primary production factors is bound to be more constrained than during the past four decades, no matter what policy configuration is chosen. The explanation of constraints on labor, natural resources and land given in chapter 6 could simply be reiterated. Regarding capital, however, several demand and supply determinants must be kept in mind.

The future demand for capital resources can be divided into six parts:

1. Consumer-related services, including housing, education, social services and various types of product services in the broad sense.
2. Measures that enhance the well-being and long-term strength of a society, including pollution control and environmental protection.
3. The easing of capacity constraints in transportation, energy generation and raw material production.
4. Implementation of programs that foster factor productivity gains.
5. Enhancement of SEI and technological progress.
6. The restructuring of output profiles to strengthen the quality and range of competitive supplies.

The claims on resources to initiate new projects to enhance factor productivity have steadily been growing in recent years. Along with the need to improve the quality of output, and hence competitiveness in foreign markets, investment demand in the material sphere has also risen. This surge has gathered strength at a time of relatively slow output growth, which has left little room for raising aggregate savings. Moreover, it has been forced to compete with an even more rapidly rising demand for capital resources in nonmaterial sectors, especially in infrastructure, transport, communication, sociocultural facilities, housing and consumer services. These may boost labor morale and improve the productive environment, but the benefits are unlikely to materialize overnight. Therefore, the outlook is for a moderate recovery in the physical supply of capital funds available for productive purposes, certainly on average below the feasible pace of total investment growth.

Though prevailing institutions and policy instruments determine feasible output combinations with given resource endowments, this environment is not altogether impervious to change. Proper policy measures can recast the development strictures embedded in factor availabilities, at least in the medium run. In fact, as most exogenous constraints are endogenous in the longer run, timely policy measures could offset some adverse developments and might even forestall their emergence.

18.2.2 External development conditions

When it comes to external conditions, it is difficult to separate exogenous constraints from those susceptible to proper policies. In parallel with the discussion of domestic factors, I find it useful to treat as exogenous the flexibility available to the CPEs in augmenting factor supply from outside the CMEA. Labor migration is usually proscribed (Brabant, 1987a, pp. 302–10). Capital inflow into Eastern Europe is not actively encouraged because policymakers fear a recurrence of the dysfunctional constraints on their economic sovereignty that appeared in the early 1980s. The CPEs are not completely averse to borrowing in financial markets, however. Indeed, the setbacks in plan implementation incurred in 1985–8 were somewhat offset through new loans. Furthermore, global financial centers are reluctant to invest in the area unless major organizational and managerial changes are enacted. Though it has recently been provided for in the modified joint venture laws of several CMEA countries, direct foreign investment is unlikely to make a quantum leap unless the members' decision-making mechanisms become more compatible with those typical of market-oriented economies.

Whereas factor mobility cannot be an expansive source of growth under the self-imposed and prevailing institutional and other features of the CPEs, trading in goods and services is largely a function of proper policies. Here too the institutional and systemic issues that confined trade in the early 1980s should be recalled. Existing economic structures are not well adapted to competing effectively in world markets, and, as recent experience has underscored, change can be sought individually or in the groupwide context only gradually. Because of their typical decision-making processes and organizational features, structural change in anticipation of or in response to shifts in real comparative costs cannot occur spontaneously in the traditional CPE but must be planned. A major dilemma thus arises. Planned structural change can ultimately succeed only if the detailed prerogatives vested in small groups of central planners are devolved; that is, if they yield some measure of economic sovereignty to economic agents, in part to bolster participation in international trade. Opening up such communication channels may entail other transitions that decision makers still perceive as inimical to a socialist society.

In addition to the overall external economic outlook, the conditions for medium-term regional cooperation will be greatly affected by regional output constraints for basic materials and by limitations on boosting export revenues from traditional manufactures – to date the backbone of the intra-CMEA commodity exchange pattern. Compared to the CMEA, world demand is more exacting and subject to stiffer competition,[2] particularly following the transformations in trade markets that occurred in the mid-1970s.[3] Therefore, it is more difficult to earn convertible currency than to raise an equivalent TR amount at prevailing exchange rates, even though for some CPEs the gap has considerably narrowed in recent years. Unless regional trading, financial and other cooperation mechanisms are re-vamped, this compounds the already substantial restrictions on attaining more suitable production modes, renewing capital assets, shifting economic structures and redesigning trade patterns.

18.3 TOWARD A RENEWAL OF POLICIES AND INSTITUTIONS

The above backdrop suggests that the CPEs should recast their growth ambitions in line with gains in factor productivity feasible under prevailing or changing institutions and policies. Though the legacies from the past as they affect factor supplies – as well as those legacies embedded in existing policies, institutions and instruments – pose formidable impediments to more buoyant factor productivity growth, some positive measures can nonetheless be taken. Modifying existing policy instruments and reshaping the supporting institutions will definitely create room for maneuvering. For example, capital replacement can be rationalized, the investment process can be accelerated, better use and proper maintenance of existing facilities are entirely possible and some assets are fungible. These and other modifications can be variously achieved, but one of the more productive ways would be by formulating a structural adjustment policy in a truly regional approach. Such growth intensification ranks high among the policy priorities of individual CPEs, some of whom will undoubtedly reap con-siderable future benefits. Two sets of circumstances hamper implementing these intentions. One derives from the state of these economies or from the cumulative legacies of past policy mistakes. Furthermore, most CPEs have a highly confined market, and the CMEA itself cannot provide sufficient support for ambitious national reforms without itself undergoing substantial transformation, which will be discussed in the next sections.

In light of the setbacks encountered in the early 1980s, several CPE policy-makers have stressed that resuming faster growth at a fairly steady pace critic-ally depends on bolstering factor productivity through growth intensification. This is admittedly reminiscent of the involved debates of the 1960s. However, the determination with which a new strategy is now being envisioned is much more convincing than in the past. The stance by key policymakers that such policies hinge on devolving decision making to local planning agents has been strengthened. The conviction that a shift in the direction of policies and management requires adequate material incentives to bolster centrally set guidelines has also been growing. Furthermore, many policymakers admit that it is difficult to engineer a strong and sustainable boost to factor productivity solely on the basis of national productive forces. Trade in general and CMEA economic intercourse in particular deserve special attention.

How best to reshape the CPEs in the years ahead fundamentally depends on the unique circumstances present at this particular juncture in Eastern Europe's postwar economic evolution. These special features critically hinge on the apparent commitment of many CPEs, most notably including the USSR, to enact positive domestic adjustment policies as well as to seek regional supports. Especially important in this drive has been the determination by current Soviet leaders to tackle the root causes of the USSR's growth slowdown. The spirit of renewal in the Soviet Union has cross-fertilized the development ambitions of other CMEA leaders, including through a transformation of traditional regional cooperation practices, which may eventually promote SEI into a significant growth determinant.

Given the debates around the two recent economic summits, the concurrent and subsequent meetings of the CCS and the ensuing Council Sessions (see chapter 6), there is now hope that new economic policies, more subtle and differentiated policy instruments and restructured supporting institutions will soon slowly emerge throughout Eastern Europe. But such transformations will need to affect more than just the domain of policy design. Perhaps more critical will be fresh approaches in the variety and reach of the instruments by which policymakers guide domestic and regional economic decisions. This in turn depends on the degree of trade dependence or policy autonomy desired.

Three important features of the CPEs have been crystallizing around recent developments. For one, as summarized in section 18.5, an unequivocal tendency throughout Eastern Europe has emerged for pursuing more active policies in areas other than central planning. A second major consideration has been the perception that economic planning cannot be settled in detail at the central level forever. This realization is somewhat associated with the growing complexity of economic structures and with the greater differentiation of domestic policy priorities away from the simple requirement to maximize industrial growth *per se*. This reformulation of economic decision making has proposed revamping the MFT's control and regulation of external commerce. Also, in view of important shifts in WMPs and TRPs, managers have become increasingly confronted with the problem of how to ensure stability without stifling activity in the economy as a whole. Trade prices are being factored into domestic prices with a minimum of delay, especially in Bulgaria, Hungary and Poland.

These observations point to the presence of instances in which pivotal CPE policy objectives and instruments have been undergoing major perturbations. Unfortunately, these changes have not yet been integrated into a coherent, well-planned strategy for structural change. Given the growing strains in CMEA economic relations and that the new leadership in the Soviet Union is determined to correct several major factors behind the economic slowdown, a significant transformation of the traditional cooperation mechanisms may well be in the offing.

18.4 LOOKING OUTWARD OR TURNING INWARD?

Individually and as a group, the CPEs could counteract the negative effects of the aforementioned external pressures through broad import substitution, vigorous export promotion or by raising their external debt. Conceivably, growth intensification could be pursued in isolation.[4] A conscious inward-turning by magnifying the import curbs enacted since the late 1970s could ease the constraints emanating from the payments deficit and the debt. But such a policy shift is unlikely to yield sustainable results because national markets in Eastern Europe are too small. Even the USSR needs to procure foodstuffs and technology from abroad. In other words, it is hard to see how a strong and sustainable boost to factor productivity might be independently engineered.

Owing to their size and resource endowment, in the years ahead most of the smaller CPEs will, for two reasons, need to diversify their procurements of fuels and raw materials. The region's output is likely at best to only show modest gains, even if present constraints can be eased. Also, output levels can only be sustained at sharply rising costs. To diversify sources of imports, the one viable strategy is all-around export promotion. This requires that structural adjustments be made to enable trade advantages to be exploited, not only by marshaling opportunities in the CMEA but also by adopting a suitable global trade profile. While true that prevailing circumstances confine the CPEs' maneuverability in enacting remedial policies, the circumstances vary among countries. At least conceptually, reformers certainly agree that the strategy should be directed at actively exploring external markets and strengthening the competitive position of their economies. However, I fear that the CPE leadership is not yet willing to freely adjust to global competition and cannot, either, for long afford to muddle through or simply bulge the external debt. The range of alternatives is thus largely conditioned by the need to gradually restructure the traditional intra-CMEA trade pattern as the foundation of genuine SEI. For this to be feasible, the smaller CPEs must make the main CMEA producer of hard goods, especially energy, sufficiently interested in expanding production and regional trade.

While true that the USSR has been deriving a substantial proportion of its convertible currency earnings from fuels that it cannot possibly forgo in the short run without reshaping its import profile, this is neither a compelling nor a logical argument for advising the CPEs to vigorously explore East-West ties. I see at least two reasons for this. First, owing to the palpable adjustments that are required, any attempt to rapidly switch markets entails a sharp recession, which CPE leaders cannot, from a sociopolitical and strategic standpoint, afford. But neither is it desirable to prolong the current economic malaise. Second, the argument that the USSR could not, under any circumstance, be persuaded to supply Eastern Europe with what it needs, possibly by diverting goods earmarked for DMEs, is implausible. But I recognize that the CPEs have set limits on the opportunity cost they are willing to incur for the sake of CMEA cohesiveness, including adhering to quantum targets when terms of trade shift and balance-of-payments disturbances thus arise.

In contrast to the thesis that the prevailing CMEA trade pattern cannot be sustained, I should like to briefly restate an alternative elaborated elsewhere (Brabant, 1987a, pp. 399–401; Brabant, 1987c, pp. 97–9). It rests on the conjecture that the foundations of a more buoyant near-term growth pattern must be solidified through a multipronged approach. Mechanisms must be found to sustain the exchange of the bulk of primary goods and fuels most CPEs need against manufactures that they can produce with some degree of comparative advantage. Short-term diversion of this trade to third markets can be entertained only at great cost in terms of a ballooning foreign debt or sizable cuts in the population's standard of living – both are ill affordable at this stage. At the same time, real cost structures should be enhanced to regulate demand and supply, and especially to foster the modernization of manufacturing sectors. Although initially focused on intragroup trade and the coordination of investments among the CPEs, this strategy also recognizes the necessity of encouraging the *gradual* substitution of imports from DEs for domestic and regional production processes that are intensive in labor and primary goods and to supply local markets with sophisticated manufactures from DMEs without greatly straining external payments. As such, East-West and East-South commerce constitutes a central pivot of the above scenario. To modernize manufacturing branches, including to meet Soviet demands, Eastern Europe especially cannot forgo imports of selective technology that cannot otherwise be procured. This hardening of the product mix offered may require even more convertible currency imports than those already embodied in its CMEA exports. Any misalignment in relative TRPs should be rectified by modifying policy instruments rather than through administrative intervention.

Such a strategy embodies a demanding policy agenda and no easy solution of the implied dilemmas is at hand. To maintain the attractiveness of the traditional CMEA trading pattern, measures should be enacted that induce producers to foster output for economic reasons. Eastern European countries must face the fact that the era of facile exchange of below-standard manufactures for fuels and primary goods is a relic of the past and that the type of exchange they previously wedded themselves to cannot be further perpetuated.

Perhaps the major thread that links the story outlined above is dual-spun. Countries appear to realize that resuming faster growth depends on enacting domestic and regional structural adjustment policies. In this strategy, forging greater regional economic cohesion is critical if constraints on more buoyant future growth policies are to be counteracted. Moreover, it would be a serious mistake to assume that the preference for CMEA cooperation, over and above the possibilities of domestic expansion and of economic relations with third partners, is indiscriminate. There is undoubtedly a strong preference for CMEA collaboration in certain areas. But there are also other endeavors for which absolute regional sovereignty would impose too high a price. In other words, among the range of preferences for SEI arrangements, there must be a turning point that separates those regional endeavors the CPEs will fully finance and those for which they may, at best, prefer to pay partially. That is, given their national and regional preferences, the CPEs cannot be expected to ignore their dynamic comparative advantages (Fröhlich, 1987; Grote and Kühn, 1986).

18.5 RESUMING FASTER ECONOMIC GROWTH

On the strength of the arguments presented in section 18.2, most CPEs appear to have little capacity for accelerating the pace of growth through probable factor growth or redistribution. In fact, it will be very difficult to slow down or reverse the redistribution required by the social and other commitments made during the past fifteen years. It is doubtful whether the adverse production impact of unfulfilled expectations on effective labor availability can be avoided. The only way out, then, is by gradually increasing policy maneuverability. Improved economic performance through shifts in the methods and goals of economic policies is critical in this regard. Similar hindrances seemingly reside in the system-specific features of CPE policies, institutions and instruments that are not well geared toward spontaneously propping up reform measures.

Boosting factor productivity levels is to some degree a function of proper incentives. These in turn critically hinge on shifts in economic mechanisms. Modifications in policy instruments and their supporting institutions can render the development environment more sensitive to the preconditions necessary for factor productivity growth. As detailed elsewhere (see Brabant, 1987a, pp. 403–7; Brabant, 1987c), moving away from the CPE context to a more decentralized environment that enhances lower-level decision making and accountability not only requires proper macroeconomic policies and institutions but also well-defined behavioral rules for integrating the decisions of decentralized agents with economywide ambitions. These measures should primarily focus on indirect coordination instruments and supporting institutions, including those in the CPEs' regional organizations. Other institutions as well may be required to formulate appropriate monetary, fiscal and income policies that support indirect economic coordination.

Looking at the individual CPE, the most important levers to be activated are wholesale prices (which must be anchored to trade prices), effective exchange and interest rates, wage compensation based on performance, much more active consumer prices, greater coordination of the economy as a whole according to clearly identified parameters that are set in line with social profitability criteria and more active credit policies. Perhaps of the utmost importance is rule certainty for all economic agents. This presupposes that the room allowed for lower-level decision making be clearly delineated and that the interests of economic agents be reflected in the criteria by which they reach their decisions. If the basic premises of the socialist economy can be separated from its more incidental features, such modifications in the 'economic mechanisms' of the CPEs are entirely plausible.

It would be unwise to advocate a greater parameterization of the CPEs' economic environment without addressing the need to transform domestic and regional institutions. Medium- to long-term structural policy issues should become the primary concern of each planning center. Included should be such issues as income distribution, aggregate savings and investment, the nonmaterial sphere, productive infrastructure and, especially, the evolving situation of the economy. Most other decisions can be reached at the enterprise level through macroeconomic guidance, which would include income, monetary and fiscal problems. It is also crucial to foster greater competition, if not within each economy then at least among CMEA members and, where possible, also with enterprises of third markets. Trade guidance can be provided indirectly through an effective tariff policy, the abolition of nonparametric subsidies and taxes that buffer domestic from foreign prices and an active exchange rate policy.

In recognition of some of the obstacles identified here, since the mid-1980s the CPEs have been seriously concerned about economic reforms. To summarize in just a few paragraphs the domestic reforms that various CPEs are currently implementing or contemplating is obviously a daunting task. Although divergent approaches can be utilized for 'intensifying economic activity,' some pointers can be identified by elaborating on the key indicators in the national economies that should have some counterpart in the CMEA economic mechanism.

18.5.1 Autonomy of enterprise decision making

One critical reform lever is the devolution of decision-making authority and responsibility from the higher levels (planning offices, branch ministries and possibly the associations) to the ultimate economic units. In principle, there is substantial consensus about the degree to which entrepreneurial decision making should be devolved to the firm, subject to macroeconomic guidance rules. Firms need greater latitude in setting input and output mixes and prices, in determining individual wages and bonuses proportionate to actual profits, in borrowing from banks at realistic scarcity interest rates and in taking greater entrepreneurial risk, with rewards particularly accruing for technological progress. To what extent this is actually being realized in the various reforms is a different matter of course. Especially important to consider is that the transition phase of this devolution has only recently been initiated and that these microeconomic aspects of the *perestrojka* are largely still on the drafting board. For well-known reasons, firms do not seem to be very keen on assuming full responsibility on a *chozrasčët* basis.

18.5.2 Role of the banking sector

Virtually all European CPEs, except perhaps Rumania, have slated the monobanking system for decentralization. Hungary has been the most advanced in this respect. There the central bank has largely been transformed into a bank of issue and domestic lender of last resort that controls the money supply and manages the financial and monetary system. The more practical aspects of day-to-day banking have increasingly been left to specialized banks established for particular purposes, including regular banking business, investment, foreign trade and construction. In some of these branches, multiple banks compete for business. It is important to note that these specialized institutions have been called upon to provide banking services on a commercial basis within the guidelines set by macroeconomic policy, particularly the monetary policy of the central bank. Similar objectives have been coveted in the Bulgarian reform and are currently being considered in Poland and the USSR.

So far, financial reforms have not evolved proper interest rate policies for enforcing capital scarcity and motivating agents into productive saving. In the most stalwart CPEs, including Rumania and the Soviet Union until very recently, ideological inhibitions have kept interest rates at modest levels so that economic agents obtain loans that are not in fact rationed by economic means. Rarely has there been a serious effort to control the money supply by technical-economic reasons as opposed to rather crude *obiter dicta* and order.

18.5.3 The role of prices

Price reform is one of the most complex and politically sensitive tasks for all reforming economies, not just the CPEs, and is one that has undone reforms and reformers on more than one occasion. Price reform has certainly decelerated the pace of reform in those CPEs that have insisted on introducing serious modifications in institutions, policies and mechanisms. Considerable resistance to price reform is also likely to be met with from the population, enterprises and entrenched party and trade union interests. For decades, the population in most of these countries has been coached into believing that price stability is maintained under socialism.[5] Furthermore, low prices for essentials and high prices for all but a few primary manufactured goods have been upheld only because of governmental subsidy-*cum*-retail tax policies that are not necessarily balanced. Policymakers have found it increasingly counterproductive, as well as financially taxing, to maintain such distortions through large consumer price subsidies to avoid passing on the basic changes in trade prices (in CMEA relations and especially those incurred in relations with the West) and to command production and consumption decisions through physical appropriations. In other words, circumstances have compelled most CPEs to reevaluate their pronounced preference for stable prices. As a result, instead of the erstwhile predictable landscape of constant retail and inflexible wholesale prices with changes introduced on a comprehensive basis only after long intervals, since the late 1970s the situation has become increasingly differentiated. But price movements have varied in a noticeably distinct pattern depending on the country and the type of goods involved.

This multiplicity of approaches to pricing indicates that ample room for improvement continues to exist. A price reform has, then, several distinct aspects, including the level and structure of prices, the relationship between various domestic price tiers and the relationship between domestic and foreign trade prices. In addition, because serious sociopolitical facets of a CPE may be affected by the particular political choices made, intricate questions crop up in connection with the desired speed of price adjustment. Finally, the comprehensiveness of the reform and at what levels it should be carried out must be configured. But policymakers are weary of comprehensive price reform as this implies a redistribution of income, usually in favor of the better-to-do layers of society.[6] Yet, price reforms are essential not only for correctly assessing economic scarcities but also for providing economic agents with the guidelines necessary for decision making.

It is particularly important to distinguish between two broad types of price reform. Reforms may aim at the administrative restructuring of prices, basically so as to reset fiat prices in line with perceived domestic and import costs at a given moment in time. In some cases, however, the adaptability of the price structure over time is a major concern. In most countries, administrative restructuring has, at best, been envisaged and attained only very incompletely. Hungary alone has been committed to realizing price adaptability. Other countries (Bulgaria, Poland and the USSR) may have the same target ambition but are still far removed from anything like real implementation.

Price reform cannot be undertaken all at once without major socioeconomic shocks and disturbances that are intolerable in a socialist system. Hence, the reform is a process spread out over time, and the architecture of its intertemporal modifications is critical. In the most ambitious reforms, various price categories are usually stipulated (including fixed prices as in the traditional CPE; prices that can move up to, from or between certain limits; and free prices). Because of the dichotomy between producer and consumer prices in the CPE, these categories usually apply variously in these two spheres. Of course, a proper link between trade and domestic prices should be set.

To anchor such a link, it is critical to establish a realistic exchange rate, or a surrogate in the form of a multiplier, commercial exchange rate, internal exchange rate, reproduction coefficient or the like (Brabant, 1987a, pp. 198–207). In fact, price reform should be intimately intermeshed with the reform of the entire 'monetary-financial' sphere (Petrakov, 1987, p. 55). In most countries, such links are calculated on the basis of average ratios of some domestic prices and the prices of exported goods, usually manufactures, in the given trade structure at some discrete intervals. Such multipliers are usually set differently for broadly homogeneous currency groupings and, in many cases, for different commodity groups as well. Rarely have countries tried to let the exchange rate find its own equilibrium, with price adjustments undertaken in line with the government's pricing policy.

18.5.4 Foreign trade and payments regimes

Instead of maintaining the foreign trade and payments regime as a key pillar in support of substantial autonomy in domestic policy, most reforms seek to entrust greater responsibility, including self-financing, in trade to individual firms or to FTOs. In terms of requirements on the behavior of firms, this is quite a different environment from one in which FTOs are kept afloat through the price equalization applied to the strict provisions of BTPAs in the case of clearing trade and central prescriptions for trade with hard currency partners. Reforms usually address these two spheres separately.

Regarding convertible currency trade with MEs, producing or trading firms are permitted to autonomously engage in trade to the extent that foreign exchange can be earned from exports and made available for imports. Initially, these operations tend to be subject to export or import licenses, which are a prerequisite for obtaining the necessary foreign exchange. But this is usually transformed into foreign exchange licensing (as in Bulgaria) or auctioning (as in Poland). Most countries make an effort to take into account the real price of trade with nonsocialist economies either in the periodic resetting of domestic prices or through actual transaction prices. This is especially the case when a large share of trade in a particular product is transacted with third countries. Of necessity, real export revenues and import returns are considered when guiding the operations of autonomous trading agents. Convertible currency trade among the CMEA countries and with some other CPEs (China and Yugoslavia in particular) is usually managed separately.

Trade with clearing currency partners, particularly within the CMEA, is generally a very different story. For the isolated reforming CPE, such as Hungary for many years, there was little choice beyond buffering domestic pricing and decision making against CMEA currency and trade operations that could not be reconciled with the objectives of the new economic mechanism (see chapter 17). Now that the USSR is in the vanguard of the reform movement, the odds are better-than-even that not only will TRPs become more realistic but also that much greater scope will be allowed for direct interfirm relations so that the devolution objectives can be carried out.

18.5.5. Economic accountability

One basic objective of any economic reform is to associate enterprise autonomy with economic accountability – that is, self-financing and profitability. But the two need not coincide. Indeed, in many cases, they get divorced shortly after the reform is launched because authorities and managers tend to react to imbalances that are, in part, unleashed by the reform in ways that are reminiscent of the traditional CPE. The two can be effectively combined only if economic agents are given the proper signals and if they are then able to mold the level and composition of inputs and outputs according to what they perceive to be in their best interest. Because of the distortions in the valuation criteria typical of the CPE, enterprise accountability is generally fully attainable only after a long transition phase. With distorted prices, it would be counterproductive to expect economic agents to formulate decisions on the basis of the wrong signals and then to hold them accountable for that. One can hardly expect the right outcome for society as a whole from such instructions.

Even so, the situation is far from hopeless. Firms can be held accountable for managing capital and labor resources in a more responsible way than under strict planning, even though interest and wage rates are far from market clearing. In the same vein, enterprises *can* be asked to shoulder the burden of excessive inventories, or at least to pay more for hoarding material and capital resources than for productive resources. They can also be expected to show greater concern for proper pricing, inventory control, catering to user or final demand and so on. These partial ways of entrusting economic agents with more responsibility than they had under the central planning in vogue until recently fall well short of full-scale economic decentralization. But they do provide a useful first step in imparting meaning to the initial phases of the transition toward decentralization.

18.5.6 Interfirm cooperation

Interfirm cooperation is much more difficult to organize than is usually assumed, principally because there are so few parameters at the disposal of economic agents for devising among themselves effective wholesale trade contacts. But certainly areas of convergence can be seen. Economic agents are undoubtedly interested in endeavors on which it is hard to place a true scarcity cost in the *ex ante* sense. Research and development is one such area; at best one hopes to realize the expected gains, though the uncertainty of these is usually very high. The larger the uncertainty and the more exploratory the venture, the greater the opportunity for interfirm cooperation.

Matters are of yet another order of complexity when it comes to organizing contacts in production and marketing, though some areas of cooperation are at hand. For example, it may be beneficial to allow excess resources in one firm to be traded either intertemporally or in exchange for resources that are in relative shortage in one area provided a mutually satisfactory price can be negotiated. This is not likely to absorb all of the excesses and shortages because a price can be imputed to the uncertainty of acquiring the resources at some point in time when they might become urgently needed. But it is likely to contribute to fostering greater economic balance. Even with absolutely fixed fiat prices that are far removed from reflecting true scarcities, direct enterprise contracts may help to boost efficiency. But the potential for economic agents to make socially counterproductive microeconomic decisions is likely to be larger than otherwise or than needed.

Where precisely the drive toward interfirm negotiations may lead is anybody's guess. I suspect it is still largely a slogan. If genuine wholesale trade is to become a key component of a new development strategy, it must be given more concrete content and precise meaning in the evolving reform than has so far been done. This applies to both East-West and CMEA joint ventures or direct enterprise contacts. Regarding East-West ventures, I have the impression that the CPE is primarily intent on attracting capital, managerial expertise and technology from the West and on acquiring convertible currency through exports of the products thus generated. In contrast, the Western partner is likely to be predominantly interested in capitalizing on relatively cheap labor resources and conquering socialist markets. Particularly in the case of joint ventures with Eastern European countries, the size of the local market is not usually attractive.

18.5.7 The role of planning and macroeconomic policy

Appropriate macroeconomic policies realized within proper policy institutions are just as important as the effective introduction of indirect coordination instruments and their associated policy institutions for effective economic decentralization. Macroeconomic policies must effectively prop up and fine tune the policy instruments and, indeed, guide economic units in raising efficiency or factor productivity. Another task of macroeconomic policy – and here lies the central role of statewide planning – is structural change and revamping growth strategies, including through large-scale investment projects. Finally, central planning and macroeconomic policy need to maintain control over the so-called nonmaterial sphere; that is, all activities that are quintessentially socialistic in nature, such as education, medical care, the arts and basic infrastructure, or that are typically reserved for governmental action, such as defense.

Regarding the economic sphere as such, among the crucial macroeconomic policies that are traditionally primitive in the classical CPEs are monetary, fiscal and income policies. This backwardness stems from ideological precepts and especially the primacy of quantitative planning. The traditional management of credit in line with the so-called real bills' doctrine must be revised so that decentralized banks can grant loans that can be utilized to claim resources in the context of wholesale trading. Monetary policy should be activated and extended to many new economic activities to provide for macroeconomic stability, to allow the central bank to act as the effective lender of last resort for decentralized financial institutions, to regulate absorption that is congruent with available domestic and borrowed resources and to provide a greater diversity of assets to holders of currency balances. Such asset diversification can be created without necessarily encroaching on socialist ideology regarding property. For example, some acceptable ways in which this could be made compatible with the socialist market economy concept are examined in Nuti, 1987a.

18.6 ON A CONSTITUTIONAL FRAMEWORK FOR SEI

Given present knowledge of what may be in the offing regarding reforms, two primary characteristics must be kept in mind. First, there is every indication that the goals of the contemplated changes in economic mechanisms are unlikely to coincide throughout the region. This holds even if one only searches for the most important elements of economic policies and the functioning of economies that are, or aspire toward becoming, tightly intermeshed. Second, the process of moving toward a new configuration of policies and institutions is bound to be protracted and painful. Decision makers cannot expect a decisive lift in economic performance as a result of system tinkering in the near future, say within the next three to five years. Instead, they should be prepared to steer and nurse along their prevailing mechanisms toward a reformed economy for at least a decade, even if no further changes in the target model were to come forward in the process of implementing the reform – a highly unlikely eventuality. This imposes formidable requirements not only on the design and intentions of the reform but more importantly on how to introduce processes that may solidify, perhaps after some hesitation and further tinkering, into new institutions and mechanisms that are better suited to coordinating economic decisions than those now in place. In other words, given present expectations regarding policy commitments and the realistic chances of these reforms being implemented, considerable discord among the CPEs is likely to appear at any one point as well as over time.

In light of the importance of the CMEA in the external economic relations of the CPEs, it seems reasonable to inquire into two issues. First, what role could be assigned to the CMEA as a regional economic institution, as a forum for guiding experimentation and as a regional 'market' in support of currently unsynchronized reform attempts? Should this assistance be minimal or maximal? That is, should the CMEA buttress those CPEs embarking on the most ambitious reform while protecting those other members who choose to move ahead more slowly? Alternatively, should changes in the CMEA as a regional organization be targeted at chiefly supporting the greatest common denominator of the economic mechanisms of the various CPEs at any time, in which case features of the countries with the most conservative reform would be accommodated at the regional level?

Second, given present policy stances on economic restructuring, economic reform, modernization, *perestrojka* or whatever label is being placed on coveted structural adjustments, to what extent can one logically search for feasible and desirable adjustments in the CMEA to accommodate reforms in the member economies? These especially include the mechanisms, institutions and policies that condition the CMEA's foreign trade and exchange regimes. By necessity, this impacts on the conduct of economic relations with outside partners.

These key problems have been on the CMEA debating table for at least the last five years (see chapter 6), evidently without the members thus far concurring on the desirable interrelationship between the prevailing proclivity for economic experimentation in critical CPEs and desirable SEI reforms. Even so, as a policy goal with all its attendant institutional and behavioral repercussions, the process of reforming SEI is likely to center around direct enterprise relationships and the implementation of *Scientific-Technological Progress*, perhaps in ways not even considered when the document was approved in December 1985.

It is unfortunate that we know only the rough contours of the proposed changes that presently appear to be in various stages of gaining support and approval by the key members. At this stage, of course, these proposals are still very unofficial. Nonetheless, as it has evolved since 1949, the CMEA is not well suited to support, let alone enhance, the shifts in economic policies and policy mechanisms currently envisioned by some CPEs. Therefore, it may be useful to study the desirable modifications of cooperation mechanisms, the extent to which prevailing conditions are sufficiently mature to facilitate the swift realization of these intentions, if that, and what conditions must be fulfilled for these transformations to materialize. In this process, I assume that major CMEA members will continue with reforms and that there is no ready alternative to emphasizing SEI as a prime source of CPE domestic economic growth and of the well-being of the CMEA as a community. Developing CMEA relations will remain an implicit priority at least until the members succeed in restoring domestic and external balance in their economies at a level and structure of economic activity that enhances their competitiveness in the world economy.

Two critical features to be heeded in constructing feasible regional shifts are, first, that the CMEA area is not likely to soon become a homogeneous region in which members voluntarily engage in the redistribution of value added to the degree they have done so domestically, and, second, that there is no parallel at the CMEA level for the latent power of central decision makers in individual CPEs, in spite of the paramount role of the *primus inter pares*. This lack of parallelism here argues even more strongly than it did in the case of the national reform for the establishment of a proper integration framework. Because of weak internationalism and democratic centralism at the CMEA level, regional economic cohesion needs to be solidified primarily on the basis of the economic calculus. Even if countries choose to grant development assistance or to promote factor transfers for reasons other than strict material gain, the economic calculus should be more vigorously embraced so that the direct and indirect costs of political decisions can be placed in their proper perspective. This is especially critical for the self-accounting of economic units, even if the CPEs were to intensify the magnitude of plan coordination. At the very least, the economic calculus will have to be refined as a technical tool so as to distinguish more clearly between resource appropriations and performance, to weed out what is not up to par and to foster profitable processes as measured either by strictly economic yardsticks or, given the political preference for relative self-sufficiency, by the CMEA's ultimate *raison d'être*.

If the above assessment is correct, the debate on CMEA reform should focus not on whether to change the direction and methods of SEI but rather on providing answers to the following two central questions of economy policy. First, to what extent do the CPEs consciously opt to safeguard their regional economic organization and their national independence in economic affairs? Second, because this preference entails a cost in terms of economic efficiency forgone, as measured by world standards, who will be asked to shoulder this cost and according to which rules will the cost of protection or relative inefficiency be parceled out? The justification for this position runs parallel to that advanced in section 18.5 regarding the domestic economic mechanisms of the CPEs. Once an acceptable answer to these questions is negotiated and accepted, the work ahead should be of a dual but complementary nature that parallels domestic economic reforms under way in some CPEs. One strand of adaptations involves the institutional setup and management of the regional organization and its affiliates, including the way in which these organizations interact with the member countries and *vice versa*. Another set of shifts would be geared toward economic policies and policy instruments with their related institutions. At any rate, realistic CMEA reforms should reflect the pivotal features – their commonality as well as differences – in the ongoing changes in the CPEs. The positive structural adjustment policy to be embraced could be usefully anchored to a re-designed regional framework. It is here that my suggestion for developing a constitutional framework finds its justification.

I envisage (see Brabant, 1987c, 1987e, 1987f) such a compact as a firm agreement that encompasses the goals of SEI, the mechanisms to foster progress, the institutions to ensure proper functioning of the policy instruments and a transition mechanism for assisting countries that are not yet ready to initiate domestic economic reforms. If the announced intention to establish a unified market means more than paying lip service to what ultimately needs to be done, then even these countries should be able to benefit from SEI and its further progress without currently submitting to full regional competition. In other words, a constitutional framework is a set of commitments about objectives, institutions, rules and regulations to be respected by all signatories until revised at infrequent intervals. It provides the boundaries of the area within which economic agents can pursue their own or society's perceived interests.

A constitutional framework makes sense only if it encompasses the *basic* commitments regarding purposes, rules, instruments and institutions. Agreement is desirable, especially, on the ultimate purposes of integration, the distribution of the gains and benefits, even if specified only in general terms, and on the basic policy instruments to be placed at the disposal of the regional and national centers in matters intimately related to SEI. In that sense, the purposes of SEI can be kept rather vague, and it might be fruitful to draft a new version of *Integration Program* that would be tailored to the concerns of the late 1980s and beyond. The *Collective Concept* may well soon codify this strategy. In the context of the CMEA, it might extend to agreement on the areas in which regional demand and supply should focus on the needs of the region as a whole rather than on the simple sum of national demands. Agreement is required on the degree of 'separateness' from the rest of the world economy that the CPEs want to maintain and jointly support. Furthermore, it entails specifying the rules by which the gains and costs will be distributed. The cost of regional protection may be defrayed in several ways, and the CPEs may well opt for a more egalitarian and fraternal set of rules than, say, have the European Communities.

Perhaps more important than the goals is the specification of the means to be employed to enhance SEI, to assess its losses and benefits and to agree upon the rules for distributing these results. Certainly these aspects of the SEI mechanism should also be autonomous and, at least for some CPEs, intimately related to domestic policy processes so as to prevent the typical wavering and instability of past national reforms from emerging once again. This explicit reflection of preferences for regional economic autonomy may contradict the precepts held by the majority of CPEs, but they may superimpose their own national preferences and thus separate regional cooperation from the domestic mechanism. In the other CPEs, the mechanism should mesh very closely.

Regarding policy instruments, it must be emphasized that the existing SEI economic mechanism is exceedingly primitive (see Part III); it is geared more to the reciprocal exchange of physical goods and tangible services than to the enhancement of genuine integration through indirect coordination, including in the context of national, coordinated or joint planning within the CMEA. Adapting SEI mechanisms that have no direct counterpart in any of the participating CPEs is clearly meaningless. That is, regional changes ought to be synchronized with shifts in domestic economic mechanisms. I have argued elsewhere (Brabant, 1987g, 1987h) that it should coincide with the most ambitious national reform, but no country should be compelled to emulate the farthest-reaching reform.

Among the instruments and institutions that could benefit from a new approach to SEI, the role of planning should be sharply distinguished from that of market-type instruments. CPEs need to agree on the role of central planning in the regional context, including ways of harmonizing the national planning of the reformed CPEs. When it comes to ensuring preference for the region in any further attempt to raise export dependence, room exists at the CMEA level for planning structural decisions and preparing key policy alternatives. Whether this coordination becomes expressed through formalized plans, such as through the *Concerted Plan* mechanism, or is much more indicative, basically resulting from consultations, is a matter yet to be decided.

At the same time, however, the compact should establish the major instruments and supporting institutions for coordinating possibly decentralized economic decisions, particularly in connection with the anticipated project on bolstering interfirm relations. Primary issues involve regional pricing, including exchange rates, multilateral settlements and some measure of regional convertibility (see Brabant, 1987i), the role of capital and labor mobility and how these are to be guided and price harmonization. For example, interfirm contacts that preclude autonomous negotiations about prices within overall guidelines or that need to be balanced are most undesirable. A proper regional settlements mechanism could work wonders in that regard.[7] Regional pricing of critical raw materials, including fuels, may still be conducted at a relatively high rung of the planning hierarchy. But I see little potential for progress with interfirm integration in manufacturing sectors without allowing a more flexible pricing mechanism to emerge. Preferably, genuine wholesale trade should emanate directly into the domestic pricing regimes of the participating members rather than negotiated prices being buffered at the border through a particular variant of price equalization. Evidently, however, this desirable connection between domestic and trade prices depends on the contemplated changes in domestic economic mechanisms.

Finally, some agreement must be reached on the available room for policy maneuvering within the region so as to support the most open economy, on which policy institutions and mechanisms can be exploited, on the degree of protection against regional competition that some members will be allowed to embrace, and on the transitory protection deemed necessary to buffer the, possibly substantial, impact of effective regional integration. In other words, the compact must ensure a functional degree of distinctiveness that can be tolerated without undermining SEI from within or even altogether preventing its emergence. Furthermore, it should determine the pace at which the transitory differentiation among the members can be gradually eliminated and how this should be done. Achieving this may require that SEI progress in several stages. The CPEs that are ready to introduce broad-based domestic economic reforms attuned to the regional economic mechanism should be able to progress faster and farther without being stymied by others, who by agreement, choose to postpone such transitions.

Perhaps the most critical element in the above agenda for reform focuses on the TRP regime. I am not advocating that it be abolished. Indeed, why should the CMEA not have its own preferences on regional protection? These may stem from myopic, second-best choices or they may be inspired by some macroeconomic constraints that policymakers perceive. But an own price regime would be desirable. Given the substantial criticism that has been leveled at the search for an independent price system since the late 1950s, is this proposition utopian or misguided? Recall that most of the proposals on the creation of a proper IPS worked out in the early 1960s and 1970s embodied serious flaws in that scant attention was paid to economic scarcity and socioeconomic preferences. But I am skeptical (Brabant, 1987b, pp. 237–44) about the argument that no IPS should be implemented at all (Hewett, 1974, p. 160). In my view, an IPS is very sensible for economies that emphatically do not wish to integrate themselves fully into the world economy. They may shun integration because they put a premium on warding off perturbations from world markets, on setting domestic prices relatively autonomously and on funneling possibly narrowly held, heavily weighted preferences into aggregate as well as microeconomic decision making. Similarly, an IPS would be warranted to the extent that the terms of trade available to CPEs through global relations are biased by various forms of discrimination.

Suggestions for a more suitable price regime abound. I do not advocate a bevy of nearly inapplicable rules and regulations. My main point on the economics and logic of instituting TRP reform hinges on the adoption of 'virtual prices,'[8] which essentially means the creation of flexible trade prices that reflect regional supply and demand of preset trade flows and, in some respect, also impact the domestic prices of at least one CPE. Such virtual prices could promote more efficient trade or at least facilitate the selection of trade processes that support domestic and external requirements for promoting swift productivity growth. In that sense, I need to touch upon the domestic counterparts of the proposal as well.

Determining the desired degree of CMEA autonomy is certainly not easy. It would not be helpful to look for an answer that is fully cast *ab initio*. An apter approach would be to rationally select the extent of separateness that the members voluntarily choose to support and fund by common means according to some rules on burden sharing. For instance, it would be exceedingly helpful if the SEI participants were to integrate their domestic pricing policies by linking flexible TRP pricing with domestic wholesale prices. This could be done in two ways. The more desirable option would be to choose a certain level of prices based on an IPS convention; to introduce those prices into the domestic economy, at least to the degree that the individual participants choose not to additionally superimpose their national preferences; and, at least intermittently, to let regionwide imbalances propel changes in quantities or prices, or both. A more explicit recognition of the indirect taxes and subsidies – regional tariffs, if you will – implied in this attitude could render a regional price system perfectly compatible with the aspirations of the CPEs and their desire to continue to interact with world markets.

The observer of today's CMEA scene undoubtedly has reason for a degree of guarded optimism concerning prospects for meaningful change in the SEI mechanisms. This expectation extends well beyond the wildest hope that could have been reasonably entertained as recently as two or three years ago. That is not to say that I expect swift movement in the economic mechanism of SEI and that the CMEA is now poised for rapid progress. Past experience proves sobering in this regard. In fact, I do not even subscribe to the notion that all European CPEs can realistically be expected to engage in genuine wholesale trade except marginally in the near future. Under the circumstances, it might be worthwhile to rethink the integration mechanism and make allowance for countries being on different integration stages in accordance with predetermined modalities, which is what now appears to be contemplated (see chapter 6).

In contrast with previous reform experiments and the way blueprints on the debating table have fared in the past, the above propositions may sound like wishful thinking given that the chances of any of them being soon implemented are slim. But it also seems rather improper at this stage *only* to look backwards. The recent renewal of the commanding heights in some CPEs, and that yet to come elsewhere in Eastern Europe, offers the promise of a new beginning and a new opportunity for rethinking basic issues, including technical problems that are at the heart of regional integration issues. The economic calculus *in se* presents such a technical set of topics. In the CPE context, it has often been overburdened with philosophical or ideological impediments that in fact ignore sheer technique as one important aspect of economics. I feel that the new leadership in Eastern Europe is likely to be more favorably disposed toward separating the technical from the philosophical and ideological aspects of economics, if only to obtain a proper menu of choices. Even so, I am not very confident that some of the above recommendations will appear any time soon on the highest policy agenda. In light of recent policy discussions, however, grounds do exist for being moderately optimistic that some of these reform items may emerge, though probably only very gradually as none of the essential prerequisites is yet in place.

NOTES

1. For a broader examination, see Brabant, 1987a, pp. 385–417; Brabant, 1987c; Wallace and Clarke, 1986, pp. 115–33.
2. This is perhaps the crucial explanation for the declining market shares of CPEs in Western Europe in contrast to what some developing market-oriented economies have accomplished. For some useful measurements, see Poznański, 1985, 1986a.
3. The chances for boosting East-West and East-South trade are elaborated on in Brabant, 1987c, pp. 93–6.
4. For a thoughtful evaluation of the inward-turning and outward-looking policy options available to the CPEs, see Köves, 1981, 1985.
5. In fact, prices should decline with positive gains in productivity according to the orthodox labor theory of value (for an explanation and references to the literature, see Brabant, 1987b, pp. 34–62). Miastkowski, 1980, has an interesting dissertation on that and related price topics.
6. But this effect can be offset by compensating households for the lost price subsidy through income transfers from, say, income taxes. Of course, this presupposes a well-developed fiscal policy, which is not typically a feature of the CPEs, even not in Hungary.
7. This should not be tailored from the start to full-fledged convertibility but rather set in motion the process of moving toward multilateralism through limited and partial convertibility. I have developed one proposal that simulates and adapts the mechanism used in the 1950s in the context of the EPU with a transformed TR (see Brabant, 1987i).
8. To the best of my recollection, this expression was first used in the context of CMEA price reforms in Neustadt, 1968, p. 223.

APPENDIX 1 THE CMEA SUMMIT MEETINGS[1]

Date	Place	Main purpose
1. 5–8 January 1949[2]	Moscow	Establishment of an institutionalized form of regional economic cooperation, debates on purposes, instruments, institutions and policies to be elaborated under that heading.
2. ? November 1950	Hollóháza	Reinforcement of pace and scope of autarkic industrialization and joint lifting of armaments production.
3. 20–23 May 1958	Moscow	Reinvigoration of the Council, giving concrete content to economic principles of international relations among CPEs, revive trade and economic plans, the ISDL and first steps toward elaboration of *Basic Principles*.
4. 6–7 June 1962	Moscow	Endorsement of ISDL and *Basic Principles*, decision, in principle, to create common bank and monetary unit.
5. 24–26 July 1963	Moscow	Institutional reinforcement, implementation of *Basic Principles* and attempt to resolve differences in interpretation.
6. 7 July 1966	Bucharest	To set CMEA cooperation onto a new track after the ISDL failure.
7. 23–26 April 1969	Moscow	Coincident with 23rd Council Session. Mainly endorsement of new approach to SEI, commissioning *Integration Program*, establishment of IIB and related matters.

8. 12–14 June 1984	Moscow	Structural adjustment, East-West relations, STC and SEI strategy for the 1980s and beyond.
9. 10–11 November 1986[3]	Moscow	Preparation of changes in SEI mechanism, CMEA organization, economic assistance to less-developed members, charting a program for the 1990s and beyond and invigorating *Scientific-Technological Progress*.

NOTES

1. I include here only those meetings of the CCP identified or identifiable as CMEA summit meetings; that is, deliberations concerned largely, if not exclusively, with SEI matters. Attendance at these meetings was generally confined to CMEA members (see CMEA, 1979b). But I am including meetings that took place before the christening of the CCP in 1958.
2. I am exceptionally including this meeting even though it was not a full-fledged CCP meeting, even not *avant la lettre*.
3. This is currently being referred to as a 'working meeting,' in much the same way as the 1971–3 meetings in the Krim are referred to (see CMEA, 1979b). I am not including the Krim meetings because their main purpose was not CMEA cooperation and they were not always attended by all regular CCP members.

APPENDIX 2 COUNCIL SESSIONS

Date	Place
1. 26–28 April 1949	Moscow
2. 25–27 August 1949	Sofia
3. 24–25 November 1950	Moscow
4. 26–27 March 1954	Moscow
5. 24–25 June 1954	Moscow
6. 7–11 December 1955	Budapest
7. 18–25 May 1956	Berlin
8. 18–22 June 1957	Warsaw
9. 26–30 June 1958	Bucharest
10. 11–13 December 1958	Prague
11. 13–16 May 1959	Tirana
12. 10–14 December 1959	Sofia
13. 26–29 July 1960	Budapest
14. 28 February–3 March 1961	Berlin
15. 12–15 December 1961	Warsaw
16. 7 June 1962*	Bucharest
17. 14–20 December 1962	Bucharest
18. 25–26 July 1963	Moscow
19. 28 January–2 February 1965	Prague
20. 8–10 December 1966	Sofia
21. 12–14 December 1967	Budapest
22. 21–23 January 1969	Berlin
23. 23–26 April 1969†	Moscow
24. 12–14 May 1970	Warsaw
25. 25–29 July 1971	Bucharest
26. 10–12 July 1972	Moscow
27. 5–8 June 1973	Prague
28. 18–21 June 1974	Sofia
29. 24–26 June 1975	Budapest
30. 7–9 July 1976	Berlin
31. 21–23 June 1977	Warsaw

32.	27–29 June 1978	Bucharest
33.	26–28 June 1979	Moscow
34.	17–19 June 1980	Prague
35.	2–4 July 1981	Sofia
36.	8–10 June 1982	Budapest
37.	18–20 October 1983	Berlin
38.	14 June 1984*	Moscow
39.	29–31 October 1984	Havana
40.	25–27 June 1985	Warsaw
41.	17–18 December 1985*	Moscow
42.	3–5 November 1986	Bucharest
43.	13–14 October 1987*	Moscow
44.	5–7 July 1988	Prague

NOTES

* Extraordinary Session, presumably convened at the special request of at least a majority of members, out of regular sequence.
† Special Session, presumably emphasizing the 'special' nature of the meeting, which was not only the commemorative one but also one that coincided with the economic summit.

BIBLIOGRAPHY

Abolichina, Galina A., Oleg Bakoveckij and Boris I. Medvedev, 'Susčňost' i novye formy socialističeskoj integracii', *Voprosy ėkonomiki*, 1987:1, 129–40.

Alampiev, P. M., Oleg T. Bogomolov and Jurij S. Širjaev, *Ėkonomičeskaja integracija -ob"ektivnaja potrebnost' razvitija mirovogo socializma* (Moscow: Mysl', 1971).

Apró, Antal, *Sotrudničestvo stran–členov SĖV v ėkonomičeskich organizacijach socialističeskich stran* (Moscow: Ėkonomika, 1969).

Arojo, Žak, 'Njakoi novi formi na sūtrudničestvoto meždu stranite-členki na SIV', *Meždunarodni otnošenija*, 1987:1, 55–9.

Ausch, Sándor, *Theory and practice of CMEA cooperation* (Budapest: Akadémiai Kiadó, 1972).

Ausch, Sándor and Ferenc Bartha, 'Theoretical problems of CMEA inter-trade prices', in Földi and Kiss, 1969, pp. 101–25.

Averkin, Anatolij G., *Meždunarodno-pravovye formy sovmestnoj dejatel'nosti stran-členov SĖV* (Moscow: Nauka, 1984).

Badrus, G., 'Viabilitatea deplina a principiilor fundamentale ale colaborării şi cooperării în cadrul C.A.E.R.', *Era Socialistă*, 1983: 4, 21–5.

Bagudin, Pavel D., Evgenij O. Gavrilov and Nikolaj N. Šinkov, *Sotrudničestvo stran-členov SĖV v oblasti planovoj dejatel'nosti* (Moscow: SĖV Sekretariat, 1985).

Bajbakov, Nikolaj K., 'Novoe v koordinacii narodnochozjajstvennych planov stran-členov SĖV', *Ėkonomičeskoe sotrudničestvo stran-členov SĖV*, 1976: 3, 8–12.

Bakoveckij, Oleg and Galina A. Abolichina, 'Prjamye svjazi: kursom integracii', *Ėkonomičeskaja gazeta*, 1986: 25, 21.

Ball, George W., *Diplomacy for a crowded world – an American foreign policy* (Boston, Mass.: Little, Brown & Co. 1976).

Basiuk, Jerzy, 'Ceny w handly wzajemnym krajów RWPG a ceny światowe', in Bożyk, 1974, pp. 150–73.

Basiuk, Jerzy, Mirosława Jaroszyńska and Bolesław Krawczyk, *Ceny handlu zagranicznego na rynku krajów RWPG* (Warsaw: PWE, 1975).

Bautina, Ninel' V., 'O meždunarodnych socialističeskich proizvodstvennych otnošenijach', *Mirovaja ėkonomika i meždunarodnye otnošenija*, 1968a: 4, 64–71.

Bautina, Ninel' V., 'Nekotorye osobennosti formirovanija internacional'noj stoimosti', in D'jačenko, 1968a (1968b), pp. 38–51.

Bautina, Ninel' V., *Soveršenstvovanie ėkonomičeskich vzaimootnošenij stran-členov SĖV* (Moscow: Ėkonomika, 1972).

Bautina, Ninel' V., 'Problems of equivalence', in Kiss, 1973, pp. 191–5.

Bautina, Ninel' V. and Jurij S. Širjaev, 'SĖV: problemy soveršenstvovanija ékonomičeskogo mechanizma vzaimnogo sotrudničestva', *Planovoe chozjajstvo*, 1987: 2, 108–12.

Beyer, Emma-Maria and Inge Weidemann, 'Verallgemeinerung der Erfahrungen der RGW–Länder auf dem Gebiet der wirtschaftlichen Rechnungsführung', *Wirtschaftswissenschaft*, 1987: 5, 754–6.

Bikovski, Leonid, 'Pravnoto regulirane na naučno-techničeskoto sŭtrudničestvo meždu stranite-členki na SIV', *Meždunarodni otnošenija*, 1988: 1, 39–45.

Bíró, F., 'A többoldalú hosszú távú együttműködés lehetőségei a KGST-országok élemiszer-termelésében', *Közgazdasági Szemle*, 1978: 10, 1201–10.

Biskup, J. and G. Nosiadek, 'Formy współpracy krajów RWPG w ramach międzynarodowych organizacji ekonomicznych', *Handel Zagraniczny*, 1978: 1, 10–1.

Bogomolov, Oleg T., 'The international market of the CMEA countries', in Kiss, 1973, pp. 31–6.

Bogomolov, Oleg T., 'SĖV: ėkonomičeskaja strategija 80-ch godov', *Kommunist*, 1983: 7, 72–84.

Bogomolov, Oleg T., *Strany socializma v meždunarodnom razdelenii truda* (Moscow: Nauka, 2nd edn, 1986).

Božkov, Jordan, 'Specializirovannaja produkcija vo vzaimnom éksporte', *Ėkonomičeskoe sotrudničestvo stran-členov SĖV*, 1987:1, 104–9.

Božkov, Jordan and Stefan Dulovec, 'Po puti specializacii i kooperacii proizvodstva', *Ėkonomičeskoe sotrudničestvo stran-členov SĖV*, 1985: 10, 71–4.

Bożyk, Paweł, ed., *Integracja ekonomiczna krajów socjalistycznych* (Warsaw: Książka i Wiedza, 2nd edn 1974).

Brabant, Jozef M. van, 'Long-term development credits and socialist trade', *Weltwirtschaftliches Archiv*, 1971: 107/1, 92–122.

Brabant, Jozef M. van, *Bilateralism and structural bilateralism in intra-CMEA trade* (Rotterdam: Rotterdam University Press, 1973).

Brabant, Jozef M. van, 'On the origins and tasks of the Council for Mutual Economic Assistance', *Osteuropa-Wirtschaft*, 1974a: 3, 181–209.

Brabant, Jozef M. van, 'Specialization and import-dependence of some East European countries – the case of machinery and equipment', *Jahrbuch der Wirtschaft Osteuropas – Yearbook of East-European Economics*, vol. 5 (1974b), 271–308.

Brabant, Jozef M. van, 'Zur Rolle "Ostmitteleuropas" im Rahmen des RGW', *Osteuropa-Wirtschaft*, 1976: 1, 1–20.

Brabant, Jozef M. van, *East European cooperation – the role of money and finance* (New York: Praeger, 1977).

Brabant, Jozef M. van, 'Le rouble transférable et son rôle dans le commerce Est-Ouest', in Guglielmi and Lavigne, 1978, pp. 77–105.

Brabant, Jozef M. van, 'Another look at the origins of East European cooperation', *Osteuropa-Wirtschaft*, 1979a: 4, 243–66.

Brabant, Jozef M. van, 'Specialization and trade-dependence in Eastern Europe – the case of Hungary', *Jahrbuch der Wirtschaft Osteuropas – Yearbook of East-European Economics*, vol. 8 (1979b), 213–45.

Brabant, Jozef M. van, *Socialist economic integration – aspects of contemporary economic problems in Eastern Europe* (New York: Cambridge University Press, 1980).

Brabant, Jozef M. van, 'Target programming – a new instrument of socialist economic integration?' *Jahrbuch der Wirtschaft Osteuropas – Yearbook of East-European Economics*, vol. 9/1 (1981), 141–84.

Brabant, Jozef M. van, 'Socialist economic integration and the global economic recession', *Osteuropa-Wirtschaft*, 1984a: 3, 192–212.

Brabant, Jozef M. van, 'CMEA institutions and policies versus structural adjustment – a comment' (manuscript presented to the Conference on the Soviet Union and Eastern Europe in the World Economy, Washington, D.C., 18–19 October 1984b).

Brabant, Jozef M. van, 'The USSR and socialist economic integration – a comment', *Soviet Studies*, 1984c: 1, 127–38.

Brabant, Jozef M. van, 'Entstehung und Aufgaben des Rates für gegenseitige Wirtschaftshilfe', in Haberl and Niethammer, 1986, pp. 552–74.

Brabant, Jozef M. van, *Adjustment, structural change, and economic efficiency – aspects of monetary cooperation in Eastern Europe* (New York: Cambridge University Press, 1987a).

Brabant, Jozef M. van, *Regional price formation in Eastern Europe – on the theory and practice of trade pricing* (Dordrecht: Kluwer Academic Publishers, 1987b).

Brabant, Jozef M. van, 'Economic adjustment and the future of socialist economic integration', *Eastern European Politics and Society*, 1987c: 1, 75–112.

Brabant, Jozef M. van, 'The CMEA summit and socialist economic integration – a perspective', *Jahrbuch der Wirtschaft Osteuropas – Yearbook of East-European Economics*, vol. 12/1 (1987d), 129–60.

Brabant, Jozef M. van, 'Economic reform and monetary cooperation in the CMEA' (paper prepared for the Conference on Financial Reforms in Eastern Europe, Istituto Universitario Europeo, San Domenico di Fiesole (Firenze), 12–16 October 1987e).

Brabant, Jozef M. van, 'Monetarism and the future of integration in Eastern Europe' (paper prepared for the University of Minnesota, November 1987f, manuscript).

Brabant, Jozef M. van, 'Recent growth performance, economic reform, and the future of integration in Eastern Europe', *DIESA Working Paper Series*, no. 5 (1987g).

Brabant, Jozef M. van, 'A constitutional framework for economic integration in Eastern Europe?' (paper presented at Columbia University, New York, 27 April 1987h).

Brabant, Jozef M. van, 'Economic reform and convertibility in Eastern Europe' (paper presented at the Fourth Convention of the Italian Association for Comparative Economics, Sorrento, 19–20 October 1987i).

Brabant, Jozef M. van, 'Economic disequilibrium and the centrally planned economies – Kornai versus Portes' (manuscript, 1988a).

Brabant, Jozef M. van, 'Production specialization in the CMEA – concepts and empirical evidence', *Journal of Common Market Studies*, 1988b: 3, 287–315.

Brabant, Jozef M. van, 'On the economics of scientific-technological cooperation in Eastern Europe' (paper presented at the Symposium on Civilian Science in the CMEA, Brussels, 28–30 September 1988c).

Brabant, Jozef M. van, 'Scientific-technological cooperation in Eastern Europe – its organization' (paper presented at the Symposium on Civilian Science in the CMEA, Brussels, 28–30 September 1988d).

Brabant, Jozef M. van, 'Integration reform – new horizons for the CMEA and east-west economic relations?' (paper presented at the Conference on The Political Economy of Greater East-West Economic Cooperation, Middlebury, Vt., 22–24 September 1988e).

Brabant, Jozef M. van, 'Regional integration, economic reforms, and convertibility', *Jahrbuch der Wirtschaft Osteuropas – Yearbook of East–European Economics*, vol. 13/1 (1988f), forthcoming.

Brabant, Jozef M. van, 'Wither the CMEA? – reconstructing socialist economic integration' (paper presented to the AAASS meetings in Honolulu, 18–21 November 1988g).

Brabant, Jozef M. van, *The centrally planned economies in international economic organizations* (manuscript, 1989).

Brada, Josef C., 'Soviet subsidization of Eastern Europe: the primacy of economics over politics', *Journal of Comparative Economics*, 1985: 1, 80–92.

Brada, Josef C. and José A. Méndez, 'An estimate of the dynamic effects of economic integration', *The Review of Economics and Statistics*, 1988: 2, 163–8.

Broner, Adam, *Economic integration in Eastern Europe* (unpublished Ph.D. dissertation, Princeton University 1975).

Broner, Adam, 'The degree of autarky in centrally planned economies', *Kyklos*, 1976: 3, 478–94.

Brunner, G., 'Etwas korrekter, bitte!' *Die Wirtschaft*, 1976: 26, 22.

Brzezinski, Zbigniew K., *The Soviet bloc – unity and conflict* (Cambridge: Harvard University Press, 1967, rev. edn).

BT, *Vŭnšna tŭrgovija na Narodna republika Bŭlgarija – statističeski danni*, . . . (Sofia: Komitet za socialna informacija pri ministerskija sŭvet, annual).

Butler, William E., *A source book on socialist international organizations* (Alphen aan den Rijn: Sijthoff & Noordhoff, 1978).

BY, *Statističeski godišnik na Narodna republika Bŭlgarija*, . . . (Sofia: Komitet za socialna informacija pri ministerskija sŭvet, annual).

Caffet, Jean-Pierre and Marie Lavigne, 'Les pays à économie centralement planifiée sont-ils protectionnistes?' in Bernard Lassudrie-Duchêne and Jean-Louis Reiffers (eds.), *Le protectionisme – croissance-limites-voies alternatives* (Paris: Economica, 1985, pp. 283–92).

Caillot, Jean, *Le C.A.E.M. – aspects juridiques et formes de coopération économique entre les pays socialistes* (Paris: Pichon & Durand-Auzias, 1971).

Carrère d'Encausse, Hélène, *Le grand frère – L'Union Soviétique et l'Europe soviétisé* (Paris: Flammarion, 1985).

Caves, Richard E., 'The economics of reciprocity: theory and evidence on bilateral trading arrangements', in Willy Sellekaerts (ed.), *Essays in honour of Jan Tinbergen – international trade and finance* (London: Macmillan, 1974, pp. 17–54).

Černianský, Viliam, *Ekonomika socialističeskoj vnešnej torgovli* (Moscow: Vneštorgizdat, 1963).

Chodow, L., 'Auf dem Wege zu gemeinsamen Strategien', *Die Wirtschaft*, 1976: 19, 23.

Chruščëv, Nikita S., 'Nasuščnye voprosy razvitija mirovoj socialističeskoj sistemy', *Kommunist*, 1962: 12, 3–26.

Čížkovský, Milan, 'K některým rysům hospodářské spolupráce mezi europejskými socialistickými státy v letech 1945–1953 (informativní přehled)', *Acta Universitatis Carolinae – Economica*, 1966: 2, 145–78.

Čížkovský, Milan, 'Les entreprises communes dans la sphère du conseil d'aide économique mutuelle', *Cahiers de Droit Européen*, 1968: 3, 289–96.

Čížkovský, Milan, 'Internationale Koordinierung der Volkswirtschaftspläne im Comecon', in J. H. Kaiser (ed.), *Planung IV* (Baden-Baden: Nomos Verlag, 1970, pp. 243–64).

Čížkovský, Milan, *Mezinárodní plánování – zkušenost a možnosti RVHP* (Prague: Academia, 1971).

Čížkovský, Milan, 'Ekonomická problematika vědeckotechnického rozvoje', *Politická Ekonomie*, 1988: 3, 287–96.

CMEA, *Sovet ekonomičeskoj vzaimopomošči – 25 let* (Moscow: SĖV Sekretariat, 1974).

CMEA, *Primernye položenija o finansirovanii i osušestvlenii rasčëtov meždunarodnych organizacij zainteresovannych stran-členov SĖV* (Moscow: SĖV Sekretariat, 1975a).

CMEA, *Sovet ėkonomičeskoj vzaimopomošči – osnovnye problemy* (Moscow: Ėkonomika, 1975b).

CMEA, *Collected reports on various activities of bodies of the CMEA* (Moscow: SĖV Sekretariat, 1976).

CMEA, 'Kommjunike o XXXI zasedanii sessii Soveta ėkonomičeskoj vzaimopomošči', *Ėkonomičeskoe sotrudničestvo stran-členov SĖV*, 1977a: 4, 84–7.

CMEA, *Osnovnye dokumenty Soveta ėkonomičeskoj vzaimopomošči – tom 2* (Moscow: SĖV Sekretariat, 3rd edn, 1977b).

CMEA, *Information on activities of the CMEA in 1977* (Moscow: SĖV Sekretariat, 1978).

CMEA, *The Council for Mutual Economic Assistance – 30 years* (Moscow: SĖV Sekretariat, 1979a).

CMEA, *Kommjunike o soveščanijach predstavitelej kommunistĭceskich i rabočich partij i glav pravitel'stv stran-členov Soveta ėkonomičeskoj vzaimopomošči o zasedanijach sessii soveta, 1949–1978 gg.* (Moscow: SĖV Sekretariat, 1979b).

CMEA, *Kommjunike o zasedanijach ispolnitel'nogo komiteta Soveta ėkonomičeskoj vzaimopomošči* (Moscow: SĖV Sekretariat, 1979c).

CMEA, *Naučno-techničeskoe sotrudničestvo stran-členov SĖV* (Moscow: SĖV Sekretariat, 1982).

CMEA, *Kursom naučno-techničeskogo progressa – 41-e (vneočerednoe) zasedanie Sessii Soveta ėkonomičeskoj vzaimopomošči* (Moscow: SĖV Sekretariat, 1986).

Conquest, Robert, *Harvest of sorrow – Soviet collectivization and the great famine* (New York: Oxford University Press, 1986).

Constantinescu, N. N., 'Considerații cu privire la dezvoltarea colaborăcii economice între țările socialiste', *Probleme Economice*, 1969a: 3, 60–70.

Constantinescu, R., 'Două decenii de activitate a Consiliului de Ajutor Economic Reciproc', *Probleme Economice*, 1969b: 1, 70–82.

Constantinescu, R., 'Sur les organisations internationales économiques et technico-scientifiques des pays socialistes', *Revue Roumaine d'Etudes Internationales*, 1973: 1, 63–88.

Crane, Keith and Deborah Skoller, *Specialization agreements in the Council for Mutual Economic Assistance* (Santa Monica, Calif.: The RAND Corp., 1988).

Csaba, László, 'Integration into the world economy and the cooperation of the CMEA countries in planning', *Osteuropa-Wirtschaft*, 1983: 2, 105–22.

Csikós-Nagy, Béla, 'Some theoretical problems of the price system of CMEA intertrade', in Földi and Kiss, 1969, pp. 127–36.

Csikós-Nagy, Béla, 'Mutual advantage in the economic cooperation', in Kiss, 1973, pp. 179–90.

Csikós-Nagy, Béla, *Socialist price theory and price policy* (Budapest: Akadémiai Kiadó, 1975).

Dedijer, Vladimir, *The battle Stalin lost – memoirs of Yugoslavia 1948–1953* (New York: Viking, 1971).

Desai, Padma, *Weather and grain yields in the Soviet Union* (Washington, D.C.: International Food Policy Research Institute, 1986).

Desai, Padma, 'Is the Soviet Union subsidizing Eastern Europe?' *European Economic Review*, 1986: 1, 107–16.

Dietz, Raimund, 'Advantages and disadvantages in Soviet trade with Eastern Europe: the pricing dimension', in JEC, 1986, pp. 263–301.

Dietzel, Dietrich, 'Wissenschaftlich-technischer Fortschritt und Wertbildungsprozeß', *Wirtschaftswissenschaft*, 1988: 7, 1045–50.

Dimov, A., 'Problemi na agrarno-promišlenata integracija na stranite-členki na SIV', *Planovo stopanstvo*, 1979: 1, 31–7.

Dimov, Ivan, 'Problemi na dŭlgostročnite celevi programi sŭtrudničestvo na stranite ot SIV', *Vŭnšna tŭrgovija*, 1978: 10, 2–6.

D'jačenko, V. P., ed., *Cenoobrazovanie na mirovom socialističeskom rynke* (Moscow: Ėkonomika, 1968a).

D'jačenko, V. P., 'Perspektivnye napravlenija soveršentsvovanija cen vo vnešnej torgovle stran SĖV', in D'jačenko, 1968a (1968b), pp. 6–23.

D'jačenko, V. P., 'Improvement of price formation in the intra-CMEA trade: a task for economic science', in Földi and Kiss, 1969, pp. 11–22.

Djilas, Milovan, *Conversations with Stalin* (Harmondsworth: Penguin, 1963).

Drewnowski, Jan, ed., *Crisis in the East European economy* (New York: St Martin's Press, and London: Croom Helm, 1982).

Dulovec, Stefan, 'Meždunarodnaja specializacija i kooperirovanie v promyšlennosti stran-členov SĖV', *Ėkonomičeskoe sotrudničestvo stran–členov SĖV*, 1983: 1, 17–19.

Durnev, Viktor, 'Sovmestnye predprijatija stran–členov SĖV', *Vnešnjaja torgovlja*, 1987: 6, 12–6.

Dymšic, V. E., 'Sotrudničestvo stran-členov SĖV v oblasti material'no-techničeskogo snabženija', *Ėkonomičeskoe sotrudničestvo stran-členov SĖV*, 1975: 4, 30–3.

Ehlert, Willi, Heinz Joswig, Willi Luchterhand and Karl-Heinz Stiemerling, eds., *Wörterbuch der Ökonomie – Sozialismus* (Berlin: Dietz, 4th edn, 1984).

El-Agraa, Ali M., ed., *International economic integration* (New York: St Martin's Press, 1982a).

El-Agraa, Ali M., 'The theory of economic integration', in El-Agraa, 1982a (1982b), pp. 10–27.

Ellman, Michael, 'Did the agricultural surplus provide the resources for the increase in investment in the USSR during the first five year plan?' *The Economic Journal*, 1975: 4, 844–64.

Ellman, Michael, 'On a mistake of Preobrazhensky and Stalin', *The Journal of Development Studies*, 1978: 3, 353–6.

Engel, H., 'Politökonomische Probleme der Bewertung wissenschaftlich-technischer Ergebnisse und Konsequenzen für ihre Preisbildung', *Wirtschaftswissenschaft*, 1988: 1, 16.

Engert, M., 'Langfristige Planung aus der Sicht der Planungszusammenarbeit zwischen den Mitgliedsländern des RGW', *Wissenschaftliche Zeitschrift der Hochschule für Ökonomie "B. Leuschner"*, 1978: 1, 21–30.

Evstigneev, Ruben M., 'Chozjajstvennye mechanizmy stran SĖV v integracija', *Voprosy ėkonomiki*, 1986: 1, 138–45.

Evstigneev, Ruben M., 'Socialističeskaja sobstvennost' i chozjajstvennyj mechanizm (opyt evropejskich stran SĖV)', *Voprosy ėkonomiki*, 1987: 1, 105–13.

Faddeev, Nikolaj V., 'Mnogostoronnee ėkonomičeskoe sotrudničestvo – važnyj faktor razvitija socialističeskich stran', in Tokareva, 1967, pp. 3–12.

Faddeev, Nikolaj V., *Sovet ėkonomičeskoj vzaimopomošči* (Moscow: Ėkonomika, 2nd edn, 1969).

Faddeev, Nikolaj V., '25 Jahre RGW – Internationale Wirtschaftsorganisation sozialistischer Länder, 1949–1974', *Einheit*, 1974a: 1, 10–23.

Faddeev, Nikolaj V., *Sovet ėkonomičeskoj vzaimopomošči – XXV* (Moscow: Ėkonomika, 3rd edn, 1974b).

Faude, Eugen, Gerhard Grote and Christa Luft, eds., *Sozialistische Außenwirtschaft* (Berlin: Die Wirtschaft, 1976).

Faude, Eugen, Gerhard Grote and Christa Luft, eds., *Sozialistische Außenwirtschaft – Lehrbuch* (Berlin: Die Wirtschaft, 1984).

Fedorowicz, Zdzisaw, 'Les problèmes actuels du rouble transférable', in Gugliel-mi and Lavigne, 1978, pp. 57–64.

Fehér, Ferenc, 'Eastern Europe's long revolution against Yalta', *Eastern European Politics and Societies*, 1988: 1, 1–34.

Fischer, M., 'Wirtschaftliche Rechnungsführung in internationalen ökonomischen Organisationen der RGW-Mitgliedsländer', *Sozialistische Finanzwirtschaft*, 1978: 10, 29–30.

Fiumel, Henryk de, 'Réflexions sur le principe de l'intérêt dans les statuts du Consell [*sic*!] d'Assistance Economique Mutuelle (C.A.E.M.)', *Polish Yearbook of International Law*, vol. 13 (1984), 69–75.

Földi, Tamás and Tibor Kiss, eds., *Socialist world market prices* (Leyden: Sijthoff, and Budapest: Akadémiai Kiadó, 1969).

Forner, Andreas, 'Zusammenhänge zwischen komparativen Vorteilen und Außen-handelsrentabilität in der sozialistischen Volkswirtschaft', *Wirtschaftswissen-schaft*, 1987: 10, 1473–82.

Frenzel, Gottfried, 'Wertrechnung und Preisrechnung in der sozialistischen Planung der UdSSR', *Statistische Hefte*, vol. 77 (1966), 74–111.

Friss, István, 'Socialističeskaja ėkonomičeskaja integracija i postroenie socializma v Vengrii', *Acta Oeconomica*, 1974: 12/1, 1–29.

Fröhlich, Gerhard, 'Zum Artikel "Komparative Vorteile und ihre Ausnutzung im Außenhandel sozialistischer Länder"', *Wirtschaftswissenschaft*, 1987: 3, 415–20.

Garbuzov, Vasilij F., 'Soveršenstvovanie valjutno-finansovych otnošenij stran-členov SĖV', in *Meždunarodnaja socialističeskaja valjuta stran-členov SĖV (Moscow: Finansy, 1973, pp. 5–13)*.

Gatzka, Rajmund A., *'Grundzüge der Entwicklung der wissenschaftlich-technischen Zusammenarbeit (WTZ) der Mitgliedsländer des RGW', Osteuropa-Recht, 1985: 1/2, 41–58.*

Georgiev, G., 'DCPS – važnaja osnova dal'nejšego rasširenija sotrudničestva NRB s bratskimi socialističeskimi stranami', *Planovoe chozjajstvo*, 1978: 9, 24–31.

Gomulka, Stanisaw, 'The Polish crisis: will it spread and what will be the outcome?' in Drewnowski, 1982, pp. 72–86.

Góra, Stanisaw and Zygmunt Knyziak, *Międzynarodowa specializacja produkcji krajów RWPG* (Warsaw: PWE, 1974).

Gorbačëv, Michail S., 'O zadačach partii po korennoj perestrojka upravlenija ėkonomikoj', *Ėkonomičeskaja gazeta*, 1987: 27, 2–9.

Gräbig, Gertrud, Gerhard Brendel and Hans-Joachim Dubrowsky, *Ware-Geld-Beziehungen in der sozialistischen Integration* (Berlin: Die Wirtschaft, 1975).

Grebennikov, P. N. and A. V. Jakovlev, 'Otnošenija obmena i ceny na mirovom socialističeskom rynke', in N. A. Čerkasov and A. N. Malafeev (eds.), *Razdelenie truda i tovarno-denežnye otnošenija v uslovijach internacionalizacii socialističeskogo proizvodstva* (Leningrad: Izdatel'stvo leningradskogo universi-teta, 1985, pp. 78–90).

Grinberg, Ruslan and Michail S. Ljubskij, 'Ceny i valjutnye otnošenija v sotrudni-čestve stran SĖV', *Voprosy ėkonomiki*, 1985: 6, 99–107.

Grinev, Vladimir S., 'Ceny vzaimnoj torgovli stran-členov SĖV i razvitie ich valjutno-finansovych otnošenij', in A. M. Alekseev *et al.* (eds.), *Meždunarodnye valjutno-finansovye i kreditnye otnošenija* (Moscow: Meždunarodnye otnošenija, 1984, pp. 313–27).

Grinev, Vladimir S., 'Perestrojka vnešneėkonomičeskogo kompleksa', *Vnešnjaja torgovlja*, 1987: 5, 2–5.

Grote, Gerhard, 'Einige theoretische und praktische Fragen des staatlichen

Monopols auf dem Gebiet der Außenwirtschaft', *Wirtschaftswissenschaft*, 1981: 2, 143–52.

Grote, Gerhard and Horst Kühn, 'Komparative Vorteile und ihre Ausnutzung im Außenhandel sozialistischer Länder', *Wirtschaftswissenschaft*, 1986: 8, 1138–56.

Guglielmi, Jean-Louis and Marie Lavigne, eds., *Unités et monnaies de compte* (Paris: Economica, 1978).

Haberl, Othmar and Lutz Niethammer, eds., *Der Marshall-Plan und die europäische Linke* (Frankfurt a.M.: Europäische Verlagsanstalt, 1986).

Haffner, Friedrich, *Das sowjetische Preissystem – Theorie und Praxis: Änderungsvorschläge und Reformmaßnahmen* (Berlin: Duncker & Humblot, 1968).

Haluška, Ivan, 'Pôsobenie cien na rozvoj priamych vzt'ahov v rámci RVHP', *Finance a Úvěr*, 1987: 5, 289–92.

Hamouz, Vratislav, 'Dynamický se rozvijející společenství', *Hospodářské Noviny*, 1982: 6, 3.

Hegemann, Margot, *Kurze Geschichte des RGW* (Berlin: VEB Deutscher Verlag der Wissenschaften, 1980).

Hertz, Frederick, *The economic problems of the Danubean states – a study in economic nationalism* (London: Gollancz, 1947).

Hewett, Edward A., *Foreign trade prices in the Council for Mutual Economic Assistance* (unpublished Ph.D. dissertation, University of Michigan, 1971).

Hewett, Edward A., *Foreign trade prices in the Council for Mutual Economic Assistance* (New York: Cambridge University Press, 1974).

Hewett, Edward A., 'A gravity model of CMEA trade', in Josef C. Brada (ed.), *Quantitative and analytical studies in east-west economic relations* (Bloomington, Ind.: International Development Research Center, 1976, pp. 1–16).

Hoensch, Jorg K., *Sowjetische Osteuropa-Politik, 1945–1975* (Düsseldorf: Droste, 1977).

Holzman, Franklyn D., 'Soviet foreign trade pricing and the question of discrimination: a customs union approach', *Review of Economics and Statistics*, 1962: 2, 134–47.

Holzman, Franklyn D., 'More on Soviet bloc trade discrimination', *Soviet Studies*, 1965: 1, 44–65.

Holzman, Franklyn D., 'Comecon: a "trade-destroying" customs union?' *Journal of Comparative Economics*, 1985: 4, 410–23.

Holzman, Franklyn D., 'The significance of Soviet subsidies to Eastern Europe', *Comparative Economic Studies*, 1986a: 1, 54–65.

Holzman, Franklyn D., 'Further thoughts on the significance of Soviet subsidies to Eastern Europe', *Comparative Economic Studies*, 1986b: 3, 59–63.

Holzman, Franklyn D., ed., *The economics of Soviet bloc trade and finance* (Boulder, Colo.: Westview Press, 1987).

Huber, Gerhard, ed., '25 Jahre zielstrebige internationale Arbeitsteilung die unsere sozialistische Staatengemeinschaft zur dynamischten Wirtschaftsregion der Welt werden ließ', *Die Wirtschaft*, 1974a: 2A, supplement.

Huber, Gerhard, 'Planung und Stimulierung der internationalen sozialistischen Spezialisierung und Kooperation', *Wirtschaftswissenschaft*, 1974b, 508–20.

HY, *Statisztikai évkönyv, . . .* (Budapest: Központi Statisztikai Hivatal, annual).

Ivanov, Jurij, 'SĚV i meždunarodnye ėkonomičeskie otnošenija', *Meždunarodnaja žizn'*, 1979: 9, 27–36.

Jacquemin, Alexis and André Sapir, 'European integration or world integration?' *Weltwirtschaftliches Archiv*, 1988: 1, 127–39.

Joint Economic Committee of the US Congress (JEC), ed., *East European economies: slow growth in the 1980's, Vol. 2, Foreign trade and international finance* (Washington, D.C.: US Government Printing Office, 1986).

Jones, A. J., 'The theory of economic integration', in J. K. Bowers (ed.), *Inflation, development and integration* (Leeds: Leeds University Press, 1979, pp. 193–213).

Kalbe, Ernstgert *et al.*, *Geschichte der sozialistischen Gemeinschaft – Herausbildung und Entwicklung des realen Sozialismus von 1917 bis zur Gegenwart* (Berlin: VEB Verlag der Wissenschaften, 1981).

Kalčev, Vasil, 'Vlijanieto na socialističeskata integracija vŭrchu vŭnšnotŭrgovskija stokoobmen', *Vŭnšna tŭrgovija*, 1983: 12, 7–10.

Kamecki, Zbigniew, 'The problem of foreign trade monopoly in a socialist economy', in Józef Sołdaczuk (ed.), *International trade and development – theory and policy* (Warsaw: PWN, 1966, pp. 11–36).

Kaplan, Karel, 'Die Entwicklung des Rates für gegenseitige Wirtschaftshilfe (RgW) in der Zeit von 1949 bis 1957 – zu einigen Fragen der Kontinuität in den Integrationsproblemen und -tendenzen' (Ebenhausen: Stiftung Wissenschaft und Politik, 1977, mimeographed).

Kaplan, Karel, *Dans les archives du comité central – 30 ans de secrets du bloc soviétique* (Paris: Michel Albin, 1978).

Kaplan, Karel, 'The Council for Mutual Economic Aid /1949–1951/ – /excerpts of documents with commentary/ (Frankfurt a.M.: 1979 mimeographed).

Kaser, Michael C., 'Les préoccupations actuelles du Comécon', *Projet*, 1966: 7, 815–26.

Kaser, Michael C., *Comecon – integration problems of the planned economies* (London: Oxford University Press, 2nd edn, 1967).

Kerner, Antonín and Jan Trubač, 'Základní rysy metodologie společného plánování', *Acta Universitatis Carolinae – Oeconomica*, 1975: 2, 101–15.

Kirillin, V. I., 'Aktual'nye problemy povyšenija effektivnosti naučno-techničeskogo sotrudničestva stran-členov SĖV', *Ėkonomičeskoe sotrudničestvo stran-členov SĖV*, 1977: 5, 32–5.

Kiss, Tibor, *International division of labour in open economies – with special regard to the CMEA* (Budapest: Akadémiai Kiadó, 1971).

Kiss, Tibor, ed., *The market of socialist economic integration – selected conference papers* (Budapest: Akadémiai Kiadó, 1973).

Kiss, Tibor, 'Nemzetközi tervezési együttműködés és KGST-ben', *Közgazdasági Szemle*, 1975: 6, 736–53.

Klawe, Andrzej J., 'Ceny w handlu międzynarodowym krajów RWPG', *Sprawy Międzynarodowe*, 1976: 2, 90–8.

Klepacki, Zbigniew M., 'Membership and other forms of participation of states in the activities of the socialist economic, scientific and technical intergovernmental organizations', *Polish Yearbook of International Law*, vol. 7 (1975), 45–64.

Knyziak, Zygmunt, 'Ceny w handlu wzajemnym krajów RWPG a ceny krajowe', in Bożyk, 1974, pp. 174–88.

Kohlmey, Gunther, *Der demokratische Weltmarkt – Entstehung, Merkmale und Bedeutung für den sozialistischen Aufbau* (Berlin: Die Wirtschaft, 1955).

Kohlmey, Gunther, ed., *RGW-DDR – 25 Jahre Zusammenarbeit* (Berlin: Akademie-Verlag, 1974).

Konovalova, N. A., 'Učët transportnogo faktora pri soveršenstvovanii vnešnetorgovych cen', in D'jačenko, 1968a (1968), pp. 135–49.

Konstantinov, Jurij A., 'Finansi na meždunarodnite specializirane ikonomičeski organizacii', *Finansi i kredit*, 1977: 2, 3–14; 1977: 3, 3–14; 1977: 4, 3–12.

Konstantinov, Jurij A., *Meždunarodnaja valjutnaja sistema stran-členov SĖV* (Moscow: Finansy i statistika, 1982).

Konstantinov, Jurij A., 'Valjutnaja sistema socialističeskogo gosudarstva', *Finansy SSSR*, 1984: 4, 28–35.

Konstantinov, Jurij A., 'Prjamye svjazi v ramkach SĖV: ich valjutno-finansovoe obespečenie', *Finansy SSSR*, 1987: 4, 54–60.

Korbonski, Andrzej, 'Détente, east-west trade, and the future of economic integration in Eastern Europe', *World Politics*, 1976: 4, 568–89.

Kormnov, Jurij F., *Specializacija i kooperacija proizvodstva stran SĖV v uslovijach socialističeskoj ėkonomičeskoj integracii* (Moscow: Ėkonomika, 1972).

Kormnov, Jurij F., 'Dolgosročnye celevye programmy sotrudničestva stran SĖV', *Voprosy ėkonomiki*, 1977a: 1, 86–94.

Kormnov, Jurij F., 'Meždunarodnye dolgosročnye celevye programmy sotrudničestva stran SĖV', in R. N. Evstigneev (ed.), *Kompleksnye programmy razvitija v stranach SĖV* (Moscow: Mysl', 1977b, pp. 188–213).

Kostecki, Maciej M., 'State trading in industrialized and developing countries', *Journal of World Trade Law*, 1978: 3, 187–207.

Köves, András, 'Befelé vagy kifelé fordulás – qondolatok a KGST-országok külgazdasági stratégiájáról', *Közgazdasági Szemle*, 1981: 7/8, 878–95.

Köves, András, 'Implicit szubvenciók és a KGST-n belüli gazdasági kapcsolatok néhány kérdése (Megjegyzések Michael Marrese és Jan Vanous elemzéseihez*)', *Közgazdasági Szemle*, 1984: 10, 1235–44.

Köves, András, *The CMEA countries in the world economy: turning inwards or turning outwards* (Budapest: Akadémiai Kiadó, 1985).

Kowalewski, Jósef, 'Współpraca przemysłowa krajów RWPG – na przykładzie przemysłu elektromaszynowego', *Handel Zagraniczny*, 1980a: 11, 16–21, 25.

Kowalewski, Józef, *Współpraca przemysłowa krajów RWPG* (Warsaw: PWE, 1980b).

Kowalik, Tadeusz, *On crucial reform of real socialism* (Vienna: Forschungsberichte des Wiener Instituts für Internationale Wirtschaftsvergleiche, no. 122, October 1986).

Koz'menko, Vasilij, 'Transportnyj faktor i cenoobrazovanie na rynke stran SĖV', *Vnešnjaja torgovlja*, 1986: 1, 25–8.

Kraus, Josef, 'Cenová tvorba zemědělsko-potravinářských výrobků v obchodě zemí RVHP', *Zahraniční Obchod*, 1985: 9, 9–12.

Kunz, Willy, ed., *Sozialistische ökonomische Integration* (Berlin: Die Wirtschaft, 1982).

Kuznecov, V., 'Soveršenstvovanie ėkonomičeskoj dejatel'nosti – byt' li u nas valjutnomu rynku?' *Ėkonomičeskaja gazeta*, 1988: 26, 21.

Kuznecova, N., 'Razvitie proizvodstvennoj specializacii i kooperacii v mašinostroenii stran-členov SĖV', *Vestnik statistiki*, 1981: 3, 44–52.

Lavigne, Marie, *Le Comécon – le programme du comécon et l'intégration socialiste* (Paris: Cujas, 1973).

Lavigne, Marie, 'Les transferts de technologie entre pays socialistes européens', *Mondes en Développement*, 1976, reproduced in *Problèmes Economiques*, no. 1515 (23 March 1977), 24–30.

Lavigne, Marie, 'The Soviet Union inside Comecon', *Soviet Studies*, 1983: 2, 135–53.

Lavigne, Marie, *The evolution of CMEA institutions and policies and the need for structural adjustment* (paper presented to the Conference on the Soviet Union and Eastern Europe in the World Economy, Washington, D.C., 18–19 October 1984).

Lehmann, Gudrun, 'Zu einigen theoretischen und praktischen Fragen der Bildung und der Leitung gemeinsamer Betriebe von Mitgliedsländern des RGW', *Wirtschaftswissenschaft*, 1973: 9, 1312–30.

Lehmann, Gudrun 'Planungszusammenarbeit in internationalen ökonomischen Organisationen der RGW-Länder', *Volkswirtschaftsplanung – Beiträge zur Theorie und Praxis*, 1977: 10.

Lér, Ondřej, 'Komplexní program vědeckotechnického pokroku zemí RVHP – význam organizací-koordinátorů', *Svět Hospodářství*, 1986: 42, 1.

Leznik, A., 'Upravlenie meždunarodnoj naučno-proizvodstvennoj kooperaciej stran SĖV', *Planovoe chozjajstvo*, 1987: 4, 23–30.

Ljutov, Atanas, 'Economic integration and the socialist international market', in Kiss, 1973, pp. 49–55.

Lukin, Lev I., 'Pervoe desjatiletie Soveta ėkonomičeskoj vzaimopomošči', *Voprosy istorii*, 1974: 4, 39–57.

Lukin, Lev I., 'Statističeskoe issledovanie socialističeskoj ėkonomičeskoj integracii', *Vnešnjaja torgovlja*, 1981: 11, 37–41.

Lundestad, Geir, 'Der Marshall-Plan und Osteuropa', in Haberl and Niethammer, 1986, pp. 59–74.

Marczewski, Jean, *Planification et croissance économique des démocraties populaires* (Paris: Presses Universitaires de France, 1956).

Marer, Paul, *Foreign trade prices in the Soviet bloc – a theoretical and empirical study* (unpublished Ph.D. dissertation, University of Pennsylvania, 1968a).

Marer, Paul, 'Foreign trade prices in the Soviet bloc', *ASTE Bulletin*, 1968b: 2, 1–11.

Marer, Paul, *Postwar pricing and price patterns in socialist foreign trade (1946–1971)* (Bloomington, Ind.: IDRC, 1972).

Marer, Paul, 'The political economy of Soviet relations with Eastern Europe', in Sarah M. Terry (ed.), *Soviet policy in Eastern Europe* (New Haven-London: Yale University Press, 1984, pp. 155–88).

Marer, Paul and John Michael Montias, 'The Council for Mutual Economic Assistance', in El-Agraa, 1982a (1982), pp. 102–38.

Marques-Méndes, José A., *Economic integration and growth in Europe* (London: Croom Helm, 1987).

Marrese, Michael, 'CMEA: effective but cumbersome political economy', *International Organization*, 1986: 2, 287–327.

Marrese, Michael and Jan Vaňous, *Soviet subsidization of trade with Eastern Europe – a Soviet perspective* (Berkeley, Calif.: Institute of International Studies, 1983a).

Marrese, Michael and Jan Vaňous, 'Unconventional gains from trade', *Journal of Comparative Economics*, 1983b: 4, 382–99.

Marrese, Michael and Jan Vaňous, *The content and controversy of Soviet trade relations with Eastern Europe* (unpublished manuscript, April 1986).

Matějka, Karel, *RVHP dokumenty – vědeckotechnická spolupráce ČSSR se socialistickými státy – I. díl* (Prague: Československá obchodní a průmyslová komora, 1985a).

Matějka, Karel, *RVHP dokumenty – vědeckotechnická spolupráce ČSSR se socialistickými státy – II. díl* (Prague: Československá obchodní a průmyslová komora, 1985b).

Matlin, Anatolij M., 'Zakon stoimosti i planovoe cenoobrazovanie', *Voprosy ėkonomiki*, 1985: 11, 76–87.

Mayes, David G., 'The problems of the quantitative estimation of integration effects', in El-Agraa, 1982a (1982), pp. 28–43.

Mazanov, Georgij, *Meždunarodnye rasčёty stran-členov SĖV* (Moscow: Finansy, 1970).

Meißner, Boris, 'Sowjetische Hegemonie und osteuropäische Föderation', in Gilbert Ziebura (ed.), *Nationale Souveränität oder übernationale Integration?* (Berlin: Colloquium Verlag, 1966, pp. 57–85).

Meister, Manfred, *Die Vervollkommnung der Valutapreisbildung durch Anwendung ökonomisch-mathematischen Methoden* (unpublished doctoral dissertation, Hochschule für Ökonomie 'Bruno Leuschner', 1975).

Mendershausen, Horst, 'Terms of trade between the Soviet Union and smaller communist countries', *Review of Economics and Statistics*, 1959: 2, 106–18.

Mendershausen, Horst, 'Terms of Soviet satellite trade', *Review of Economics and Statistics*, 1960: 2, 152–63.

Menžinskij, V. I., ed., *Meždunarodnye organizacii socialističeskich stran* (Moscow: Meždunarodnye otnošenija, 1971).

Mervart, Josef, 'Bedeutung und Entwicklung der Preise im internationalen Handel', *Wirtschaftswissenschaftliche Informationen*, nos. 26–29 (1963).

Miastkowski, Lech, 'Zmiany struktury i poziomu cen detalicznych w gospodarce socjalistycznej', *Ekonomista*, 1980: 4, 893–915.

Mikesell, R. F., *Foreign exchange in the postwar period* (New York: Twentieth Century Fund, 1954).

Mirošničenko, A., 'Meždunarodnoe razdelenie truda vo mašinostroenii stran-členov SĖV', *Voprosy ėkonomiki*, 1970: 7, 105–11.

Mirov, G. and I. Dimov, 'Sŭvmestnite dŭlgosročni programi na stranite-členki na SIV', *Planovo stopanstvo*, 1977: 2, 27–35.

Mitrofanova, Nina M., 'O vzaimosvjazi vnutrennich i vnešnetorgovych cen v evropejskich socialističeskich stranach', *Planovoe chozjajstvo*, 1973: 9, 90–7.

Mitrofanova, Nina M., 'Perspektivy dal'nejšego soveršenstvovanija vnešnetorgovych cen socialističeskich stran', *Planovoe chozjajstvo*, 1974: 4, 41–9.

Mitrofanova, Nina M., 'Ob ėkonomičeskoj prirode kontraktnych cen vo vzaimnom sotrudničestve stran SĖV', *Izvestija akademii nauk SSSR – serija ėkonomičeskaja*, 1977: 5, 116–24.

Mitrofanova, Nina M., *Ceny v mechanizme ėkonomičeskogo sotrudničestva stran-členov SĖV* (Moscow: Nauka, 1978).

Mitrofanova, Nina M. and A. L. Starikova, 'Problemy cen na meždunarodnom rynke SĖV', in V. M. Šastitko (ed.), *Meždunarodnyj rynok SĖV v uslovijach integracii* (Moscow: Nauka, 1980, pp. 164–86).

Monkiewicz, Jan, 'Scientific and technological integration of CMEA countries. Directions of evolution', *Studies in International Relations*, 1975: 6, 88–100.

Montias, John M., 'Planning with material balances in Soviet-type economies', *American Economic Review*, 1959: 5; reprinted in Alex Nove and D. Mario Nuti (eds.), *Socialist economies* (Harmondsworth: Penguin, 1959, pp. 223–51).

Montias, John M., *Economic development in communist Rumania* (Cambridge, Mass.: The M.I.T. Press, 1967).

Montias, John M., 'Socialist industrialization and trade in machinery products: an analysis based on the experience of Bulgaria, Poland, and Rumania', in Alan A. Brown and Egon Neuberger (eds.), *International trade and central planning – an analysis of economic interactions* (Berkeley, Calif: University of California Press, 1968, pp. 130–58).

Montias, John M., 'The structure of Comecon trade and the prospects of east-west exchanges', in Joint Economic Committee of the US Congress (ed.), *Reorientation and commercial relations of the economies of Eastern Europe* (Washington, D.C.: Superintendent of Documents, 1974, pp. 662–81).

Morozov, Vladimir, 'Perspektivnye formy sotrudničestvo stran-členov SĖV', *Voprosy ėkonomiki*, 1974: 6, 95–103.

Neumann, Gerd, *Die ökonomischen Entwicklungsbedingungen des RGW – Versuch einer wirtschaftshistorischen Analyse – Band I: 1945–1958* (Berlin: Akademie-Verlag, 1980).

Neustadt, Alojz, 'External economic relations and the system of management in Czechoslovakia', *Bulletin of the Research Institute for Economic Planning*, 1968: 2 215–34.

Neustadt, Alojz, 'Construction of international prices on the socialist world market', *Czechoslovak Economic Papers*, no. 20 (1982), 65–85.

Neustadt, Alojz, 'Zdokonalení tvorby kontraktních cen – předpoklad širokého rozvoje přímých vztahů mezi hospodářským organizacemi členských států RVHP', *Finance a Úvěr*, 1987: 4, 253–66.

Nosiadek, Grzegorz, 'Polska w RWPG – powiązania specjalizacyjne i kooperacyjne', *Rynki Zagraniczne*, 1988: 124, 3.

Novák, Stanislav, 'Zapojení Československa do mezinárodní specializace a kooperace výroby členských zemí RVHP', *Zahraniční Obchod*, 1984: 4, 6–10.

Nuti, D. Mario, *Financial innovation under market socialism* (Florence: European University Institute, Working Paper no. 87/285, 1987a).

Nuti, D. Mario, 'Alternative definitions and measures of disequilibrium and shortage in centrally planned economies' (San Domenico di Fiesole, Istituto Universitario Europeo, manuscript 1987b).

Nyers, Rezső, 'A KGST többoldalú integrációs intezkedéseinek hatása a magyar népgazdaságra az 1976-1980-as években', *Közgazdasági Szemle*, 1977: 4, 423–9.

Organy, 'Orgány Rady Vzájemné Hospodářské Pomoci', *Zahraniční Obchod*, 1978: 11/12, insert.

Padoa-Schioppa, Tommaso *et al.*, *Efficiency, stability, and equity – a strategy for the evolution of the economic system of the European Community* (Oxford: Oxford University Press, 1987).

Panjuškin, Dmitrij, 'Sozdanie sovremennych mašin i oborudovanija – zadača obščaja', *Ekonomičeskoe sotrudničestvo stran-členov SEV*, 1987: 6, 49–54.

Pechlivanov, Vasil, 'Vŭprosi na cenoobrazuvaneto pri vnosnite stoki v stranite-členki na SEI', *Vŭnšna tŭrgovija*, 1981: 3, 9–13.

Pechlivanov, Vasil, Stefan Krŭstev and Vasil Christov, *Sbližavane na vŭtrešnoto cenoobrazuvane na stranite-členki na SEI* (Varna: Bakalov, 1978).

Pécsi, Kálmán, *A KGST termelési integrácio közgazdasági kérdései* (Budapest: Közgazdasági és Jógi Könyvkiadó, 1977).

Pécsi, Kálmán, *Economic questions of production integration within the CMEA* (Budapest: Hungarian Scientific Council for World Economy, 1978).

Pécsi, Kálmán, 'Nekotoryje problemy ustanovlenija cen vo vzaimnoj torgovle', *Mirovaja ekonomika i meždunarodnye otnošenija*, 1979: 9, 93–101.

Pekšev, Ju., 'Novaja forma sotrudničestva stran SEV v oblasti planovoj dejatel'nosti', *Vnešnjaja torgovlja*, 1978a: 11, 2–11.

Pekšev, Ju., 'Soveršenstvovanie sovmestnoj planovoj dejatel'nosti socialističeskich gosudarstv', *Voprosy ekonomiki*, 1978b: 5, 89–98.

Pekšev, Ju., 'Integracija stran SEV v sel'skom chozjajstve i piščevoj promyšlennosti', *Vnešnjaja torgovlja*, 1979a: 7, 2–6, 16.

Pekšev, Ju., 'Novyje gorizonty sotrudničestva', *Ekonomičeskaja gazeta*, 1979b: 24, 20.

Pelzman, Joseph, 'Trade integration in the Council for Mutual Economic Assistance, 1954–1970', *ACES Bulletin*, 1976a: 3, 39–59.

Pelzman, Joseph, *Economic integration in C.M.E.A.* (Columbia, S.C.: University of South Carolina School of Business Administration, Working Papers in Economics, no. 10, 1976b).

Pelzman, Joseph, 'Trade creation and trade diversion in the Council for Mutual Economic Assistance, 1954–1970', *American Economic Review*, 1977: 4, 713–22.

Pěnkava, Jaromír, 'Zdokonalování cenove tvorby v procesu socialistické ekonomicke integrace členských států RVHP', *Finance a Úvěr*, 1975: 10, 649–57.

Petrakov, Nikolaj Ja., 'Cena – ryčag upravlenija', *Ekonomičeskaja gazeta*, 1986: 16, 10.

Petrakov, Nikolaj Ja., 'Planovaja cena v sisteme upravlenija narodnym chozjajstvom', *Voprosy ekonomiki*, 1987: 1, 44–55.

Petřivalský, Jiří, 'Problems of an own price basis – related questions of economic and foreign exchange policy', in Földi and Kiss, 1969, pp. 127–36.

Petrova, M., 'Dŭlgosročni celevi programi za sŭtrudničestvo meždu stranite-členki na SIV', *Vŭnšna tŭrgovija*, 1979: 3, 2–6.

PI, *Rocznik statystyczny inwestycji i srodków trwałych*, . . . (Warsaw: Główny Urząd Statystyczny, annual until 1974).

Pilat, Vasile and Daniel Dăianu, 'Some problems of the development of European socialist economies', *Revue Roumaine d'Etudes Internationales*, 1984: 3, 245–61.

Popov, Konstantin I., 'Ob ob″ektivnych osnovach postroenija sistemy cen v torgovle meždu socialističeskimi stranami', *Voprosy èkonomiki*, 1968a: 8, 67–75.

Popov, Konstantin I., *Razvitie èkonomičeskich svjazej stran socializma (analyz praktiki i teoretičeskich problem)* (Moscow: Mysl′, 1968b).

Popov, Konstantin I., 'Modern theories of building up price systems in trade between socialist countries', in Douglas C. Hague (ed.), *Price formation in various economies* (London: Macmillan, 1969, pp. 145–50).

Poznański, Kazimierz, *Competitiveness of Polish industry* (paper presented at the Workshop on the Polish Economy and Debt, Washington, D.C., 21–22 October 1985).

Poznański, Kazimierz, 'Competition between Eastern Europe and developing countries in the western market for manufactured goods', in Joint Economic Committee of the US Congress (ed.), *East European Economies: slow growth in the 1980s, vol 2*, (Washington, D.C.: US Government Printing Office, 1986a, pp. 62–90).

Poznański, Kazimierz, *Implicit trade subsidies: discussion of methodology and new evidence* (Troy, N.Y.: Rensselaer Polytechnic Institute, unpublished MS, 1986b).

Proft, Gerhard, Hannelore Liebsch and Klaus Werner, *Planung in der sozialistischen ökonomischen Integration* (Berlin: Staatsverlag, 1973).

PT, *Rocznik statystyczny handlu zagranicznego*, . . . (Warsaw: Główny Urząd Statystyczny, annual).

Ptaszek, Jan, 'Postępy współpracy', *Życie Gospodarcze*, 1972: 38, 5.

PY, *Rocznik statystyczny*, . . . (Warsaw: Główny Urząd Statystyczny, annual).

Rácz, Margit, 'A summary analysis', in András Inotai (ed.), *The Hungarian enterprise in the context of intra-CMEA relations* (Budapest: Hungarian Scientific Council for World Economy, 1986).

Rand, *Directory of specialization agreements within the Council for Mutual Economic Assistance (CMEA)* (Santa Monica, Calif.: The Rand Corporation, working draft, 1986).

Rózański, Henryk, 'Początki RWPG', *Polityka*, 1987: 19, 13–5.

Rusmich, Ladislav, 'Tovarno-denežnye aspekty perestrojki mechanizma integracii', *Èkonomičeskoe sotrudničestvo stran-členov SÈV*, 1988: 3, 51–6.

Rüster, Lothar, ed., *Musterdokumente des RGW für die wissenschaftlich-technische Zusammenarbeit* (Berlin: Staatsverlag, 1987).

Rutkowski, Jerzy, 'Stabilność i elastyczność cen w obrotach wzajemnych krajów RWPG', *Handel Zagraniczny*, 1977: 1, 3–8.

RY, *Anuarul statistic al Republicii Socialiste România*, . . . (Bucharest: Direcţia Centrală di Statistică, 1986).

Rybakov, Oleg, 'Eščë raz o novom podchode k ravitiju èkonomičeskogo sotrudničestva SSSR s socialističeskimi stranami', *Planovoe chozjajstvo*, 1988: 4, 65–75.

Rybalko, G., 'Aktivnaja rol′ valjutnogo mechanizma', *Èkonomičeskaja gazeta*, 1987: 11, 20.

Rybalko, G., 'Konvertabel′nost′ rublja v povestke dnja', *Èkonomičeskaja gazeta*, 1988: 9, 20.

Šalamanov, S., 'Meždunarodnata socialističeska integracija na ikonomikata – važen faktor za razvitieto na N.R. Bŭlgarija', in Žak Arojo (ed.), *Marksistko-leninskata ikonomičeska teorija i aktualnite problemi na razvitieto na N.R. Bŭlgarija* (Sofia: BKP, 1971), pp. 5–49.

Šamraj, Jurij, 'Voprosy soveršenstvovanija sistemy ustanovlenija cen na gotovye izdelija vo vzaimnoj torgovle stran-členov SĖV', *Vnešnjaja torgovlja*, 1981a: 1, 34–40.

Šamraj, Jurij, 'Voprosy soveršenstvovanija sistemy ustanovlenija cen no gotovye izdelija vo vzaimnoj torgovle stran-členov SĖV', *Vnešnjaja torgovlja*, 1981b: 2, 30–3.

Šanina, Valentina A., 'Voprosy cenoobrazovania na vnešnetorgovye perevozki meždu stranami-členami SĖV', *Ėkonomičeskie nauki*, 1973: 10, 84–9.

Šarenkov, S. and B. Djakin, 'Meždunarodnyj sojuz novogo typa', *Ėkonomičeskie nauki*, 1979: 3, 5–10.

Savov, Michail N., 'Sovet ėkonomičeskoj vzaimopomošči (osnovnye celi, principy, funkcii i struktura)', *Izvestija akademii nauk SSSR—serija ėkonomičeskaja*, 1973: 4, 49–62.

Savov, Michail N., *Razvitie na vŭnšnata tŭrgovija meždu NRD i SSSR v uslovijata na integracijata* (Varna: Bakalov, 1977).

Savov, Michail N. and N. Veličkov, 'Specializacijata na proizvodstvoto i cenite v tŭrgovijata meždu socialističeskite strani', *Planovoto stopanstvo i statistika*, 1966: 7, 12–22.

Scheller, J., 'Internationale Wirtschaftsgemeinschaft – ein sich entwickelnder Typ internationaler Wirtschaftsorganisation', *DDR Aussenwirtschaft*, 1978: 17, supplement, 5–10.

Schelling, Gerhard, 'Zum Problem der Preisbildung wissenschaftlich-technischer Ergebnisse', *Wirtschaftswissenschaft*, 1988: 7, 1051–6.

Schiavone, G., *The institutions of Comecon* (London: Macmillan, 1981).

Schneider, Wolfgang, 'Zu einigen Fragen der Anwendung internationaler Ware-Geld-Beziehungen in der Forschungskooperation der Mitgliedsländer des RGW', *Wissenschaftliche Zeitschrift der Hochschule für Ökonomie 'Bruno Leuschner'*, 1984: 1, 92–6.

Semënov, A., 'Novaja stupen' sotrudničestva', *Mirovaja ėkonomika i meždunarodnye otnošenija*, 1978: 9, 100–9.

Semrádová, L., 'Nový orgán RVHP: stálá komise RVHP pro spolupráci v oblasti zdravotnictví', *Zahraniční Obchod*, 1975: 12, 16–7.

Sil'vestrov, S., 'O prjamych svjazjach predprijatij v socialističeskom sodružestve', *Voprosy ėkonomiki*, 1987: 3, 127–30.

Širjaev, Jurij S., 'Sovmestnaja planovaja dejatel'nost' – osnova ėkonomičeskogo mechanisma socialističeskoj integracii', *Planovoe chozjajstvo*, 1977: 5, 63–8.

Širjaev, Jurij S., 'Naučno-techničeskij progress i socialističeskaja integracija', *Voprosy ėkonomiki*, 1986: 5, 129–36.

Širjaev, Jurij S., 'KGST-reform közben', *Magyar Hírlap*, 21 February 1987 (1987a), 5.

Širjaev, Jurij S., 'Perestrojka i monopolija na vnešneėkonomičeskie svjazi', *Meždunarodnaja žizn'*, 1987b: 5, 13–20.

Širjaev, Jurij S., 'Problemy razrabotki i realizacii novoj strategii sotrudničestva i razvitija stran-členov SĖV', *Ėkonomika i matematičeskie metody*, 1987c: 5, 785–94.

Sitaru, Dragos-Alexandru, 'Les organisations économiques internationales à caractère non-gouvernemental constituées dans le cadre du C.A.E.M.', *Revue Roumaine d'Etudes Internationales*, 1987: 5, 451–74.

Škarenkov, Jurij, 'Prjamye svjazy – instrument intencifikacii vnešneėkonomičeskoj dejatel'nosti', *Vnešnjaja torgovlja*, 1987: 8, 2–5.

Sláma, Jiří, 'Die politische und wirtschaftliche Integration Osteuropas in der Stalinära' (Munich: Osteuropa-Institut, 1979, typescript).

Smith, Arthur J., 'The Council for Mutual Economic Assistance in 1977: new economic power, new political perspectives and some old and new problems', in Joint Economic Committee of the US Congress (ed.), *East European economies post-Helsinki* (Washington, D.C.: US Government Printing Office, 1977, pp. 152–73).

Smith, A., 'Is there a Romanian economic crisis? The problem of energy indebtedness', in Drewnowski 1982, pp. 103–30.

Sobell, Vladimir, *The red market – industrial co-operation and specialisation in Comecon* (Aldershot: Gower, 1984).

Sobell, Vladimir, 'Technology flows within Comecon and channels of communication', in Ron Amann and Julian Cooper (eds.), *Technological progress and Soviet development* (Oxford: Blackwell, 1986, pp. 135–52).

Sorokin, Gennadij M., 'Problemy ėkonomičeskoj integracii stran socializma', *Voprosy ėkonomiki*, 1968: 12, 77–86.

Sorokin, Gennadij M., 'Leninskie principy sotrudničestva socialističeskich stran', *Planovoe chozjajstvo*, 1969: 3, 3–11.

Špaček, Petr, *Platebně úvěrový mechanismus v RVHP* (Prague: Academia, 1981).

Špaček, Petr, 'MBHS – základní článek platebního a úvěrového mechanismu členských státu RVHP', *Finance a Úvěr*, 1984: 7, 433–40.

Špaček, Petr, 'Posílit úlohu kolektivní měny', *Svět Hospodářství*, 1985: 17, 1.

Spiller, Hans, 'Rechtsprobleme der Finanzierung internationaler Wirtschaftsorganisationen', *Staat und Recht*, 1978: 5, 431–41.

Spulber, Nicholas, *The economics of communist Eastern Europe* (New York: Wiley, 1957).

Stalin, Josif V., *Economic problems of socialism in the USSR* (Moscow: Progress, 1953).

Stancu, Ştefan, 'Un eveniment remarcabil în dezvoltarea colaborării si cooperării economice dintre ţările membre ale C.A.E.R.', *Revista Economică*, 1978: 27, 24–6.

Stancu, Ştefan, 'Direcţii ale dezvoltării colaborării economice şi a cooperării in producţie între ţările membre ale C.A.E.R.', *Revista Economică*, 1980: 27, 26–7.

Stepanenko, Stanislav I., *SEV: meždunarodnoe sotrudničestvo v oblasti nauki i techniki* (Moscow: Meždunarodnye otnošenija, 1985).

Štrougal, L., 'Iz vystuplenija', *Ėkonomičeskoe sotrudničestvo stran-členov SĖV*, 1977: 4, 76–9.

Sweezy, Paul M., *The theory of capitalist development– principles of Marxian political economy* (New York: Modern Reader Paperback, 1968).

Syčёv, Vjačeslav V., 'Novye rubeži naučno-techničeskogo progressa stran-členov SĖV', *Planovoe chozjajstvo*, 1986a: 4, 41–51.

Syčёv, Vjačeslav V., 'Kursom intensifikacii sotrudničestva', *Ėkonomičeskaja gazeta*, 1986b: 48, 23.

Syčёv, Vjačeslav V., 'Novye rubeži naučno-techničeskogo sotrudničestvo', *Ėkonomičeskoe sotrudničestvo stran-členov SĖV*, 1986c: 1, 14–9.

Syčёv, Vjačeslav V., 'SĖV: integracija v dejstvii – kursom intensifikacii sotrudničestva', *Ėkonomičeskaja gazeta*, 1987a:48, 23.

Szawlowski, Richard, 'L'évolution du C.O.M.E.C.O.N. 1949–1963', *Annuaire français de droit international*, vol. 9 (1963), 670–94.

Szawlowski, Richard, *The system of the international organizations of the communist countries* (Leyden: Sijthoff, 1976).

Szita, J., 'A szocialista gazdasági integráció utján', *Közgazdasági Szemle*, 1976: 9, 1005–29.

Tarnovskij, Oleg I. and Nina M. Mitrofanova, *Stoimost' i cena na mirovom socialističeskom rynke* (Moscow: Nauka, 1968).

Teichmanowa, Eufemia, 'Koszt transportu w obrotach towarowych między krajami RWPG', *Handel Zagraniczny*, 1976: 11, 37–9.

Tokareva, Praskov'ja A., ed., *Mnogostoronnee ėkonomičeskoe sotrudničestvo socialističeskich gosudarstv – sbornik dokumentov* (Moscow: Juridičeskaja literatura, 1967).

Tokareva, Praskov'ja A., ed., *Mnogostoronnee ėkonomičeskoe sotrudničestvo socialističeskich gosudarstv – sbornik dokumentov* (Moscow: Juridičeskaja literatura, 1972, 2nd edn).

Tokareva, Praskov'ja A., ed., *Učreždenie mežgosudarstvennych ėkonomičeskich oganizacii stran-členov SĖV* (Moscow: Juridičeskaja literatura, 1976a).

Tokareva, Praskov'ja A., ed., *Mnogostoronnee ėkonomičeskoe sotrudničestvo socialističeskich gosudarstv (dokumenty za 1972–1975gg.)* (Moscow: Juridičeskaja literatura, 1976b, 3rd edn).

Tokareva, Praskov'ja A., *Meždunarodnyj organizacionno-pravovoj mechaniszm socialističeskoj ėkonomičeskoj integracii* (Moscow: Nauka, 1980).

Tokareva, Praskov'jaa A., ed., *Mnogostoronnee ėkonomičeskoe sotrudničestvo socialističeskich gosudarstv – dokumenty 1975–1980* (Moscow: Juridičeskaja literatura, 1981, 4th edn).

UN, 'Note on the institutional developments in the foreign trade of the Soviet Union and Eastern European countries', *Economic Bulletin for Europe*, 1968: 1, 43–52.

UN, 'Recent changes in the organization of foreign trade in the centrally planned economies', *Economic Bulletin for Europe*, 1973: 1, 36–49.

Uschakow, Alexander, *Integration im RGW (COMECON) – Dokumente* (Baden-Baden: Nomos, 1983a).

Uschakow, Alexander, 'Probleme der politischen Kooperation und Integration in Osteuropa', in *Moderne Welt – Jahrbuch für Ost-West Fragen 1983* (1983b), pp. 191–206.

Usenko, E. T., ed., *Pravovye formy organizacii sovmestnych proizvodstv stran-členov SĖV* (Moscow: Nauka, 1985a).

Usenko, E. T., 'Ėkonomičeskoe soveščanie stran-členov SĖV nekotorye pravovye problemy socialističeskoj integracii i sochranenija mira', *Sovetskoe gosudarstvo i prava*, 1985b: 6, 90–8.

Uspenskij, V. A. and A. Ju. Ždanov, 'Važnyj faktor ukreplenija sotrudničestva stran-členov SĖV', *Den'gi i kredit*, 1987: 4, 20–7.

Válek, Vratislav, 'Mezinárodní hospodářská organizace členských států RVHP a problematika devizového plánovaní v ČSSR', *Plánované Hospodářství*, 1978: 2, 36–45.

Válek, Vratislav, 'Mezinárodní ekonomické organizace členských států RVHP', *Svět Hospodářství*, 1979a : 4, supplement.

Válek, Vratislav, 'Společné podniky členských států RVHP', *Mezinárodní Vztahy*, 1979b : 3, 38–48.

Válek, Vratislav, *Společná investiční členských států RVHP* (Prague: SNTL, 1984).

Vel'jaminov, Georgij M., 'Meždunarodnye ėkonomičeskie organizacii socialističeskich stran', *Bjulleten' inostrannoj kommerčeskoj informacii – priloženie*, 1977: 1, 3–37.

Vel'jaminov, Georgij M., 'Pravovye osnovy sotrudničestva stran–členov SĖV na sovremennom ėtape', *Vnešnjaja torgovlja*, 1986: 2, 18–21.

Vorkauf, H., 'Studie zu Problemen der Entwicklung des abgestimmten Planes mehrseitiger Integrationsmaßnahmen zu einer qualitativ neuen Form der Planungszusammenarbeit der RGW-Länder', *Volkswirtschaftsplanung – Beiträge zur Theorie und Praxis*, 1977: 4, 1–28.

Vorotnikov, V. V. and N. R. Lopuchova, *Meždunarodnye ėkonomičeskie organizacii stran-členov SĖV* (Moscow: SĖV Sekretariat, 1985).

Vostavek, Jaroslav, 'Směnitelnost zrcadlim ekonomiky', Hospodářské Noviny, 1987: 17, 3.

Wallace, William V. and Roger A. Clarke, Comecon, trade and the west (London: Frances Pinter, 1986).

Wasilkowski, A., 'Coordination of national economic plans of the member countries of CMEA', Polish Yearbook of International Law, vol. 4 (1971), 37–48.

Weiss, G., 'Zielstrebig auf dem Weg der sozialistischen ökonomischen Integration', Einheit, 1978: 9, 929–34.

Wiles, Peter J., Communist international economics (Oxford: Blackwell, 1968).

Wiles, Peter J., 'Introduction', in Drewnowski 1982, pp. 7–17.

Zacharov, G., 'Po valjutnym koefficientam', Ėkonomičeskaja gazeta, 1987: 29, 21.

Zápotocký, Evžen, et al., Mezinárodní hospodářské vztahy – II. socialismus (Prague: SPN, 1977).

Zápotocký, Evžen, et al., Mezinárodní hospodářské vztahy – II. socialismus (Prague: SNTL–ALFA, 1980).

Želev, G. E., Problemy vosproizvodstva i meždunarodnogo razdelenija truda v stranach-členach SĖV (Moscow: Ėkonomika, 1971).

Zerev, Nikolaj, 'Ikonomičeski problemi na meždunarodnite naučno-proizvodstveni obedinenija', Ikonomika, 1987: 8, 25–36.

Zolotarëv, Vladimir I., Mirovoj socialističeskij rynok (Moscow: Meždunarodnye otnošenija, 1970).

Zschiedrich, Harald, 'Internationale Wirtschaftsvereinigungen der RGW-Mitgliedsländer', Deutsche Aussenpolitik, 1975: 11, 1678–87.

Zverev, A., 'Valjutnye fondy i otčislenija', Ėkonomičeskaja gazeta, 1987: 31, 21.

INDEX